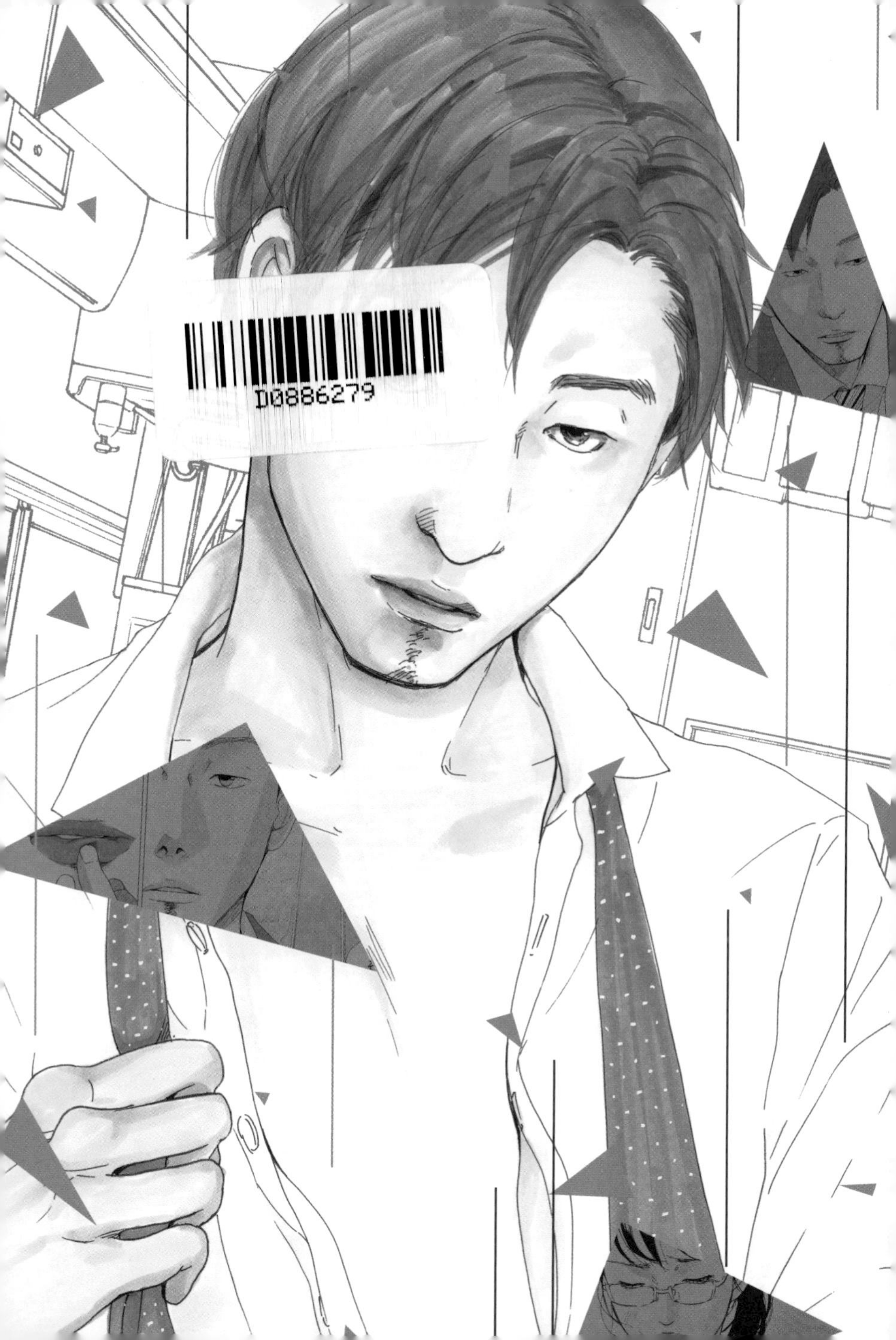

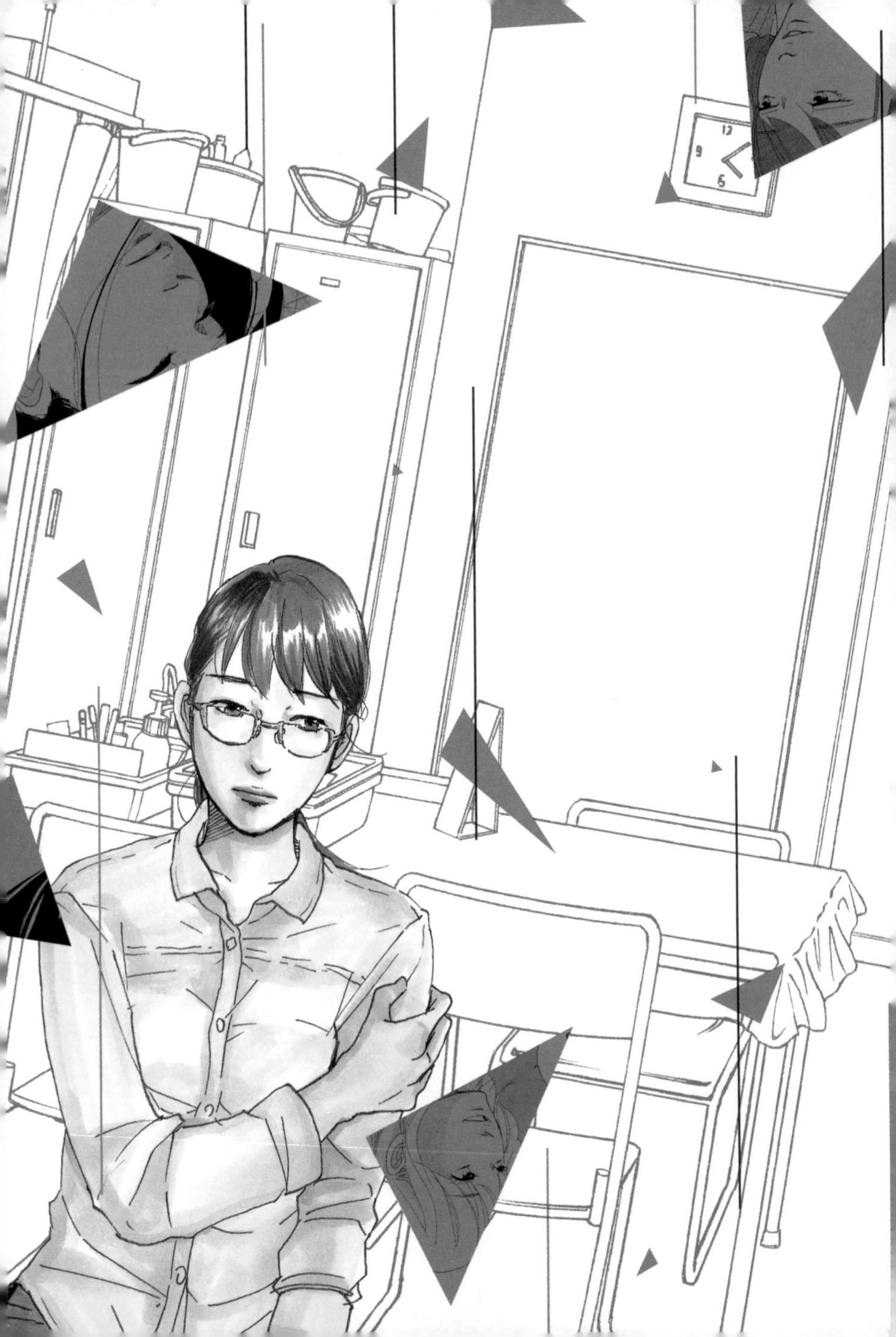

Sensei's Pious Lie

Akane Torikai

②

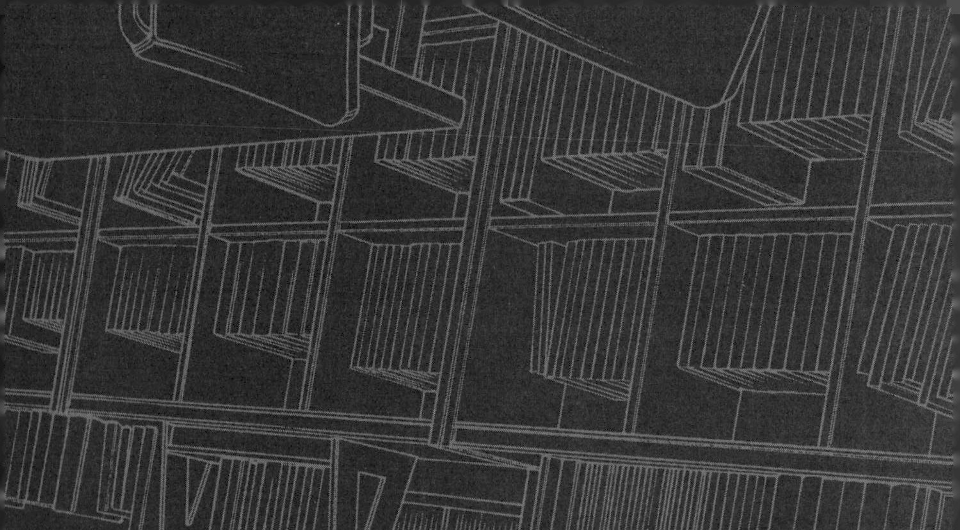

CONTENTS

WARNING: Includes graphic depictions of sexual violence

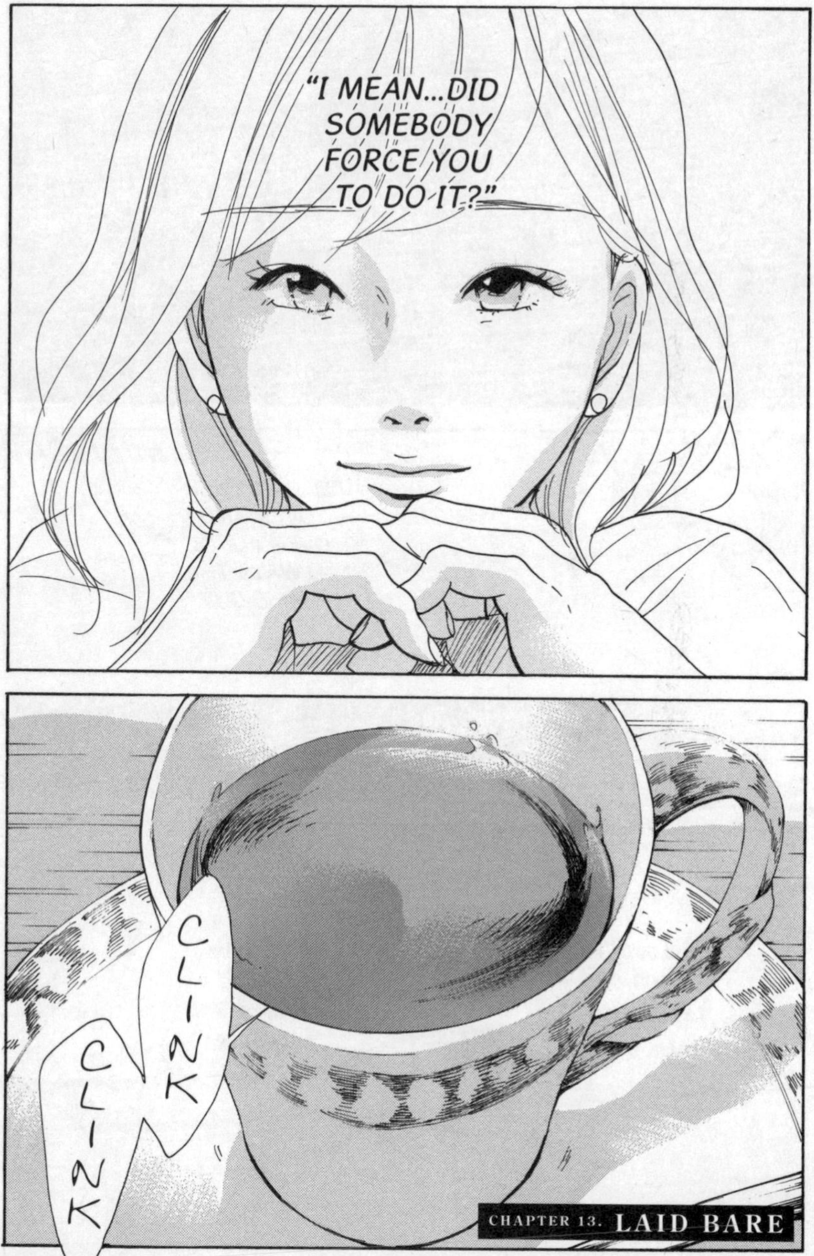
"I MEAN...DID SOMEBODY FORCE YOU TO DO IT?"
CLINK
CLINK
CHAPTER 13. LAID BARE

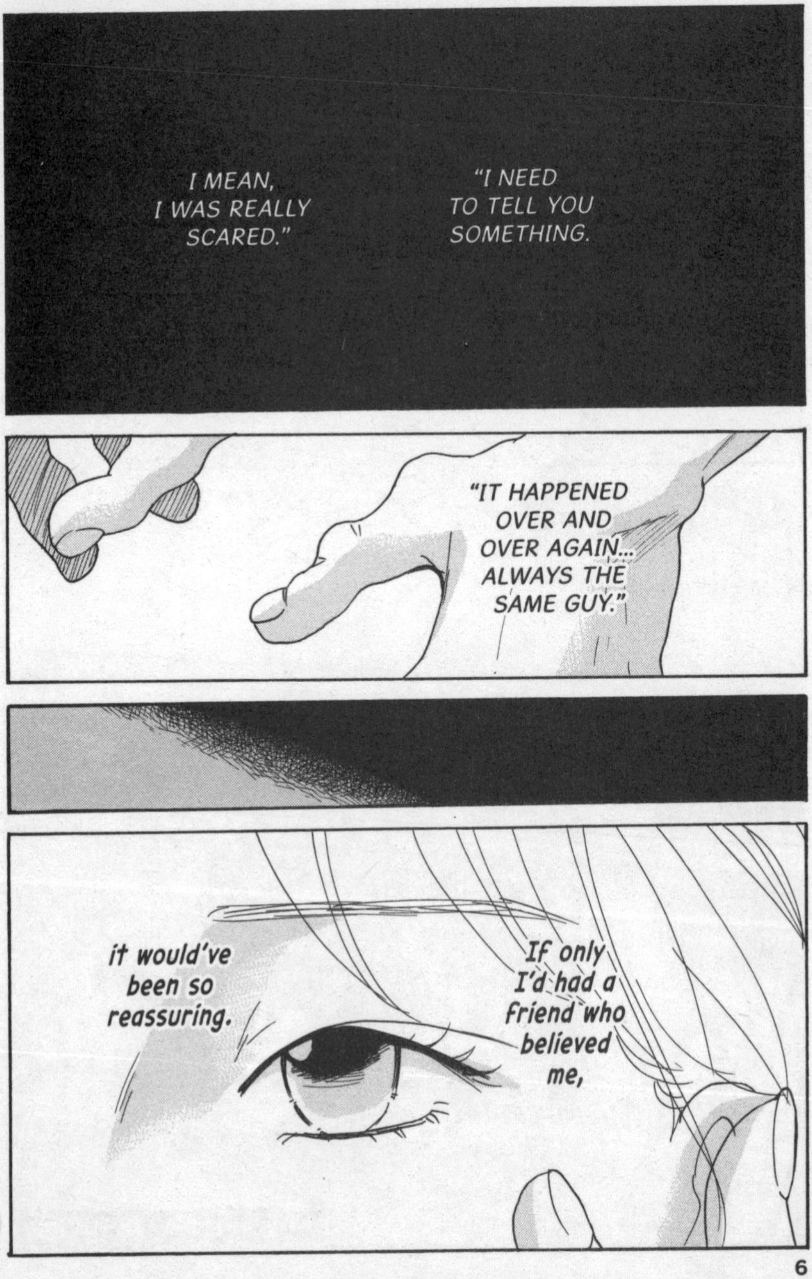
"I NEED TO TELL YOU SOMETHING.
I MEAN, I WAS REALLY SCARED."
"IT HAPPENED OVER AND OVER AGAIN... ALWAYS THE SAME GUY."
If only I'd had a friend who believed me,
it would've been so reassuring.

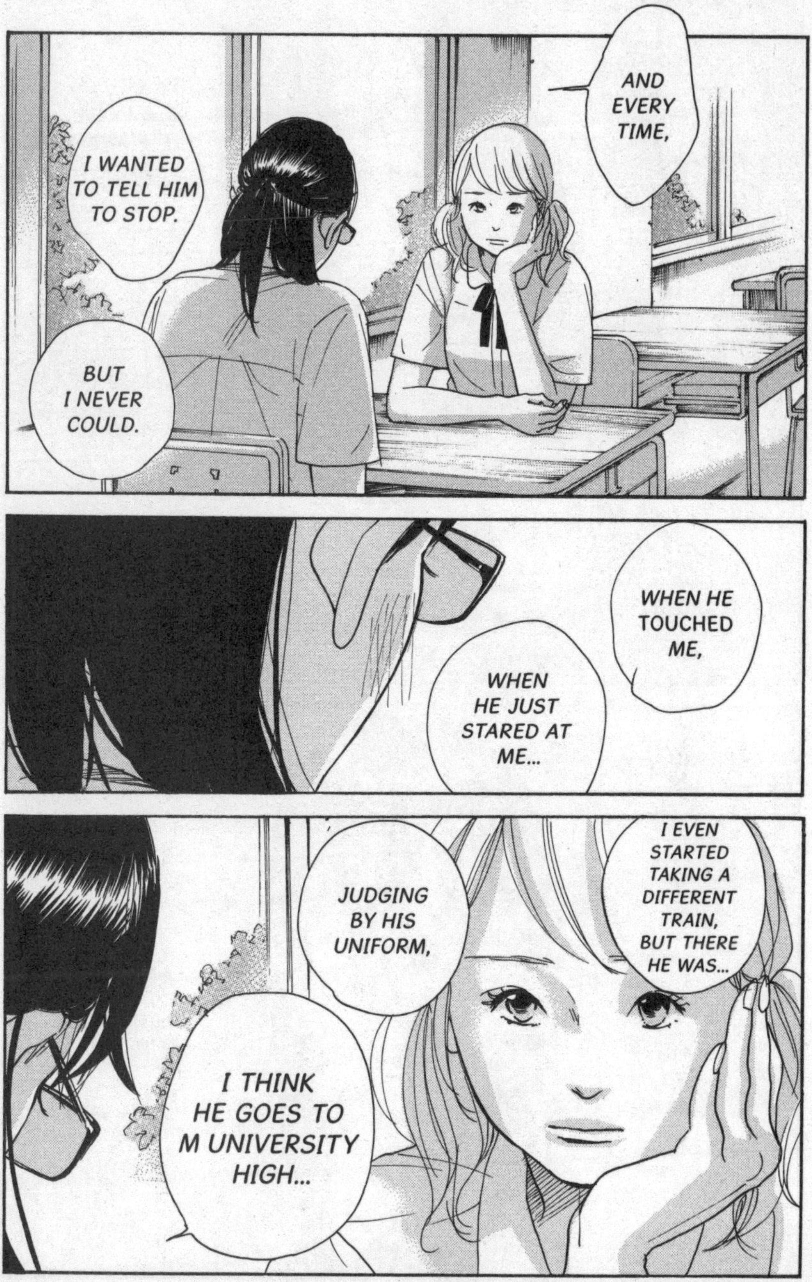
AND EVERY TIME,
I WANTED TO TELL HIM TO STOP.
BUT I NEVER COULD.
WHEN HE TOUCHED ME,
WHEN HE JUST STARED AT ME...
I EVEN STARTED TAKING A DIFFERENT TRAIN, BUT THERE HE WAS...
JUDGING BY HIS UNIFORM,
I THINK HE GOES TO M UNIVERSITY HIGH...

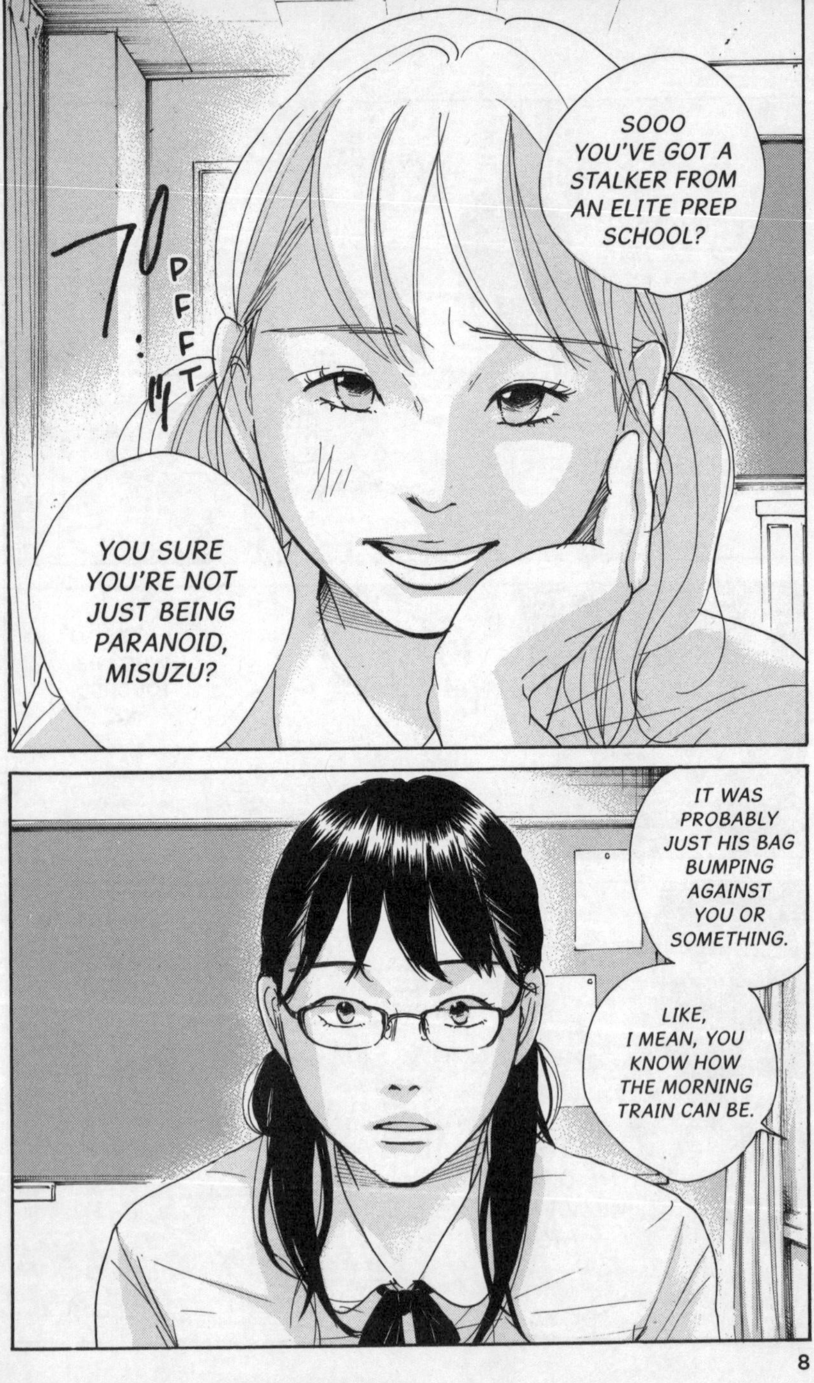
SOOO YOU'VE GOT A STALKER FROM AN ELITE PREP SCHOOL?
PFFFT
YOU SURE YOU'RE NOT JUST BEING PARANOID, MISUZU?
IT WAS PROBABLY JUST HIS BAG BUMPING AGAINST YOU OR SOMETHING.
LIKE, I MEAN, YOU KNOW HOW THE MORNING TRAIN CAN BE.

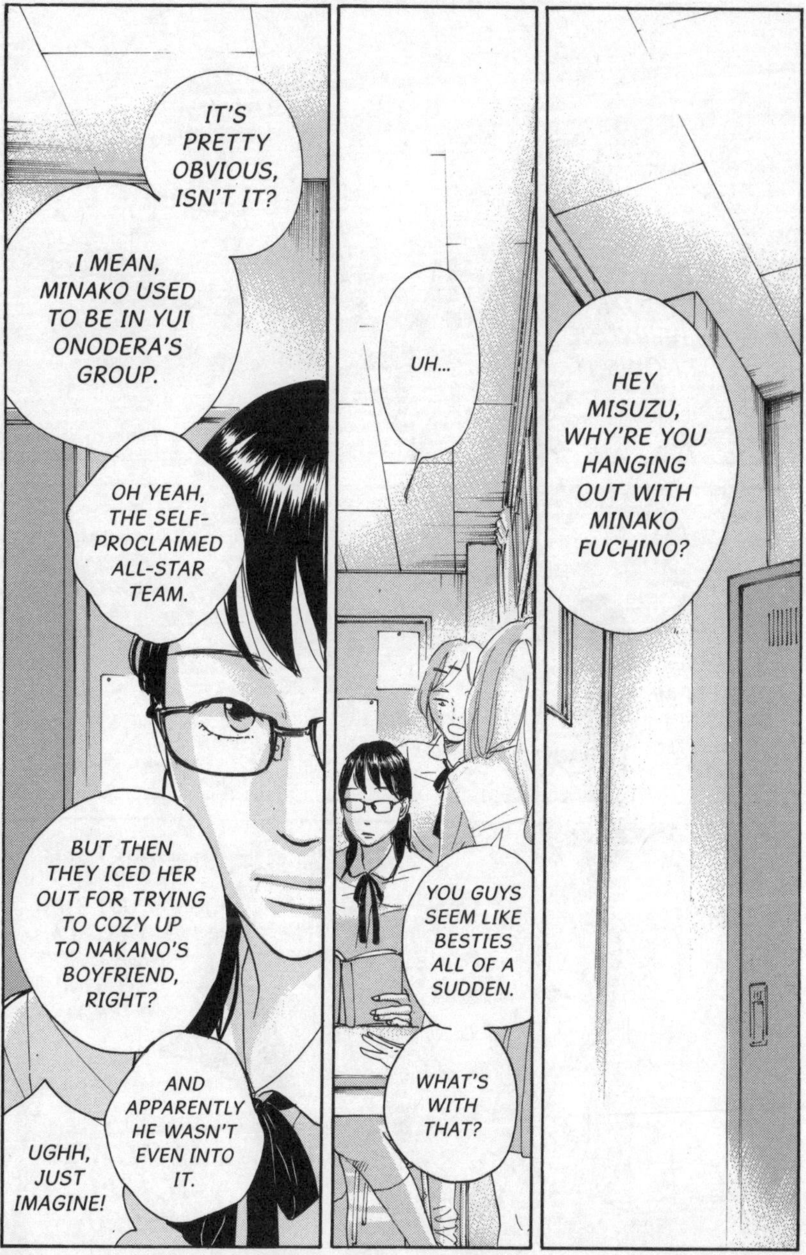
HEY MISUZU, WHY'RE YOU HANGING OUT WITH MINAKO FUCHINO?
YOU GUYS SEEM LIKE BESTIES ALL OF A SUDDEN.
WHAT'S WITH THAT?
UH...
IT'S PRETTY OBVIOUS, ISN'T IT?
I MEAN, MINAKO USED TO BE IN YUI ONODERA'S GROUP.
OH YEAH, THE SELF-PROCLAIMED ALL-STAR TEAM.
BUT THEN THEY ICED HER OUT FOR TRYING TO COZY UP TO NAKANO'S BOYFRIEND, RIGHT?
AND APPARENTLY HE WASN'T EVEN INTO IT.
UGHH, JUST IMAGINE!

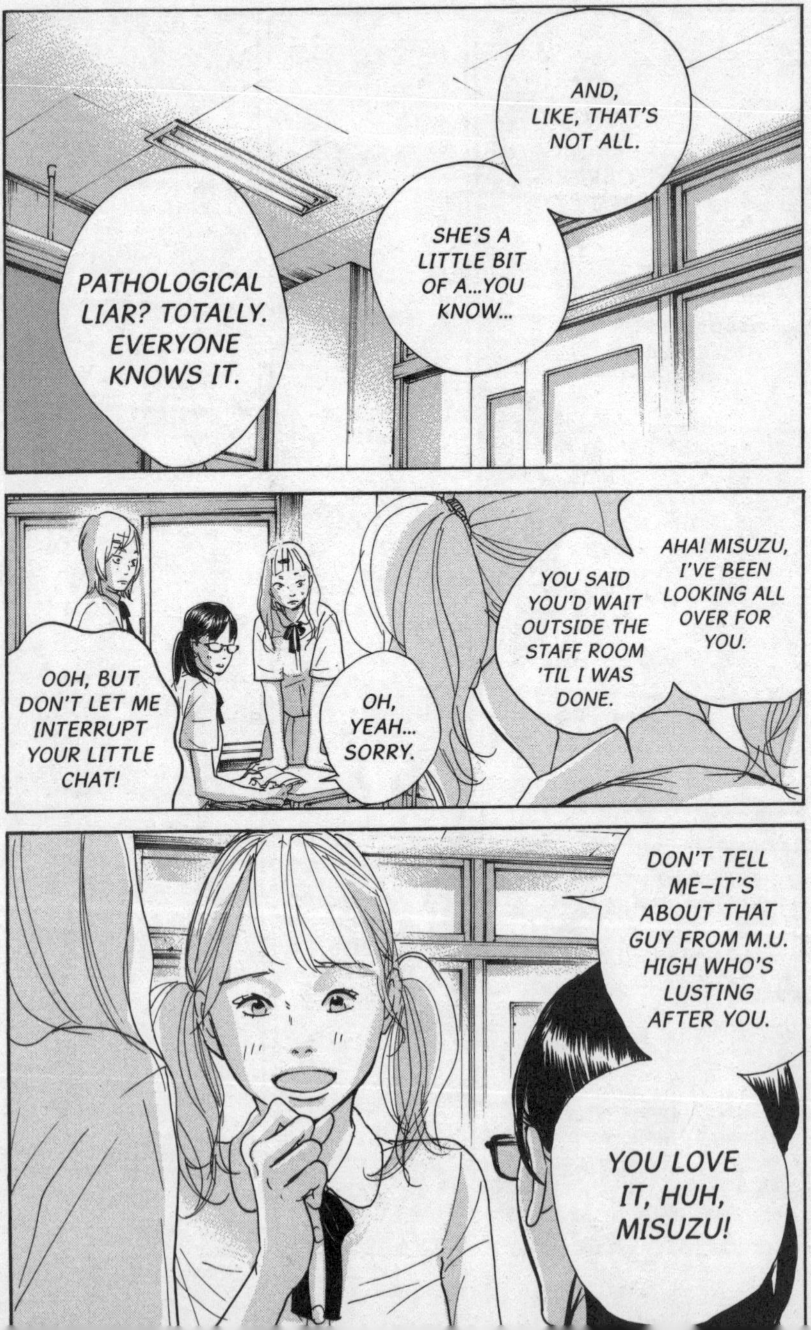
AND, LIKE, THAT'S NOT ALL.
SHE'S A LITTLE BIT OF A...YOU KNOW...
PATHOLOGICAL LIAR? TOTALLY. EVERYONE KNOWS IT.
AHA! MISUZU, I'VE BEEN LOOKING ALL OVER FOR YOU.
YOU SAID YOU'D WAIT OUTSIDE THE STAFF ROOM 'TIL I WAS DONE.
OH, YEAH... SORRY.
OOH, BUT DON'T LET ME INTERRUPT YOUR LITTLE CHAT!
DON'T TELL ME—IT'S ABOUT THAT GUY FROM M.U. HIGH WHO'S LUSTING AFTER YOU.
YOU LOVE IT, HUH, MISUZU!

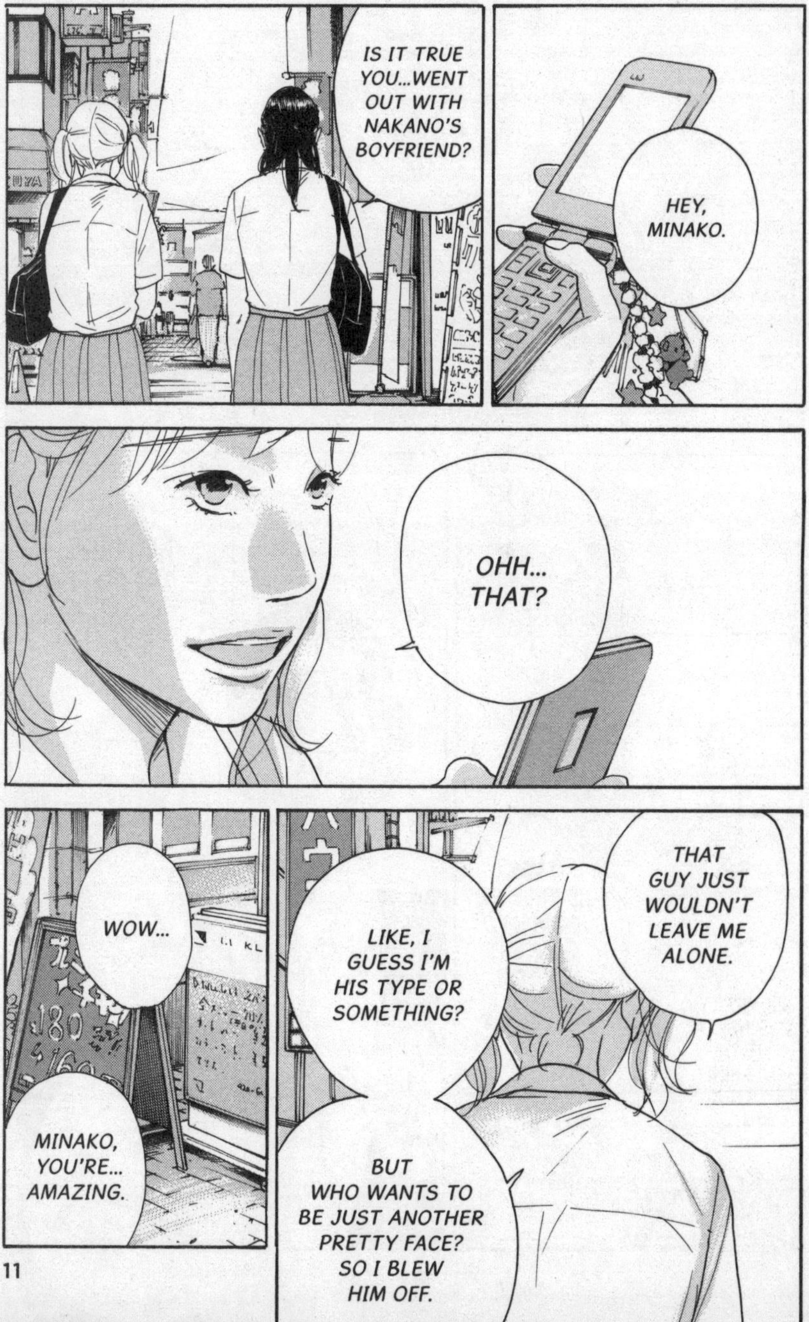
HEY, MINAKO.
IS IT TRUE YOU...WENT OUT WITH NAKANO'S BOYFRIEND?
OHH... THAT?
THAT GUY JUST WOULDN'T LEAVE ME ALONE.
LIKE, I GUESS I'M HIS TYPE OR SOMETHING?
BUT WHO WANTS TO BE JUST ANOTHER PRETTY FACE? SO I BLEW HIM OFF.
WOW...
MINAKO, YOU'RE... AMAZING.

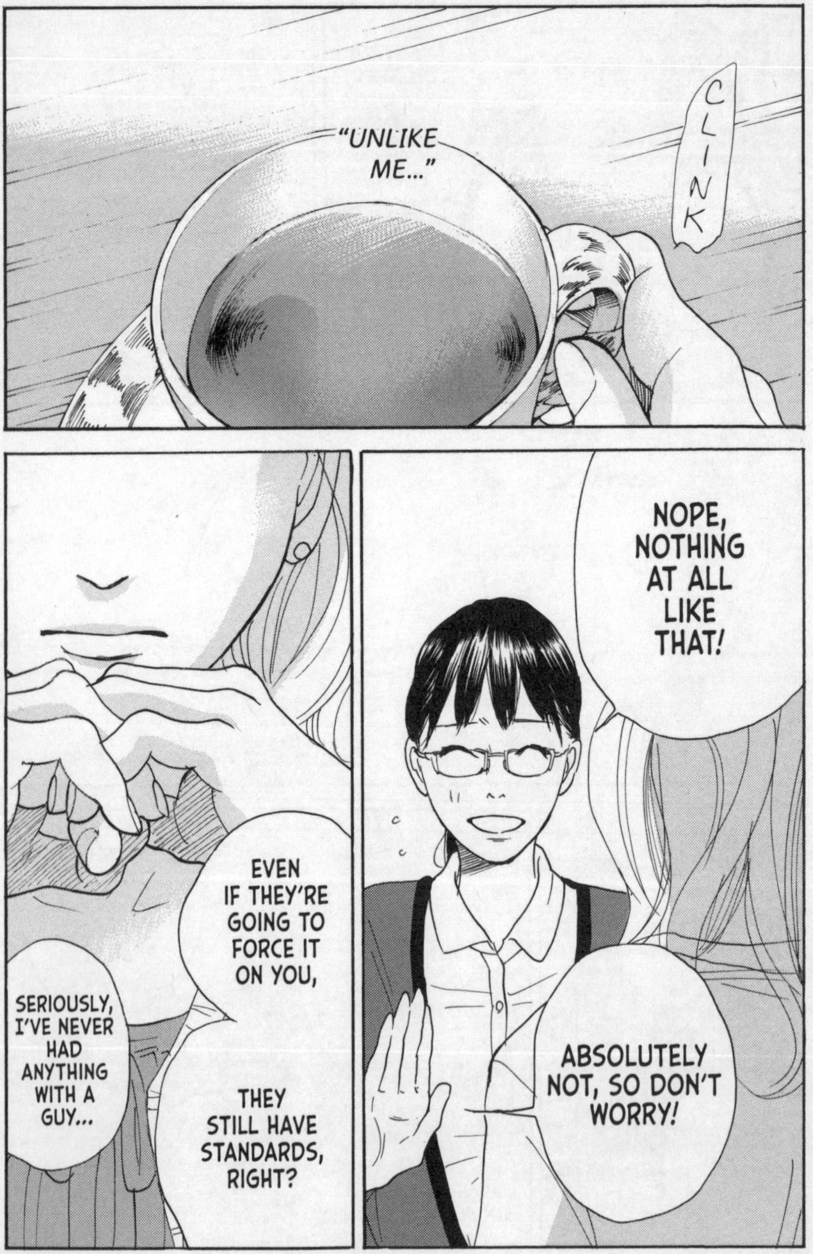
CLINK
"UNLIKE ME..."
NOPE, NOTHING AT ALL LIKE THAT!
ABSOLUTELY NOT, SO DON'T WORRY!
EVEN IF THEY'RE GOING TO FORCE IT ON YOU,
THEY STILL HAVE STANDARDS, RIGHT?
SERIOUSLY, I'VE NEVER HAD ANYTHING WITH A GUY...

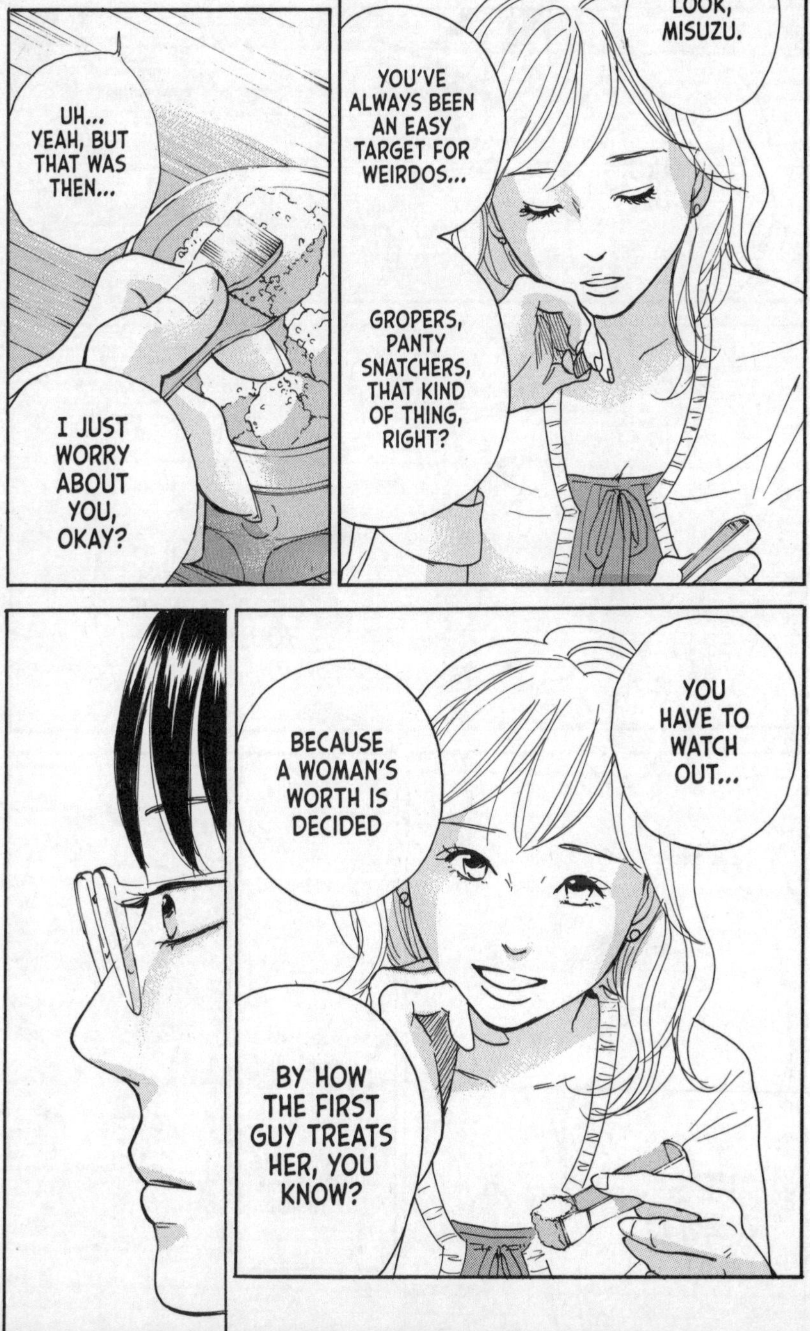
LOOK, MISUZU.
YOU'VE ALWAYS BEEN AN EASY TARGET FOR WEIRDOS...
GROPERS, PANTY SNATCHERS, THAT KIND OF THING, RIGHT?
UH... YEAH, BUT THAT WAS THEN...
I JUST WORRY ABOUT YOU, OKAY?
YOU HAVE TO WATCH OUT...
BECAUSE A WOMAN'S WORTH IS DECIDED
BY HOW THE FIRST GUY TREATS HER, YOU KNOW?

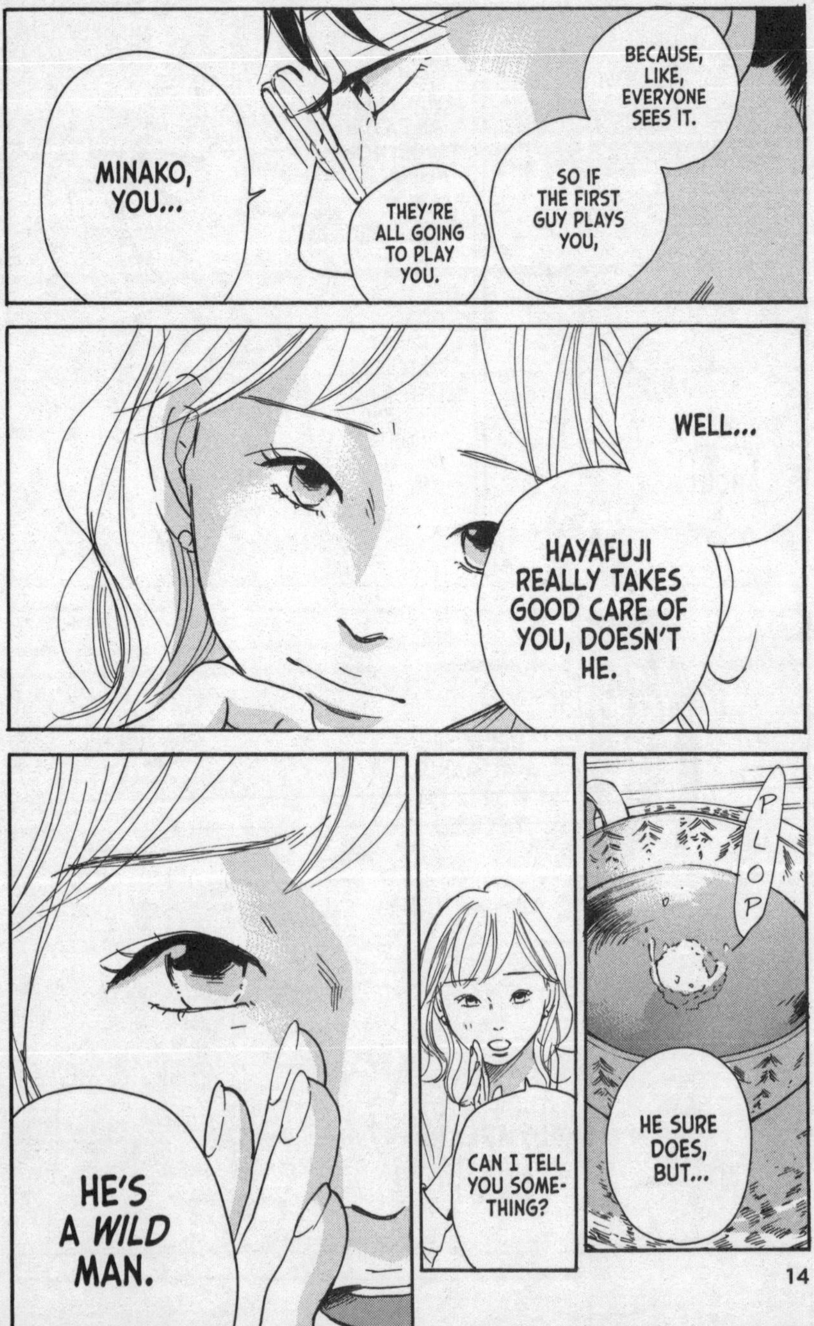
BECAUSE, LIKE, EVERYONE SEES IT.
SO IF THE FIRST GUY PLAYS YOU,
THEY'RE ALL GOING TO PLAY YOU.
MINAKO, YOU...
WELL...
HAYAFUJI REALLY TAKES GOOD CARE OF YOU, DOESN'T HE.
PLOP
HE SURE DOES, BUT...
CAN I TELL YOU SOME-THING?
HE'S A *WILD* MAN.

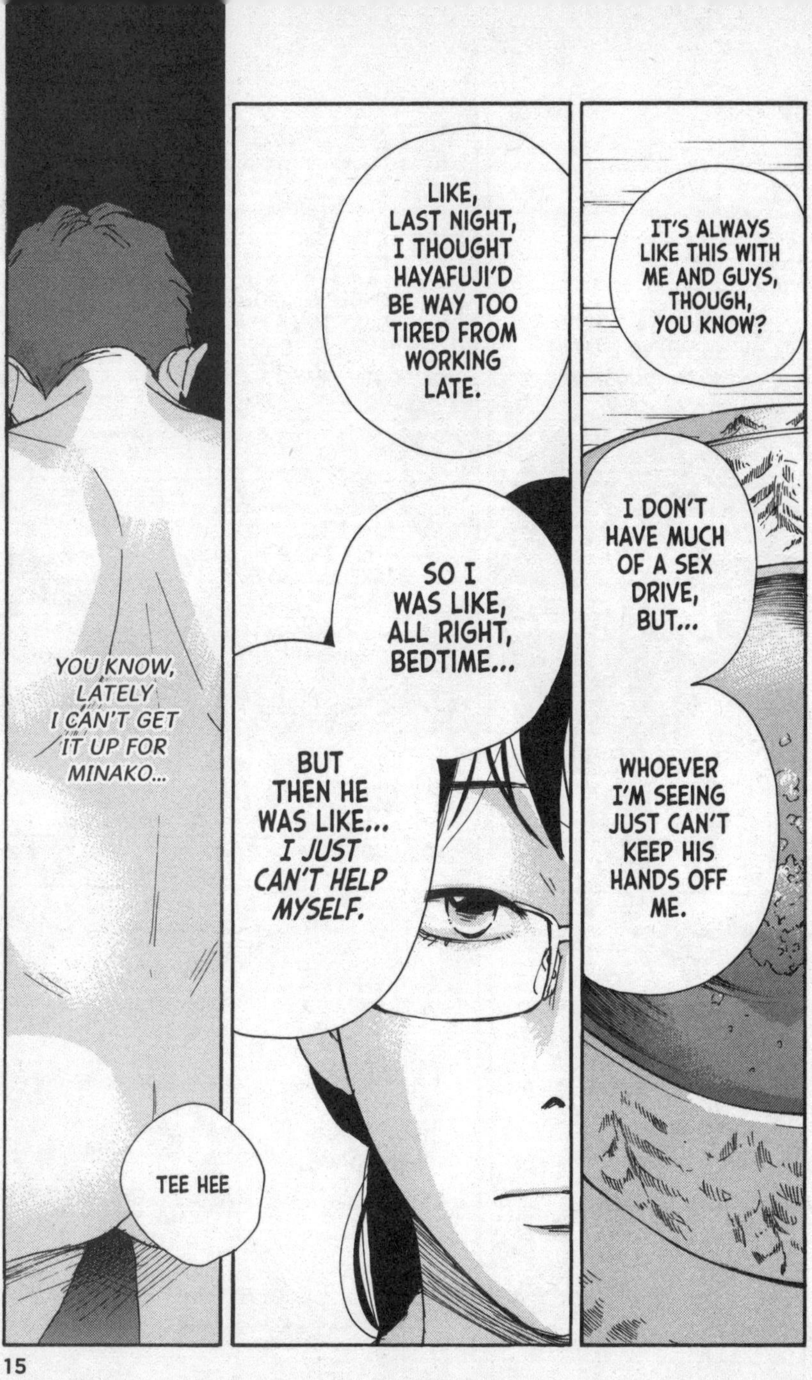
IT'S ALWAYS LIKE THIS WITH ME AND GUYS, THOUGH, YOU KNOW?
I DON'T HAVE MUCH OF A SEX DRIVE, BUT...
WHOEVER I'M SEEING JUST CAN'T KEEP HIS HANDS OFF ME.
LIKE, LAST NIGHT, I THOUGHT HAYAFUJI'D BE WAY TOO TIRED FROM WORKING LATE.
SO I WAS LIKE, ALL RIGHT, BEDTIME...
BUT THEN HE WAS LIKE... *I JUST CAN'T HELP MYSELF.*
YOU KNOW, LATELY I CAN'T GET IT UP FOR MINAKO...
TEE HEE

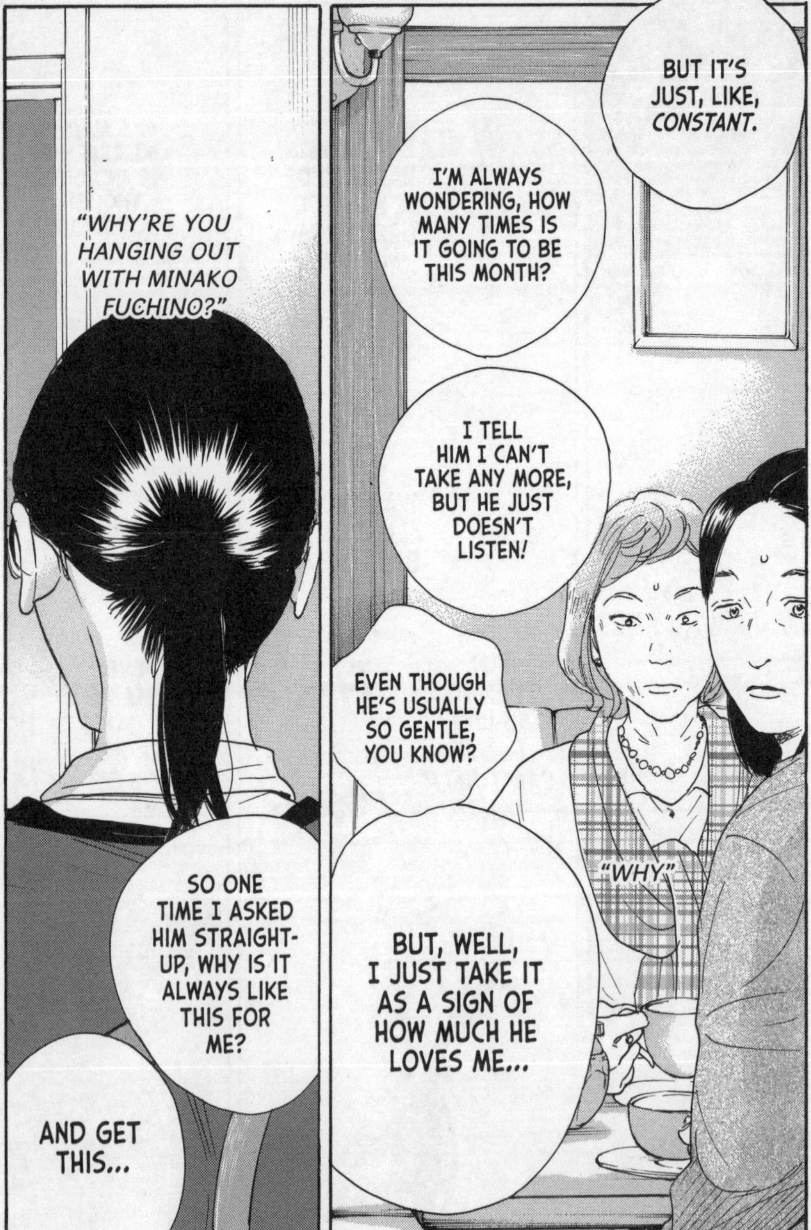
BUT IT'S JUST, LIKE, *CONSTANT.*
I'M ALWAYS WONDERING, HOW MANY TIMES IS IT GOING TO BE THIS MONTH?
I TELL HIM I CAN'T TAKE ANY MORE, BUT HE JUST DOESN'T LISTEN!
EVEN THOUGH HE'S USUALLY SO GENTLE, YOU KNOW?
"WHY"
BUT, WELL, I JUST TAKE IT AS A SIGN OF HOW MUCH HE LOVES ME...
"WHY'RE YOU HANGING OUT WITH MINAKO FUCHINO?"
SO ONE TIME I ASKED HIM STRAIGHT-UP, WHY IS IT ALWAYS LIKE THIS FOR ME?
AND GET THIS...

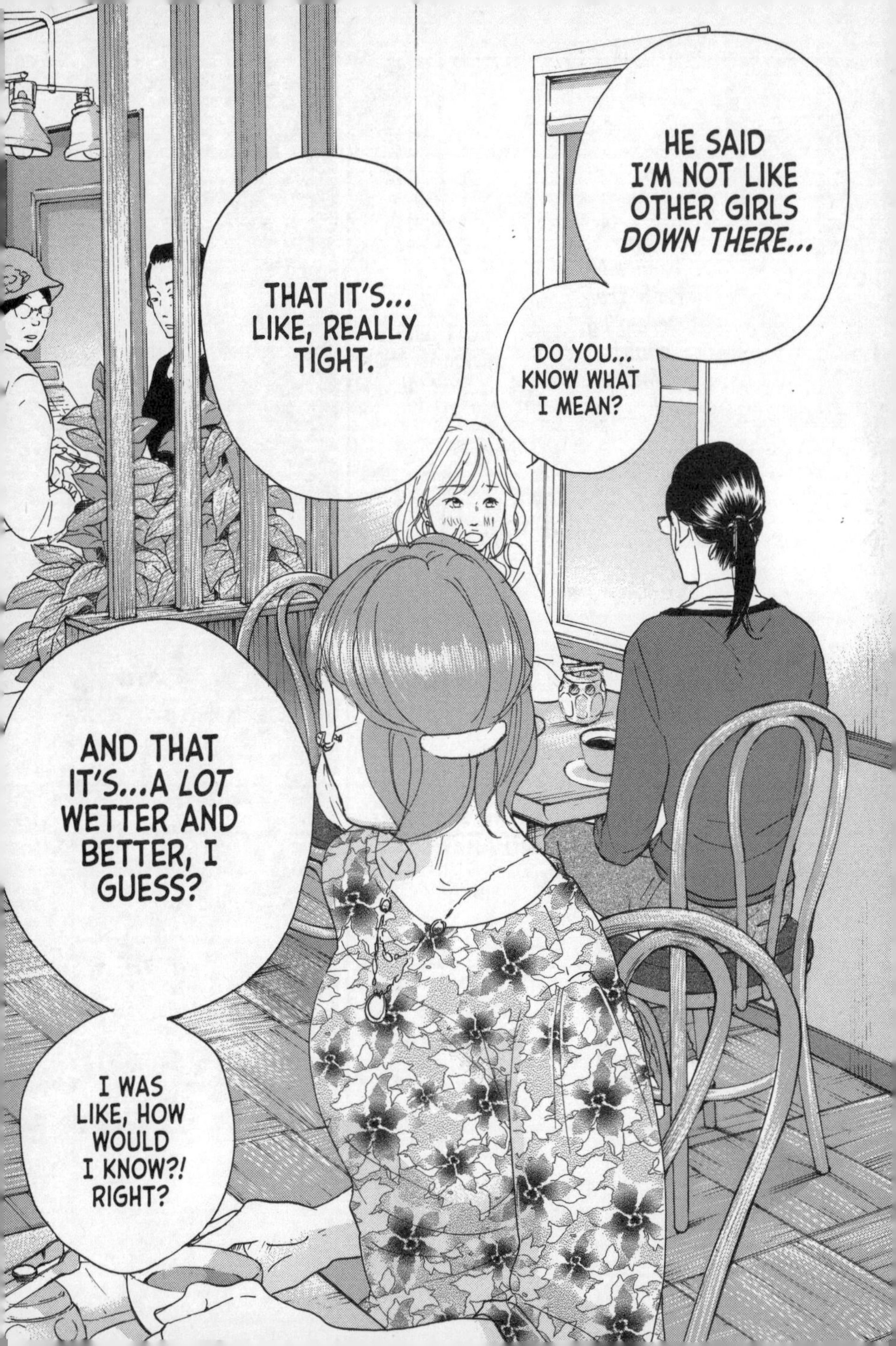
HE SAID I'M NOT LIKE OTHER GIRLS *DOWN THERE...*
DO YOU... KNOW WHAT I MEAN?
THAT IT'S... LIKE, REALLY TIGHT.
AND THAT IT'S...A *LOT* WETTER AND BETTER, I GUESS?
I WAS LIKE, HOW WOULD I KNOW?! RIGHT?

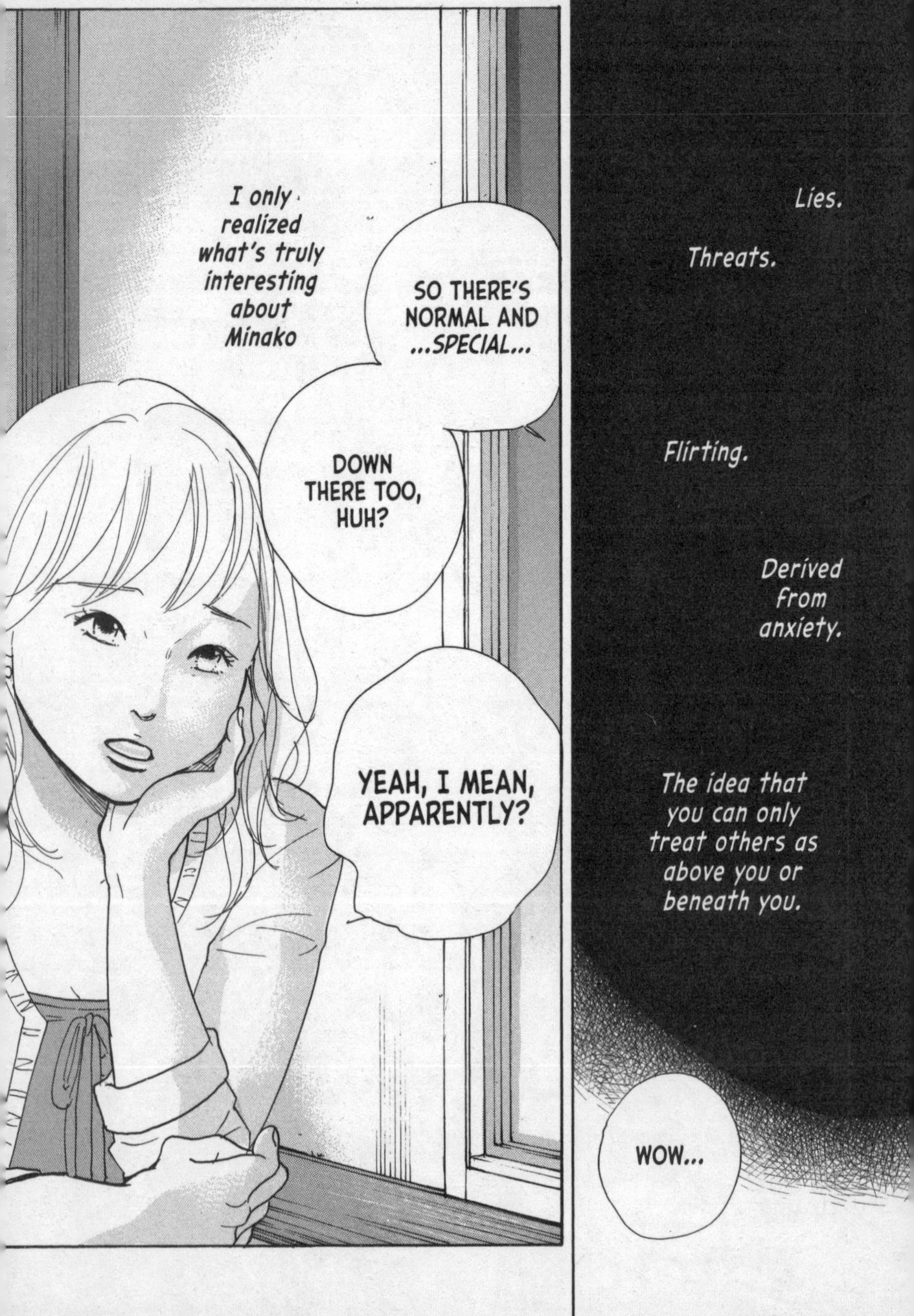
Lies.
Threats.
Flirting.
Derived from anxiety.
The idea that you can only treat others as above you or beneath you.
WOW...
SO THERE'S NORMAL AND ...SPECIAL...
I only realized what's truly interesting about Minako
DOWN THERE TOO, HUH?
YEAH, I MEAN, APPARENTLY?

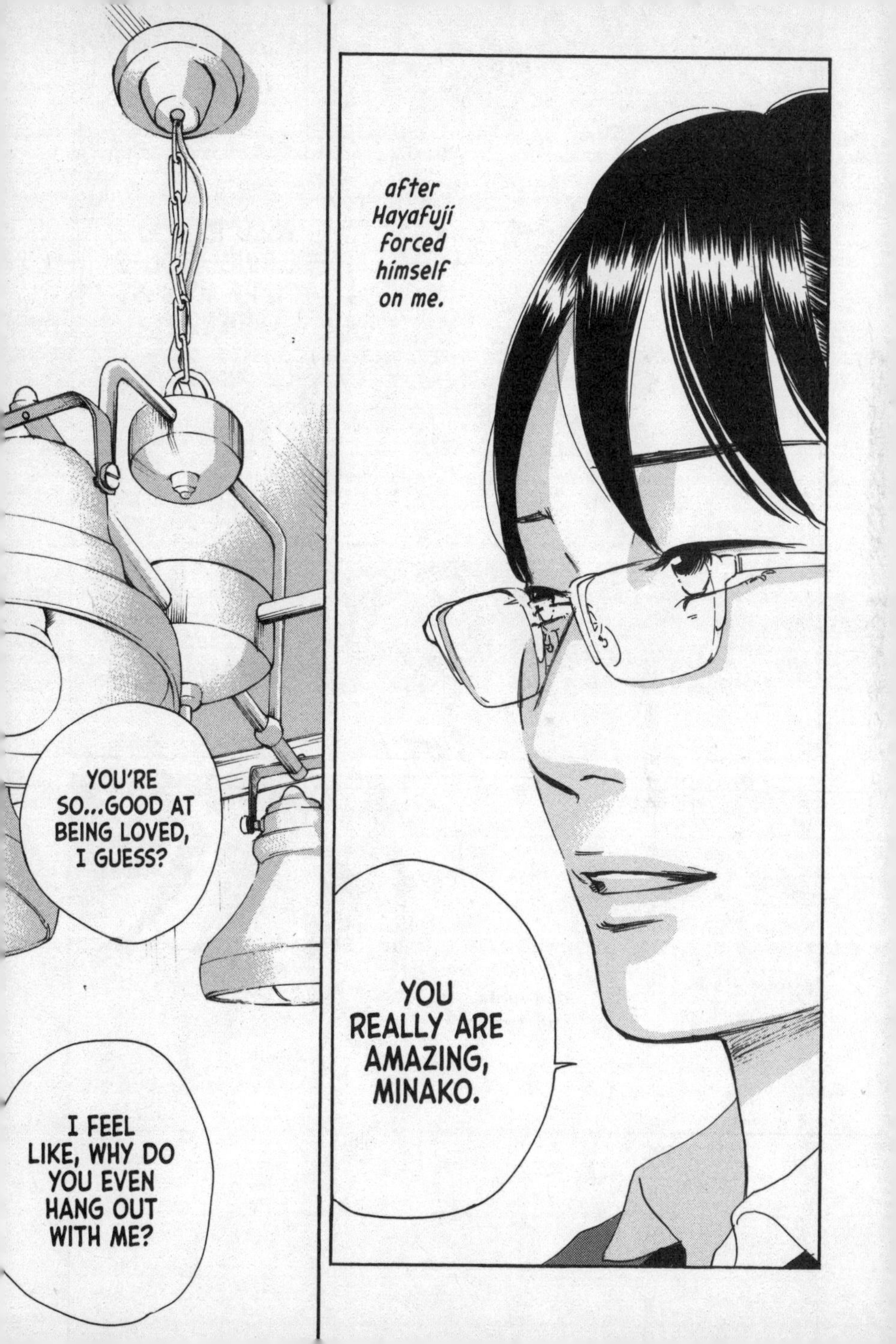
after Hayafuji forced himself on me.
YOU REALLY ARE AMAZING, MINAKO.
YOU'RE SO...GOOD AT BEING LOVED, I GUESS?
I FEEL LIKE, WHY DO YOU EVEN HANG OUT WITH ME?

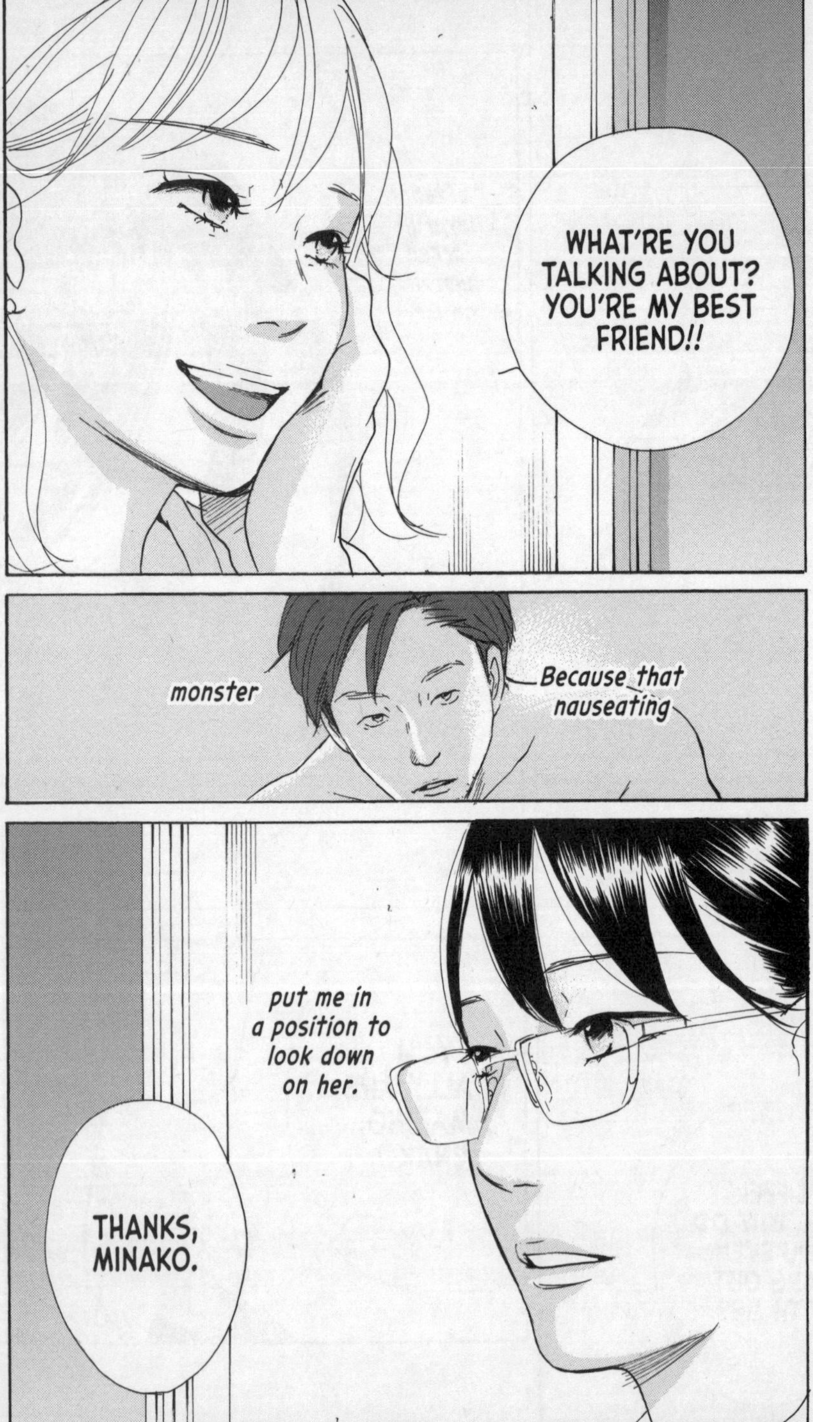
WHAT'RE YOU TALKING ABOUT? YOU'RE MY BEST FRIEND!!
Because that nauseating
monster
put me in a position to look down on her.
THANKS, MINAKO.

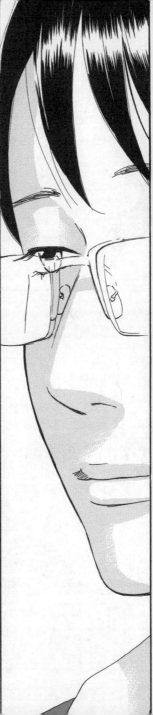

Poor
Minako.

Poor
thing.

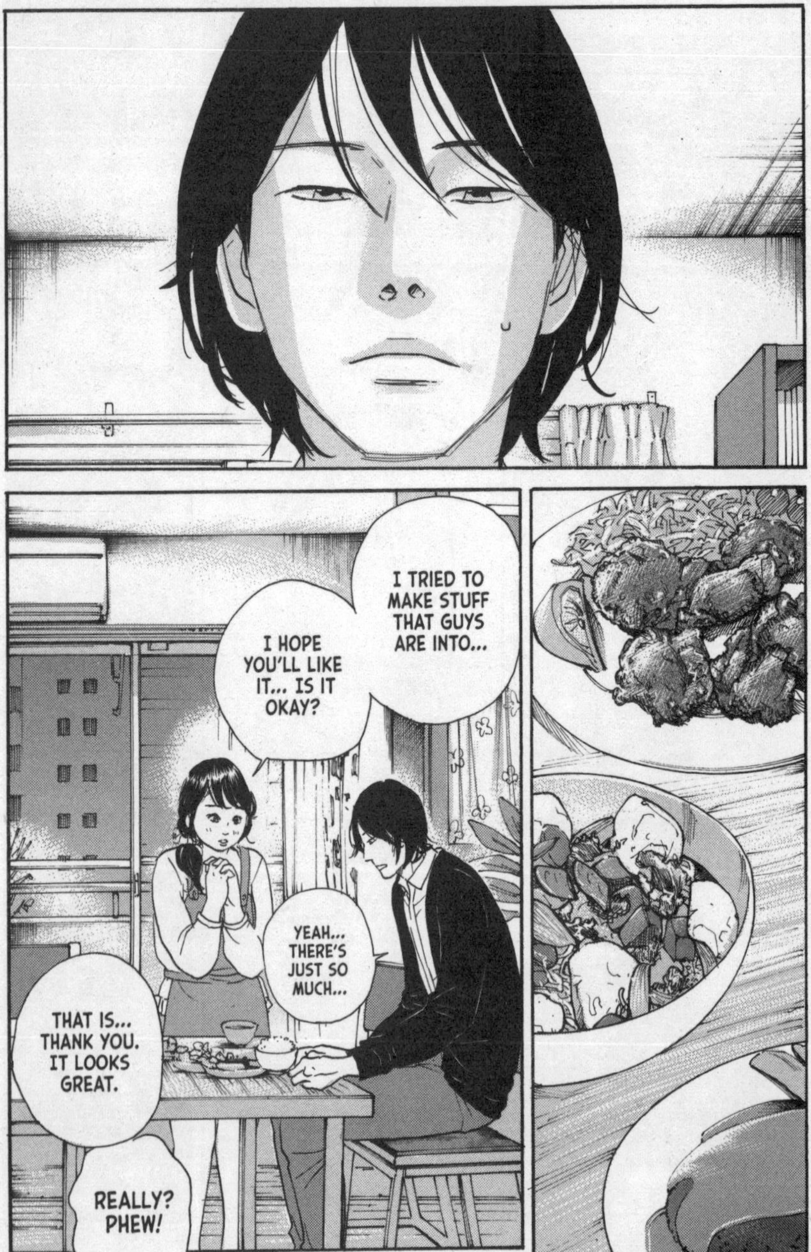
I TRIED TO MAKE STUFF THAT GUYS ARE INTO...
I HOPE YOU'LL LIKE IT... IS IT OKAY?
YEAH... THERE'S JUST SO MUCH...
THAT IS... THANK YOU. IT LOOKS GREAT.
REALLY? PHEW!

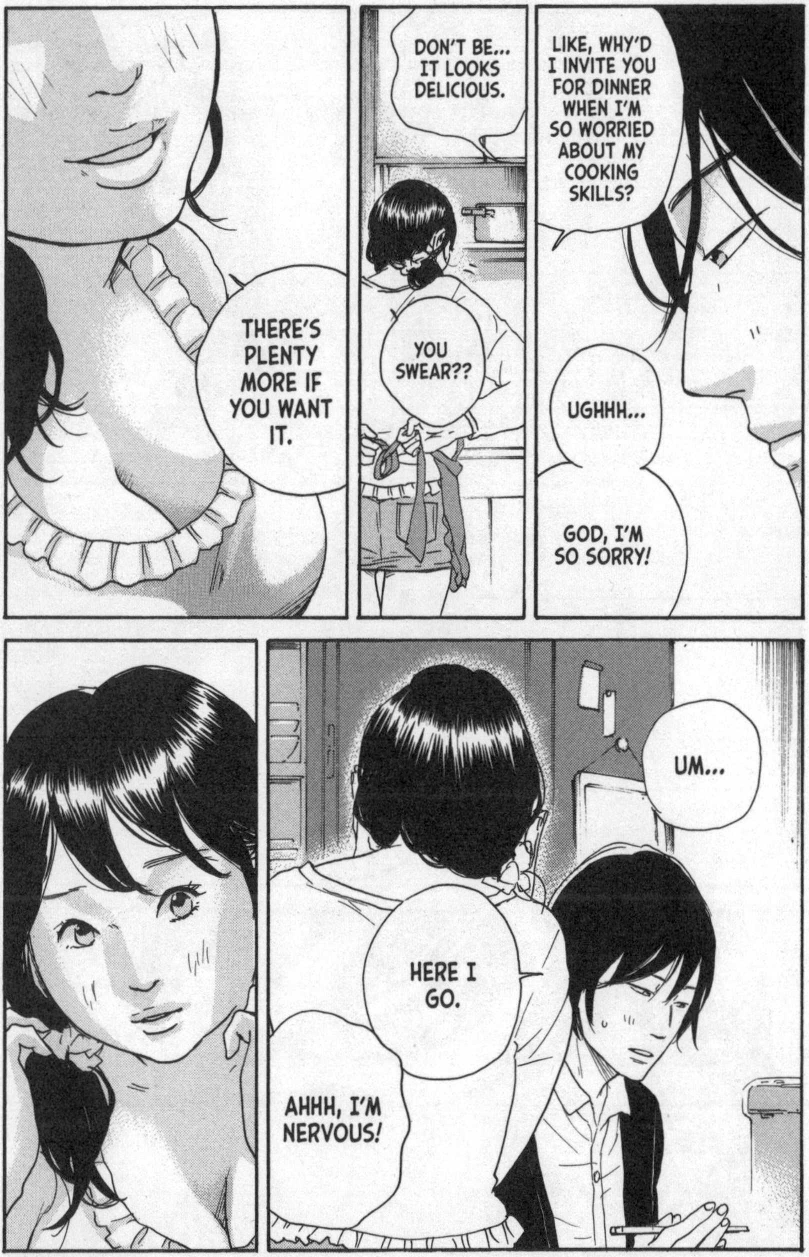
LIKE, WHY'D I INVITE YOU FOR DINNER WHEN I'M SO WORRIED ABOUT MY COOKING SKILLS?
UGHHH...
GOD, I'M SO SORRY!
DON'T BE... IT LOOKS DELICIOUS.
YOU SWEAR??
THERE'S PLENTY MORE IF YOU WANT IT.
UM...
HERE I GO.
AHHH, I'M NERVOUS!

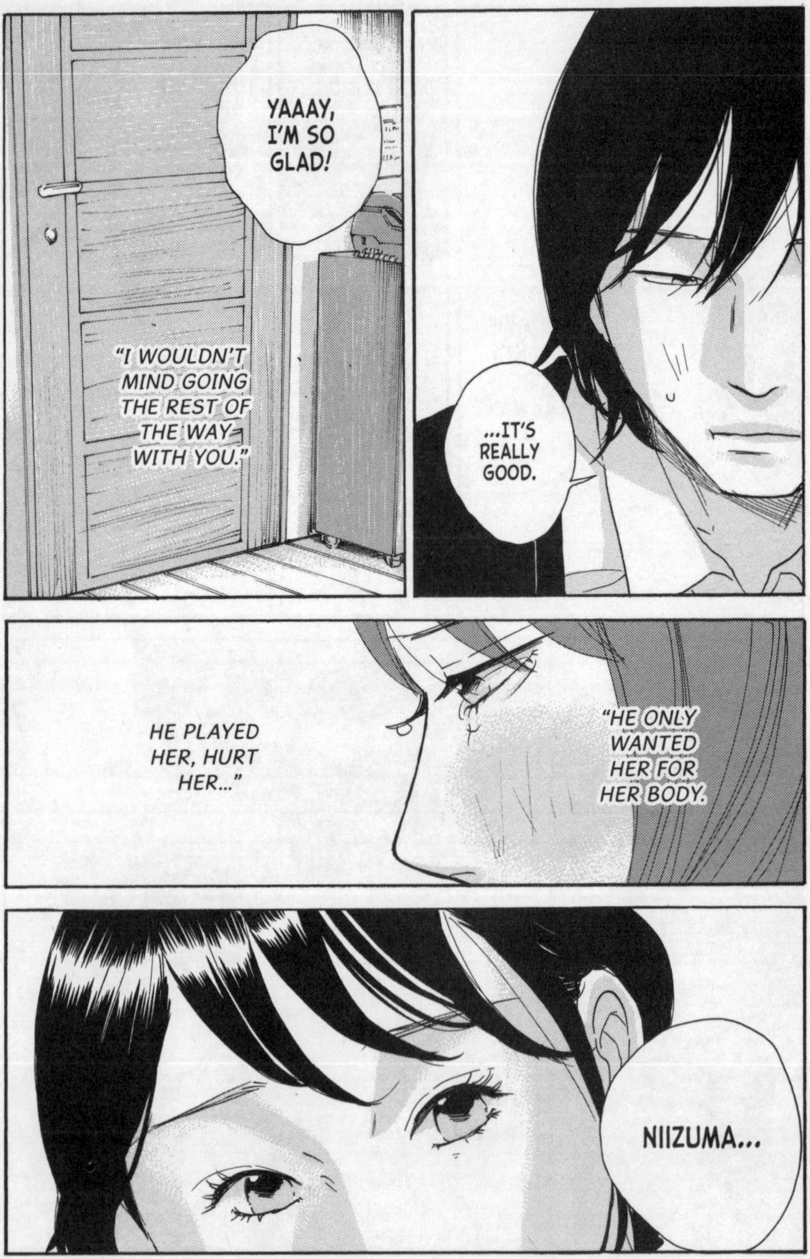
...IT'S REALLY GOOD.
YAAAY, I'M SO GLAD!
"I WOULDN'T MIND GOING THE REST OF THE WAY WITH YOU."
"HE ONLY WANTED HER FOR HER BODY.
HE PLAYED HER, HURT HER..."
NIIZUMA...

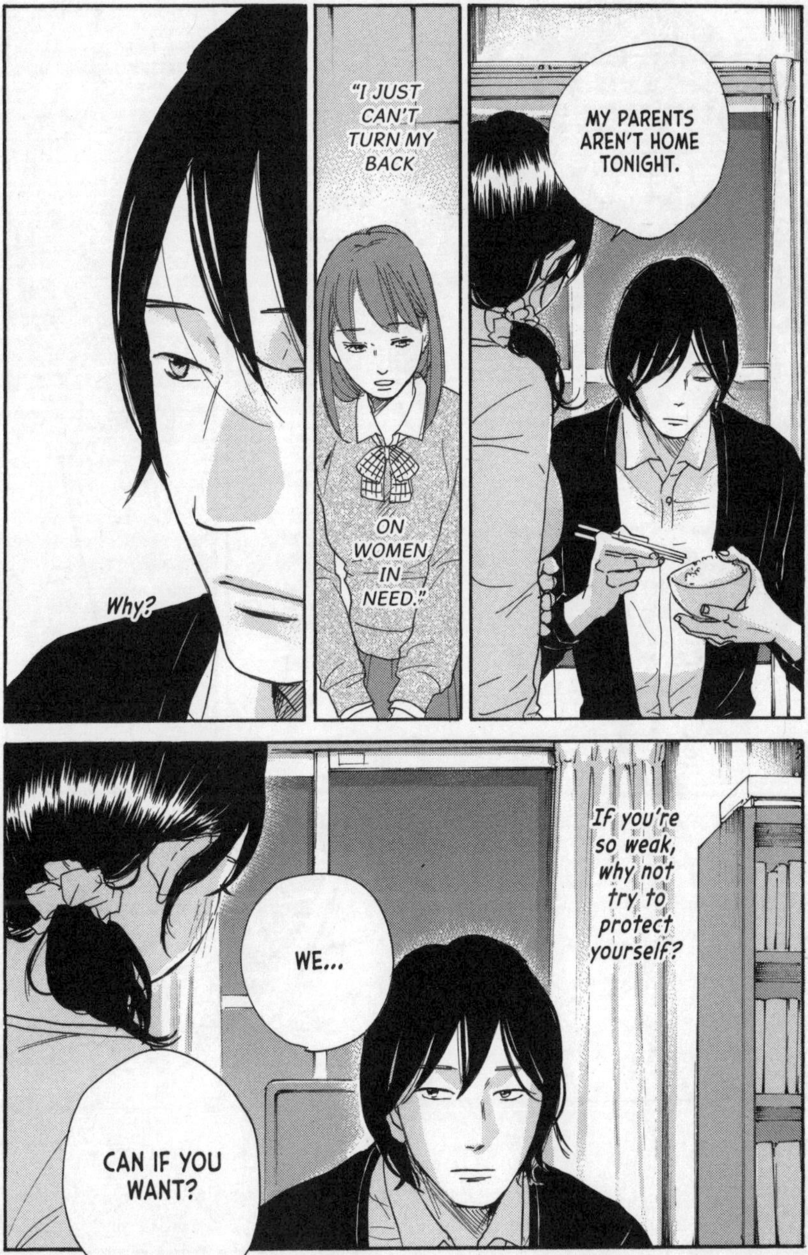
MY PARENTS AREN'T HOME TONIGHT.
"I JUST CAN'T TURN MY BACK
ON WOMEN IN NEED."
Why?
If you're so weak, why not try to protect yourself?
WE...
CAN IF YOU WANT?

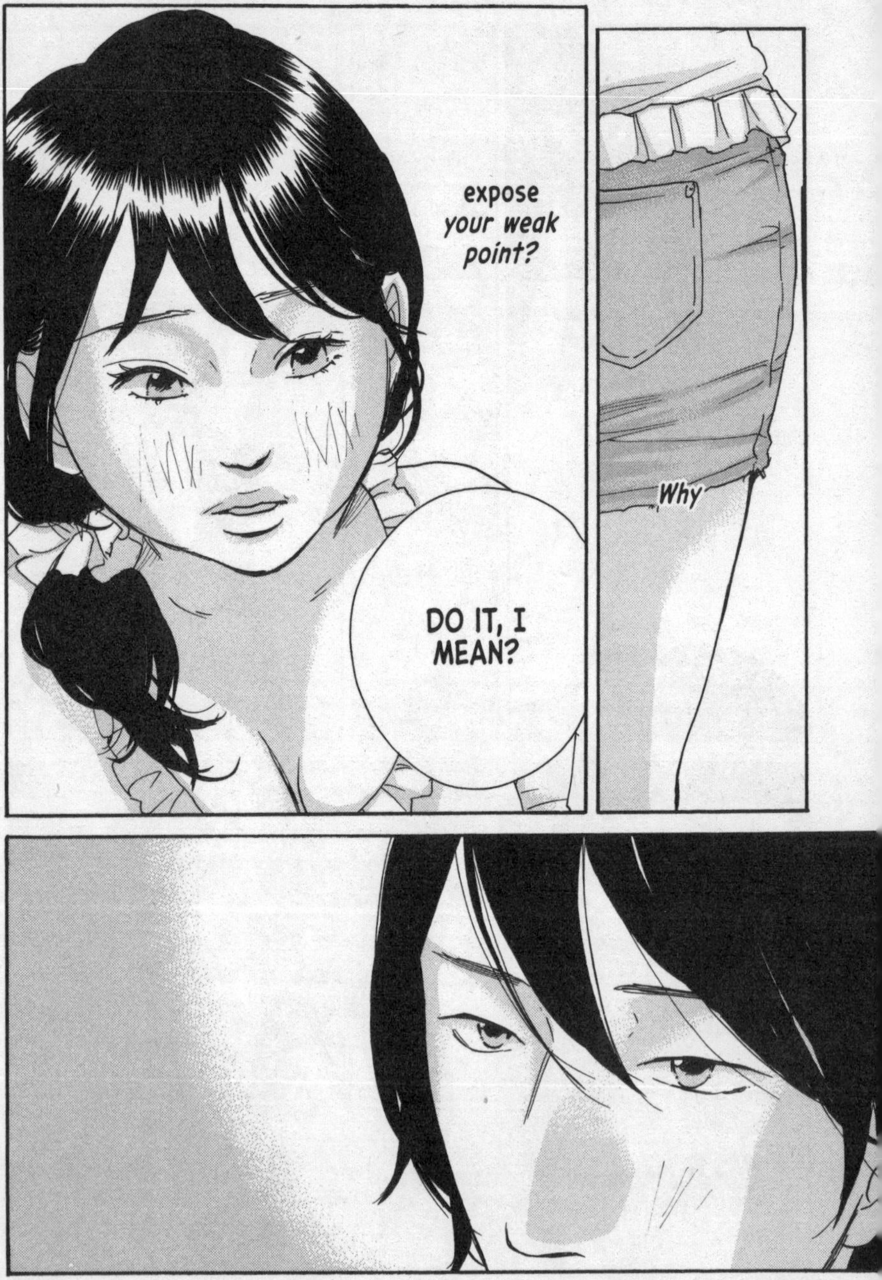
Why
expose
your weak
point?
DO IT, I
MEAN?

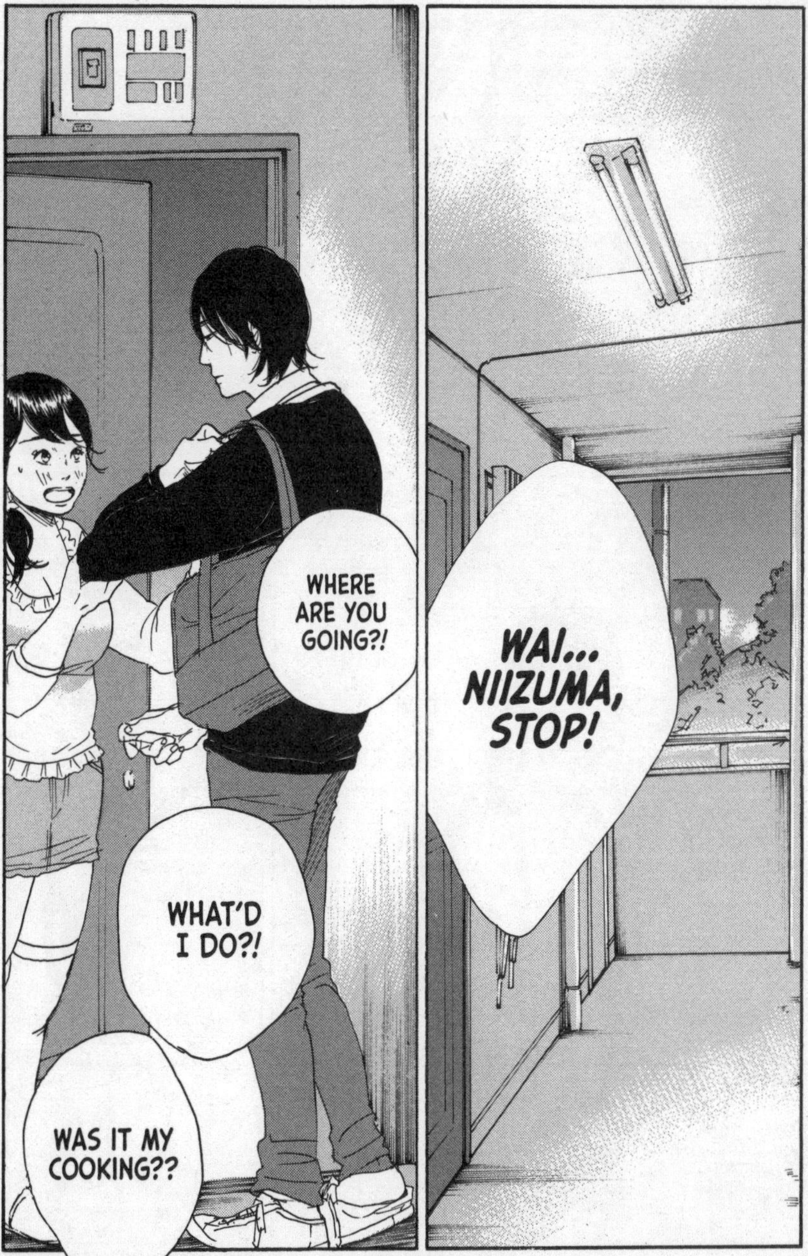
WAI... NIIZUMA, STOP!
WHERE ARE YOU GOING?!
WHAT'D I DO?!
WAS IT MY COOKING??

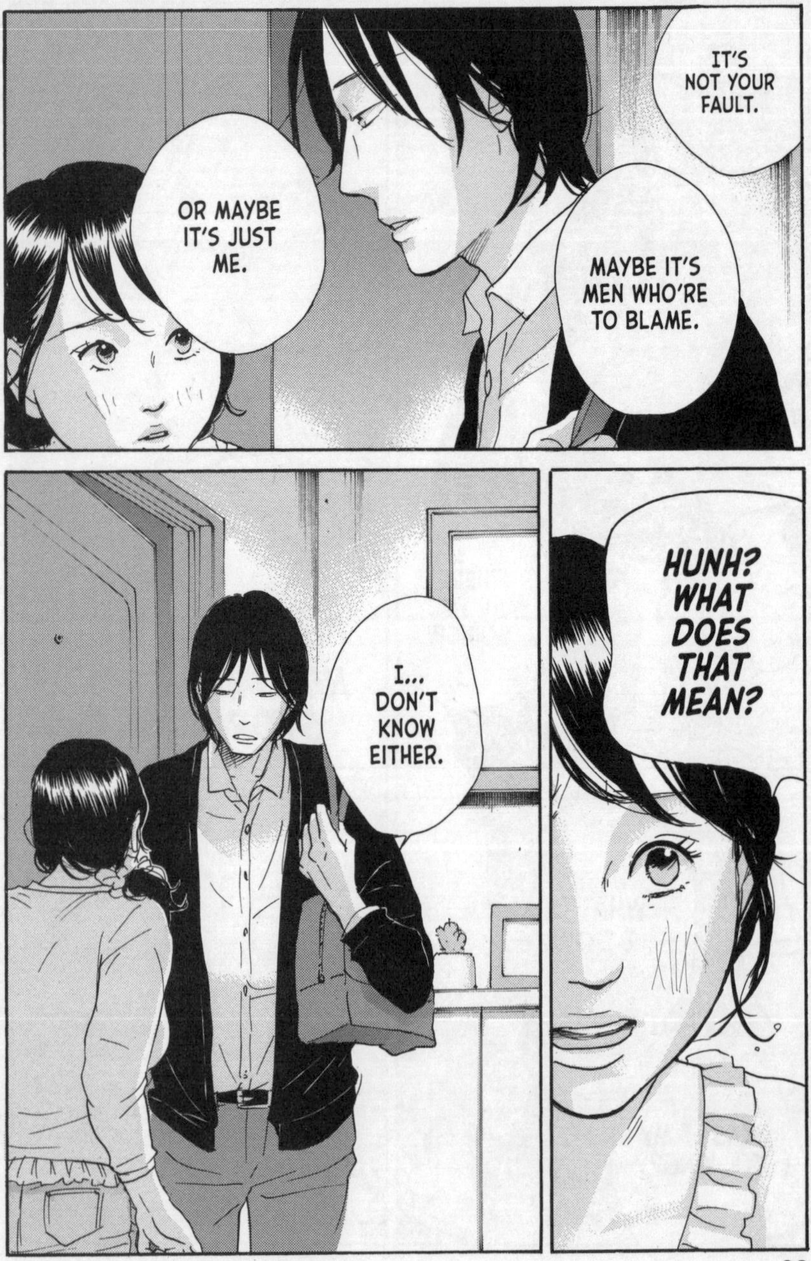
IT'S NOT YOUR FAULT.
MAYBE IT'S MEN WHO'RE TO BLAME.
OR MAYBE IT'S JUST ME.
HUNH? WHAT DOES THAT MEAN?
I... DON'T KNOW EITHER.

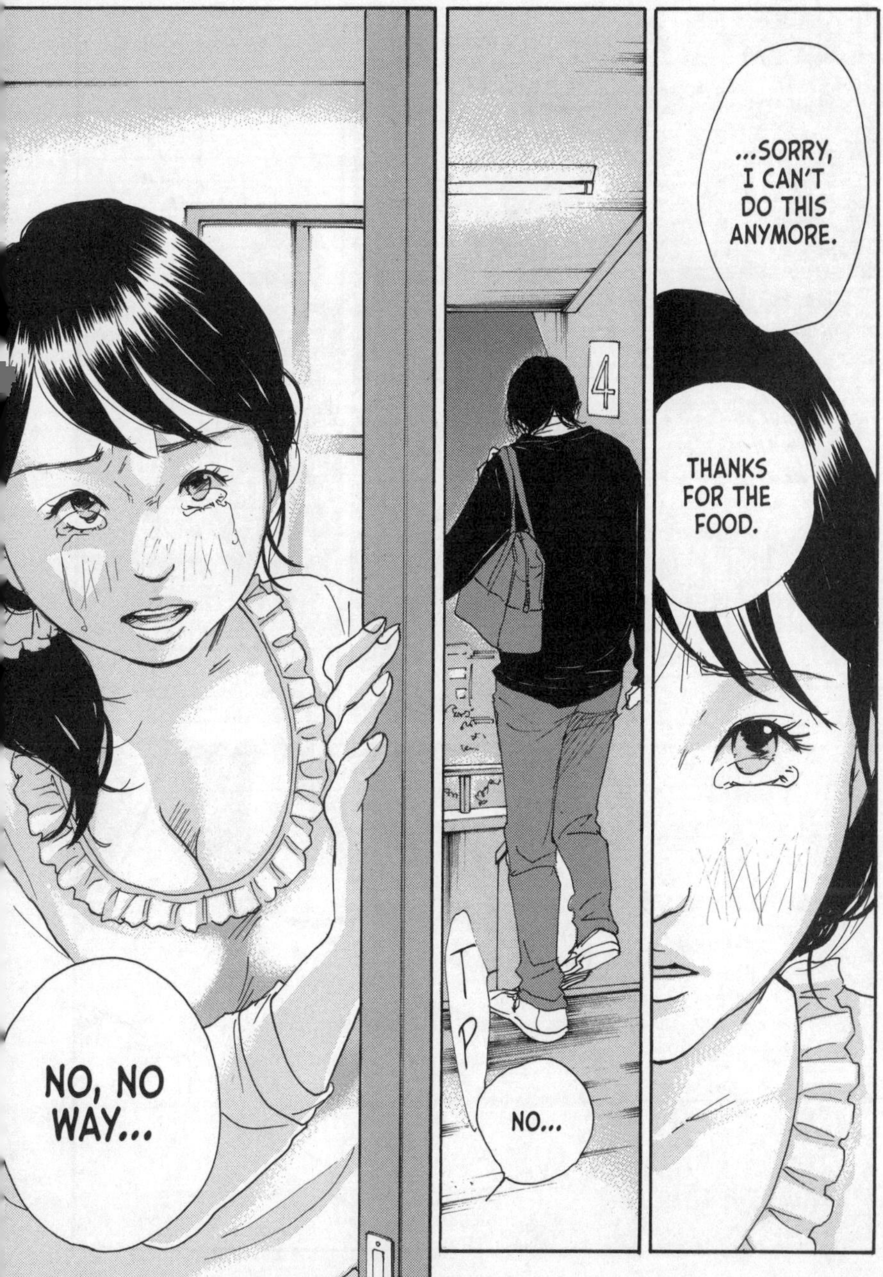
...SORRY, I CAN'T DO THIS ANYMORE.
THANKS FOR THE FOOD.
TP
NO...
NO, NO WAY...

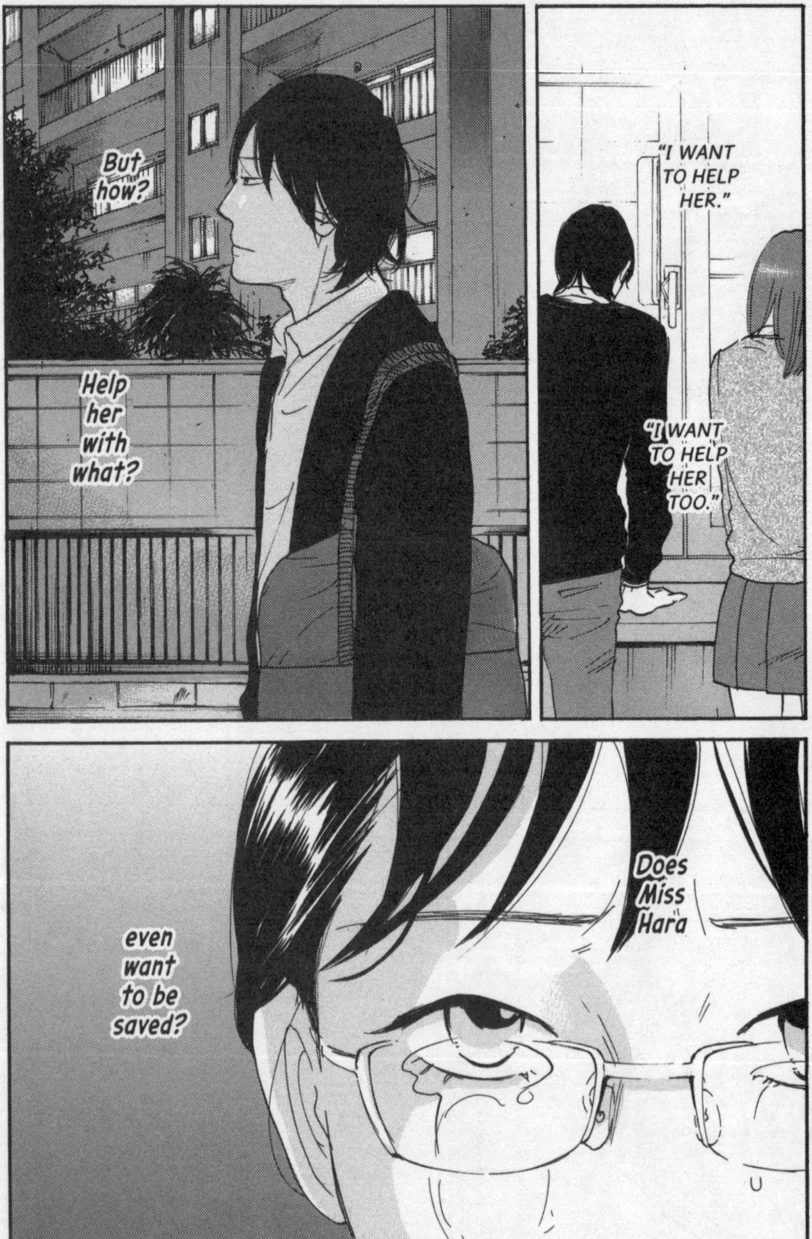
"I WANT TO HELP HER."
"I WANT TO HELP HER TOO."
But how?
Help her with what?
Does Miss Hara
even want to be saved?

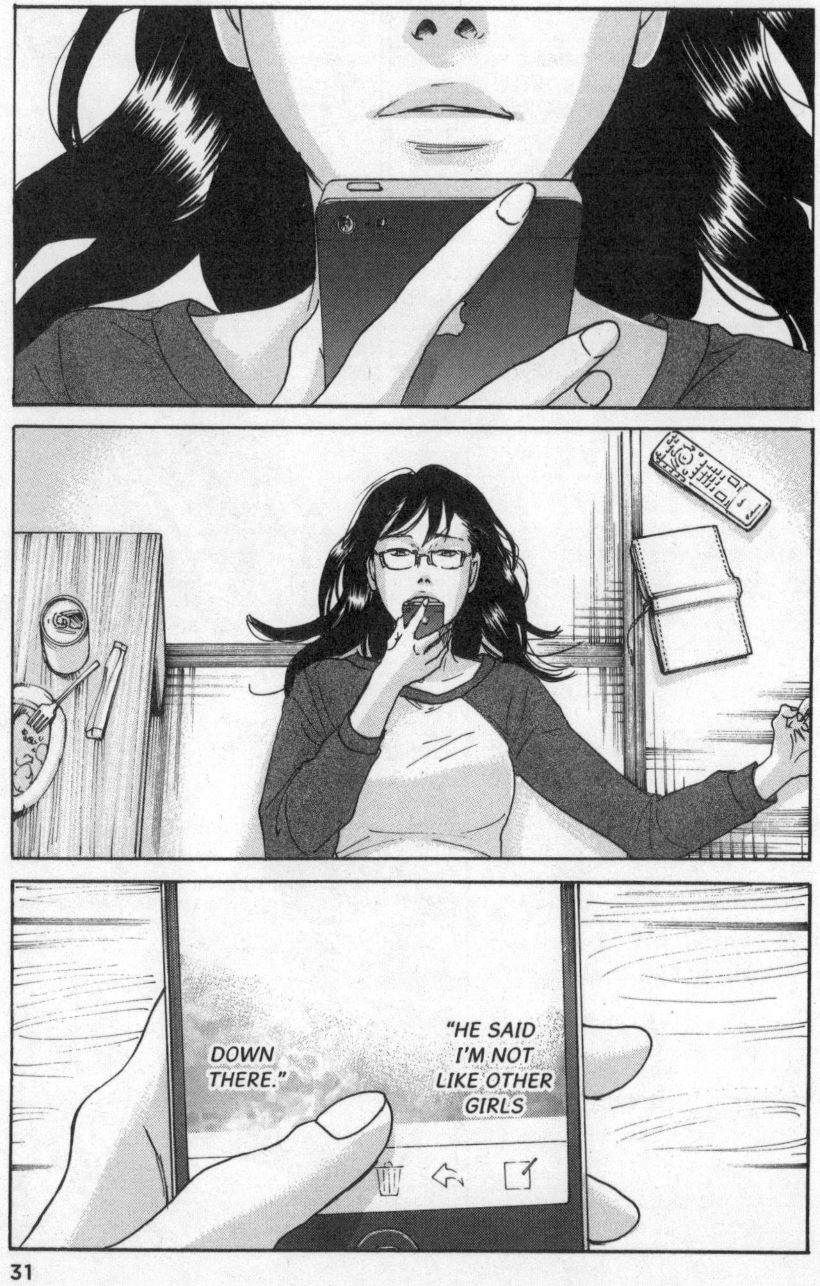
"HE SAID I'M NOT LIKE OTHER GIRLS
DOWN THERE."

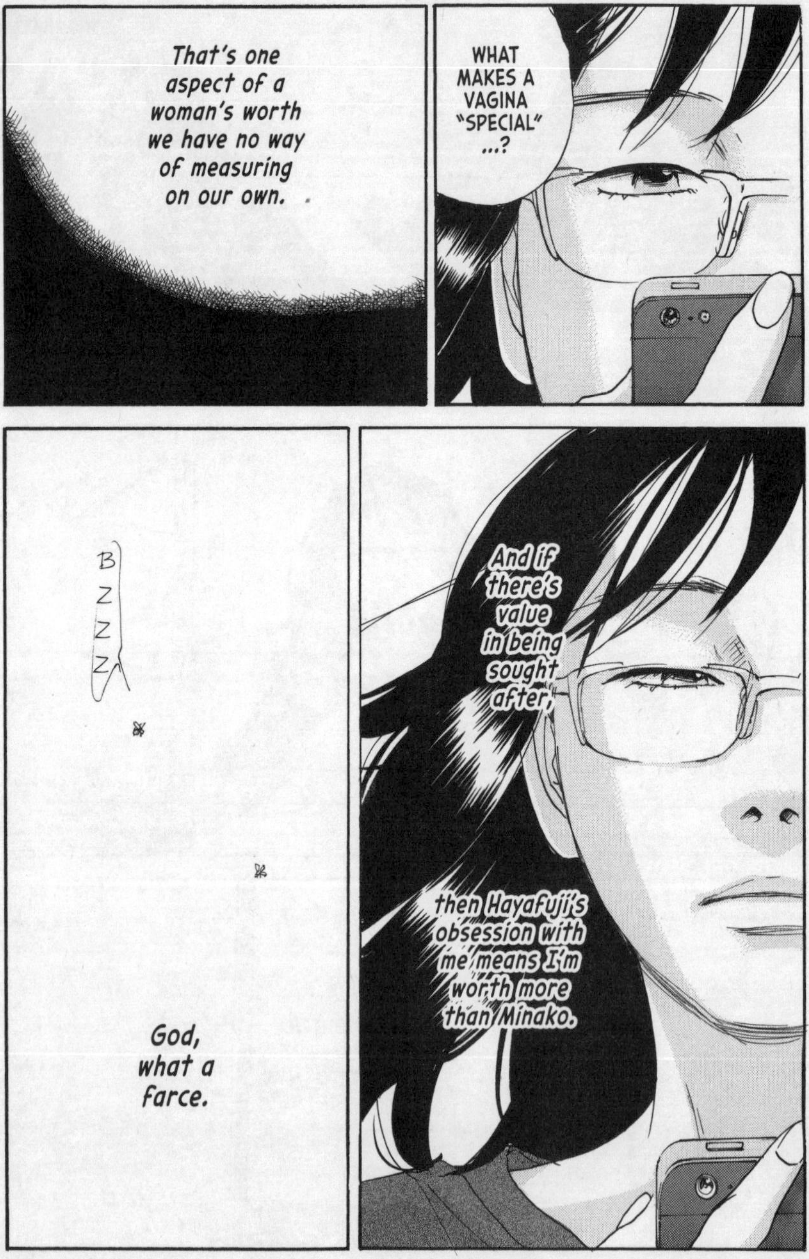
WHAT MAKES A VAGINA "SPECIAL" ...?
That's one aspect of a woman's worth we have no way of measuring on our own.
And if there's value in being sought after,
then Hayafuji's obsession with me means I'm worth more than Minako.
BZZZ
God, what a farce.

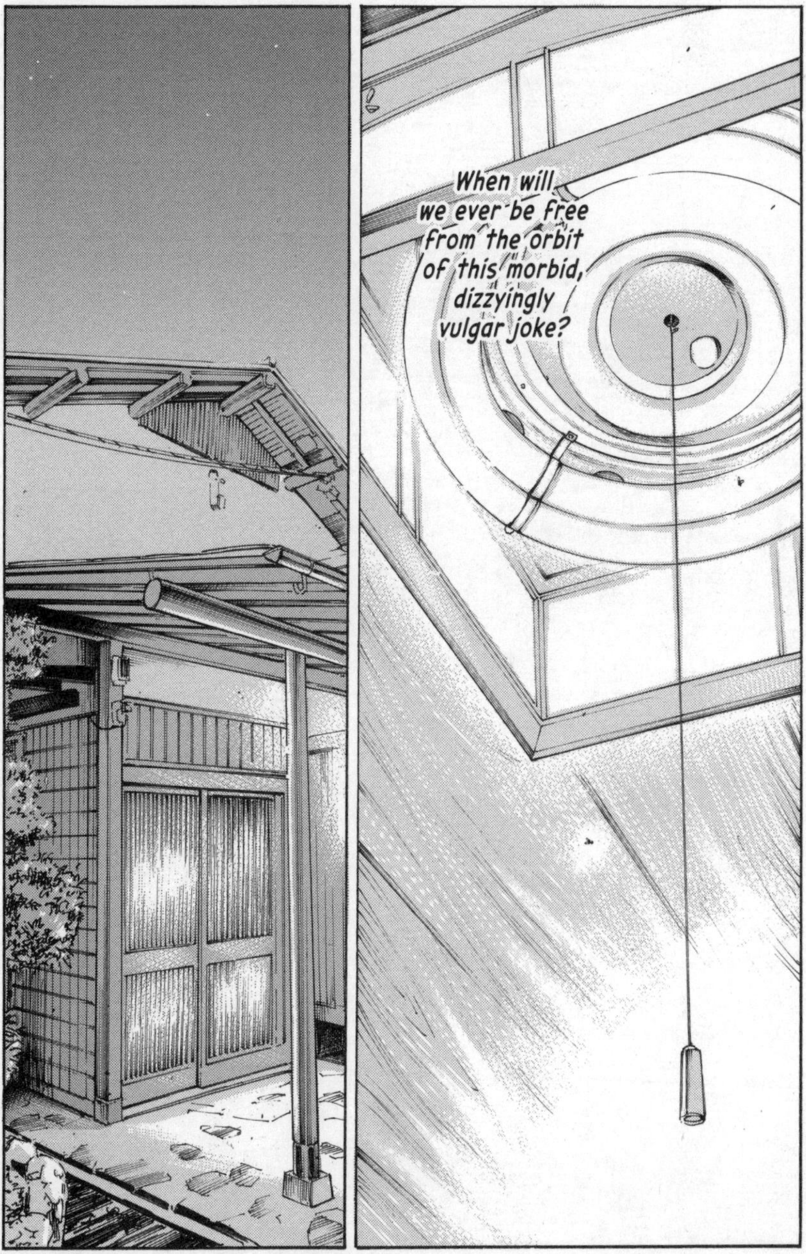
When will we ever be free from the orbit of this morbid, dizzyingly vulgar joke?

END

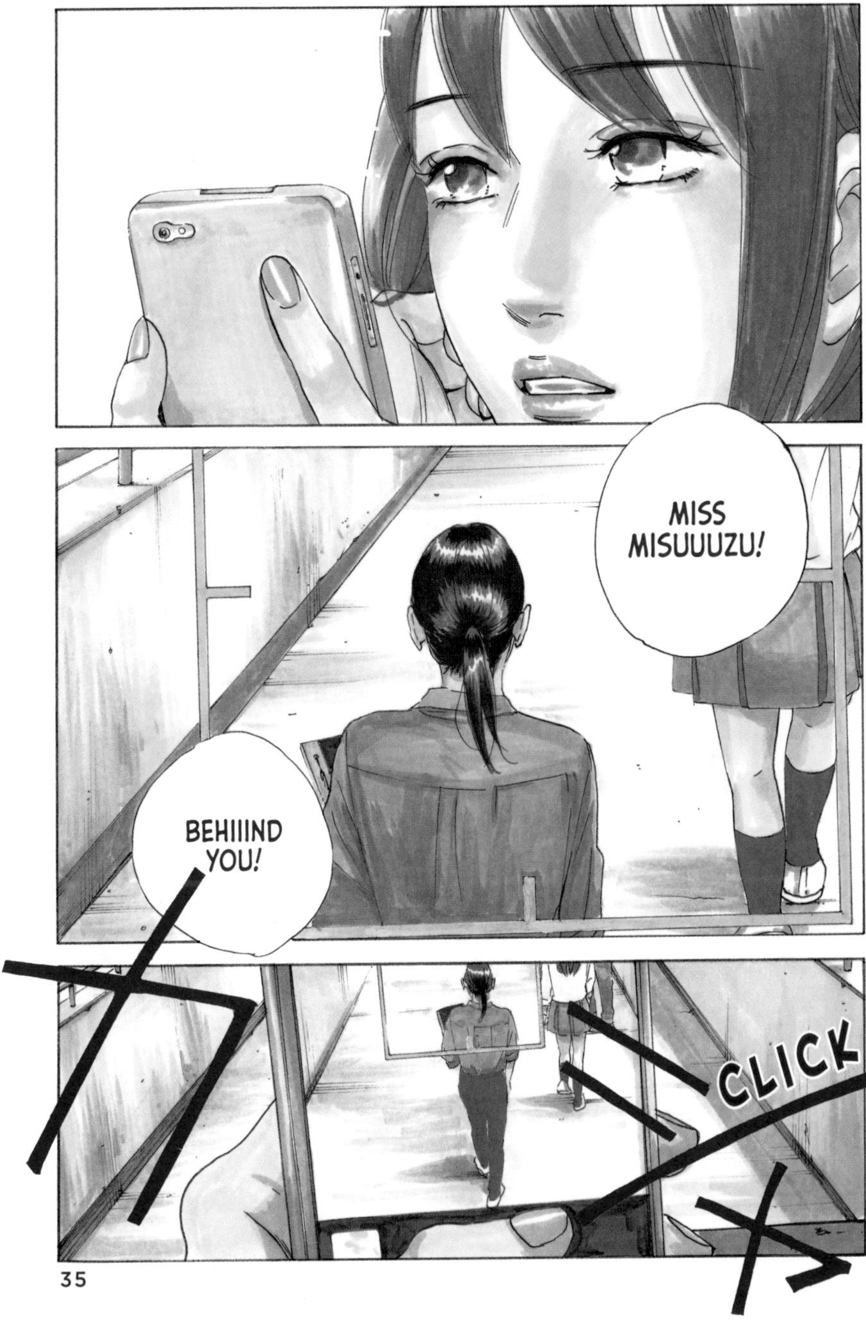
MISS MISUUUZU!
BEHIIIND YOU!
CLICK

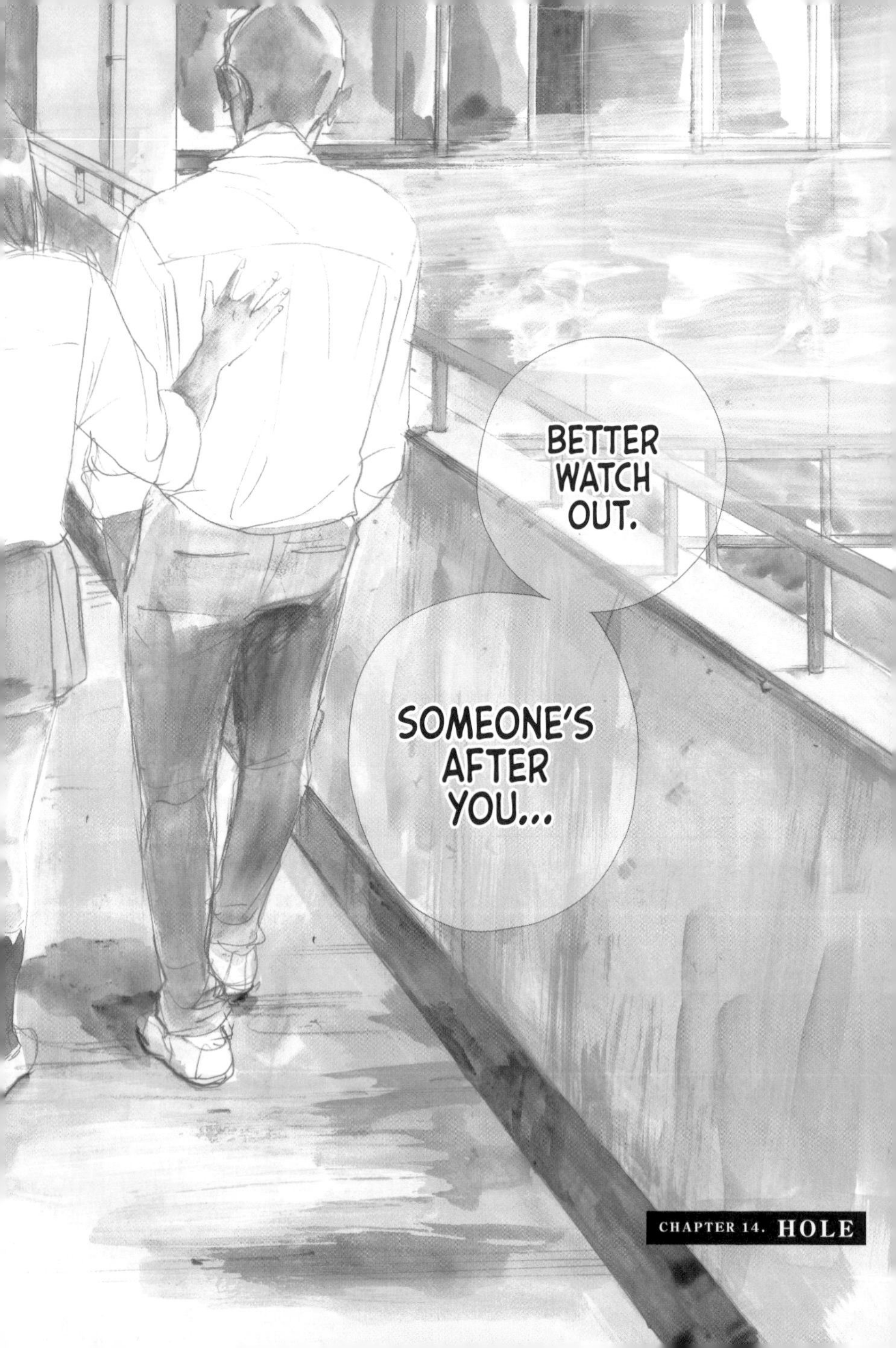
BETTER WATCH OUT.
SOMEONE'S AFTER YOU...

CHAPTER 14. HOLE

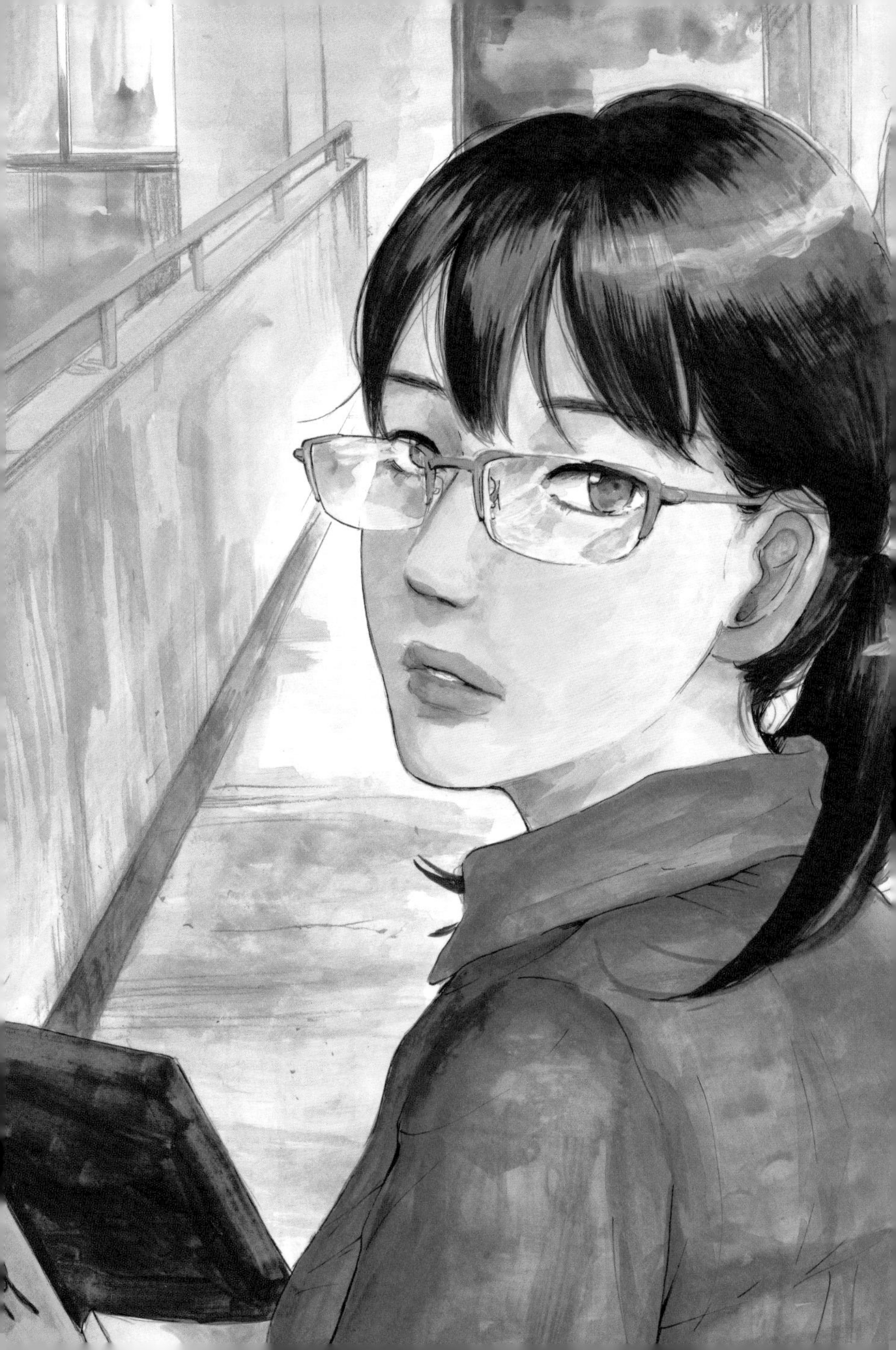

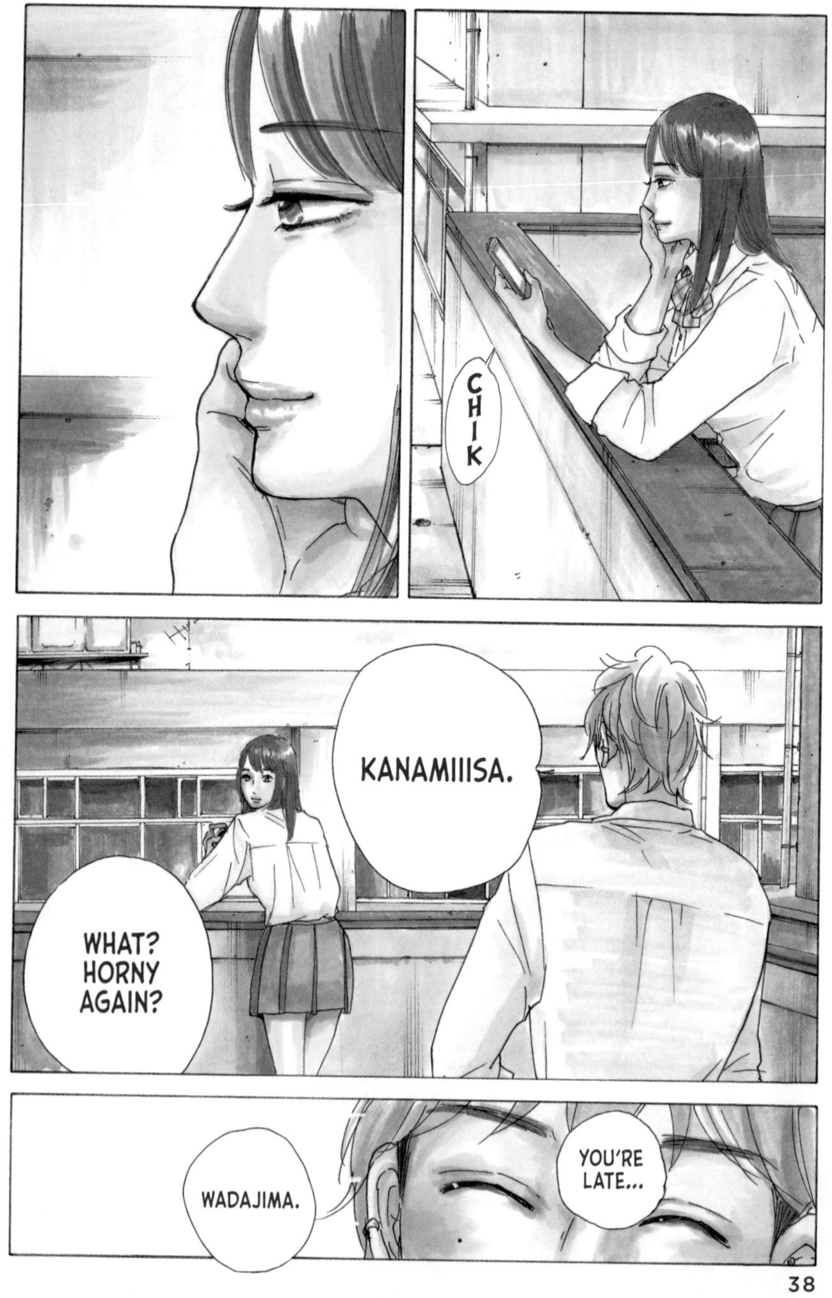
CHIK
KANAMIIISA.
WHAT? HORNY AGAIN?
YOU'RE LATE...
WADAJIMA.

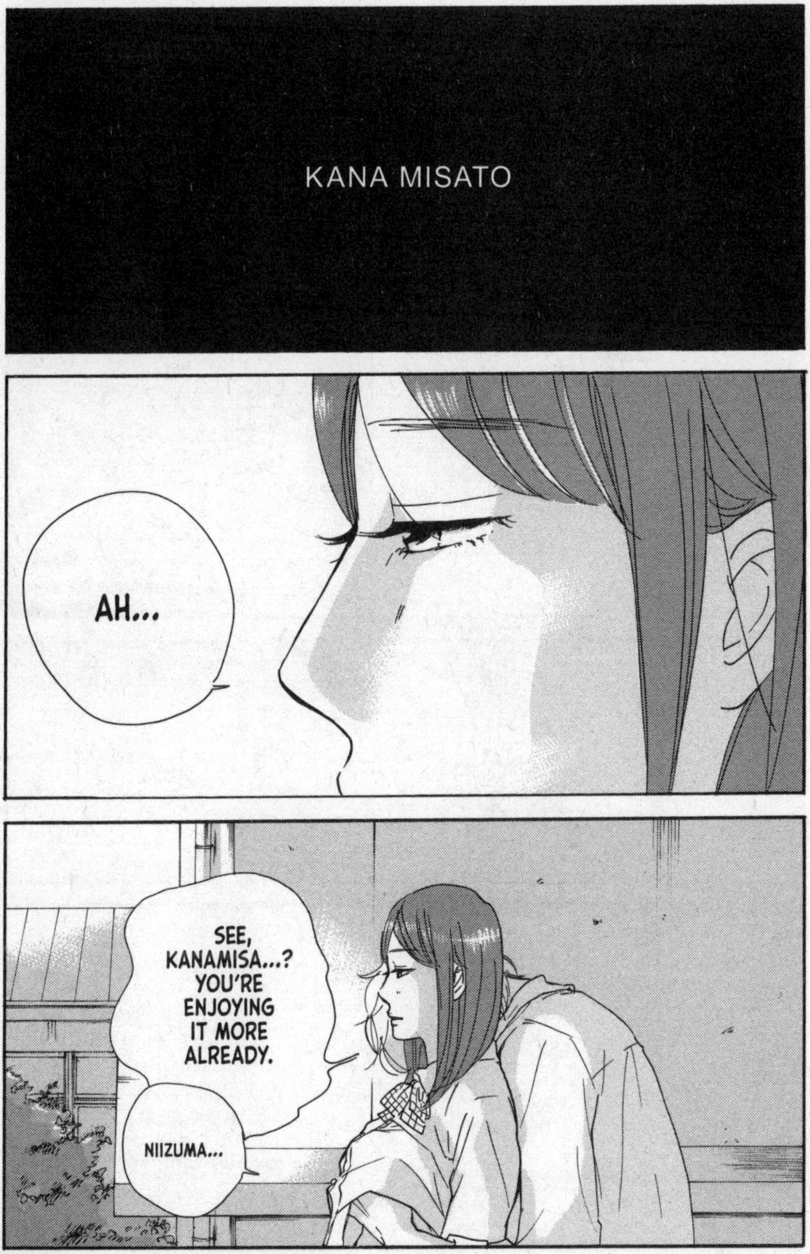
KANA MISATO
AH...
SEE, KANAMISA...? YOU'RE ENJOYING IT MORE ALREADY.
NIIZUMA...

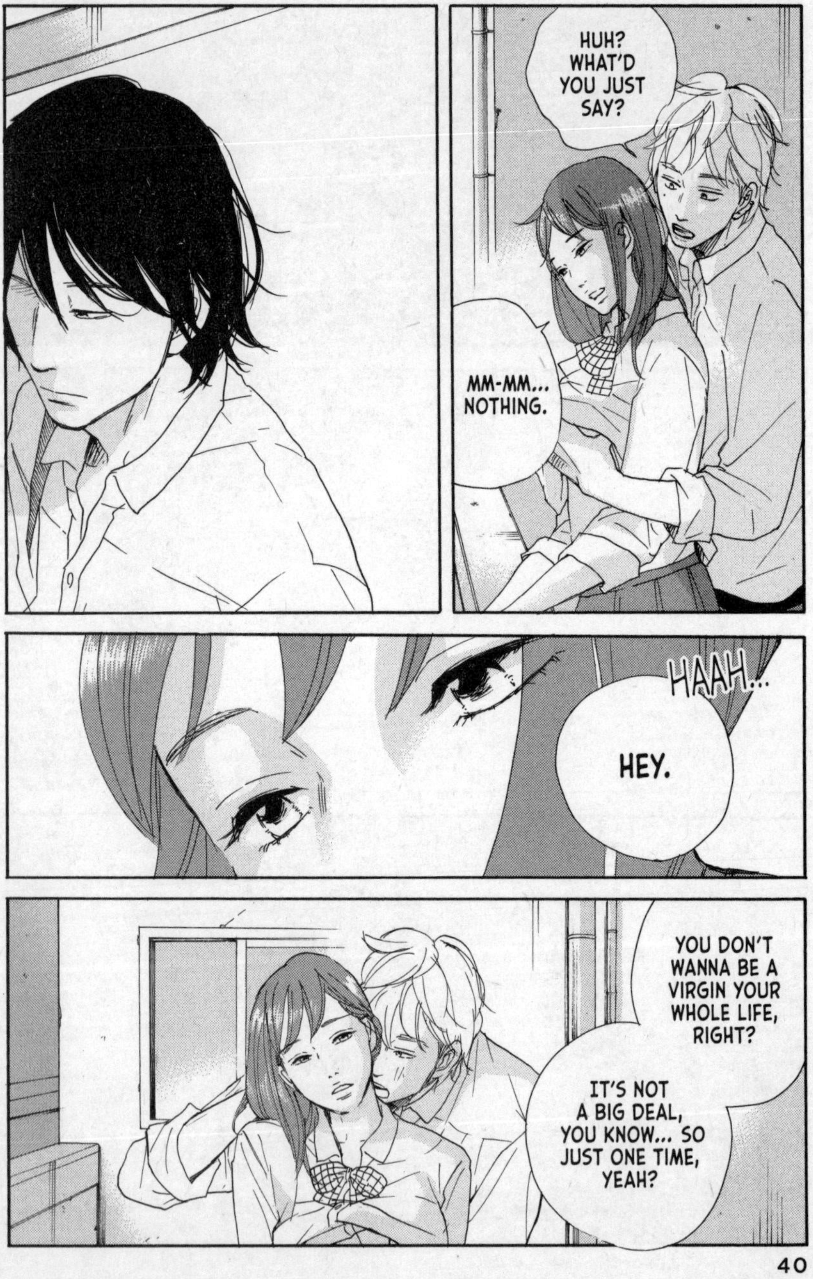
HUH? WHAT'D YOU JUST SAY?
MM-MM... NOTHING.
HAAH...
HEY.
YOU DON'T WANNA BE A VIRGIN YOUR WHOLE LIFE, RIGHT?
IT'S NOT A BIG DEAL, YOU KNOW... SO JUST ONE TIME, YEAH?

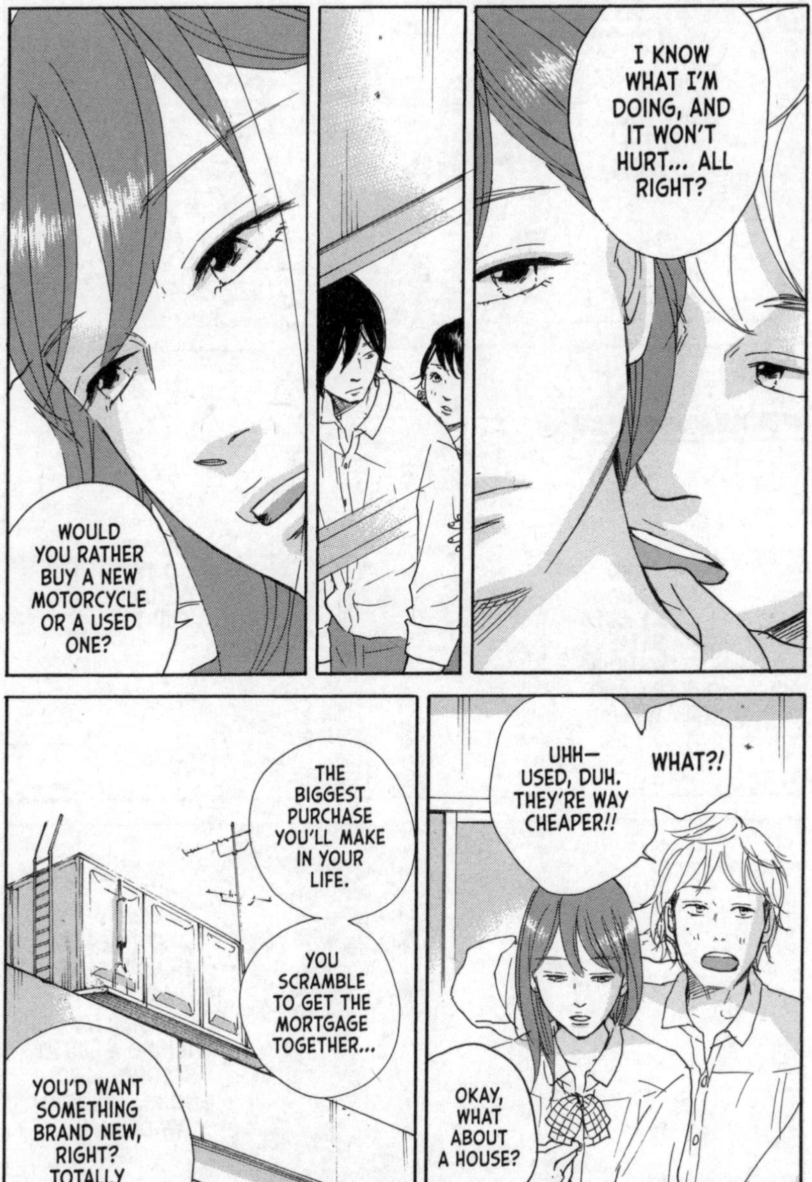
I KNOW WHAT I'M DOING, AND IT WON'T HURT... ALL RIGHT?
WOULD YOU RATHER BUY A NEW MOTORCYCLE OR A USED ONE?
WHAT?!
UHH— USED, DUH. THEY'RE WAY CHEAPER!!
OKAY, WHAT ABOUT A HOUSE?
THE BIGGEST PURCHASE YOU'LL MAKE IN YOUR LIFE.
YOU SCRAMBLE TO GET THE MORTGAGE TOGETHER...
YOU'D WANT SOMETHING BRAND NEW, RIGHT? TOTALLY UNTOUCHED.

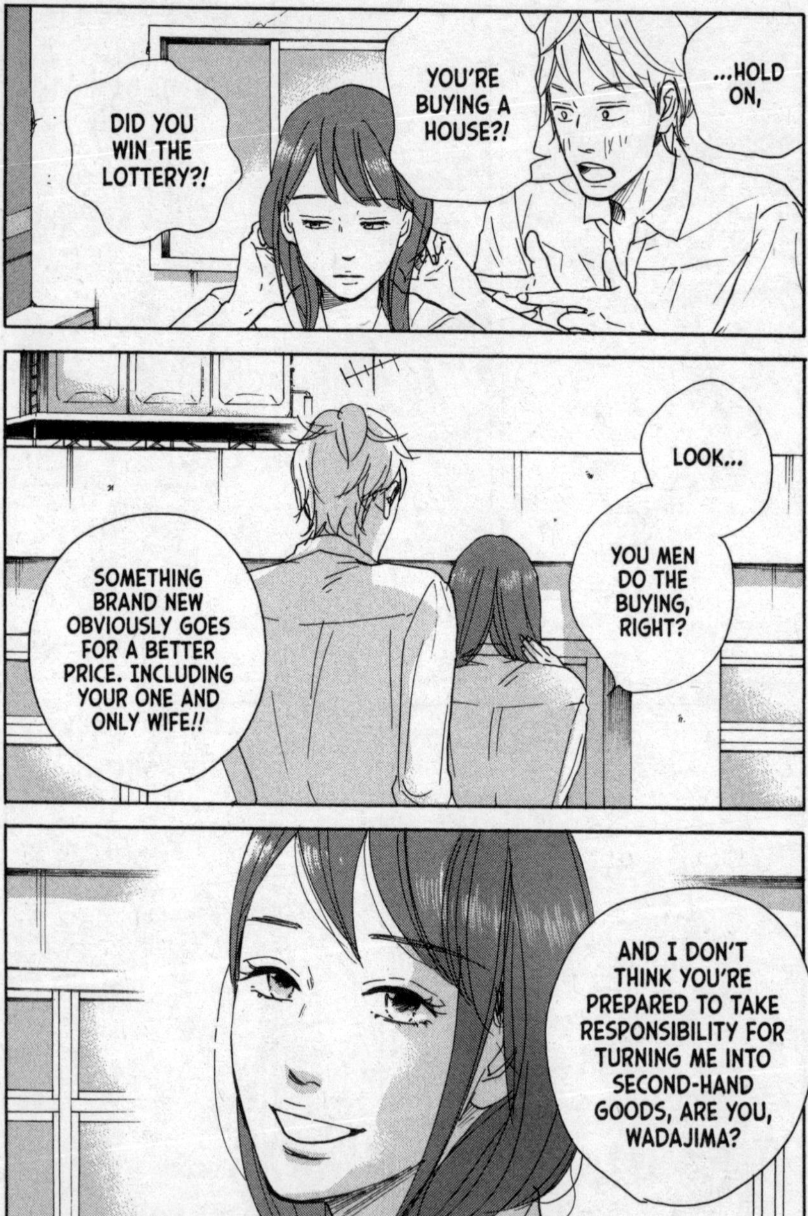
...HOLD ON,
YOU'RE BUYING A HOUSE?!
DID YOU WIN THE LOTTERY?!
LOOK...
YOU MEN DO THE BUYING, RIGHT?
SOMETHING BRAND NEW OBVIOUSLY GOES FOR A BETTER PRICE. INCLUDING YOUR ONE AND ONLY WIFE!!
AND I DON'T THINK YOU'RE PREPARED TO TAKE RESPONSIBILITY FOR TURNING ME INTO SECOND-HAND GOODS, ARE YOU, WADAJIMA?

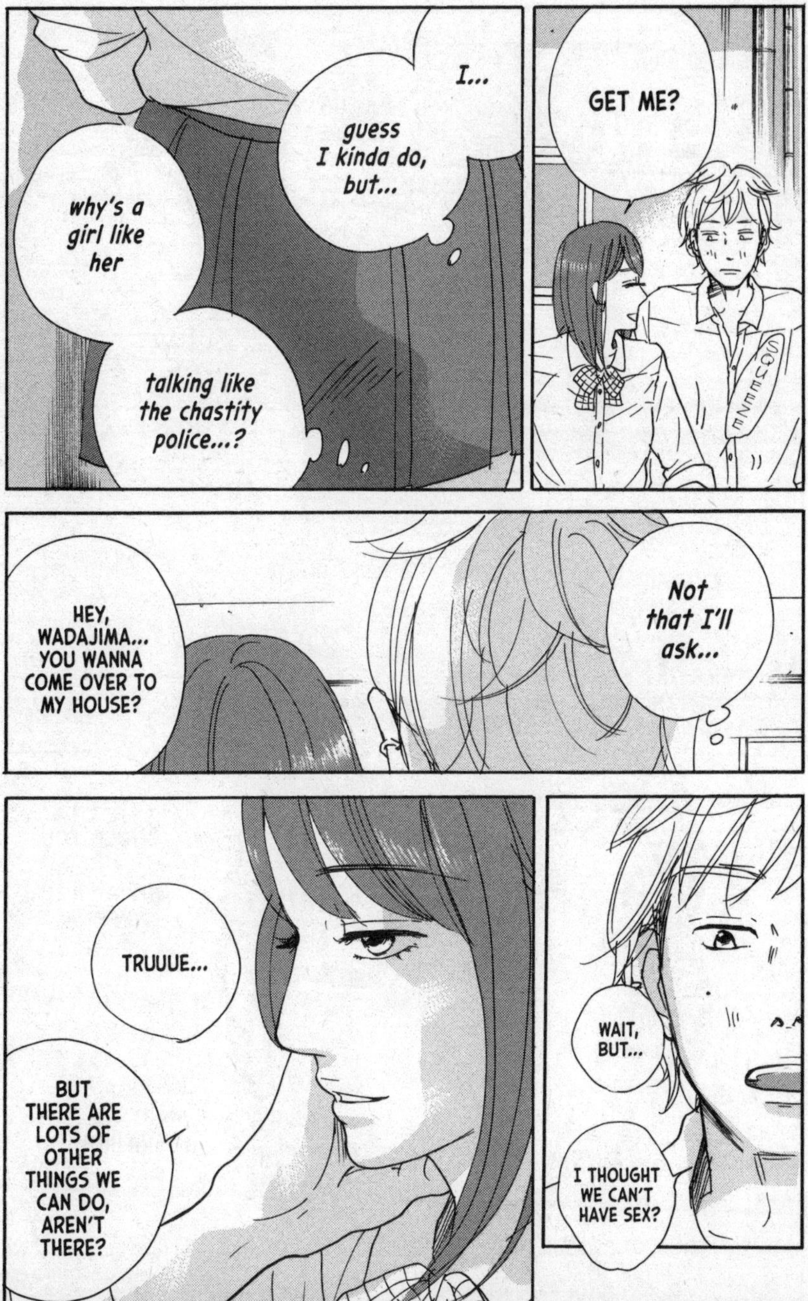
GET ME?
I...
guess I kinda do, but...
why's a girl like her
talking like the chastity police...?
Not that I'll ask...
HEY, WADAJIMA... YOU WANNA COME OVER TO MY HOUSE?
WAIT, BUT...
I THOUGHT WE CAN'T HAVE SEX?
TRUUUE...
BUT THERE ARE LOTS OF OTHER THINGS WE CAN DO, AREN'T THERE?

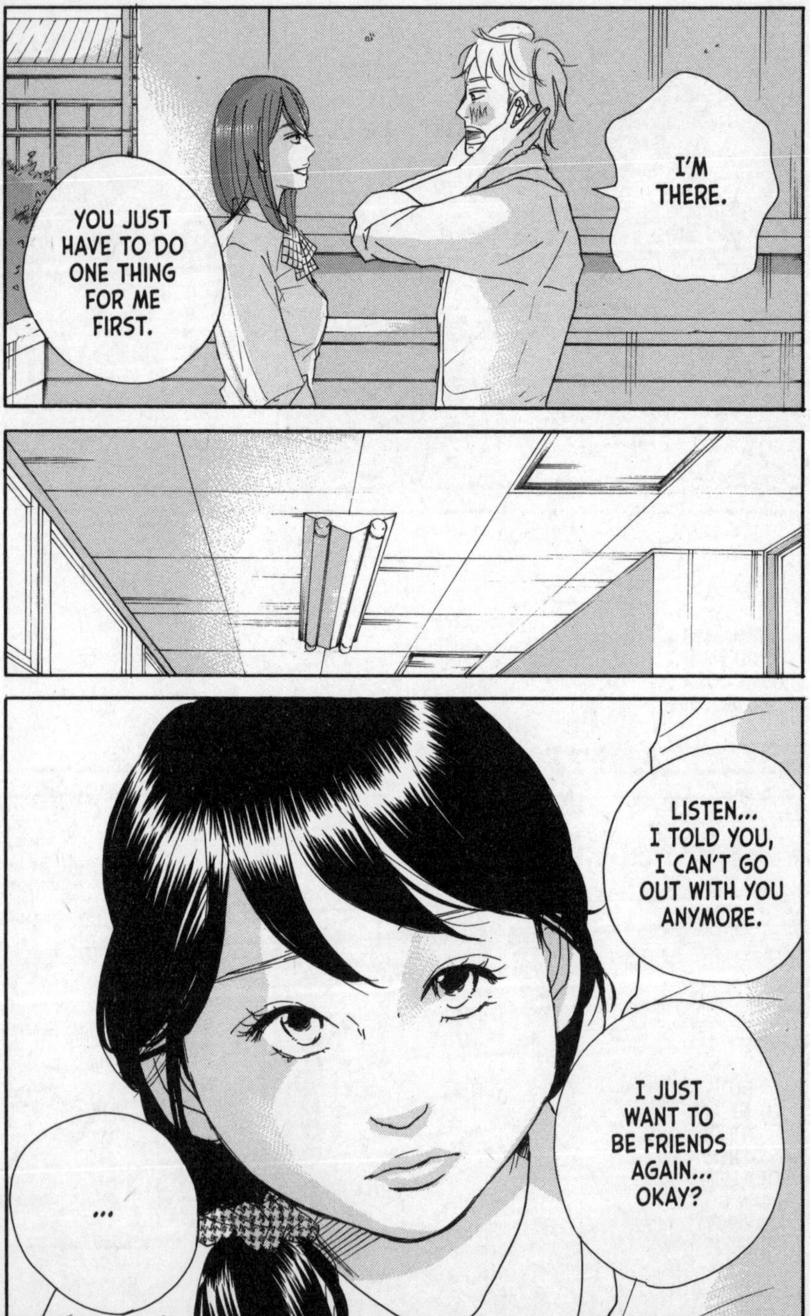
I'M THERE.
YOU JUST HAVE TO DO ONE THING FOR ME FIRST.
LISTEN... I TOLD YOU, I CAN'T GO OUT WITH YOU ANYMORE.
I JUST WANT TO BE FRIENDS AGAIN... OKAY?
...

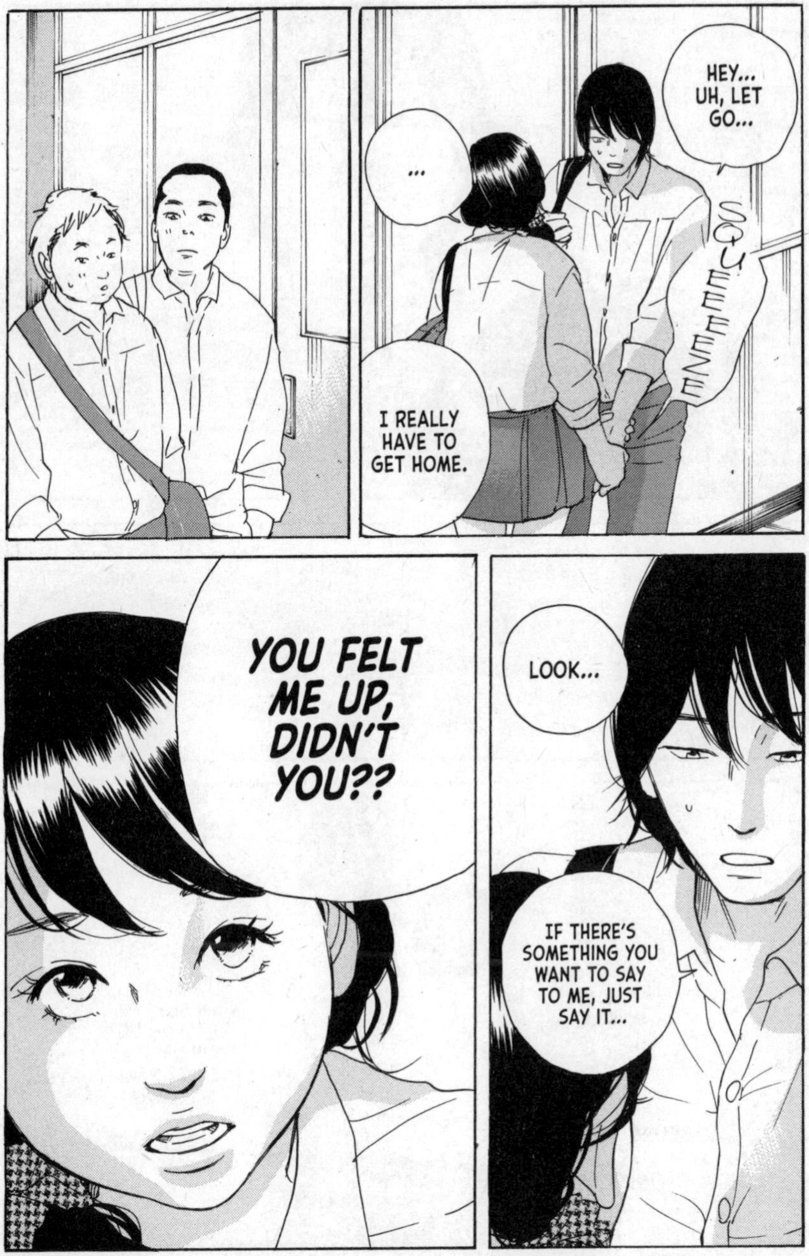
HEY... UH, LET GO...
...
SQUEEEEZE
I REALLY HAVE TO GET HOME.
LOOK...
IF THERE'S SOMETHING YOU WANT TO SAY TO ME, JUST SAY IT...
YOU FELT ME UP, DIDN'T YOU??

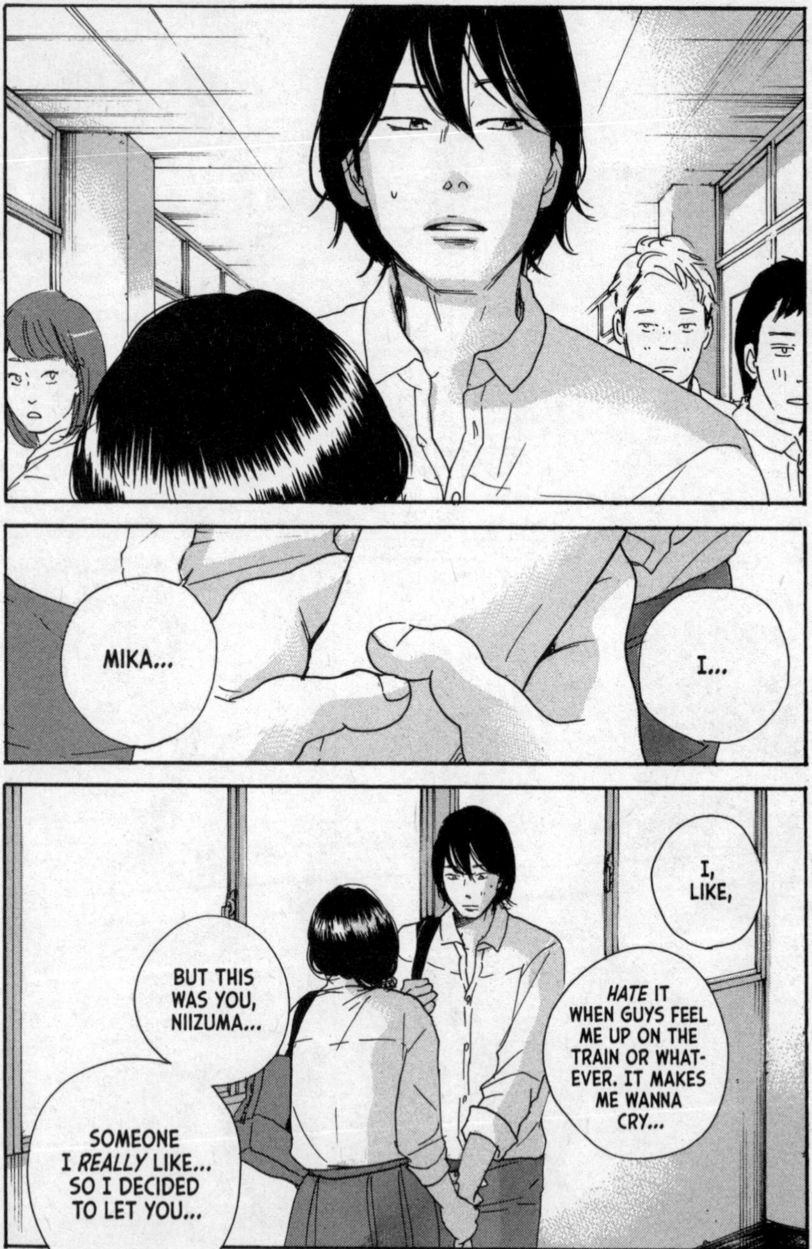
I...
MIKA...
I, LIKE,
HATE IT WHEN GUYS FEEL ME UP ON THE TRAIN OR WHAT-EVER. IT MAKES ME WANNA CRY...
BUT THIS WAS YOU, NIIZUMA...
SOMEONE I *REALLY* LIKE... SO I DECIDED TO LET YOU...

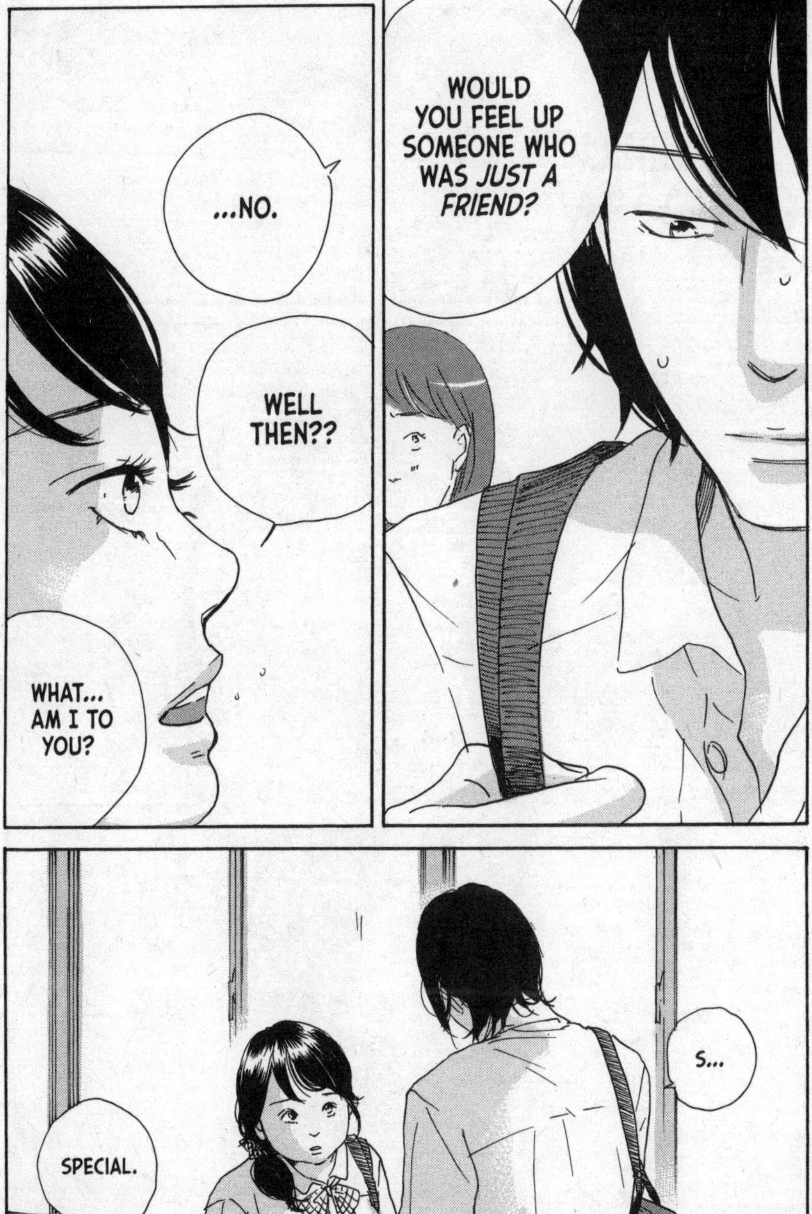
WOULD YOU FEEL UP SOMEONE WHO WAS *JUST A FRIEND?*
...NO.
WELL THEN??
WHAT... AM I TO YOU?
S...
SPECIAL.

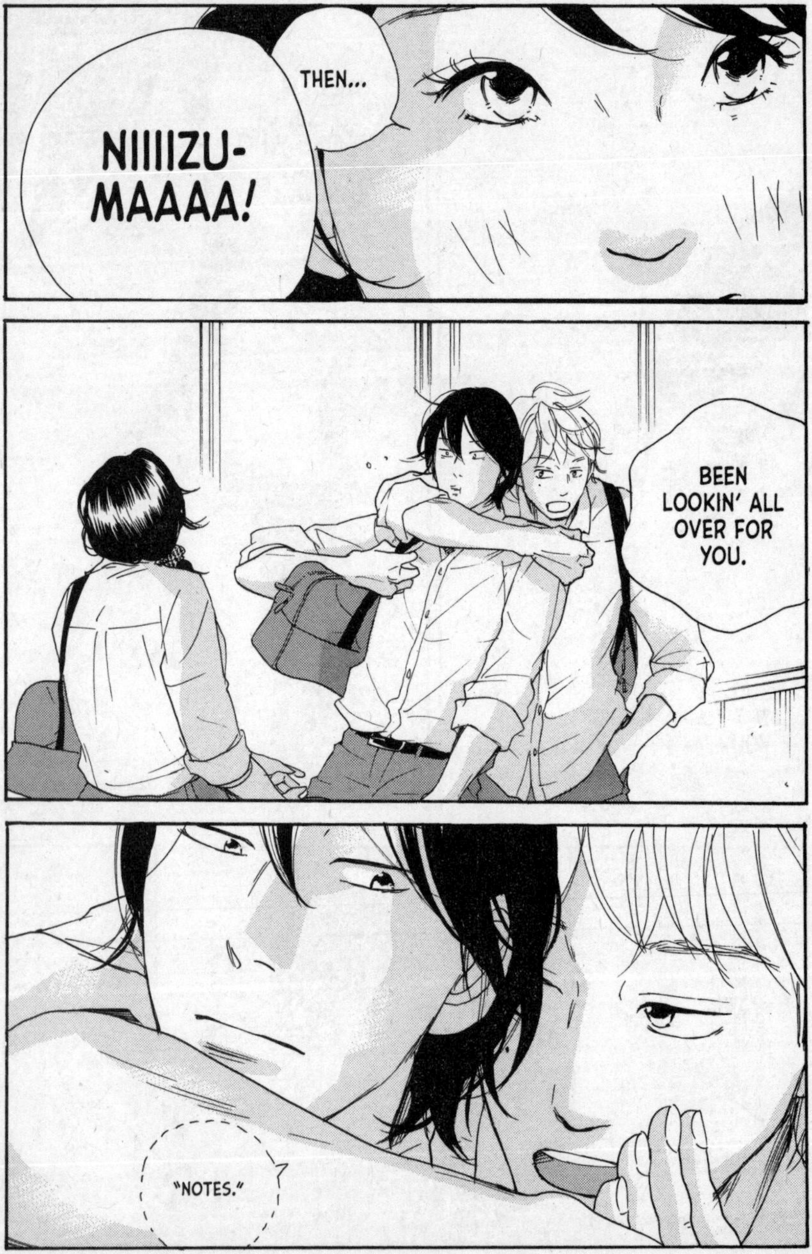
THEN...
NIIIIZU-MAAAA!
BEEN LOOKIN' ALL OVER FOR YOU.
"NOTES."

"NOTES"...
...
OH, RIGHT, I FORGOT. MY NOTES.
YEAH, THE ONES YOU *PROMISED* YOU'D LEND ME...
THOSE, YEAH... THEY'RE AT MY HOUSE.
SORRY, MIKA.
GOTTA RUUUN ♡

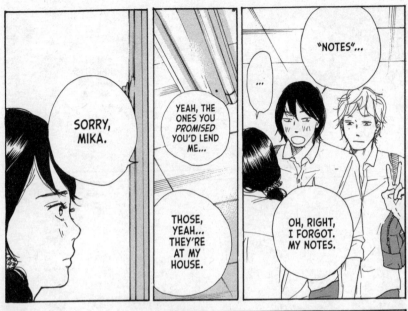

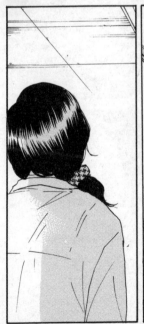

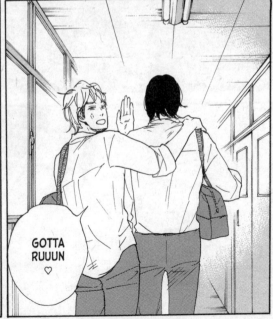

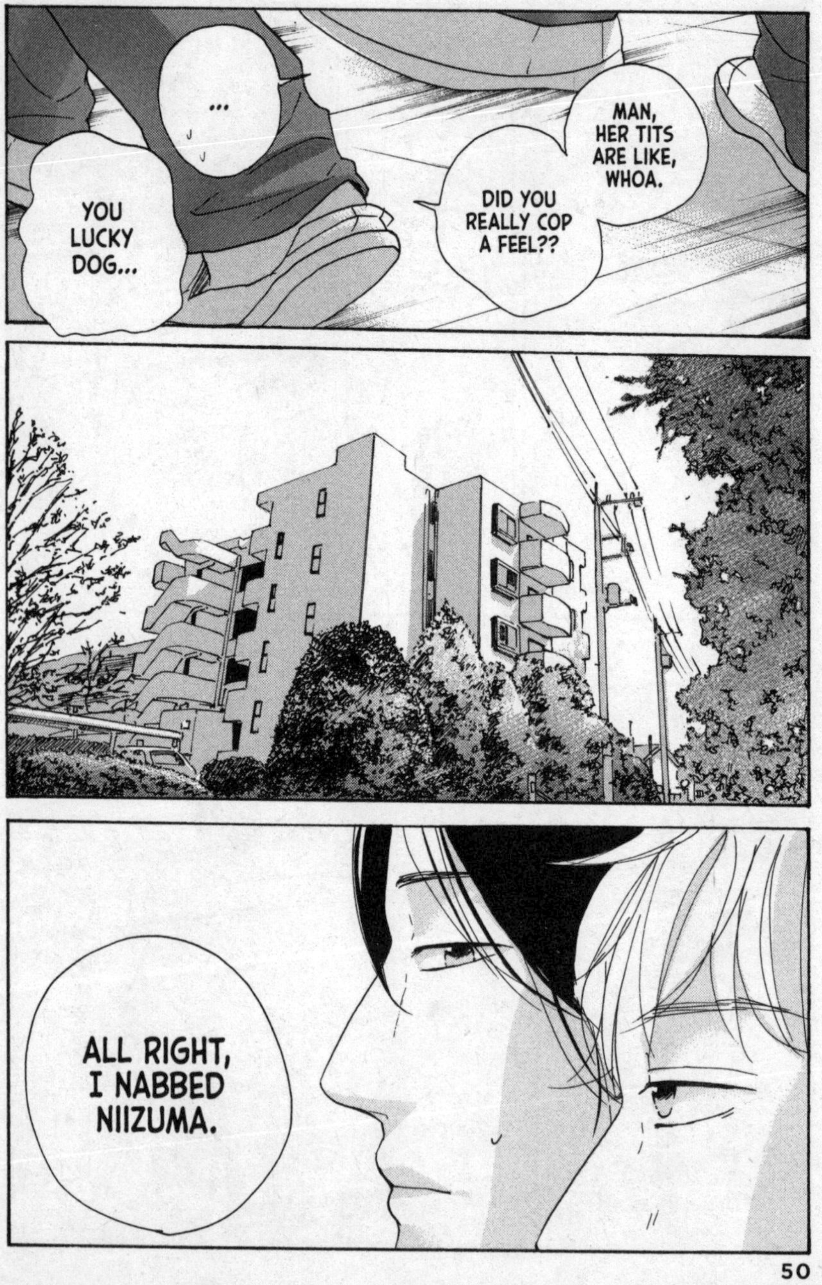
MAN, HER TITS ARE LIKE, WHOA.
DID YOU REALLY COP A FEEL??
...
YOU LUCKY DOG...
ALL RIGHT, I NABBED NIIZUMA.

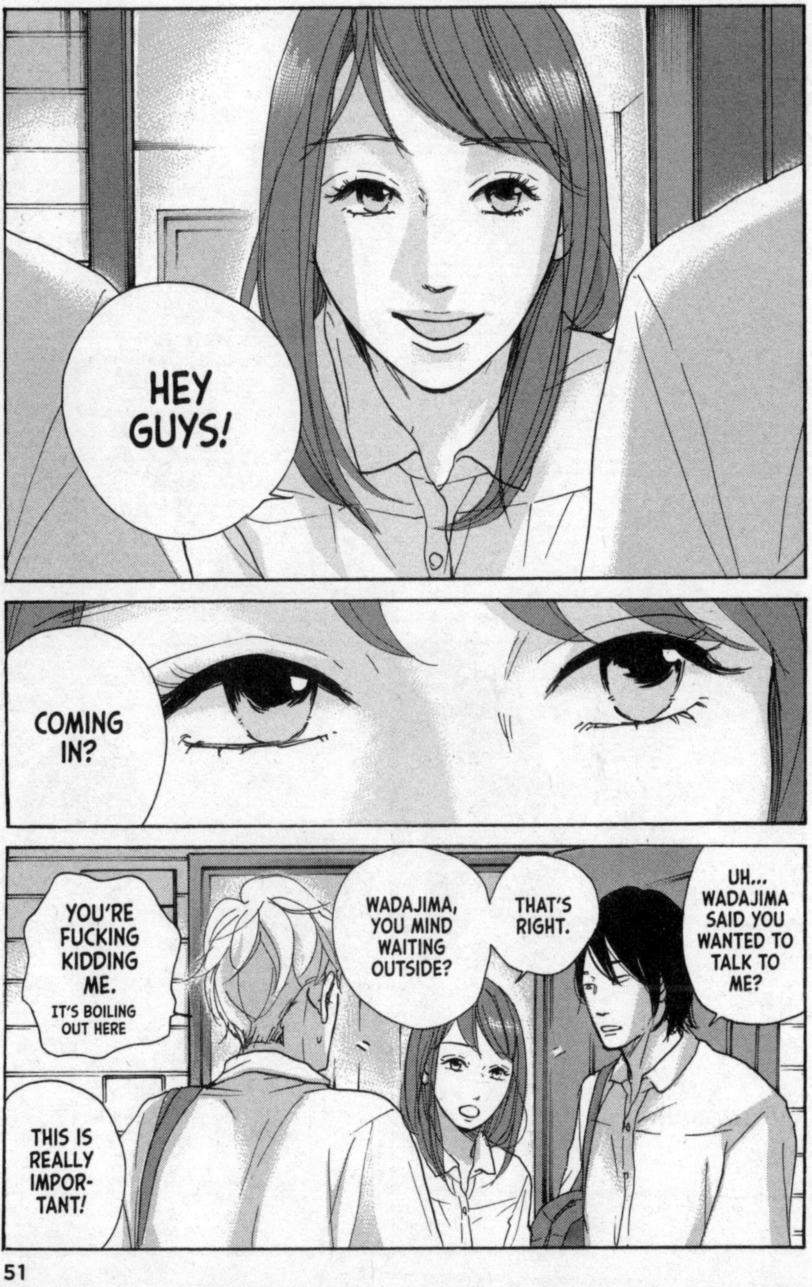
HEY GUYS!
COMING IN?
UH... WADAJIMA SAID YOU WANTED TO TALK TO ME?
THAT'S RIGHT.
WADAJIMA, YOU MIND WAITING OUTSIDE?
YOU'RE FUCKING KIDDING ME.
IT'S BOILING OUT HERE
THIS IS REALLY IMPOR-TANT!

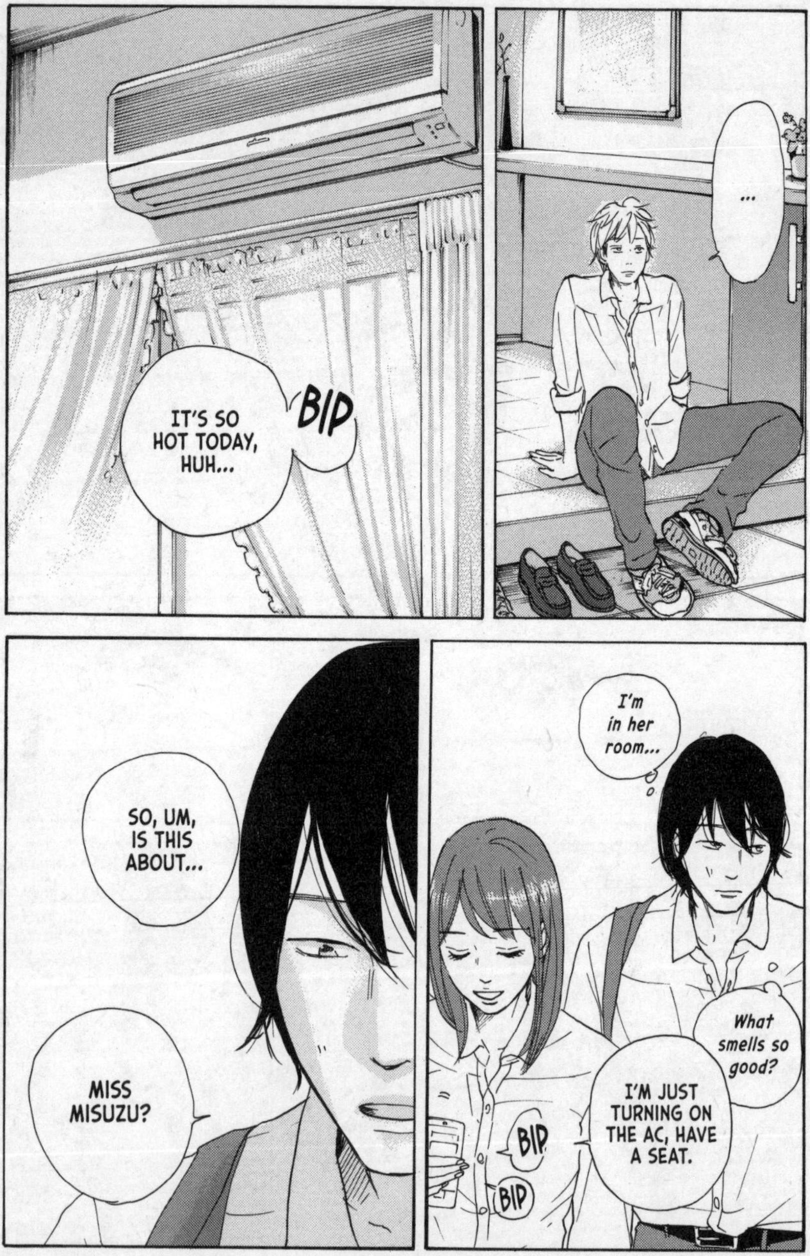
...
BIP
IT'S SO HOT TODAY, HUH...
I'm in her room...
What smells so good?
I'M JUST TURNING ON THE AC, HAVE A SEAT.
BIP
BIP
SO, UM, IS THIS ABOUT...
MISS MISUZU?

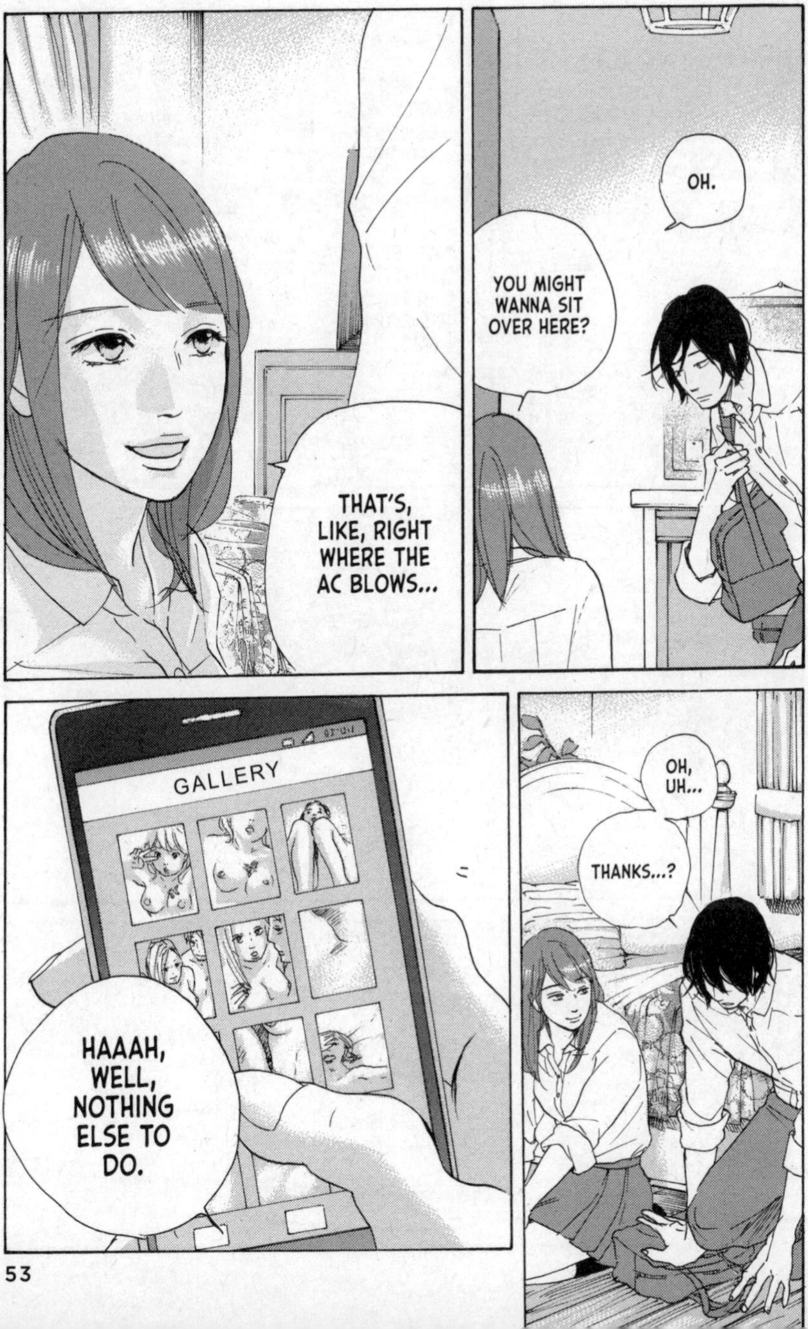
OH.
YOU MIGHT WANNA SIT OVER HERE?
THAT'S, LIKE, RIGHT WHERE THE AC BLOWS...
OH, UH...
THANKS...?
GALLERY
HAAAH, WELL, NOTHING ELSE TO DO.

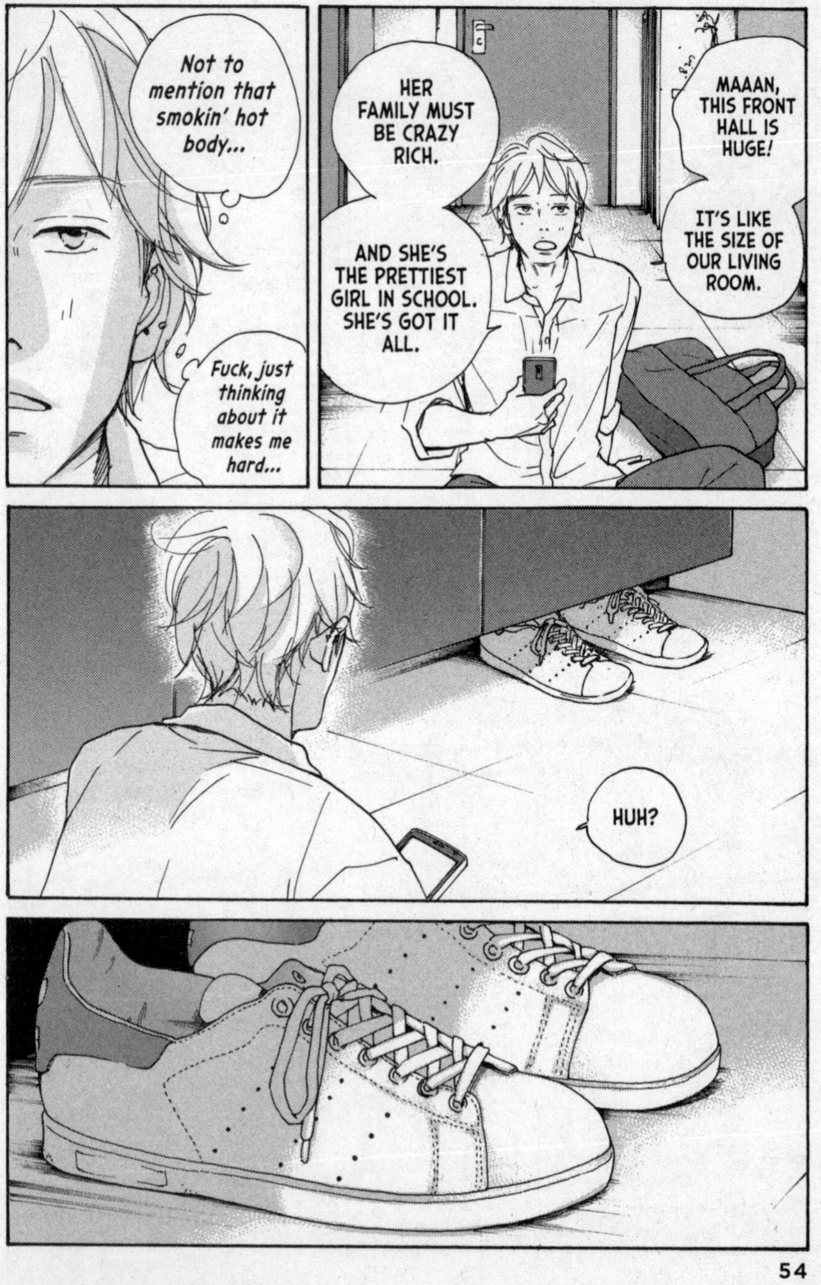
MAAAN, THIS FRONT HALL IS HUGE!
IT'S LIKE THE SIZE OF OUR LIVING ROOM.
HER FAMILY MUST BE CRAZY RICH.
AND SHE'S THE PRETTIEST GIRL IN SCHOOL. SHE'S GOT IT ALL.
Not to mention that smokin' hot body...
Fuck, just thinking about it makes me hard...
HUH?

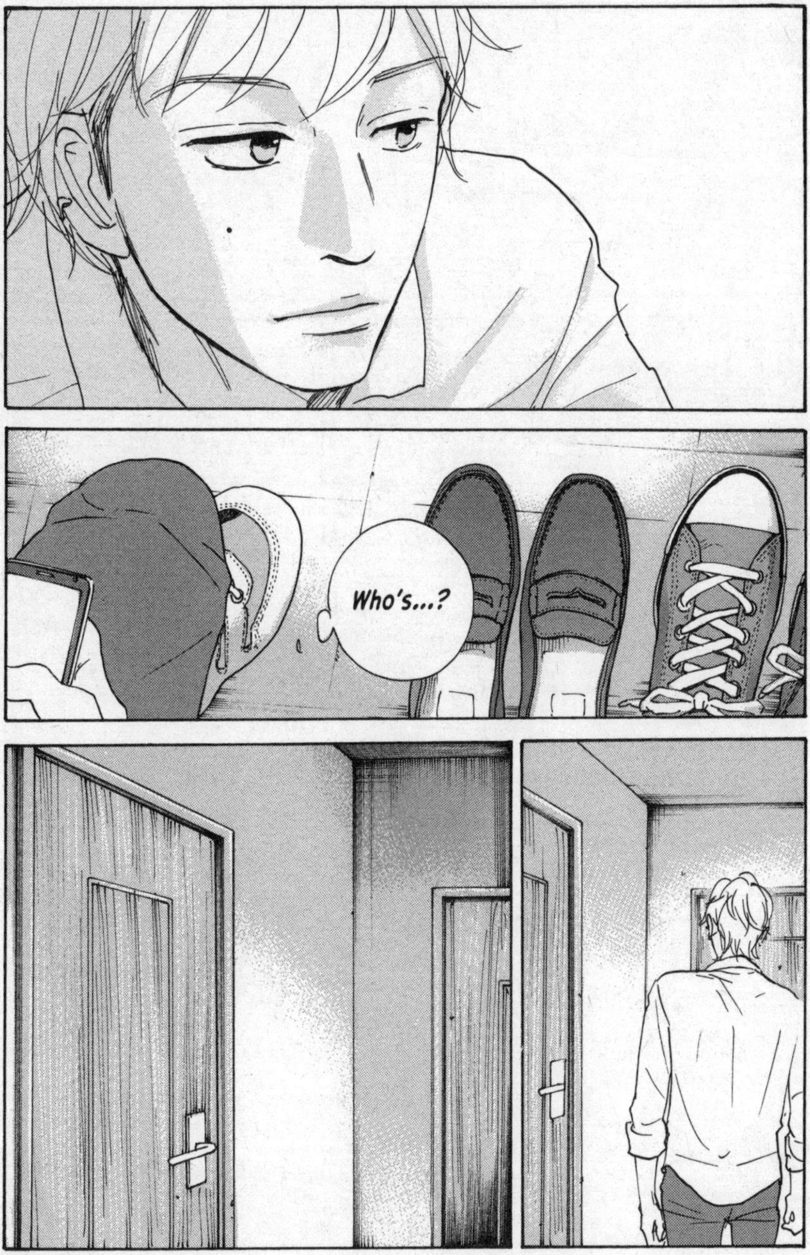
Who's...?

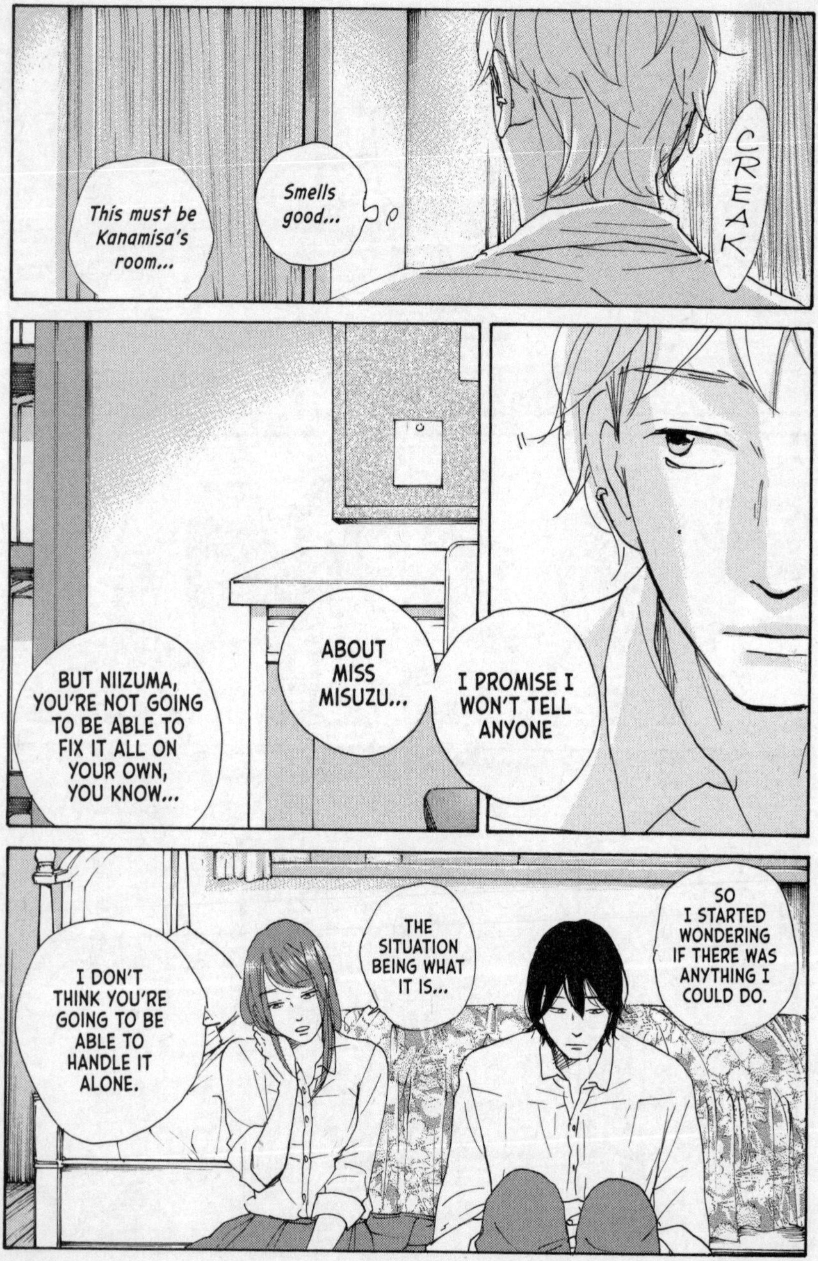
CREAK
Smells good...
This must be Kanamisa's room...
I PROMISE I WON'T TELL ANYONE
ABOUT MISS MISUZU...
BUT NIIZUMA, YOU'RE NOT GOING TO BE ABLE TO FIX IT ALL ON YOUR OWN, YOU KNOW...
SO I STARTED WONDERING IF THERE WAS ANYTHING I COULD DO.
THE SITUATION BEING WHAT IT IS...
I DON'T THINK YOU'RE GOING TO BE ABLE TO HANDLE IT ALONE.

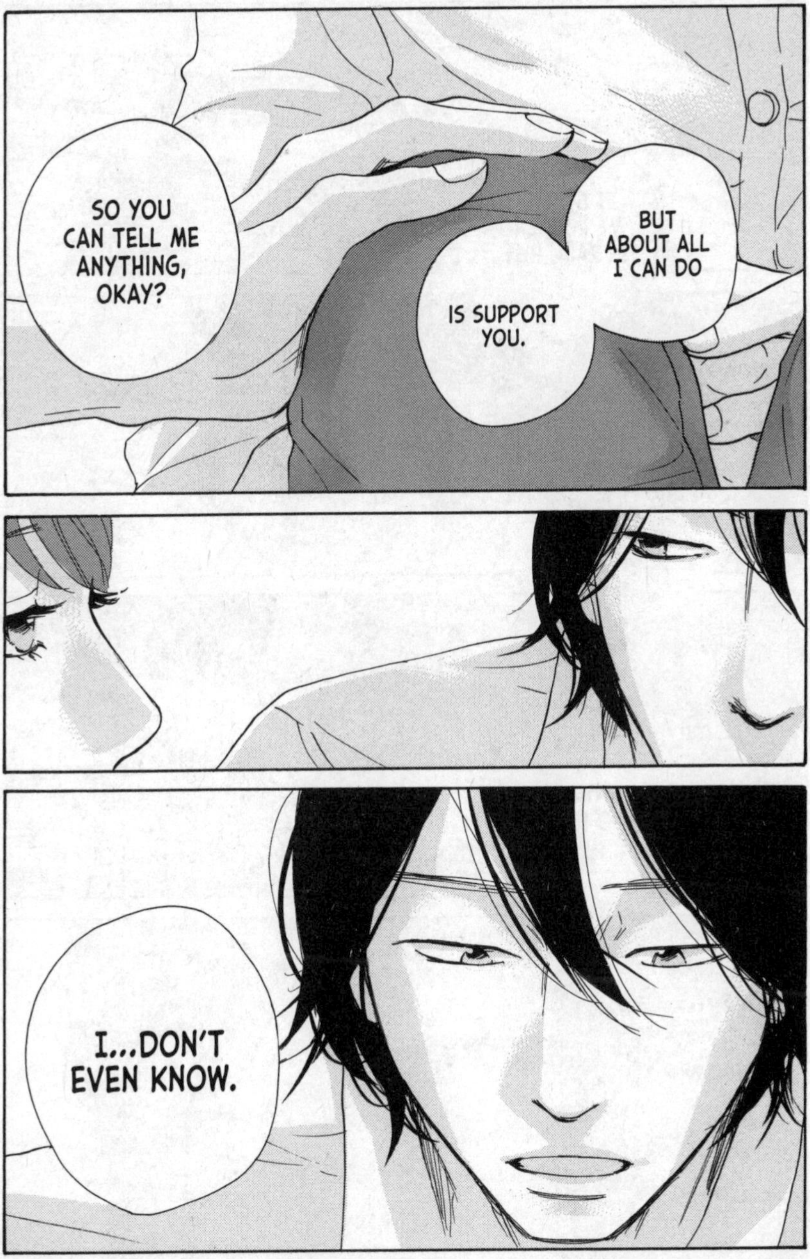
BUT ABOUT ALL I CAN DO
IS SUPPORT YOU.
SO YOU CAN TELL ME ANYTHING, OKAY?
I...DON'T EVEN KNOW.

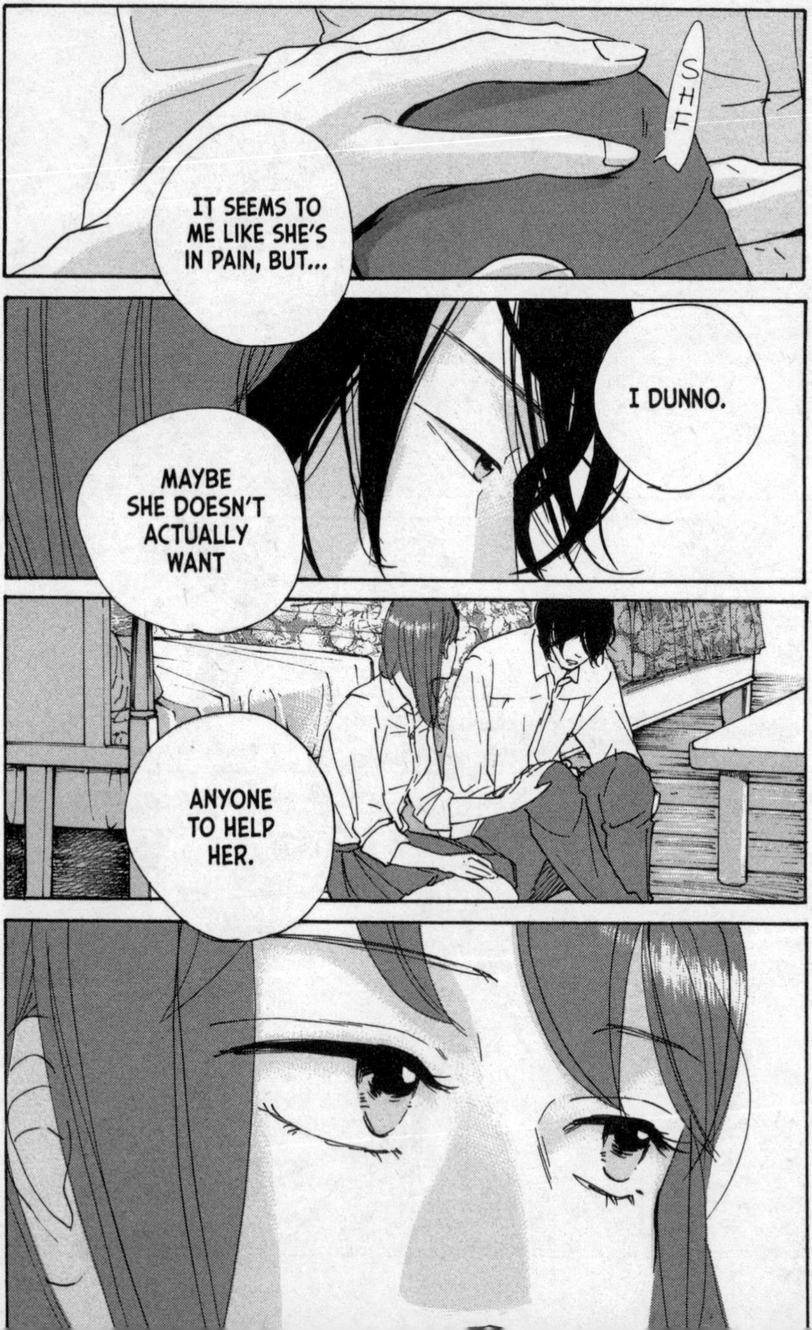
SHF
IT SEEMS TO ME LIKE SHE'S IN PAIN, BUT...
I DUNNO.
MAYBE SHE DOESN'T ACTUALLY WANT
ANYONE TO HELP HER.

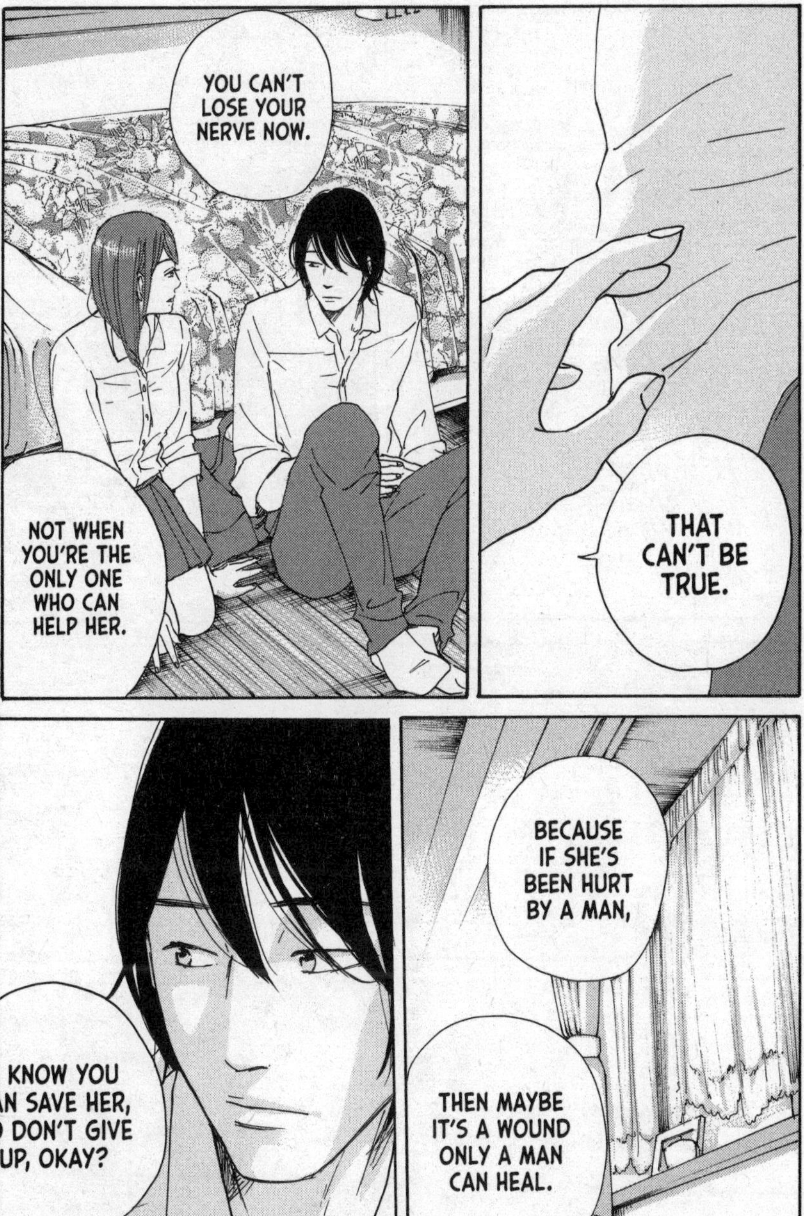
THAT CAN'T BE TRUE.
YOU CAN'T LOSE YOUR NERVE NOW.
NOT WHEN YOU'RE THE ONLY ONE WHO CAN HELP HER.
BECAUSE IF SHE'S BEEN HURT BY A MAN,
THEN MAYBE IT'S A WOUND ONLY A MAN CAN HEAL.
I KNOW YOU CAN SAVE HER, SO DON'T GIVE UP, OKAY?

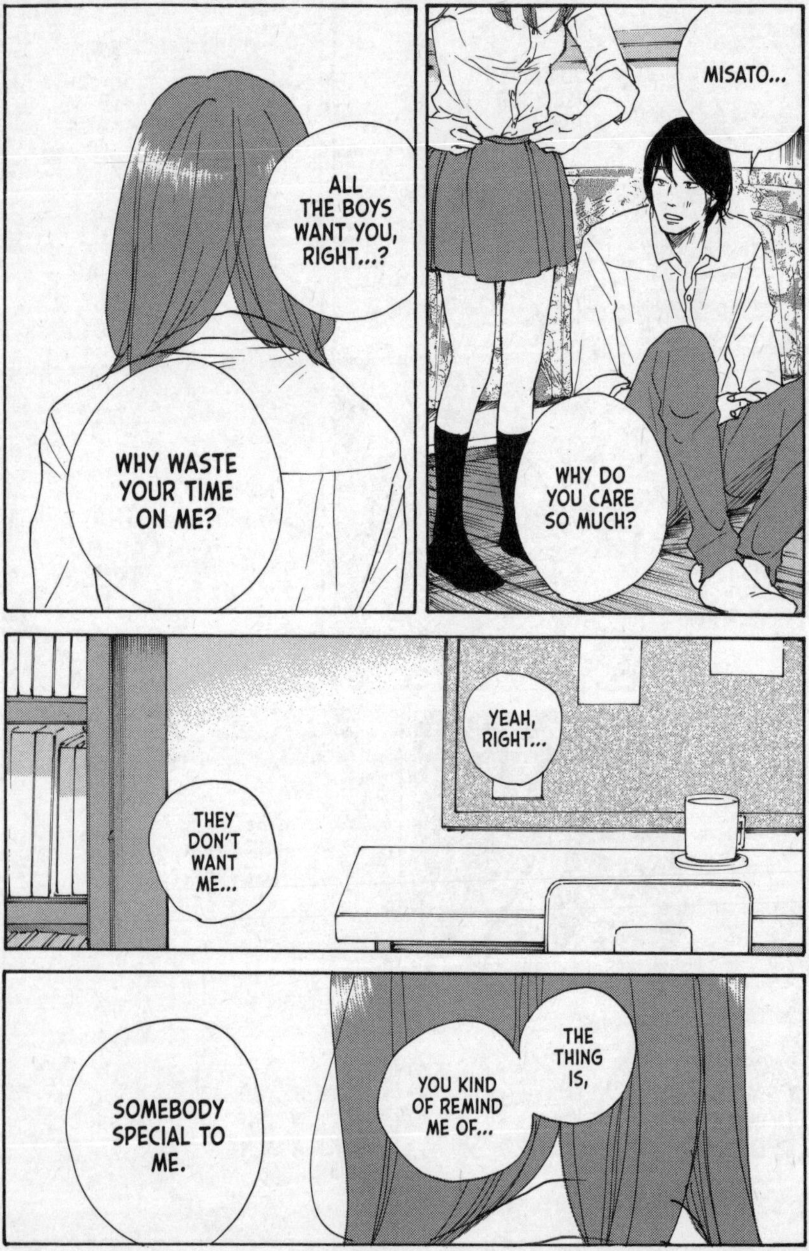
MISATO...
WHY DO YOU CARE SO MUCH?
ALL THE BOYS WANT YOU, RIGHT...?
WHY WASTE YOUR TIME ON ME?
YEAH, RIGHT...
THEY DON'T WANT ME...
THE THING IS,
YOU KIND OF REMIND ME OF...
SOMEBODY SPECIAL TO ME.

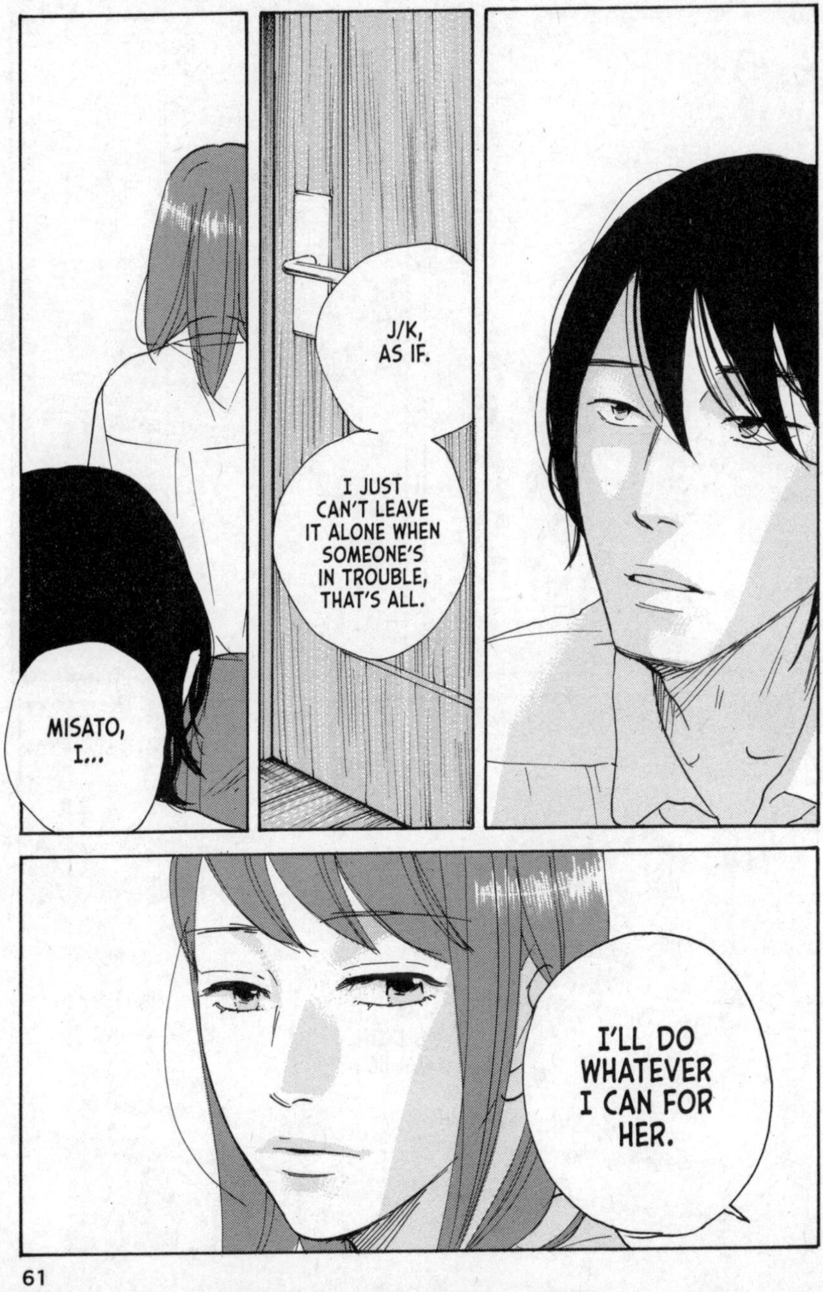
J/K, AS IF.
I JUST CAN'T LEAVE IT ALONE WHEN SOMEONE'S IN TROUBLE, THAT'S ALL.
MISATO, I...
I'LL DO WHATEVER I CAN FOR HER.

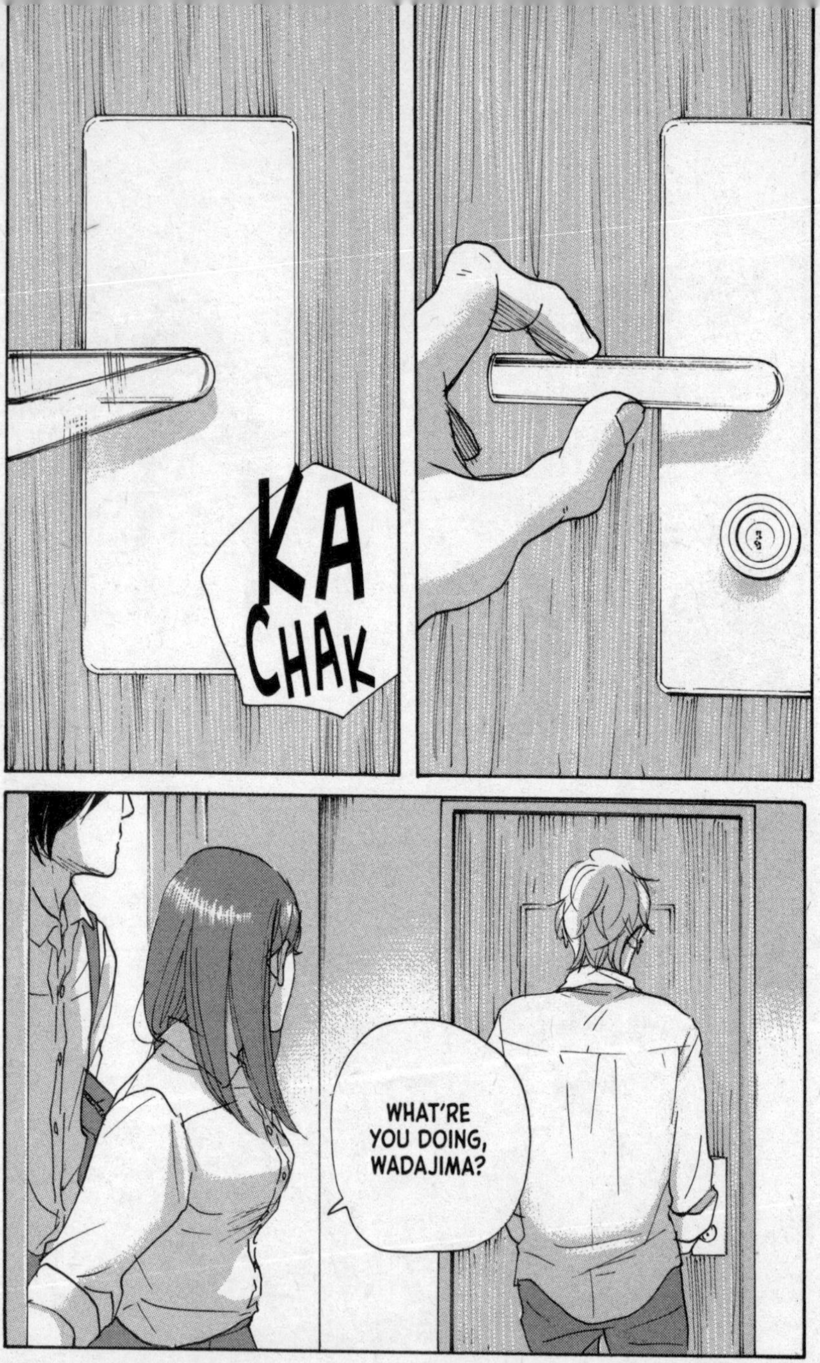
KA CHAK
WHAT'RE YOU DOING, WADAJIMA?

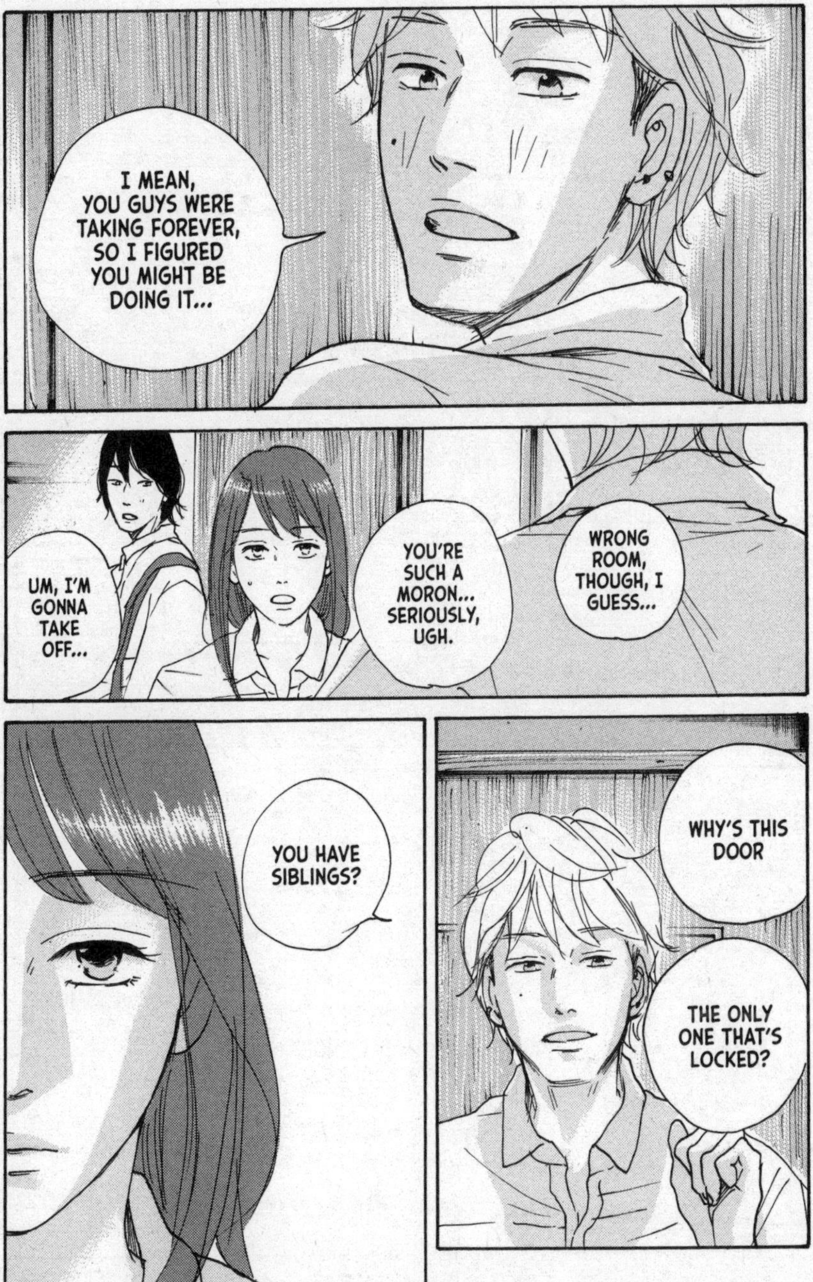
I MEAN, YOU GUYS WERE TAKING FOREVER, SO I FIGURED YOU MIGHT BE DOING IT...
WRONG ROOM, THOUGH, I GUESS...
YOU'RE SUCH A MORON... SERIOUSLY, UGH.
UM, I'M GONNA TAKE OFF...
WHY'S THIS DOOR
THE ONLY ONE THAT'S LOCKED?
YOU HAVE SIBLINGS?

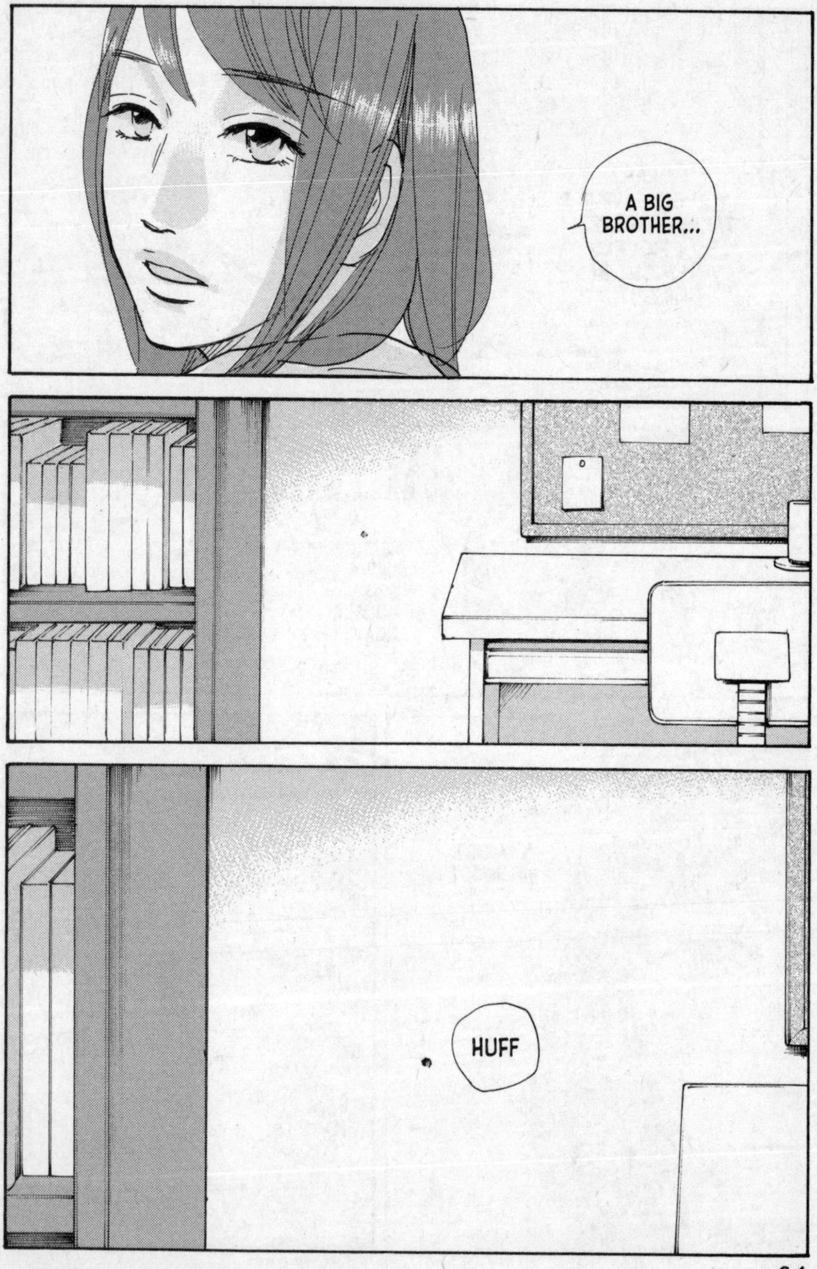
A BIG BROTHER...
HUFF

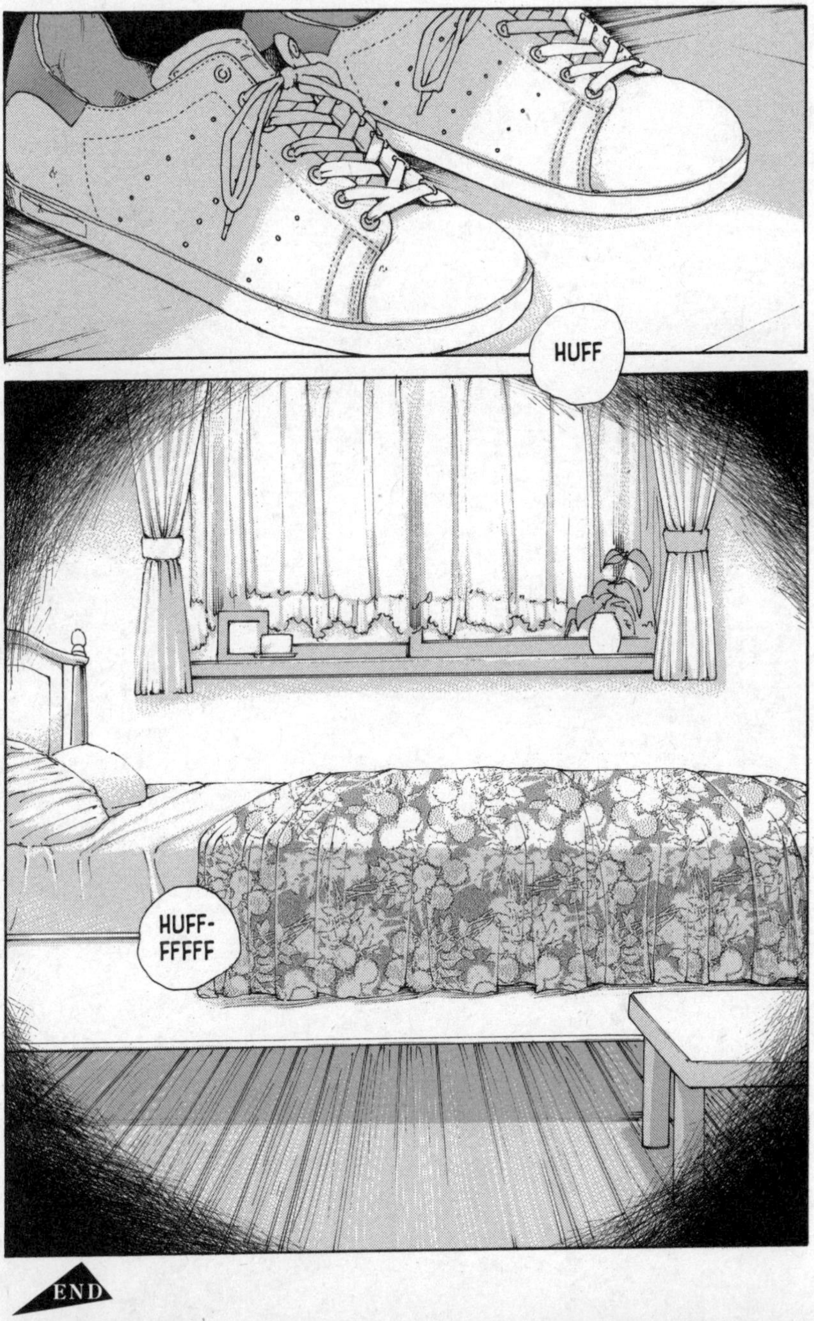
HUFF
HUFF-FFFFF

END

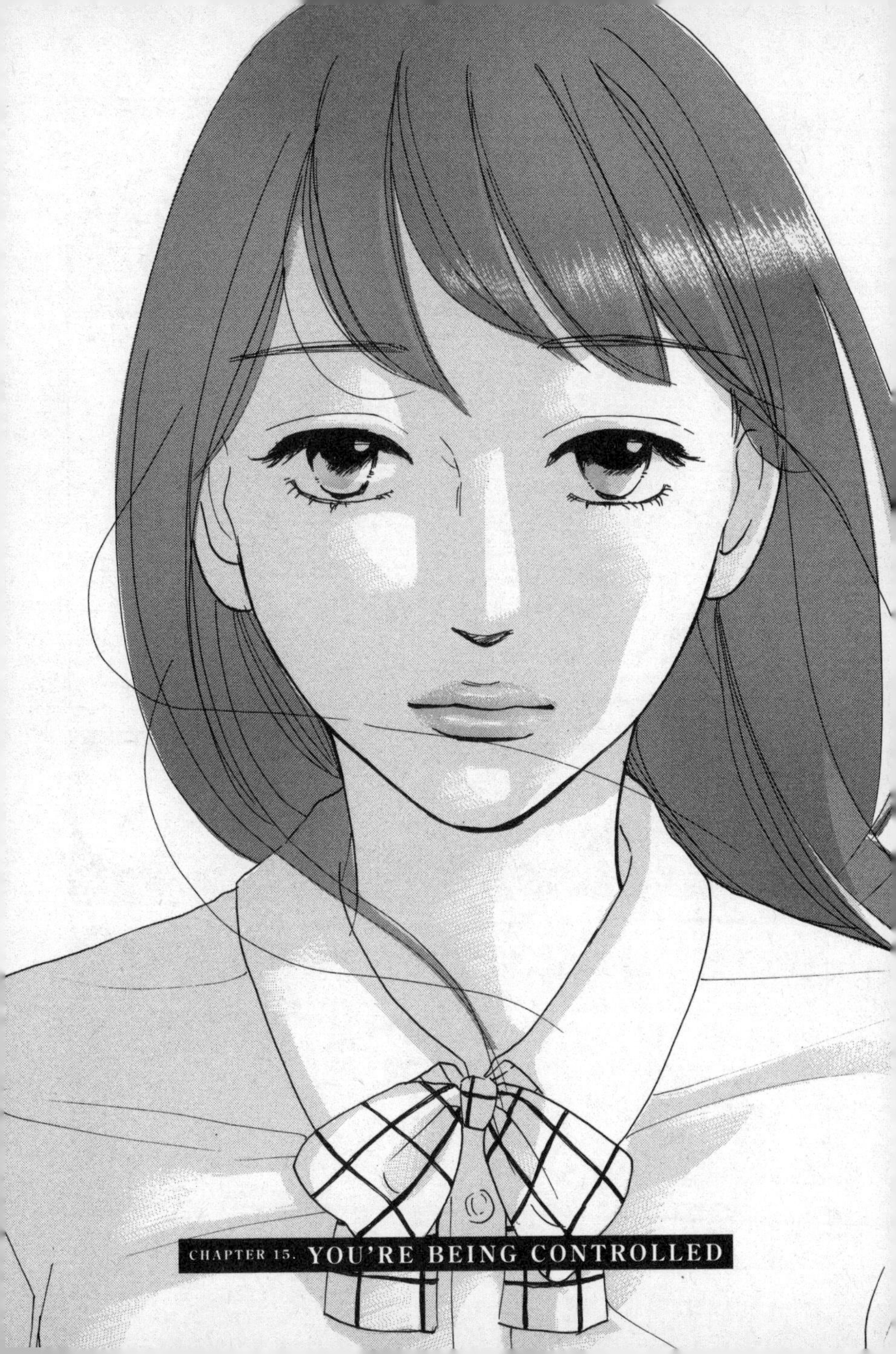
CHAPTER 15. YOU'RE BEING CONTROLLED

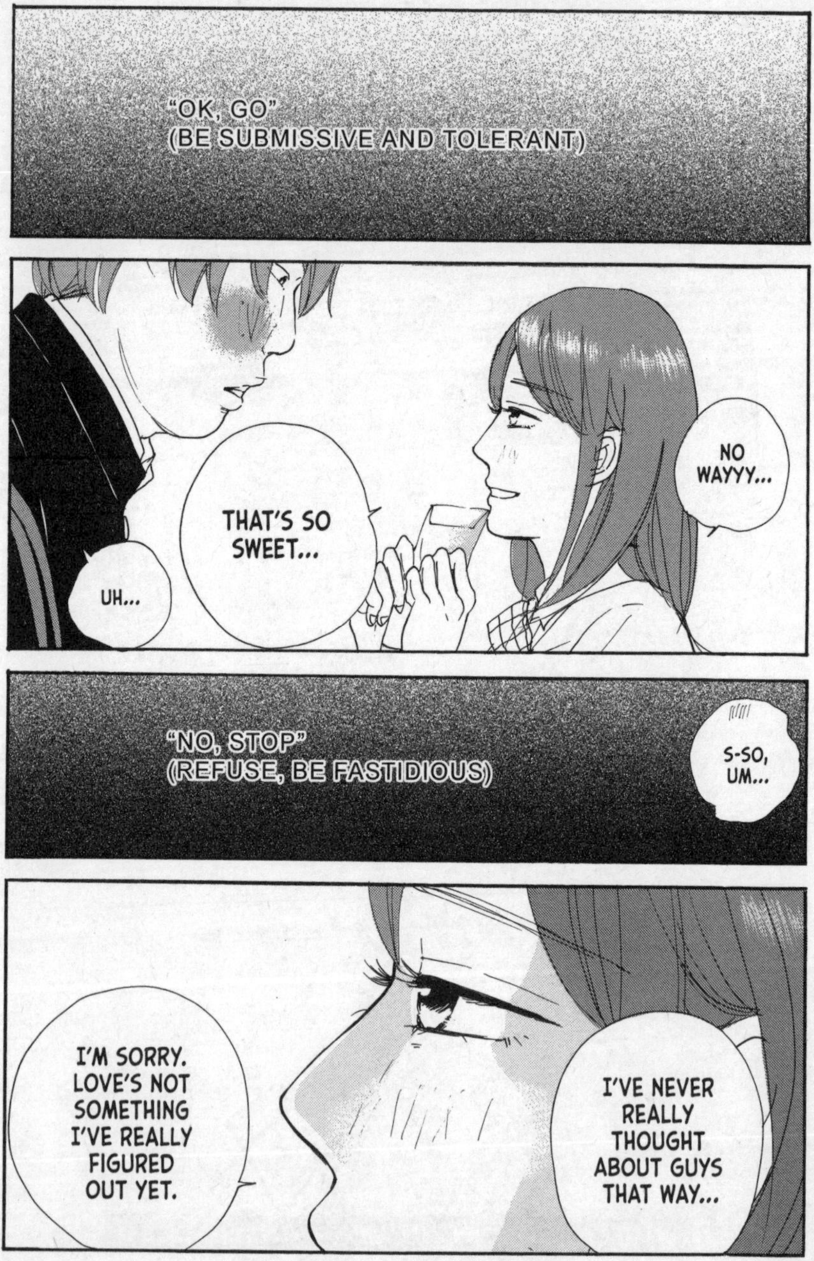
"OK, GO" (BE SUBMISSIVE AND TOLERANT)
NO WAYYY...
THAT'S SO SWEET...
UH...
S-SO, UM...
"NO, STOP" (REFUSE, BE FASTIDIOUS)
I'VE NEVER REALLY THOUGHT ABOUT GUYS THAT WAY...
I'M SORRY. LOVE'S NOT SOMETHING I'VE REALLY FIGURED OUT YET.

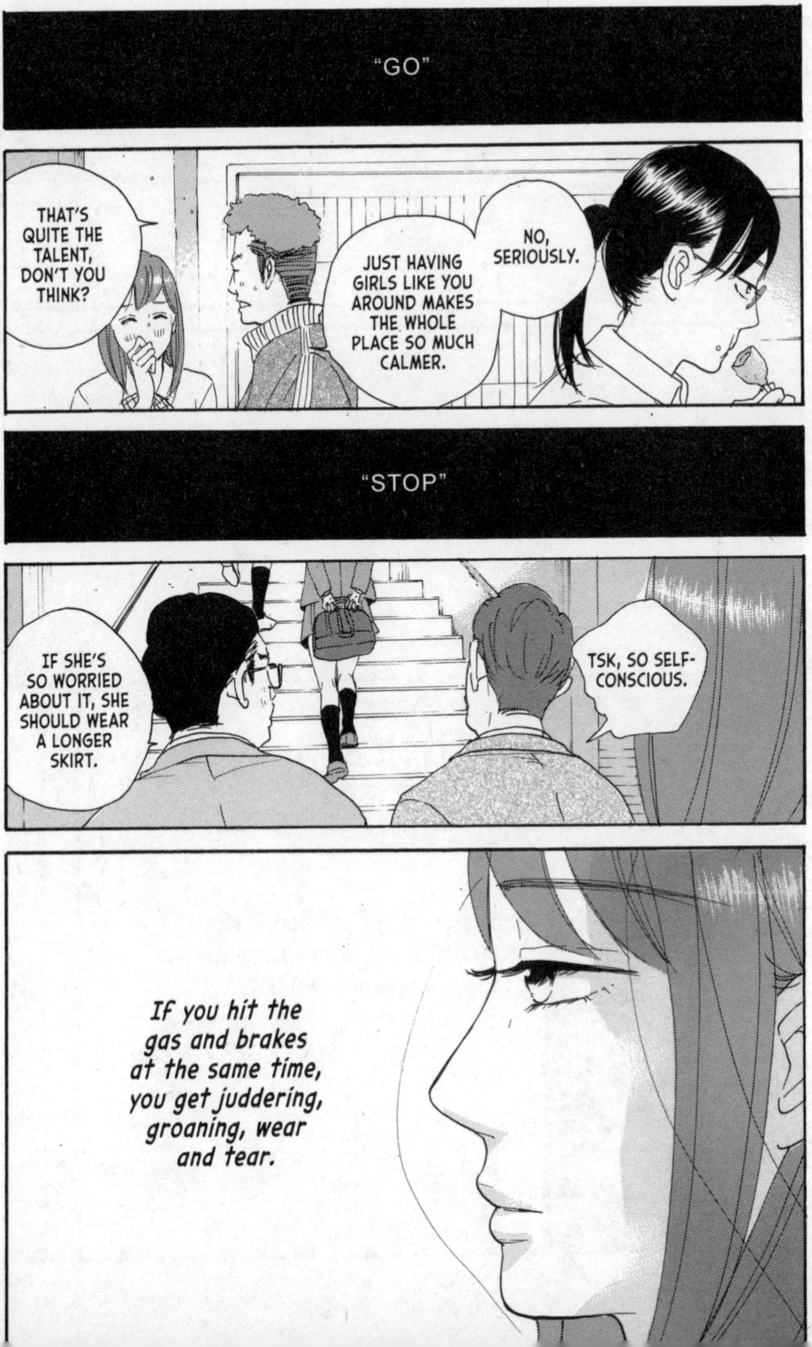
"GO"
NO, SERIOUSLY.
JUST HAVING GIRLS LIKE YOU AROUND MAKES THE WHOLE PLACE SO MUCH CALMER.
THAT'S QUITE THE TALENT, DON'T YOU THINK?
"STOP"
TSK, SO SELF-CONSCIOUS.
IF SHE'S SO WORRIED ABOUT IT, SHE SHOULD WEAR A LONGER SKIRT.
If you hit the gas and brakes at the same time, you get juddering, groaning, wear and tear.

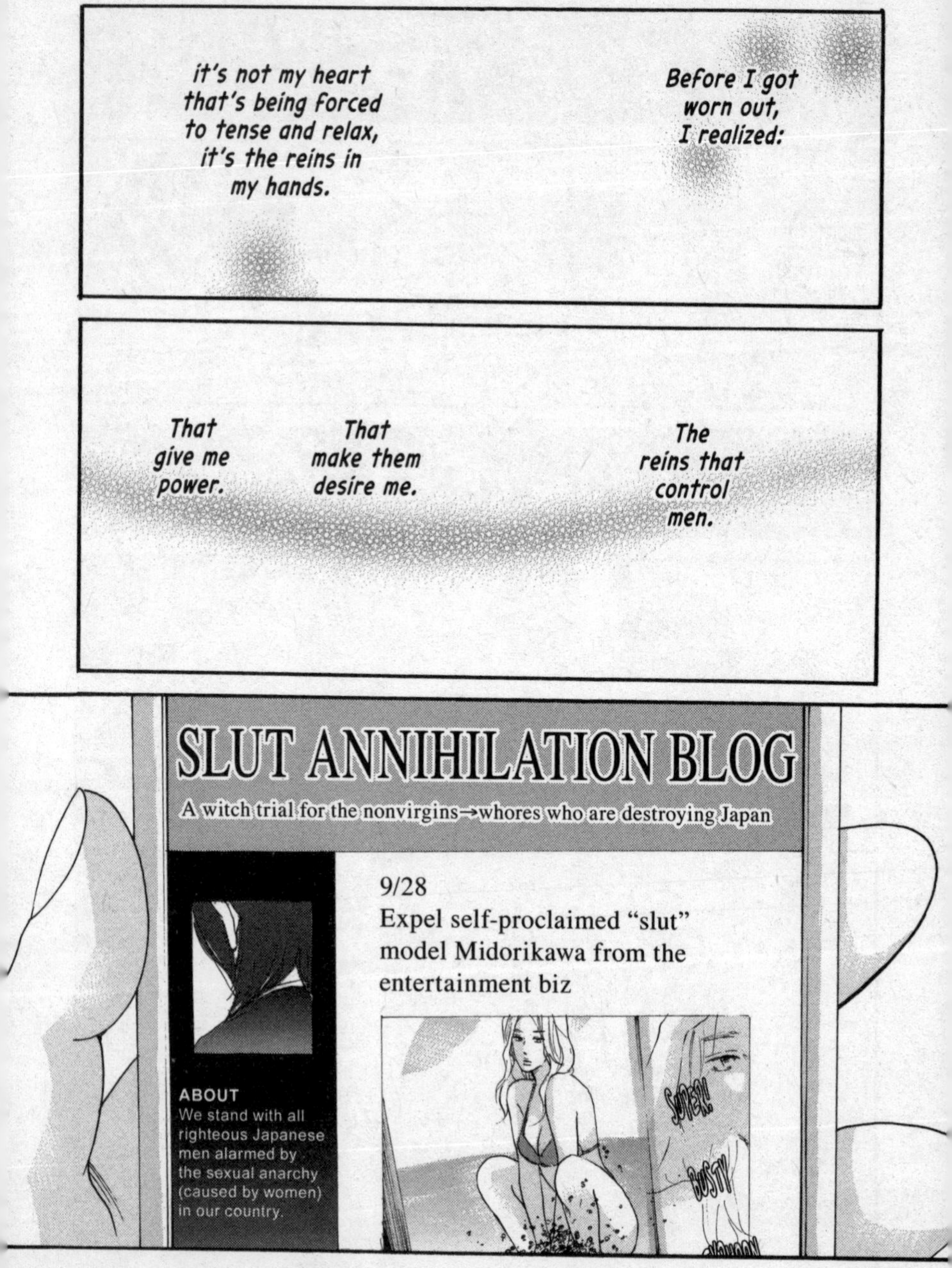
Before I got worn out, I realized:
it's not my heart that's being forced to tense and relax, it's the reins in my hands.
The reins that control men.
That make them desire me.
That give me power.
SLUT ANNIHILATION BLOG
A witch trial for the nonvirgins→whores who are destroying Japan
ABOUT
We stand with all righteous Japanese men alarmed by the sexual anarchy (caused by women) in our country.
9/28
Expel self-proclaimed "slut" model Midorikawa from the entertainment biz
SUPER!
BUSTY

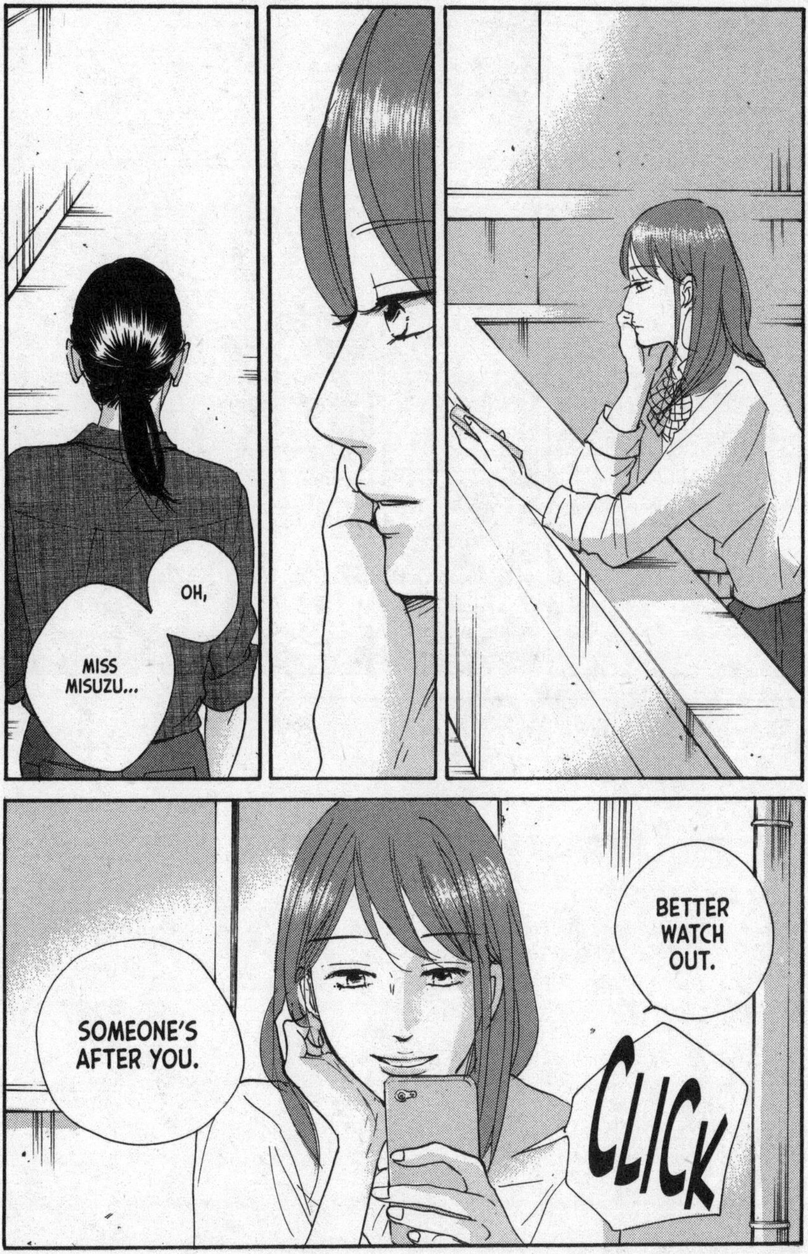
OH,
MISS MISUZU...
BETTER WATCH OUT.
SOMEONE'S AFTER YOU.
CLICK

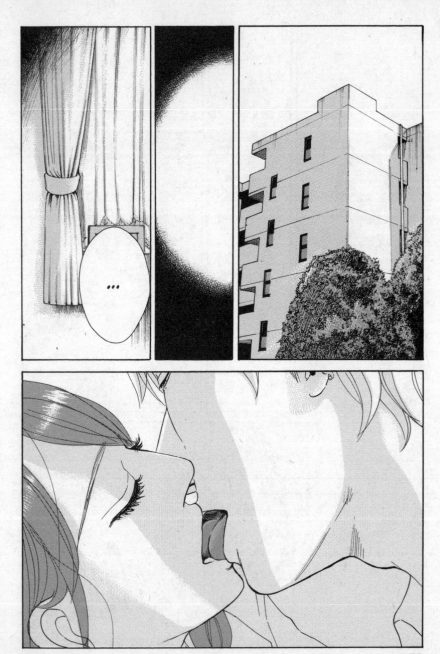

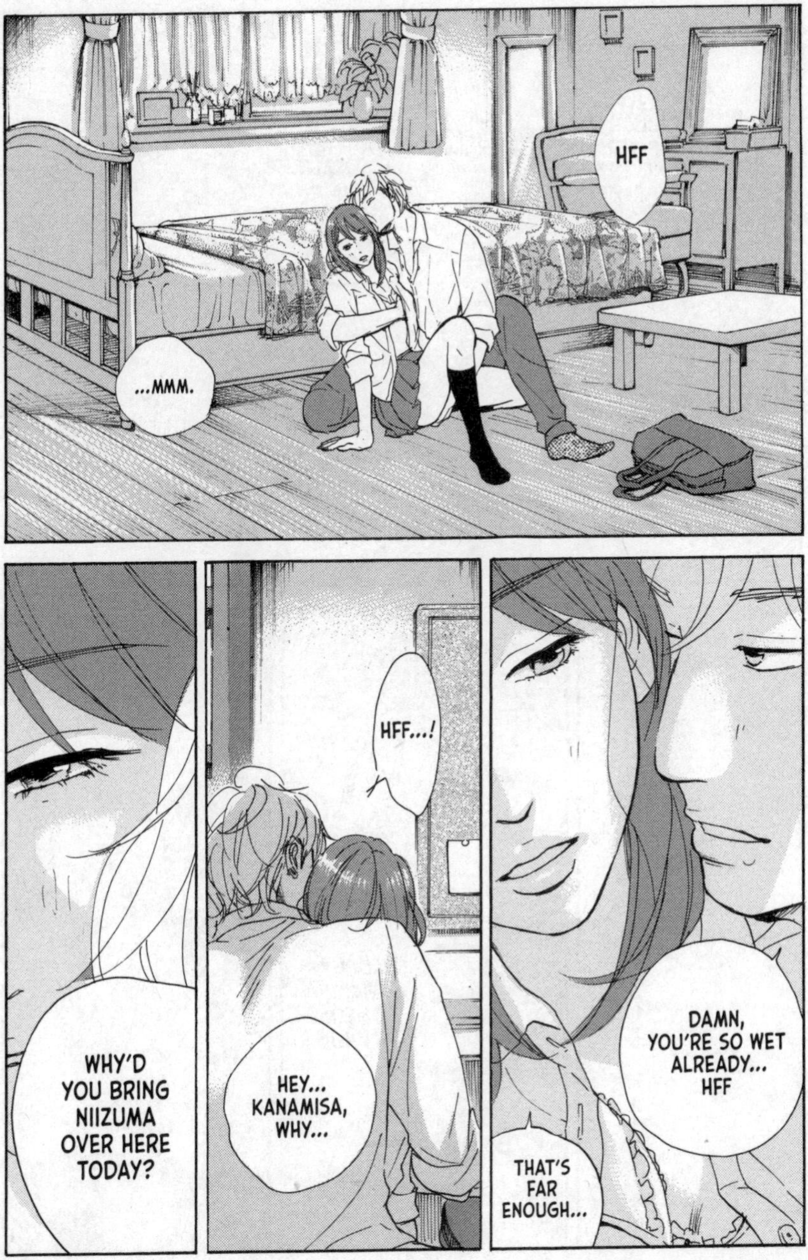
HFF
...MMM.
DAMN, YOU'RE SO WET ALREADY... HFF
THAT'S FAR ENOUGH...
HFF...!
HEY... KANAMISA, WHY...
WHY'D YOU BRING NIIZUMA OVER HERE TODAY?

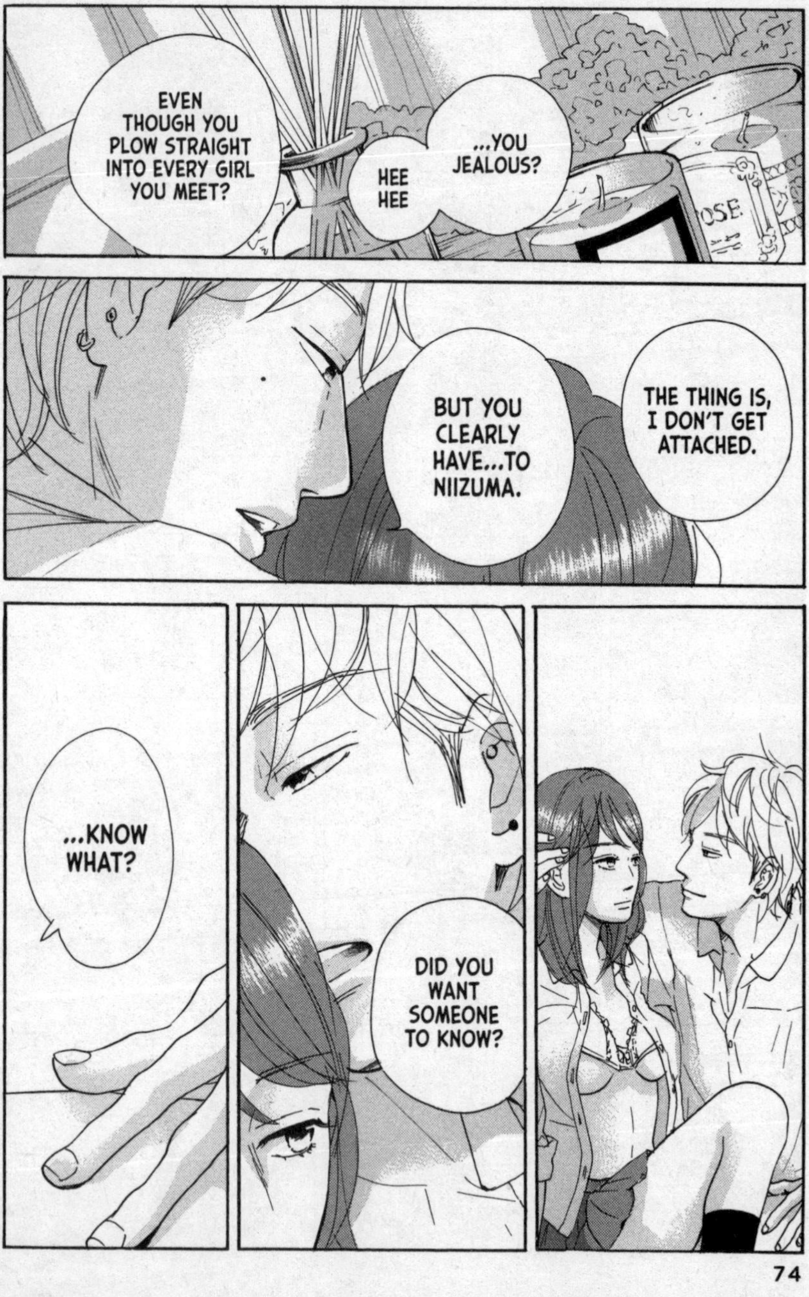
...YOU JEALOUS?
HEE HEE
EVEN THOUGH YOU PLOW STRAIGHT INTO EVERY GIRL YOU MEET?
THE THING IS, I DON'T GET ATTACHED.
BUT YOU CLEARLY HAVE...TO NIIZUMA.
DID YOU WANT SOMEONE TO KNOW?
...KNOW WHAT?

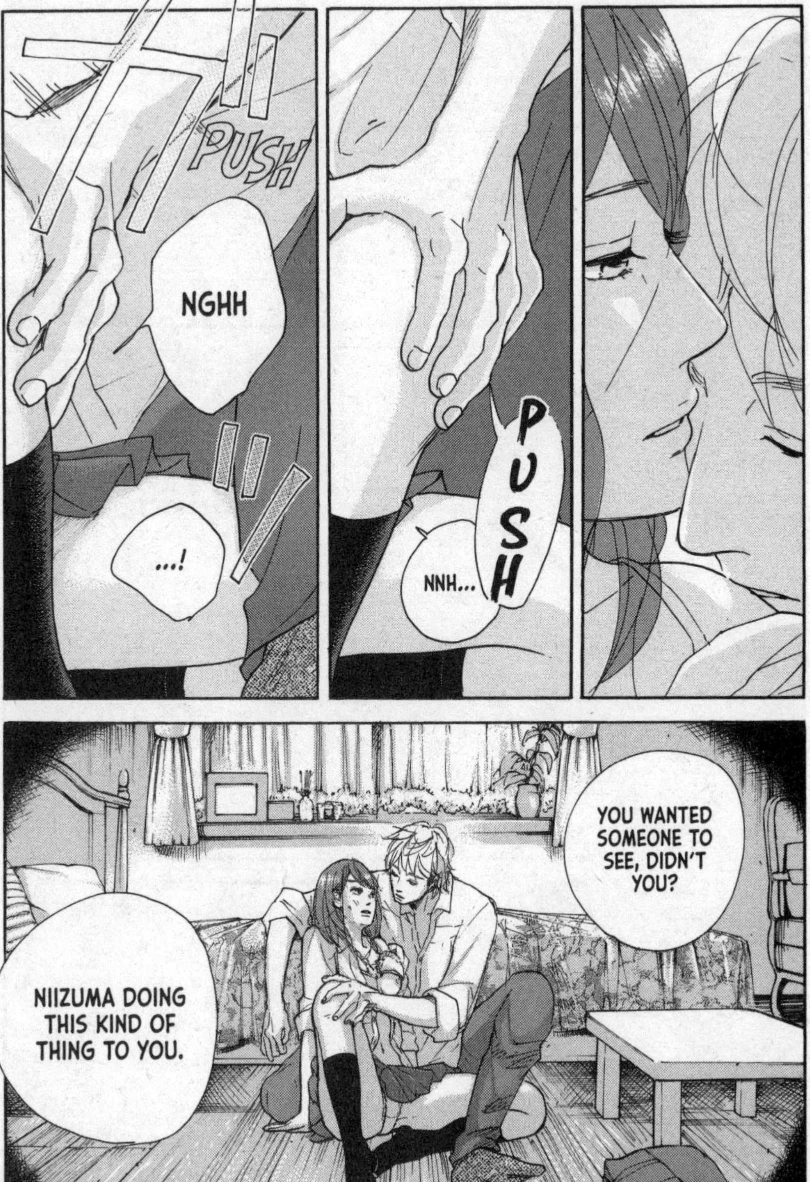
PUSH
NNH...
PUSH
NGHH
...!
YOU WANTED SOMEONE TO SEE, DIDN'T YOU?
NIIZUMA DOING THIS KIND OF THING TO YOU.

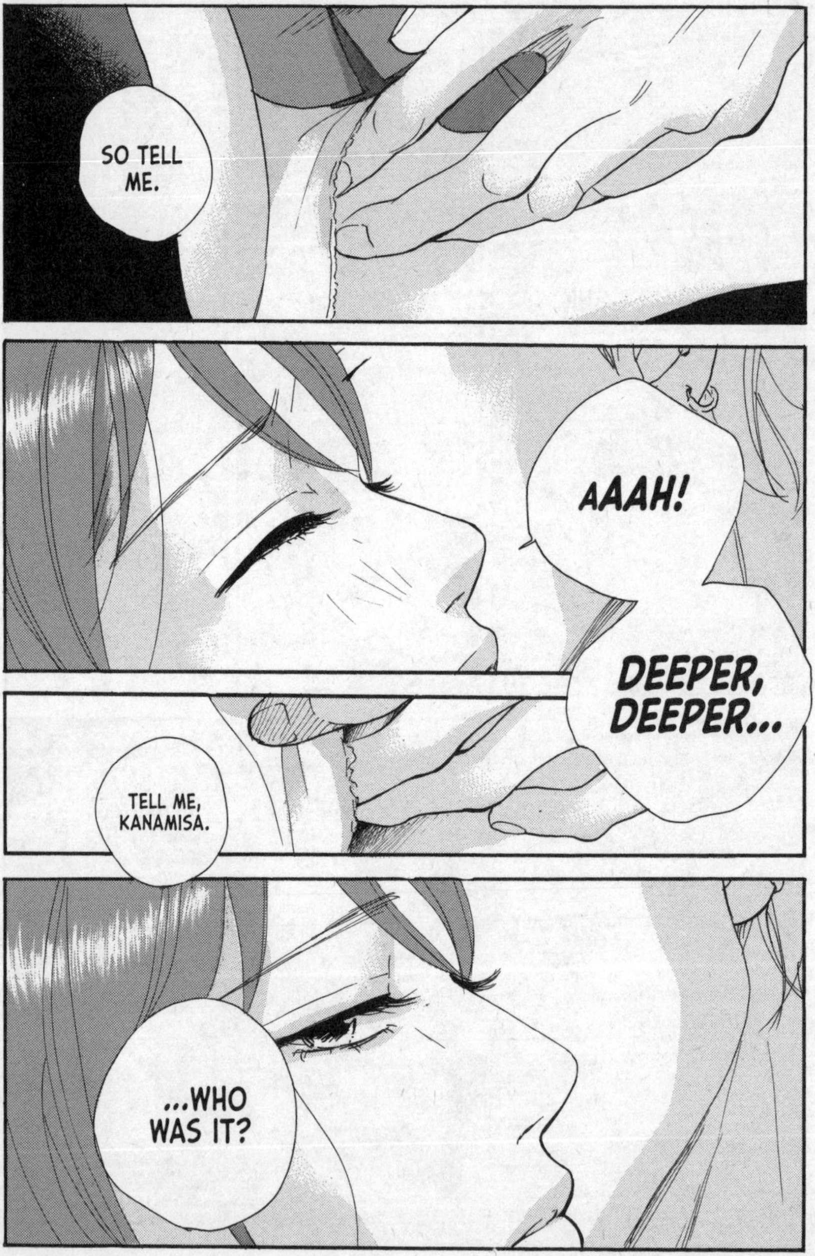
SO TELL ME.
AAAH!
DEEPER, DEEPER...
TELL ME, KANAMISA.
...WHO WAS IT?

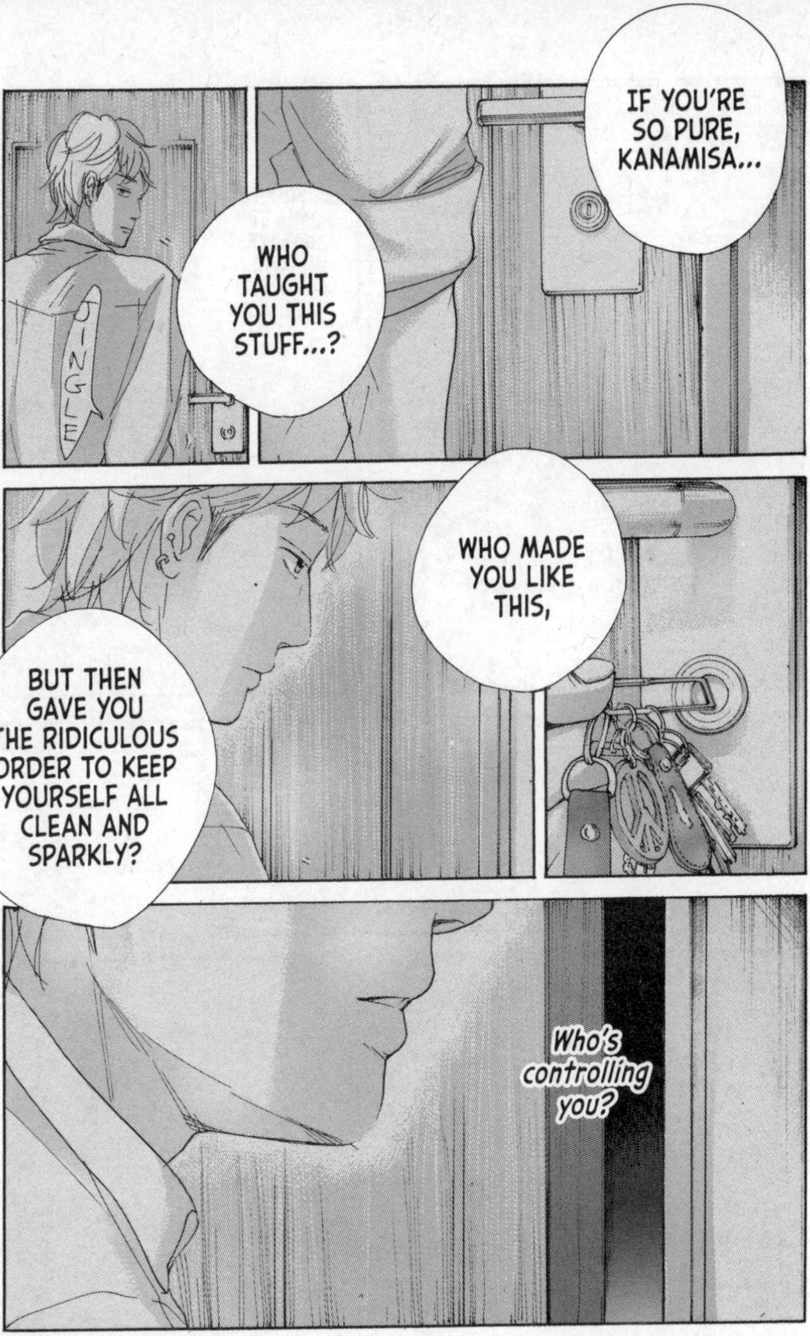
IF YOU'RE SO PURE, KANAMISA...
WHO TAUGHT YOU THIS STUFF...?
JINGLE
WHO MADE YOU LIKE THIS,
BUT THEN GAVE YOU THE RIDICULOUS ORDER TO KEEP YOURSELF ALL CLEAN AND SPARKLY?
Who's controlling you?

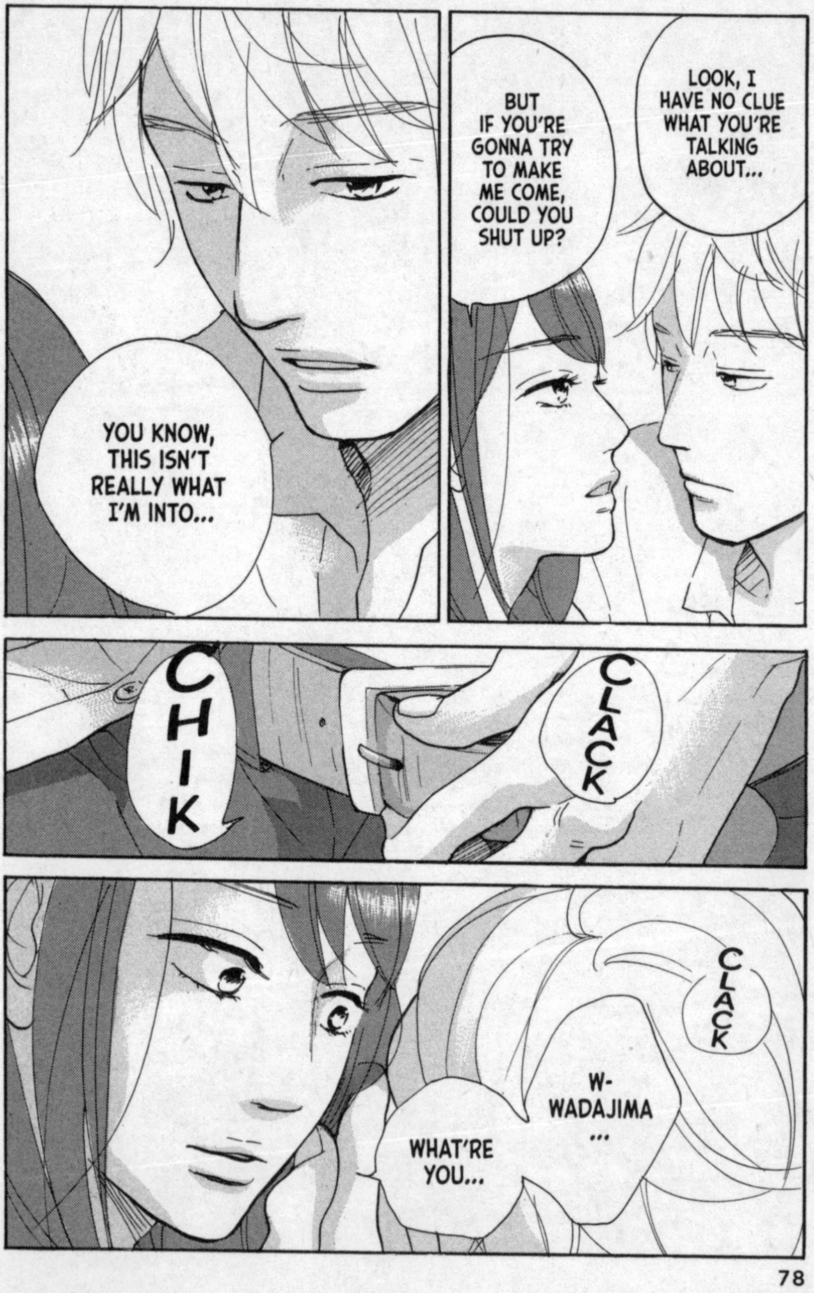
LOOK, I HAVE NO CLUE WHAT YOU'RE TALKING ABOUT...
BUT IF YOU'RE GONNA TRY TO MAKE ME COME, COULD YOU SHUT UP?
YOU KNOW, THIS ISN'T REALLY WHAT I'M INTO...
CLACK
CHIK
CLACK
W- WADAJIMA ...
WHAT'RE YOU...

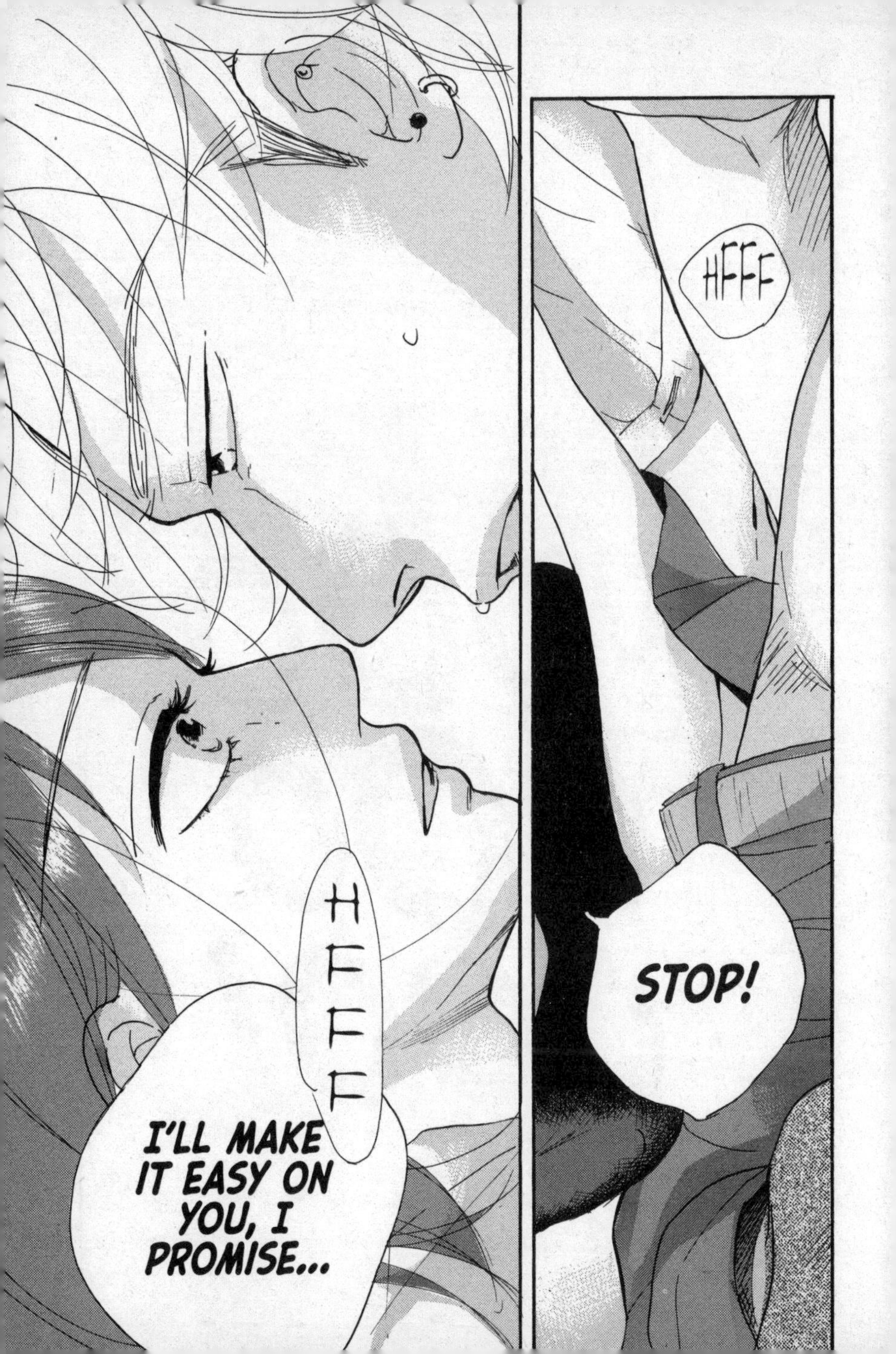
HFFF
STOP!
HFFF
I'LL MAKE IT EASY ON YOU, I PROMISE...

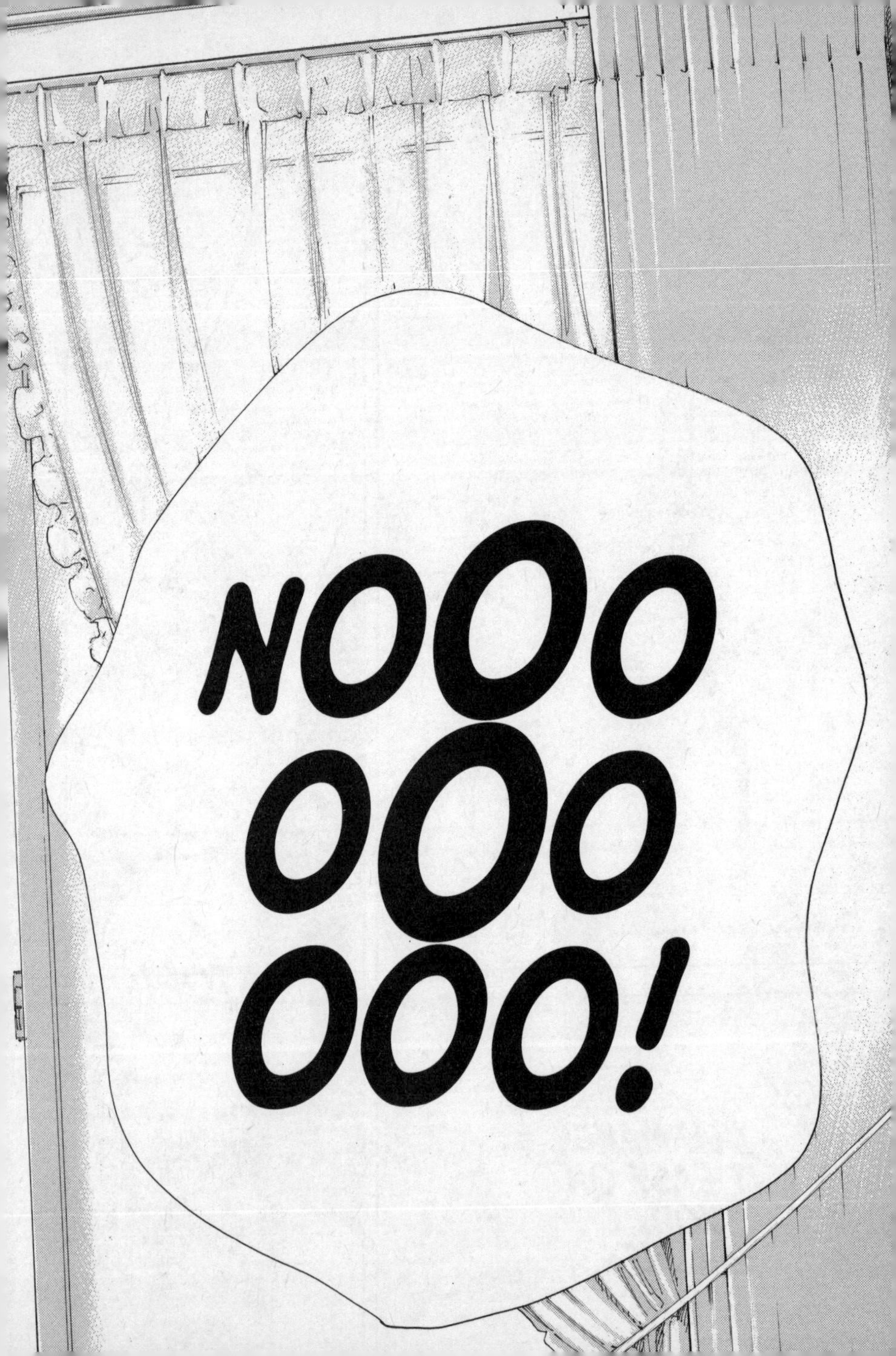
NOOOOOOOOO!

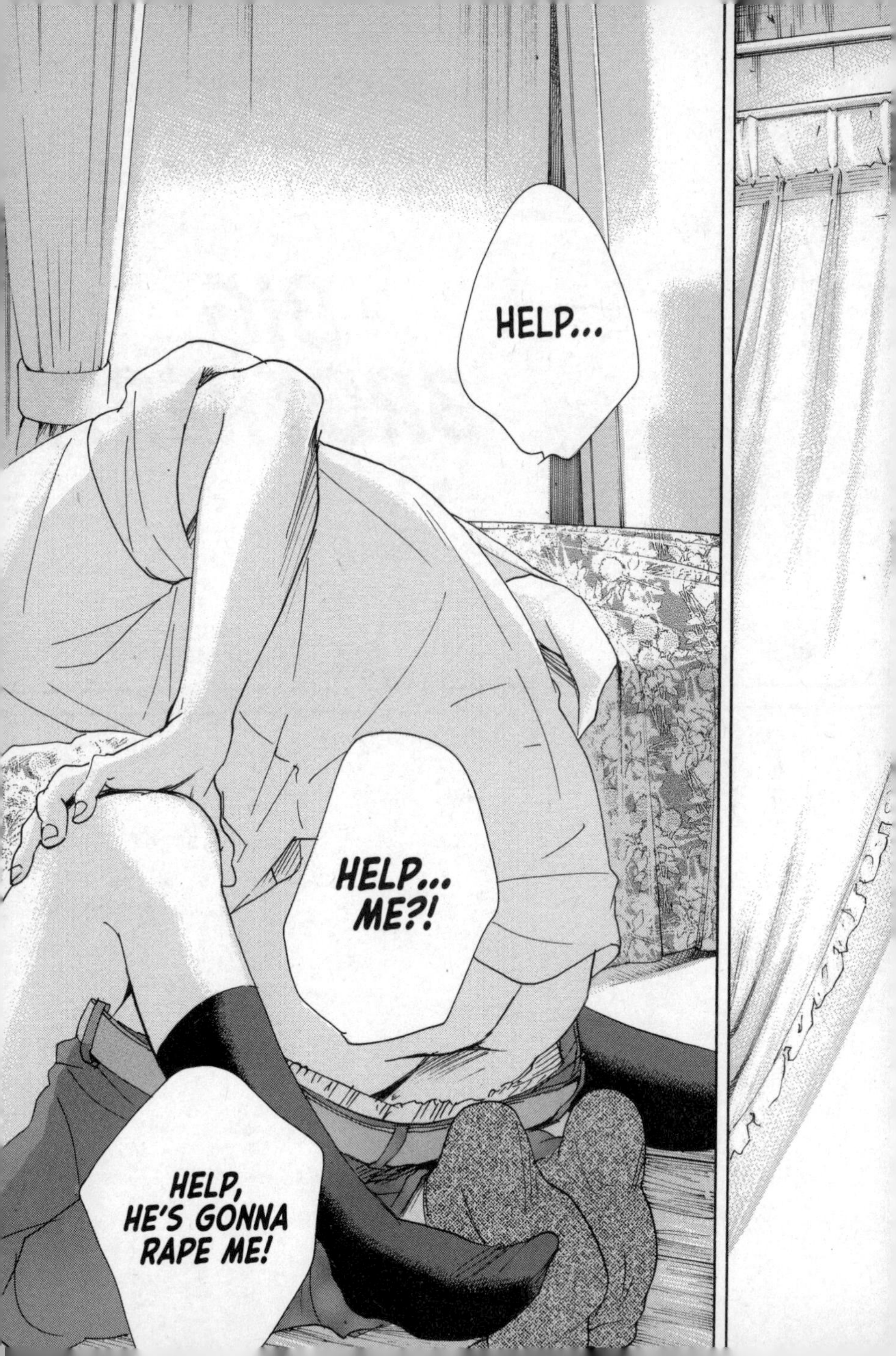
HELP...
HELP... ME?!
HELP, HE'S GONNA RAPE ME!

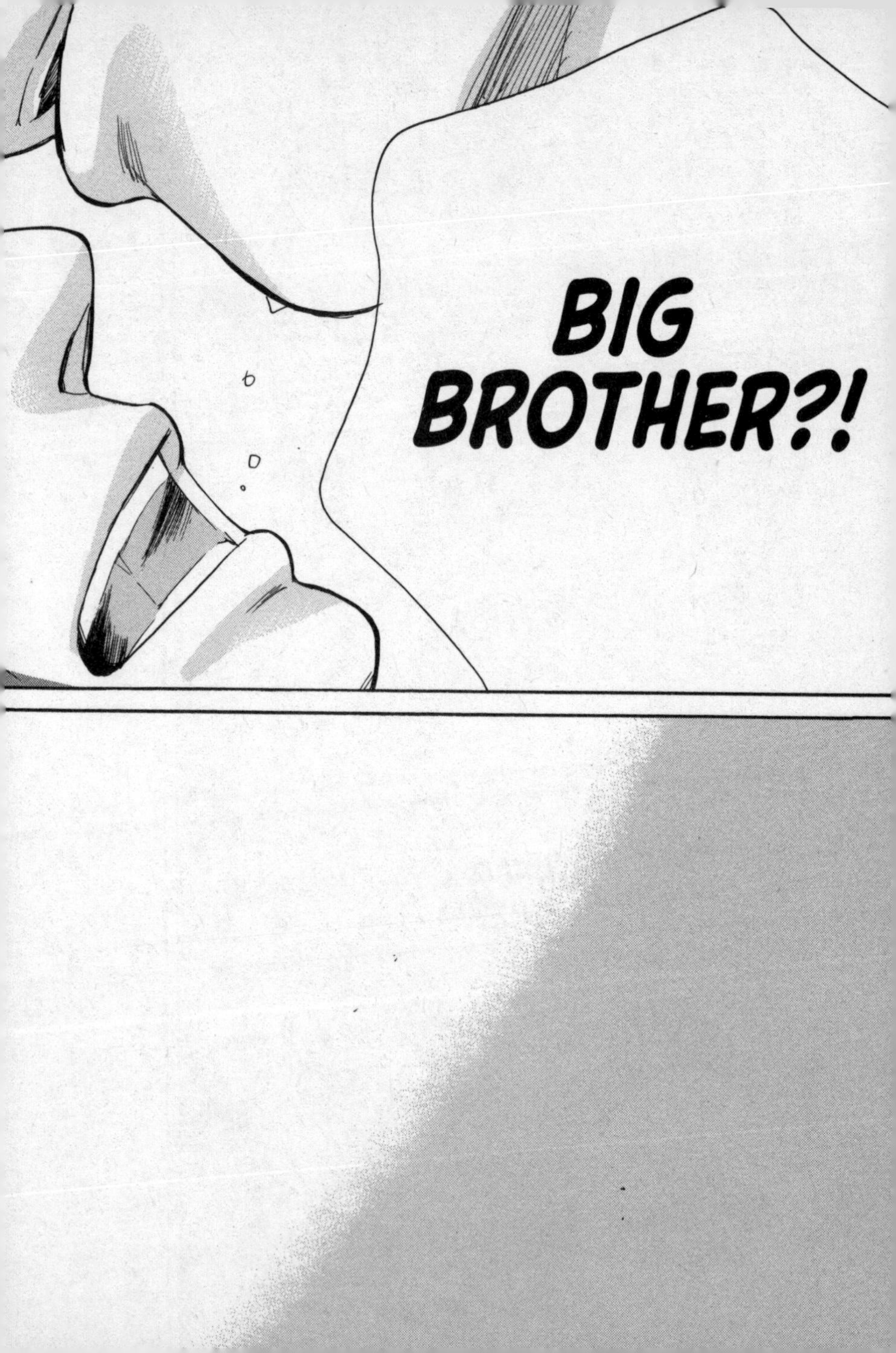
BIG BROTHER?!

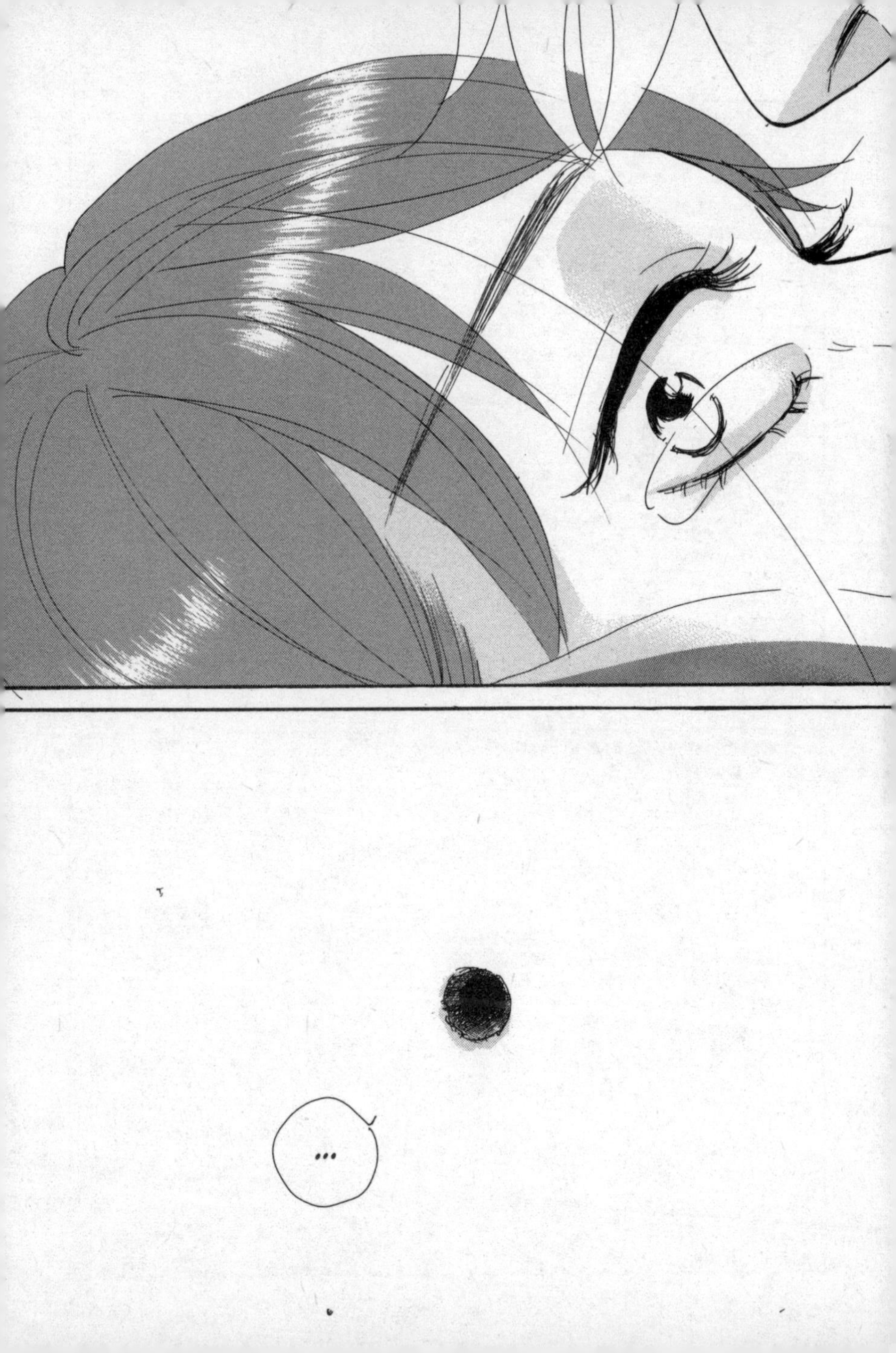
...

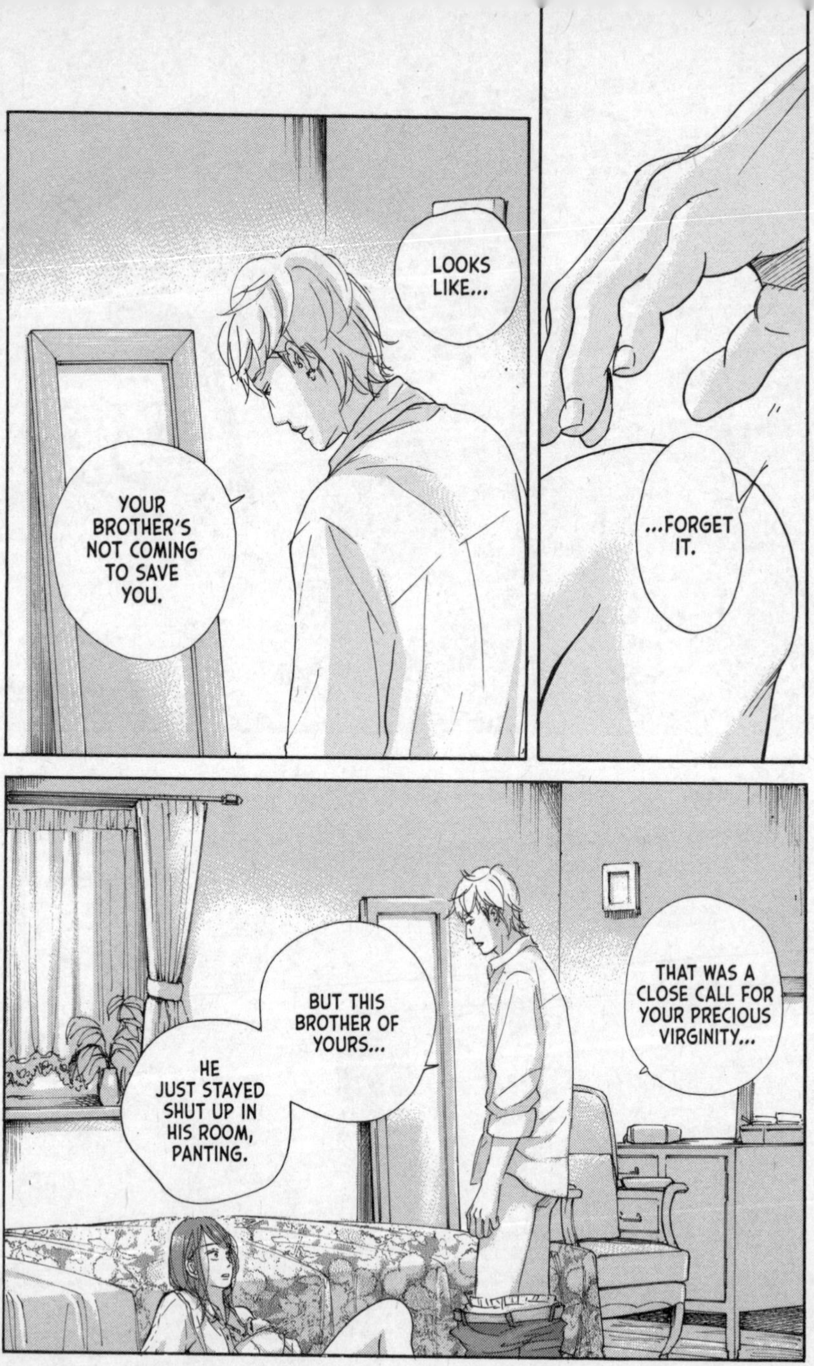
...FORGET IT.
LOOKS LIKE...
YOUR BROTHER'S NOT COMING TO SAVE YOU.
THAT WAS A CLOSE CALL FOR YOUR PRECIOUS VIRGINITY...
BUT THIS BROTHER OF YOURS...
HE JUST STAYED SHUT UP IN HIS ROOM, PANTING.

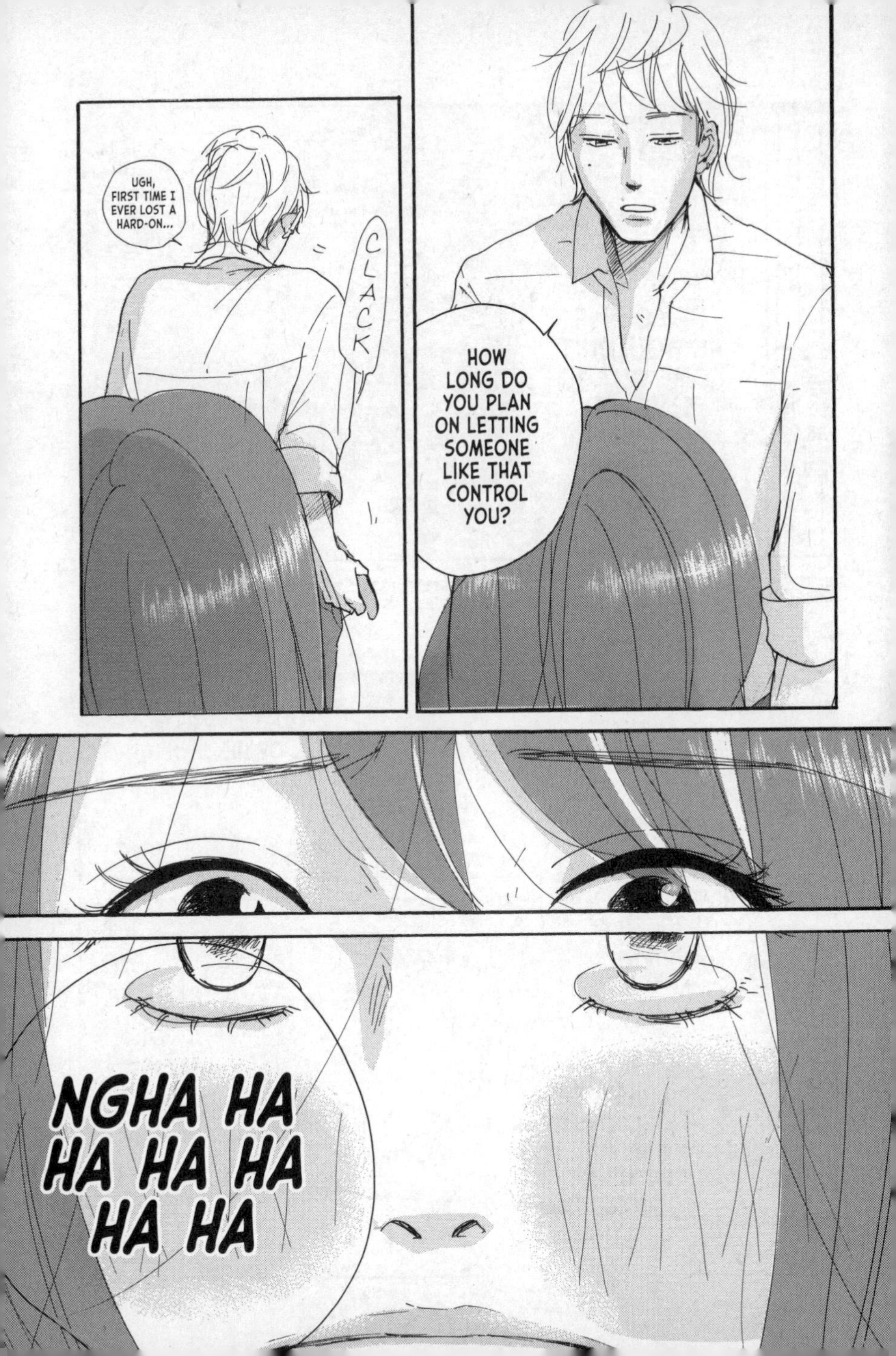
HOW LONG DO YOU PLAN ON LETTING SOMEONE LIKE THAT CONTROL YOU?
UGH, FIRST TIME I EVER LOST A HARD-ON...
CLACK
NGHA HA HA HA HA HA HA

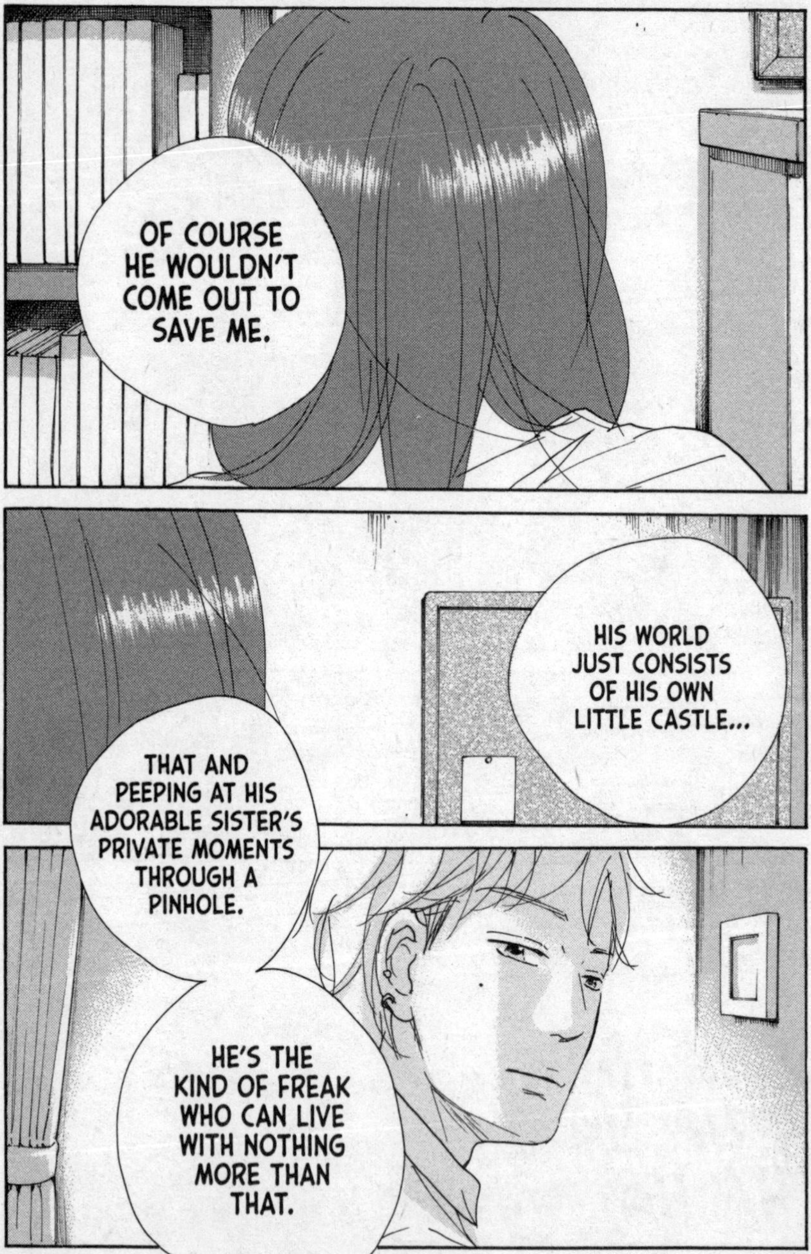
OF COURSE HE WOULDN'T COME OUT TO SAVE ME.
HIS WORLD JUST CONSISTS OF HIS OWN LITTLE CASTLE...
THAT AND PEEPING AT HIS ADORABLE SISTER'S PRIVATE MOMENTS THROUGH A PINHOLE.
HE'S THE KIND OF FREAK WHO CAN LIVE WITH NOTHING MORE THAN THAT.

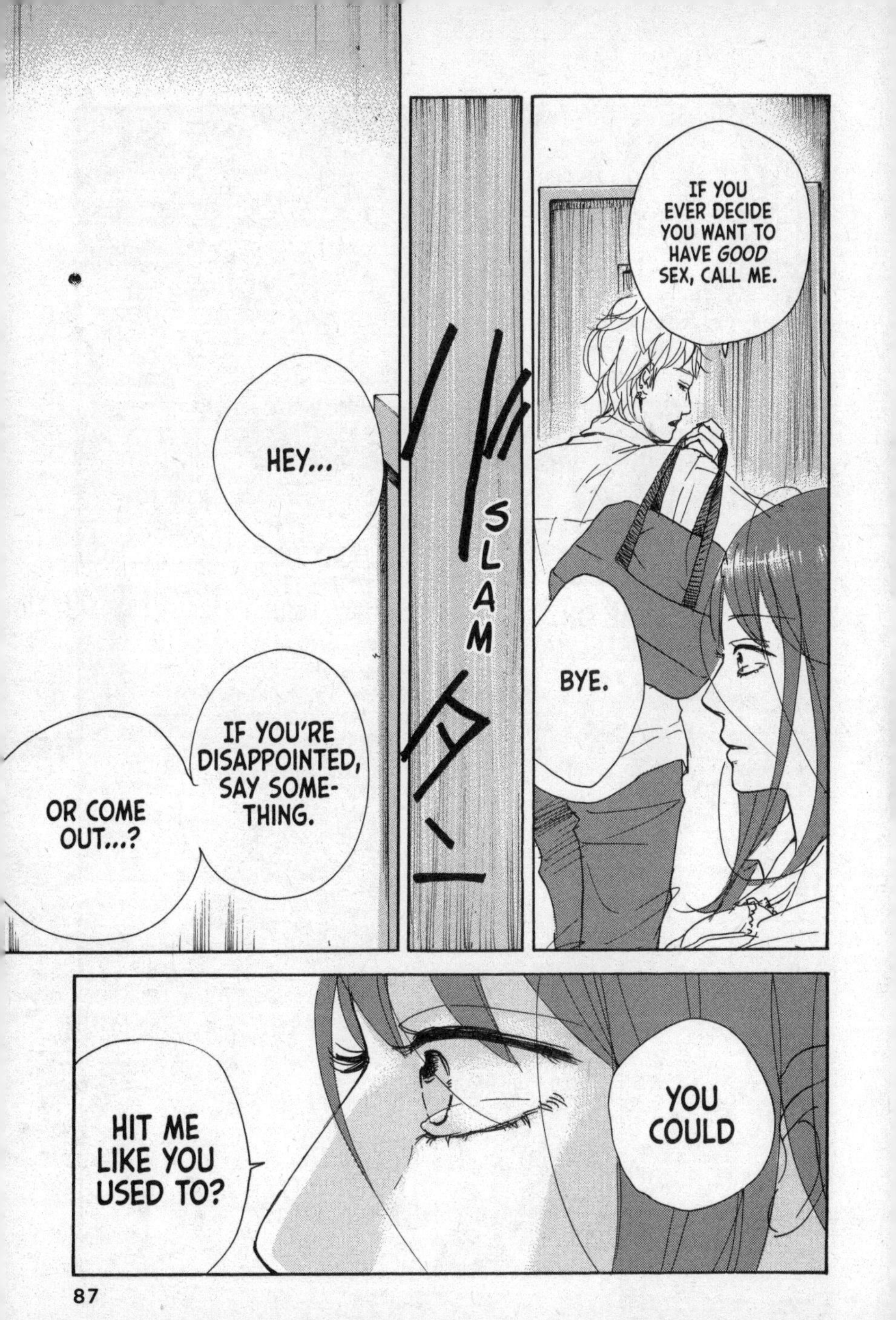
IF YOU EVER DECIDE YOU WANT TO HAVE *GOOD* SEX, CALL ME.
BYE.
SLAM
HEY...
IF YOU'RE DISAPPOINTED, SAY SOME-THING.
OR COME OUT...?
YOU COULD
HIT ME LIKE YOU USED TO?

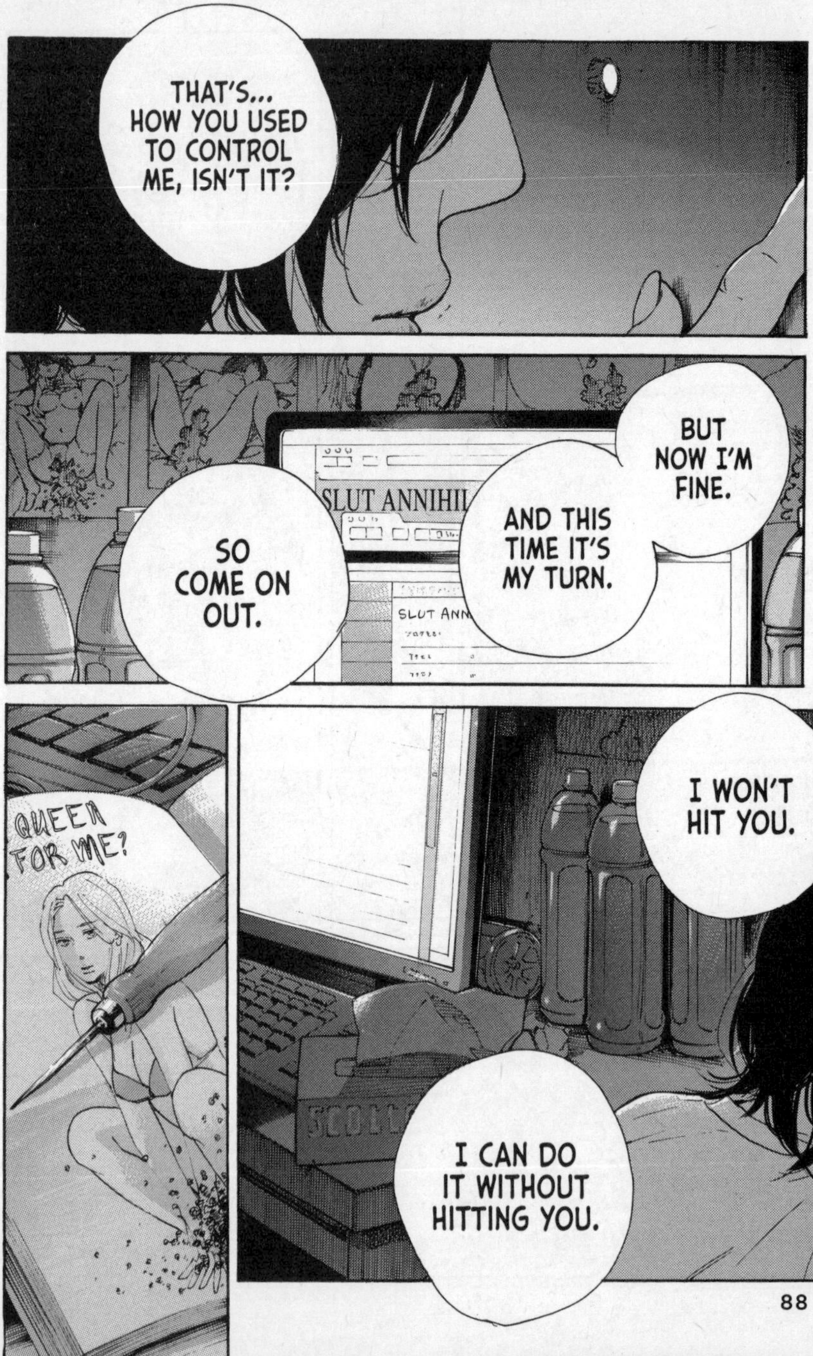
THAT'S... HOW YOU USED TO CONTROL ME, ISN'T IT?
BUT NOW I'M FINE.
AND THIS TIME IT'S MY TURN.
SO COME ON OUT.
I WON'T HIT YOU.
I CAN DO IT WITHOUT HITTING YOU.
QUEEN FOR ME?

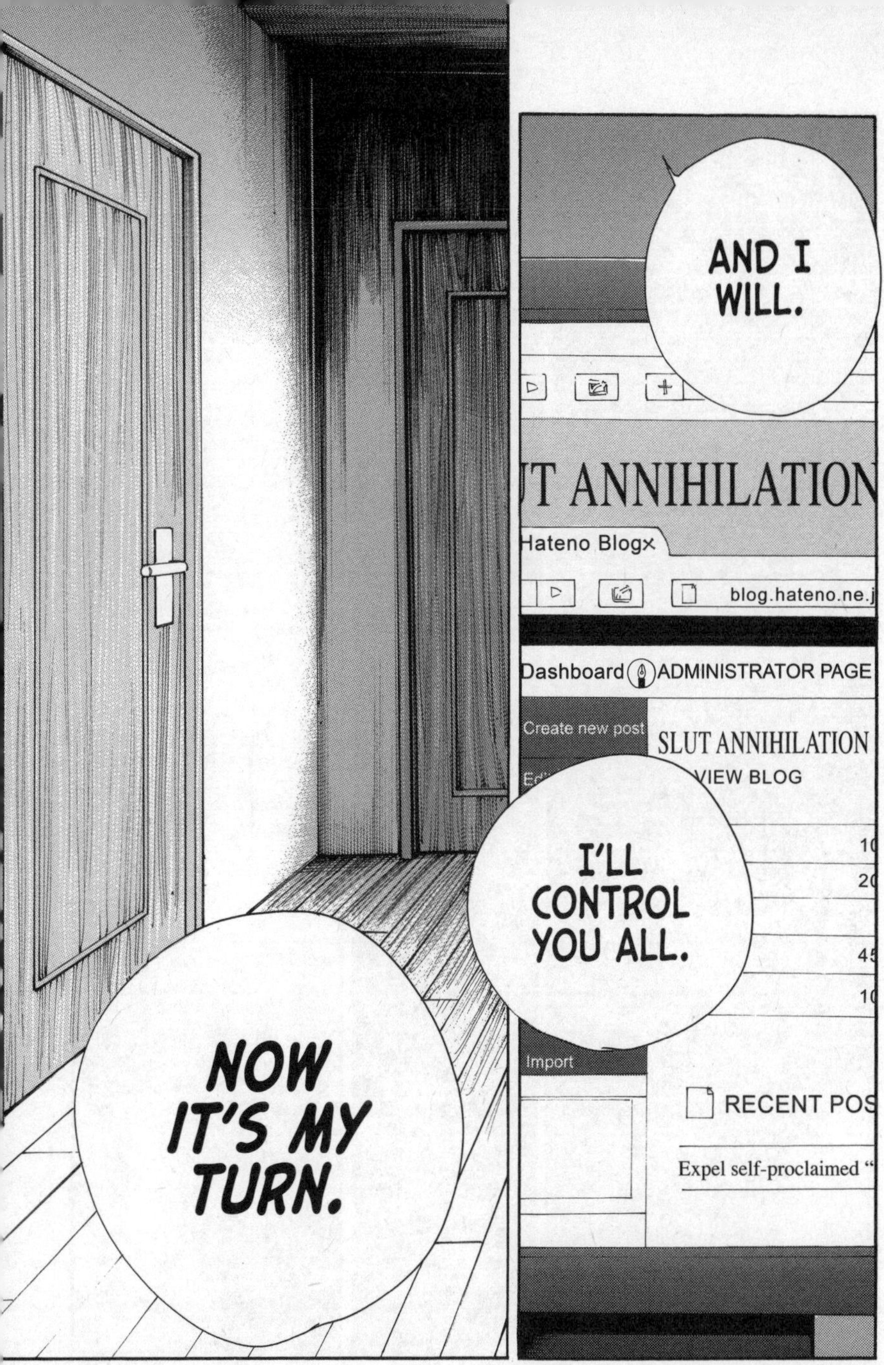

AND I WILL.
UT ANNIHILATION
Hateno Blog×
blog.hateno.ne.j
Dashboard
ADMINISTRATOR PAGE
Create new post
SLUT ANNIHILATION
VIEW BLOG
I'LL CONTROL YOU ALL.
Import
RECENT POS
Expel self-proclaimed "
NOW IT'S MY TURN.

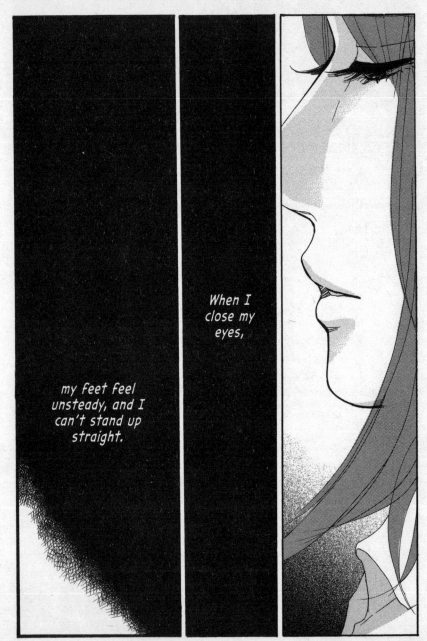

When I close my eyes,

my feet feel unsteady, and I can't stand up straight.

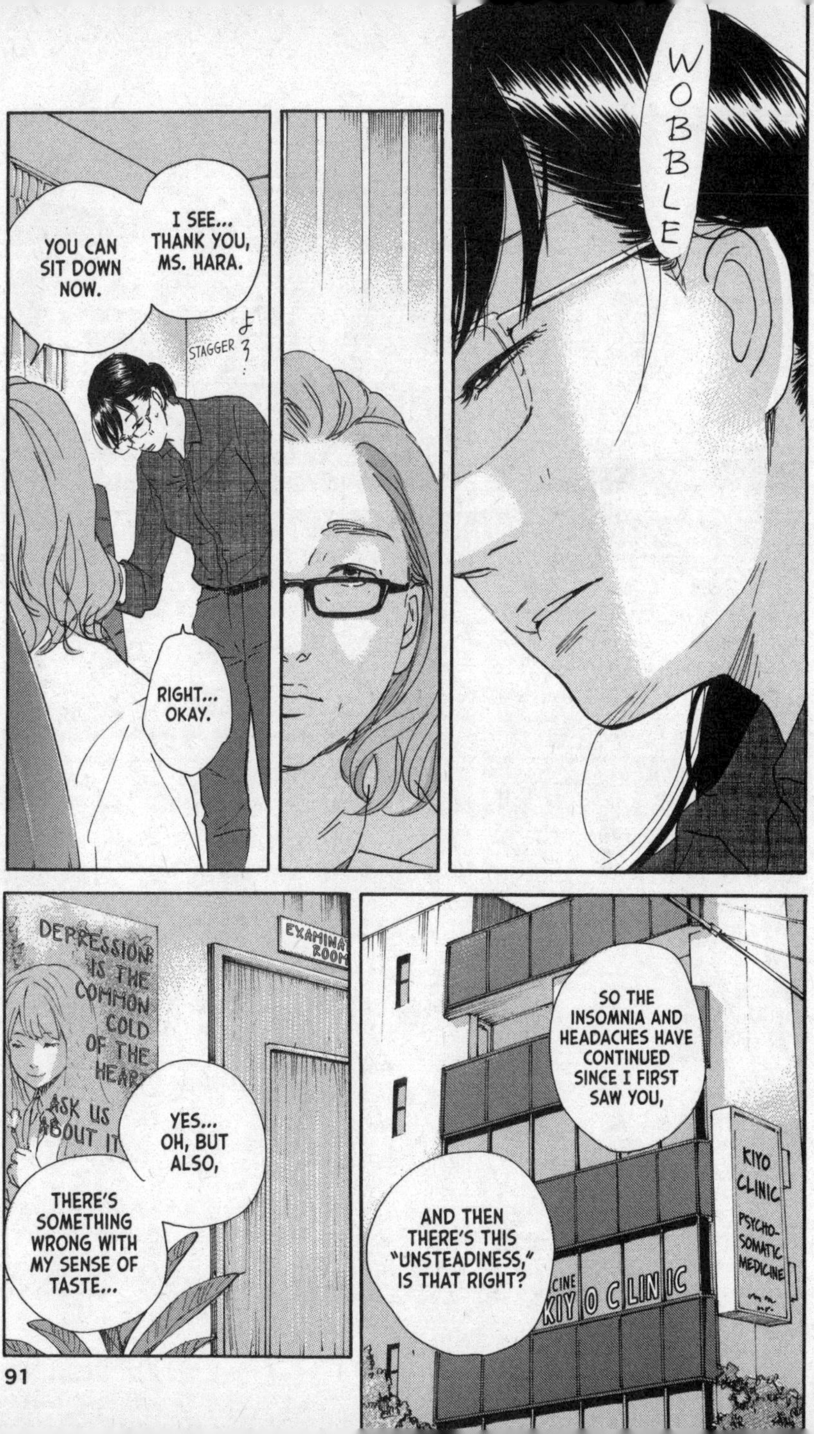
WOBBLE
I SEE... THANK YOU, MS. HARA.
YOU CAN SIT DOWN NOW.
STAGGER
よろ
RIGHT... OKAY.
SO THE INSOMNIA AND HEADACHES HAVE CONTINUED SINCE I FIRST SAW YOU,
AND THEN THERE'S THIS "UNSTEADINESS," IS THAT RIGHT?
KIYO CLINIC
PSYCHO-SOMATIC MEDICINE
CINE
KIY O C LIN IC
EXAMINAT ROOM
DEPRESSION IS THE COMMON COLD OF THE HEAR
ASK US ABOUT IT
YES... OH, BUT ALSO,
THERE'S SOMETHING WRONG WITH MY SENSE OF TASTE...

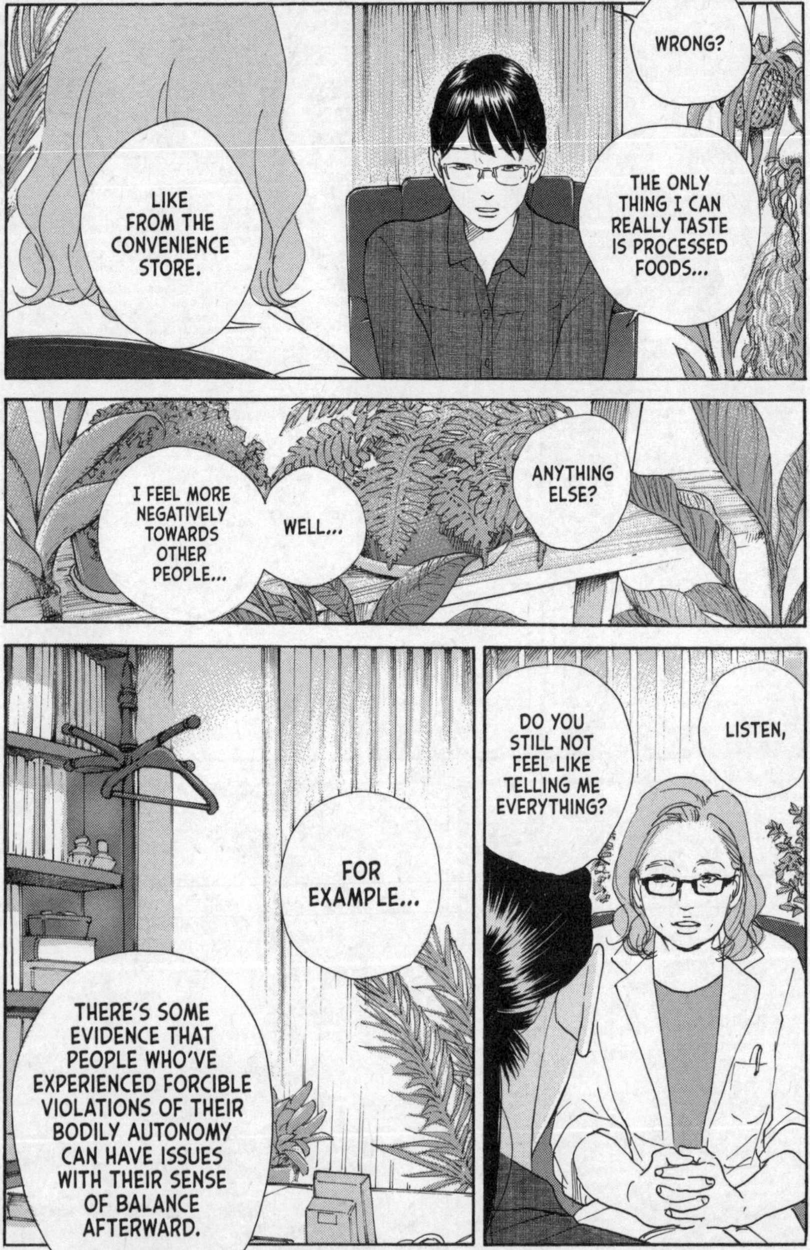
WRONG?
THE ONLY THING I CAN REALLY TASTE IS PROCESSED FOODS...
LIKE FROM THE CONVENIENCE STORE.
ANYTHING ELSE?
WELL...
I FEEL MORE NEGATIVELY TOWARDS OTHER PEOPLE...
LISTEN,
DO YOU STILL NOT FEEL LIKE TELLING ME EVERYTHING?
FOR EXAMPLE...
THERE'S SOME EVIDENCE THAT PEOPLE WHO'VE EXPERIENCED FORCIBLE VIOLATIONS OF THEIR BODILY AUTONOMY CAN HAVE ISSUES WITH THEIR SENSE OF BALANCE AFTERWARD.

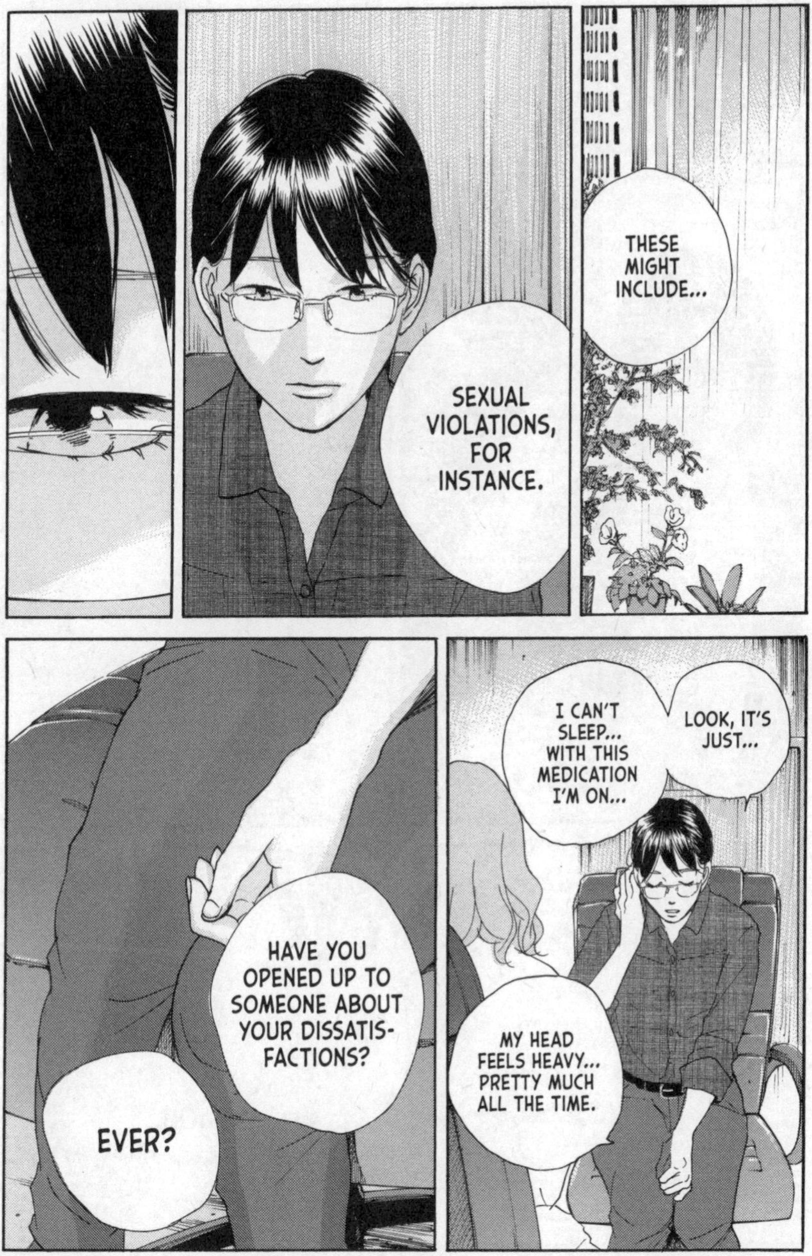
THESE MIGHT INCLUDE...
SEXUAL VIOLATIONS, FOR INSTANCE.
LOOK, IT'S JUST...
I CAN'T SLEEP... WITH THIS MEDICATION I'M ON...
MY HEAD FEELS HEAVY... PRETTY MUCH ALL THE TIME.
HAVE YOU OPENED UP TO SOMEONE ABOUT YOUR DISSATIS-FACTIONS?
EVER?

to someone?

Opened up

NO,

I DON'T REALLY—

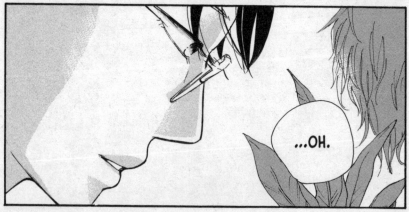

...OH.

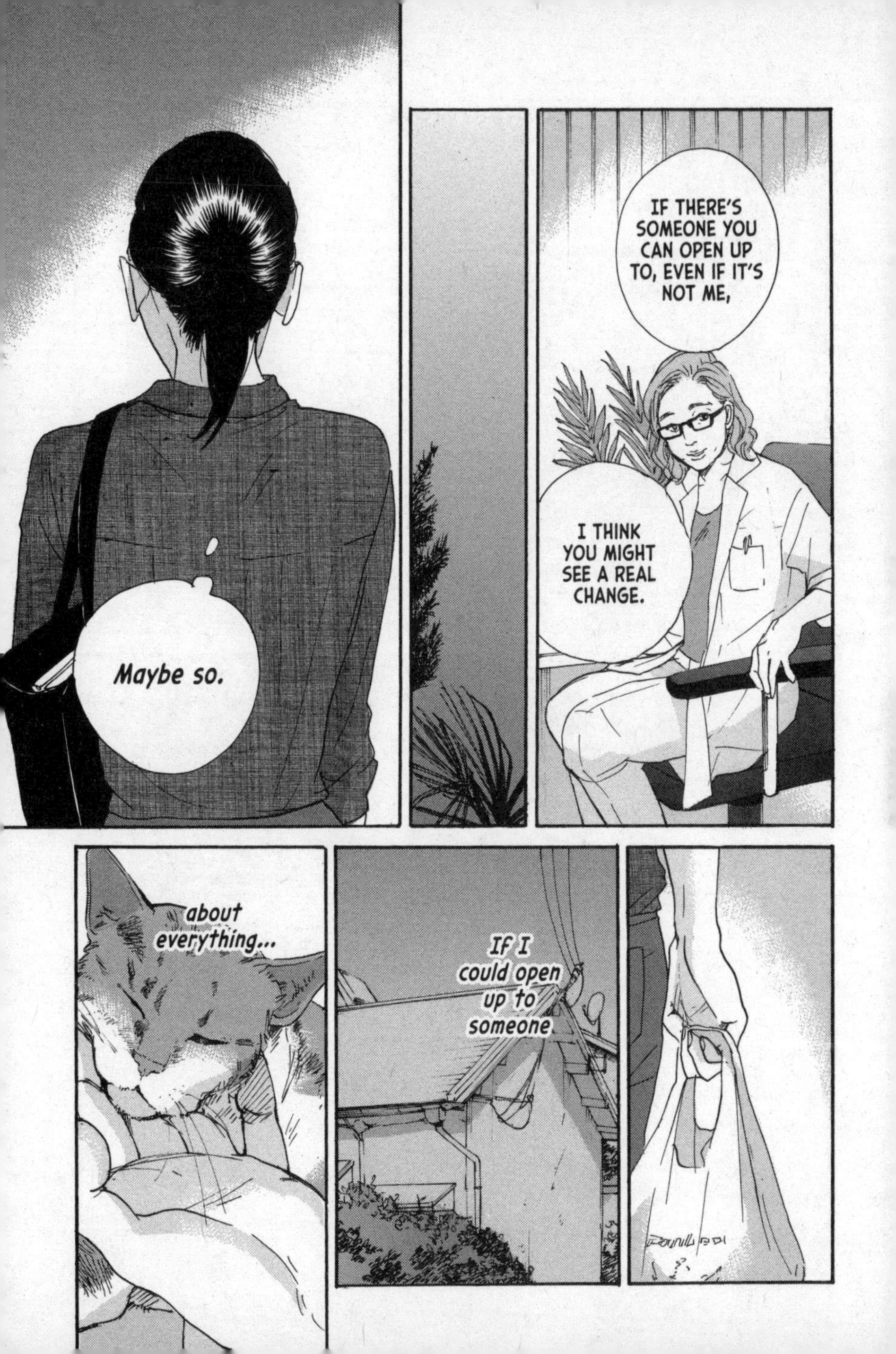
IF THERE'S SOMEONE YOU CAN OPEN UP TO, EVEN IF IT'S NOT ME,
I THINK YOU MIGHT SEE A REAL CHANGE.
Maybe so.
If I could open up to someone
about everything...

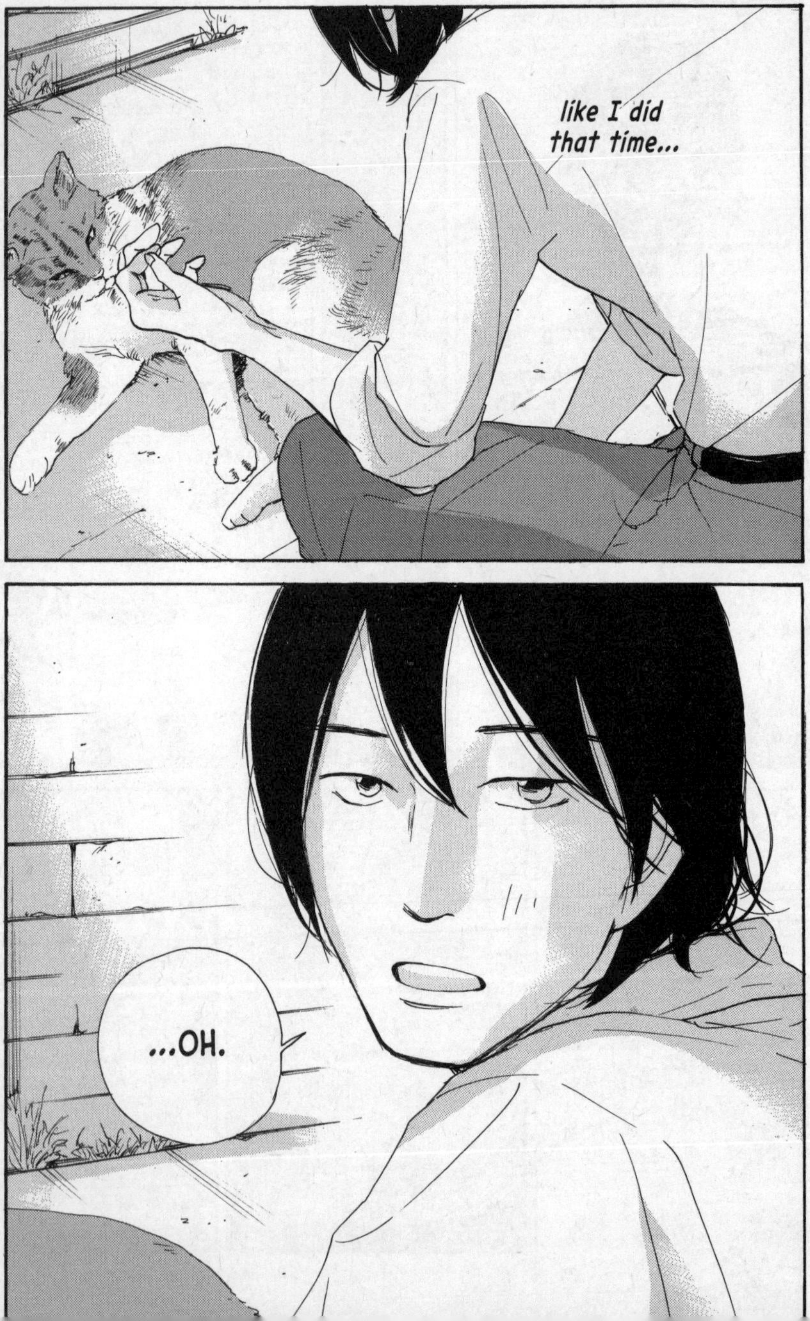
like I did that time...
...OH.

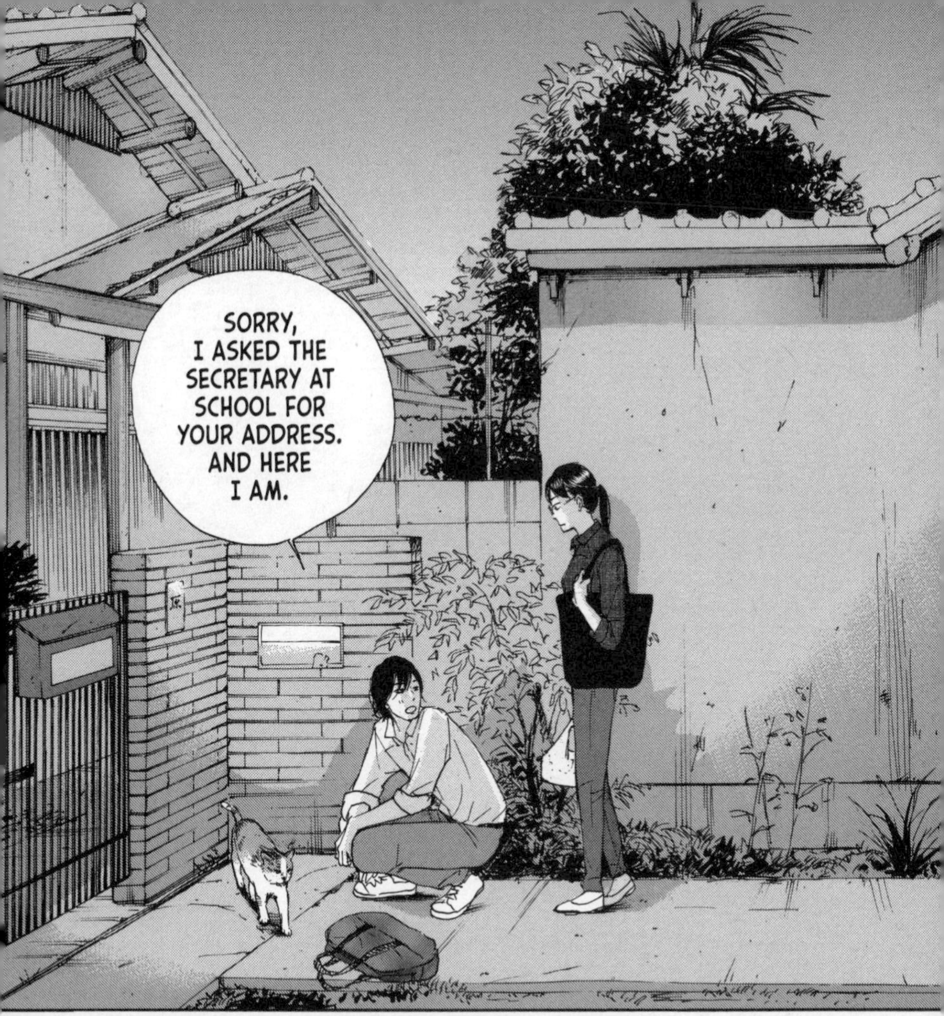
SORRY, I ASKED THE SECRETARY AT SCHOOL FOR YOUR ADDRESS. AND HERE I AM.

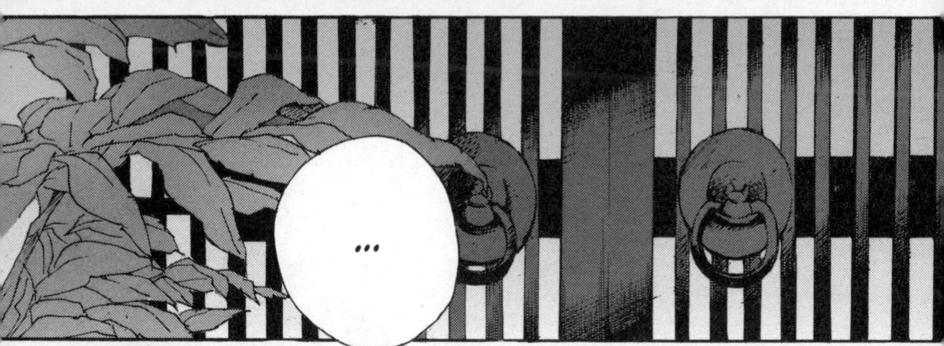
...

END

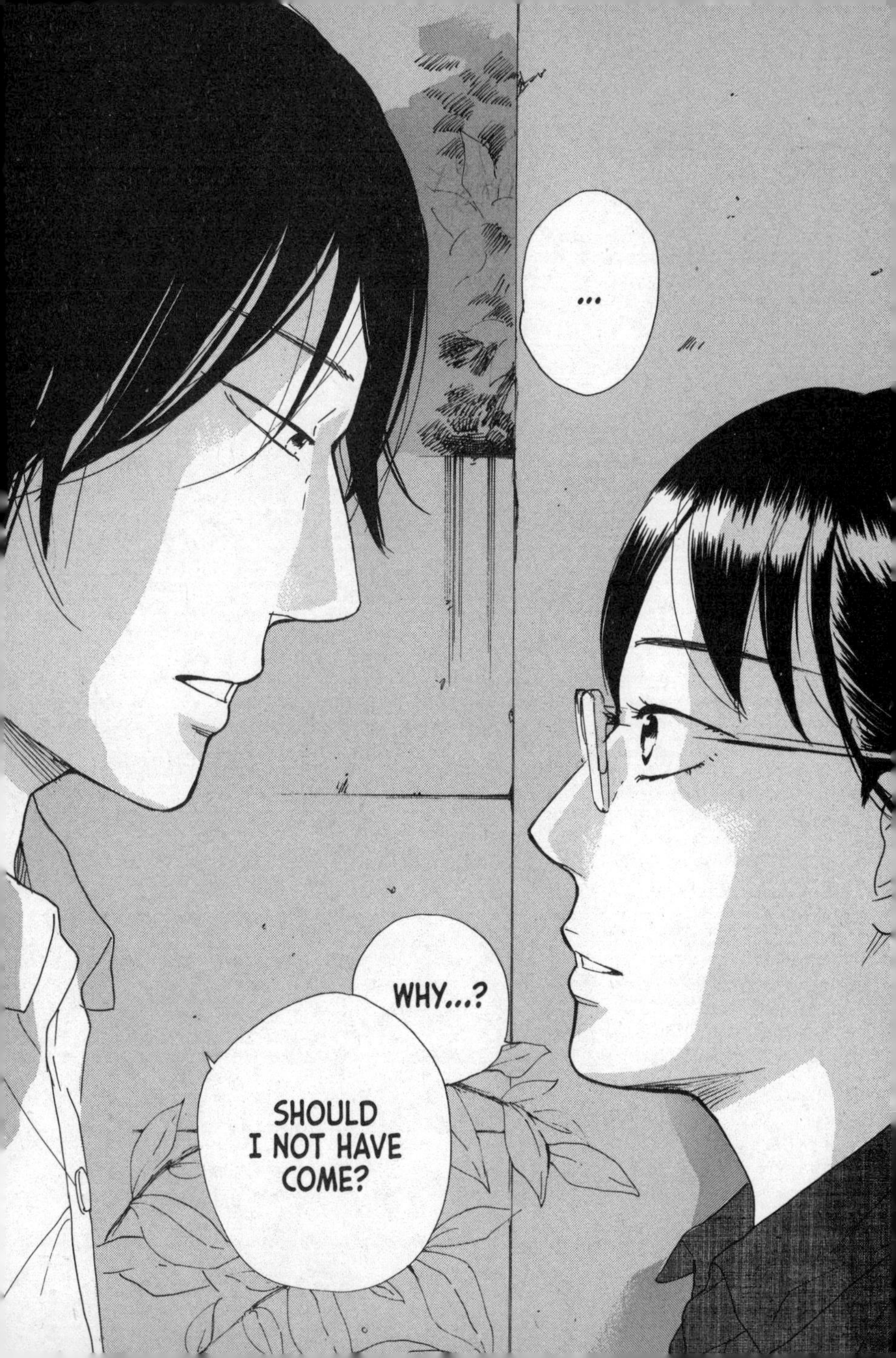
...
WHY...?
SHOULD I NOT HAVE COME?

CHAPTER 16. CALL FOR HELP IF YOU GET SCARED

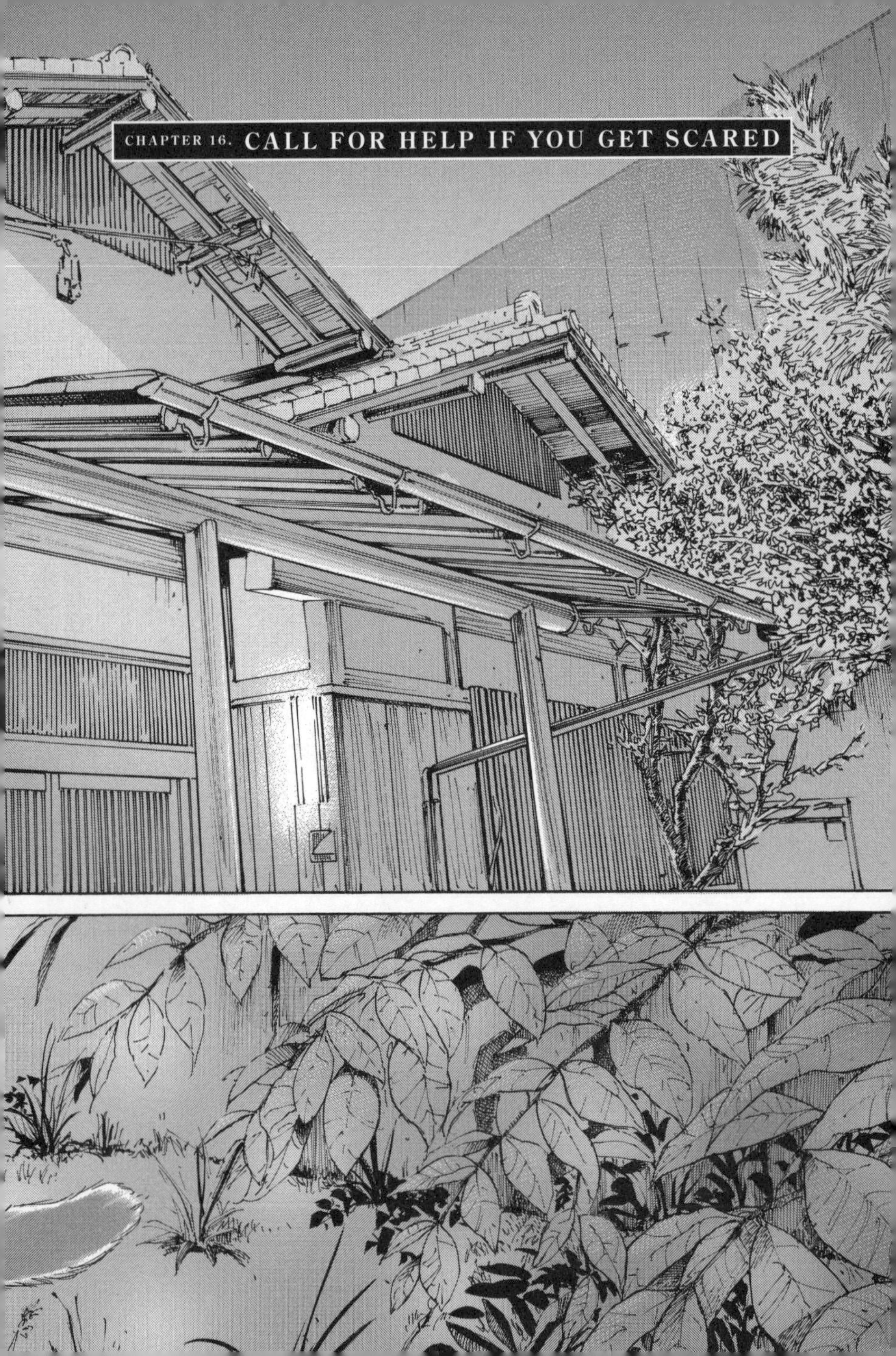

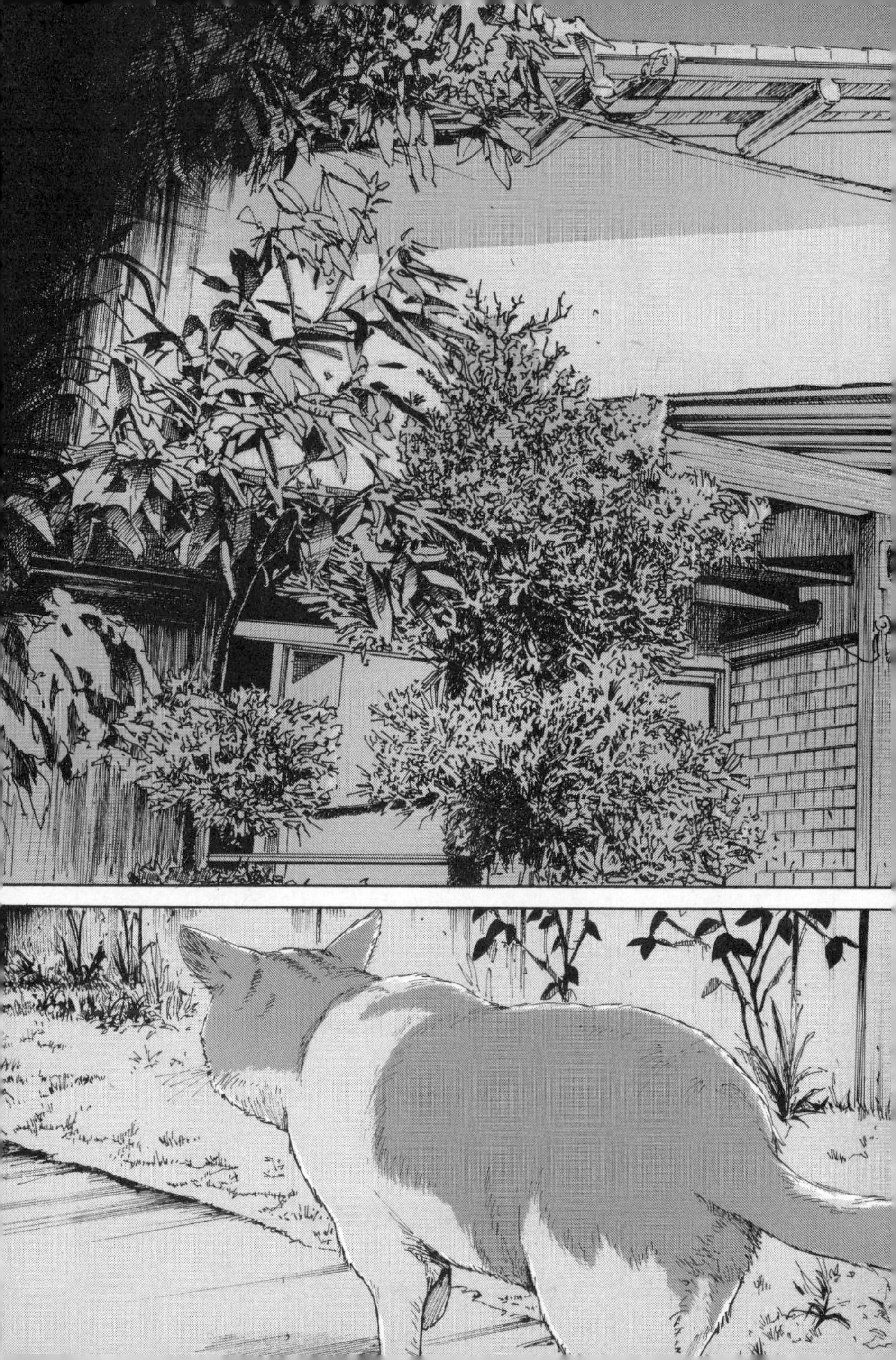

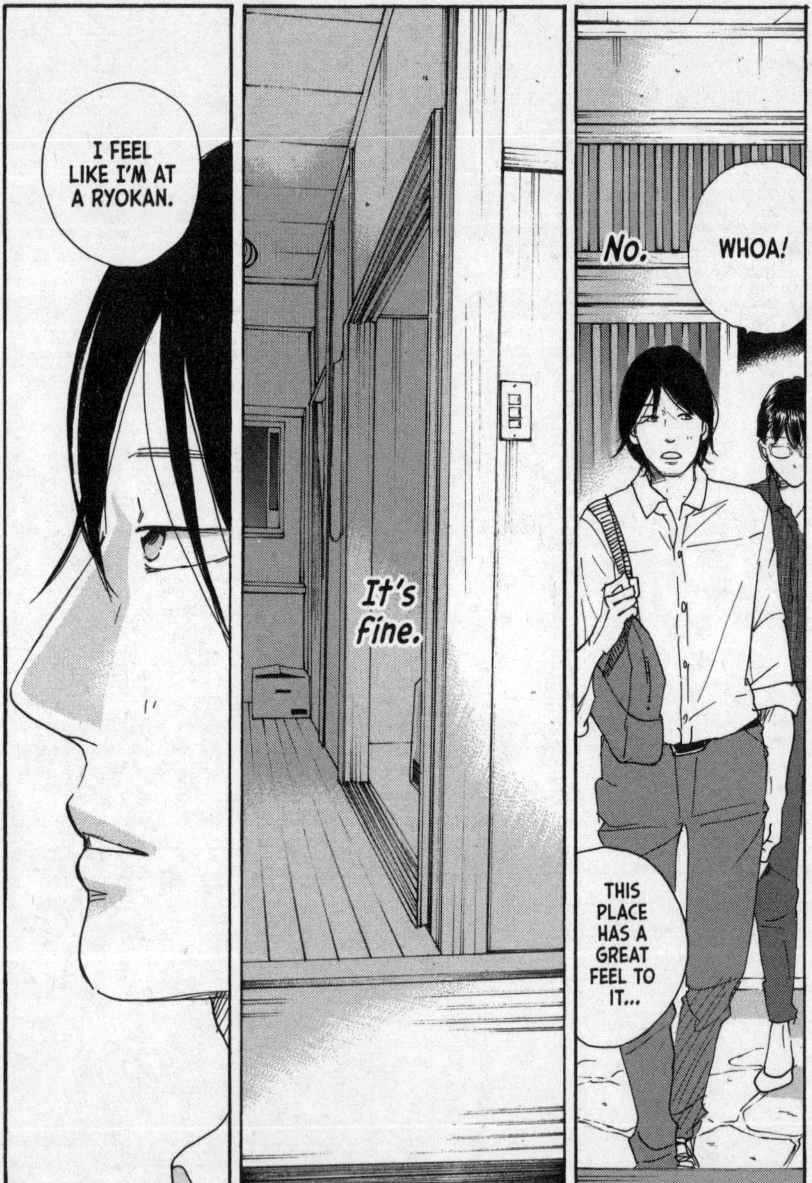
WHOA!
No.
THIS PLACE HAS A GREAT FEEL TO IT...
It's fine.
I FEEL LIKE I'M AT A RYOKAN.

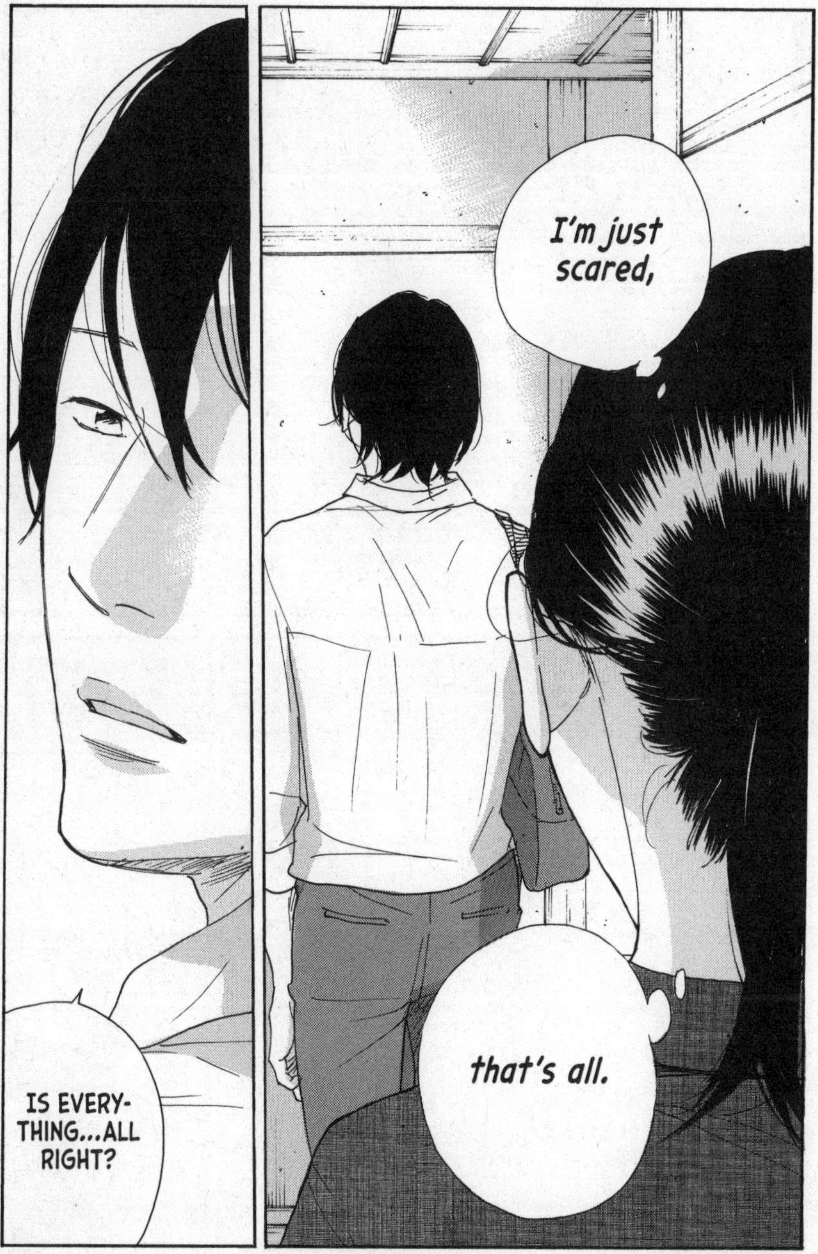
I'm just scared,
that's all.
IS EVERY-THING...ALL RIGHT?

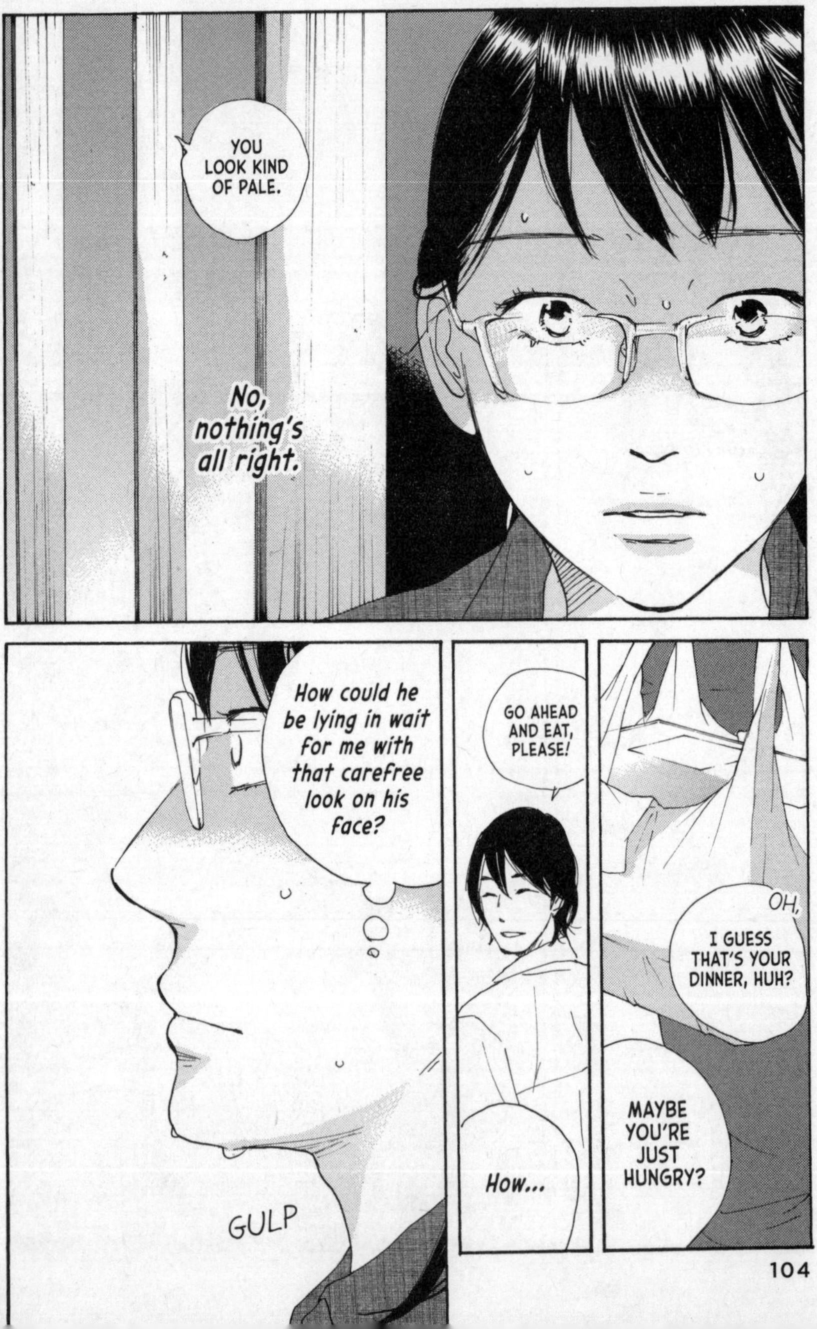
YOU LOOK KIND OF PALE.
No, nothing's all right.
OH, I GUESS THAT'S YOUR DINNER, HUH?
MAYBE YOU'RE JUST HUNGRY?
GO AHEAD AND EAT, PLEASE!
How...
How could he be lying in wait for me with that carefree look on his face?
GULP

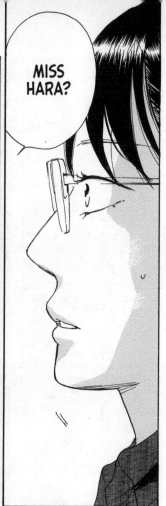

MISS HARA?

Right.

I'm his teacher, so it is all right.

W–

WAS THERE SOMETHING YOU NEEDED?

And he's my student.

I'm his teacher.

...I'LL MAKE SOME TEA.

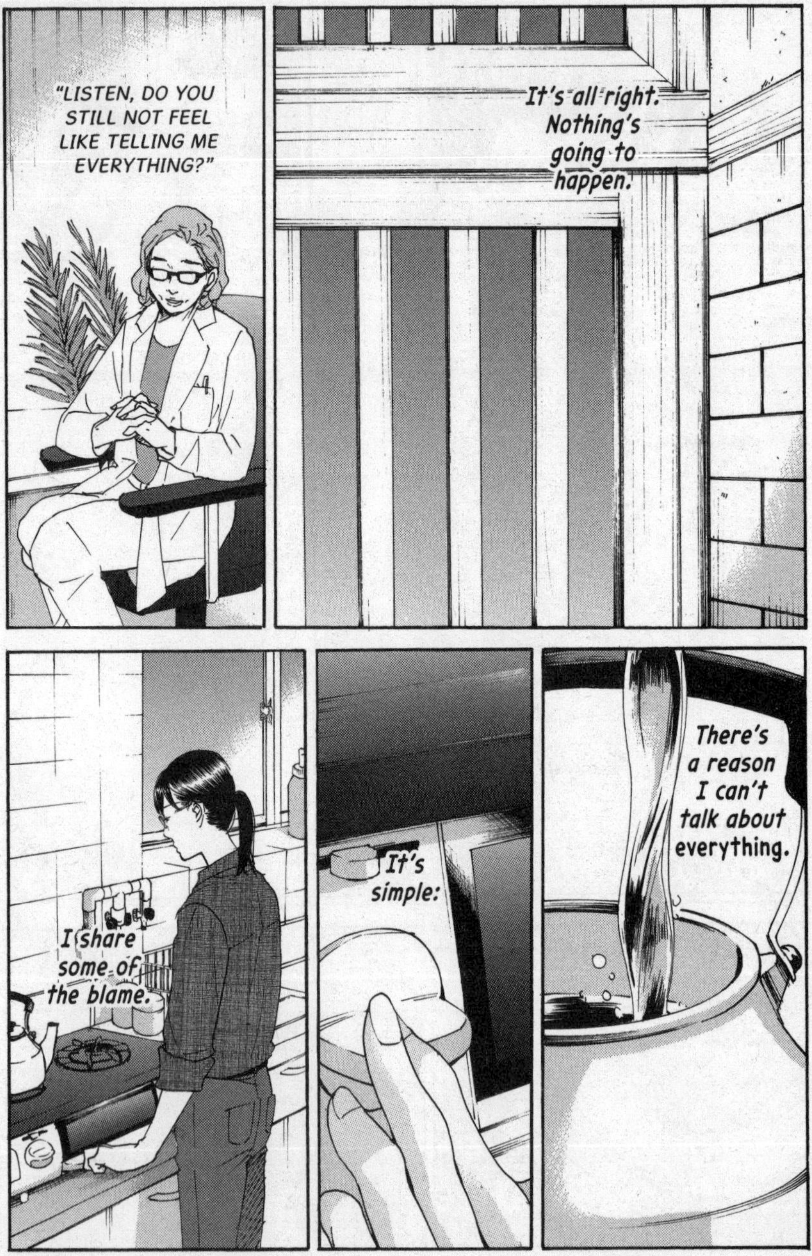
It's all right. Nothing's going to happen.
"LISTEN, DO YOU STILL NOT FEEL LIKE TELLING ME EVERYTHING?"
There's a reason I can't talk about everything.
It's simple:
I share some of the blame.

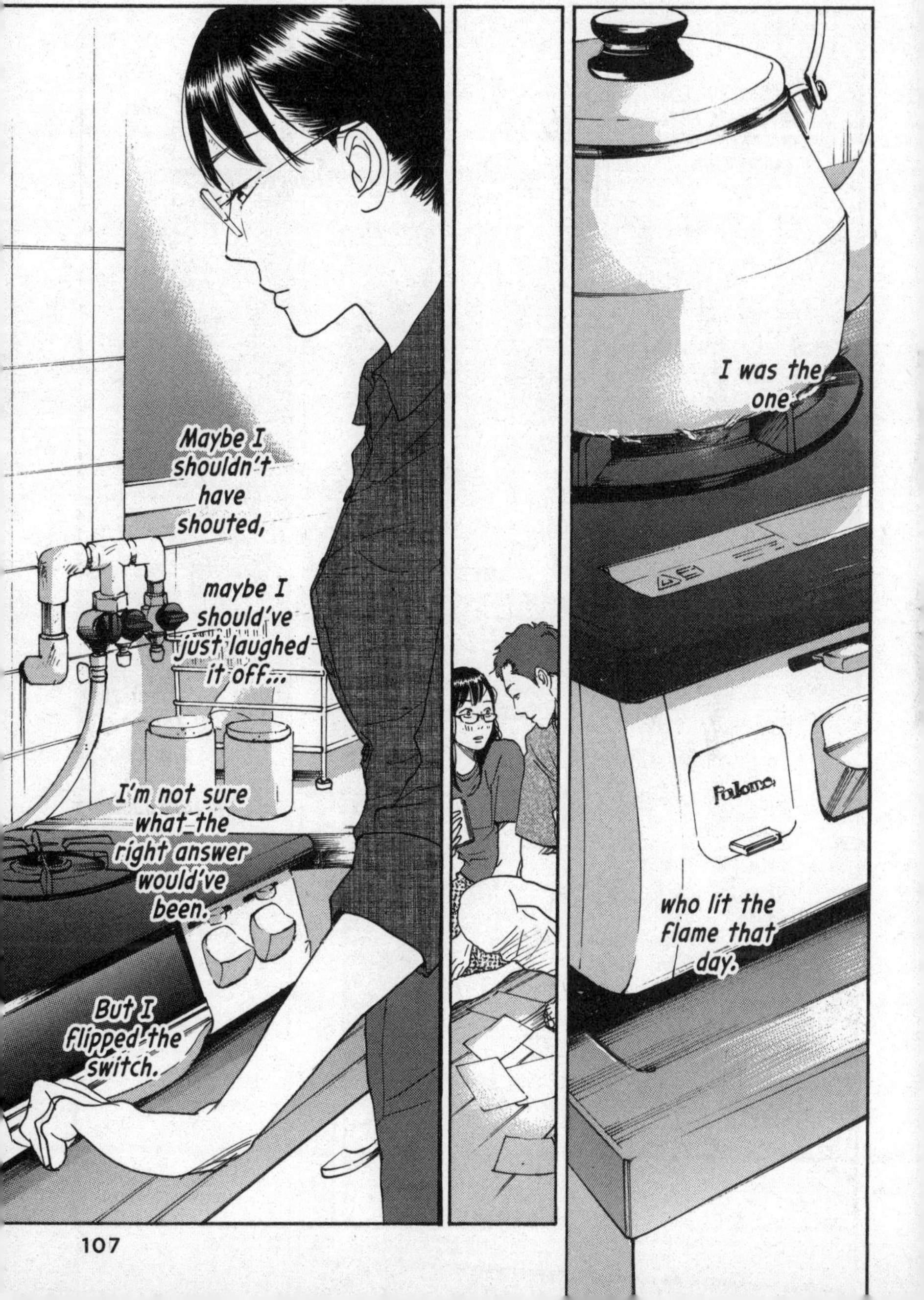
I was the one
who lit the flame that day.
Maybe I shouldn't have shouted,
maybe I should've just laughed it off...
I'm not sure what the right answer would've been.
But I flipped the switch.

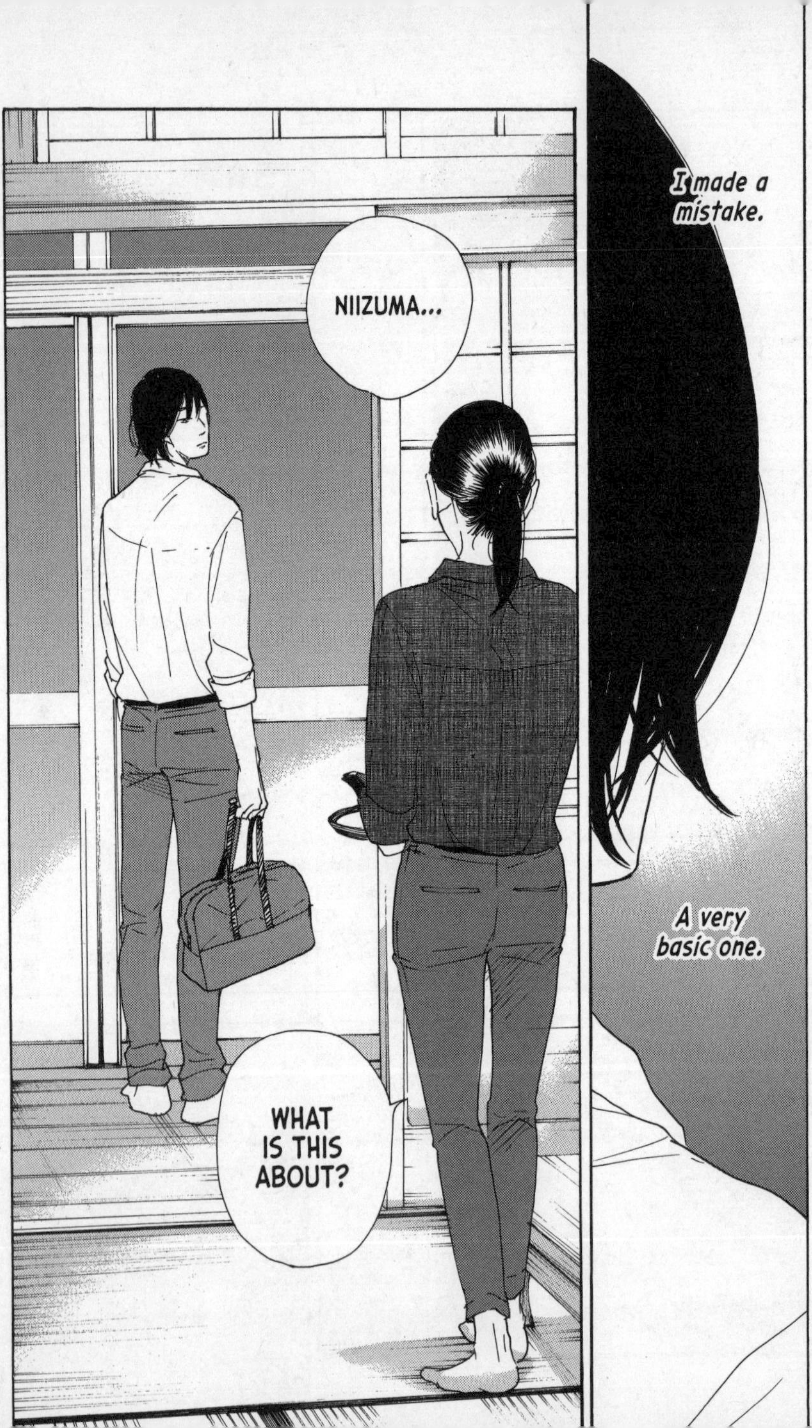
I made a mistake.
A very basic one.
NIIZUMA...
WHAT IS THIS ABOUT?

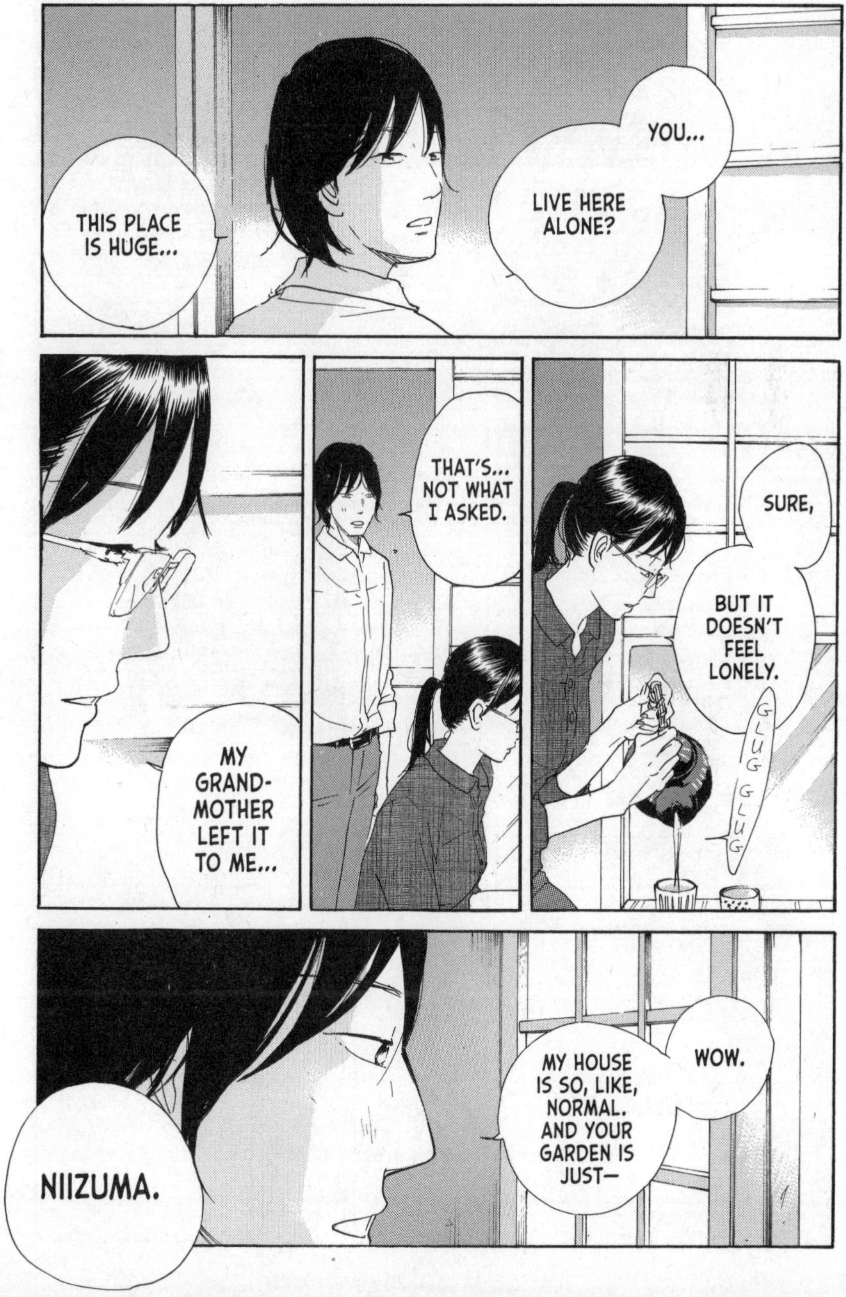
YOU...
LIVE HERE ALONE?
THIS PLACE IS HUGE...
SURE,
BUT IT DOESN'T FEEL LONELY.
GLUG GLUG
THAT'S... NOT WHAT I ASKED.
MY GRAND-MOTHER LEFT IT TO ME...
WOW.
MY HOUSE IS SO, LIKE, NORMAL. AND YOUR GARDEN IS JUST—
NIIZUMA.

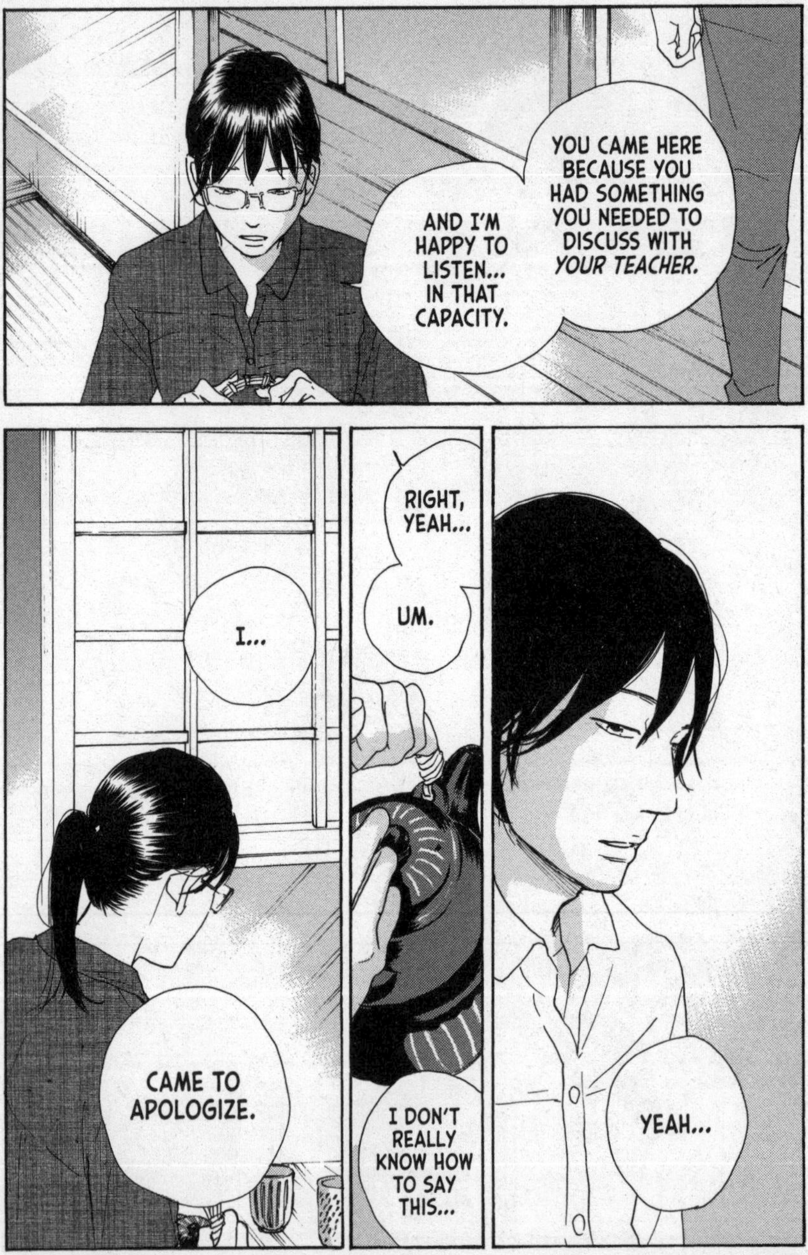
YOU CAME HERE BECAUSE YOU HAD SOMETHING YOU NEEDED TO DISCUSS WITH *YOUR TEACHER.*
AND I'M HAPPY TO LISTEN... IN THAT CAPACITY.
YEAH...
RIGHT, YEAH...
UM.
I DON'T REALLY KNOW HOW TO SAY THIS...
I...
CAME TO APOLOGIZE.

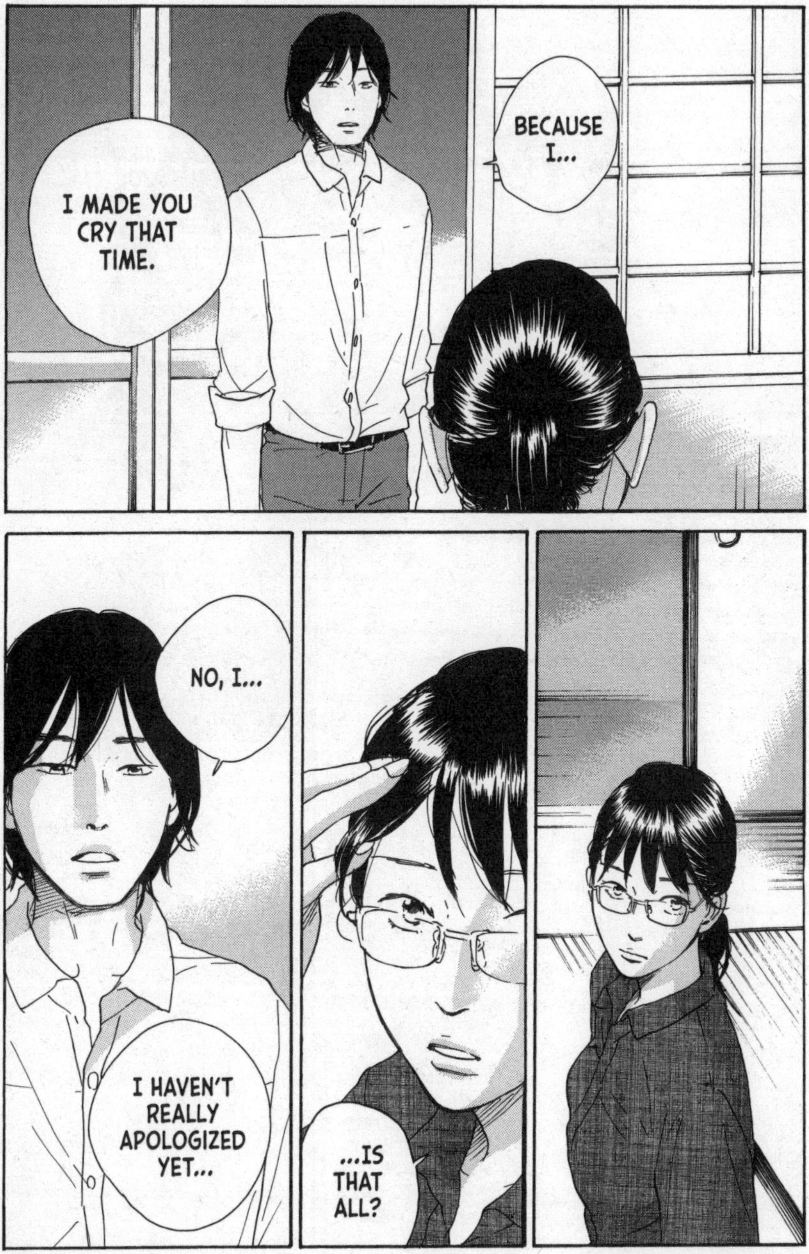
BECAUSE I...
I MADE YOU CRY THAT TIME.
...IS THAT ALL?
NO, I...
I HAVEN'T REALLY APOLOGIZED YET...

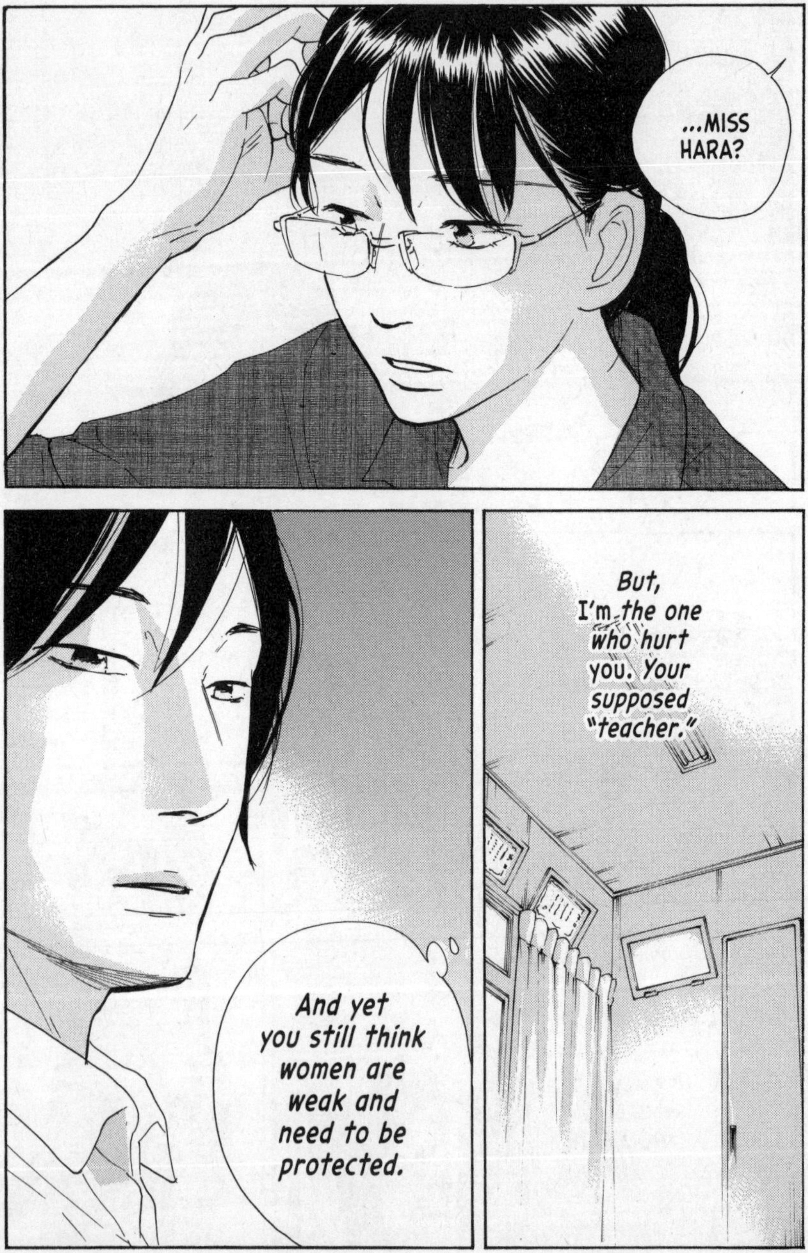
...MISS HARA?
But, I'm the one who hurt you. Your supposed "teacher."
And yet you still think women are weak and need to be protected.

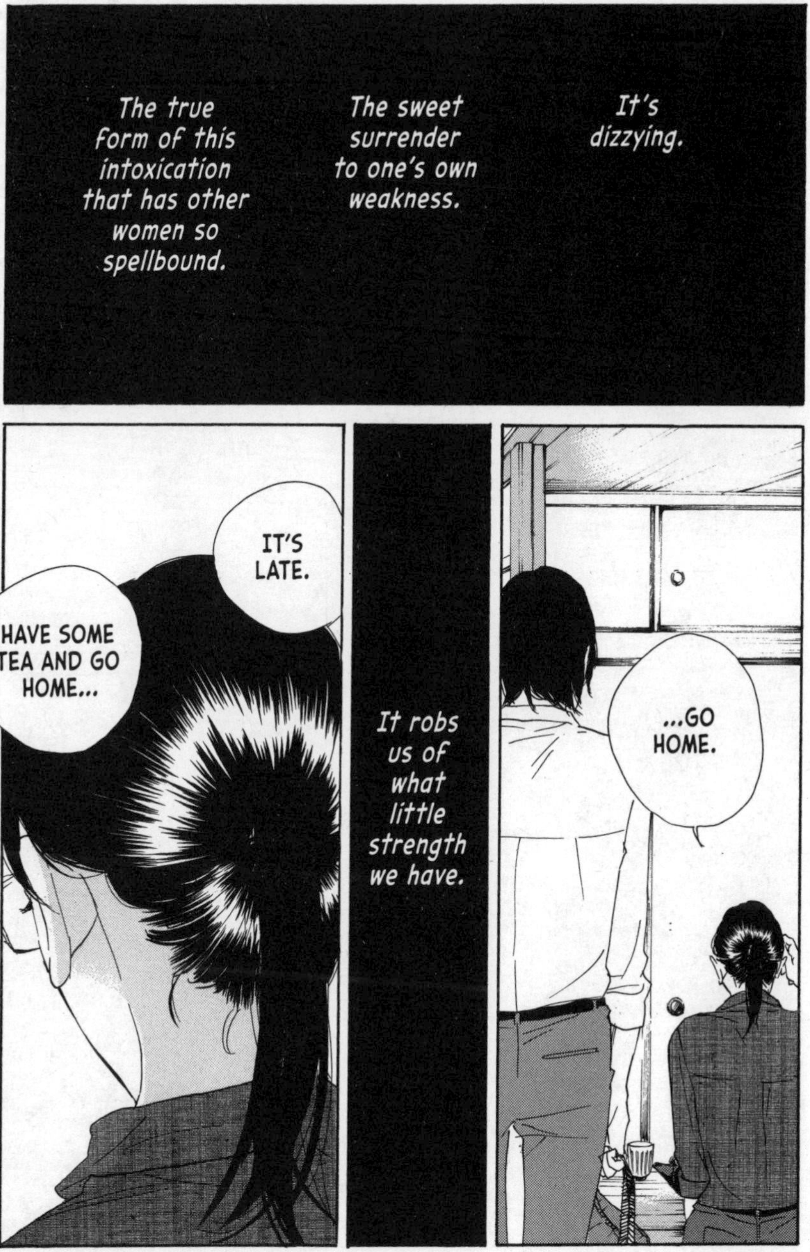
It's dizzying.
The sweet surrender to one's own weakness.
The true form of this intoxication that has other women so spellbound.
...GO HOME.
It robs us of what little strength we have.
IT'S LATE.
HAVE SOME TEA AND GO HOME...

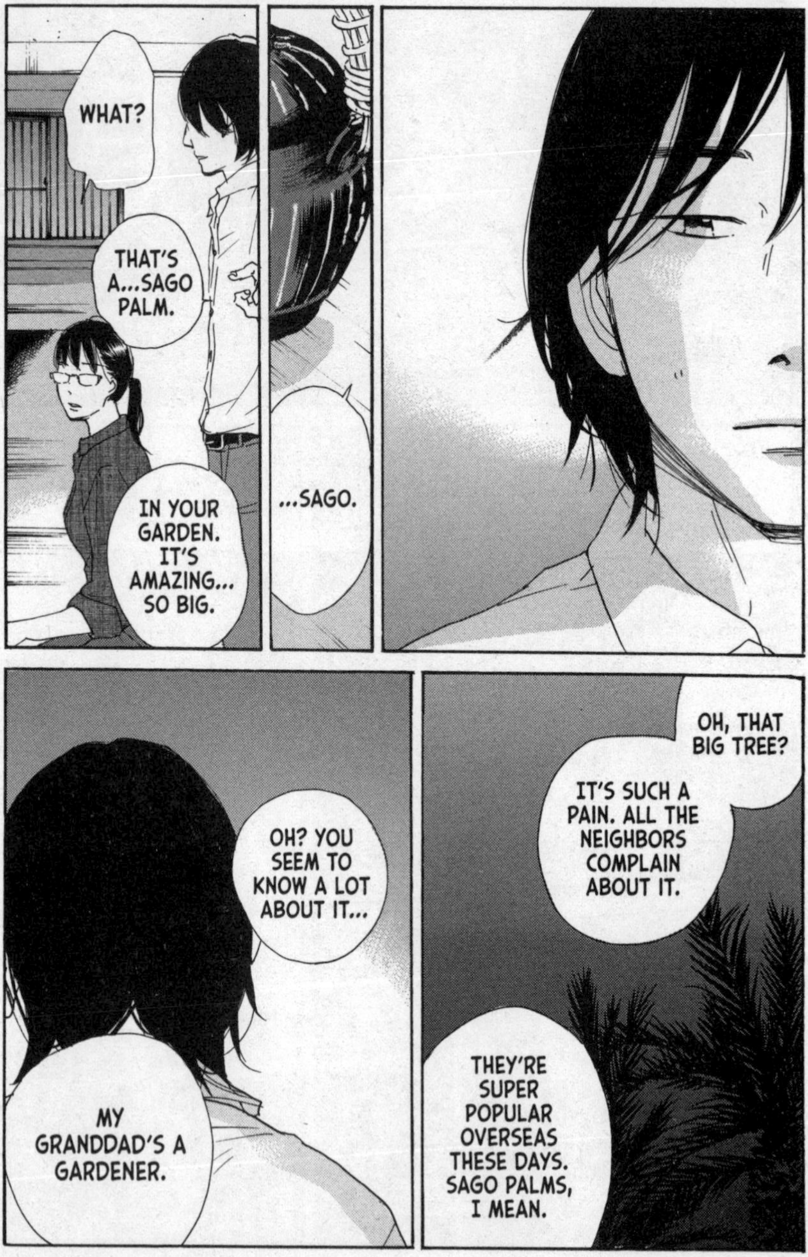
...SAGO.
WHAT?
THAT'S A...SAGO PALM.
IN YOUR GARDEN. IT'S AMAZING... SO BIG.
OH, THAT BIG TREE?
IT'S SUCH A PAIN. ALL THE NEIGHBORS COMPLAIN ABOUT IT.
THEY'RE SUPER POPULAR OVERSEAS THESE DAYS. SAGO PALMS, I MEAN.
OH? YOU SEEM TO KNOW A LOT ABOUT IT...
MY GRANDDAD'S A GARDENER.

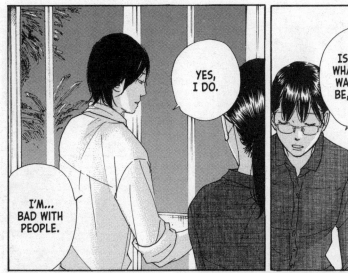

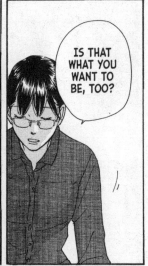

IS THAT WHAT YOU WANT TO BE, TOO?
YES, I DO.
I'M... BAD WITH PEOPLE.
I GET IT.
SO AM I...
I'd been thinking of my students like plants.
IS IT OK IF I COME OVER TO LOOK AT YOUR GARDEN AGAIN SOMETIME?

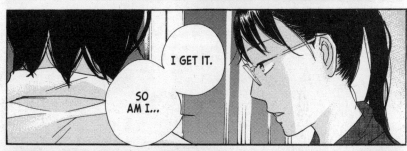

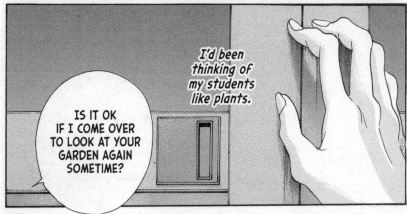

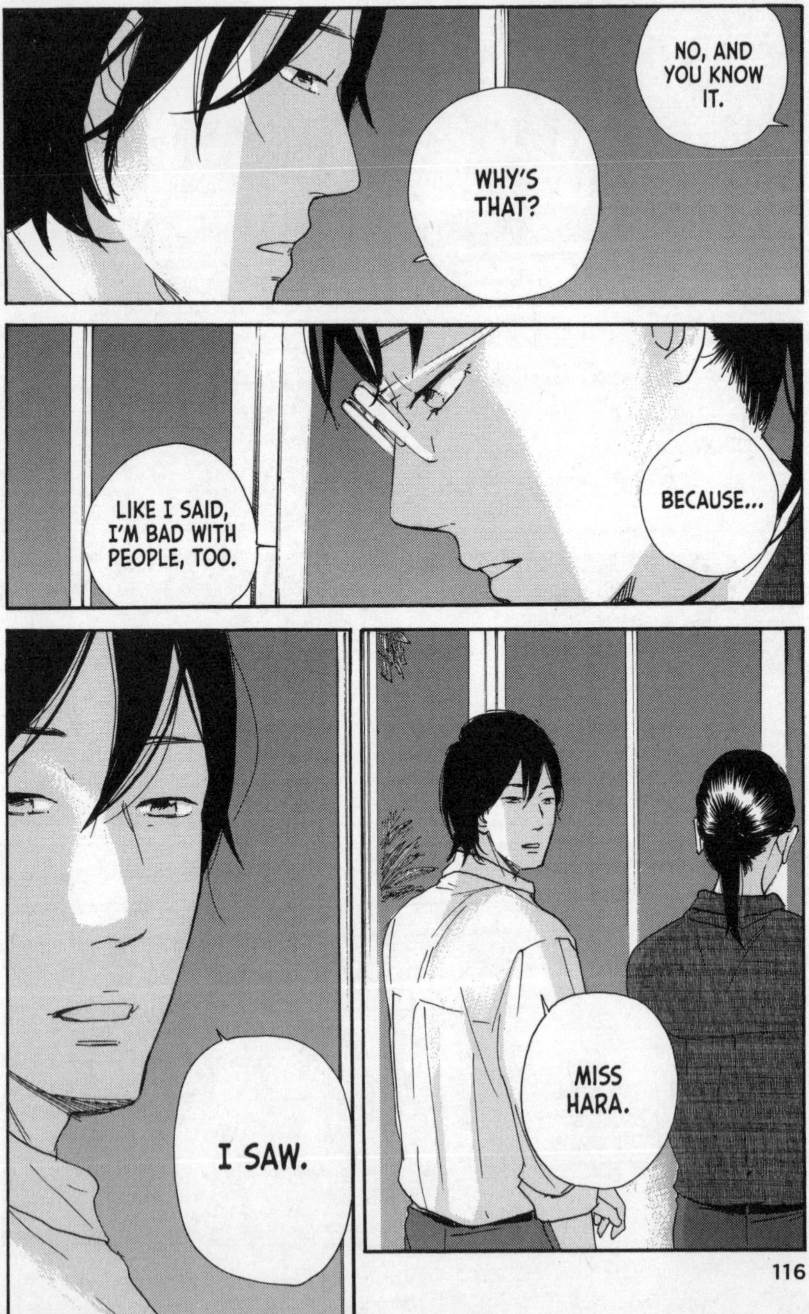
NO, AND YOU KNOW IT.
WHY'S THAT?
BECAUSE...
LIKE I SAID, I'M BAD WITH PEOPLE, TOO.
MISS HARA.
I SAW.

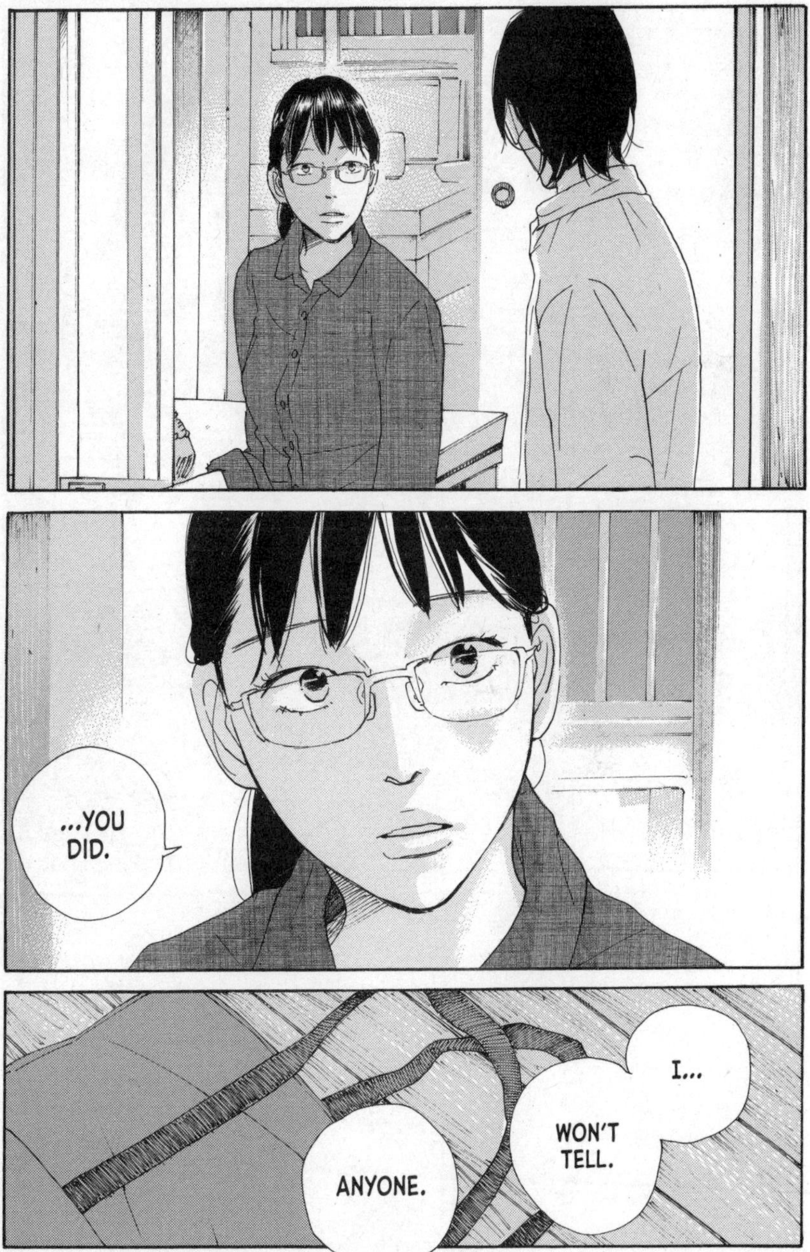
...YOU DID.
I...
WON'T TELL.
ANYONE.

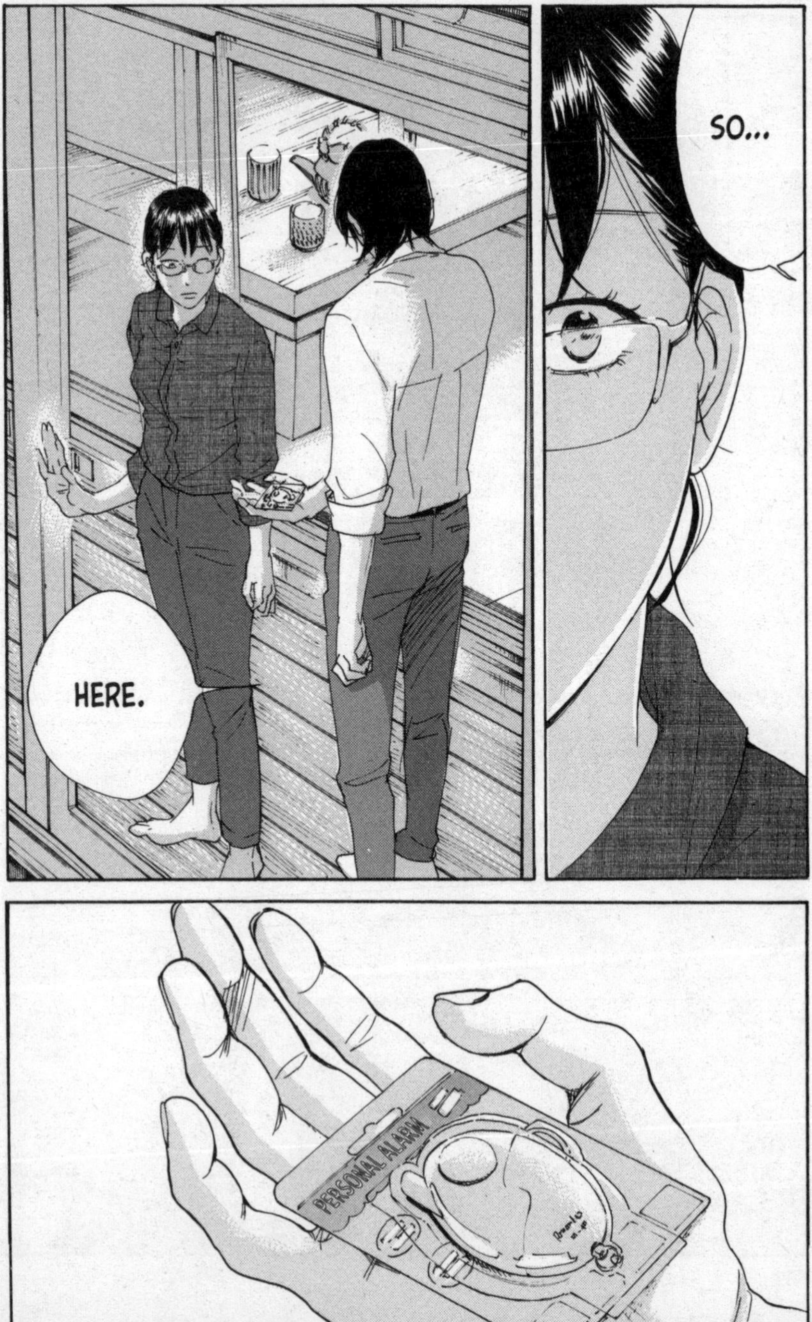
SO...
HERE.
PERSONAL ALARM

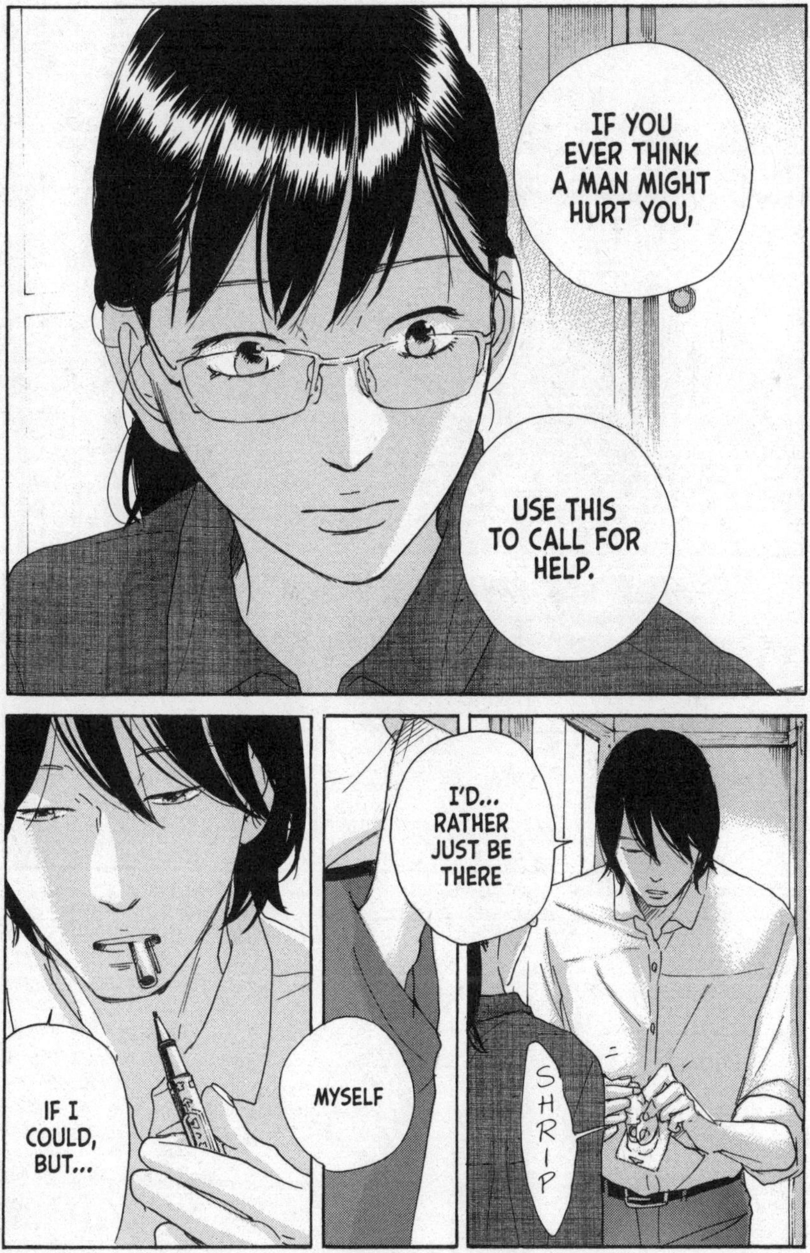
IF YOU EVER THINK A MAN MIGHT HURT YOU,
USE THIS TO CALL FOR HELP.
SHRIP
I'D... RATHER JUST BE THERE
MYSELF
IF I COULD, BUT...

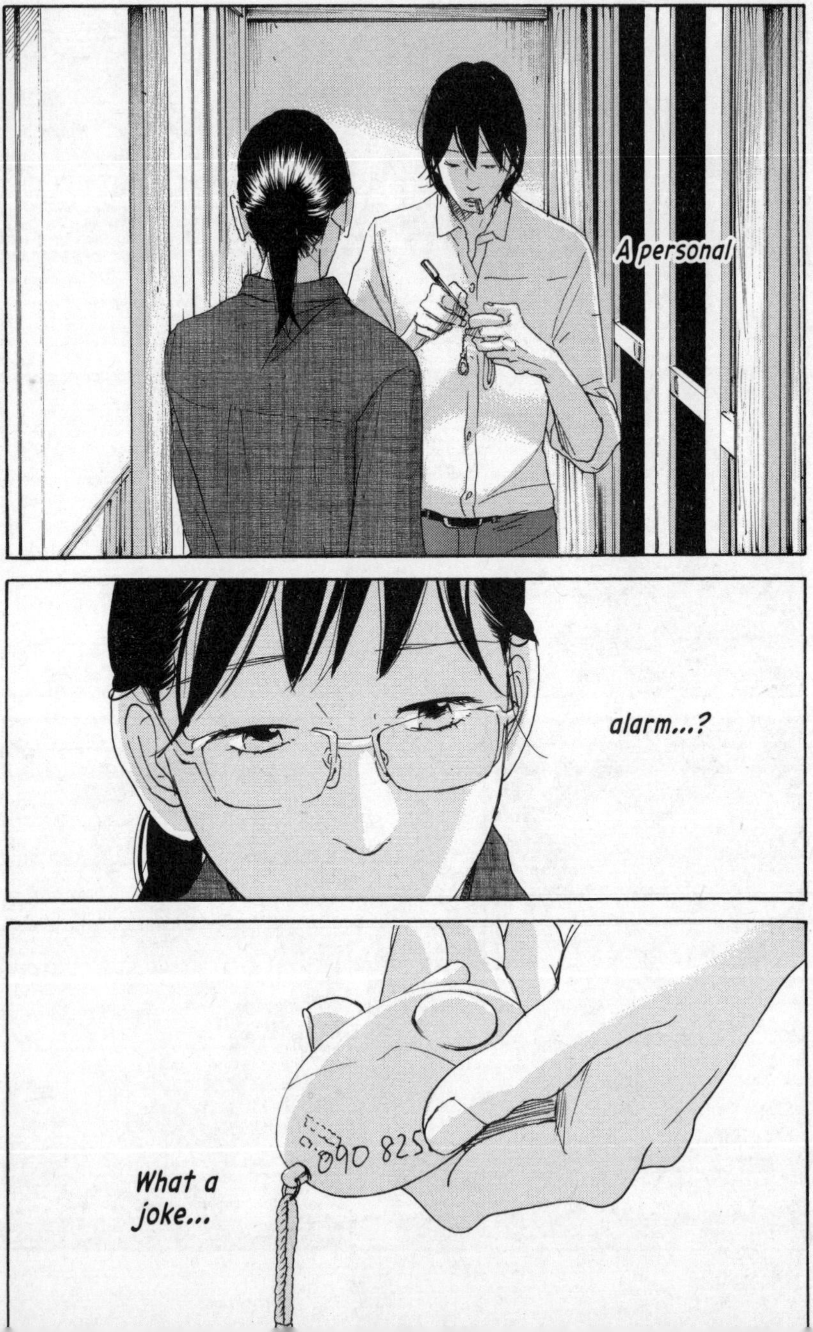
A personal
alarm...?
090 825
What a joke...

YOU SAID BEFORE THAT YOU'D BEEN... RAPED BY THAT OLDER WOMAN.

THAT YOU WERE REALLY SCARED.

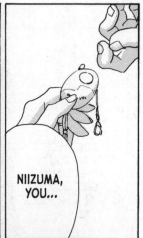

NIIZUMA, YOU...

Come on, I can't call for help.

...

I DID, YEAH.

The world isn't set up that way.

THEN IF I WERE IN YOUR SHOES,

I WOULD NEVER JUST WALTZ INTO A PLACE LIKE THIS.

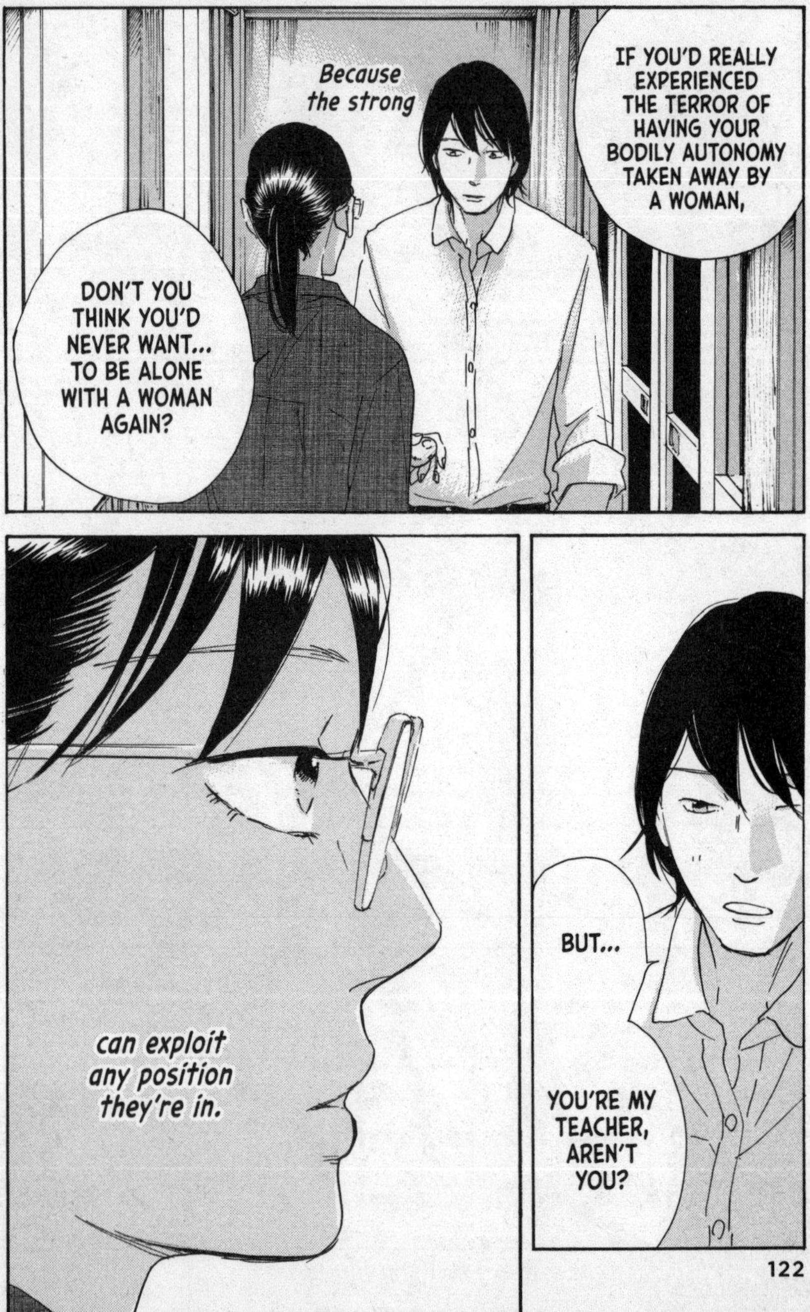
IF YOU'D REALLY EXPERIENCED THE TERROR OF HAVING YOUR BODILY AUTONOMY TAKEN AWAY BY A WOMAN,
Because the strong
DON'T YOU THINK YOU'D NEVER WANT... TO BE ALONE WITH A WOMAN AGAIN?
BUT...
YOU'RE MY TEACHER, AREN'T YOU?
can exploit any position they're in.

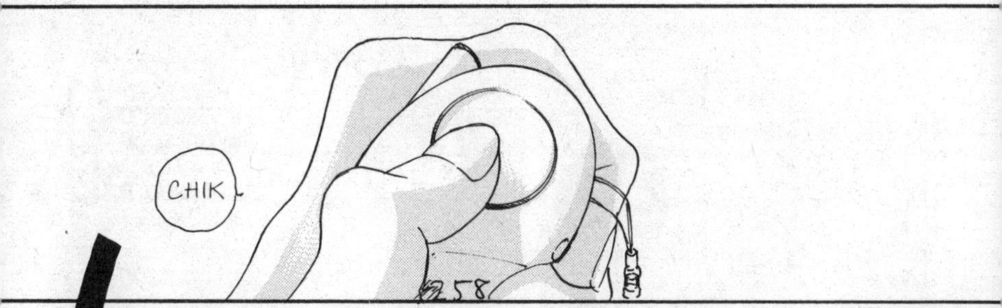
CHIK
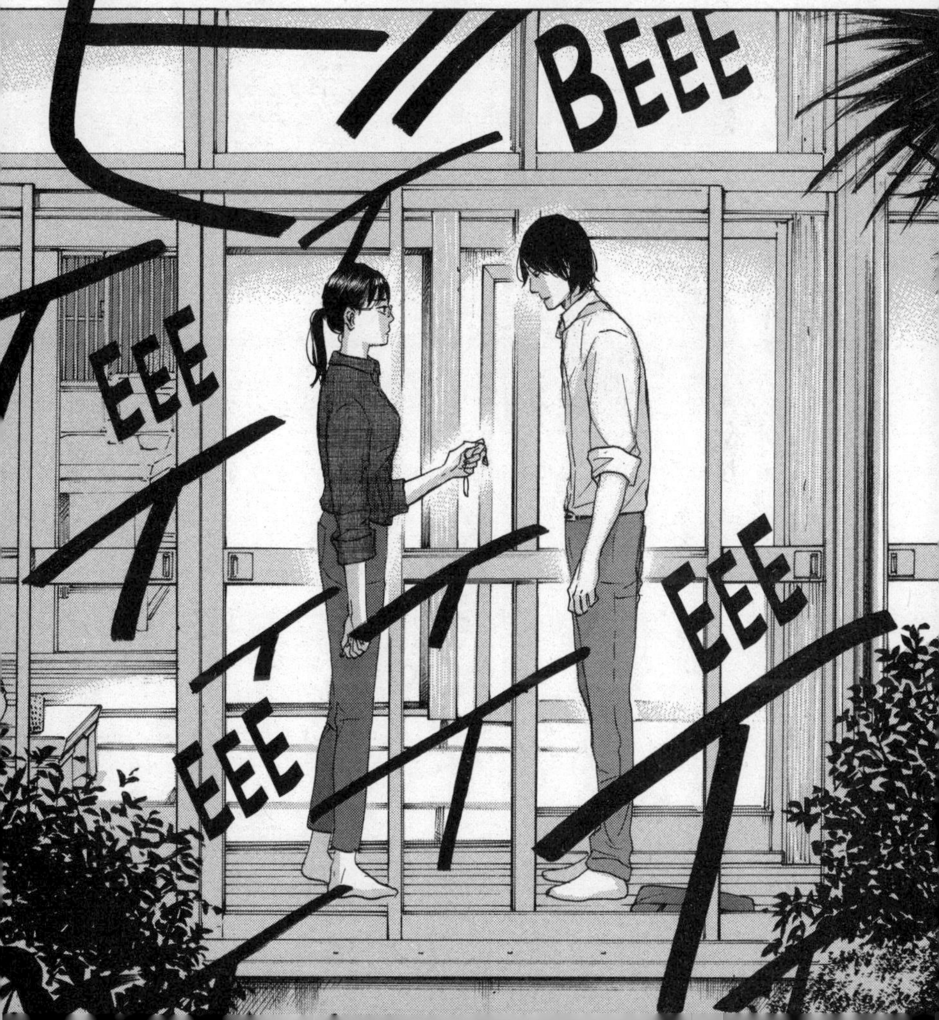
BEEE
EEE
EEE
EEE

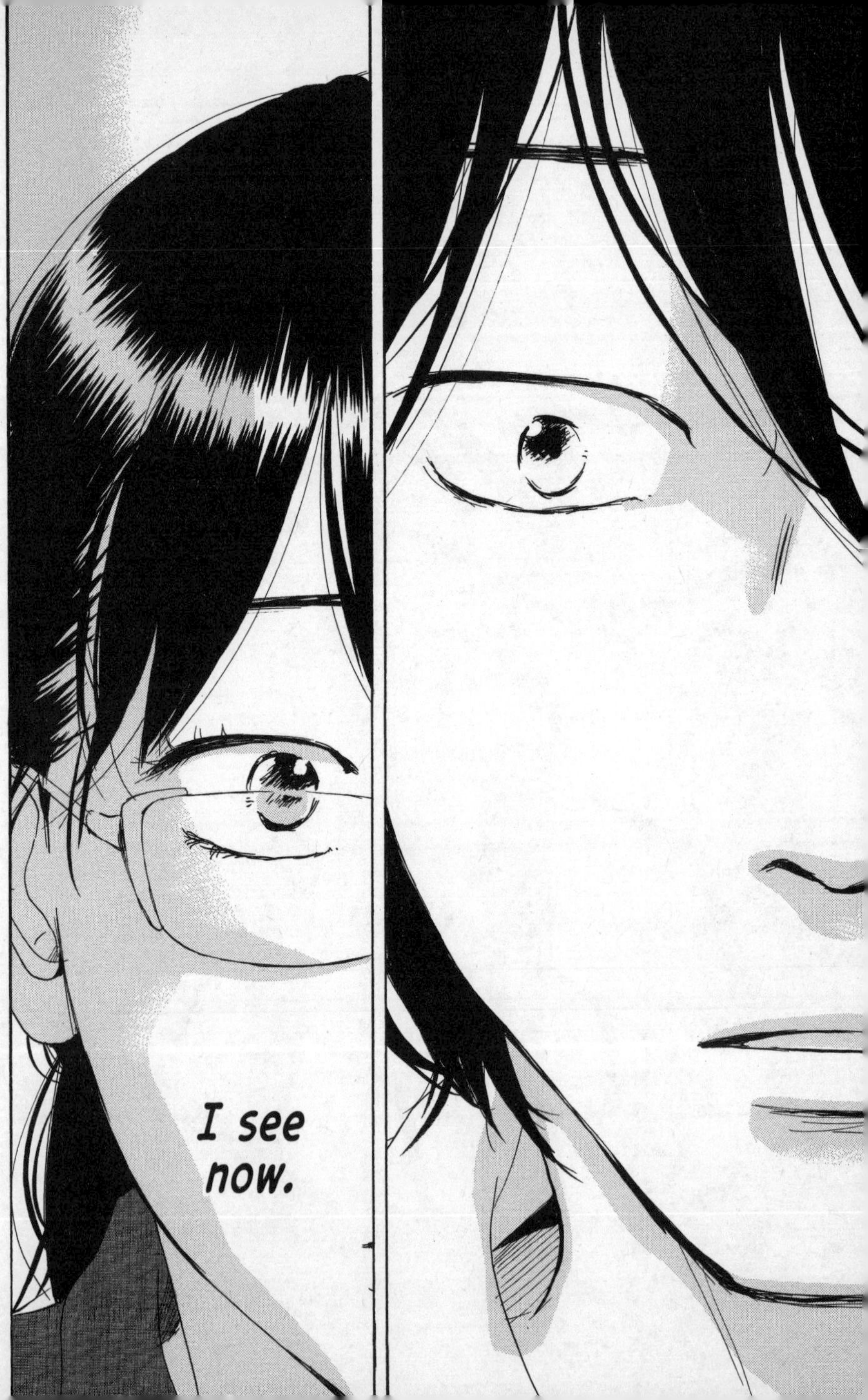
I see now.

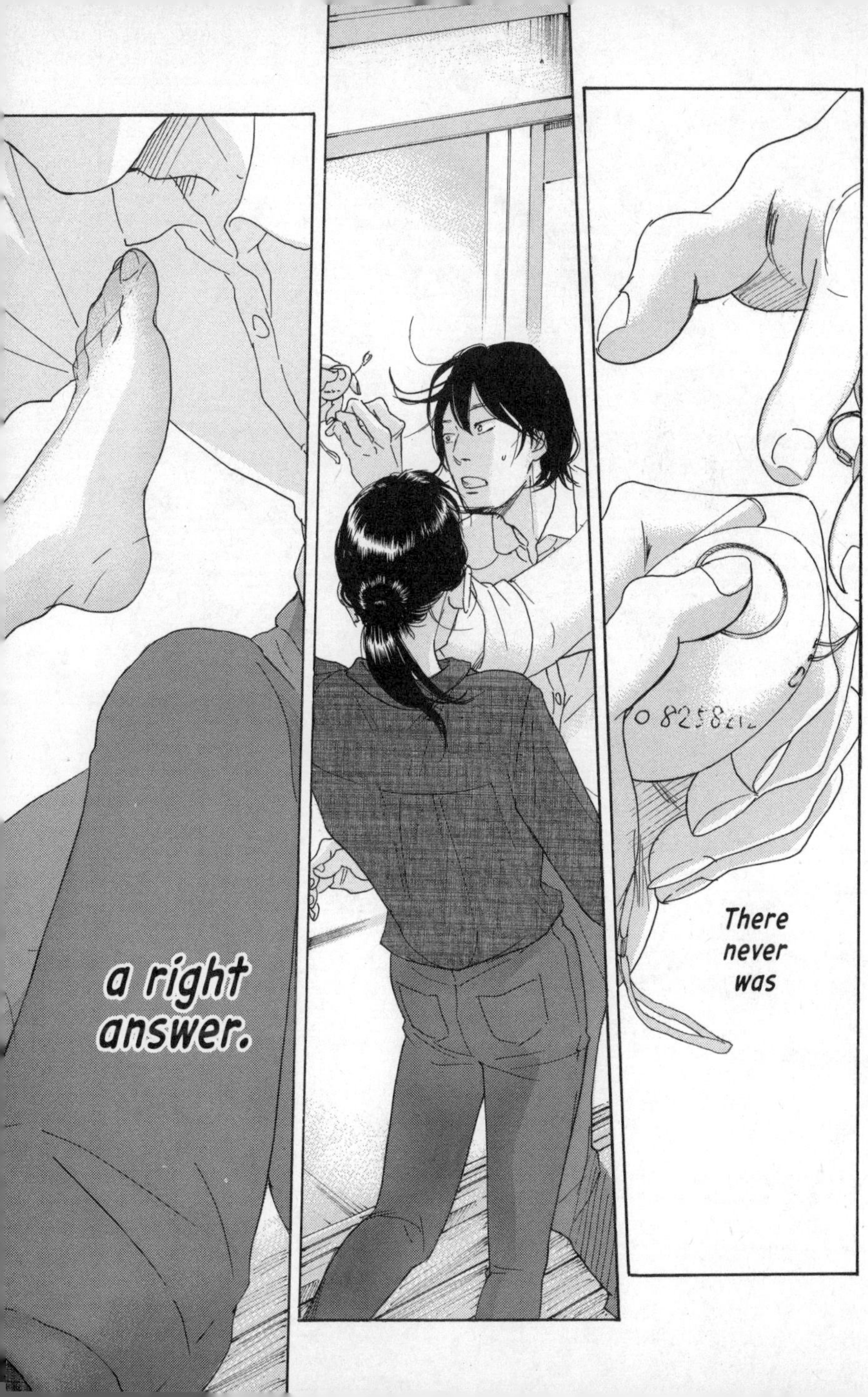
There never was
a right answer.

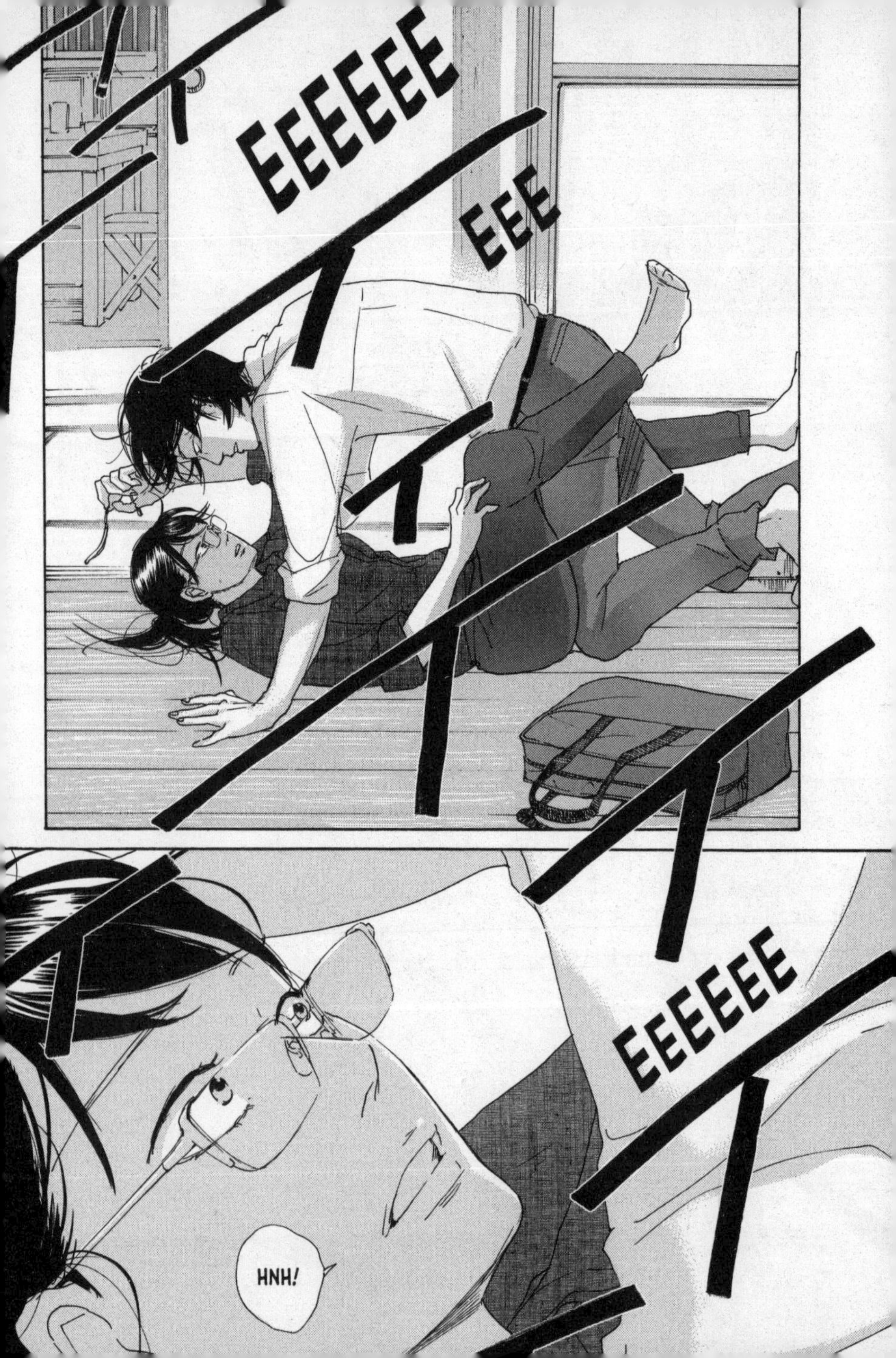
EEEEEE
EEE
EEEEEE
HNH!

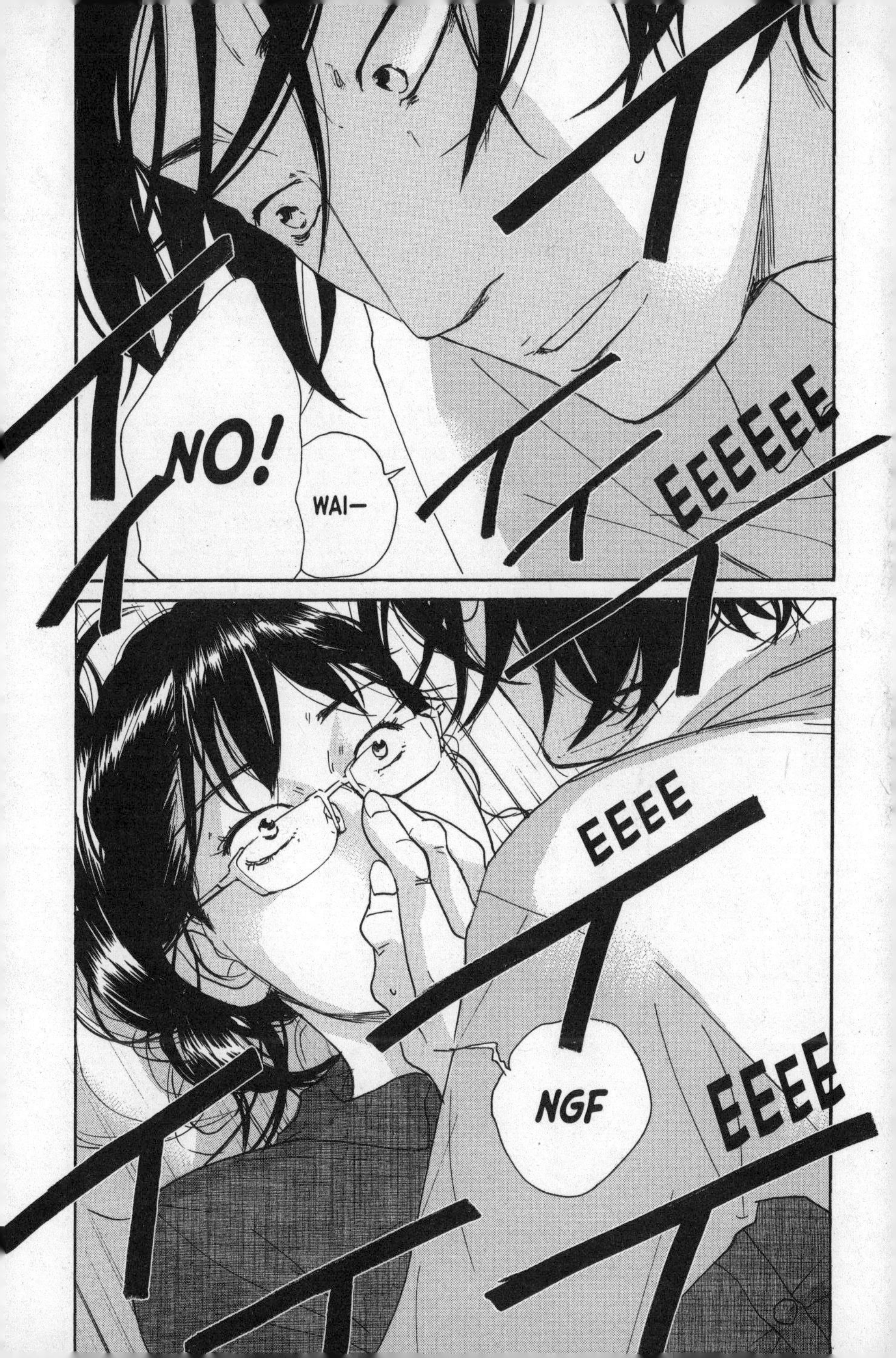
EEEEEE
WAI—
NO!
EEEE
EEEE
NGF

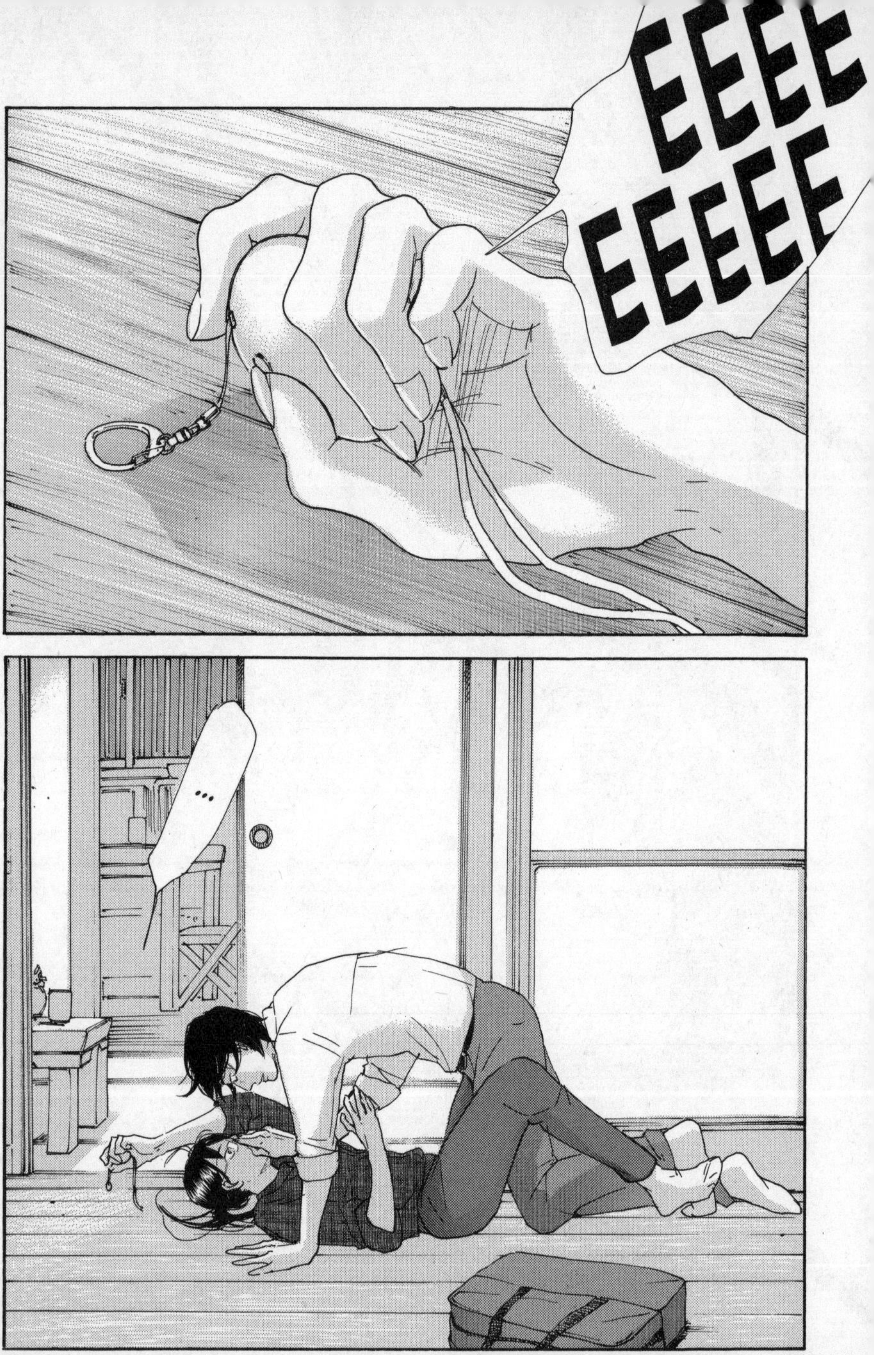
EEEE
EEEEE
...

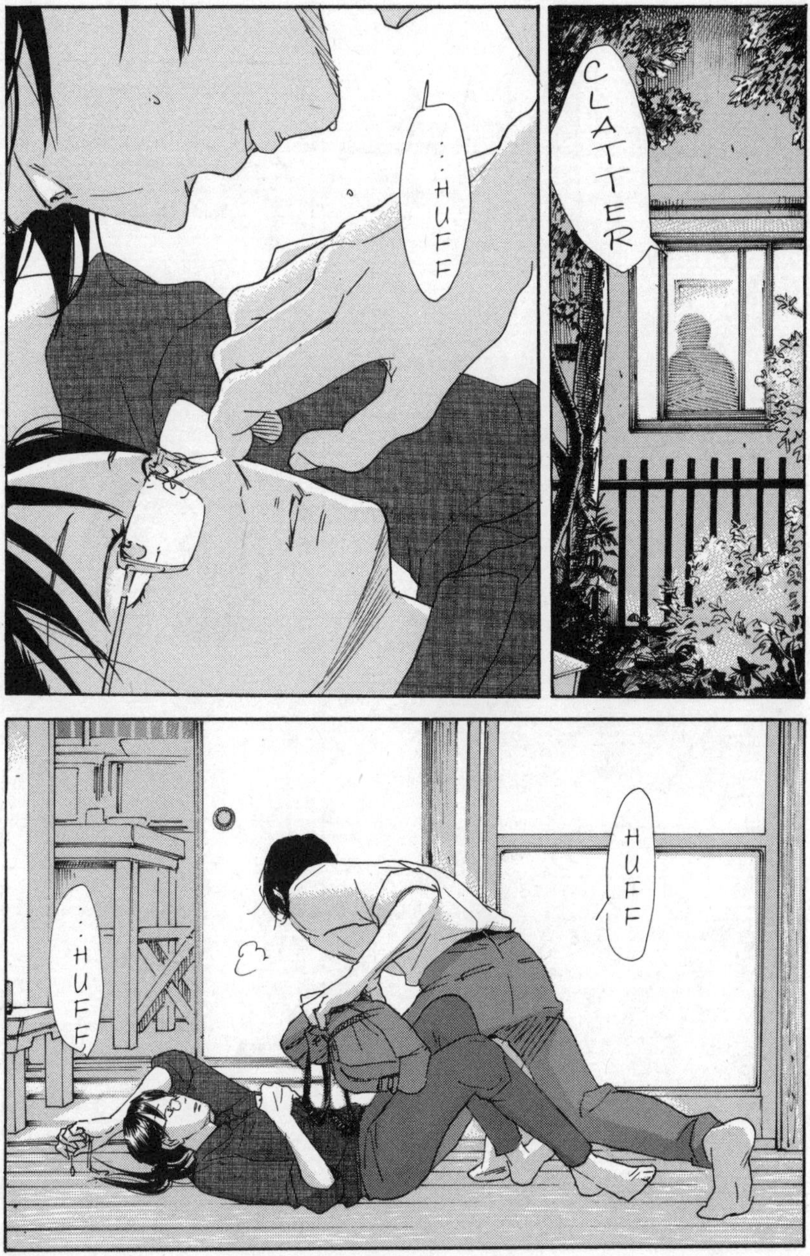
CLATTER
...HUFF
HUFF HUFF
...HUFF

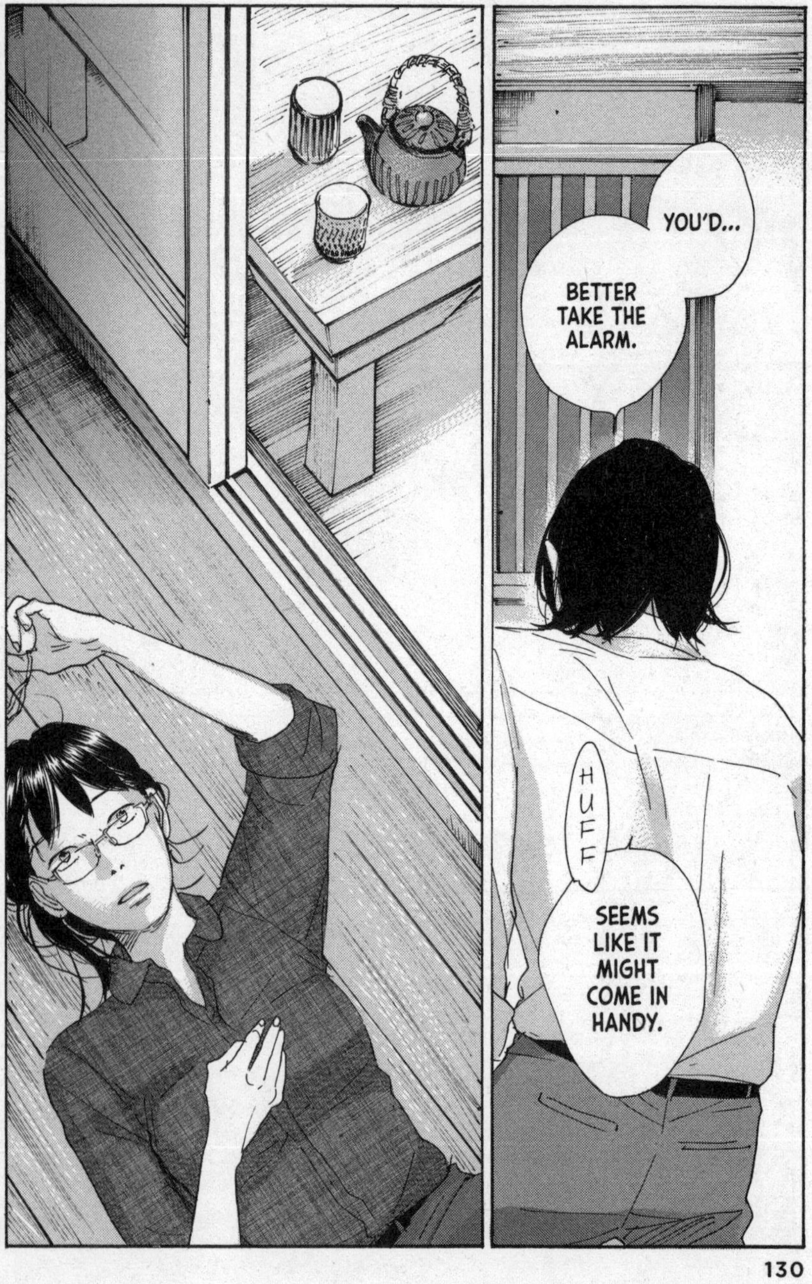
YOU'D...
BETTER TAKE THE ALARM.
HUFF
SEEMS LIKE IT MIGHT COME IN HANDY.

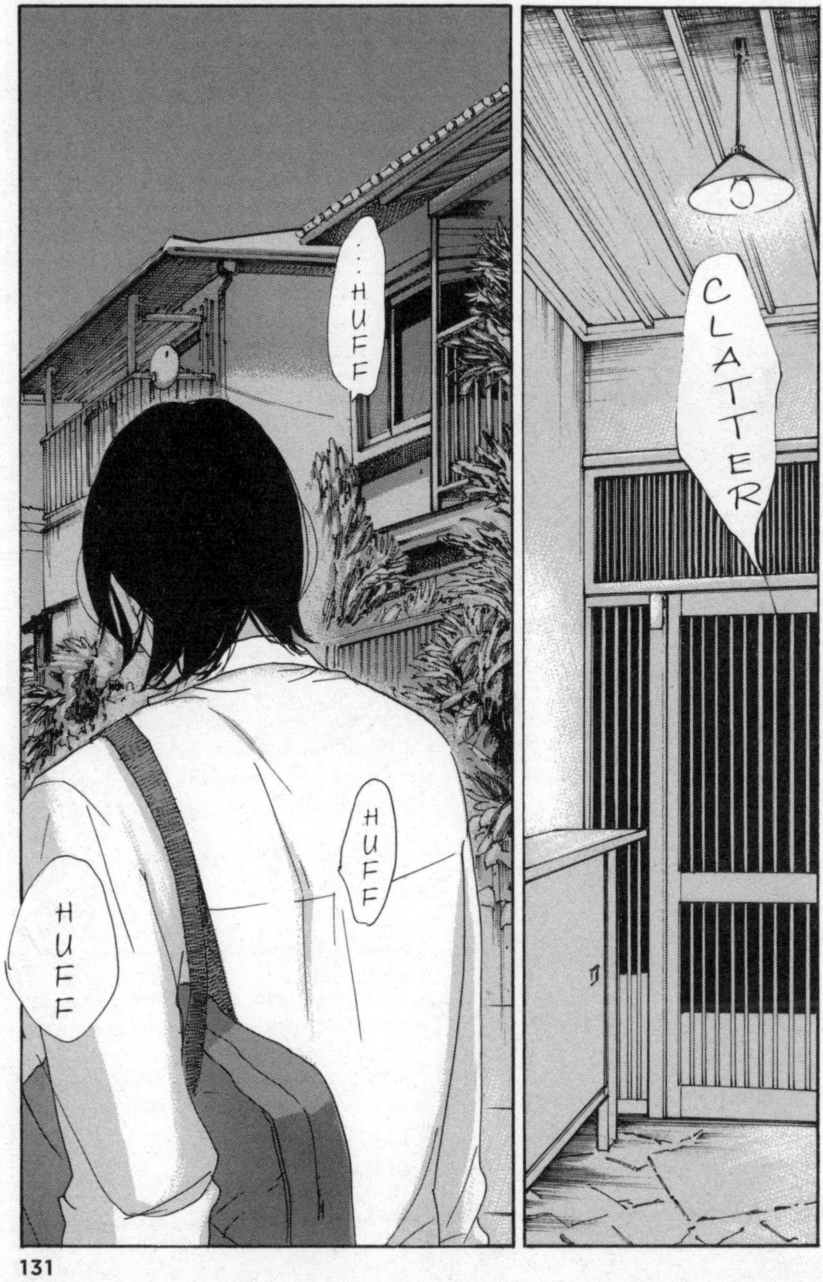
CLATTER
...HUFF
HUFF
HUFF

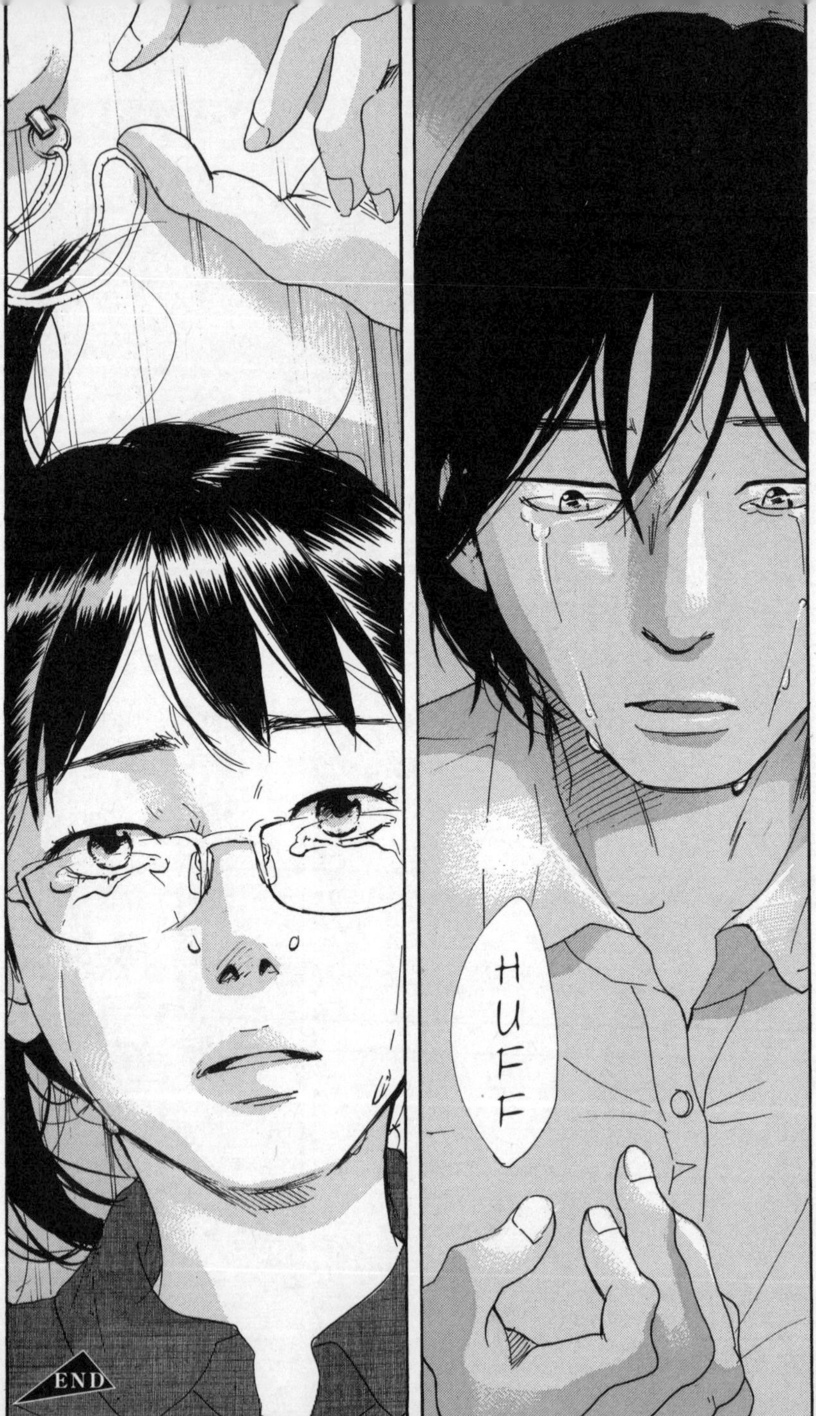
HUFF
END

CHAPTER 17. THERE WAS LOVE

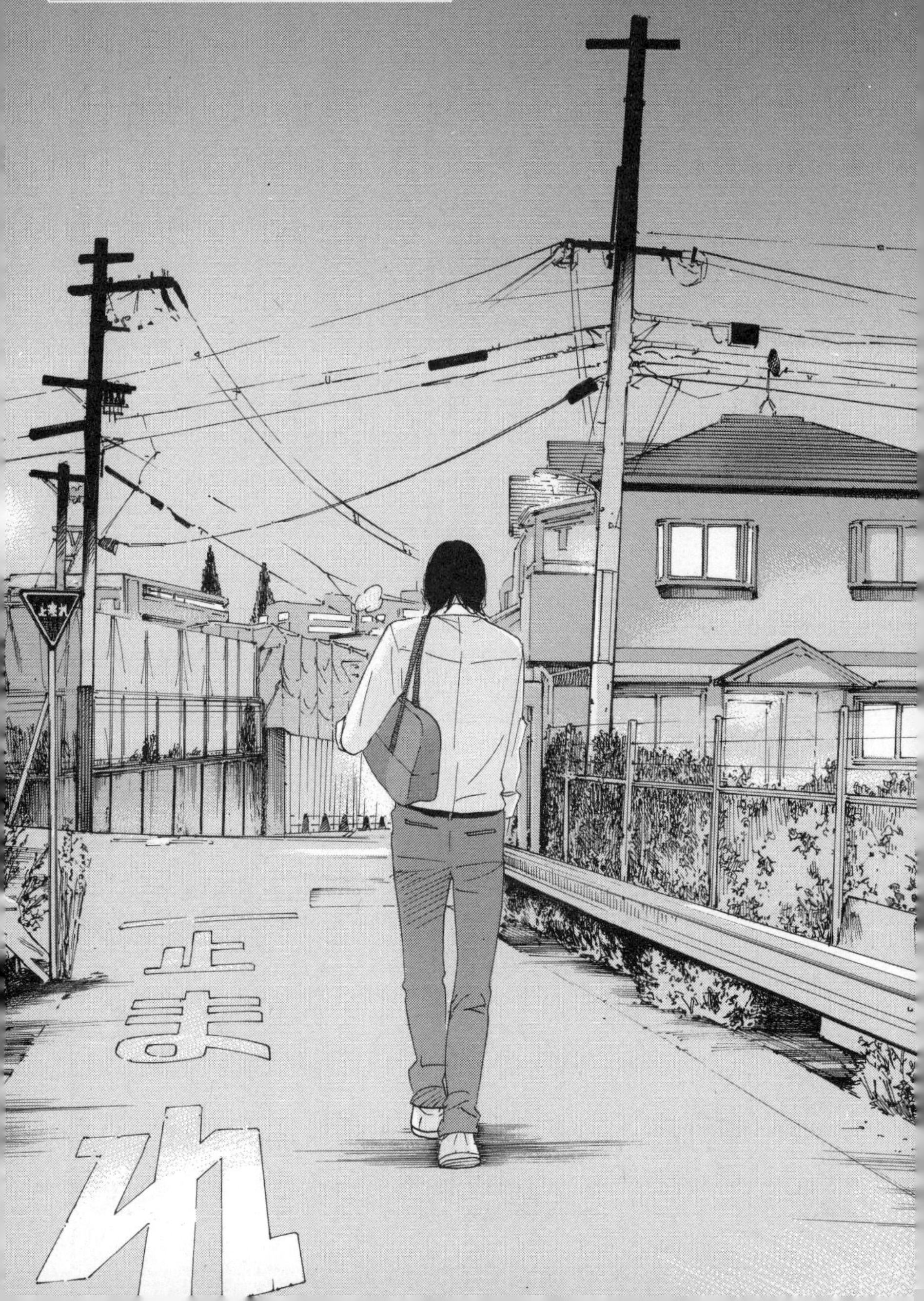
止まれ

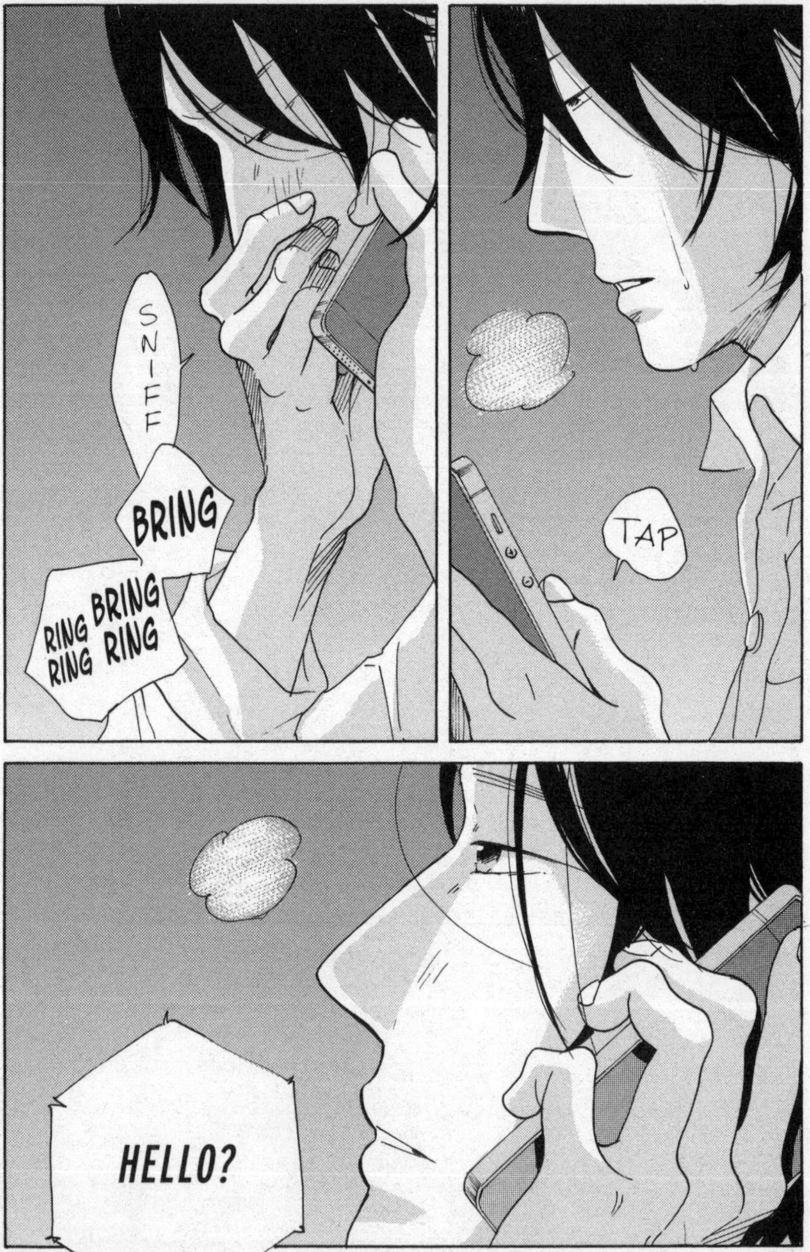
TAP
SNIFF
BRING
RING BRING RING RING
HELLO?

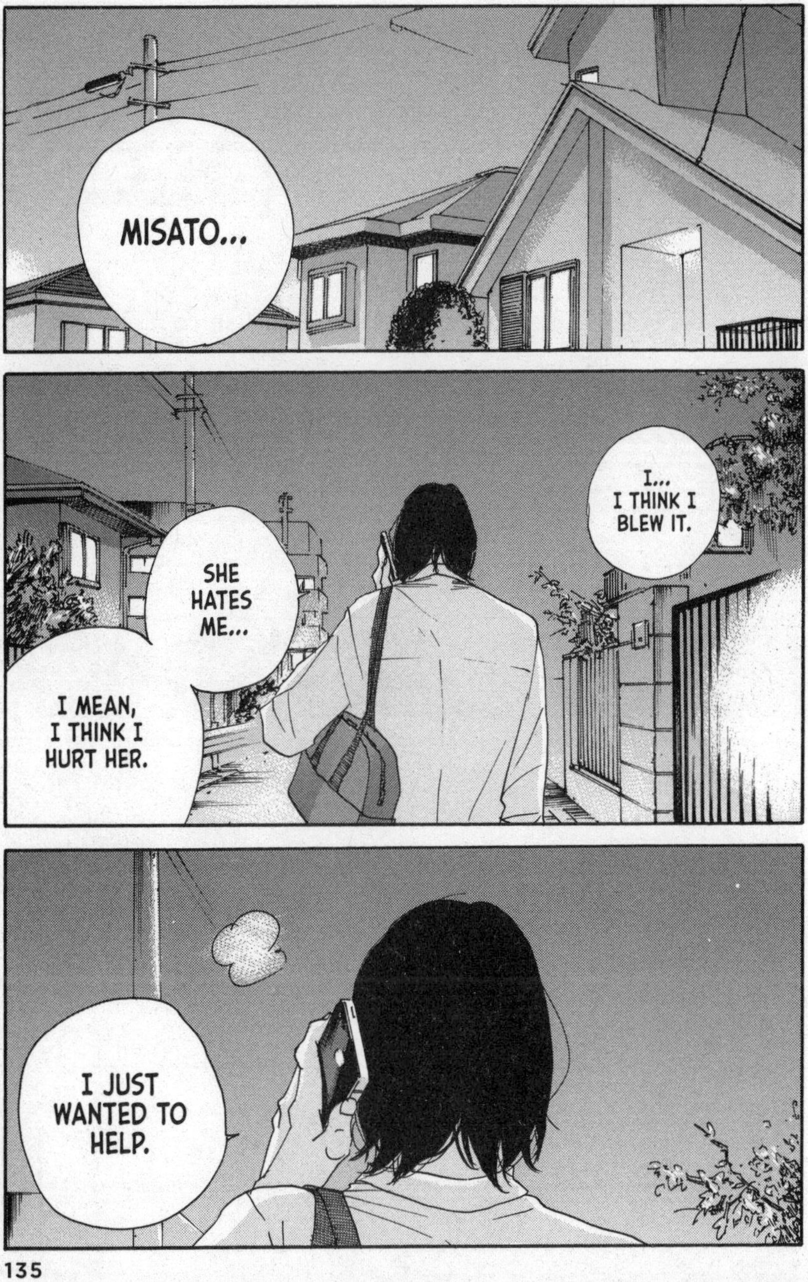
MISATO...
I... I THINK I BLEW IT.
SHE HATES ME...
I MEAN, I THINK I HURT HER.
I JUST WANTED TO HELP.

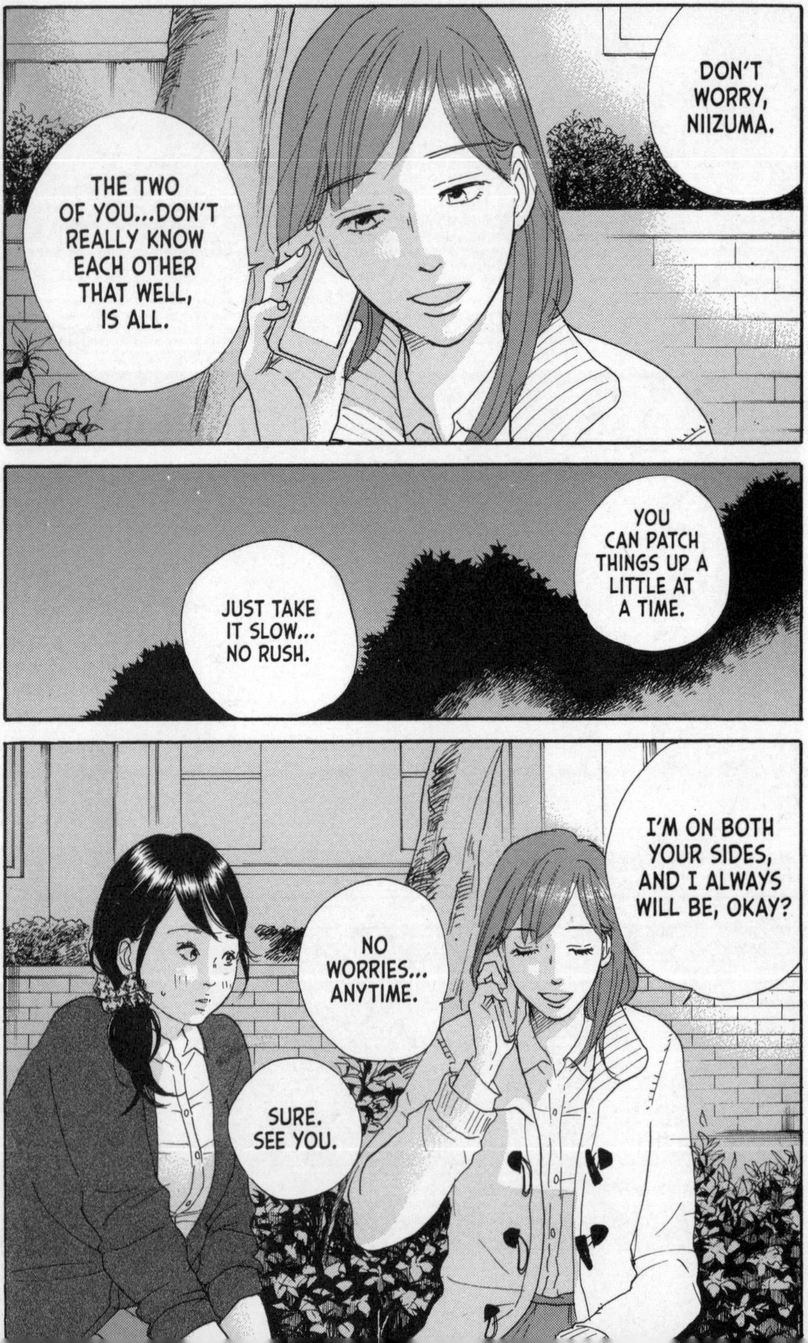
DON'T WORRY, NIIZUMA.
THE TWO OF YOU...DON'T REALLY KNOW EACH OTHER THAT WELL, IS ALL.
YOU CAN PATCH THINGS UP A LITTLE AT A TIME.
JUST TAKE IT SLOW... NO RUSH.
I'M ON BOTH YOUR SIDES, AND I ALWAYS WILL BE, OKAY?
NO WORRIES... ANYTIME.
SURE. SEE YOU.

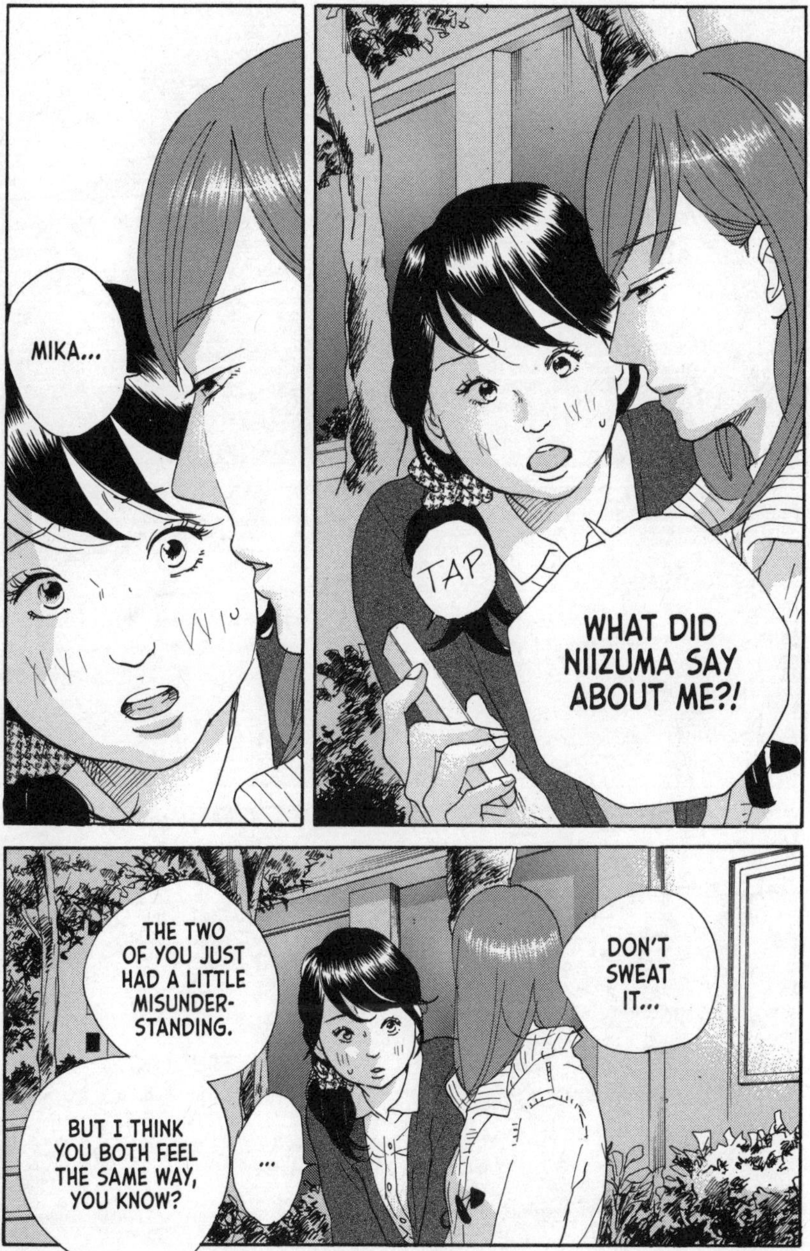
TAP
WHAT DID NIIZUMA SAY ABOUT ME?!
MIKA...
DON'T SWEAT IT...
THE TWO OF YOU JUST HAD A LITTLE MISUNDER-STANDING.
BUT I THINK YOU BOTH FEEL THE SAME WAY, YOU KNOW?
...

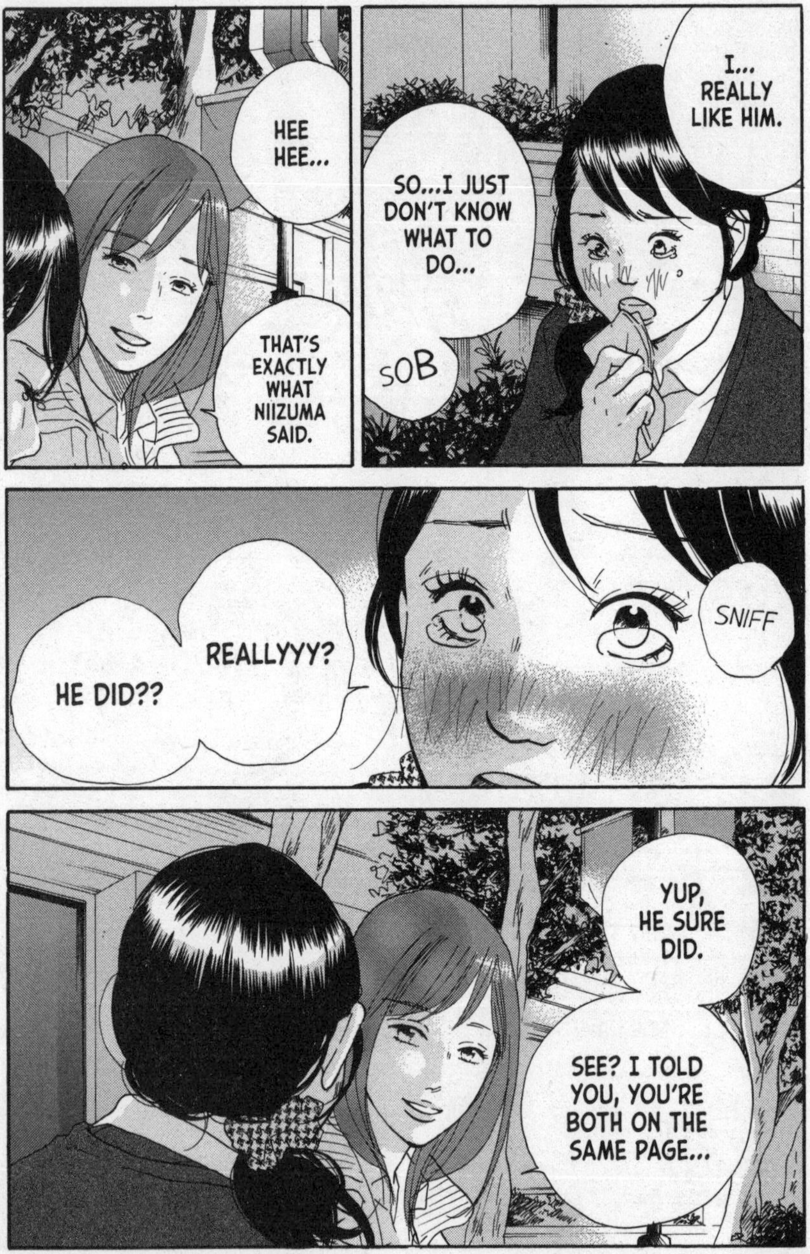
I... REALLY LIKE HIM.
SO...I JUST DON'T KNOW WHAT TO DO...
SOB
HEE HEE...
THAT'S EXACTLY WHAT NIIZUMA SAID.
SNIFF
REALLYYY?
HE DID??
YUP, HE SURE DID.
SEE? I TOLD YOU, YOU'RE BOTH ON THE SAME PAGE...

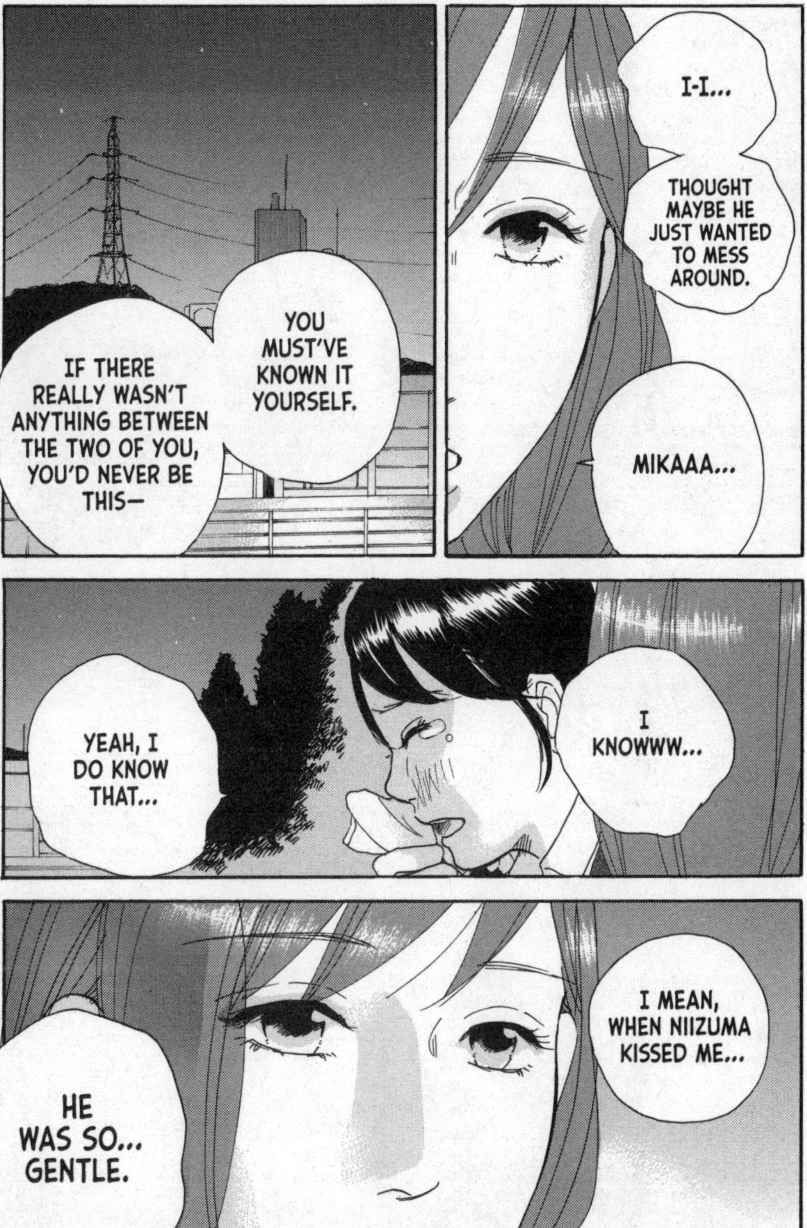
I-I...
THOUGHT MAYBE HE JUST WANTED TO MESS AROUND.
MIKAAA...
YOU MUST'VE KNOWN IT YOURSELF.
IF THERE REALLY WASN'T ANYTHING BETWEEN THE TWO OF YOU, YOU'D NEVER BE THIS—
I KNOWWW...
YEAH, I DO KNOW THAT...
I MEAN, WHEN NIIZUMA KISSED ME...
HE WAS SO... GENTLE.

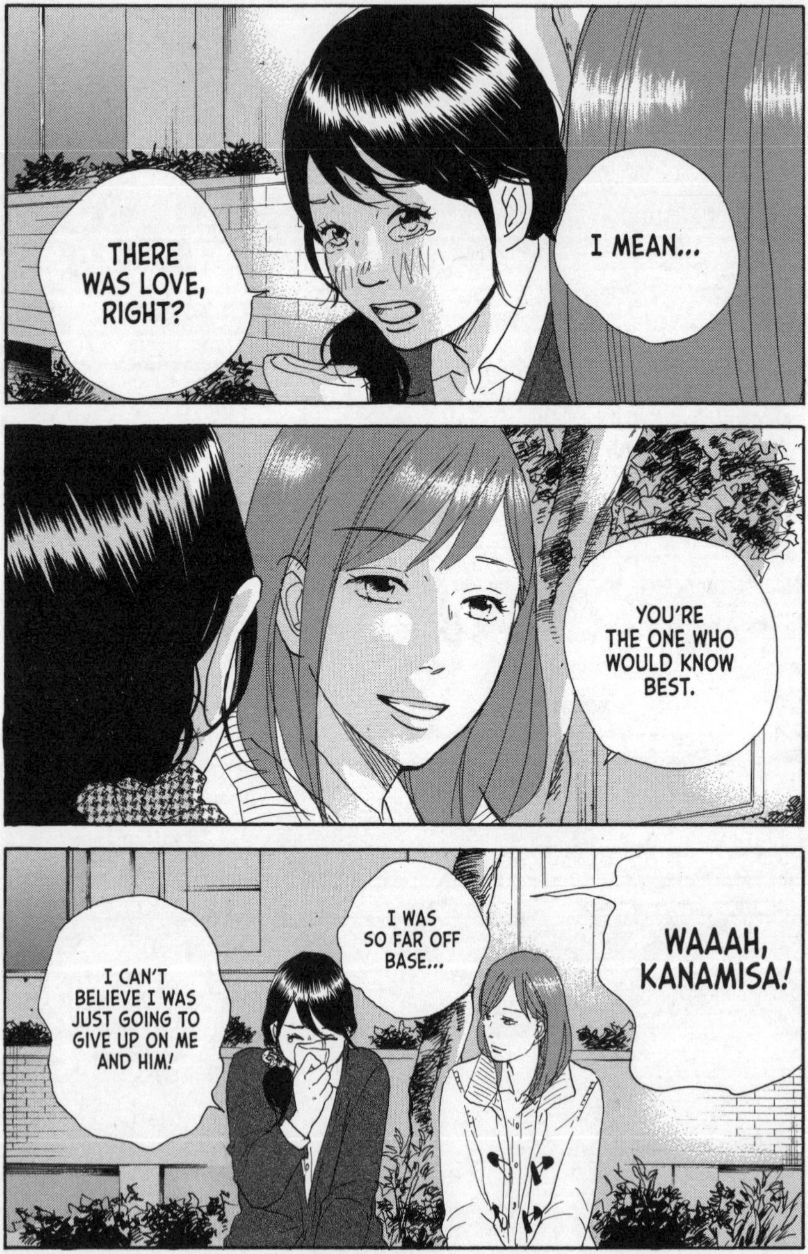
I MEAN...
THERE WAS LOVE, RIGHT?
YOU'RE THE ONE WHO WOULD KNOW BEST.
WAAAH, KANAMISA!
I WAS SO FAR OFF BASE...
I CAN'T BELIEVE I WAS JUST GOING TO GIVE UP ON ME AND HIM!

I'M...
GONNA
FIGHT
FOR US.

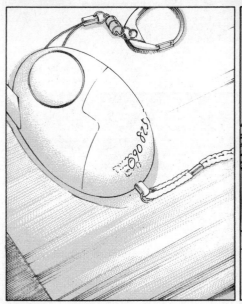

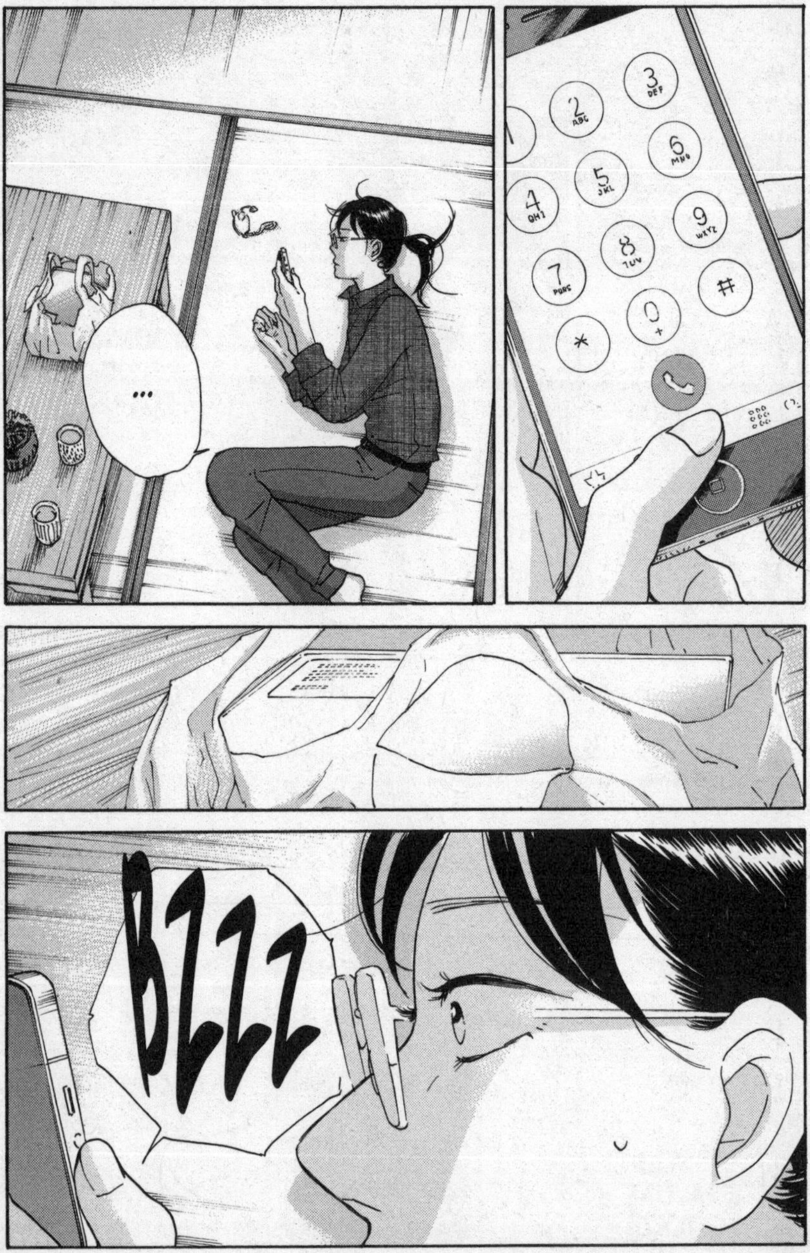
...
BZZZ

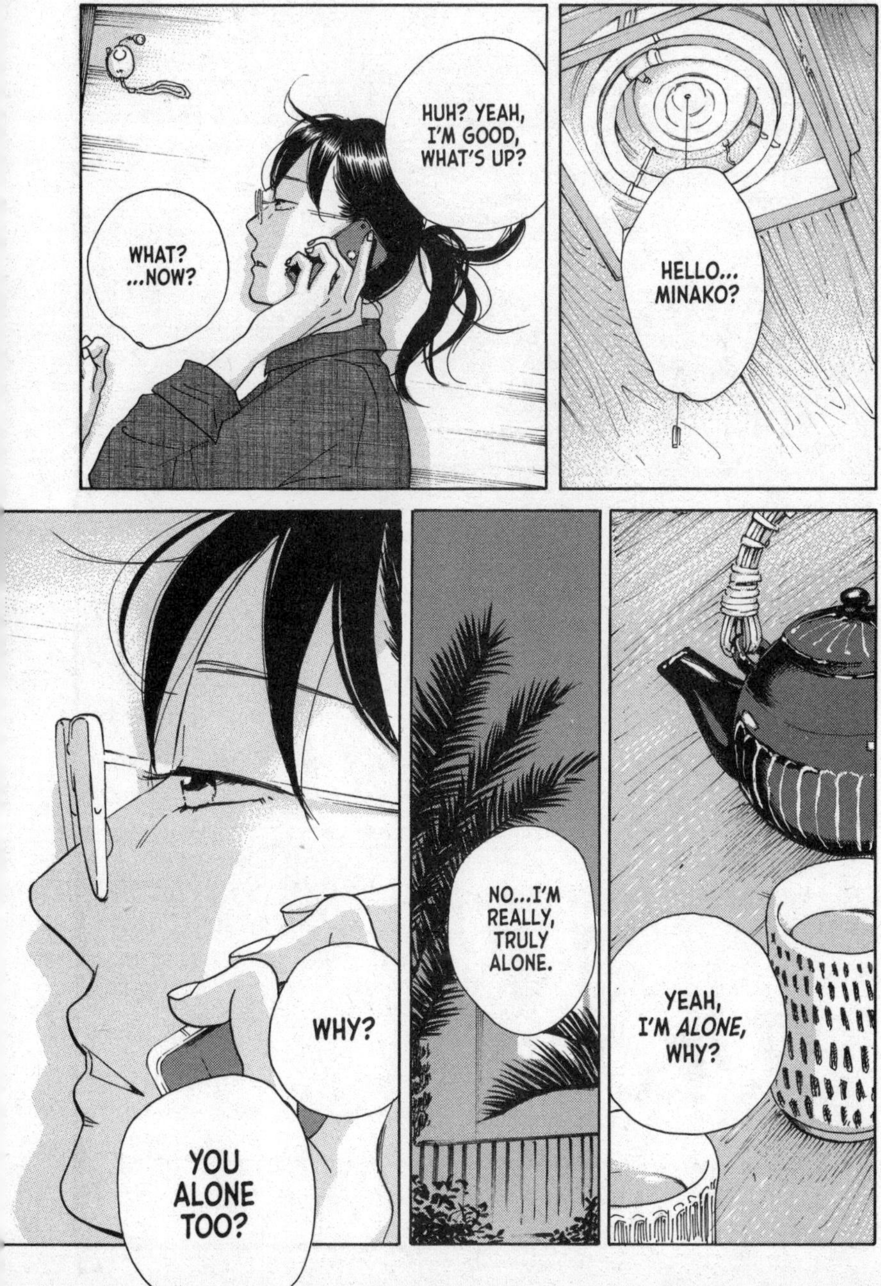
HELLO... MINAKO?
HUH? YEAH, I'M GOOD, WHAT'S UP?
WHAT? ...NOW?
YEAH, I'M *ALONE*, WHY?
NO...I'M REALLY, TRULY ALONE.
WHY?
YOU ALONE TOO?

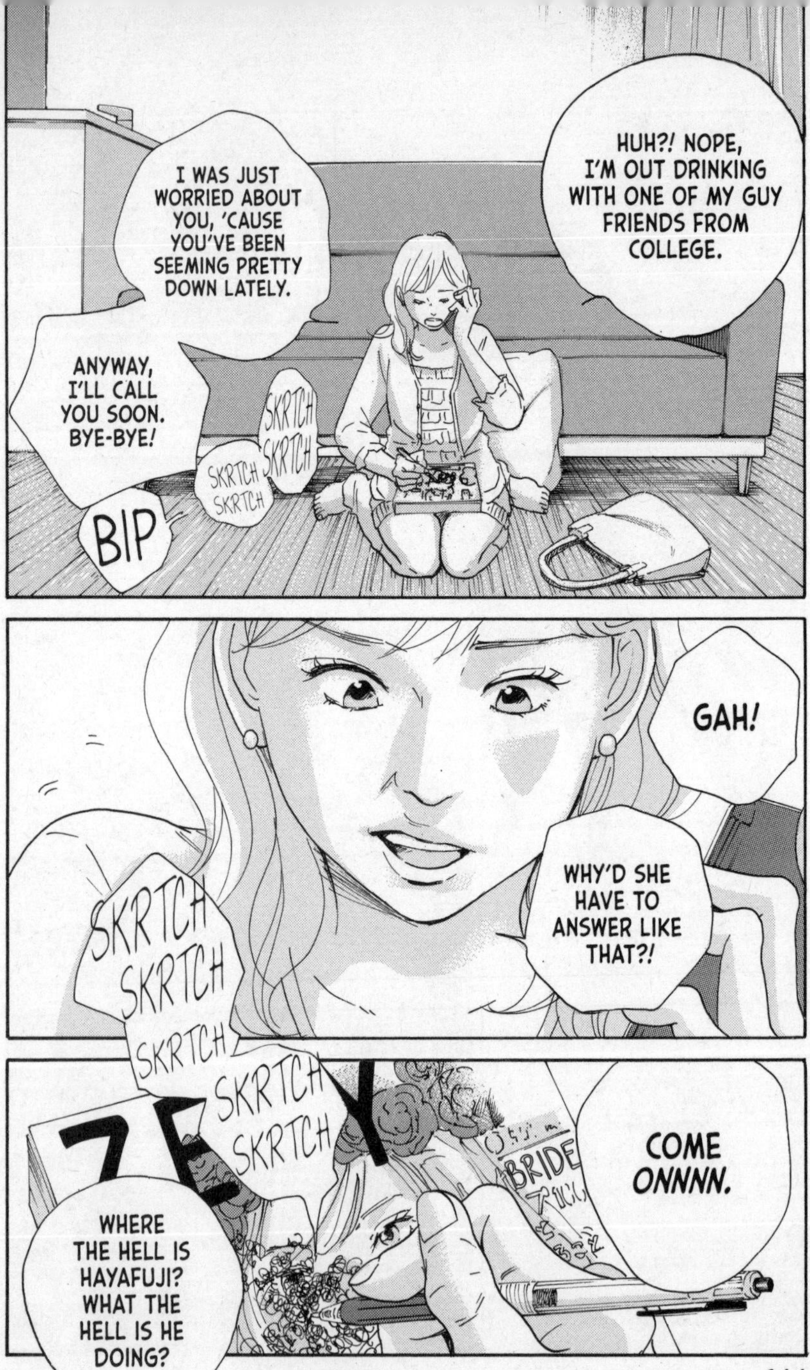
HUH?! NOPE, I'M OUT DRINKING WITH ONE OF MY GUY FRIENDS FROM COLLEGE.
I WAS JUST WORRIED ABOUT YOU, 'CAUSE YOU'VE BEEN SEEMING PRETTY DOWN LATELY.
ANYWAY, I'LL CALL YOU SOON. BYE-BYE!
SKRTCH SKRTCH
SKRTCH SKRTCH
BIP
GAH!
WHY'D SHE HAVE TO ANSWER LIKE THAT?!
SKRTCH SKRTCH SKRTCH
COME ONNNN.
SKRTCH SKRTCH
BRIDE
WHERE THE HELL IS HAYAFUJI? WHAT THE HELL IS HE DOING?

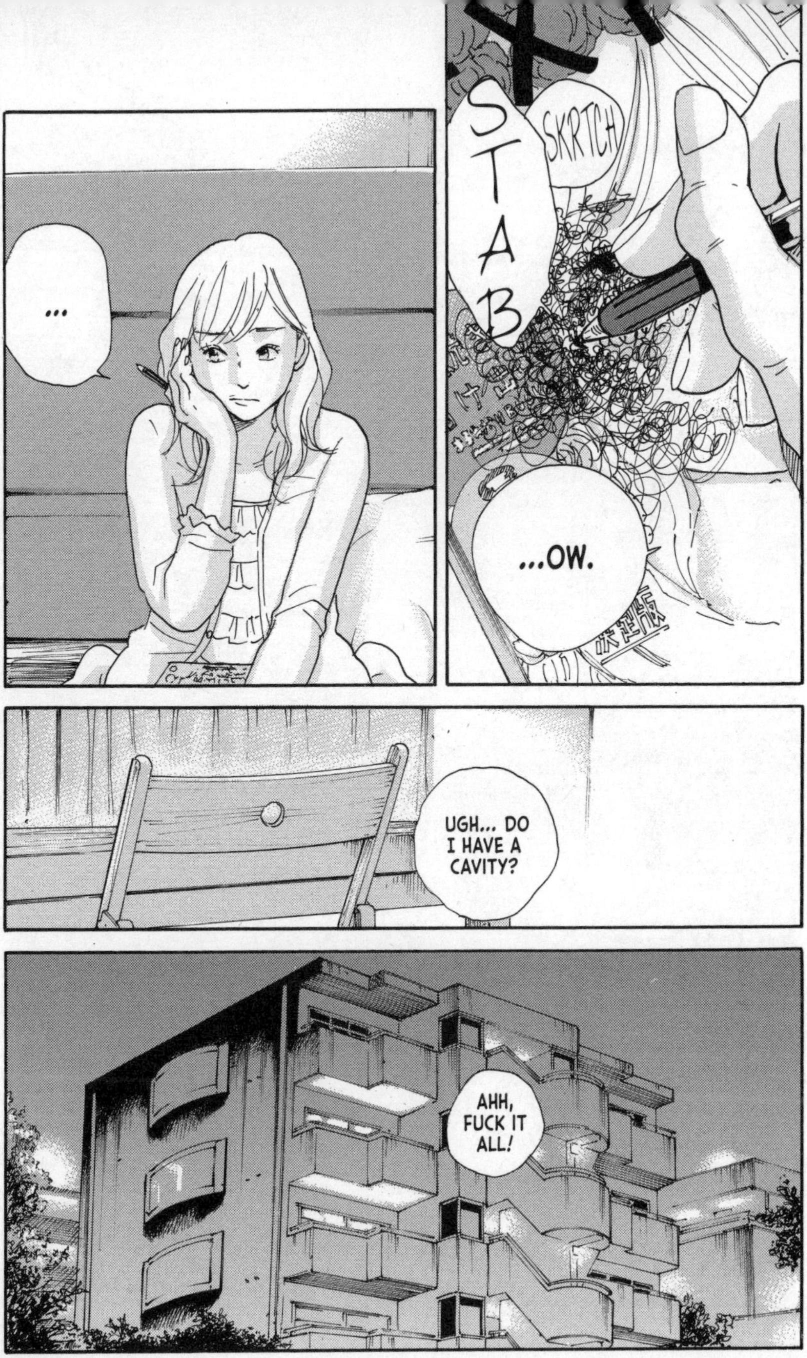
STAB
SKRTCH
...OW.
...
UGH... DO I HAVE A CAVITY?
AHH, FUCK IT ALL!

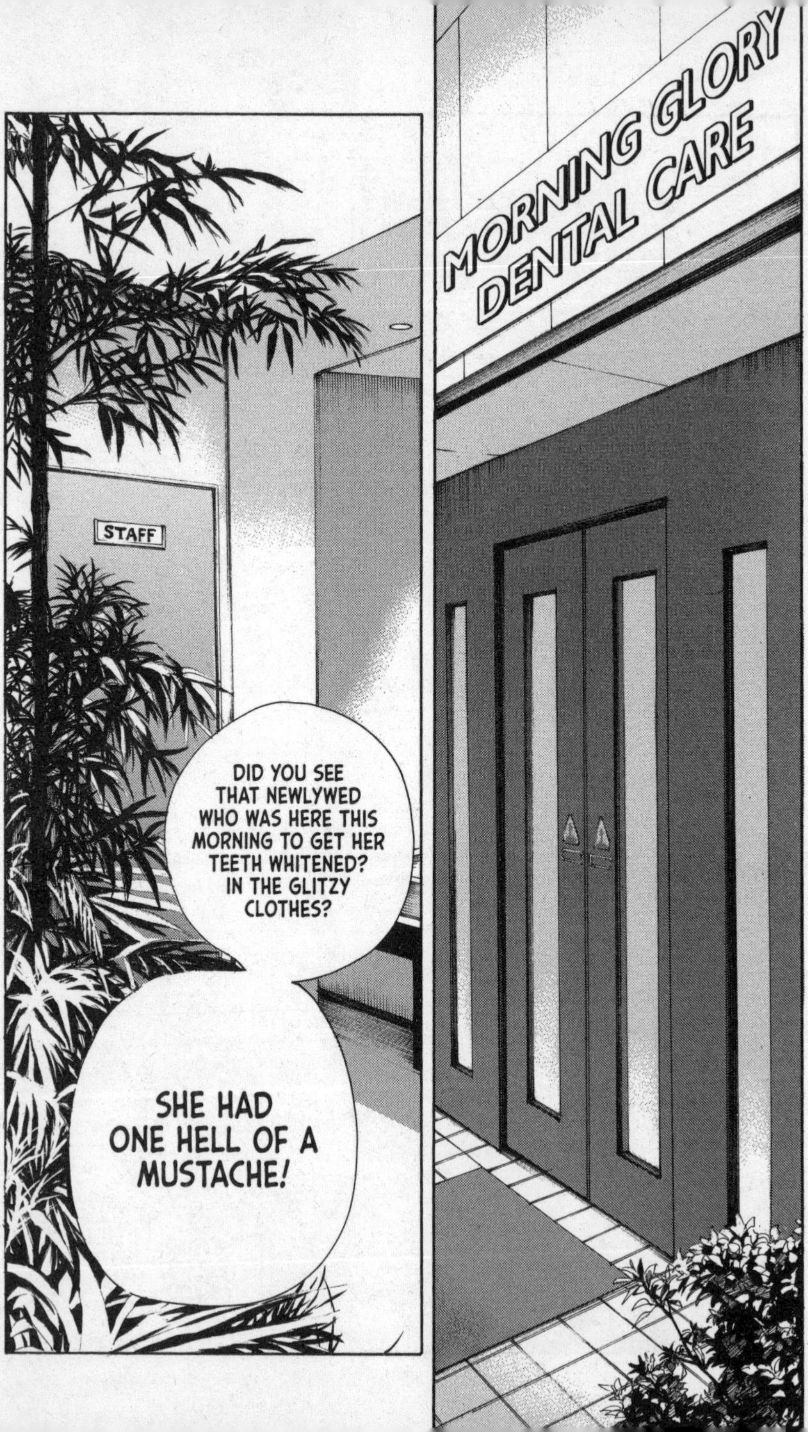
MORNING GLORY DENTAL CARE
STAFF
DID YOU SEE THAT NEWLYWED WHO WAS HERE THIS MORNING TO GET HER TEETH WHITENED? IN THE GLITZY CLOTHES?
SHE HAD ONE HELL OF A MUSTACHE!

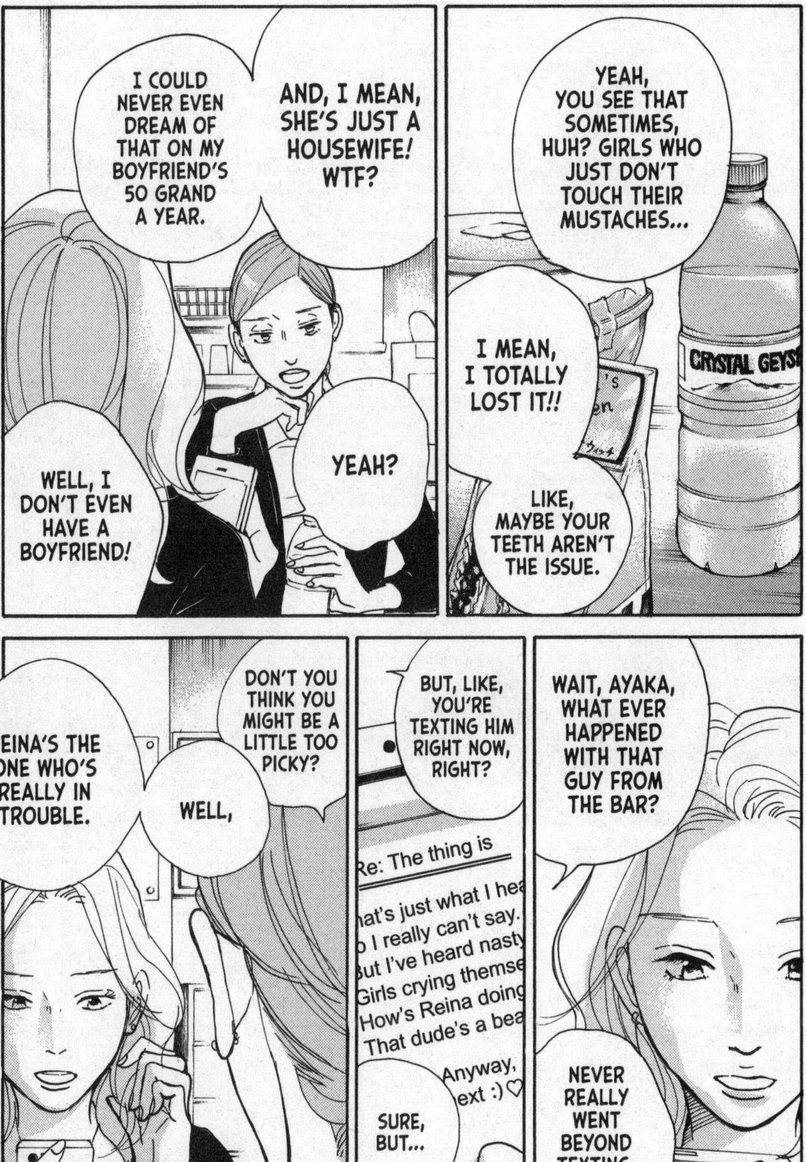
YEAH, YOU SEE THAT SOMETIMES, HUH? GIRLS WHO JUST DON'T TOUCH THEIR MUSTACHES...
CRYSTAL GEYSE
I MEAN, I TOTALLY LOST IT!!
LIKE, MAYBE YOUR TEETH AREN'T THE ISSUE.
AND, I MEAN, SHE'S JUST A HOUSEWIFE! WTF?
I COULD NEVER EVEN DREAM OF THAT ON MY BOYFRIEND'S 50 GRAND A YEAR.
YEAH?
WELL, I DON'T EVEN HAVE A BOYFRIEND!
WAIT, AYAKA, WHAT EVER HAPPENED WITH THAT GUY FROM THE BAR?
NEVER REALLY WENT BEYOND TEXTING, AS YOU CAN SEE.
BUT, LIKE, YOU'RE TEXTING HIM RIGHT NOW, RIGHT?
Re: The thing is
hat's just what I hea
o I really can't say.
But I've heard nasty
Girls crying themse
How's Reina doing
That dude's a bea
Anyway,
ext :)♡
SURE, BUT...
DON'T YOU THINK YOU MIGHT BE A LITTLE TOO PICKY?
WELL,
REINA'S THE ONE WHO'S REALLY IN TROUBLE.

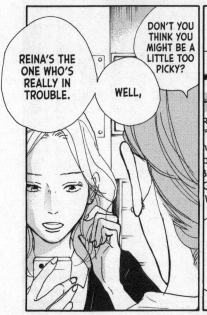

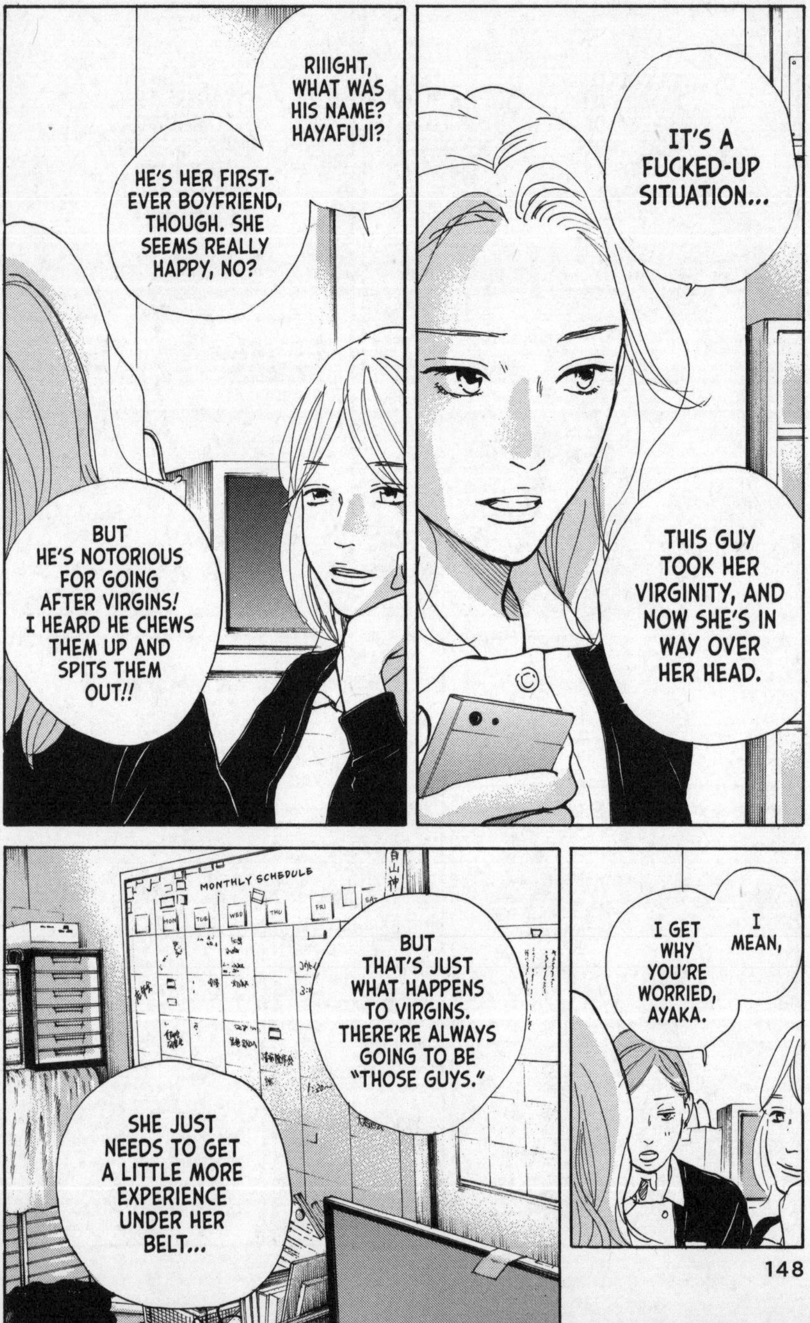
IT'S A FUCKED-UP SITUATION...
THIS GUY TOOK HER VIRGINITY, AND NOW SHE'S IN WAY OVER HER HEAD.
RIIIGHT, WHAT WAS HIS NAME? HAYAFUJI?
HE'S HER FIRST-EVER BOYFRIEND, THOUGH. SHE SEEMS REALLY HAPPY, NO?
BUT HE'S NOTORIOUS FOR GOING AFTER VIRGINS! I HEARD HE CHEWS THEM UP AND SPITS THEM OUT!!
I MEAN,
I GET WHY YOU'RE WORRIED, AYAKA.
MONTHLY SCHEDULE
BUT THAT'S JUST WHAT HAPPENS TO VIRGINS. THERE'RE ALWAYS GOING TO BE "THOSE GUYS."
SHE JUST NEEDS TO GET A LITTLE MORE EXPERIENCE UNDER HER BELT...

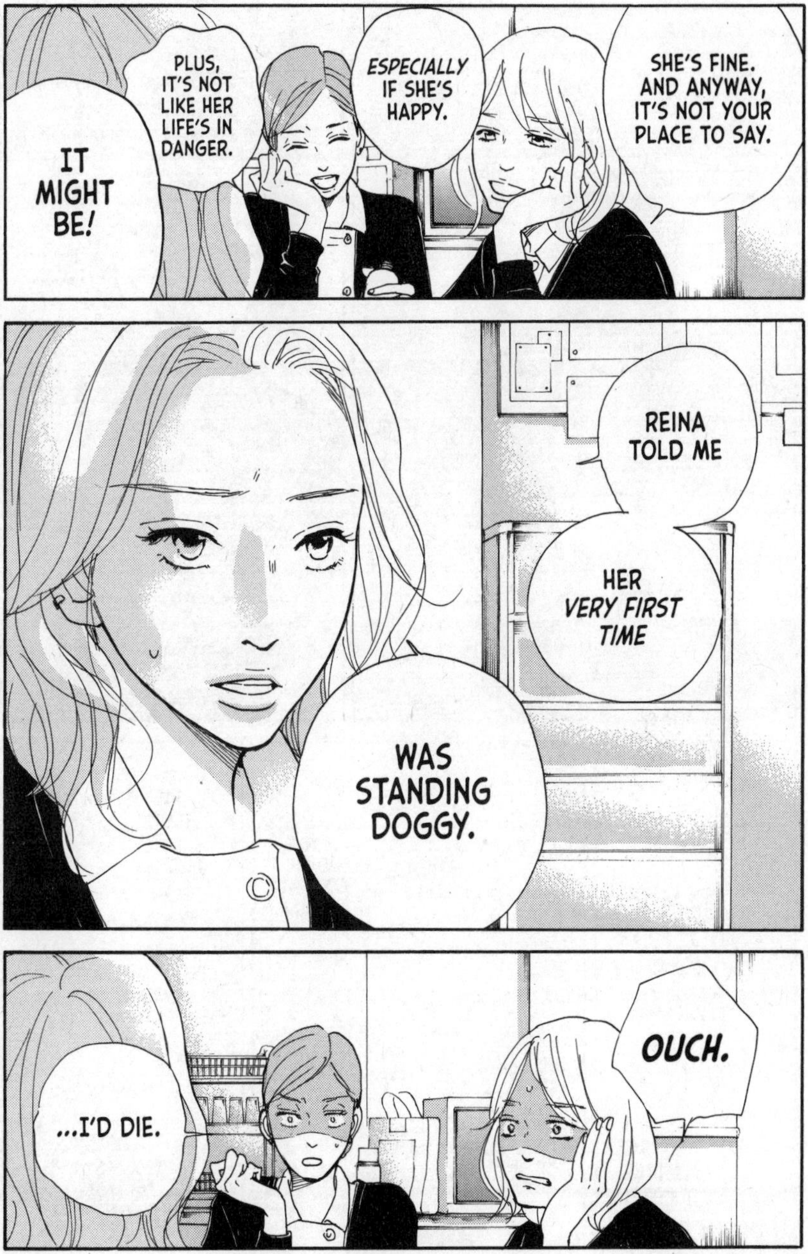
SHE'S FINE. AND ANYWAY, IT'S NOT YOUR PLACE TO SAY.
ESPECIALLY IF SHE'S HAPPY.
PLUS, IT'S NOT LIKE HER LIFE'S IN DANGER.
IT MIGHT BE!
REINA TOLD ME
HER *VERY FIRST* TIME
WAS STANDING DOGGY.
OUCH.
...I'D DIE.

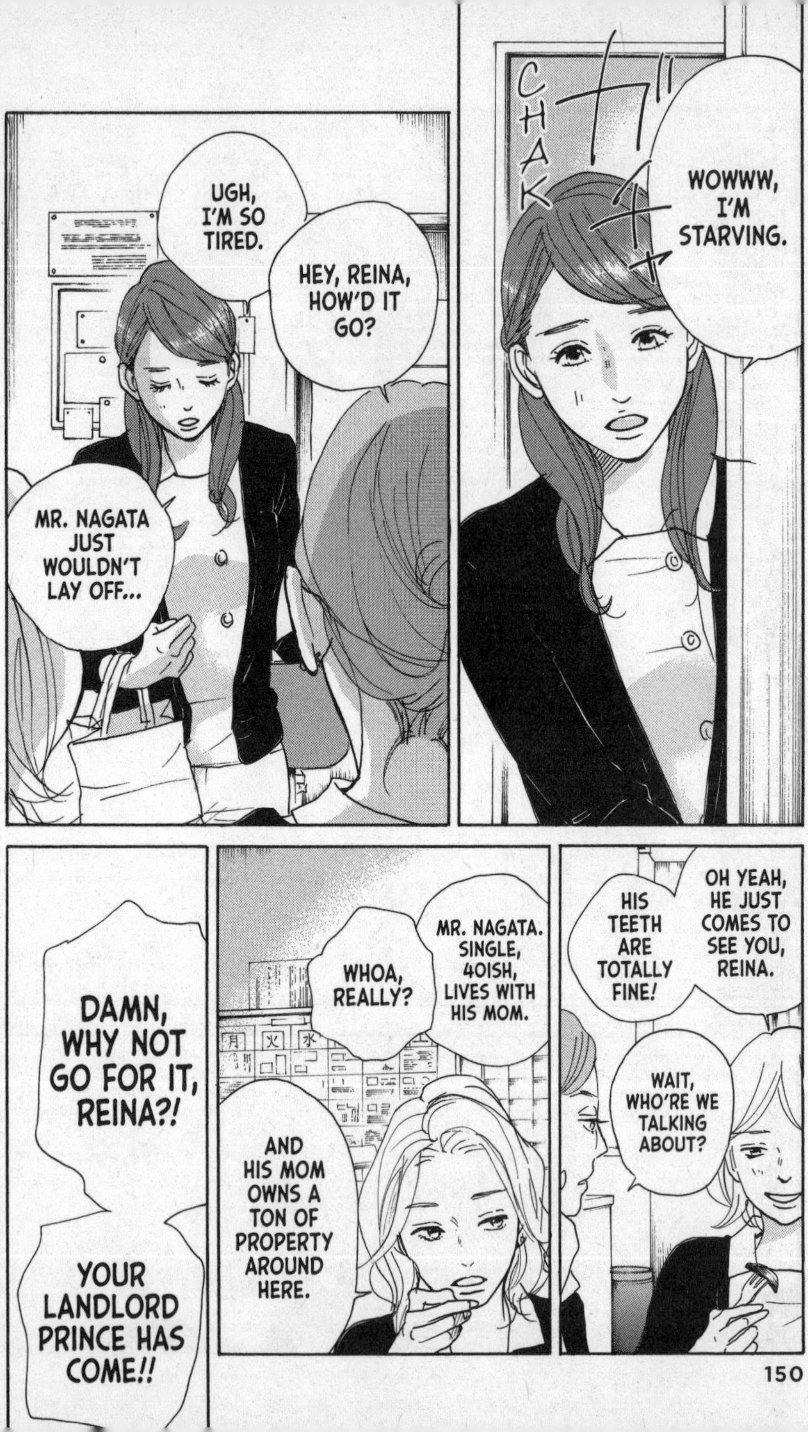
CHAK
WOWWW, I'M STARVING.
HEY, REINA, HOW'D IT GO?
UGH, I'M SO TIRED.
MR. NAGATA JUST WOULDN'T LAY OFF...
OH YEAH, HE JUST COMES TO SEE YOU, REINA.
HIS TEETH ARE TOTALLY FINE!
WAIT, WHO'RE WE TALKING ABOUT?
MR. NAGATA. SINGLE, 40ISH, LIVES WITH HIS MOM.
WHOA, REALLY?
AND HIS MOM OWNS A TON OF PROPERTY AROUND HERE.
DAMN, WHY NOT GO FOR IT, REINA?!
YOUR LANDLORD PRINCE HAS COME!!

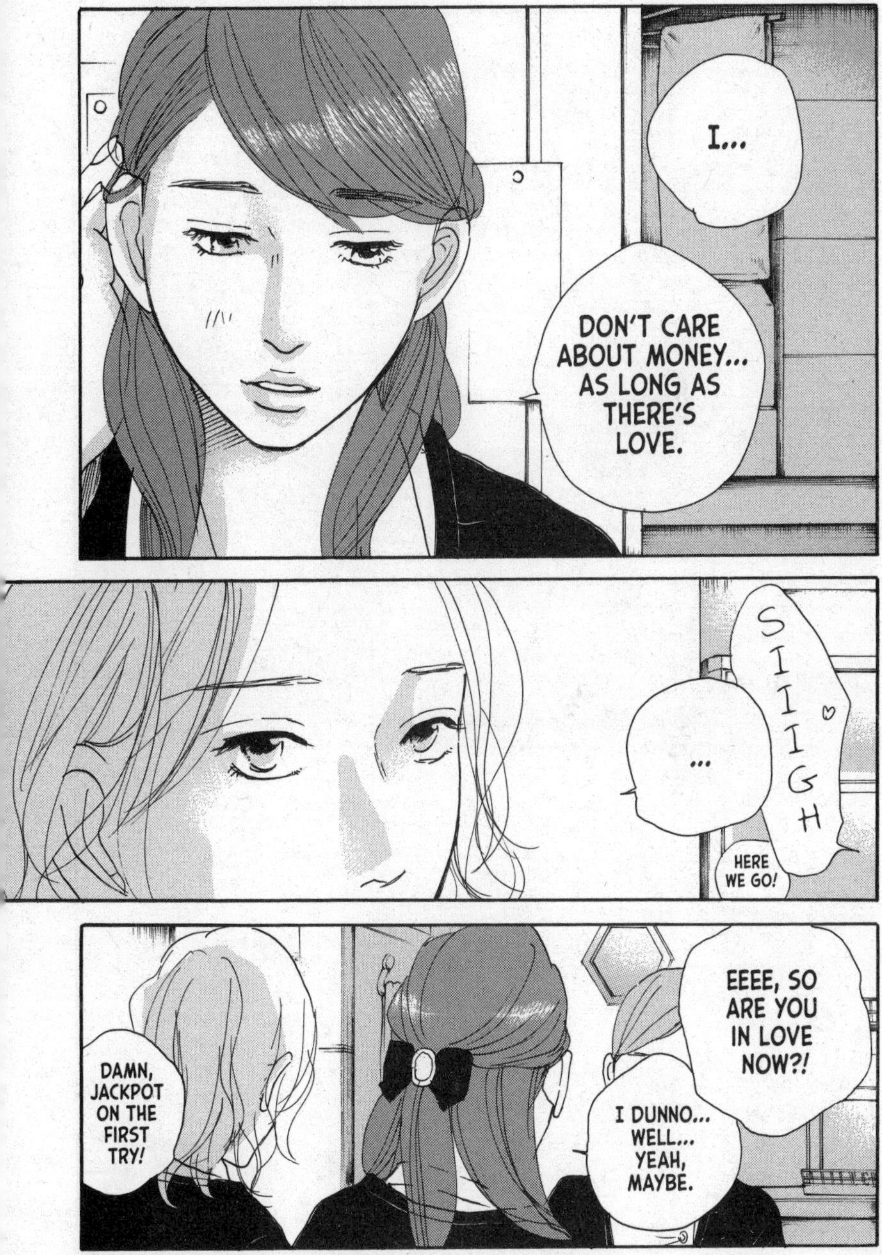
I...
DON'T CARE ABOUT MONEY... AS LONG AS THERE'S LOVE.
SIIIGH
...
HERE WE GO!
EEEE, SO ARE YOU IN LOVE NOW?!
I DUNNO... WELL... YEAH, MAYBE.
DAMN, JACKPOT ON THE FIRST TRY!

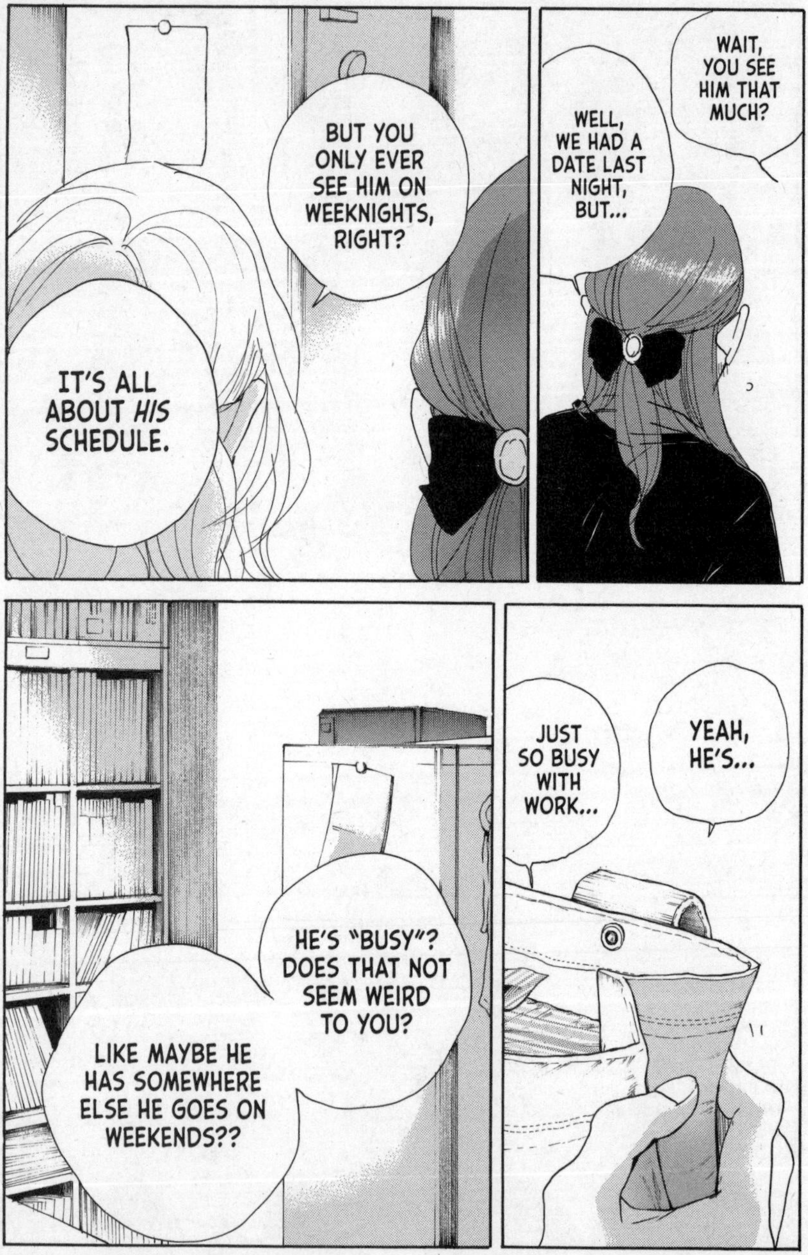
WAIT, YOU SEE HIM THAT MUCH?
WELL, WE HAD A DATE LAST NIGHT, BUT...
BUT YOU ONLY EVER SEE HIM ON WEEKNIGHTS, RIGHT?
IT'S ALL ABOUT *HIS* SCHEDULE.
YEAH, HE'S...
JUST SO BUSY WITH WORK...
HE'S "BUSY"? DOES THAT NOT SEEM WEIRD TO YOU?
LIKE MAYBE HE HAS SOMEWHERE ELSE HE GOES ON WEEKENDS??

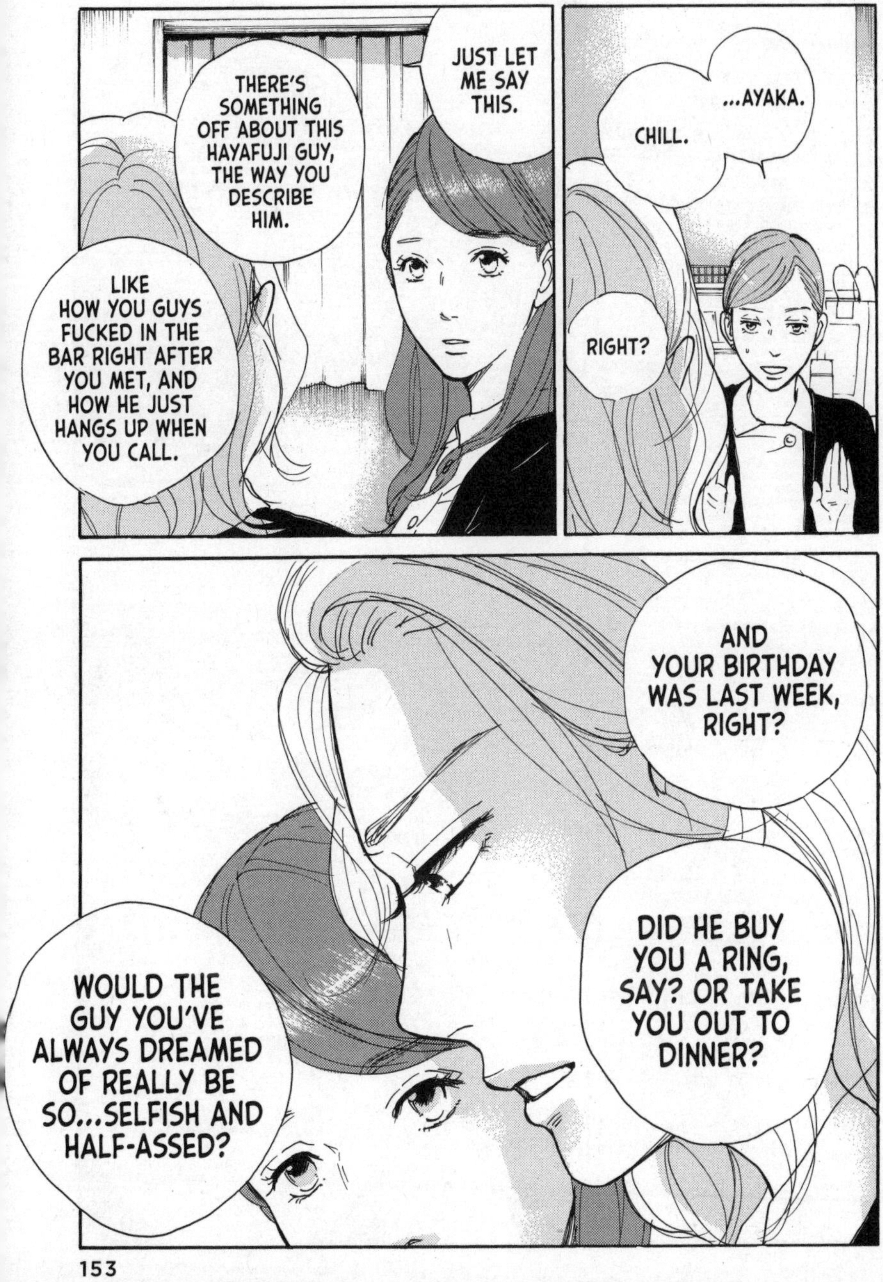
...AYAKA.
CHILL.
RIGHT?
JUST LET ME SAY THIS.
THERE'S SOMETHING OFF ABOUT THIS HAYAFUJI GUY, THE WAY YOU DESCRIBE HIM.
LIKE HOW YOU GUYS FUCKED IN THE BAR RIGHT AFTER YOU MET, AND HOW HE JUST HANGS UP WHEN YOU CALL.
AND YOUR BIRTHDAY WAS LAST WEEK, RIGHT?
DID HE BUY YOU A RING, SAY? OR TAKE YOU OUT TO DINNER?
WOULD THE GUY YOU'VE ALWAYS DREAMED OF REALLY BE SO...SELFISH AND HALF-ASSED?

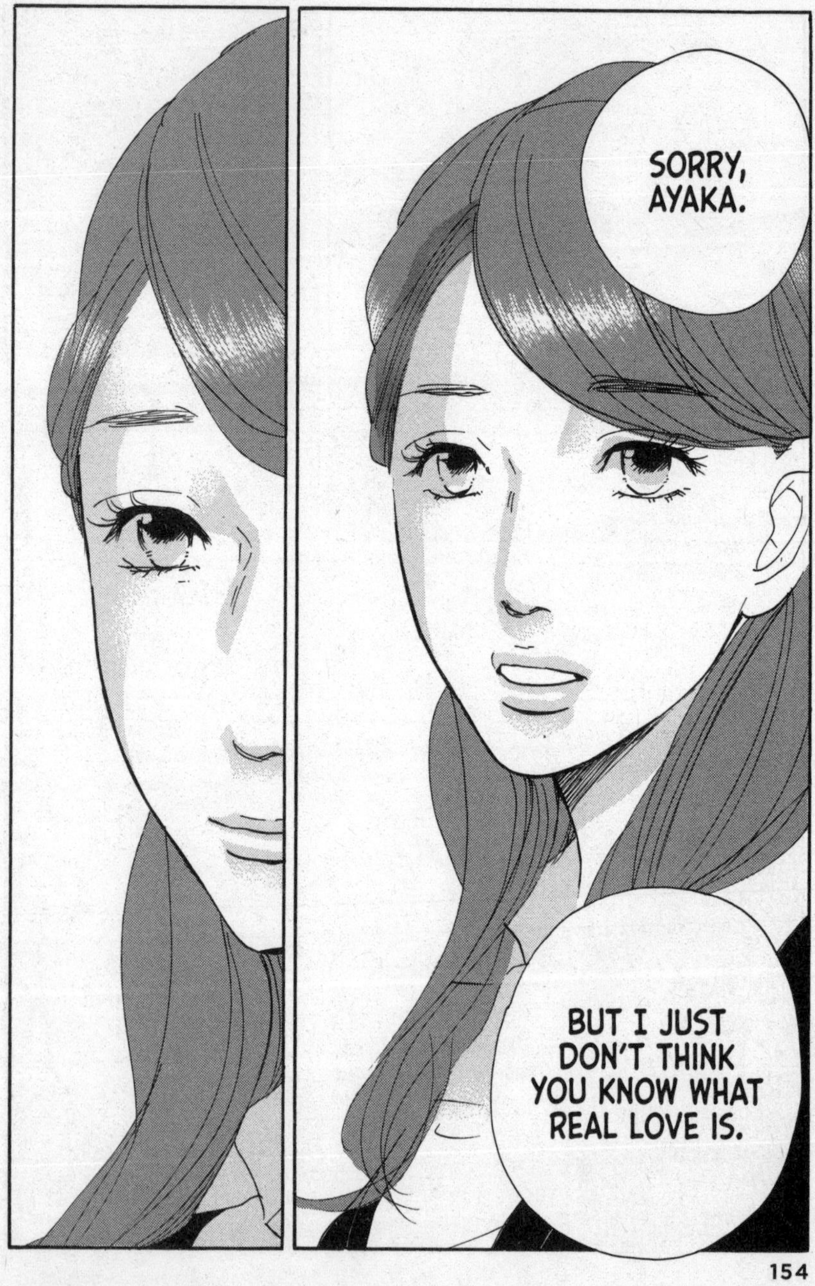
SORRY, AYAKA.
BUT I JUST DON'T THINK YOU KNOW WHAT REAL LOVE IS.

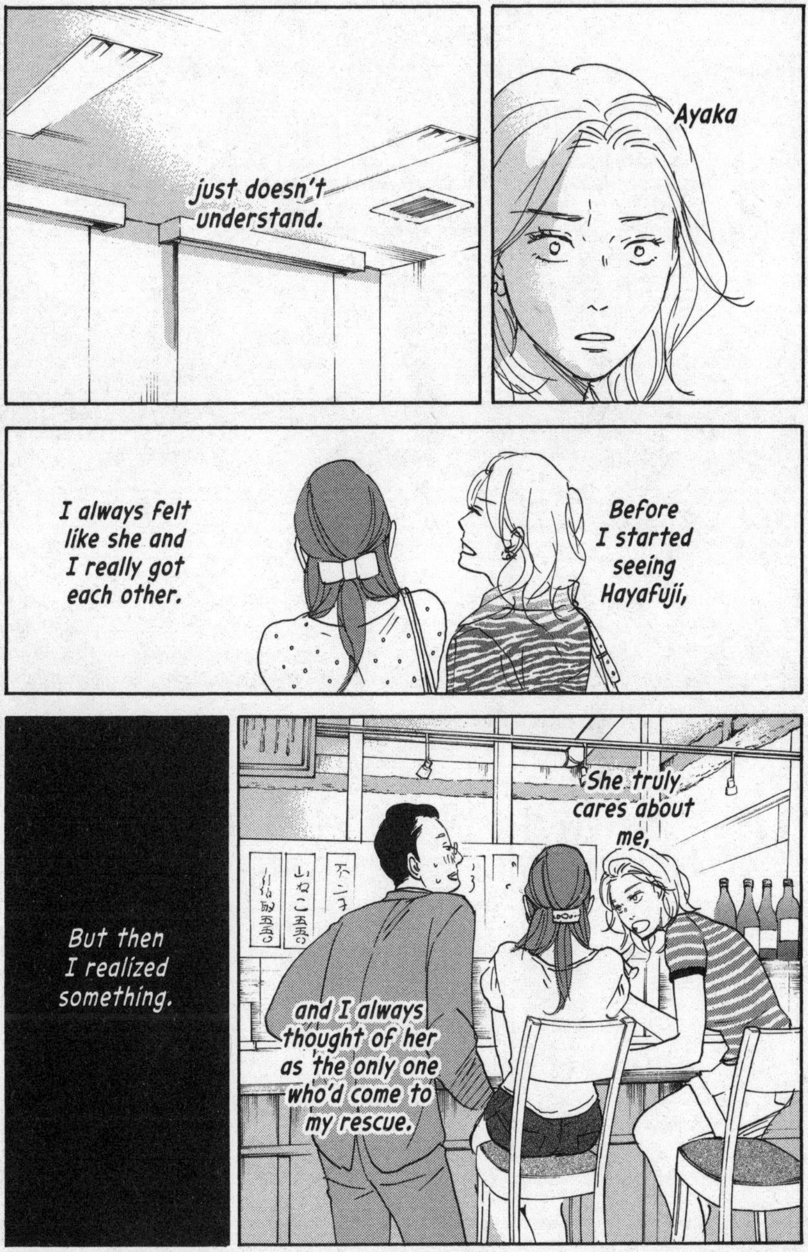
Ayaka
just doesn't understand.
Before I started seeing Hayafuji,
I always felt like she and I really got each other.
She truly cares about me,
and I always thought of her as the only one who'd come to my rescue.
But then I realized something.

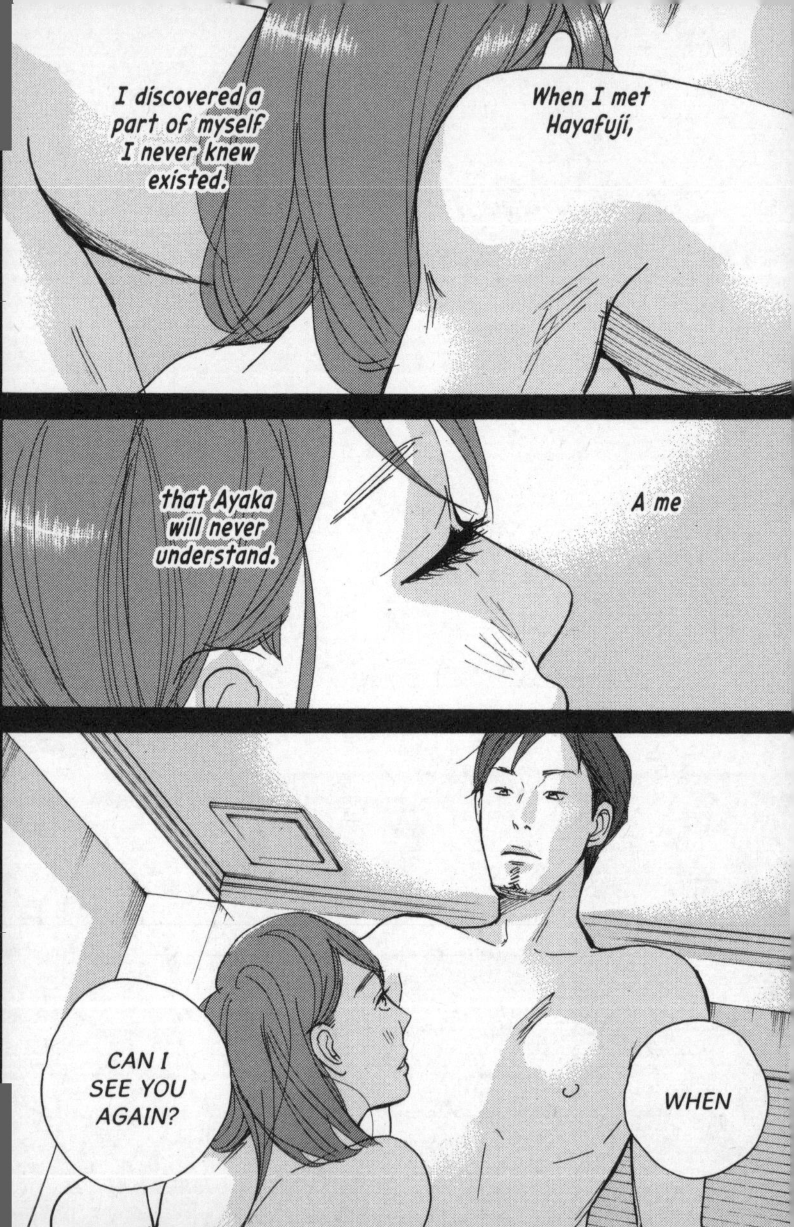
When I met Hayafuji,
I discovered a part of myself I never knew existed.
A me
that Ayaka will never understand.
WHEN
CAN I SEE YOU AGAIN?

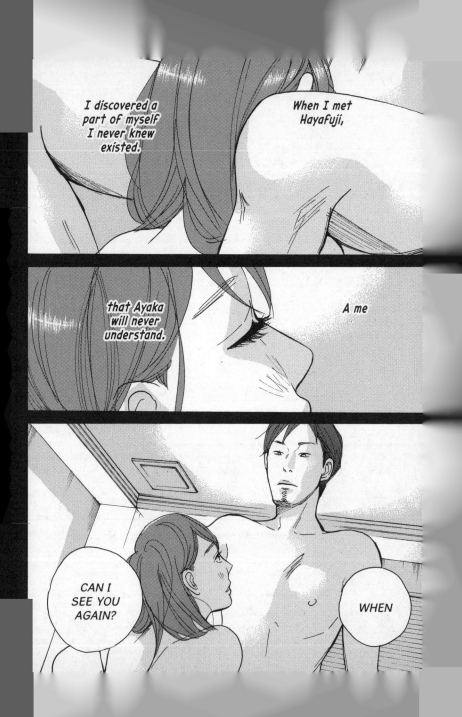

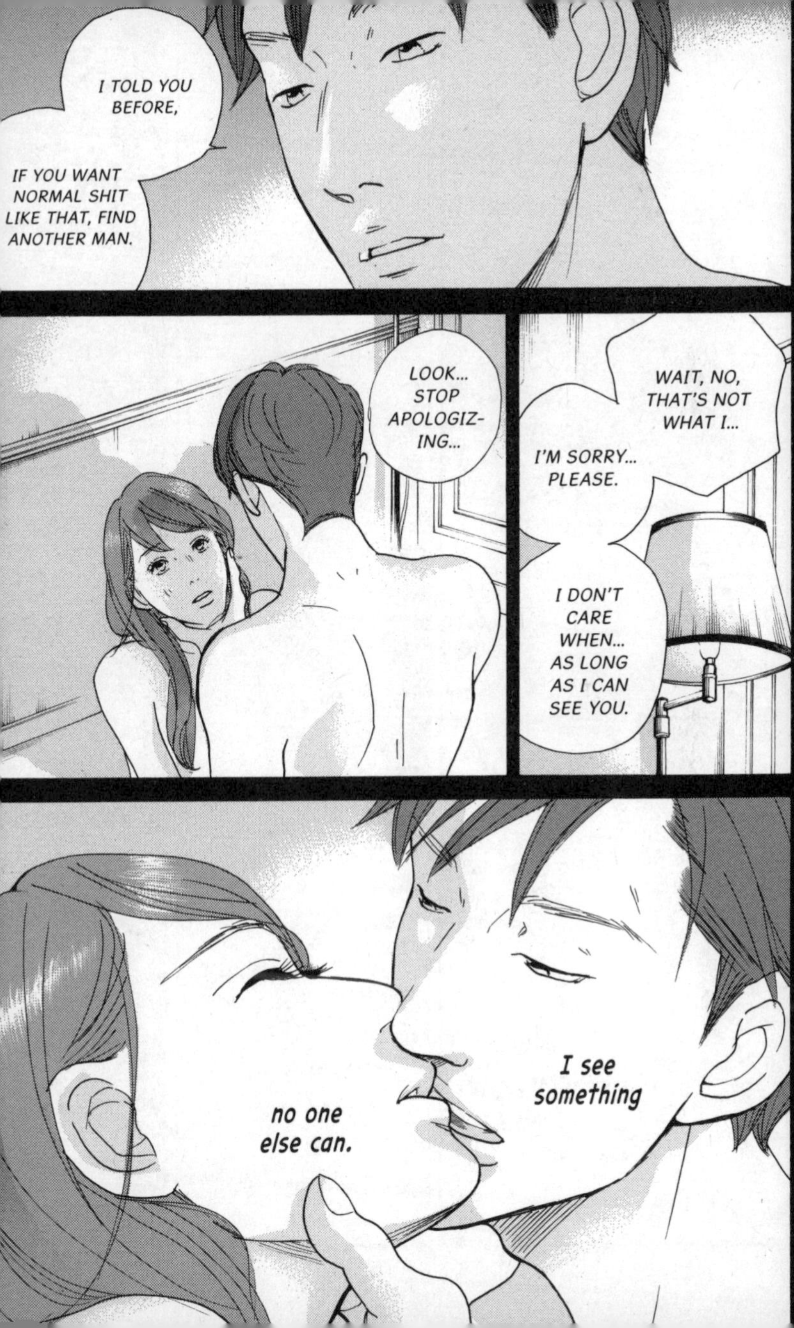
I TOLD YOU BEFORE,
IF YOU WANT NORMAL SHIT LIKE THAT, FIND ANOTHER MAN.
WAIT, NO, THAT'S NOT WHAT I...
I'M SORRY... PLEASE.
I DON'T CARE WHEN... AS LONG AS I CAN SEE YOU.
LOOK... STOP APOLOGIZ-ING...
I see something
no one else can.

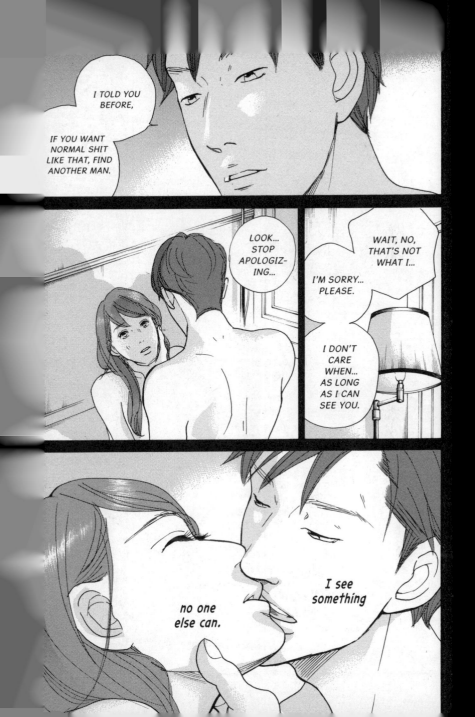

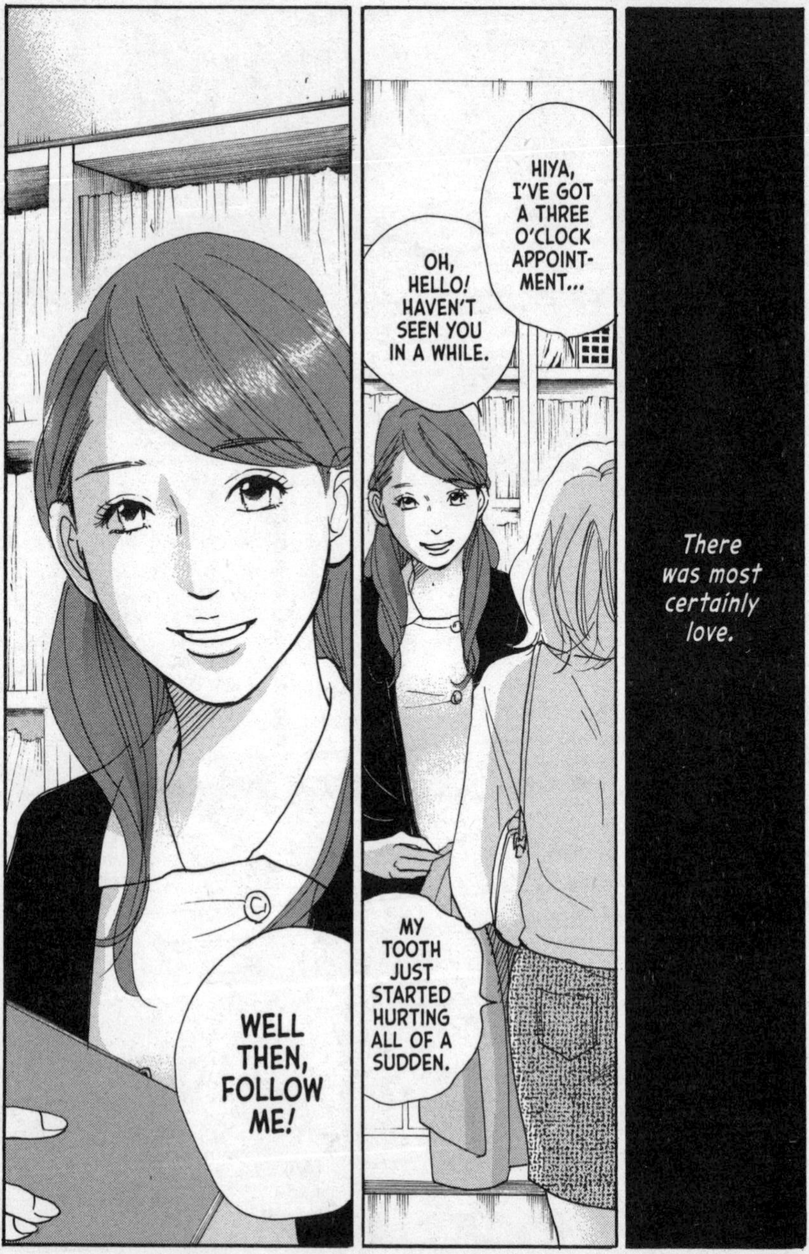
There was most certainly love.
HIYA, I'VE GOT A THREE O'CLOCK APPOINT-MENT...
OH, HELLO! HAVEN'T SEEN YOU IN A WHILE.
MY TOOTH JUST STARTED HURTING ALL OF A SUDDEN.
WELL THEN, FOLLOW ME!

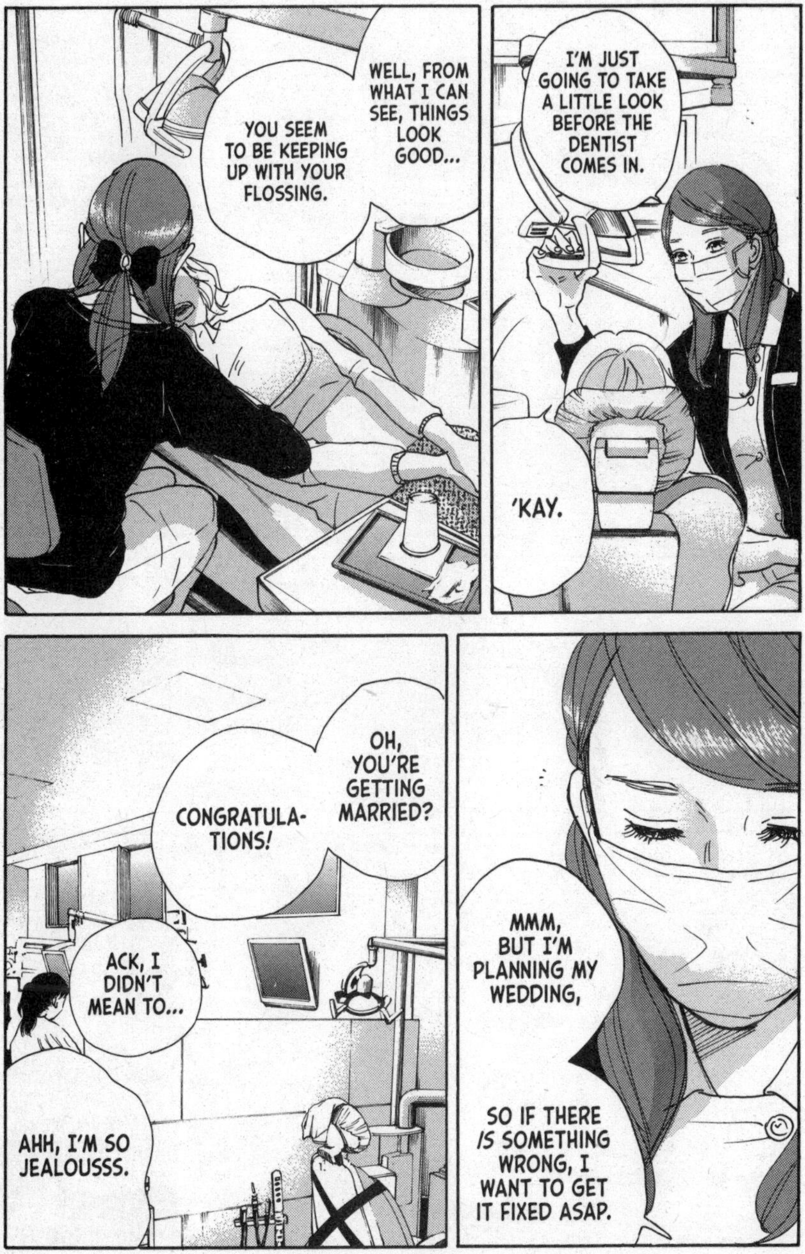
I'M JUST GOING TO TAKE A LITTLE LOOK BEFORE THE DENTIST COMES IN.
'KAY.
WELL, FROM WHAT I CAN SEE, THINGS LOOK GOOD...
YOU SEEM TO BE KEEPING UP WITH YOUR FLOSSING.
MMM, BUT I'M PLANNING MY WEDDING,
SO IF THERE *IS* SOMETHING WRONG, I WANT TO GET IT FIXED ASAP.
OH, YOU'RE GETTING MARRIED?
CONGRATULA-TIONS!
ACK, I DIDN'T MEAN TO...
AHH, I'M SO JEALOUSSS.

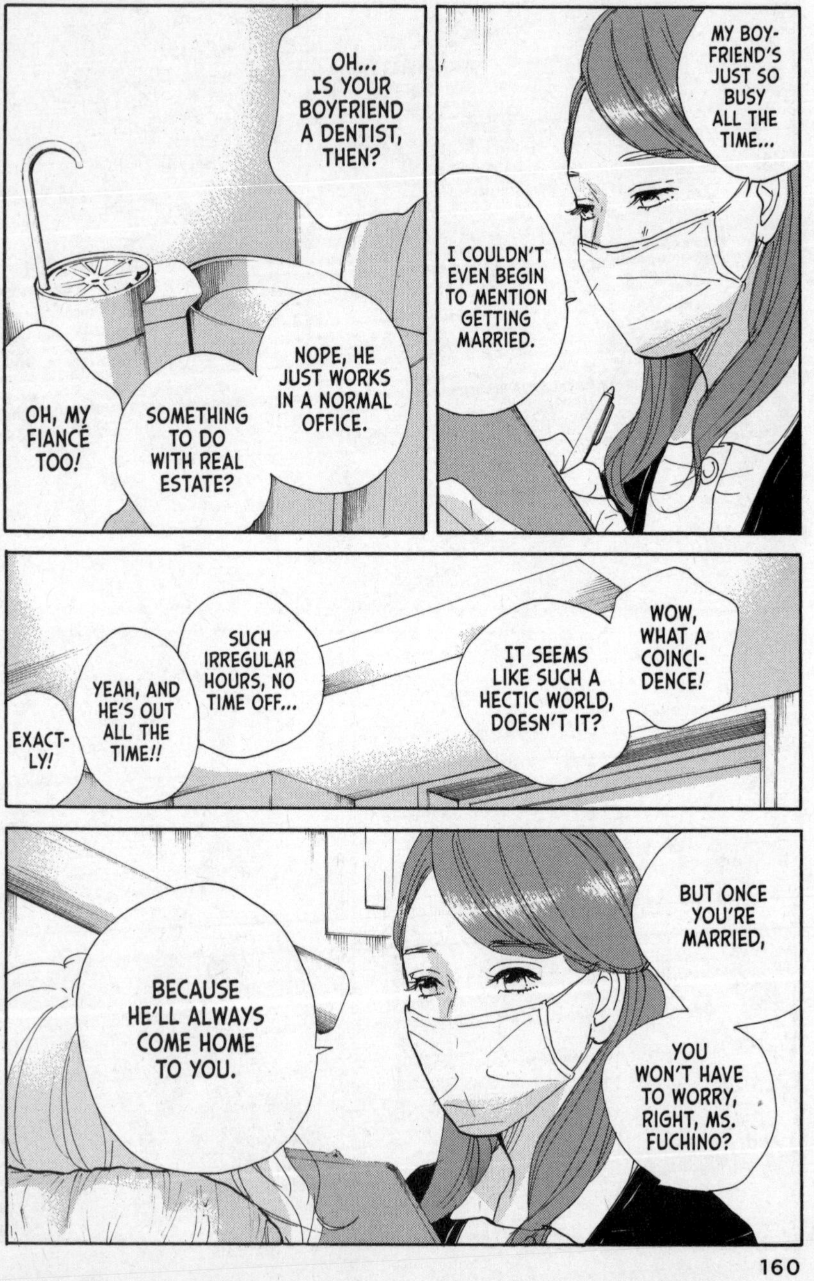
MY BOYFRIEND'S JUST SO BUSY ALL THE TIME...
I COULDN'T EVEN BEGIN TO MENTION GETTING MARRIED.
OH... IS YOUR BOYFRIEND A DENTIST, THEN?
NOPE, HE JUST WORKS IN A NORMAL OFFICE.
SOMETHING TO DO WITH REAL ESTATE?
OH, MY FIANCÉ TOO!
WOW, WHAT A COINCIDENCE!
IT SEEMS LIKE SUCH A HECTIC WORLD, DOESN'T IT?
SUCH IRREGULAR HOURS, NO TIME OFF...
YEAH, AND HE'S OUT ALL THE TIME!!
EXACTLY!
BUT ONCE YOU'RE MARRIED,
YOU WON'T HAVE TO WORRY, RIGHT, MS. FUCHINO?
BECAUSE HE'LL ALWAYS COME HOME TO YOU.

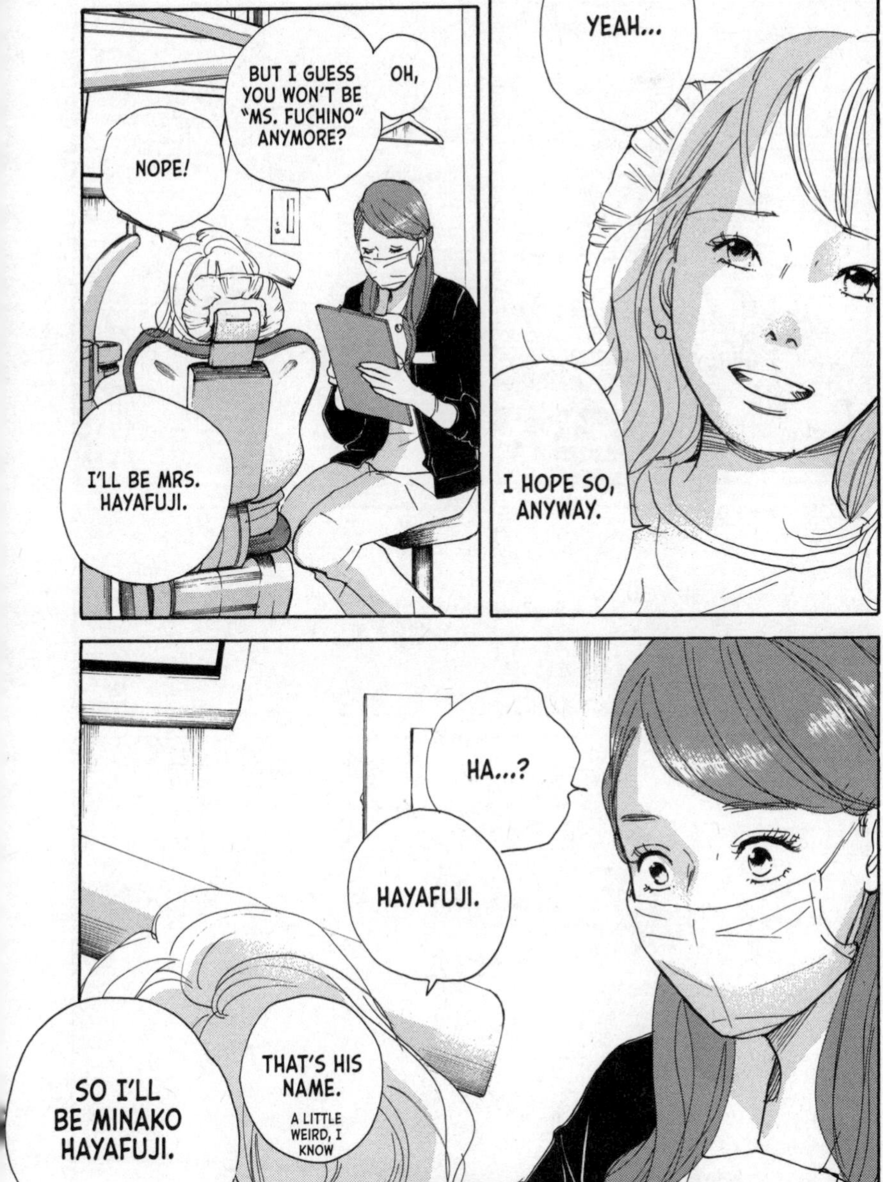
YEAH...
I HOPE SO, ANYWAY.
OH, BUT I GUESS YOU WON'T BE "MS. FUCHINO" ANYMORE?
NOPE!
I'LL BE MRS. HAYAFUJI.
HA...?
HAYAFUJI.
THAT'S HIS NAME.
A LITTLE WEIRD, I KNOW
SO I'LL BE MINAKO HAYAFUJI.

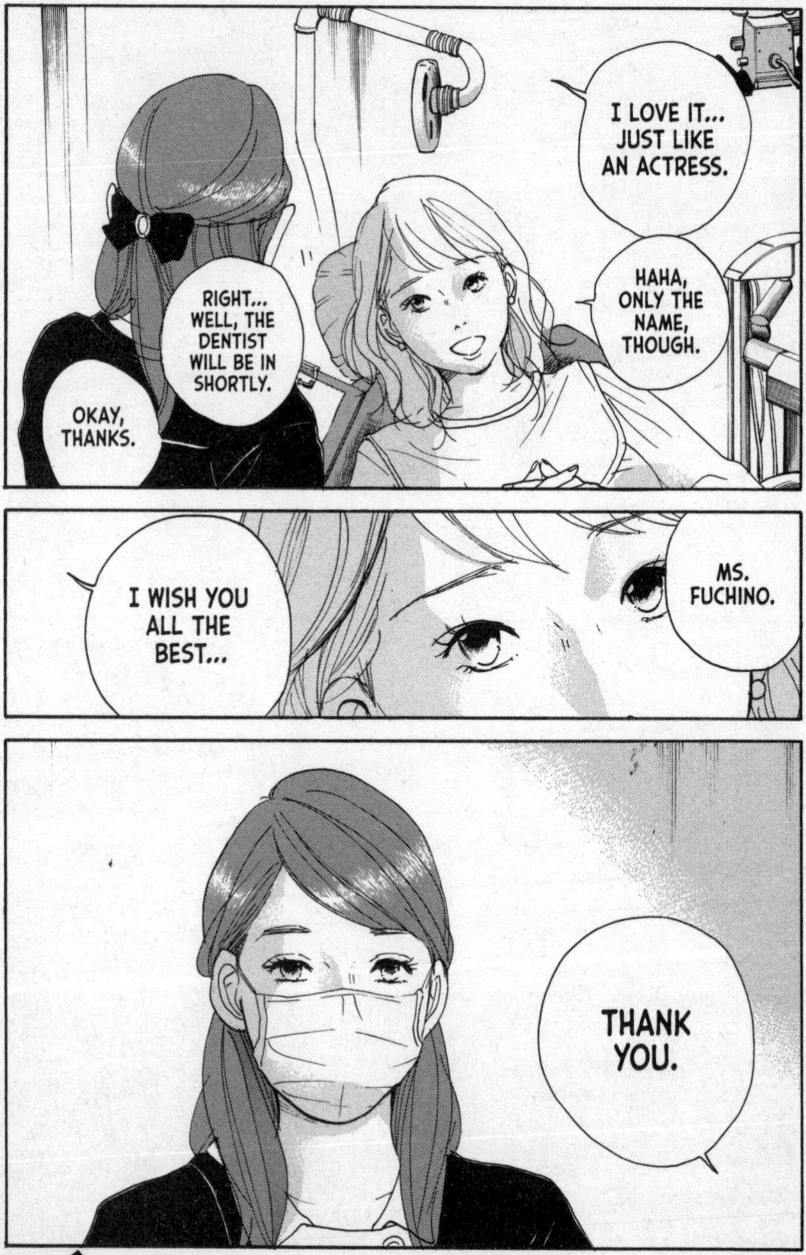
I LOVE IT... JUST LIKE AN ACTRESS.
HAHA, ONLY THE NAME, THOUGH.
RIGHT... WELL, THE DENTIST WILL BE IN SHORTLY.
OKAY, THANKS.
MS. FUCHINO.
I WISH YOU ALL THE BEST...
THANK YOU.

END

CHAPTER 18. SOMEONE I'M WORRIED ABOUT

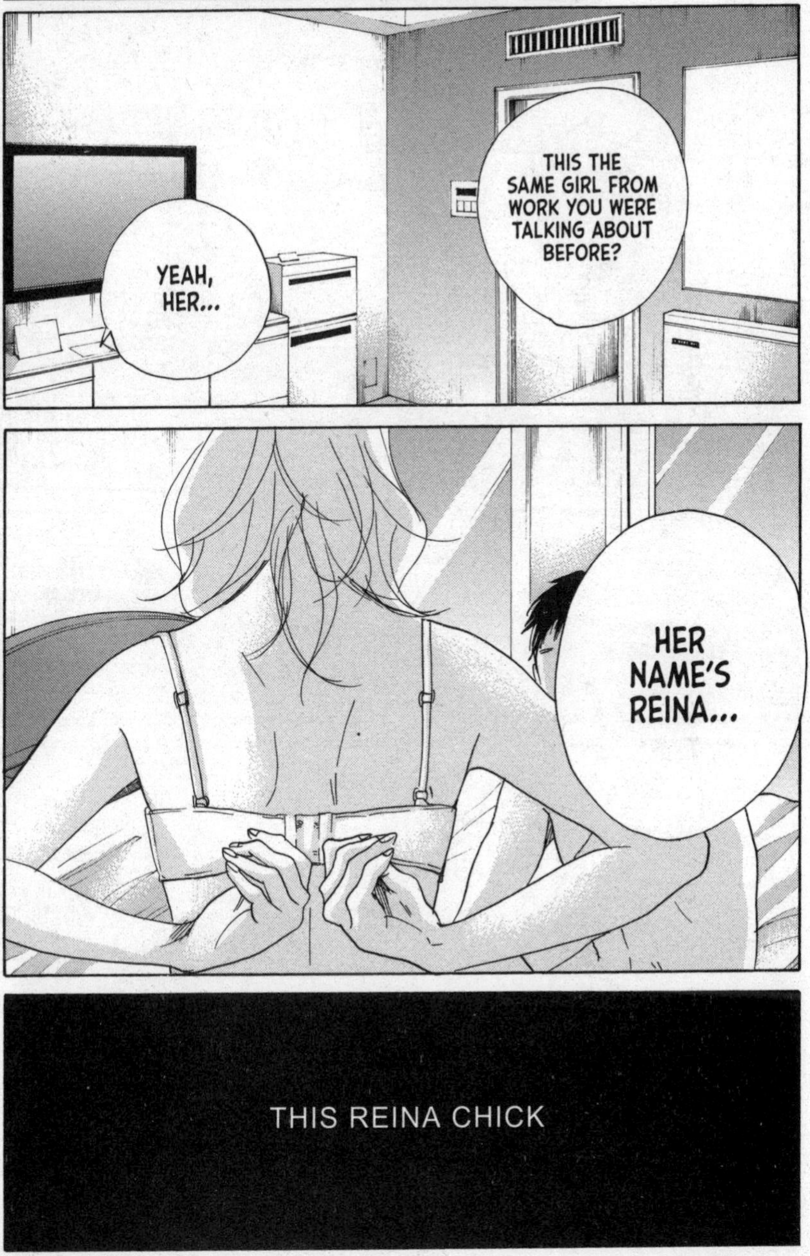
THIS THE SAME GIRL FROM WORK YOU WERE TALKING ABOUT BEFORE?
YEAH, HER...
HER NAME'S REINA...
THIS REINA CHICK

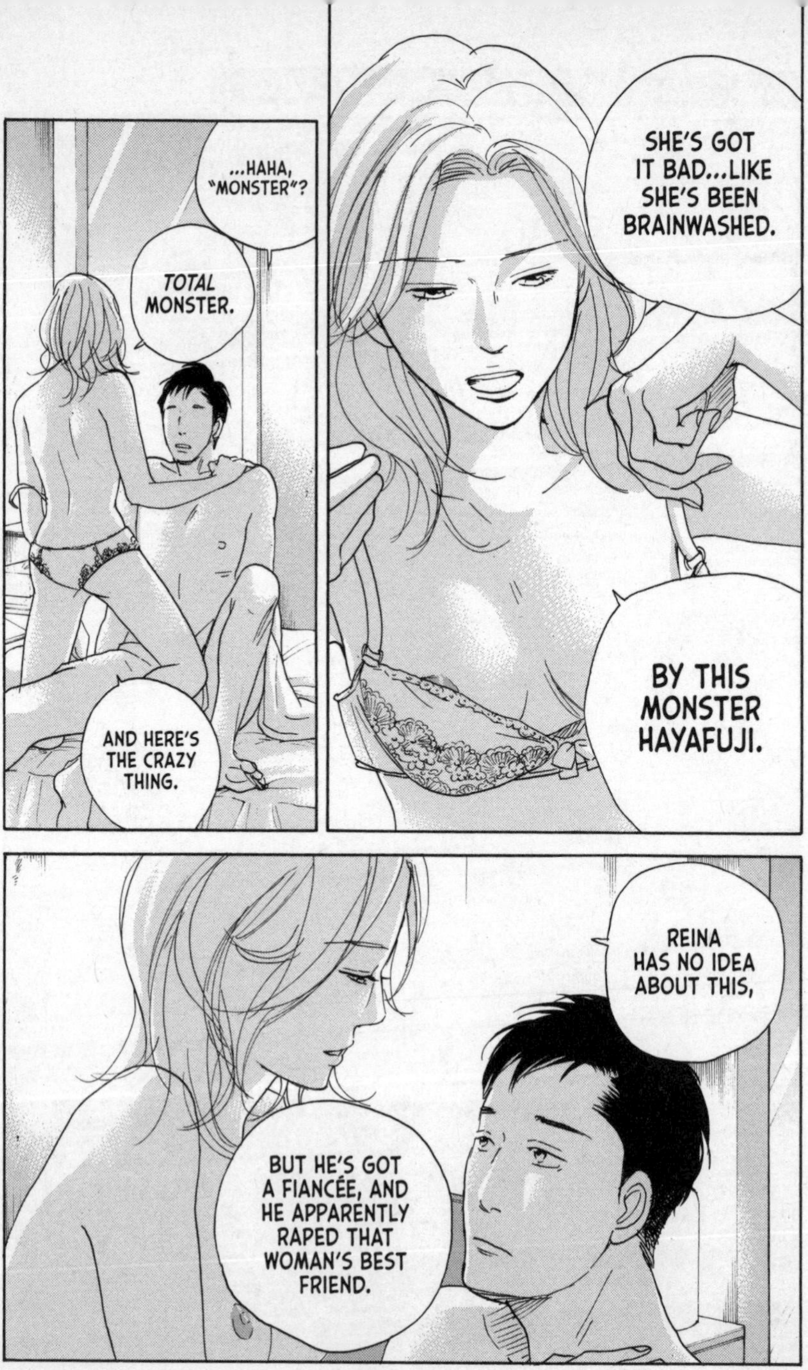
SHE'S GOT IT BAD...LIKE SHE'S BEEN BRAINWASHED.
BY THIS MONSTER HAYAFUJI.
...HAHA, "MONSTER"?
TOTAL MONSTER.
AND HERE'S THE CRAZY THING.
REINA HAS NO IDEA ABOUT THIS,
BUT HE'S GOT A FIANCÉE, AND HE APPARENTLY RAPED THAT WOMAN'S BEST FRIEND.

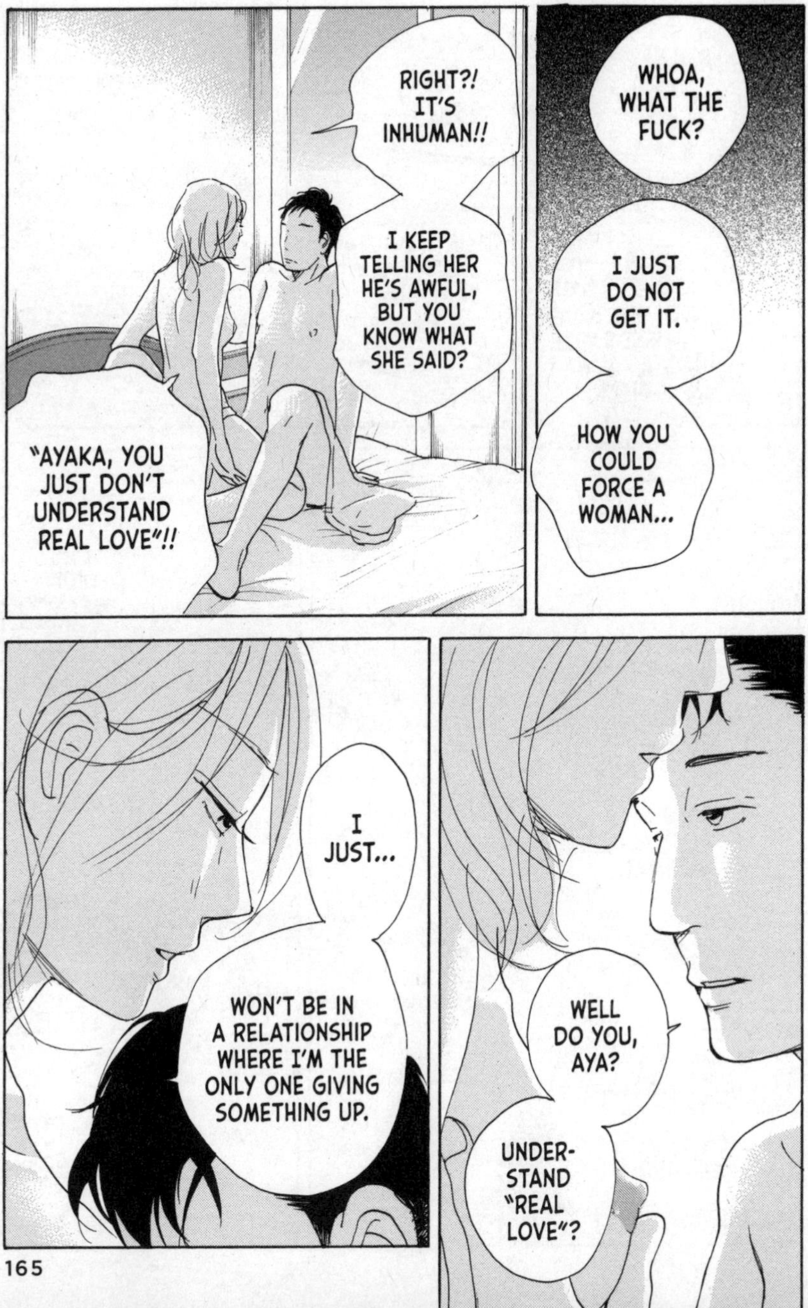
WHOA, WHAT THE FUCK?
I JUST DO NOT GET IT.
HOW YOU COULD FORCE A WOMAN...
RIGHT?! IT'S INHUMAN!!
I KEEP TELLING HER HE'S AWFUL, BUT YOU KNOW WHAT SHE SAID?
"AYAKA, YOU JUST DON'T UNDERSTAND REAL LOVE"!!
WELL DO YOU, AYA?
UNDER-STAND "REAL LOVE"?
I JUST...
WON'T BE IN A RELATIONSHIP WHERE I'M THE ONLY ONE GIVING SOMETHING UP.

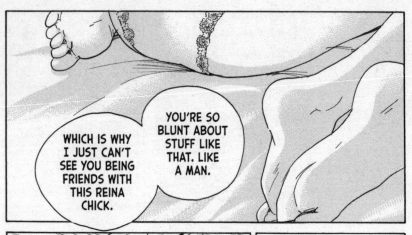

YOU'RE SO BLUNT ABOUT STUFF LIKE THAT. LIKE A MAN.
WHICH IS WHY I JUST CAN'T SEE YOU BEING FRIENDS WITH THIS REINA CHICK.
SORRY... DIDN'T MEAN TO SOUND LIKE A MAN.
I MEANT IT AS A GOOD THING...
I KNOW.
BUT SERIOUSLY.
REINA'S, LIKE, *SUCH* A GIRL!
SHE'S A TOTAL DOORMAT.
I CAN'T LET SOME AWFUL GUY TAKE ADVANTAGE OF HER.

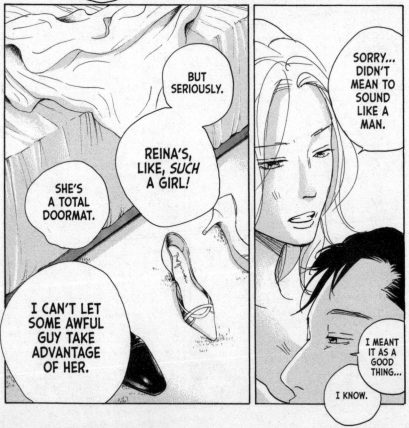

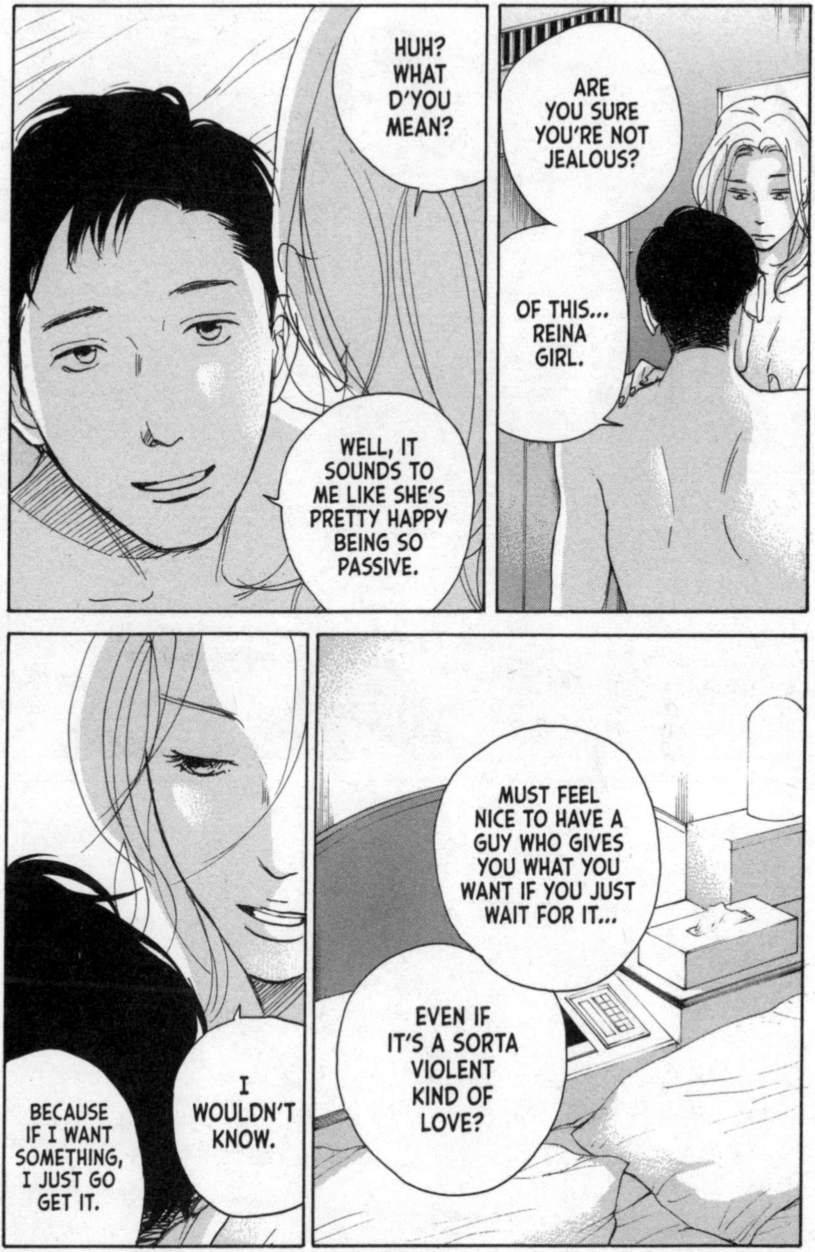
ARE YOU SURE YOU'RE NOT JEALOUS?
OF THIS... REINA GIRL.
HUH? WHAT D'YOU MEAN?
WELL, IT SOUNDS TO ME LIKE SHE'S PRETTY HAPPY BEING SO PASSIVE.
MUST FEEL NICE TO HAVE A GUY WHO GIVES YOU WHAT YOU WANT IF YOU JUST WAIT FOR IT...
EVEN IF IT'S A SORTA VIOLENT KIND OF LOVE?
I WOULDN'T KNOW.
BECAUSE IF I WANT SOMETHING, I JUST GO GET IT.

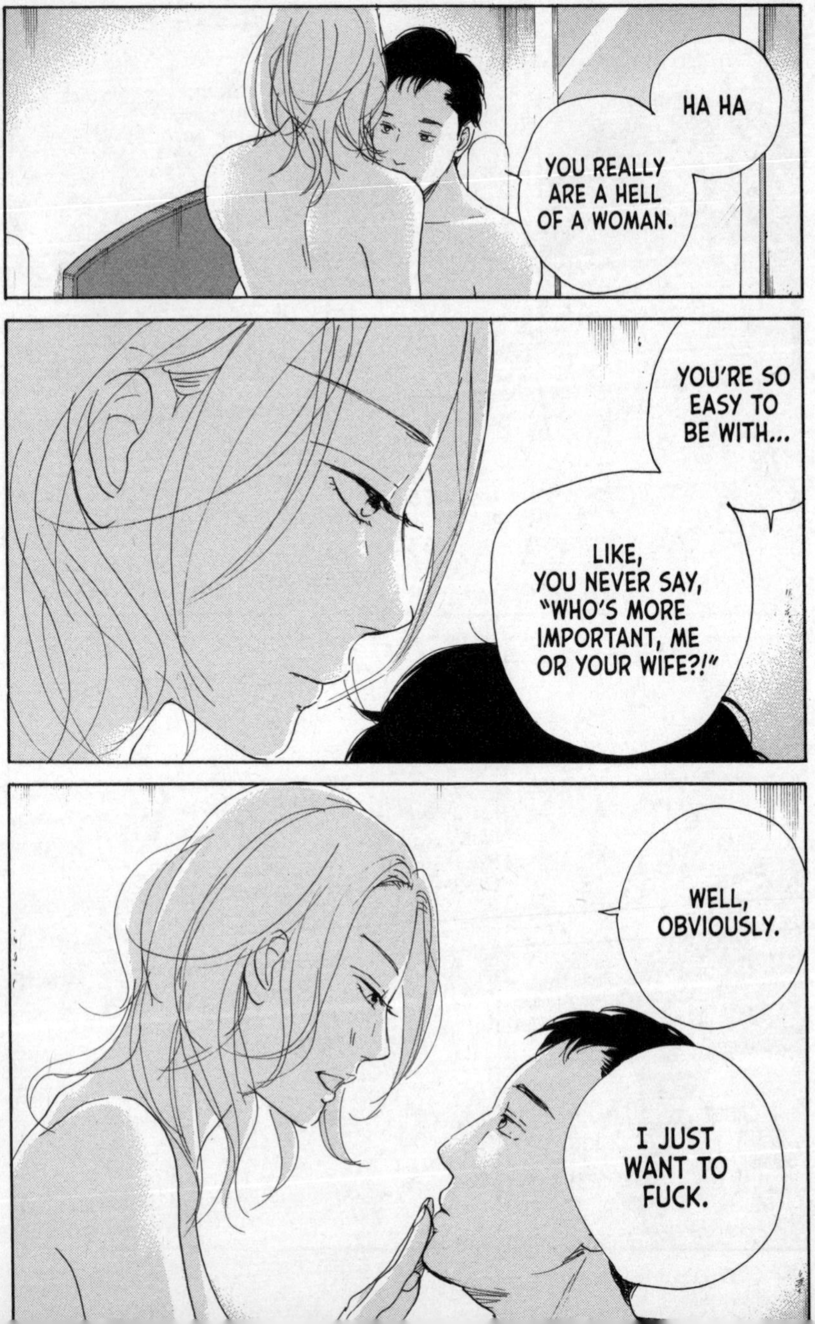
HA HA
YOU REALLY ARE A HELL OF A WOMAN.
YOU'RE SO EASY TO BE WITH...
LIKE, YOU NEVER SAY, "WHO'S MORE IMPORTANT, ME OR YOUR WIFE?!"
WELL, OBVIOUSLY.
I JUST WANT TO FUCK.

MM

UNH

AHH

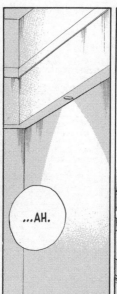

...AH.

YOU THINK YOU'RE SO SLICK...

AND THAT'S EXACTLY WHAT I LIKE ABOUT YOU.

I'd never get carried away with a guy like that.

Because I'm the one who chooses.

HAAAH...

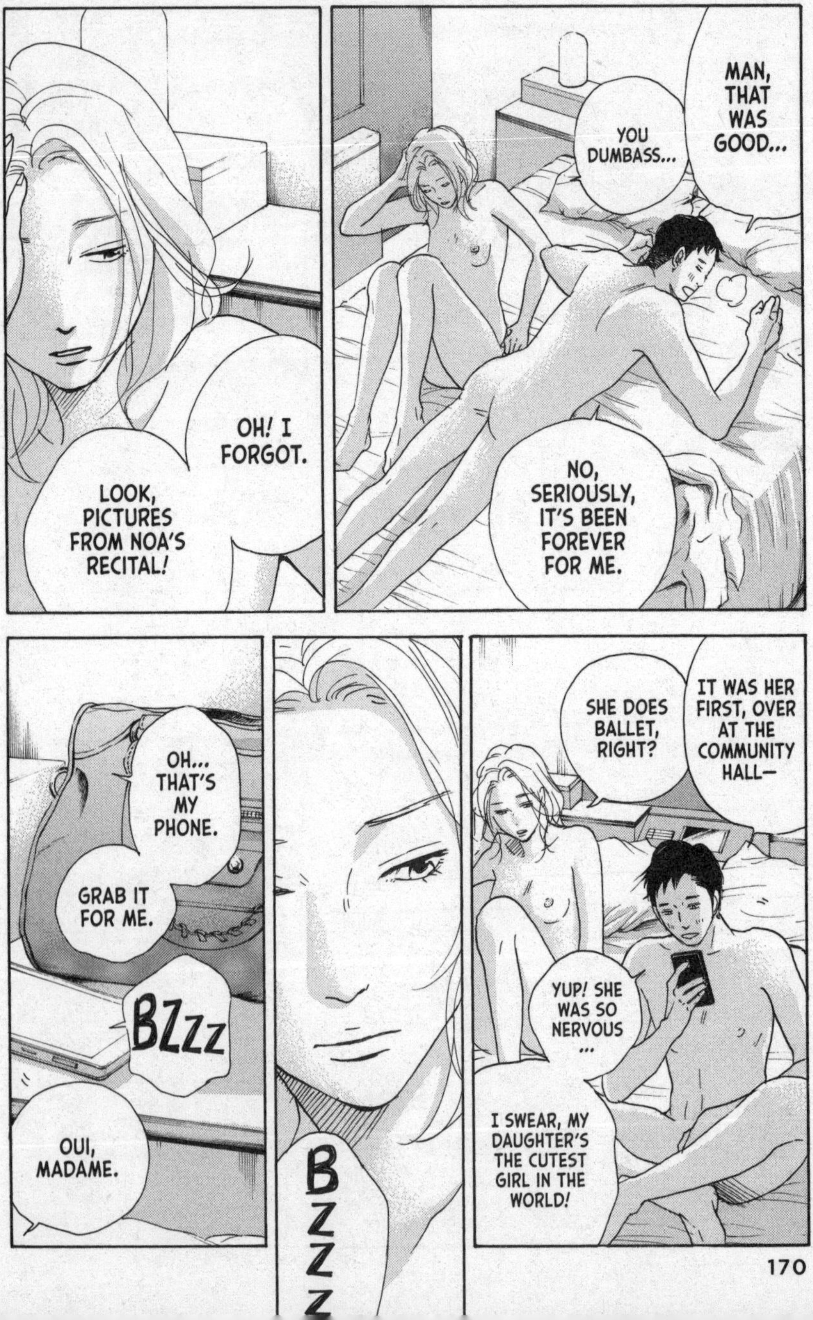

MAN, THAT WAS GOOD...
YOU DUMBASS...
NO, SERIOUSLY, IT'S BEEN FOREVER FOR ME.
OH! I FORGOT.
LOOK, PICTURES FROM NOA'S RECITAL!
IT WAS HER FIRST, OVER AT THE COMMUNITY HALL—
SHE DOES BALLET, RIGHT?
YUP! SHE WAS SO NERVOUS ...
I SWEAR, MY DAUGHTER'S THE CUTEST GIRL IN THE WORLD!
BZZZ
OH... THAT'S MY PHONE.
GRAB IT FOR ME.
BZzz
OUI, MADAME.

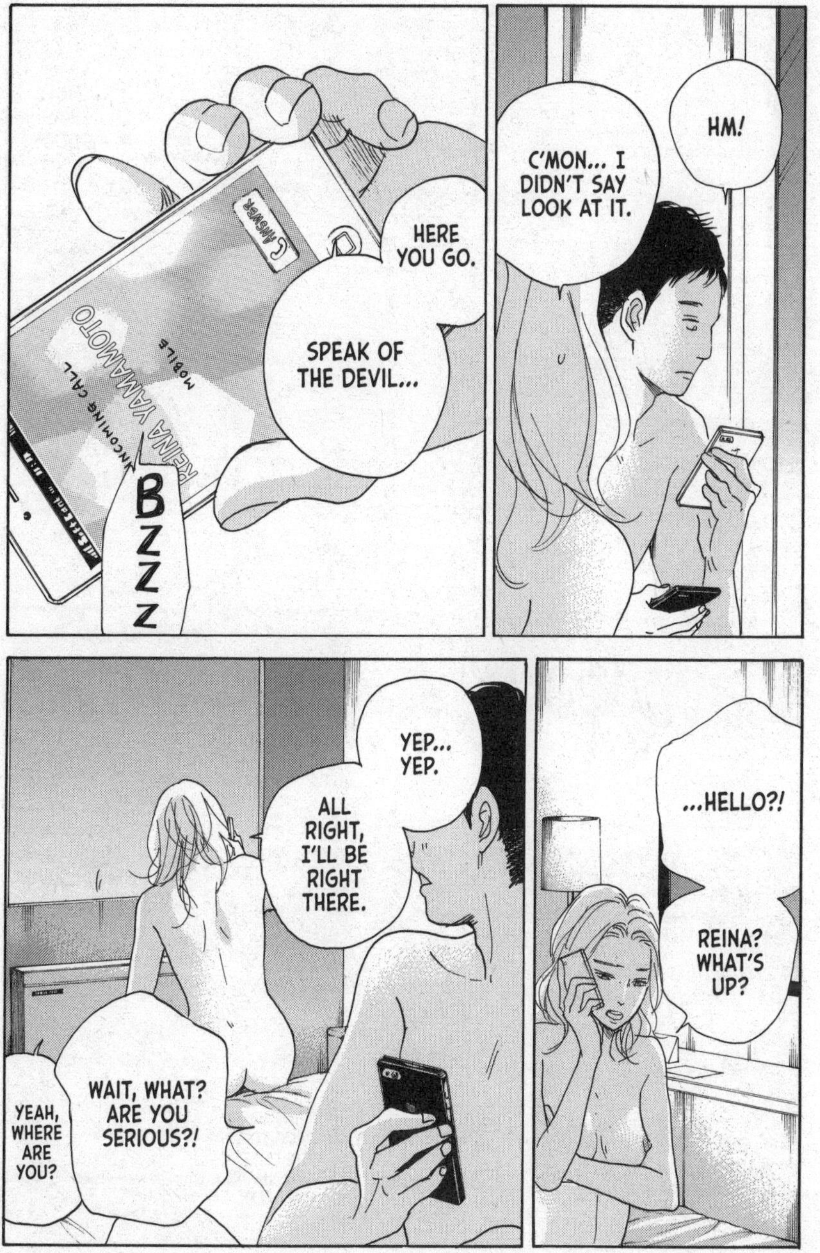
HM!
C'MON... I DIDN'T SAY LOOK AT IT.
HERE YOU GO.
SPEAK OF THE DEVIL...
REINA YAMAMOTO
MOBILE
INCOMING CALL
BZZZ
...HELLO?!
REINA? WHAT'S UP?
YEP... YEP.
ALL RIGHT, I'LL BE RIGHT THERE.
WAIT, WHAT? ARE YOU SERIOUS?!
YEAH, WHERE ARE YOU?

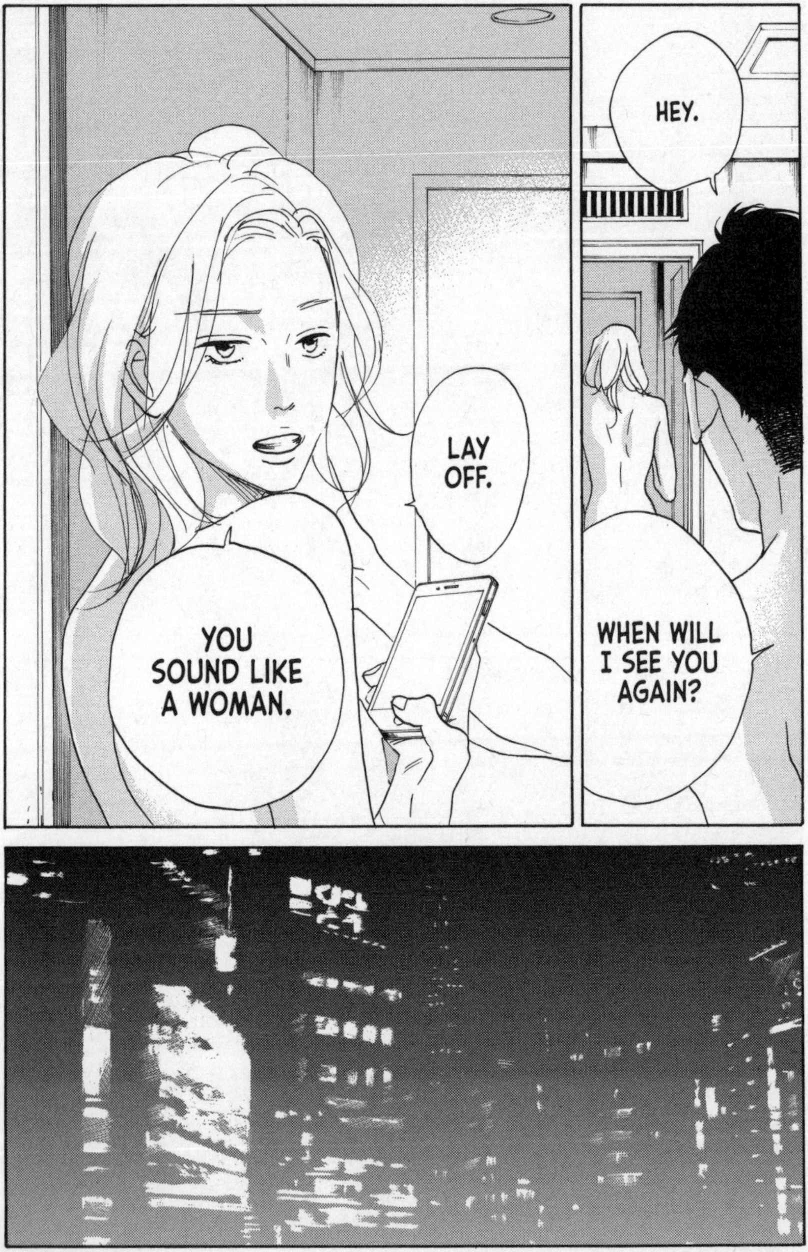
HEY.
WHEN WILL I SEE YOU AGAIN?
LAY OFF.
YOU SOUND LIKE A WOMAN.

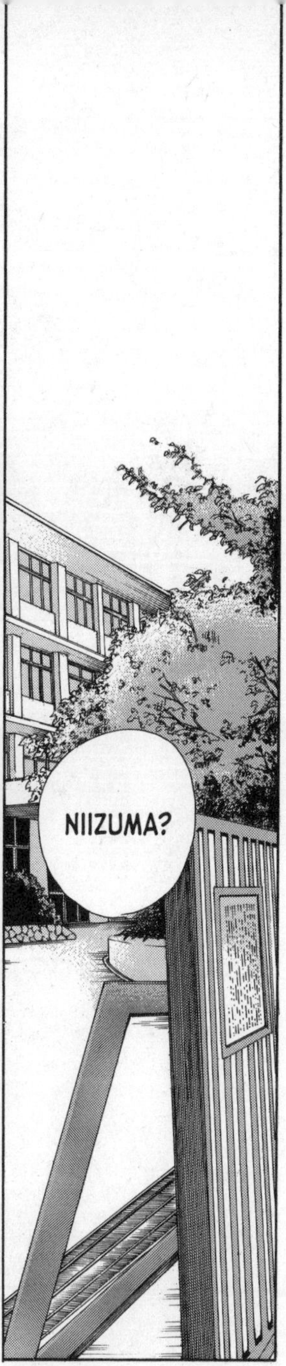
NIIZUMA?

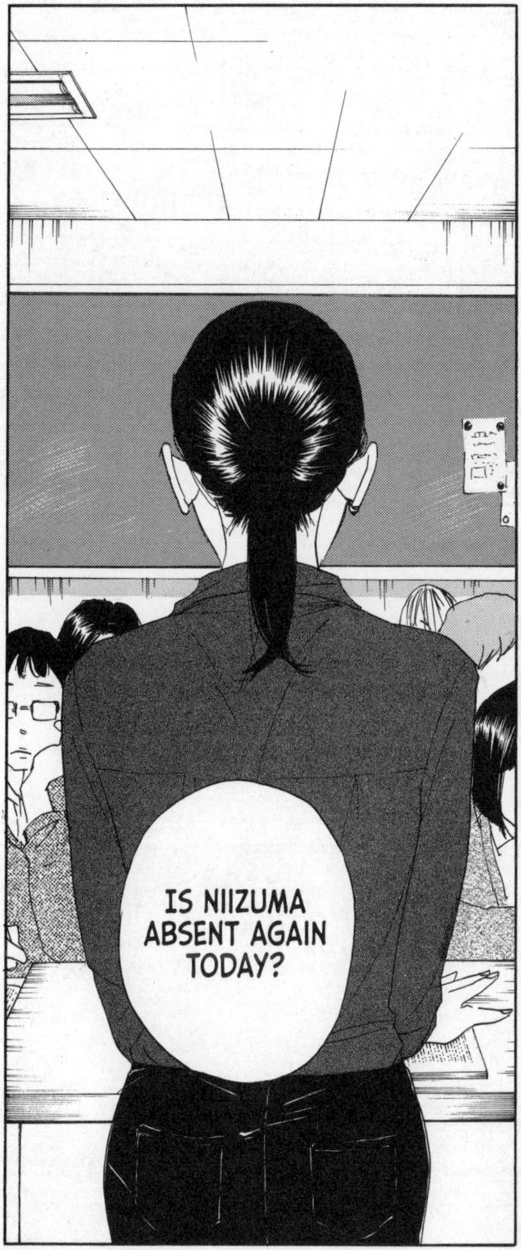
IS NIIZUMA ABSENT AGAIN TODAY?

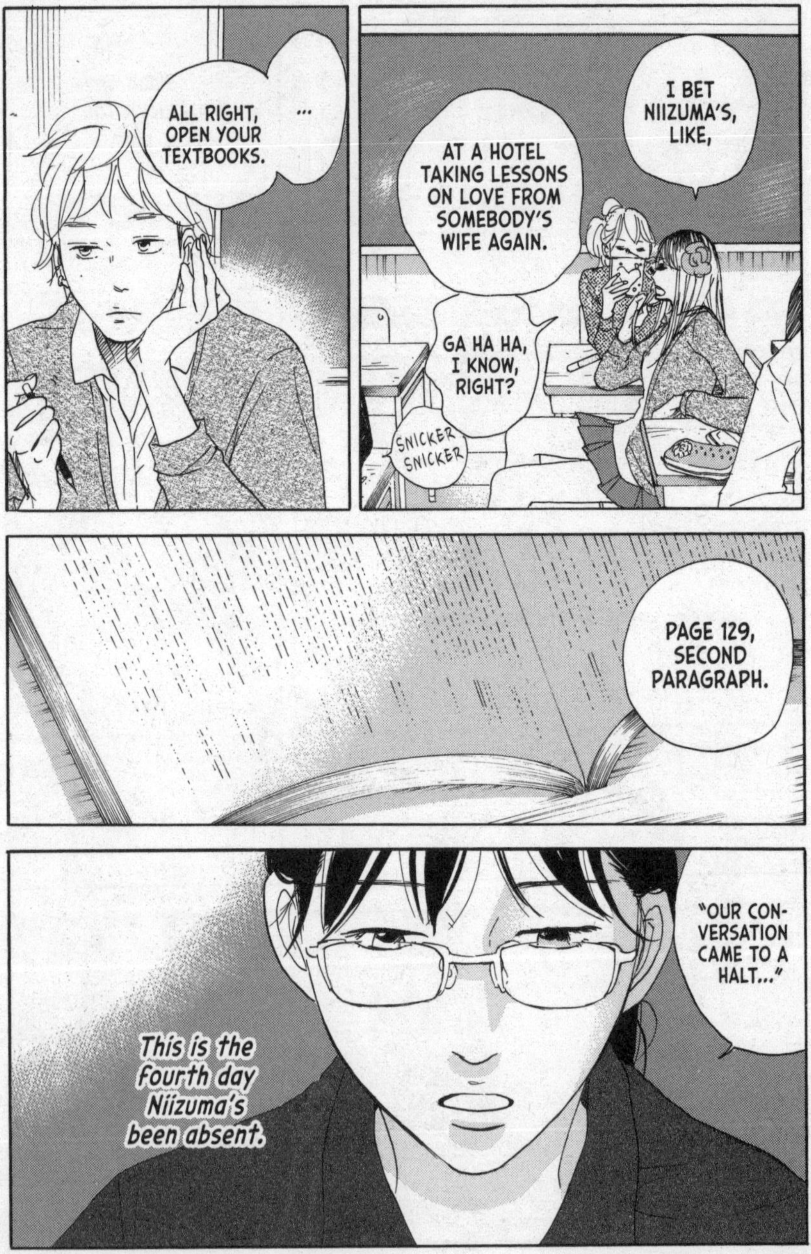
I BET NIIZUMA'S, LIKE,
AT A HOTEL TAKING LESSONS ON LOVE FROM SOMEBODY'S WIFE AGAIN.
GA HA HA, I KNOW, RIGHT?
SNICKER SNICKER
...
ALL RIGHT, OPEN YOUR TEXTBOOKS.
PAGE 129, SECOND PARAGRAPH.
"OUR CON-VERSATION CAME TO A HALT..."
This is the fourth day Niizuma's been absent.

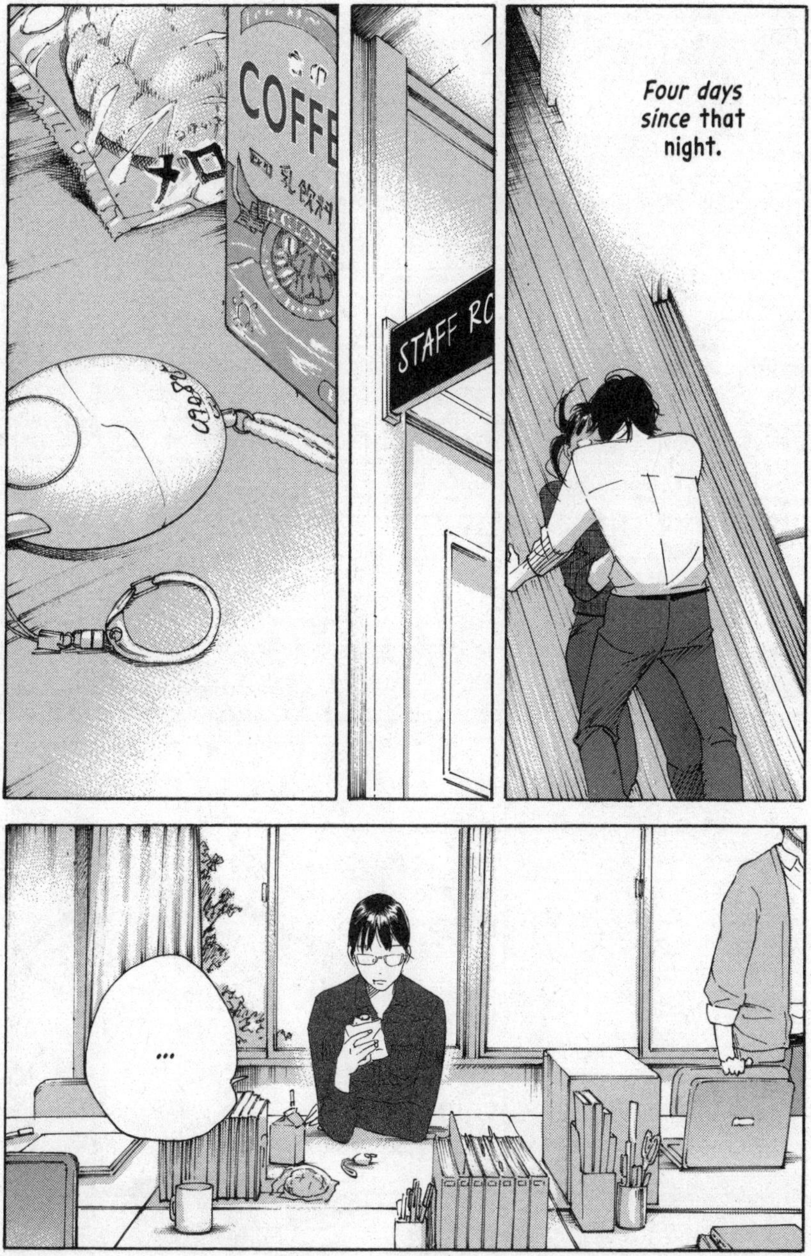
Four days since that night.
STAFF RC
COFFE
メロ
...

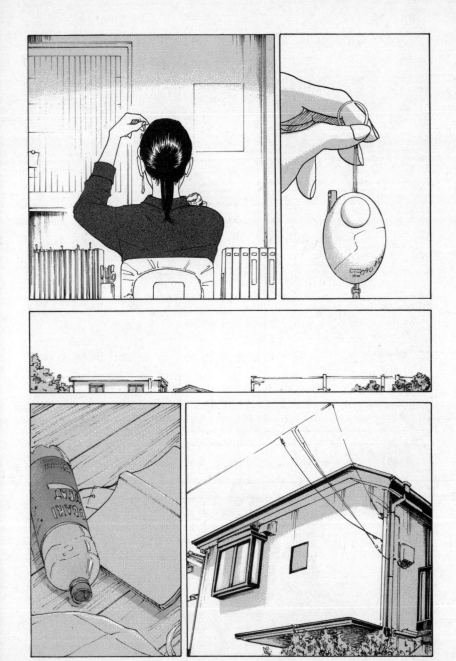

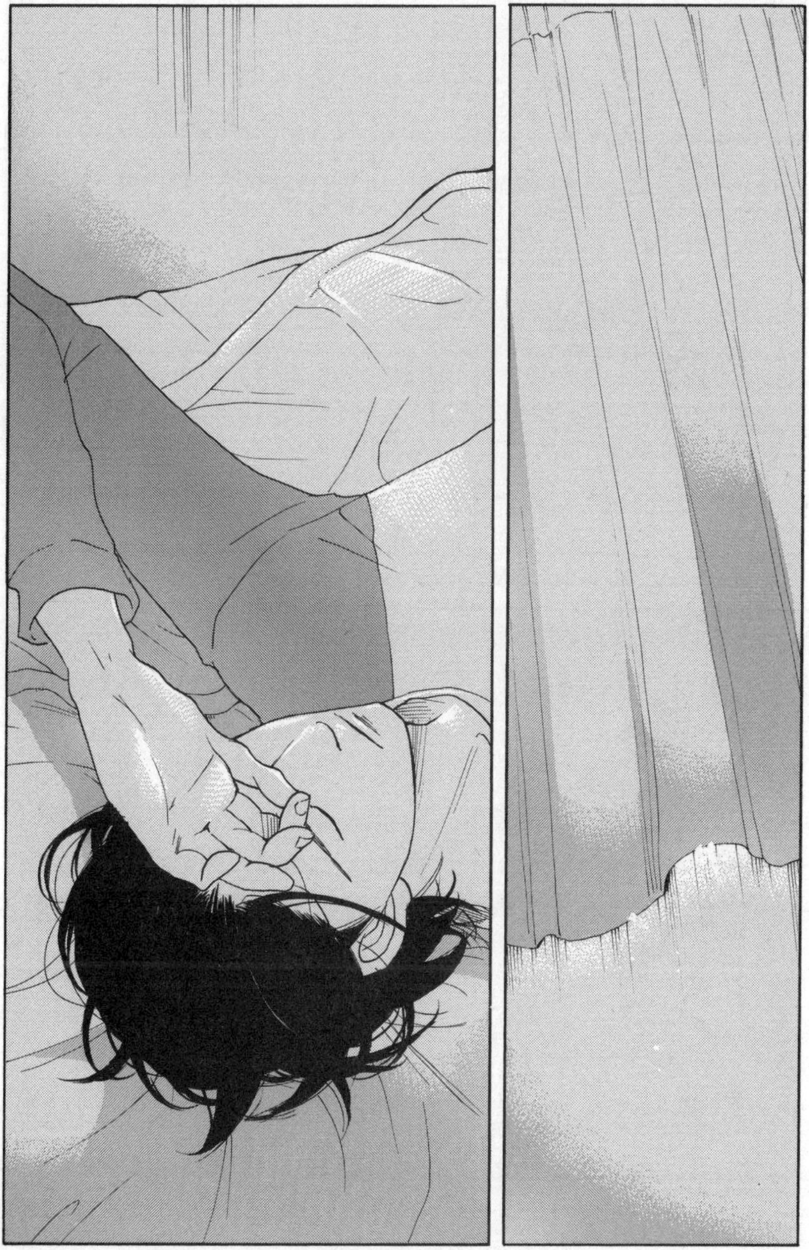

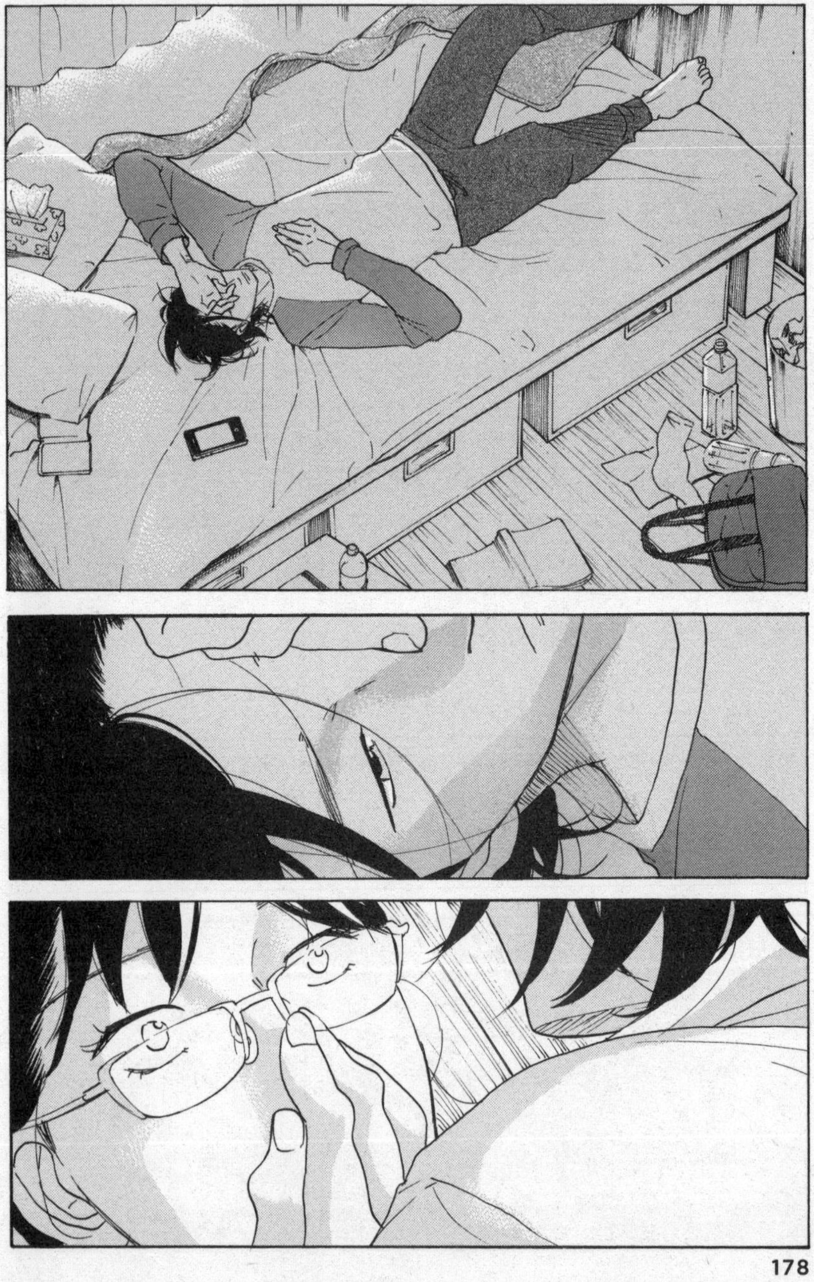

I hurt her.

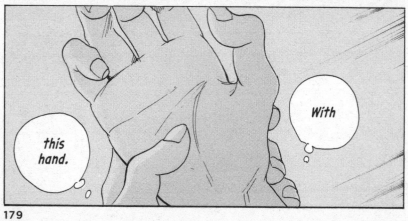

this hand.

With

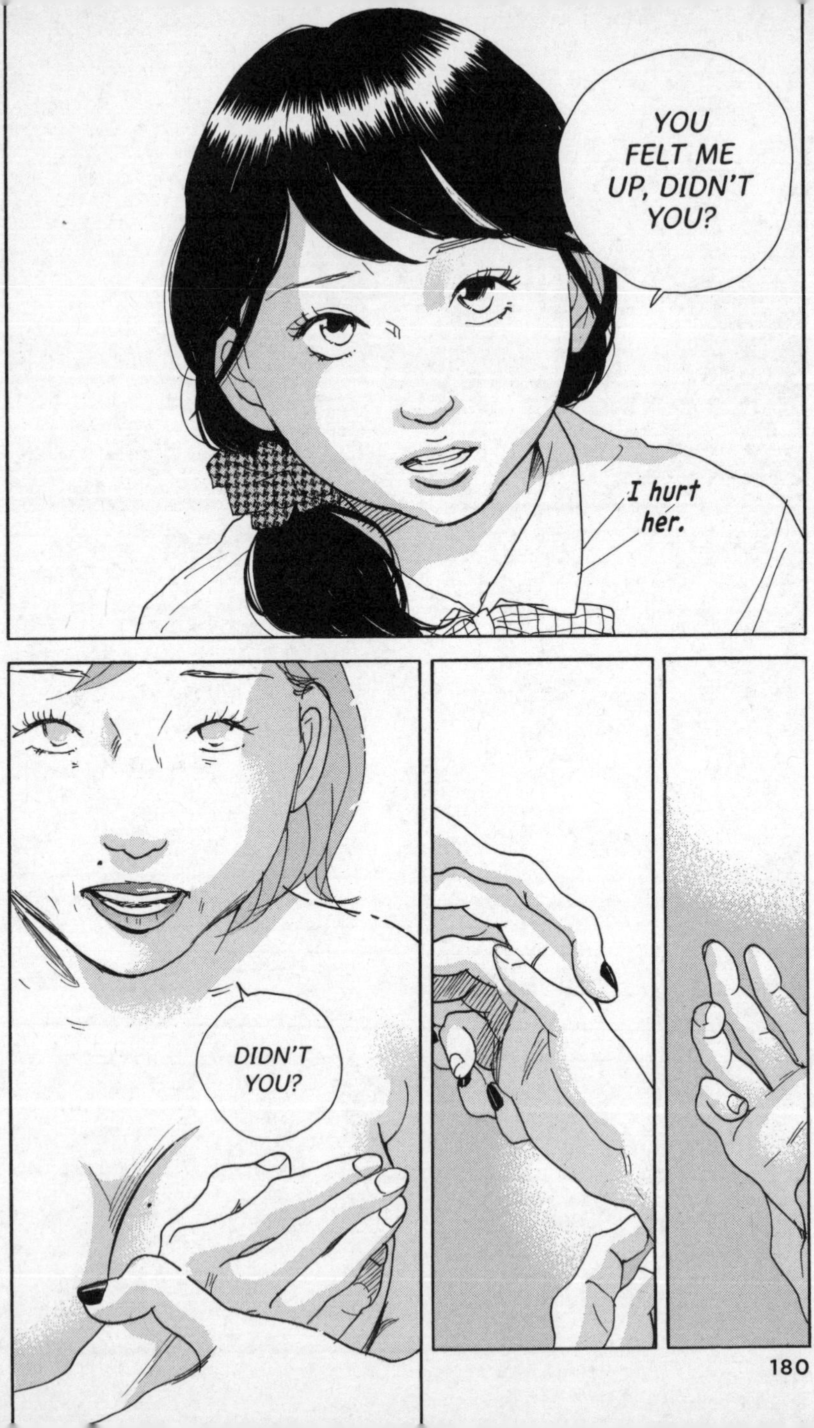
YOU FELT ME UP, DIDN'T YOU?
I hurt her.
DIDN'T YOU?

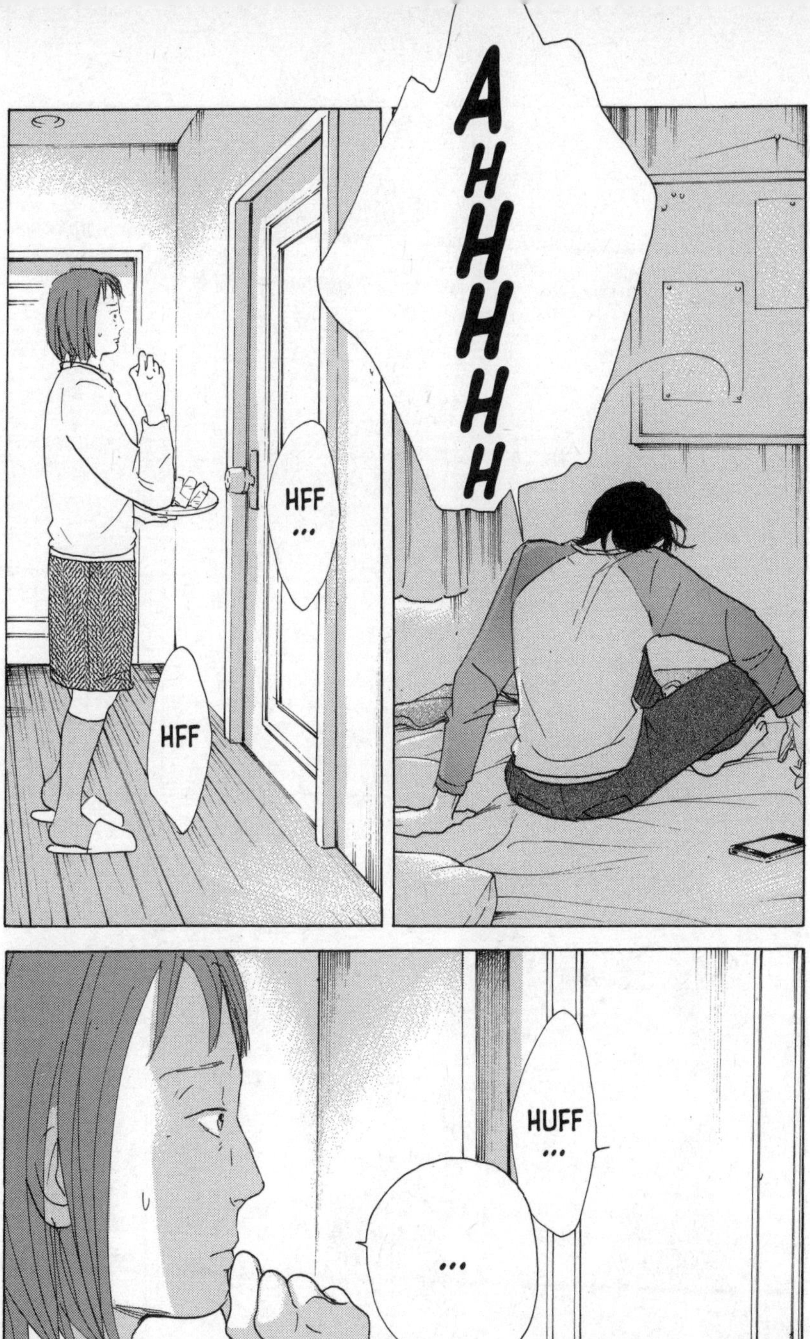
AHHHHH
HFF ...
HFF
HUFF ...
...

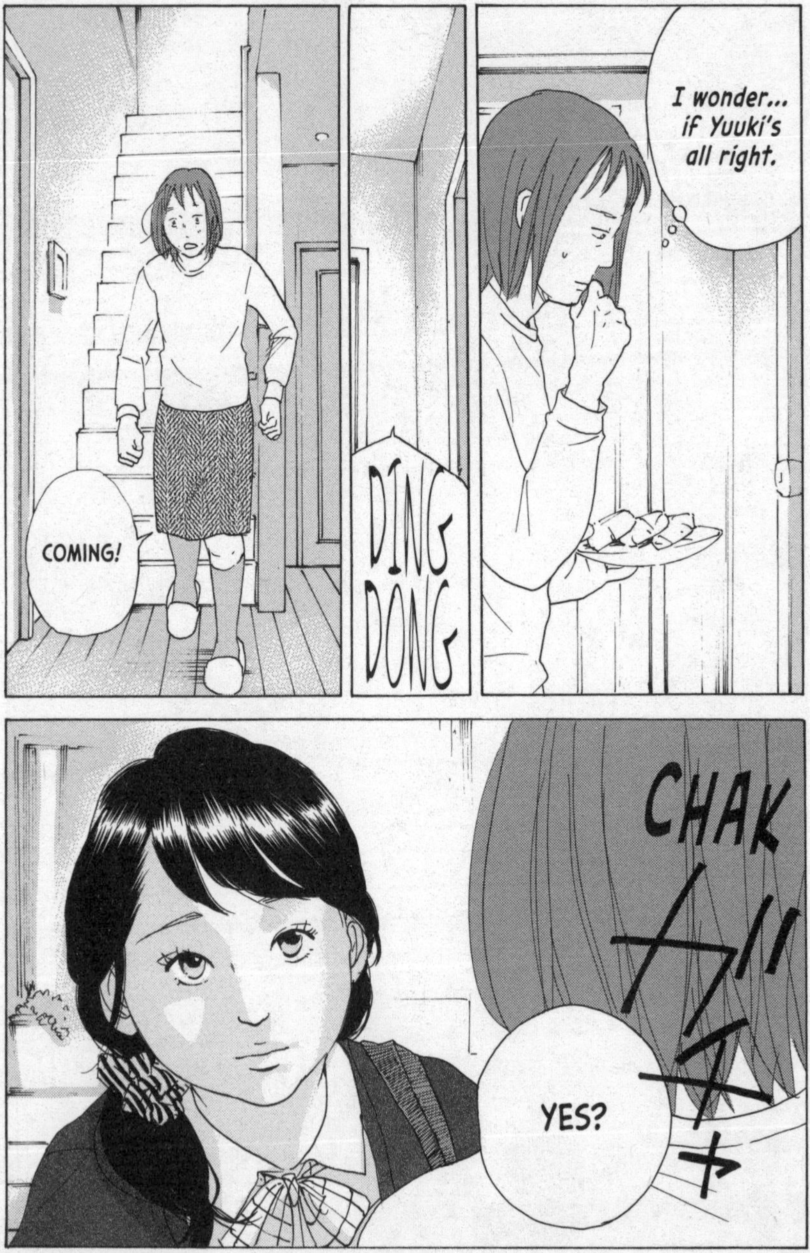
I wonder... if Yuuki's all right.
DING DONG
COMING!
CHAK
ガチャ
YES?

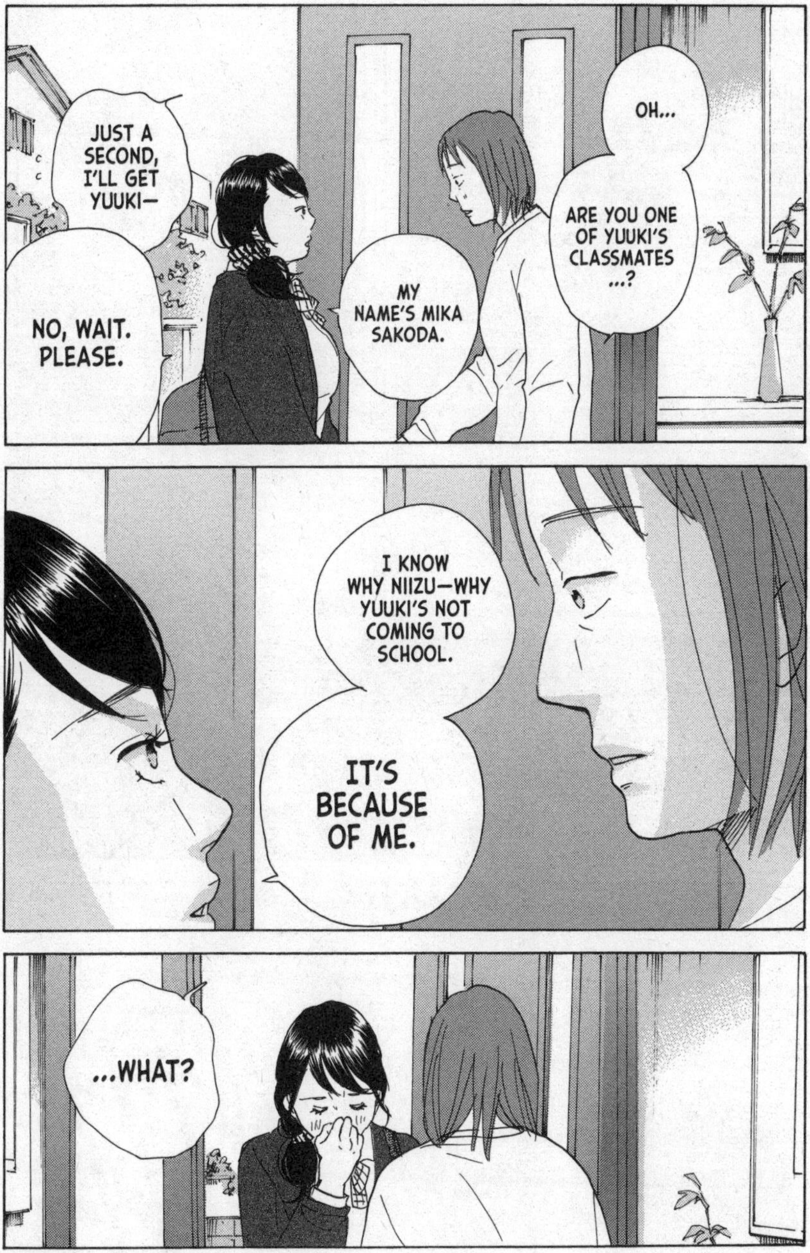
OH...
ARE YOU ONE OF YUUKI'S CLASSMATES ...?
MY NAME'S MIKA SAKODA.
JUST A SECOND, I'LL GET YUUKI—
NO, WAIT. PLEASE.
I KNOW WHY NIIZU—WHY YUUKI'S NOT COMING TO SCHOOL.
IT'S BECAUSE OF ME.
...WHAT?

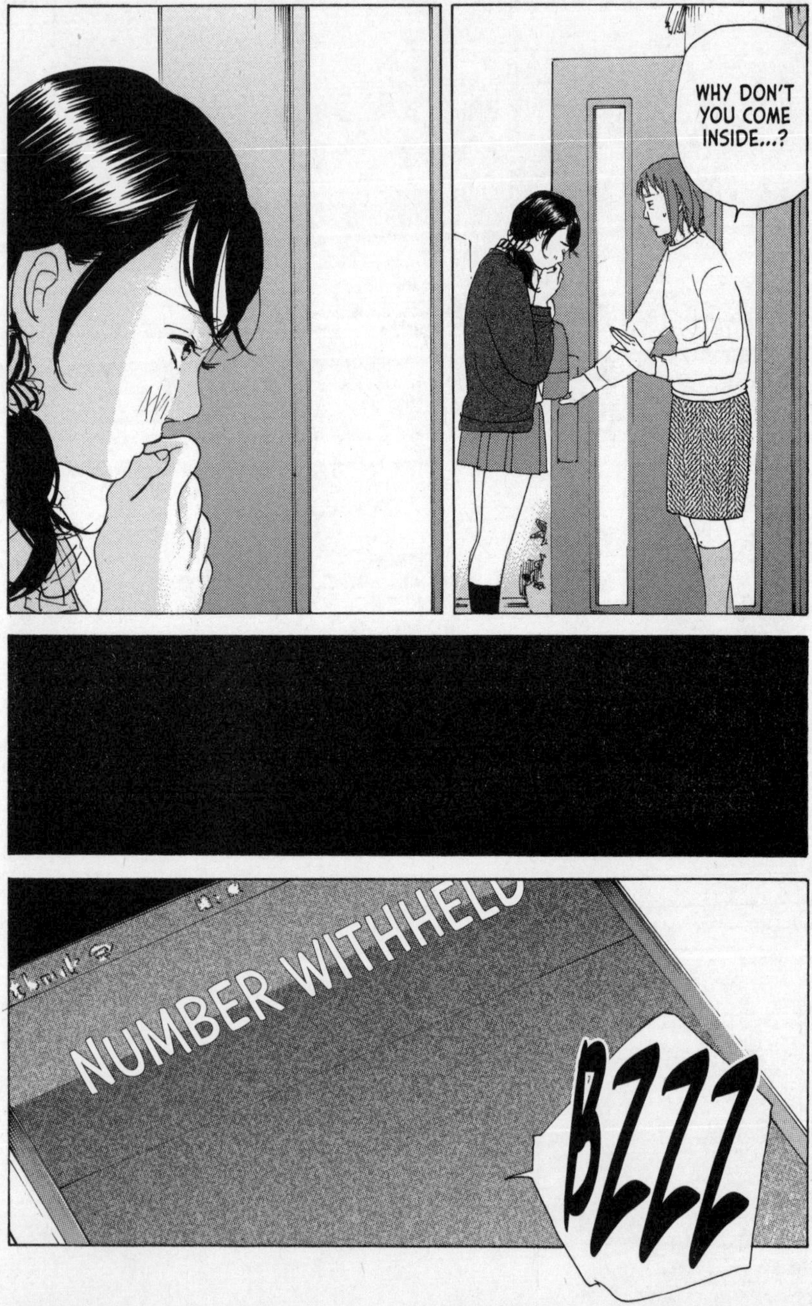
WHY DON'T YOU COME INSIDE...?
NUMBER WITHHELD
BZZZ

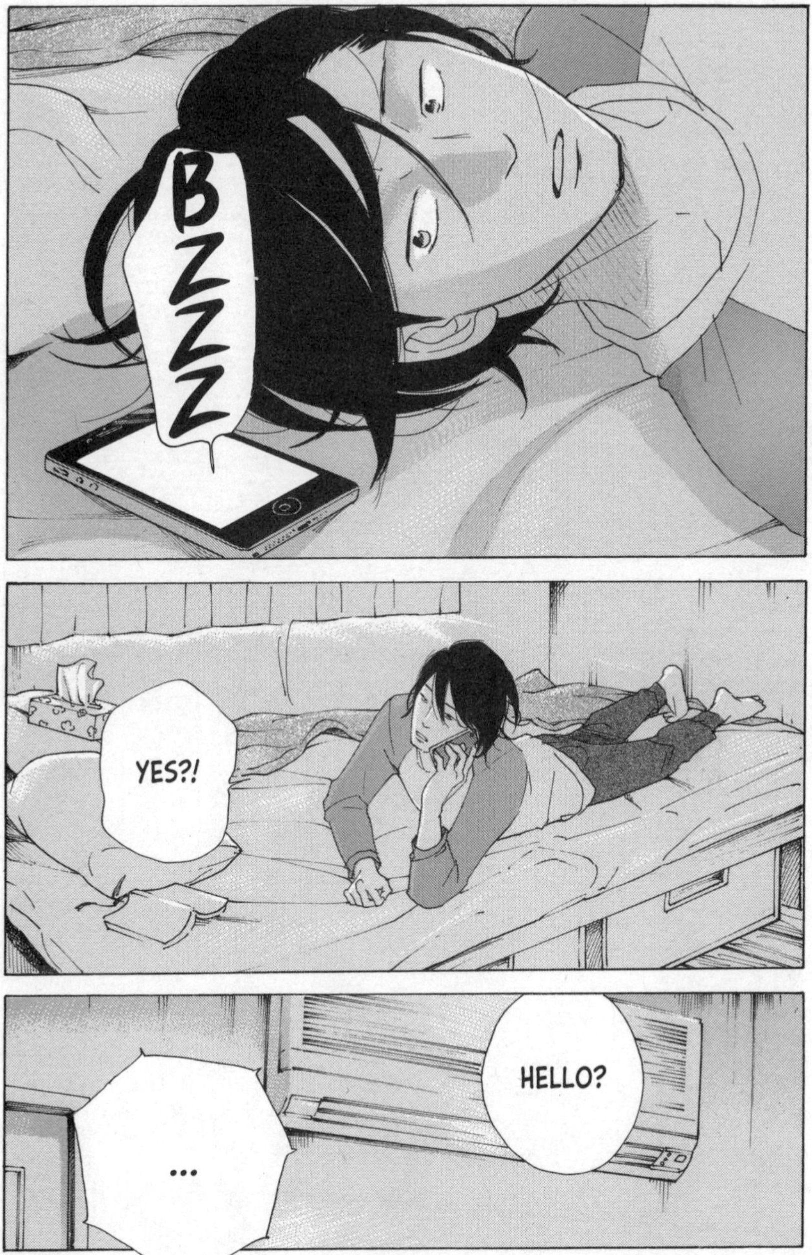
BZZZ
YES?!
HELLO?
...

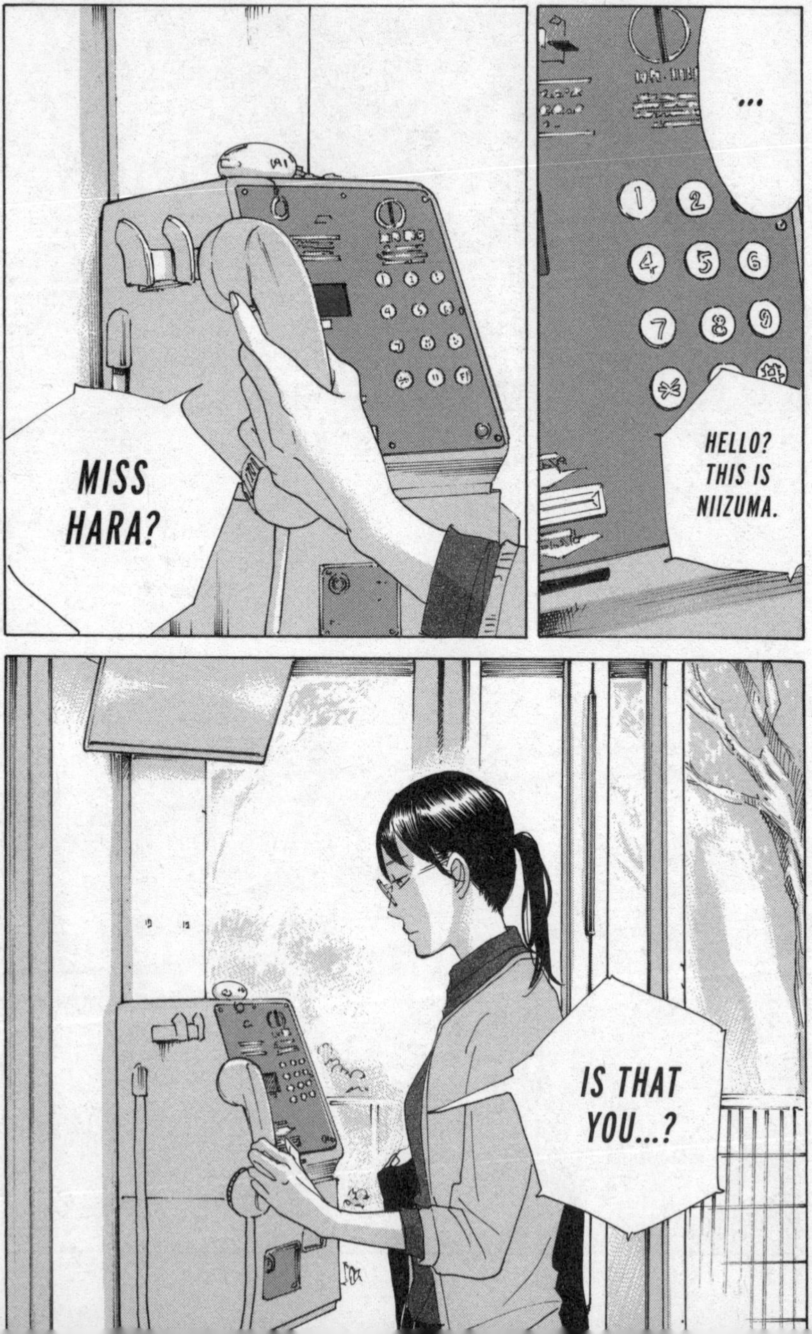
...
HELLO? THIS IS NIIZUMA.
MISS HARA?
IS THAT YOU...?

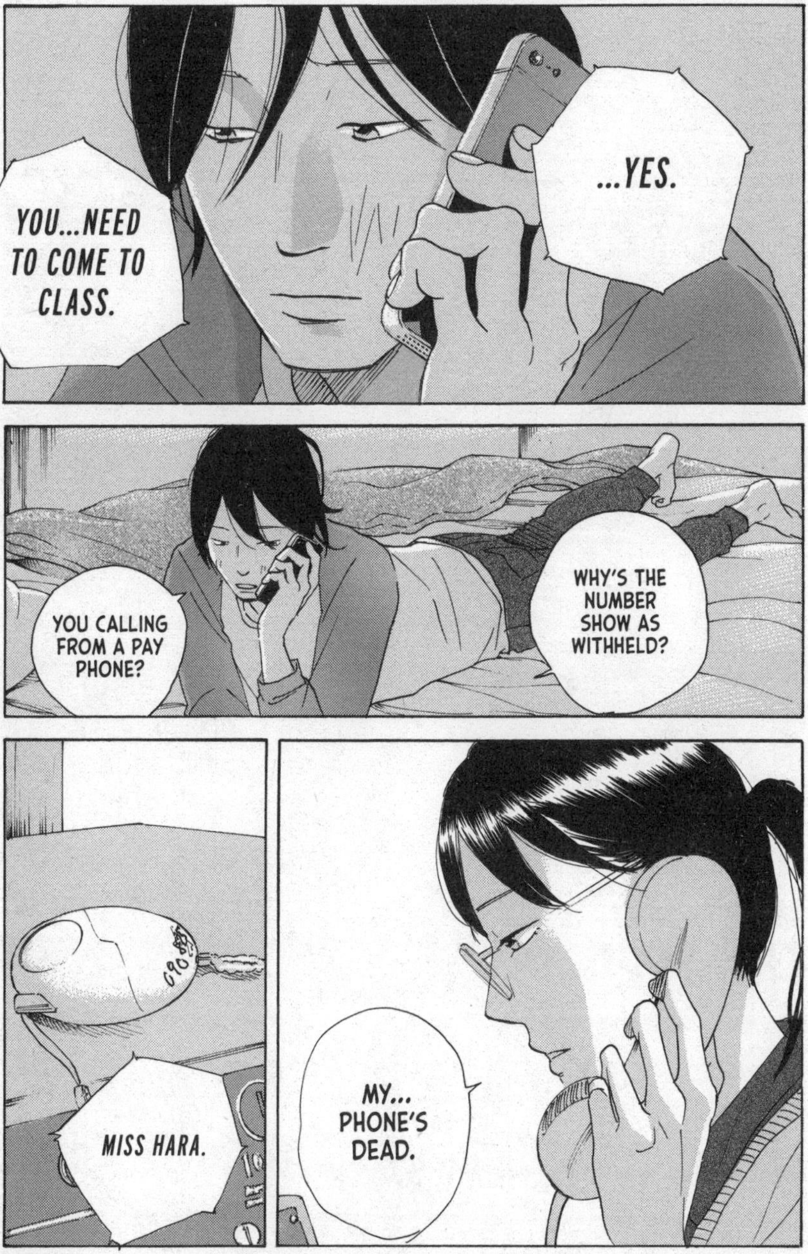
...YES.
YOU...NEED TO COME TO CLASS.
WHY'S THE NUMBER SHOW AS WITHHELD?
YOU CALLING FROM A PAY PHONE?
MY... PHONE'S DEAD.
MISS HARA.

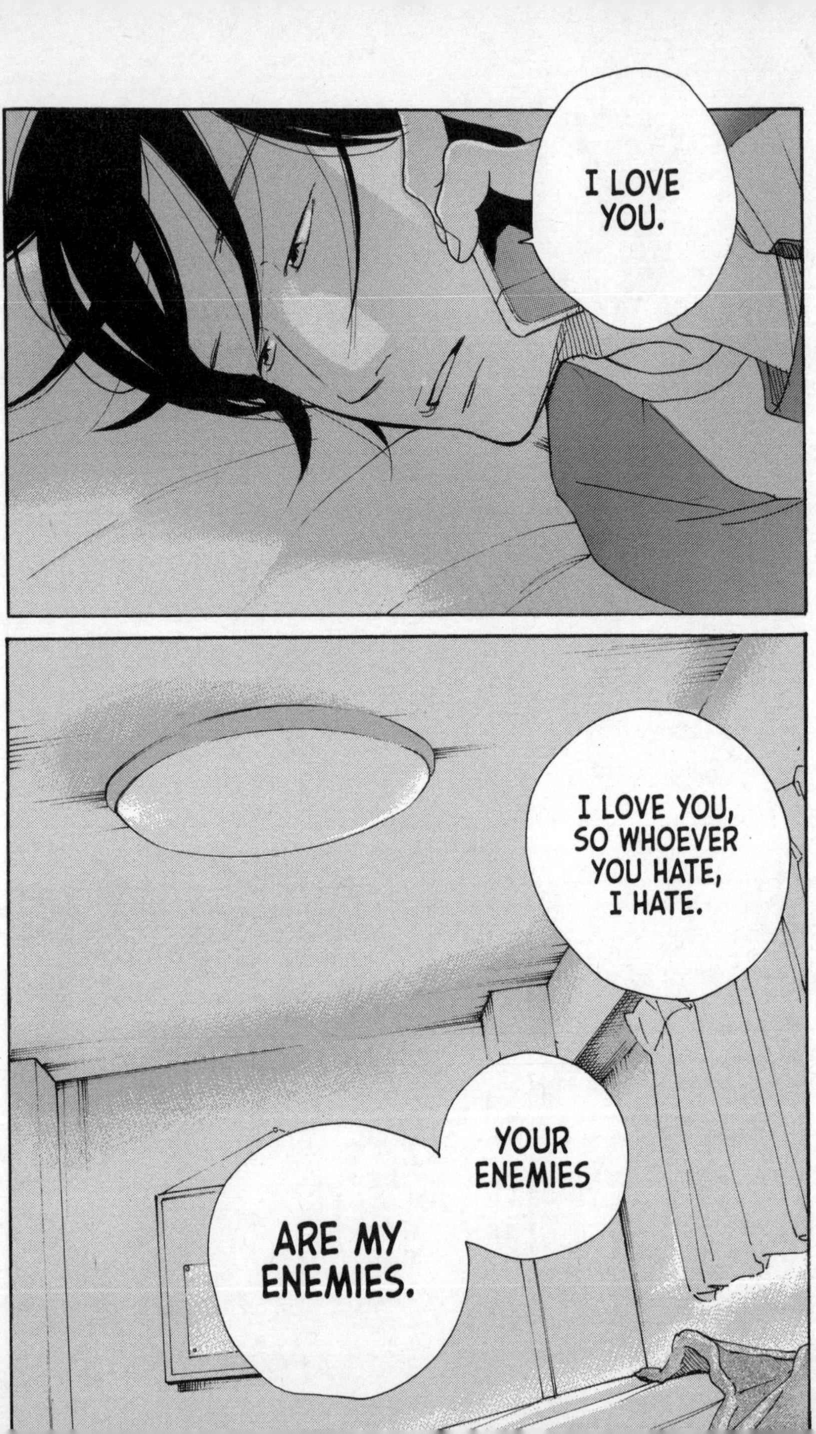
I LOVE YOU.
I LOVE YOU, SO WHOEVER YOU HATE, I HATE.
YOUR ENEMIES
ARE MY ENEMIES.

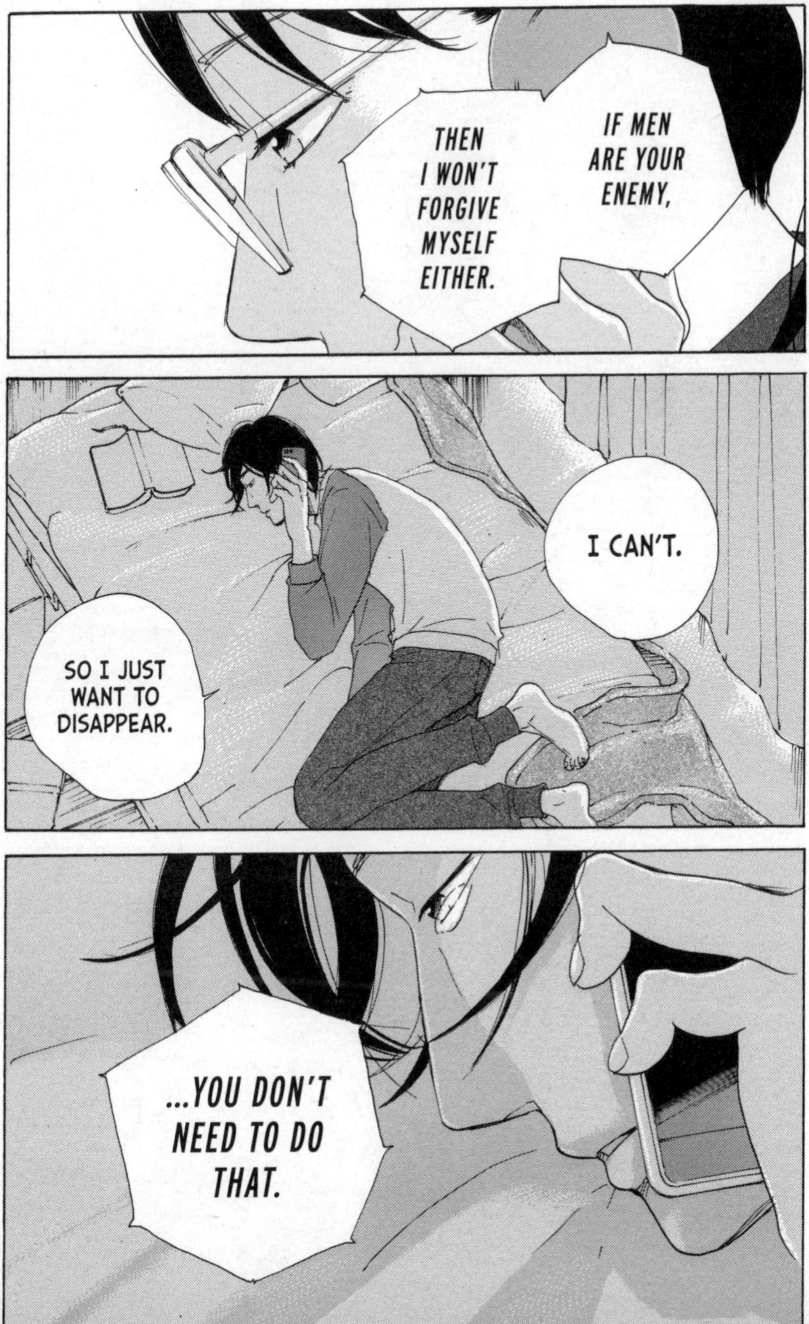
IF MEN ARE YOUR ENEMY,
THEN I WON'T FORGIVE MYSELF EITHER.
I CAN'T.
SO I JUST WANT TO DISAPPEAR.
...YOU DON'T NEED TO DO THAT.

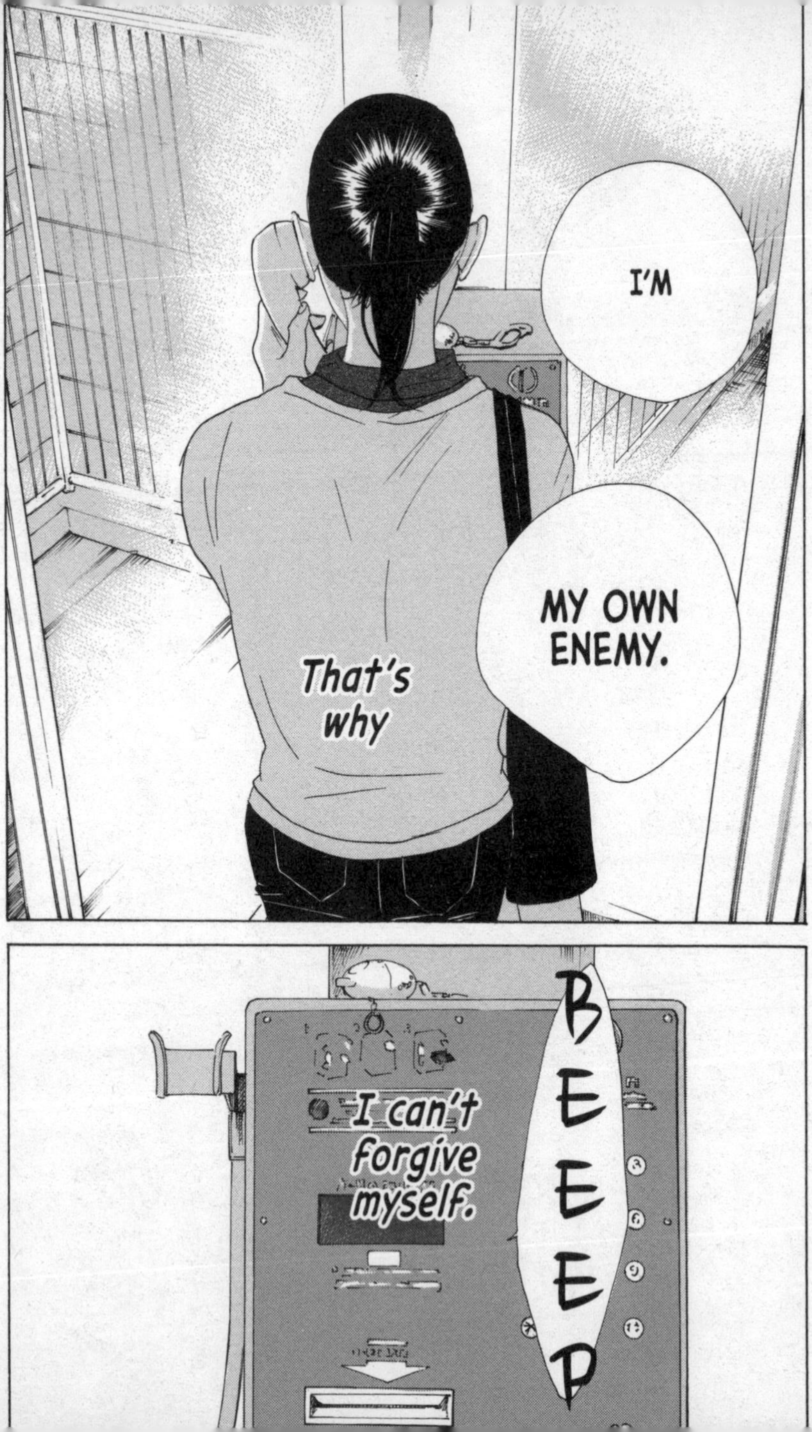
I'M
MY OWN ENEMY.
That's why
BEEEP
I can't forgive myself.

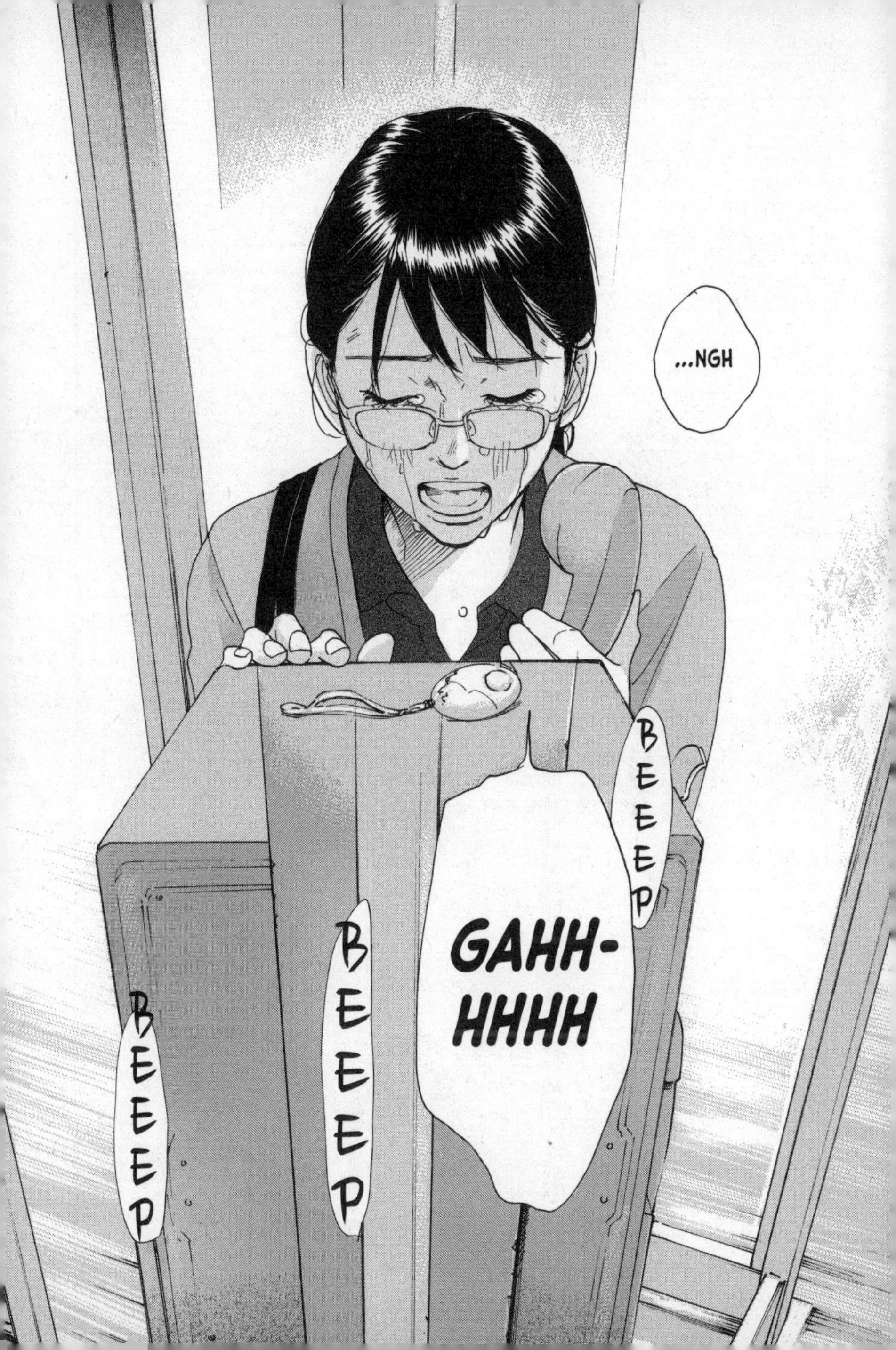
...NGH
BEEEP
GAHH-HHHH
BEEEP
BEEEP

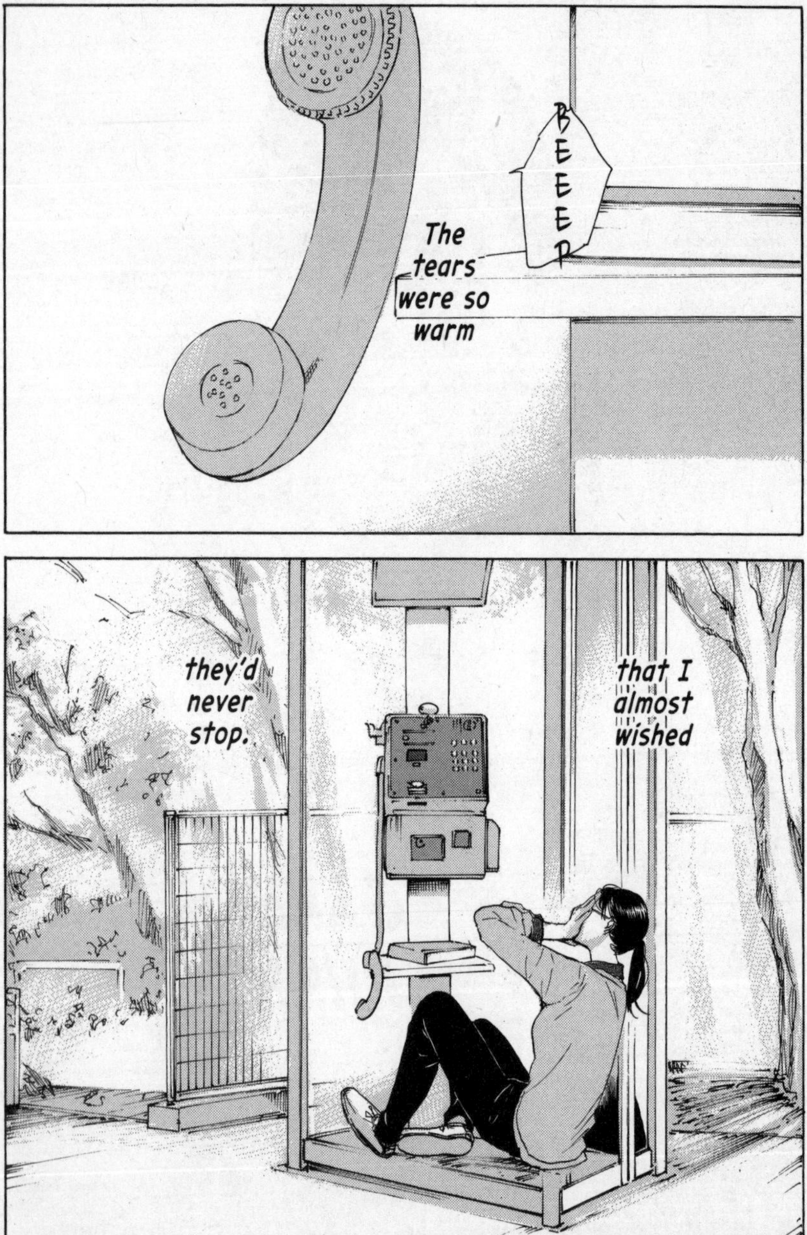
BEEEP
The tears were so warm
that I almost wished
they'd never stop.

END

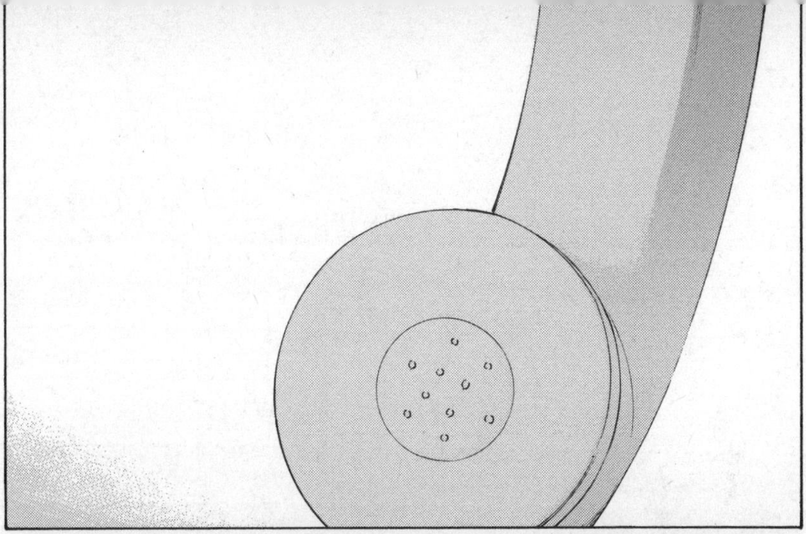

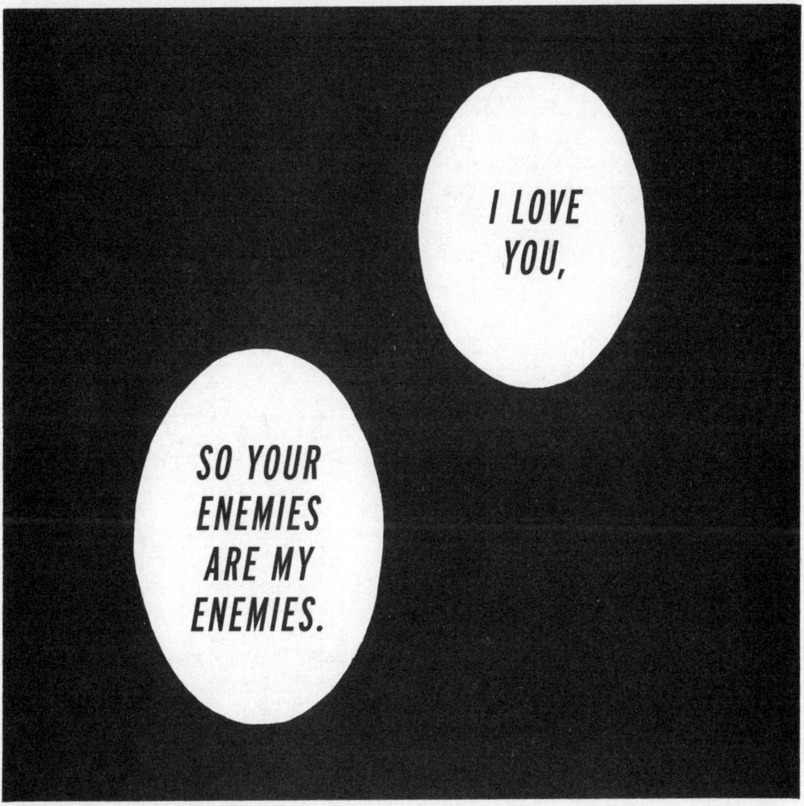
I LOVE YOU,
SO YOUR ENEMIES ARE MY ENEMIES.

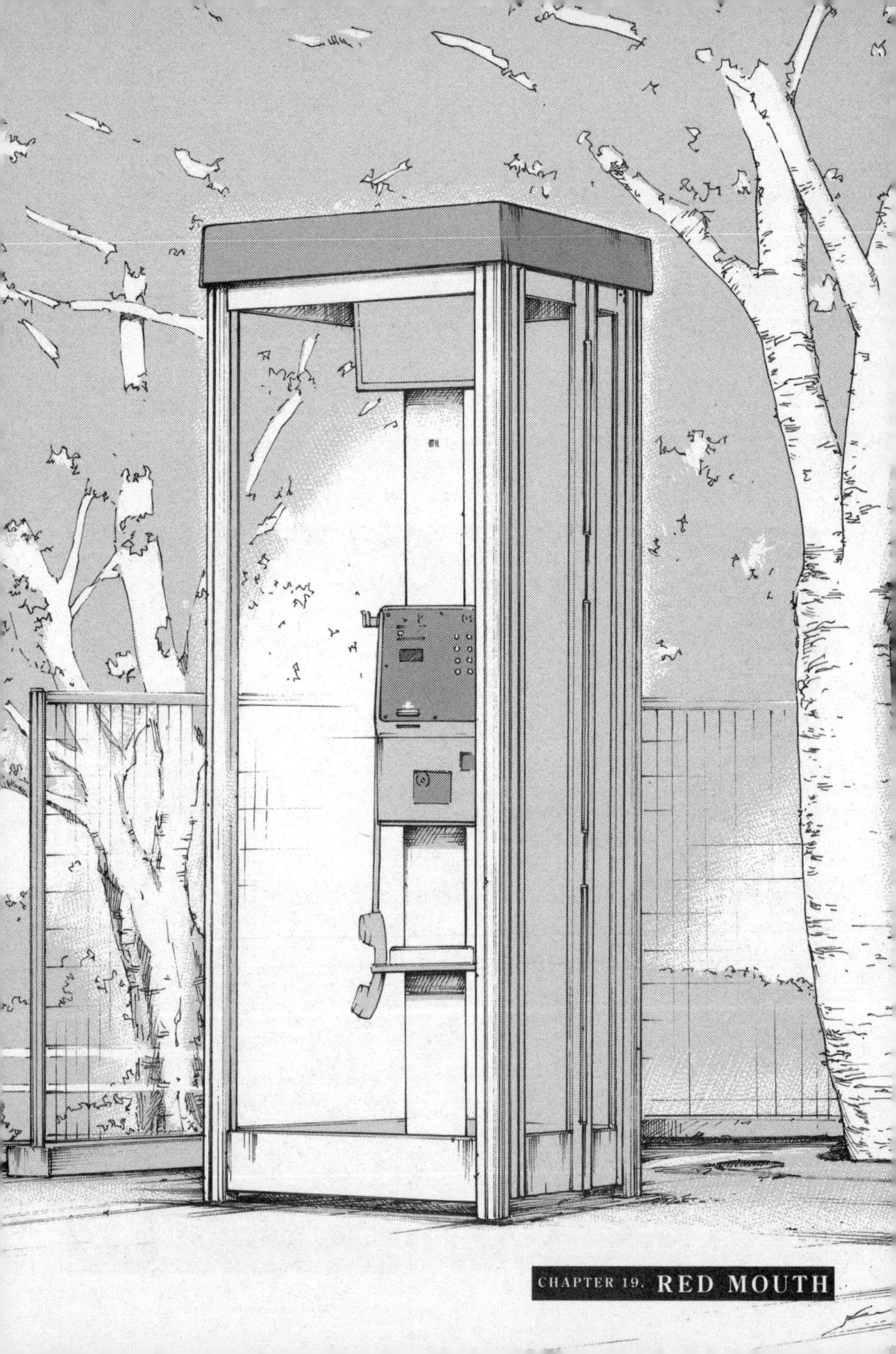

CHAPTER 19. RED MOUTH

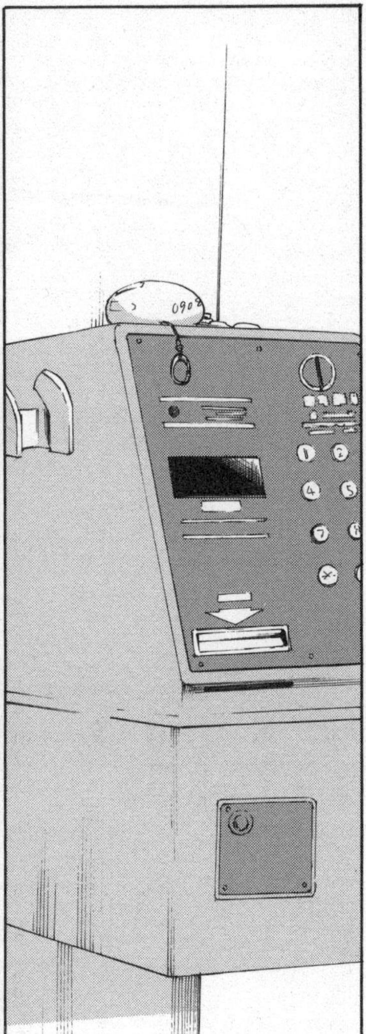

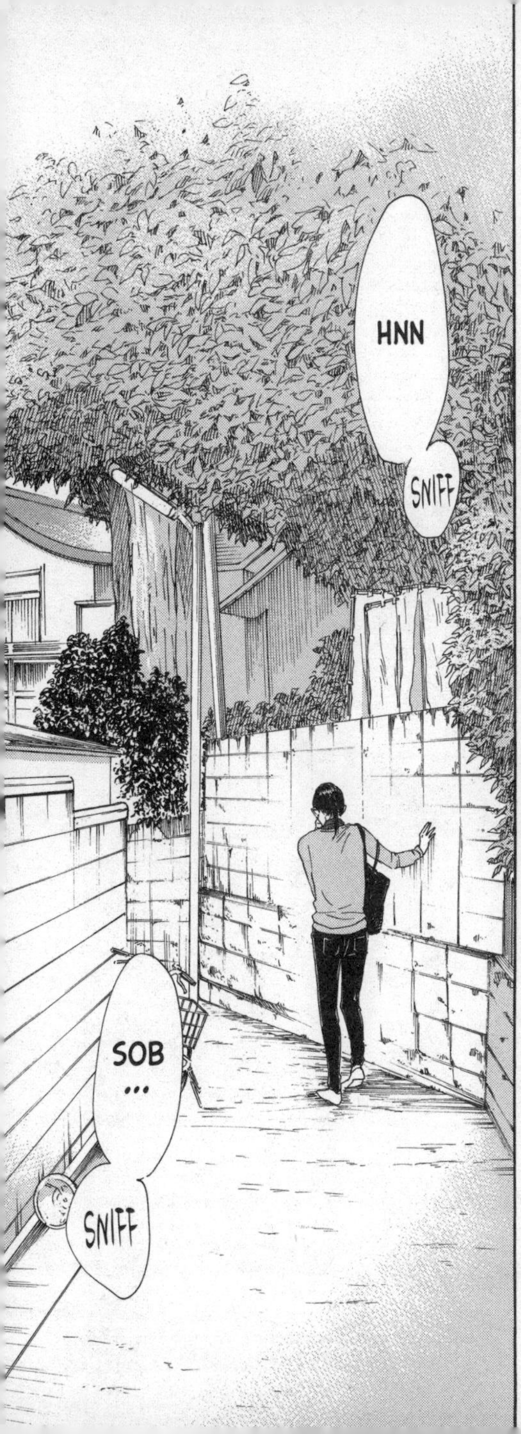
HNN
SNIFF
SOB ...
SNIFF

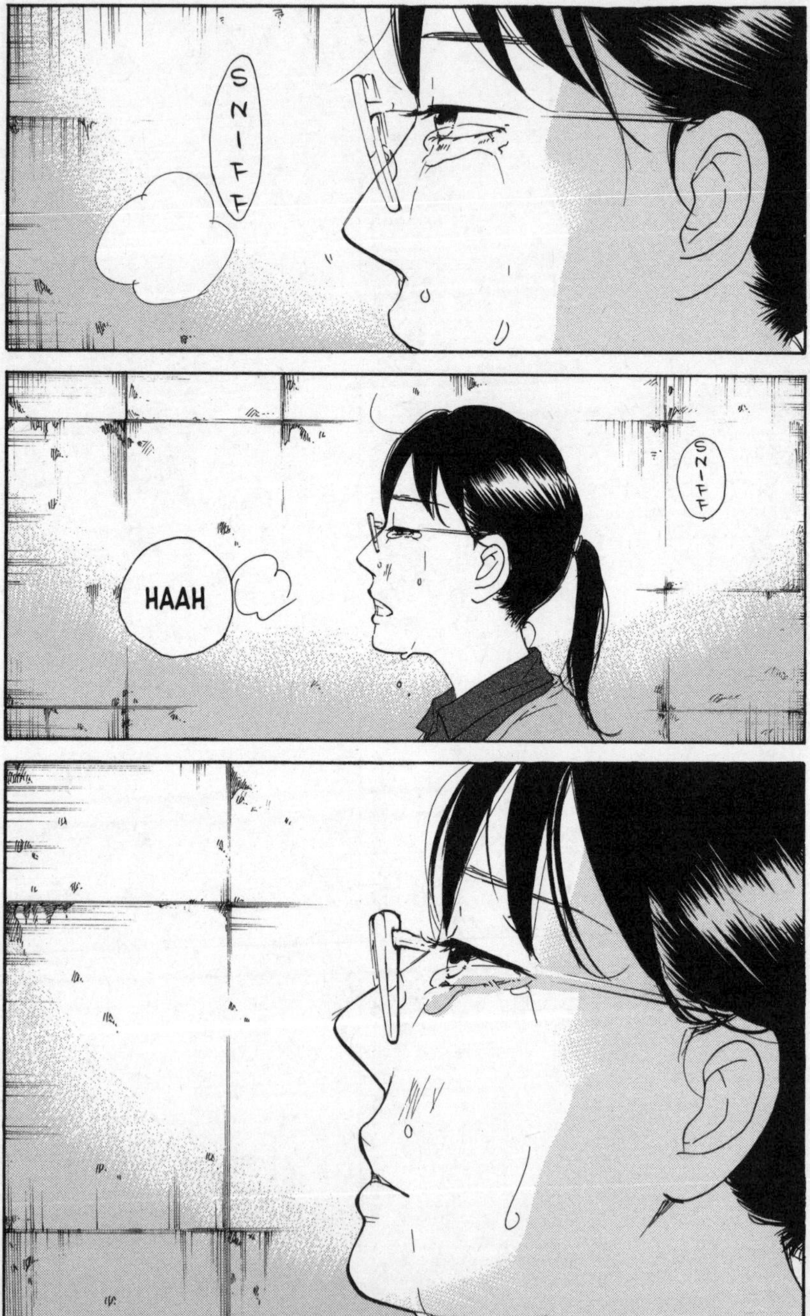
SNIFF
SNIFF
HAAH

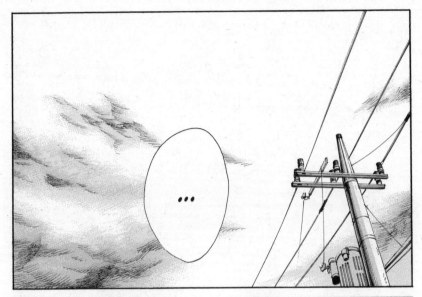

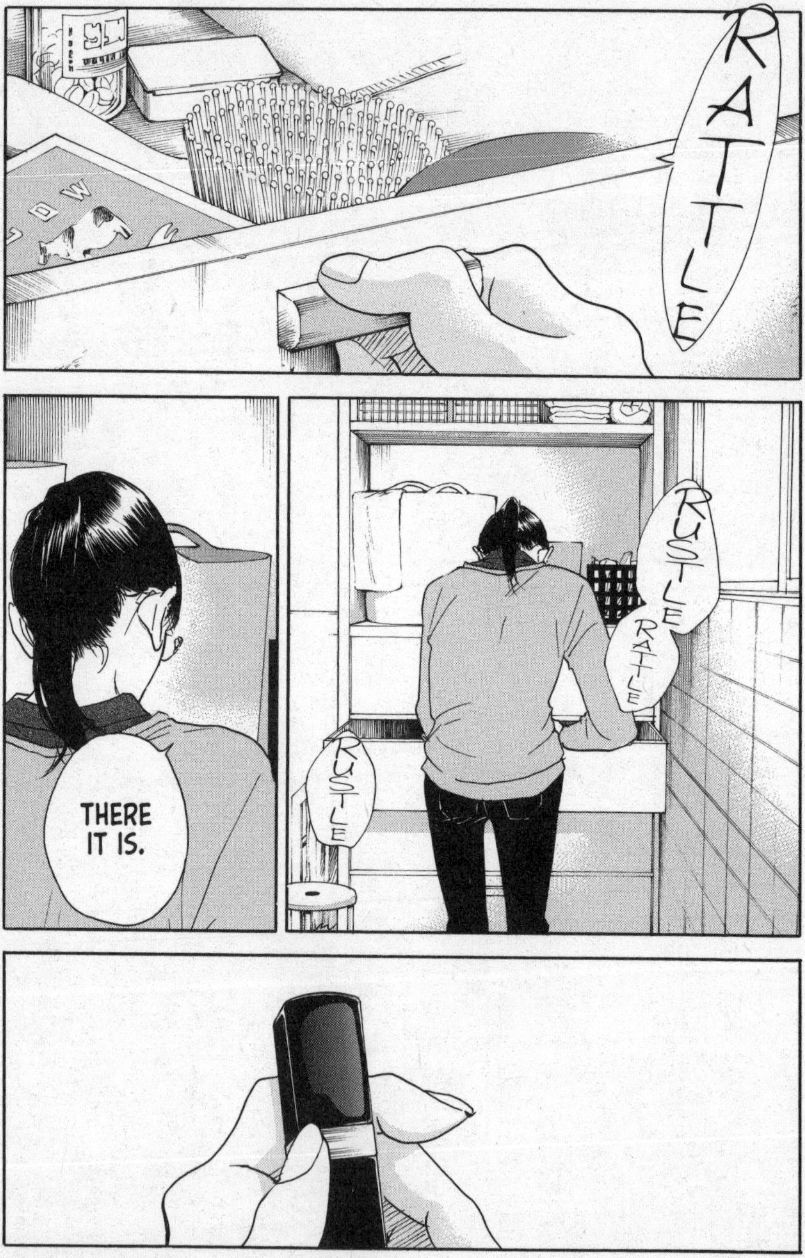
RATTLE
RUSTLE
RATTLE
RUSTLE
THERE IT IS.

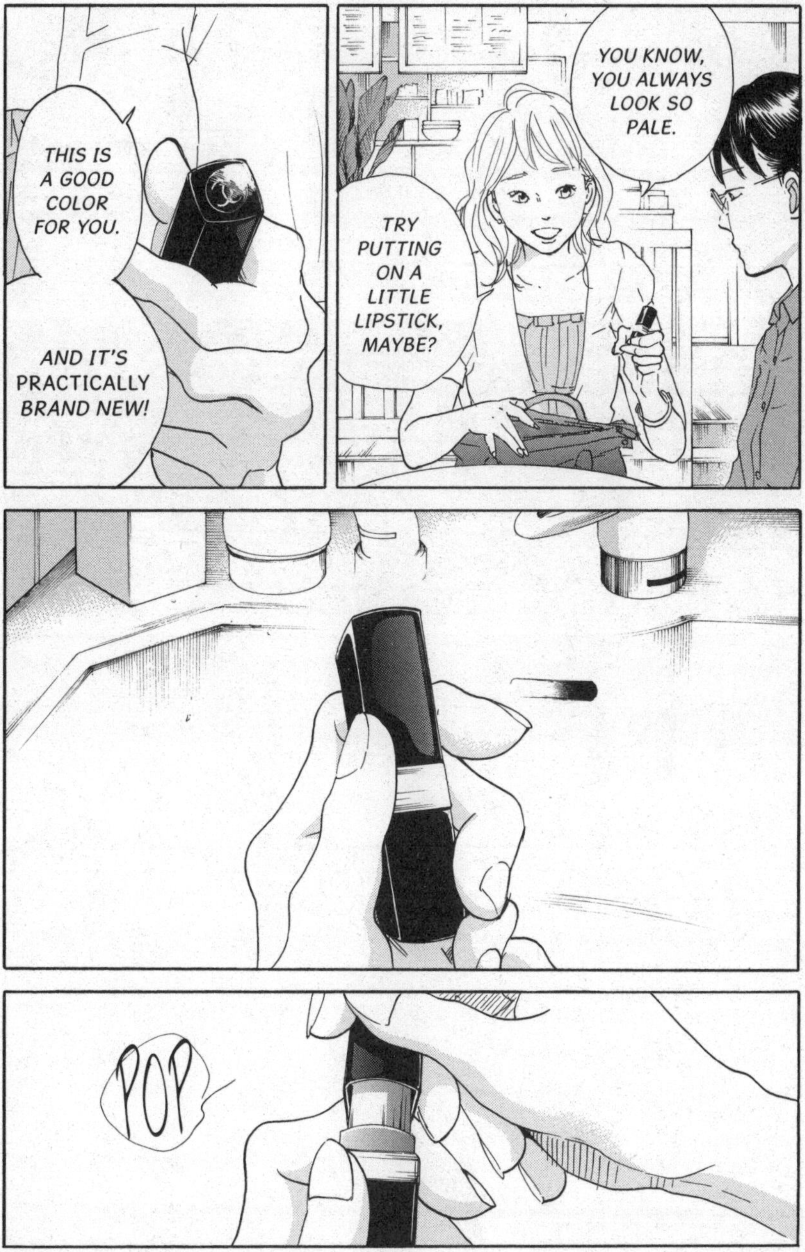
YOU KNOW, YOU ALWAYS LOOK SO PALE.
TRY PUTTING ON A LITTLE LIPSTICK, MAYBE?
THIS IS A GOOD COLOR FOR YOU.
AND IT'S PRACTICALLY BRAND NEW!
POP

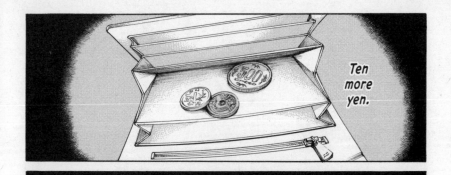

Ten
more
yen.

If I'd had ten
more yen,
I might've said
something.

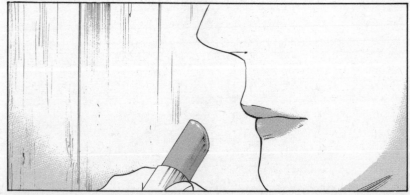

200

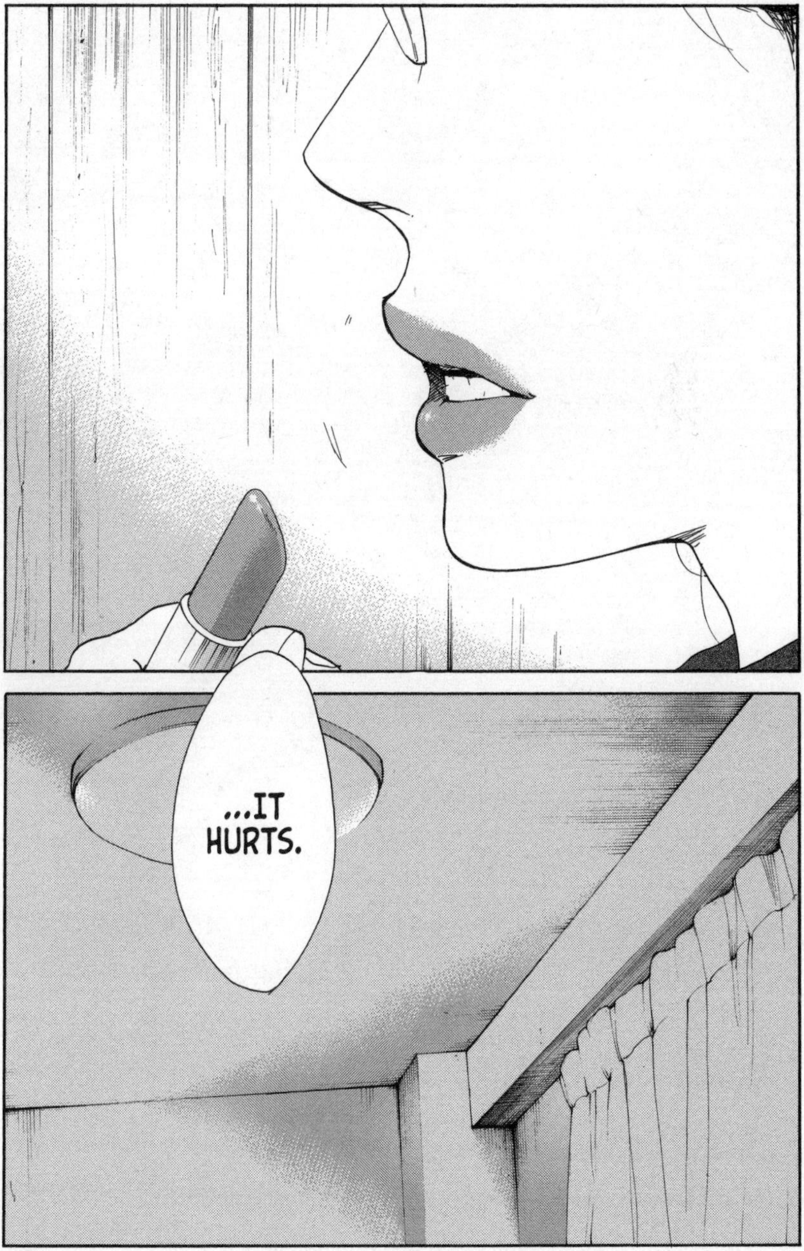
...IT
HURTS.

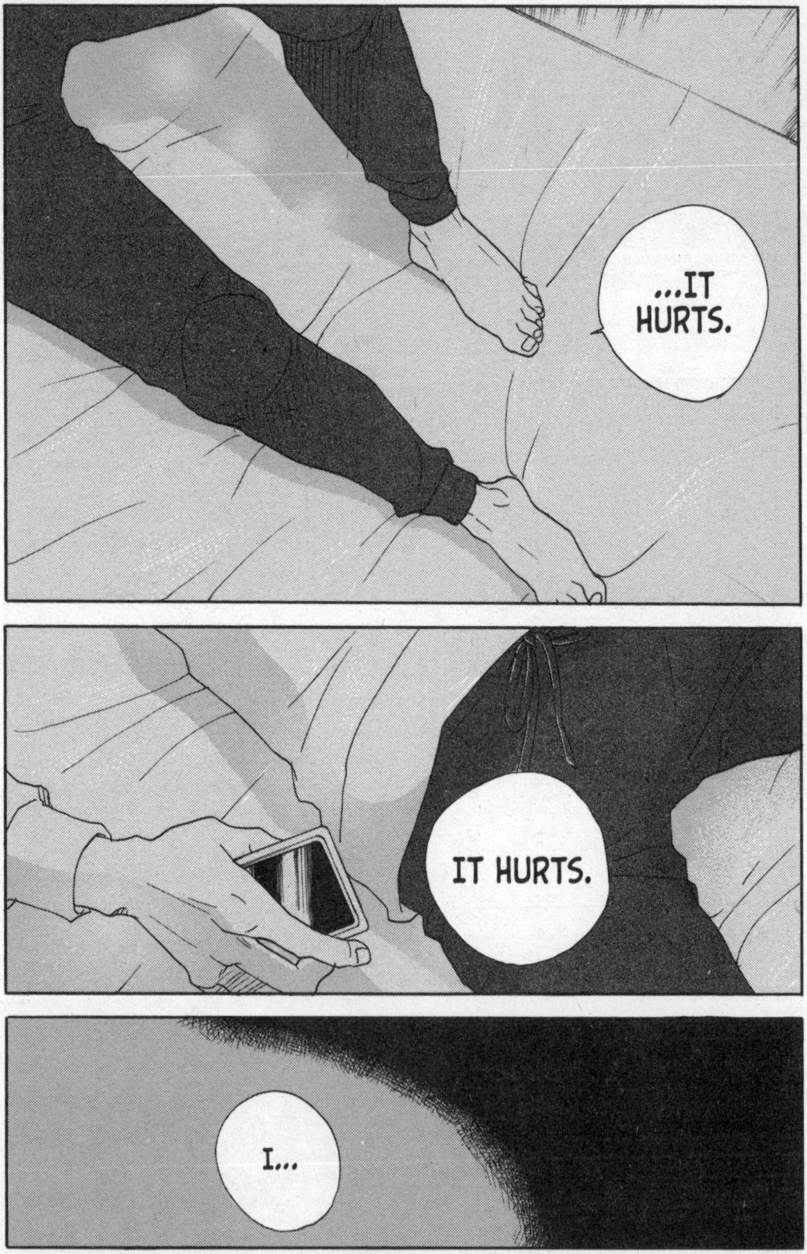
...IT HURTS.
IT HURTS.
I...

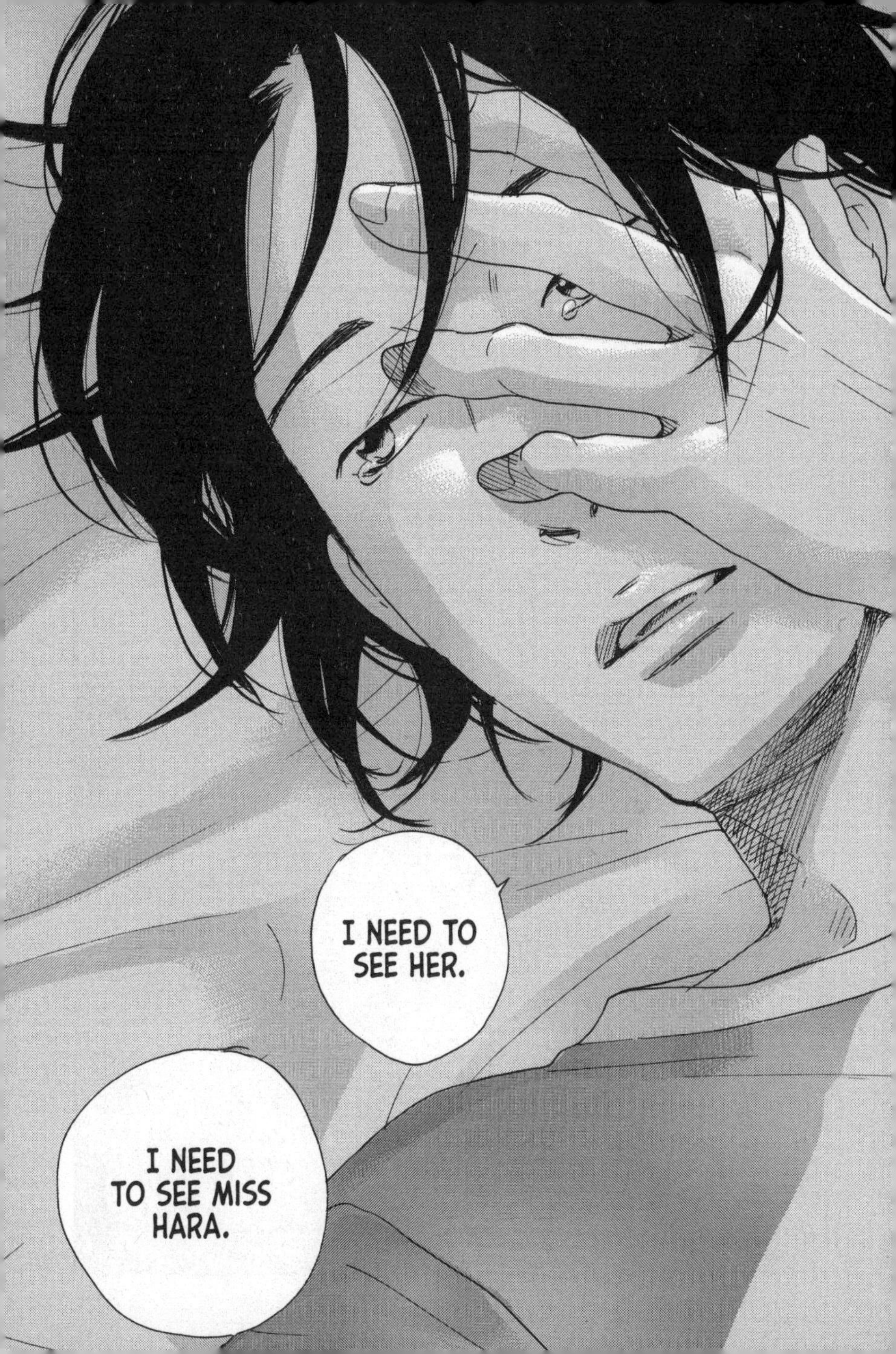
I NEED TO SEE HER.
I NEED TO SEE MISS HARA.

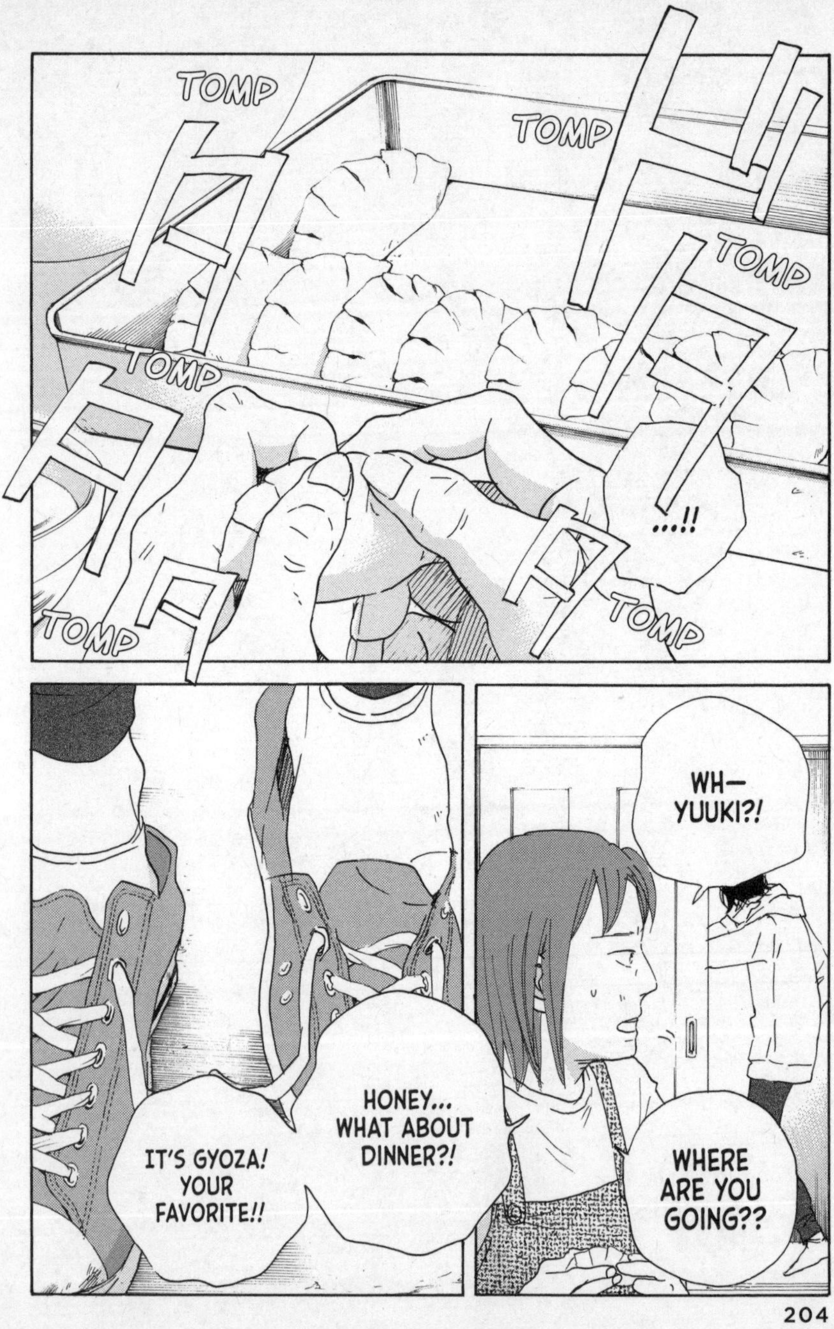
TOMP
TOMP
TOMP
TOMP
TOMP
TOMP
...!!
WH— YUUKI?!
WHERE ARE YOU GOING??
HONEY... WHAT ABOUT DINNER?!
IT'S GYOZA! YOUR FAVORITE!!

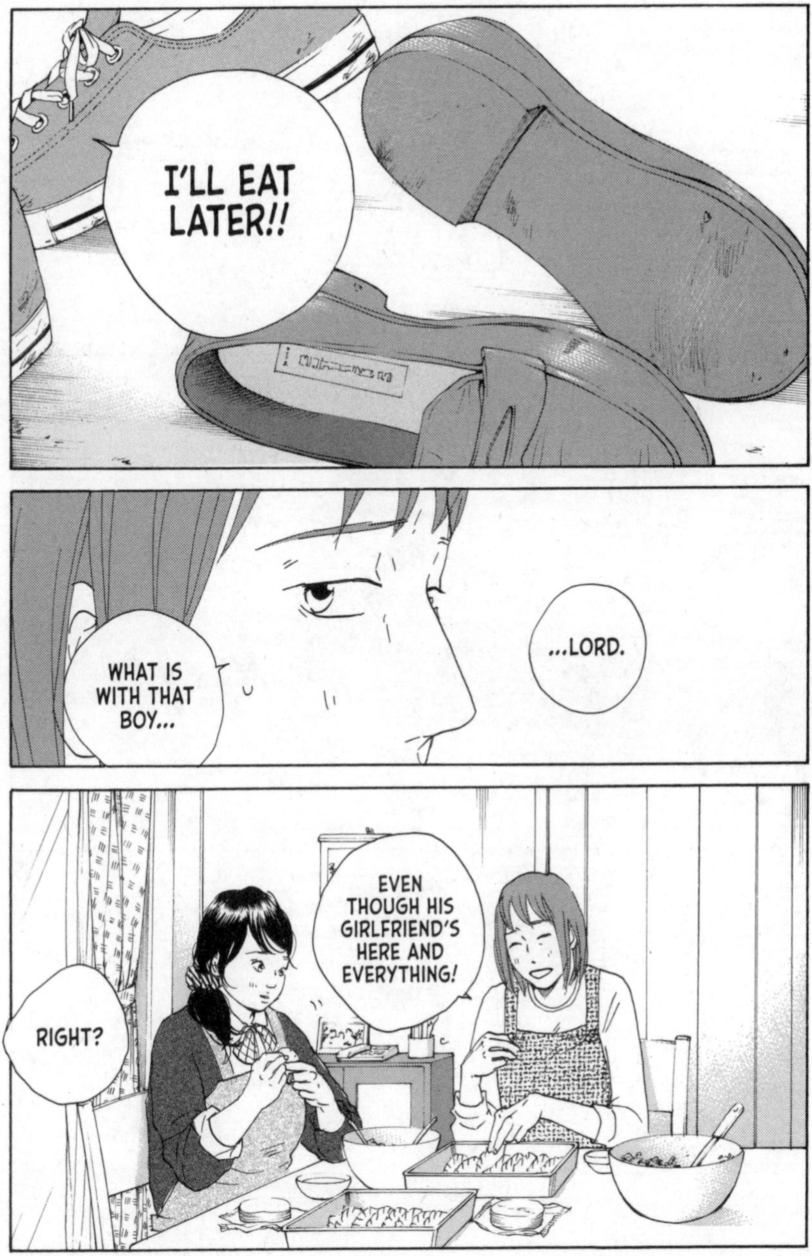
I'LL EAT LATER!!
...LORD.
WHAT IS WITH THAT BOY...
EVEN THOUGH HIS GIRLFRIEND'S HERE AND EVERYTHING!
RIGHT?

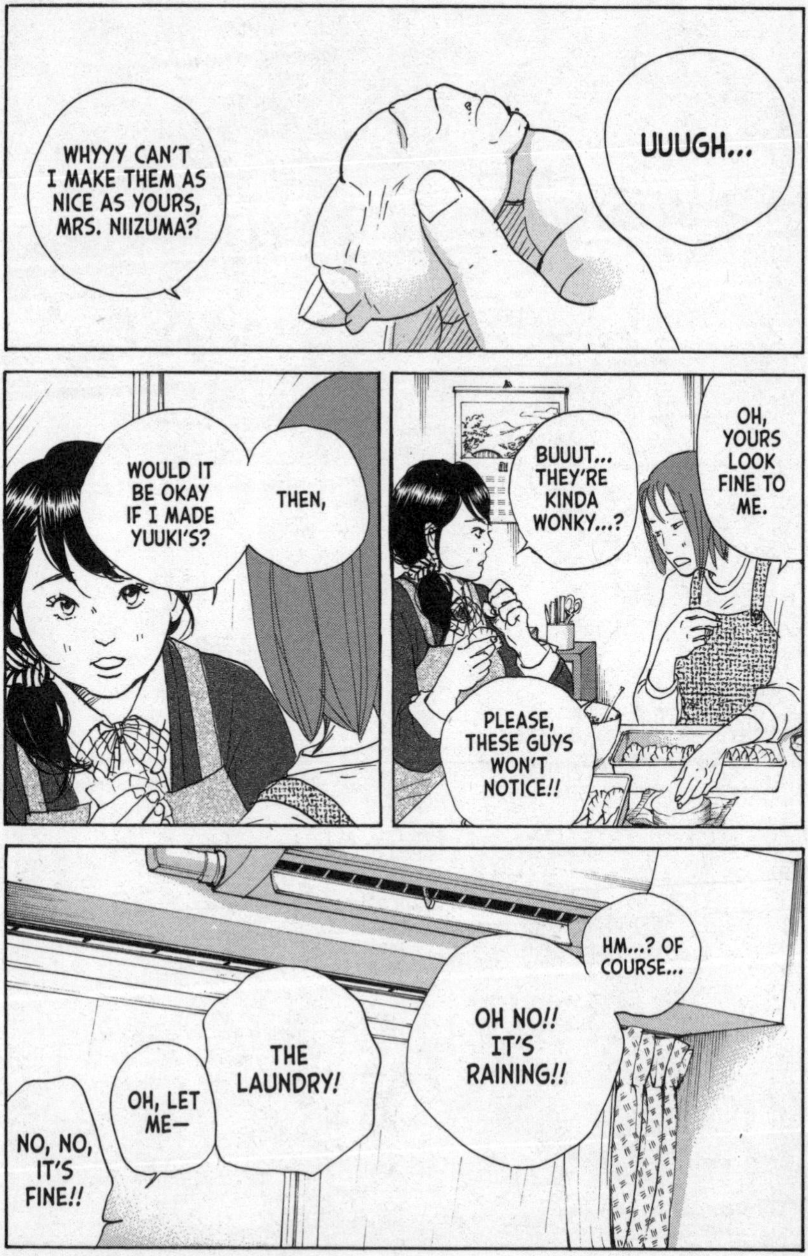
UUUGH...
WHYYY CAN'T I MAKE THEM AS NICE AS YOURS, MRS. NIIZUMA?
OH, YOURS LOOK FINE TO ME.
BUUUT... THEY'RE KINDA WONKY...?
PLEASE, THESE GUYS WON'T NOTICE!!
THEN,
WOULD IT BE OKAY IF I MADE YUUKI'S?
HM...? OF COURSE...
OH NO!! IT'S RAINING!!
THE LAUNDRY!
OH, LET ME—
NO, NO, IT'S FINE!!

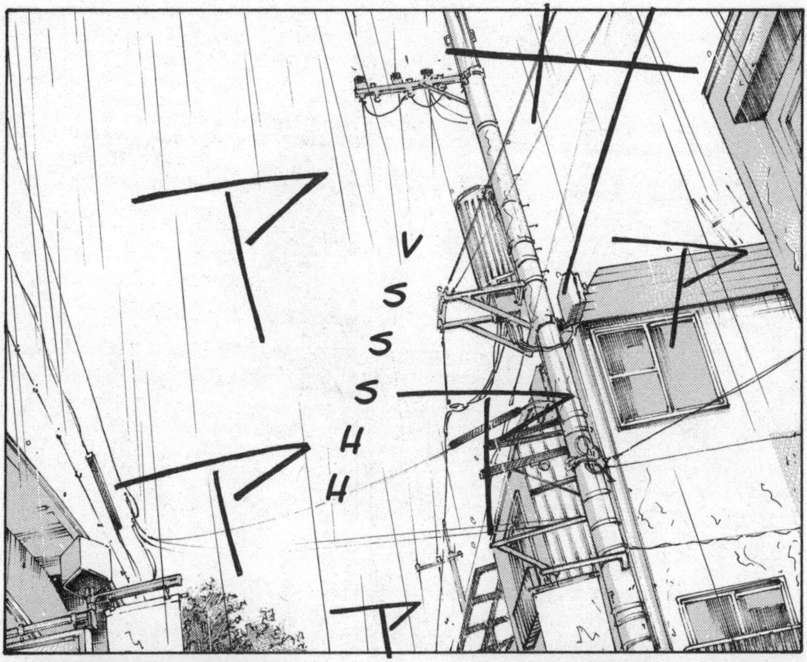
VSSSHH

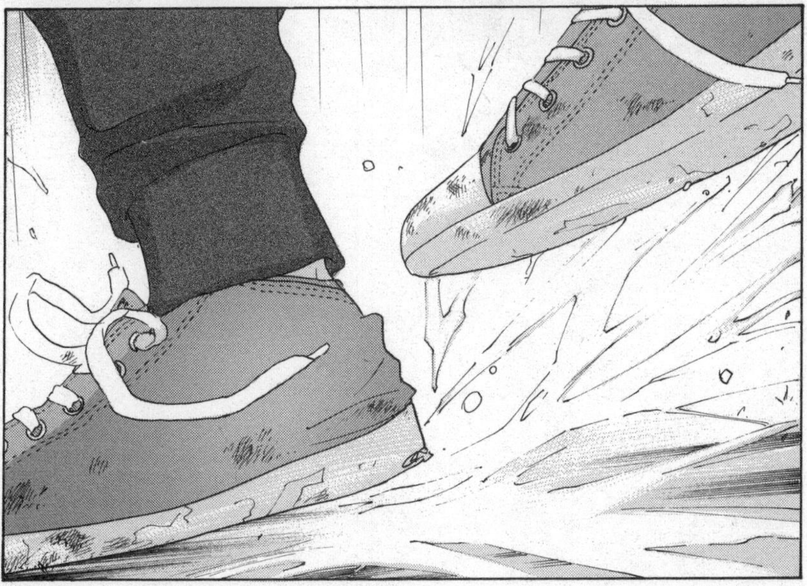

I thought
I'd keep
getting
smaller
and smaller
until I just
disappeared.

Until
today,

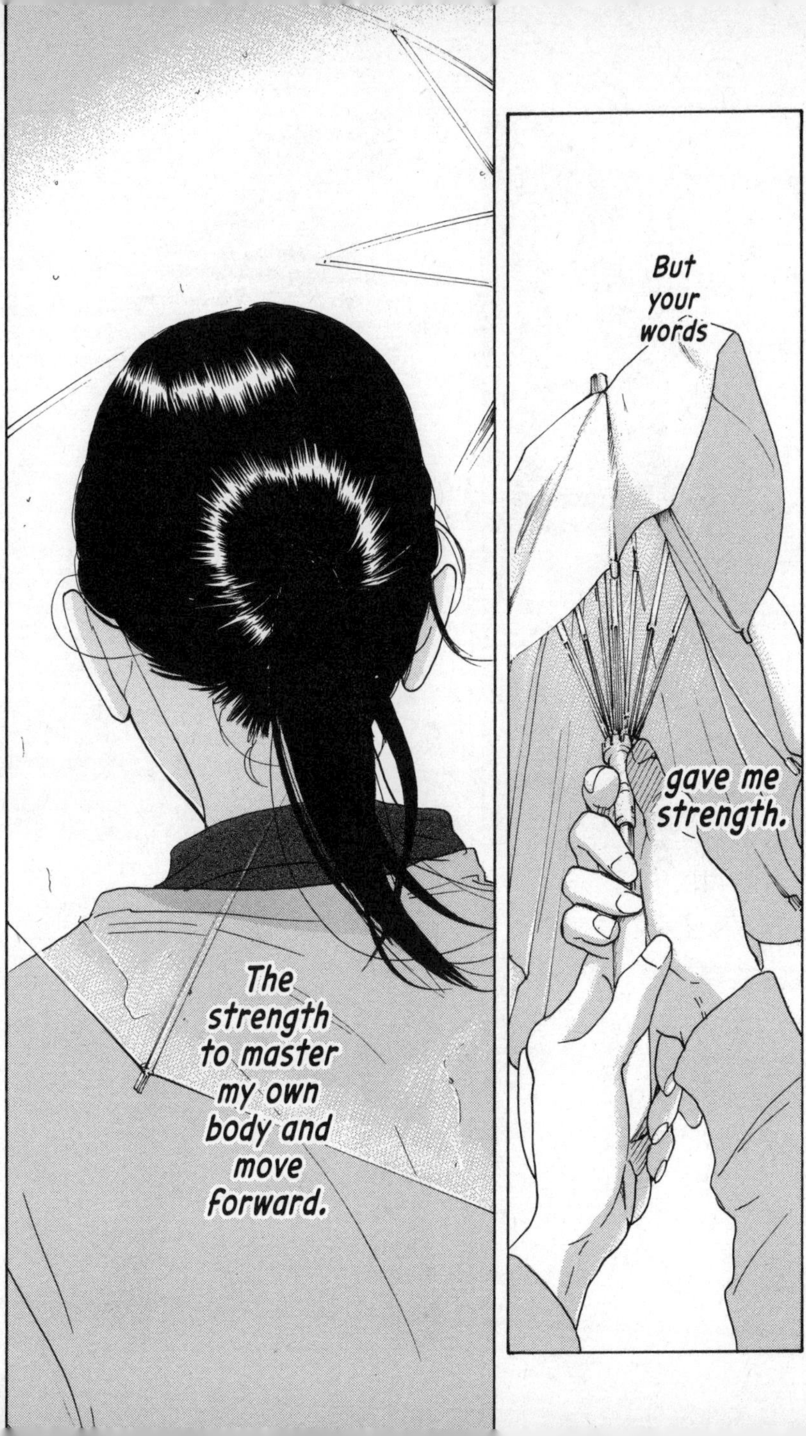
But your words
gave me strength.
The strength to master my own body and move forward.

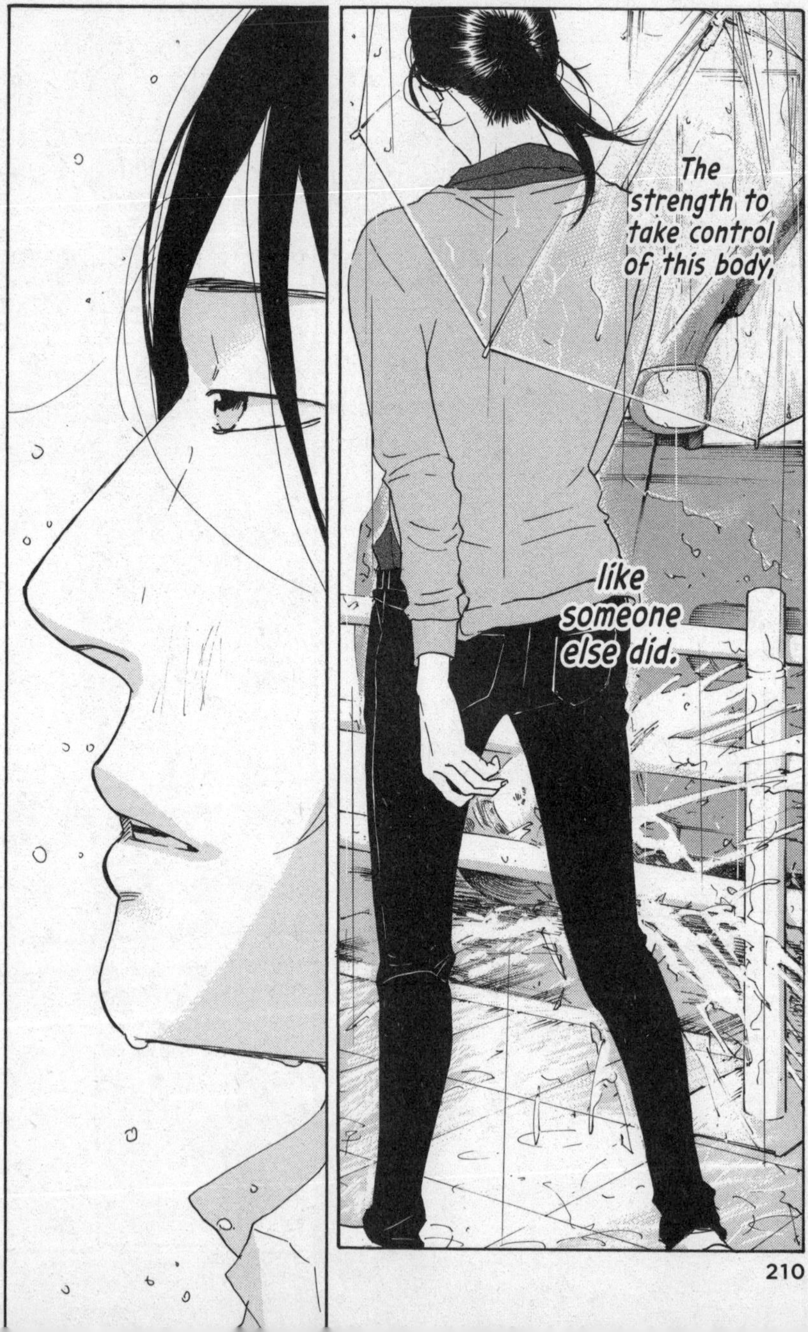
The strength to take control of this body,
like someone else did.

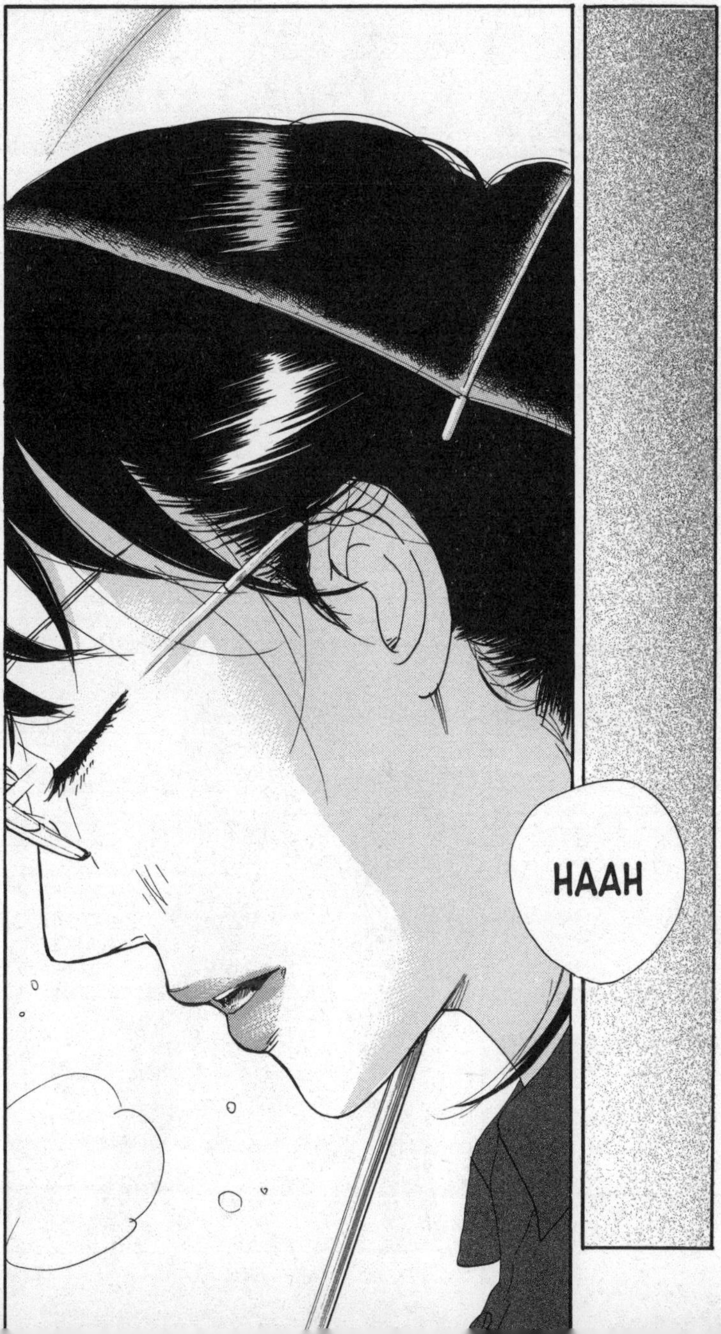
HAAH

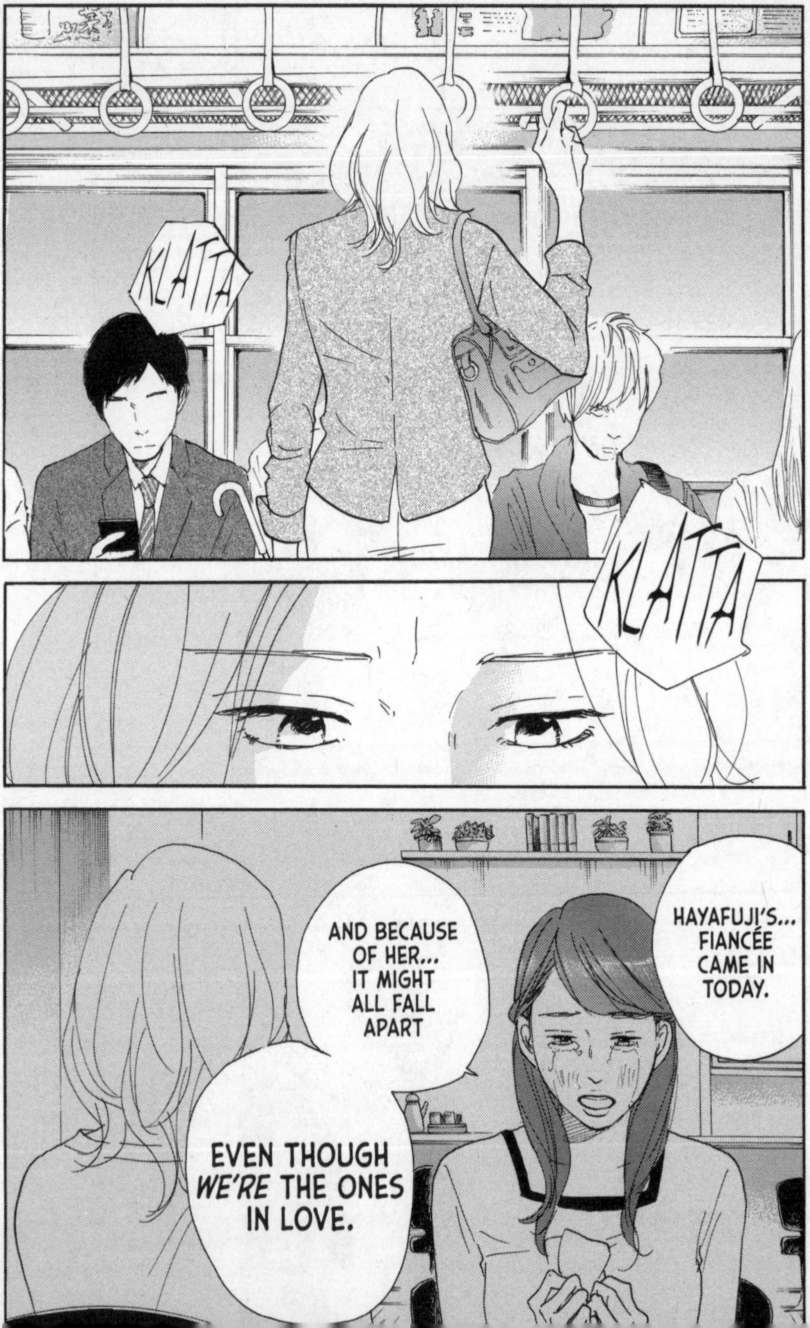
KLATTA
KLATTA
HAYAFUJI'S... FIANCÉE CAME IN TODAY.
AND BECAUSE OF HER... IT MIGHT ALL FALL APART
EVEN THOUGH *WE'RE* THE ONES IN LOVE.

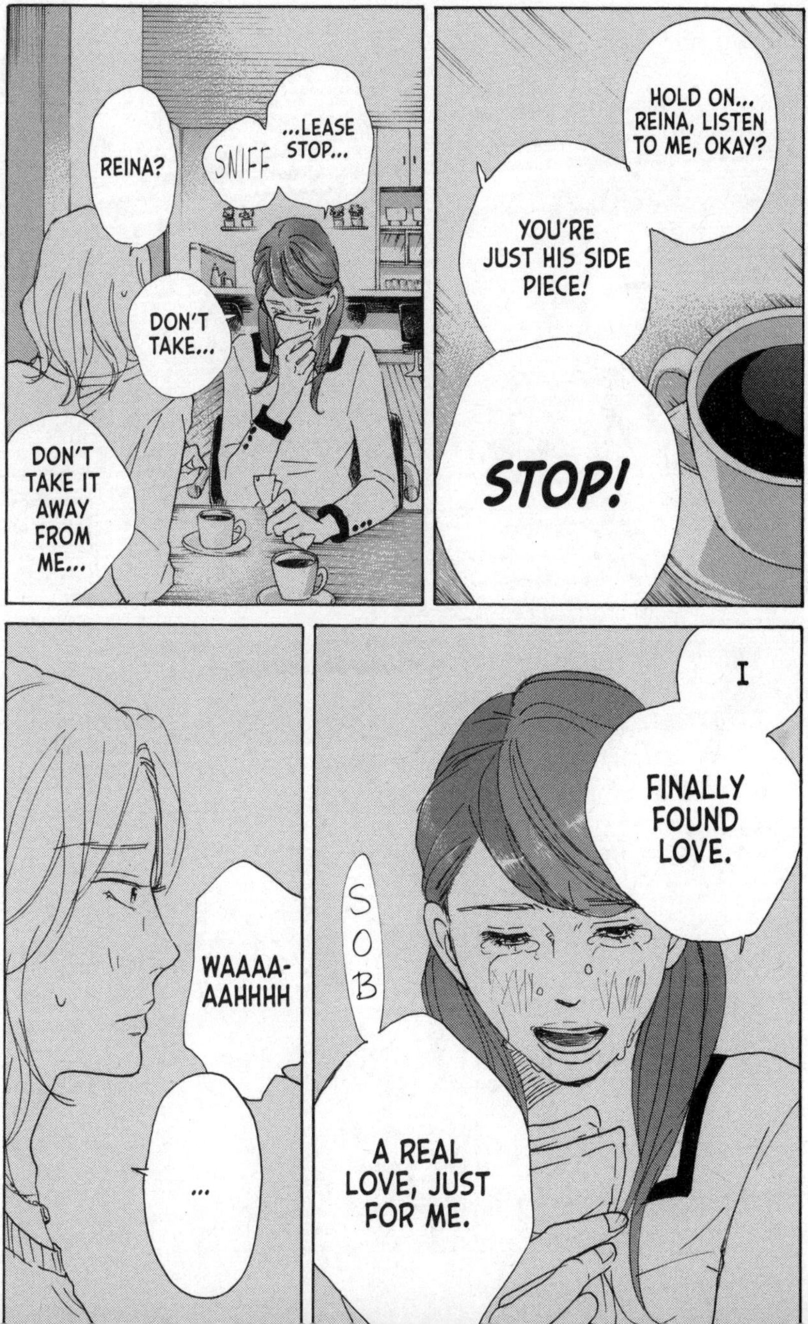
HOLD ON... REINA, LISTEN TO ME, OKAY?
YOU'RE JUST HIS SIDE PIECE!
STOP!
...LEASE STOP...
SNIFF
REINA?
DON'T TAKE...
DON'T TAKE IT AWAY FROM ME...
I
FINALLY FOUND LOVE.
SOB
A REAL LOVE, JUST FOR ME.
WAAAA-AAHHHH
...

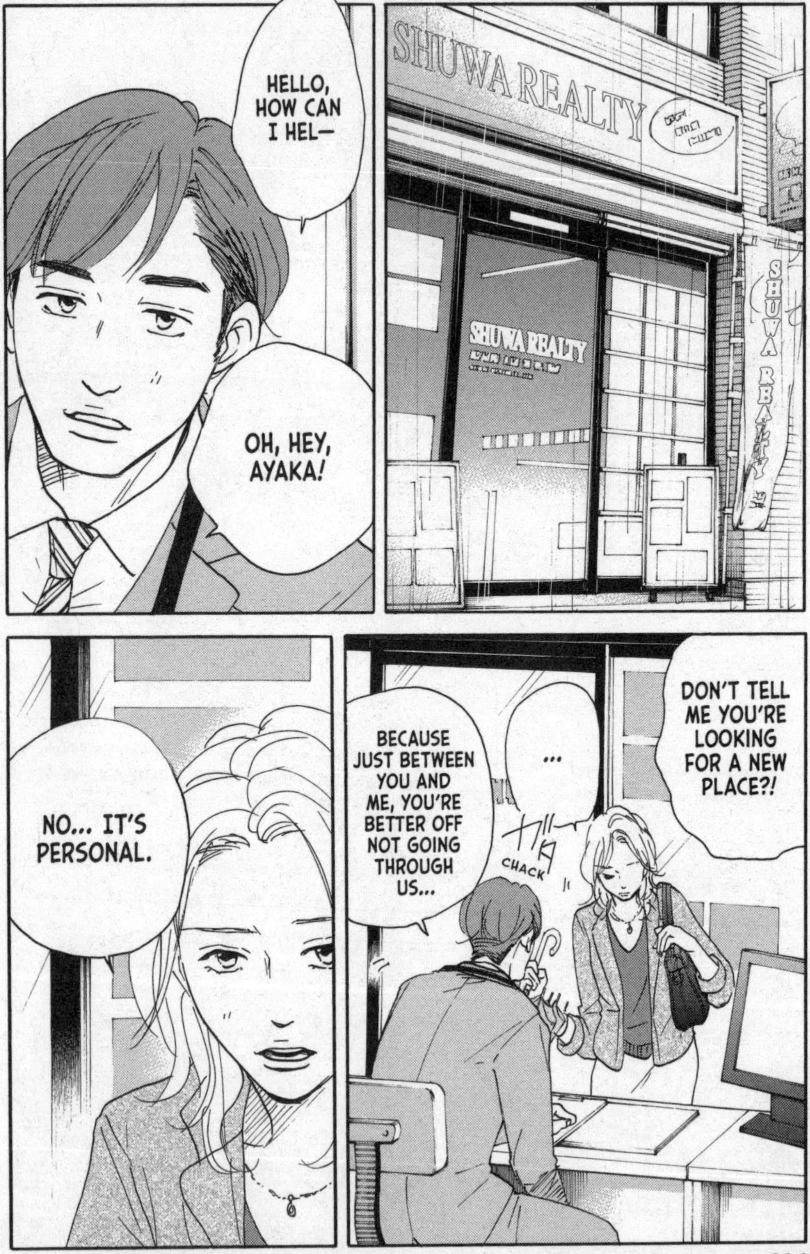
SHUWA REALTY
SHUWA REALTY
SHUWA REALTY
HELLO, HOW CAN I HEL—
OH, HEY, AYAKA!
DON'T TELL ME YOU'RE LOOKING FOR A NEW PLACE?!
...
BECAUSE JUST BETWEEN YOU AND ME, YOU'RE BETTER OFF NOT GOING THROUGH US...
CHACK
NO... IT'S PERSONAL.

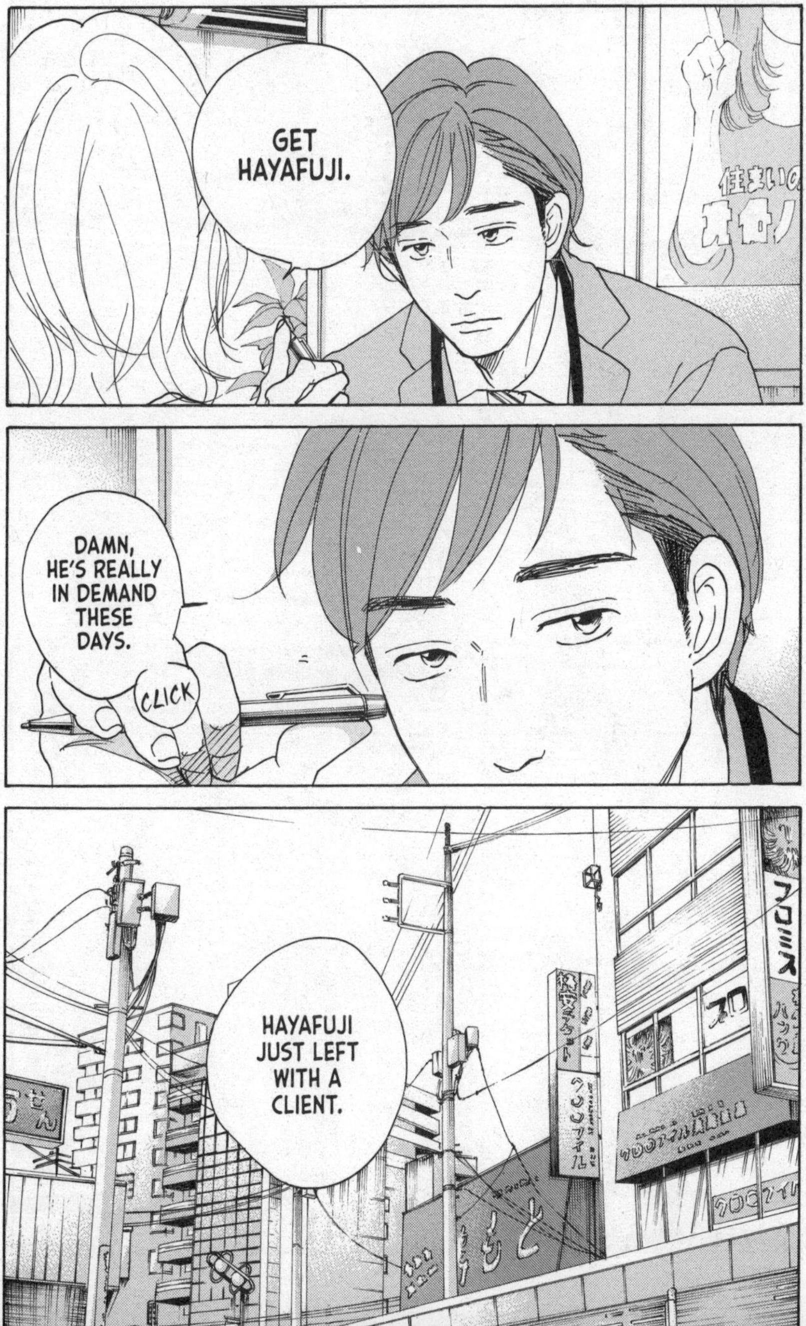
GET HAYAFUJI.
DAMN, HE'S REALLY IN DEMAND THESE DAYS.
CLICK
HAYAFUJI JUST LEFT WITH A CLIENT.

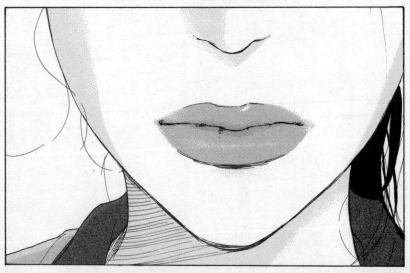

216

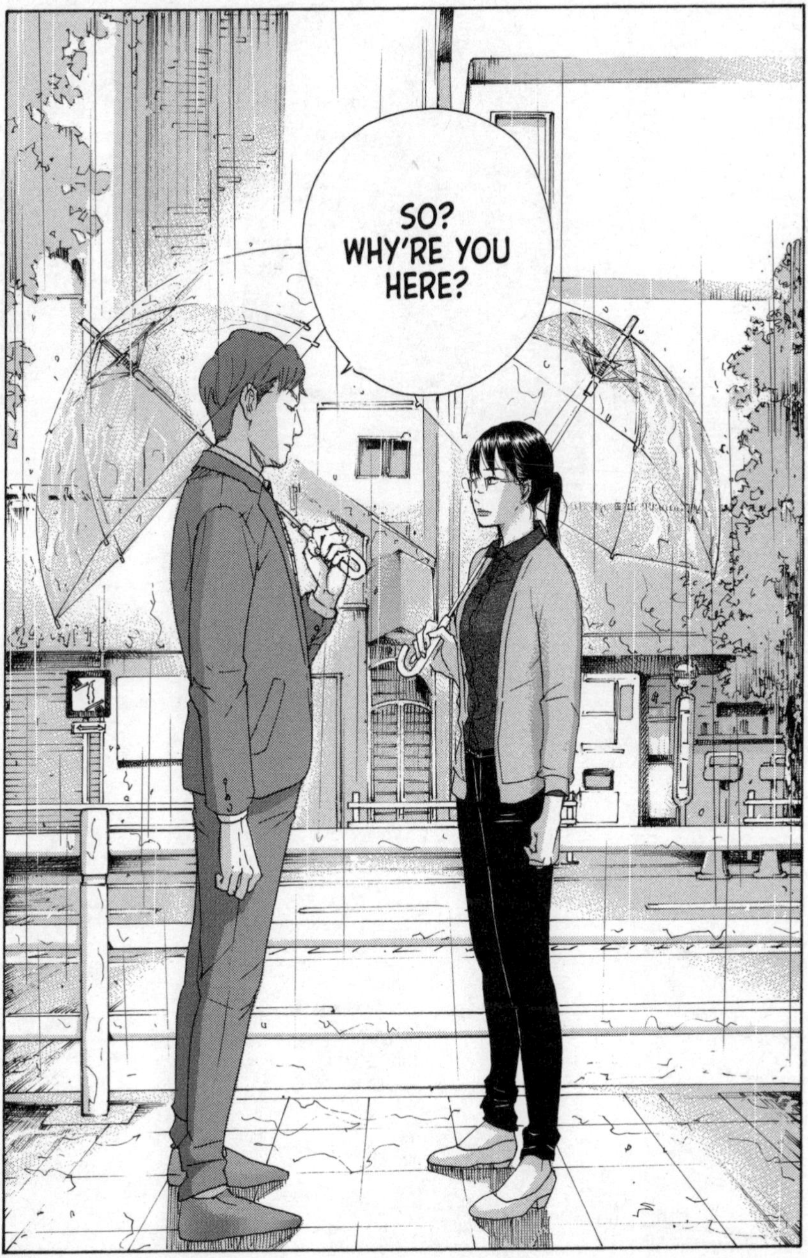
SO? WHY'RE YOU HERE?

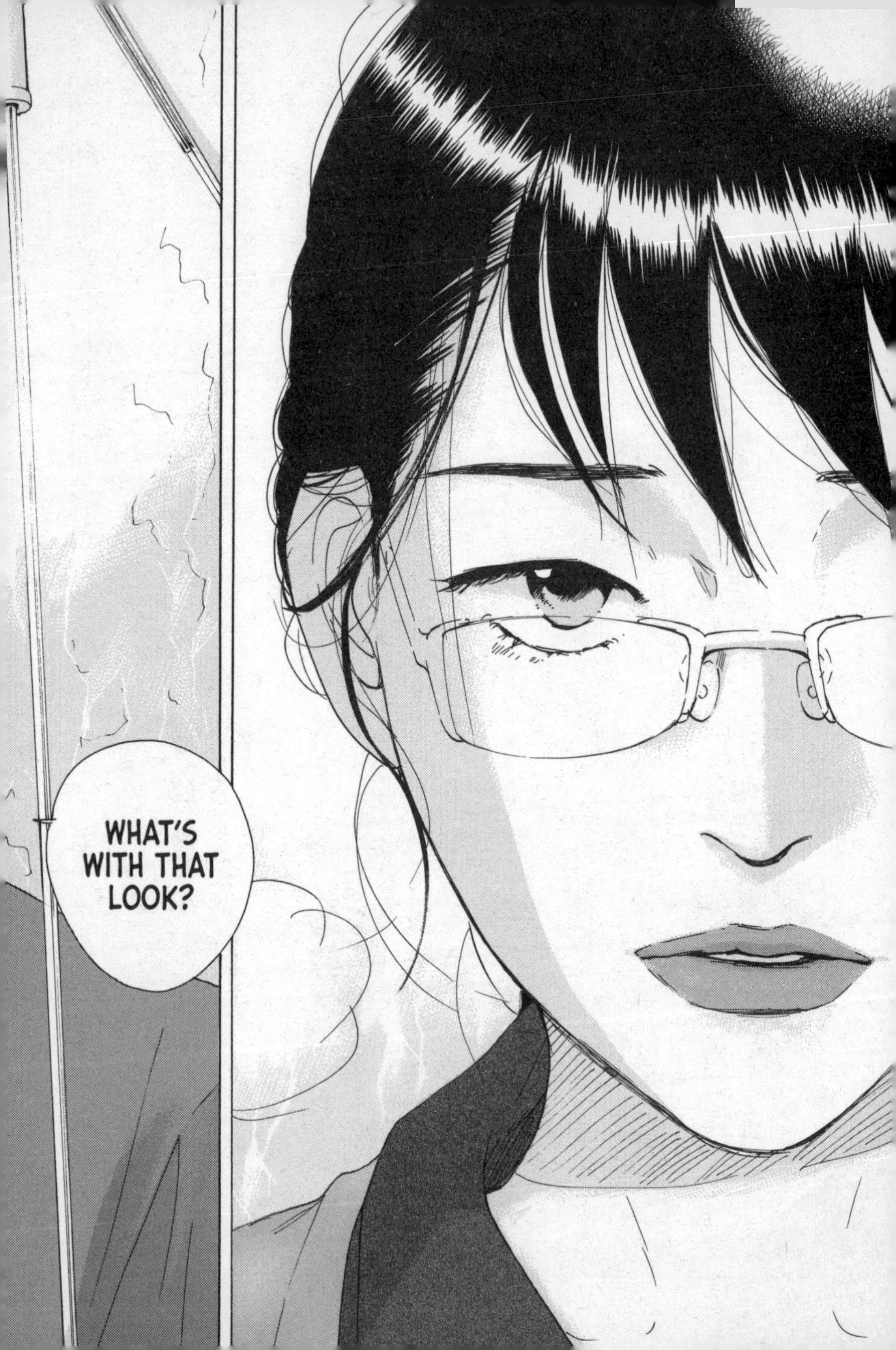
WHAT'S
WITH THAT
LOOK?

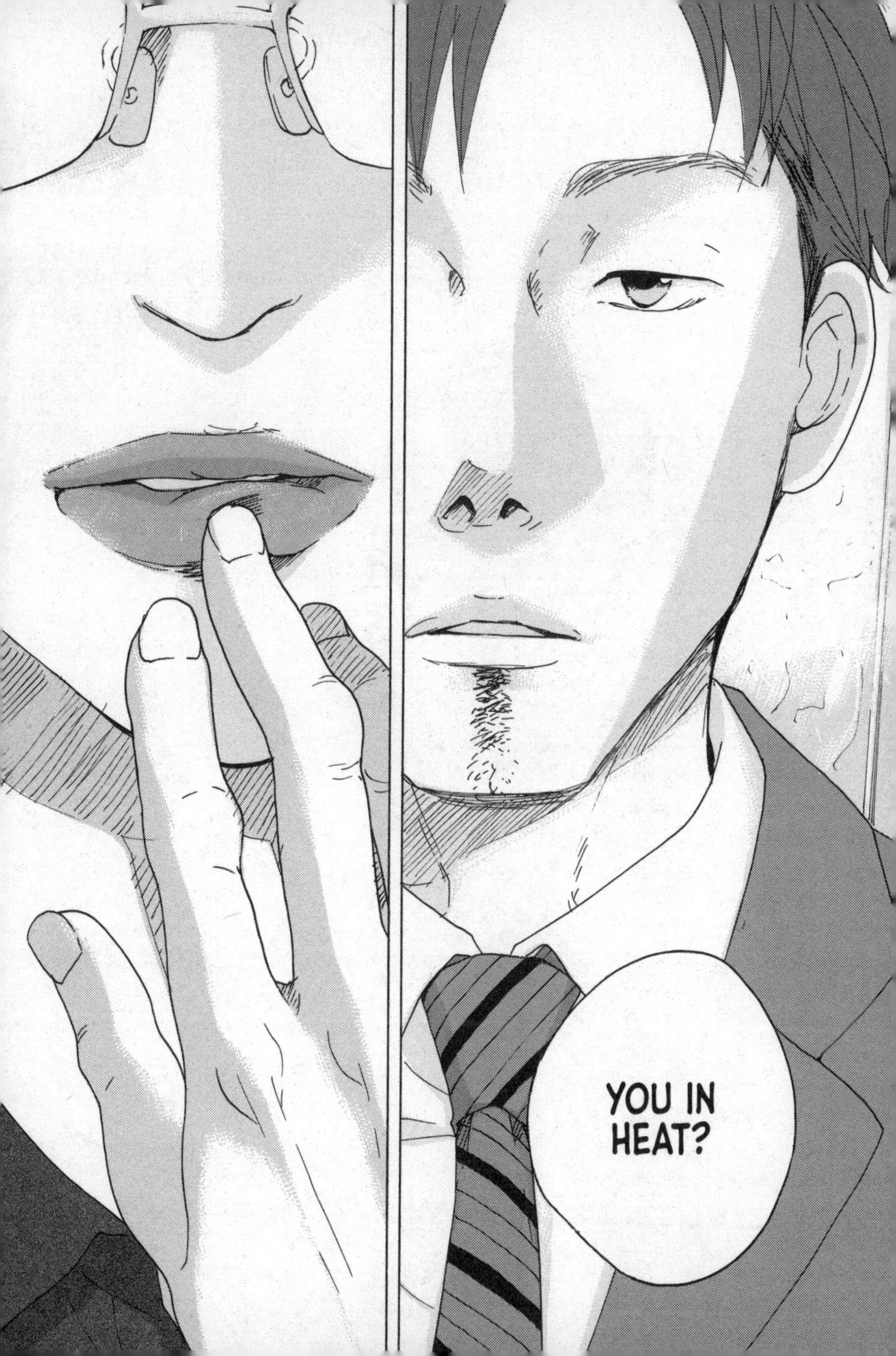
YOU IN HEAT?

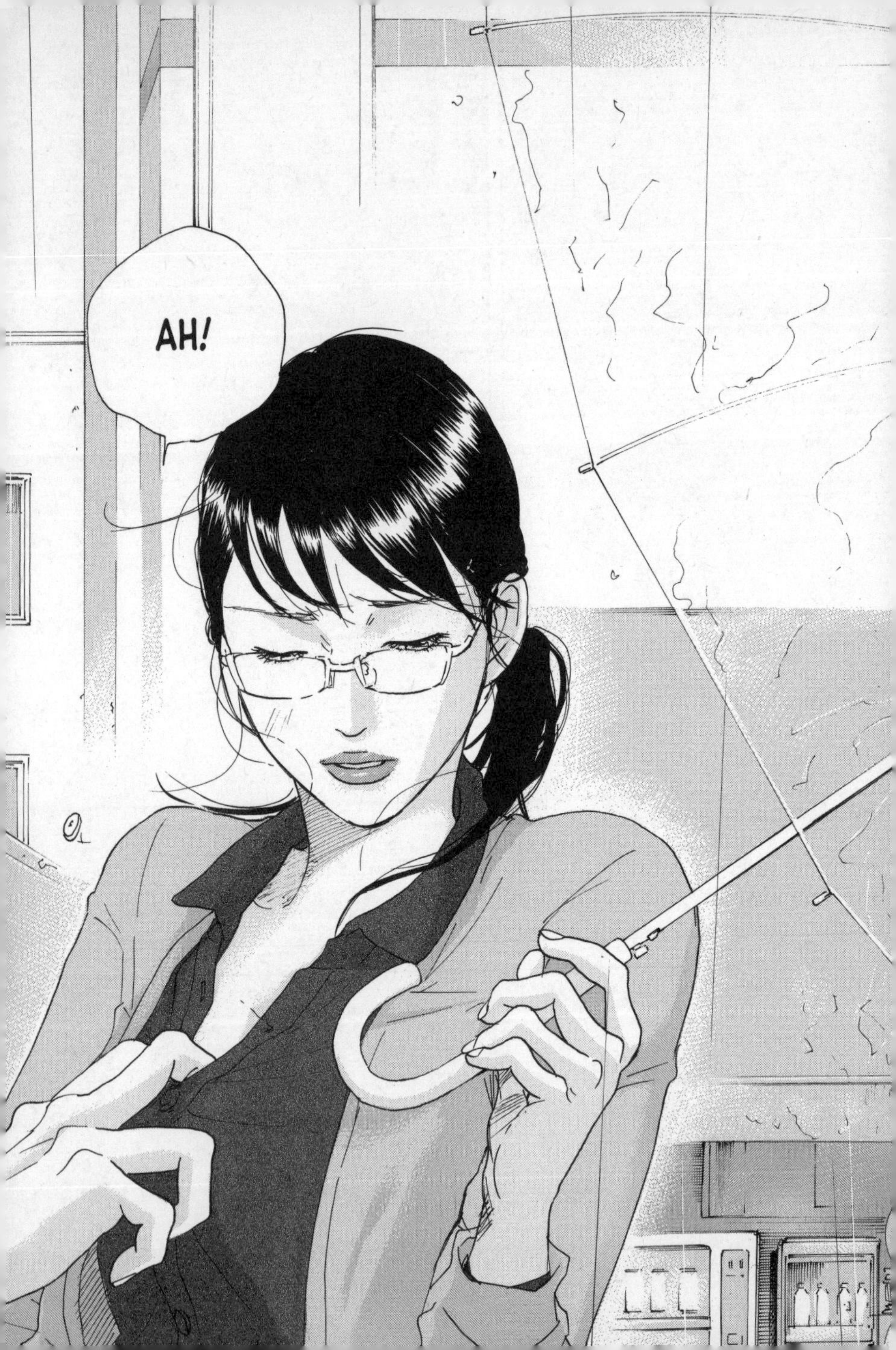
AH!

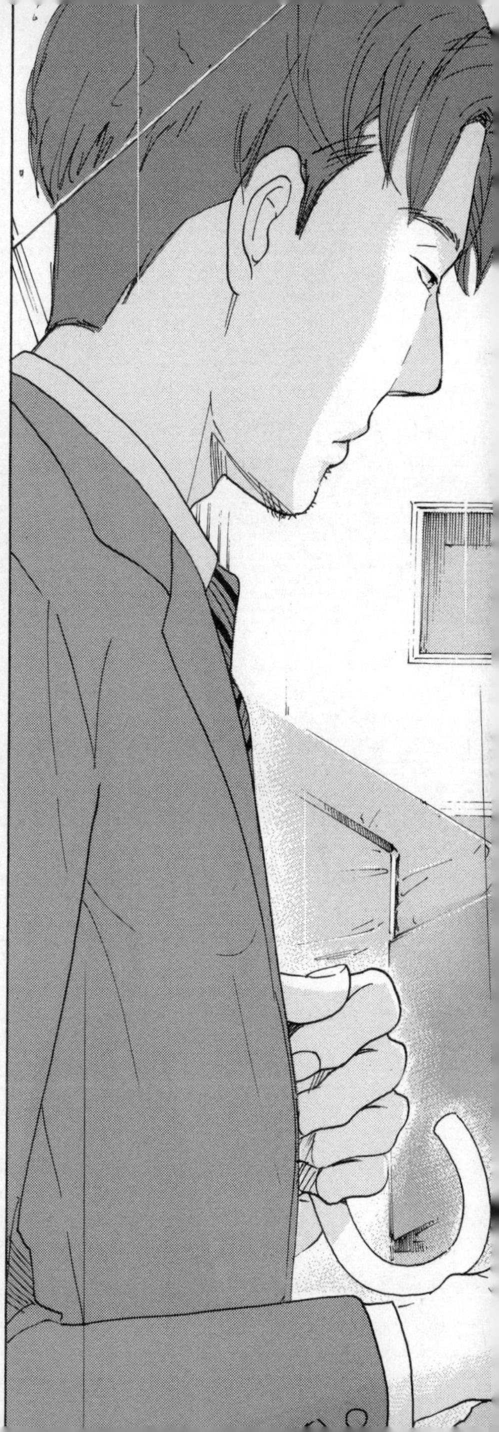

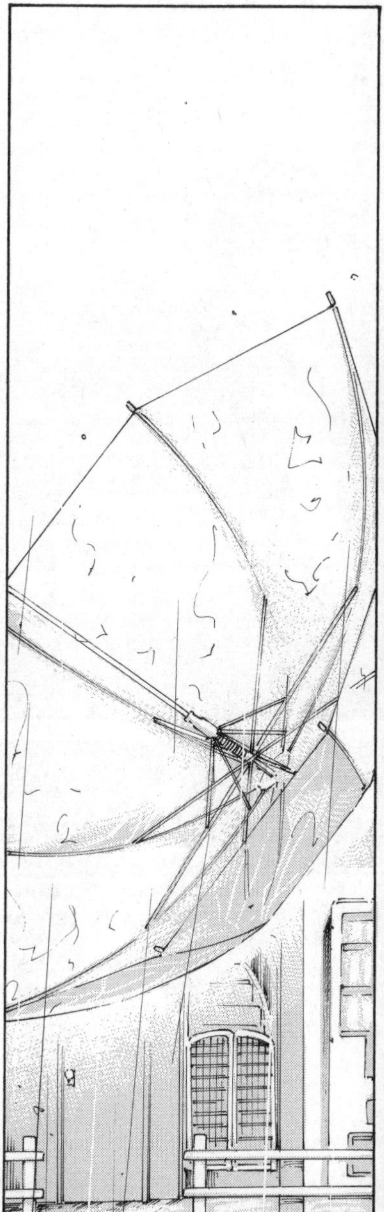

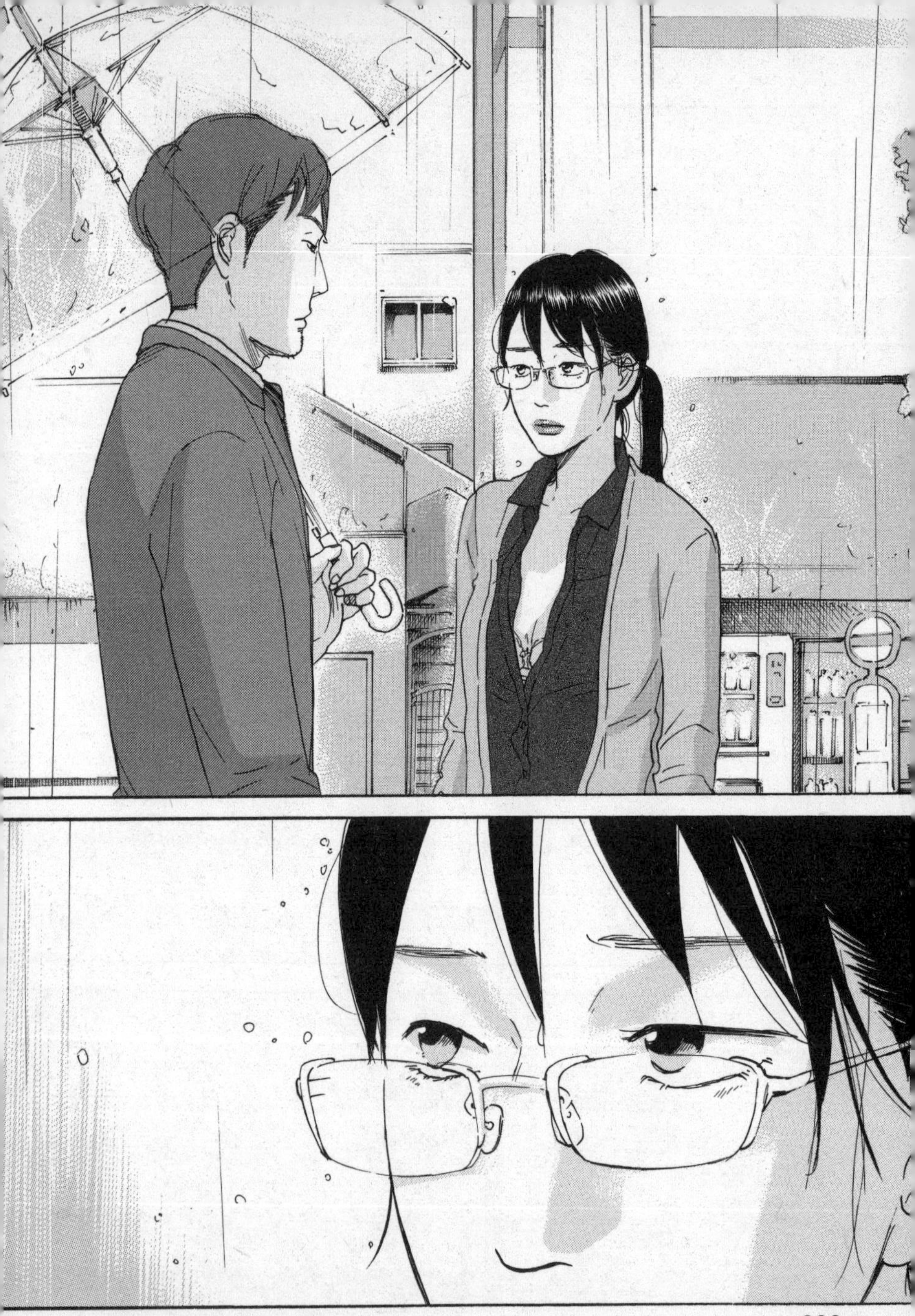

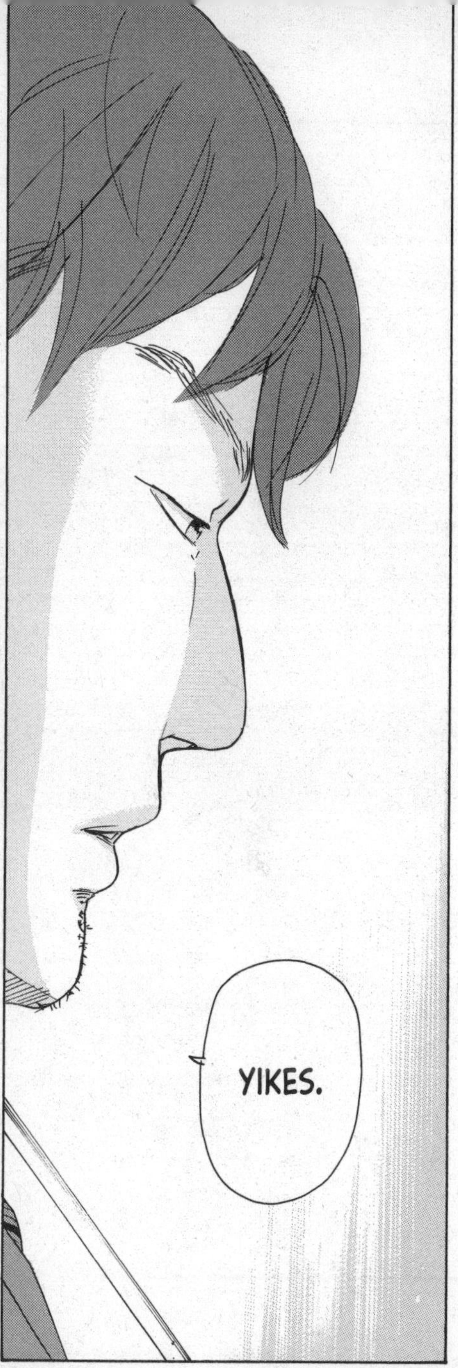
YIKES.
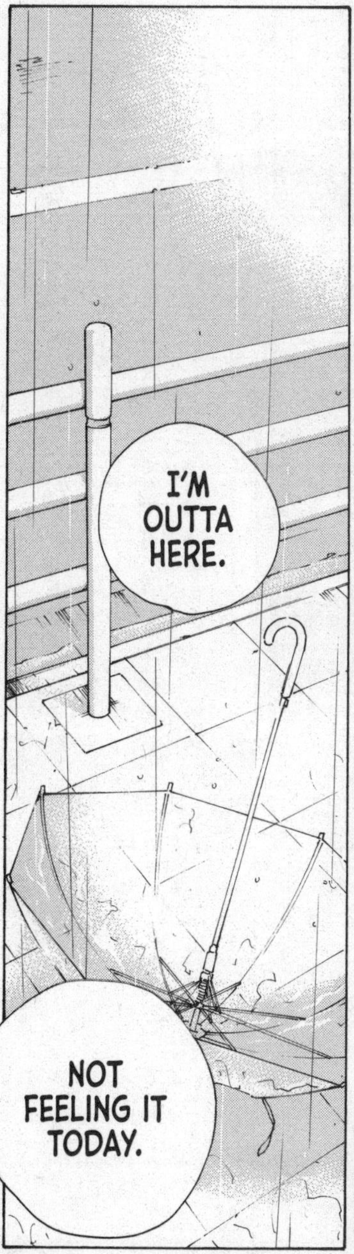
I'M OUTTA HERE.
NOT FEELING IT TODAY.

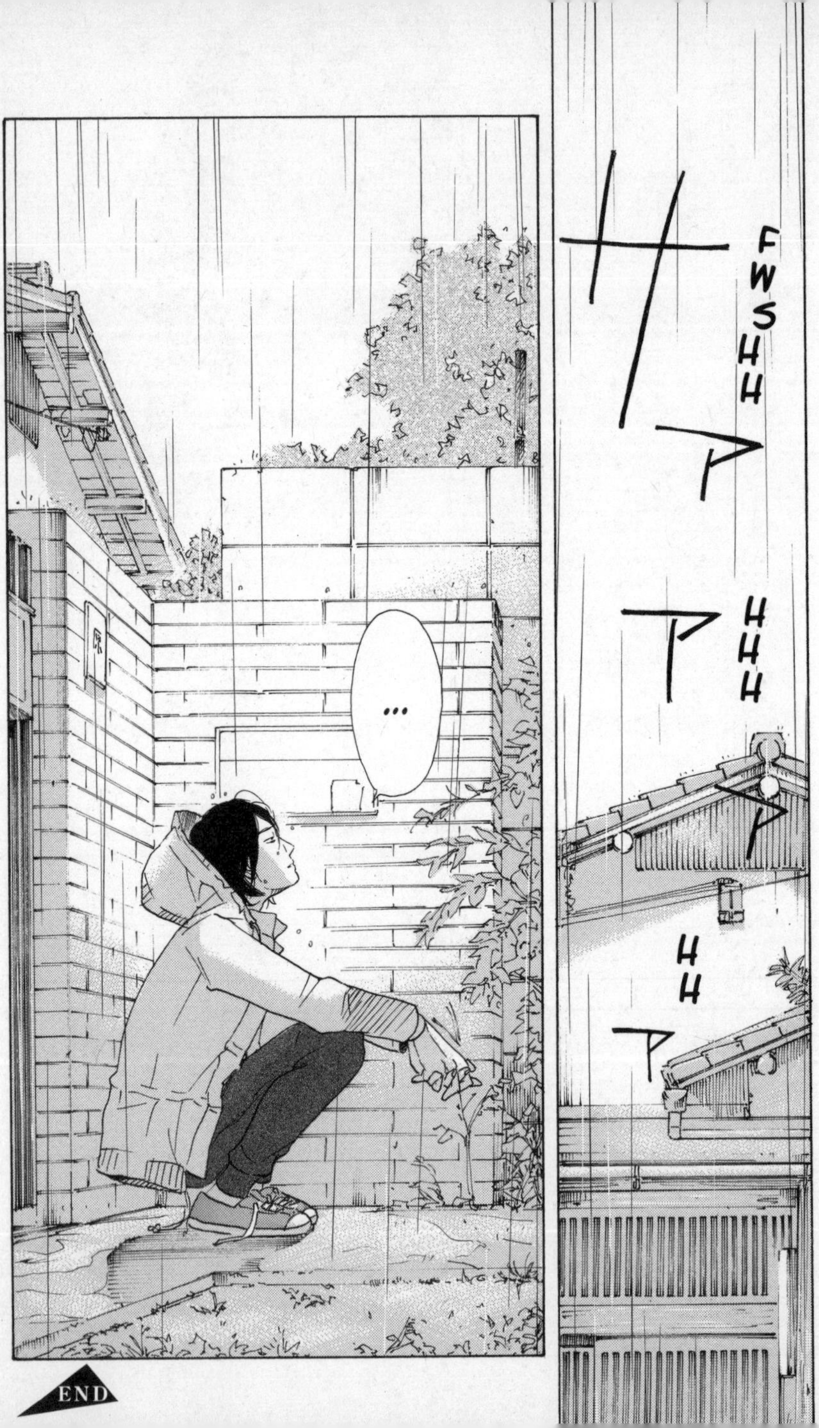

サアアアア
FWSHH
HHHH
HH
...
END

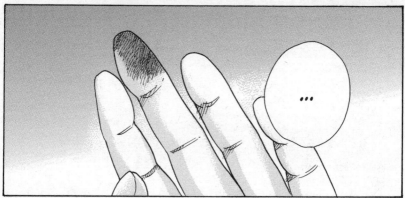

...

WIPE

SHIT.

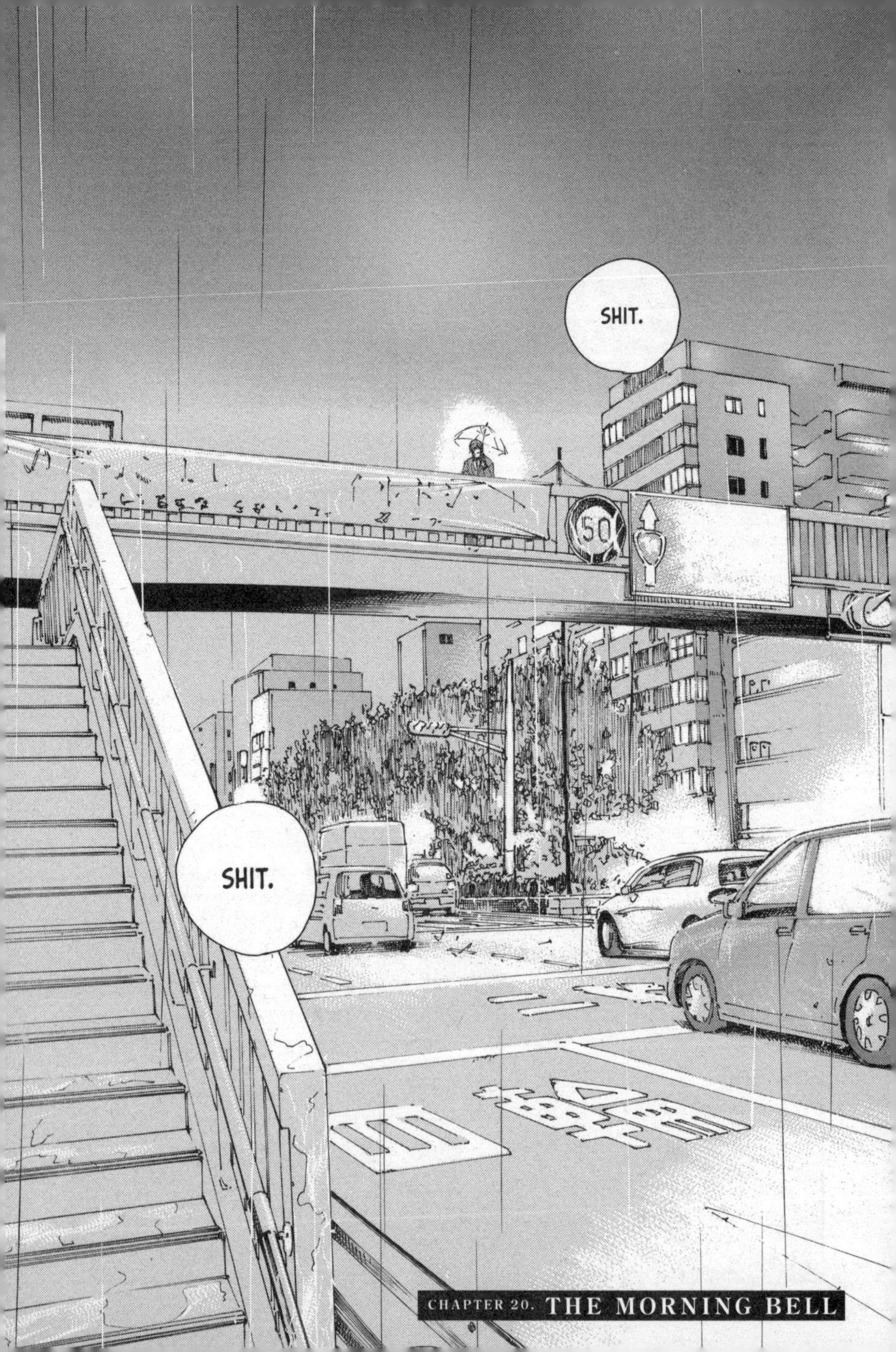
SHIT.
SHIT.

CHAPTER 20. THE MORNING BELL

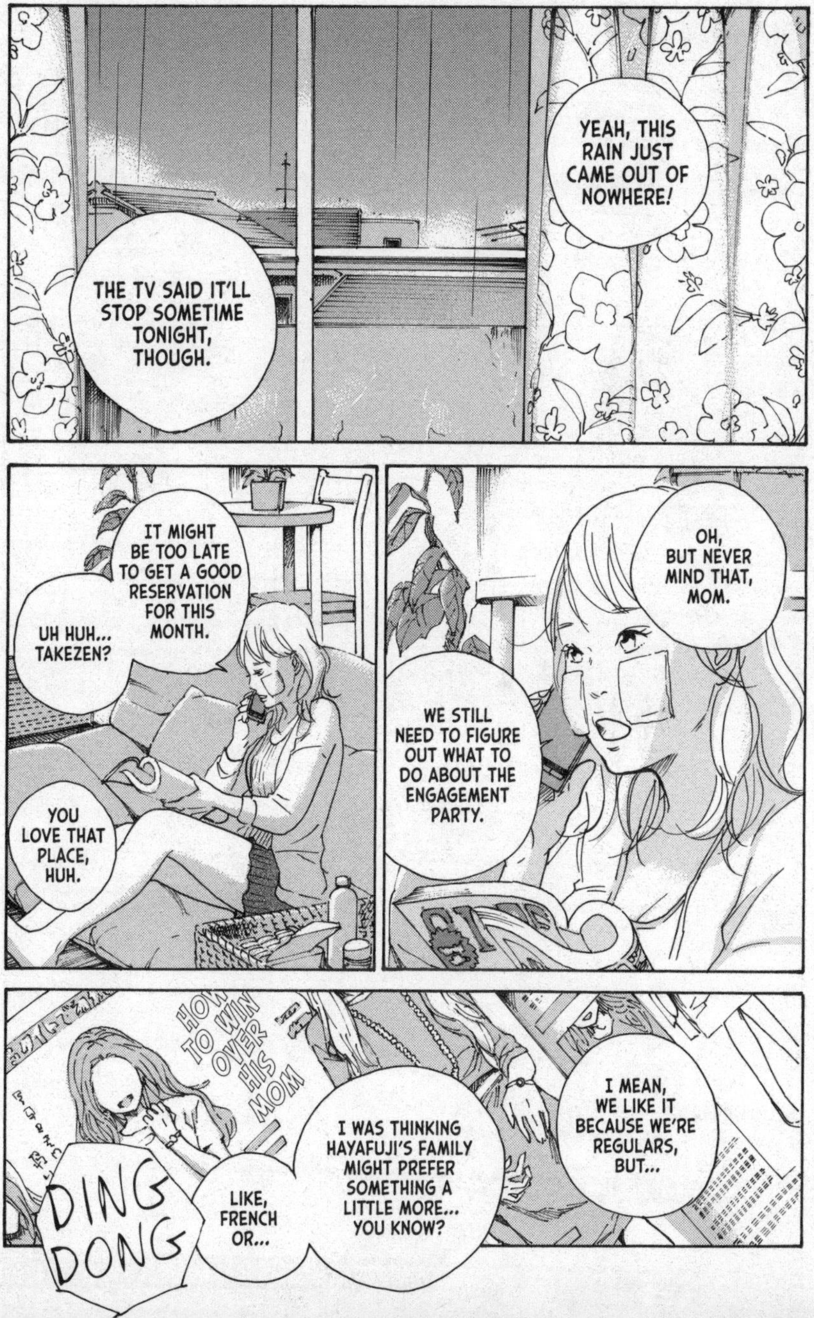
YEAH, THIS RAIN JUST CAME OUT OF NOWHERE!
THE TV SAID IT'LL STOP SOMETIME TONIGHT, THOUGH.
OH, BUT NEVER MIND THAT, MOM.
WE STILL NEED TO FIGURE OUT WHAT TO DO ABOUT THE ENGAGEMENT PARTY.
IT MIGHT BE TOO LATE TO GET A GOOD RESERVATION FOR THIS MONTH.
UH HUH... TAKEZEN?
YOU LOVE THAT PLACE, HUH.
I MEAN, WE LIKE IT BECAUSE WE'RE REGULARS, BUT...
I WAS THINKING HAYAFUJI'S FAMILY MIGHT PREFER SOMETHING A LITTLE MORE... YOU KNOW?
HOW TO WIN OVER HIS MOM
LIKE, FRENCH OR...
DING DONG

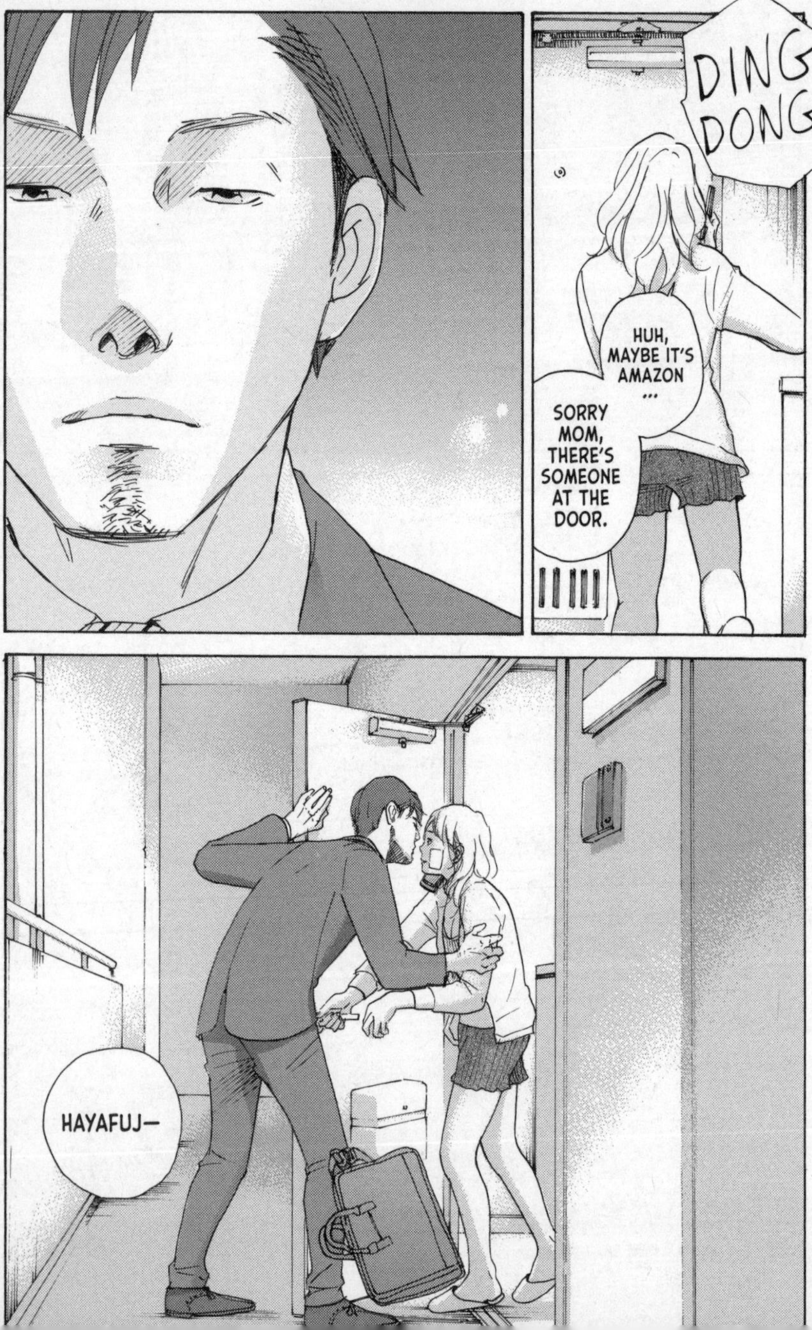
DING DONG
HUH, MAYBE IT'S AMAZON ...
SORRY MOM, THERE'S SOMEONE AT THE DOOR.
HAYAFUJ—

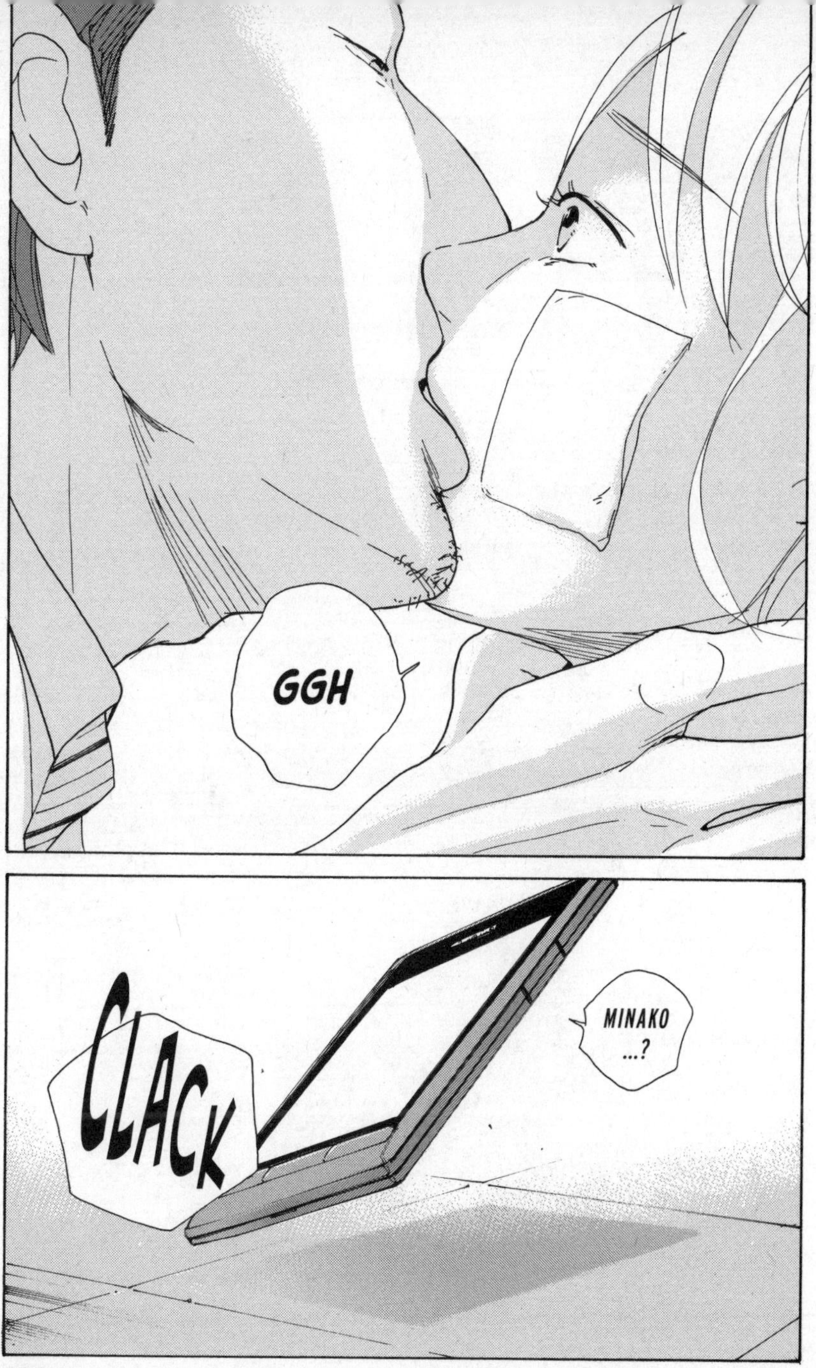
GGH
CLACK
MINAKO ...?

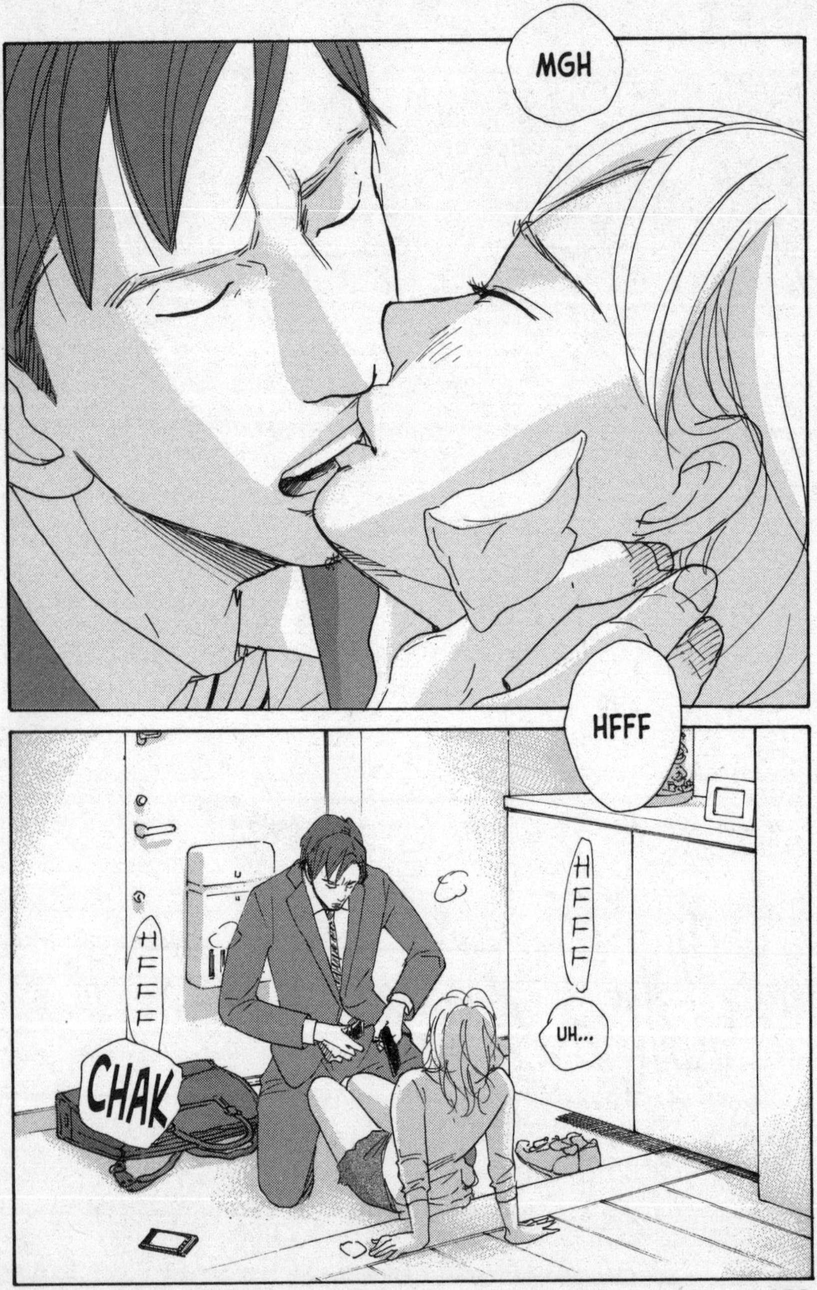
MGH
HFFF
HFFF
UH...
HFFF
CHAK

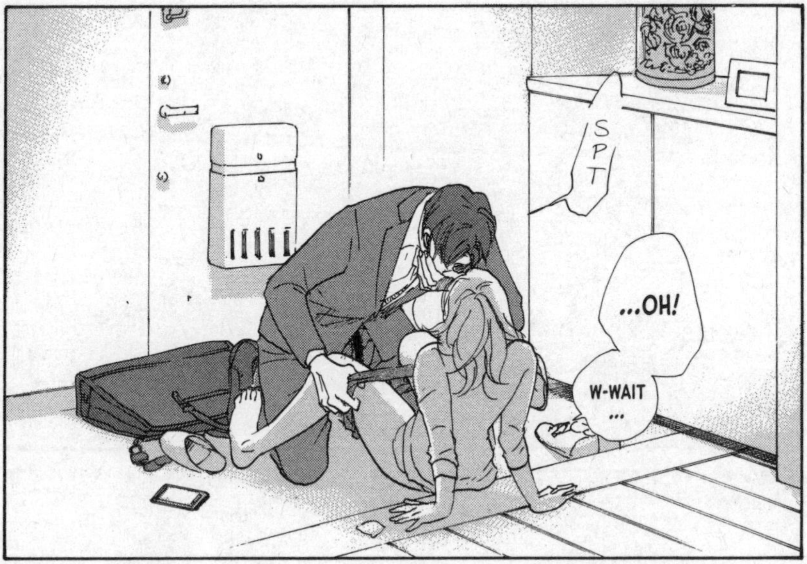
SPT
...OH!
W-WAIT ...

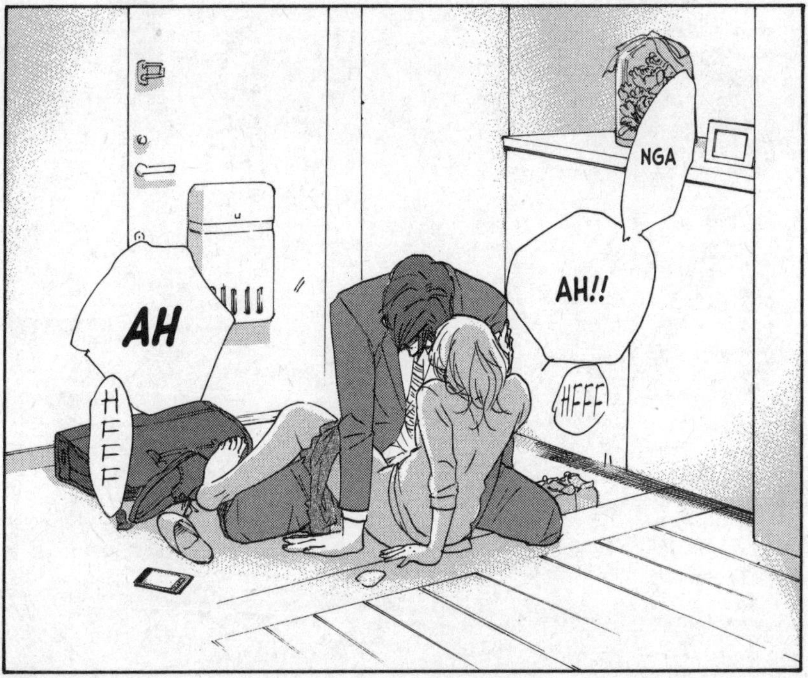
NGA
AH!!
HFFF
AH
HFFF

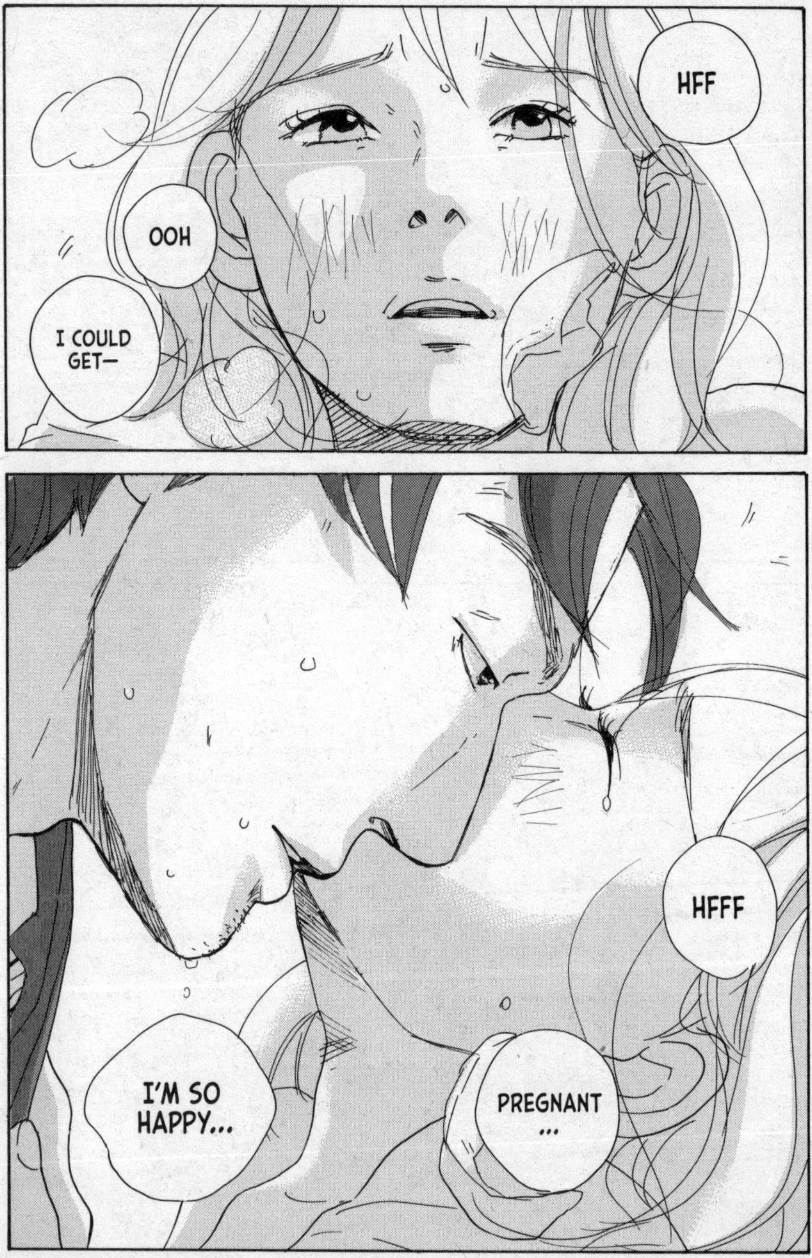
HFF
OOH
I COULD GET—
HFFF
PREGNANT ...
I'M SO HAPPY...

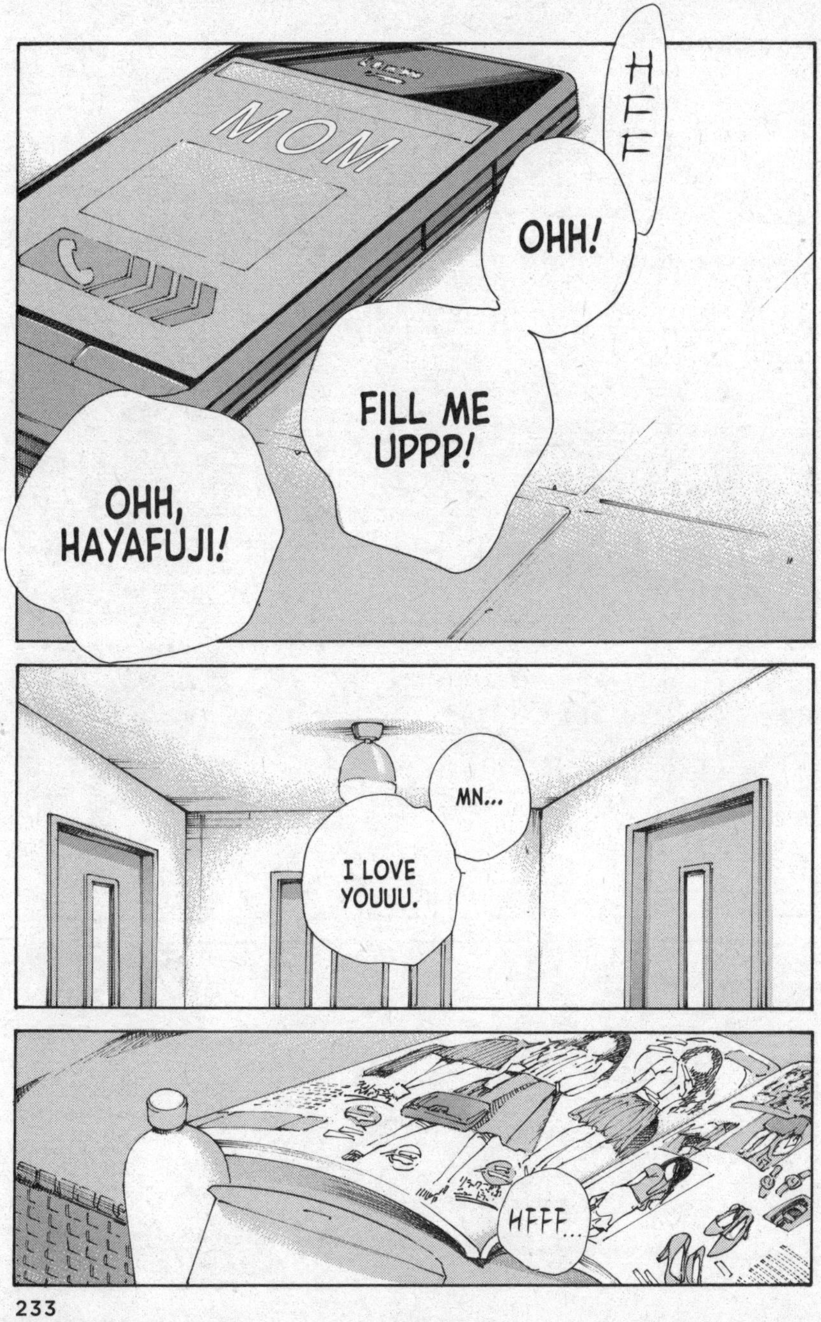
HFF
MOM
OHH!
FILL ME UPPP!
OHH, HAYAFUJI!
MN...
I LOVE YOUUU.
HFFF...

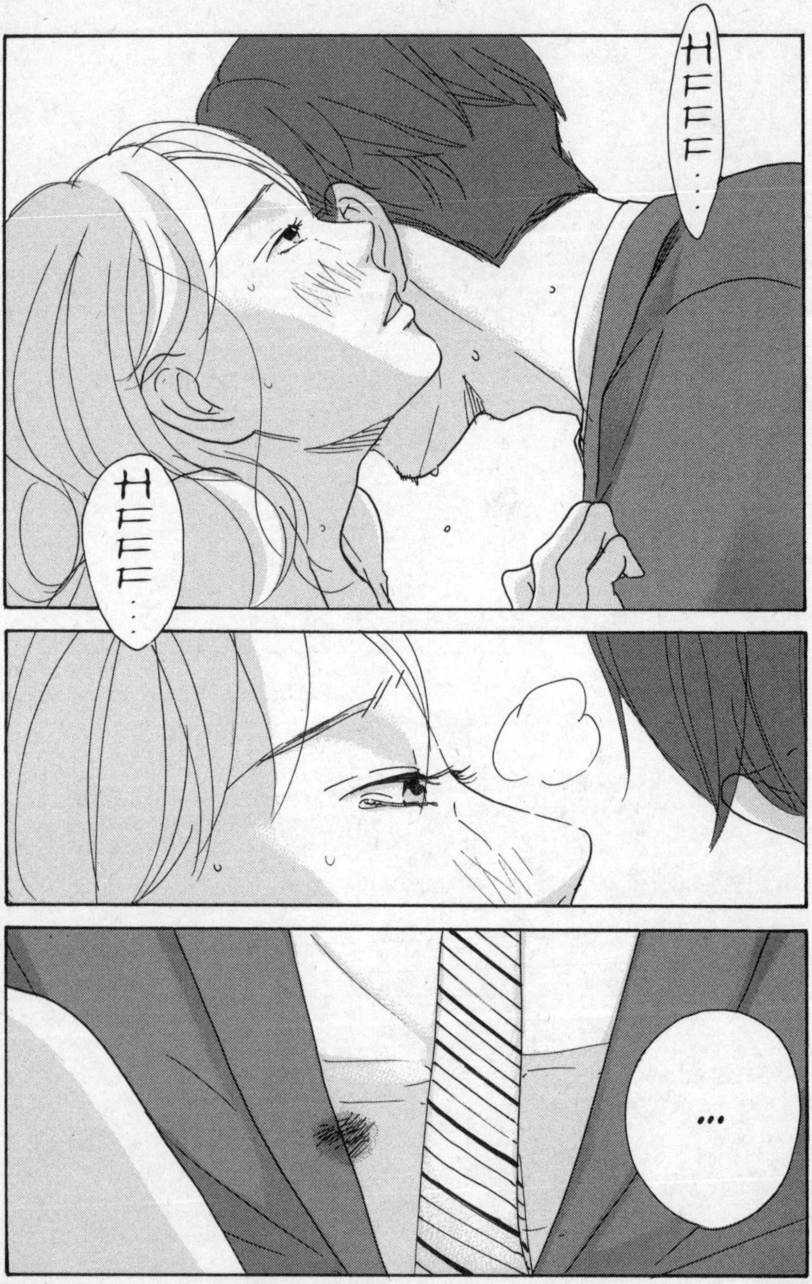
HFFF...
HFFF...
...

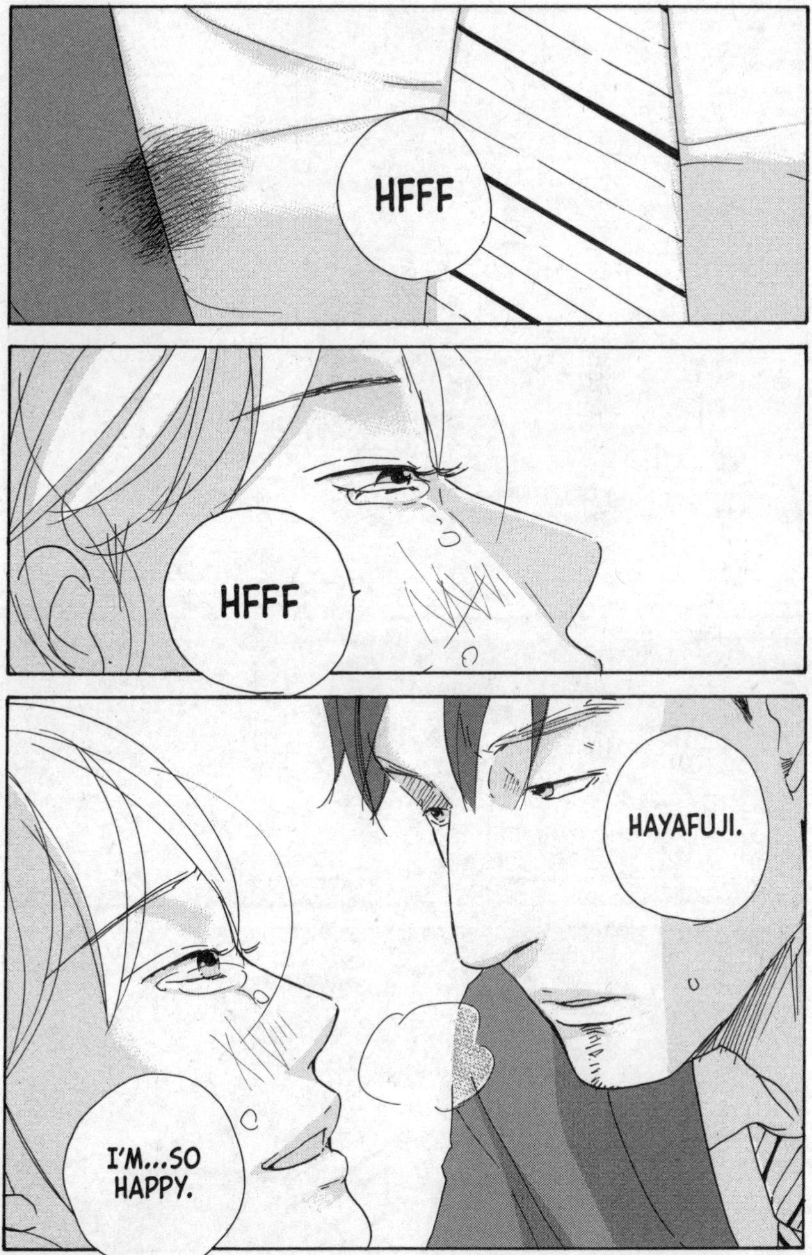
HFFF
HFFF
HAYAFUJI.
I'M...SO HAPPY.

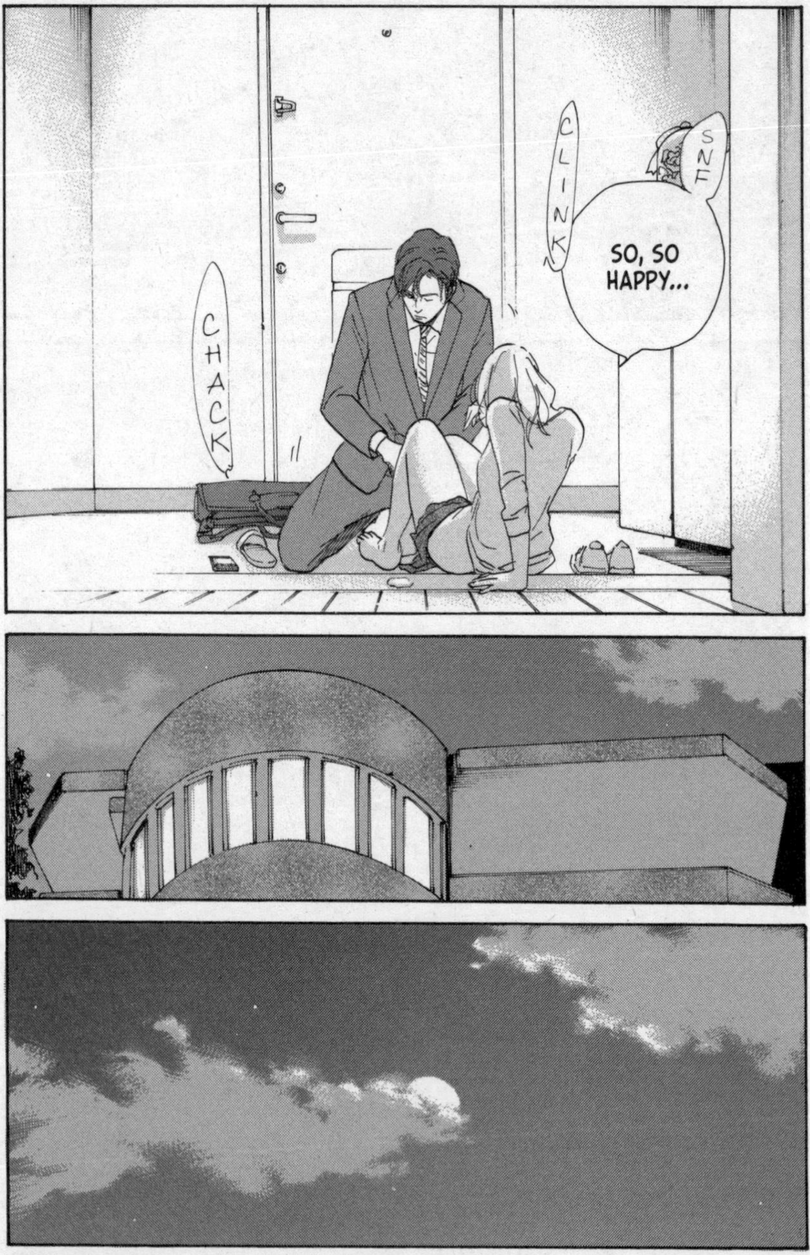
SNF
SO, SO HAPPY...
CLINK
CHACK

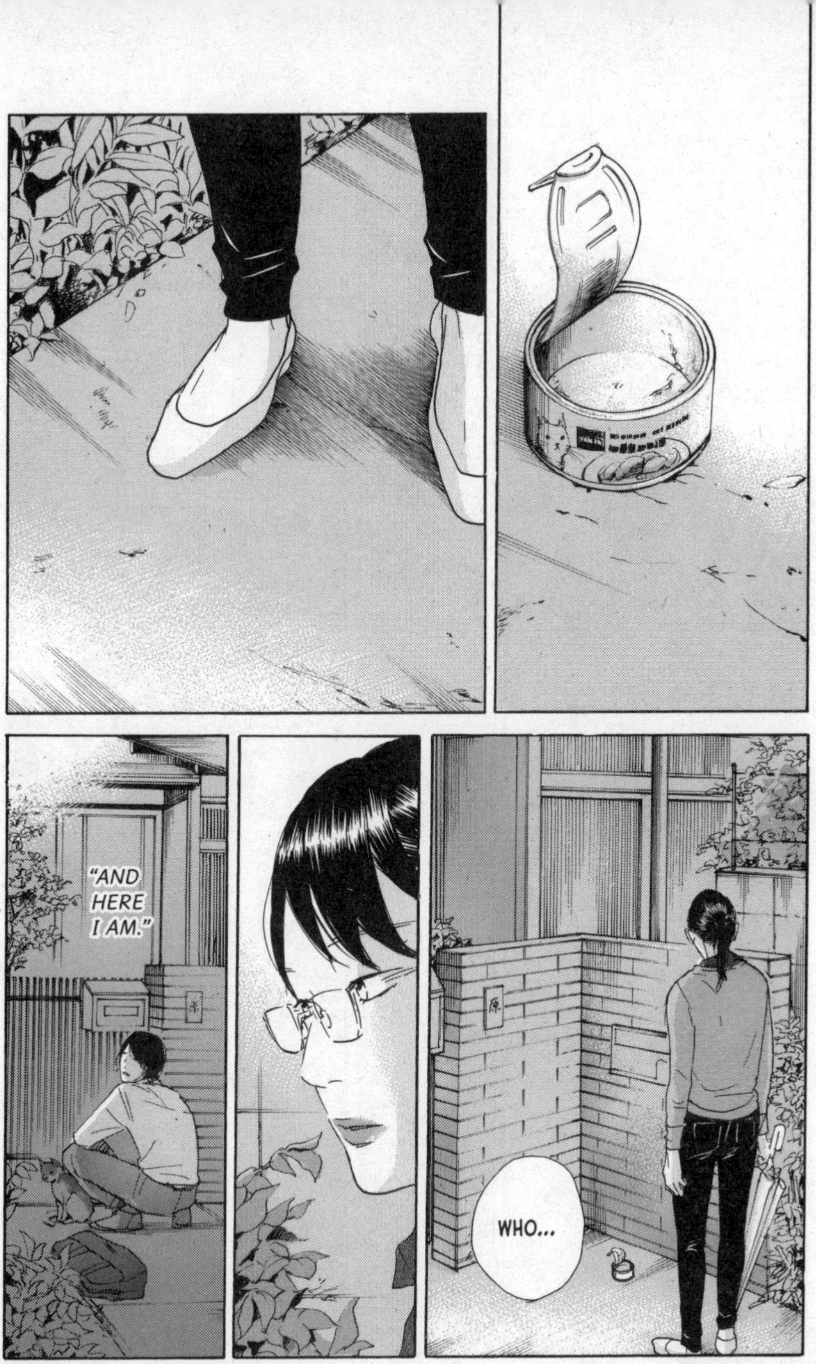
WHO...
"AND HERE I AM."

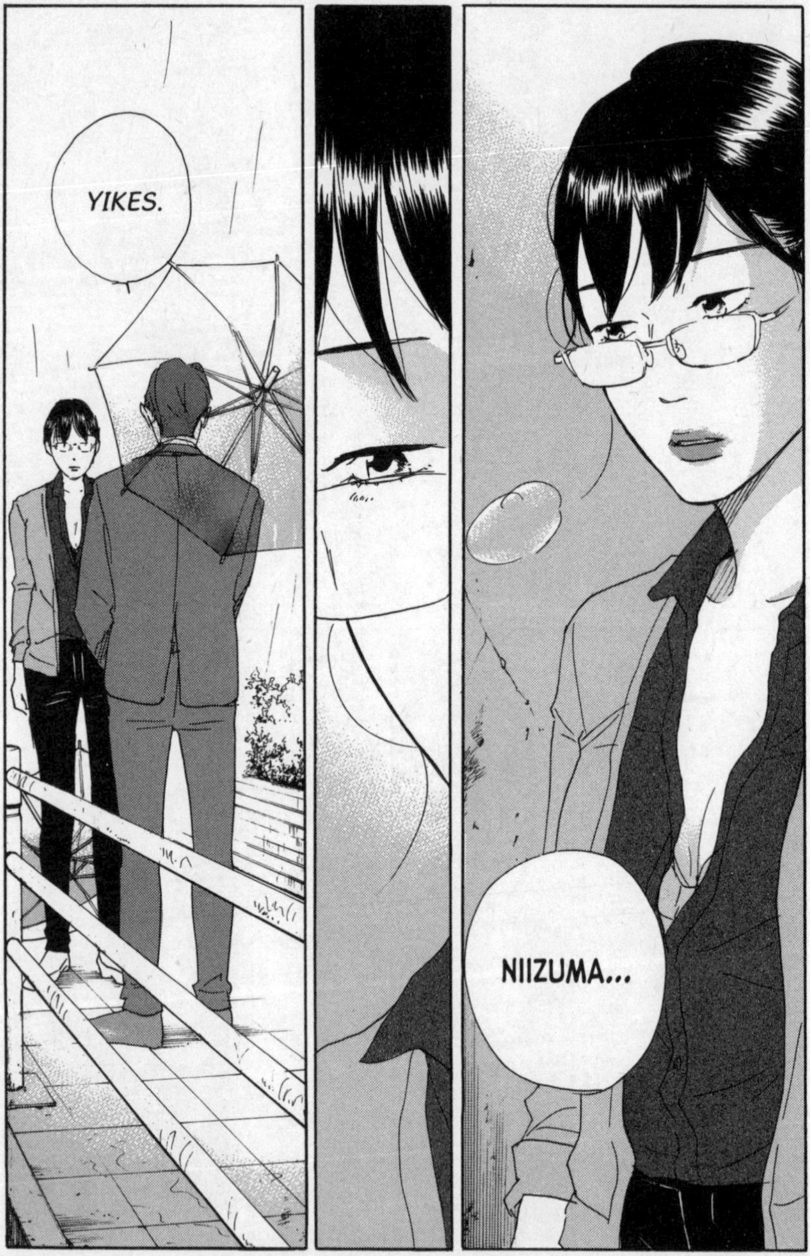
NIIZUMA...
YIKES.

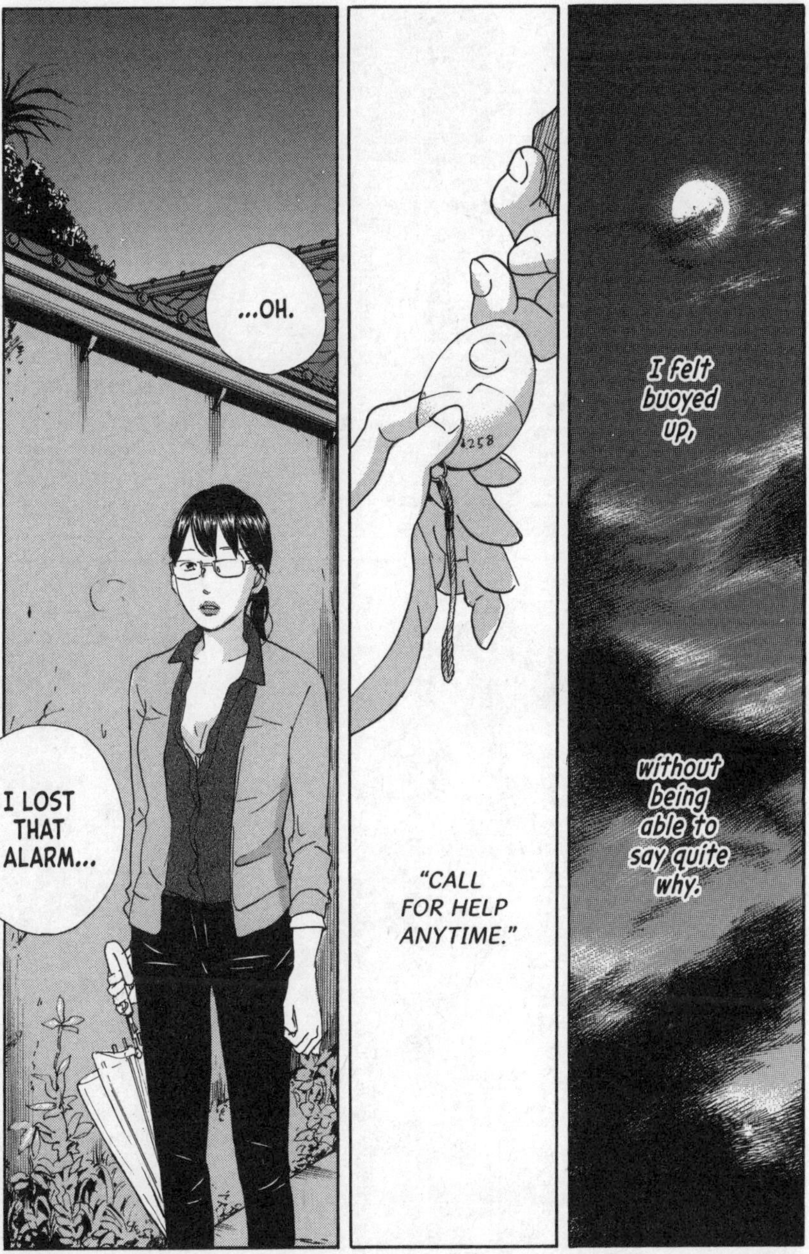
I felt buoyed up,
without being able to say quite why.
"CALL FOR HELP ANYTIME."
...OH.
I LOST THAT ALARM...

And

I may have lost his voice, too.

SO, YOU WENT AND MADE GYOZA WITH NIIZUMA'S MOM,

SINCE HE'S GONE INTO RECLUSE MODE?

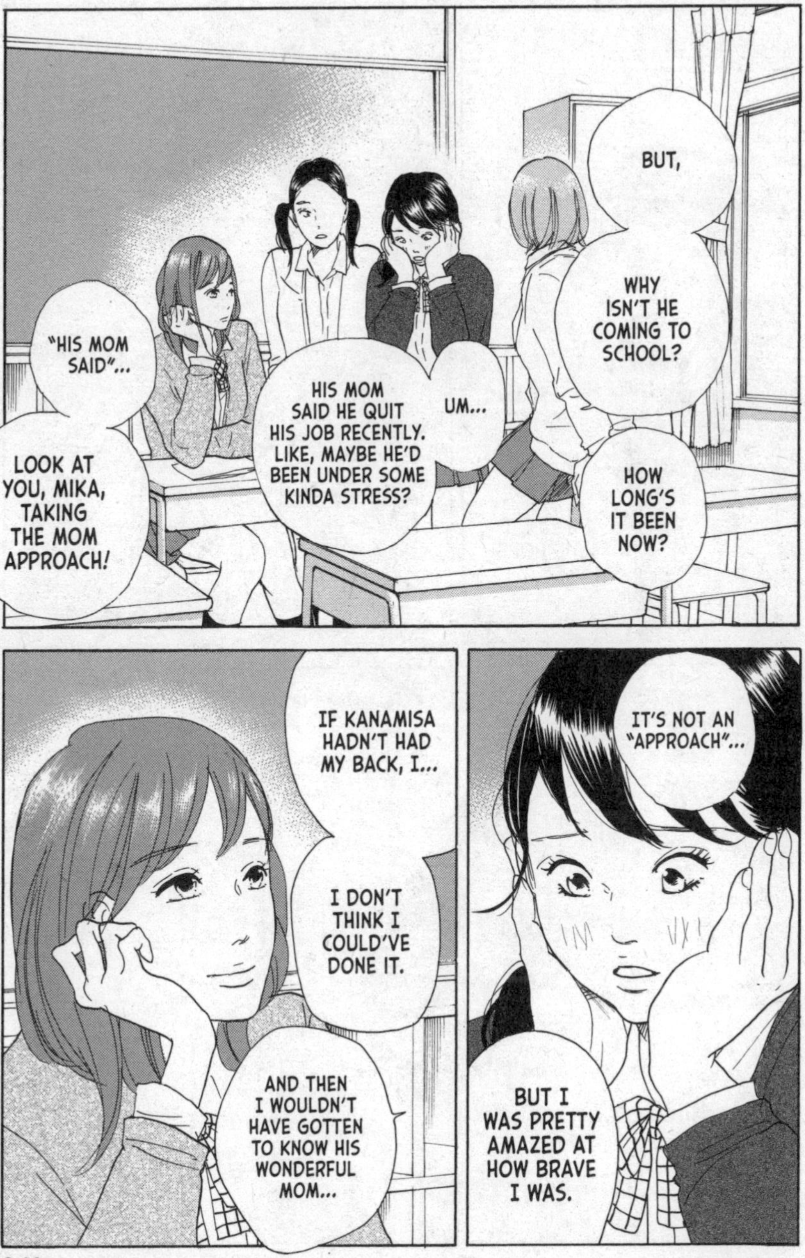
BUT,
WHY ISN'T HE COMING TO SCHOOL?
HOW LONG'S IT BEEN NOW?
UM...
HIS MOM SAID HE QUIT HIS JOB RECENTLY. LIKE, MAYBE HE'D BEEN UNDER SOME KINDA STRESS?
"HIS MOM SAID"...
LOOK AT YOU, MIKA, TAKING THE MOM APPROACH!
IT'S NOT AN "APPROACH"...
BUT I WAS PRETTY AMAZED AT HOW BRAVE I WAS.
IF KANAMISA HADN'T HAD MY BACK, I...
I DON'T THINK I COULD'VE DONE IT.
AND THEN I WOULDN'T HAVE GOTTEN TO KNOW HIS WONDERFUL MOM...

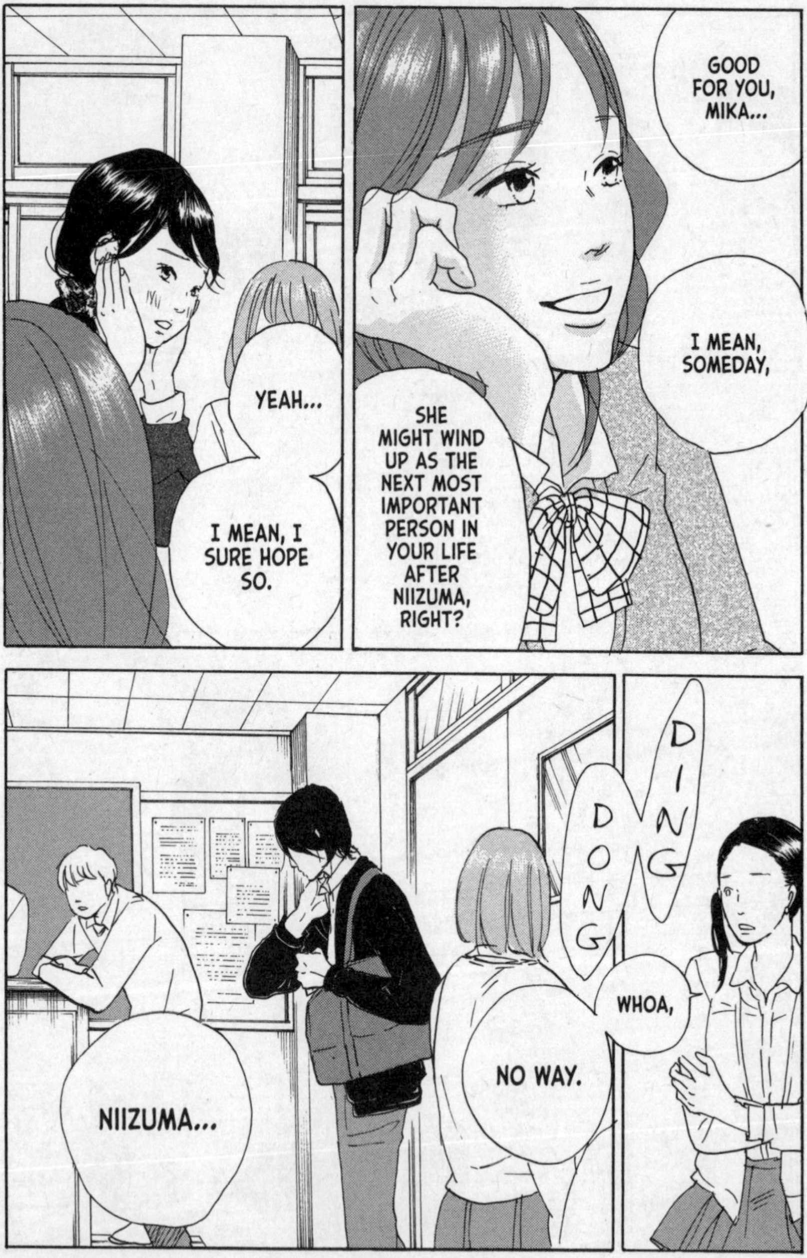
GOOD FOR YOU, MIKA...
I MEAN, SOMEDAY,
SHE MIGHT WIND UP AS THE NEXT MOST IMPORTANT PERSON IN YOUR LIFE AFTER NIIZUMA, RIGHT?
YEAH...
I MEAN, I SURE HOPE SO.
DING
DONG
WHOA,
NO WAY.
NIIZUMA...

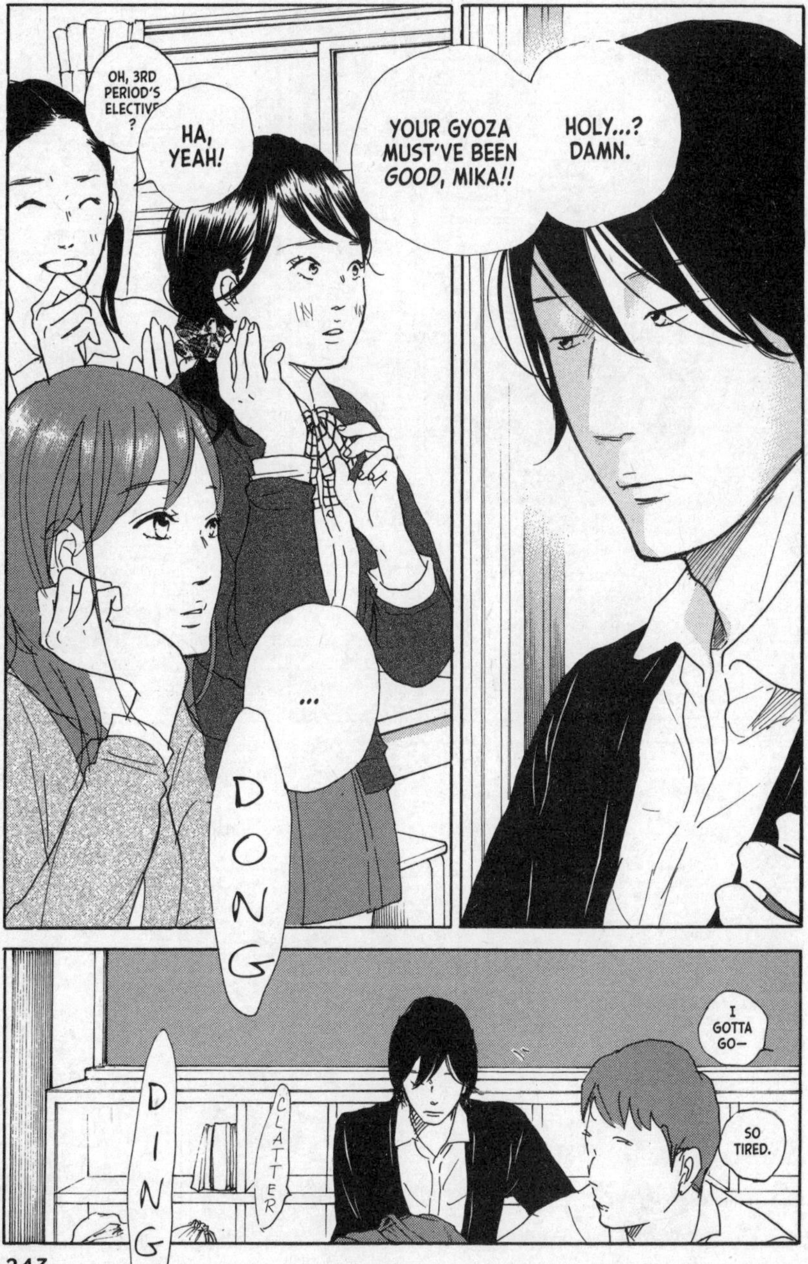
HOLY...? DAMN.
YOUR GYOZA MUST'VE BEEN GOOD, MIKA!!
OH, 3RD PERIOD'S ELECTIVE?
HA, YEAH!
...
DONG
I GOTTA GO—
SO TIRED.
CLATTER
DING

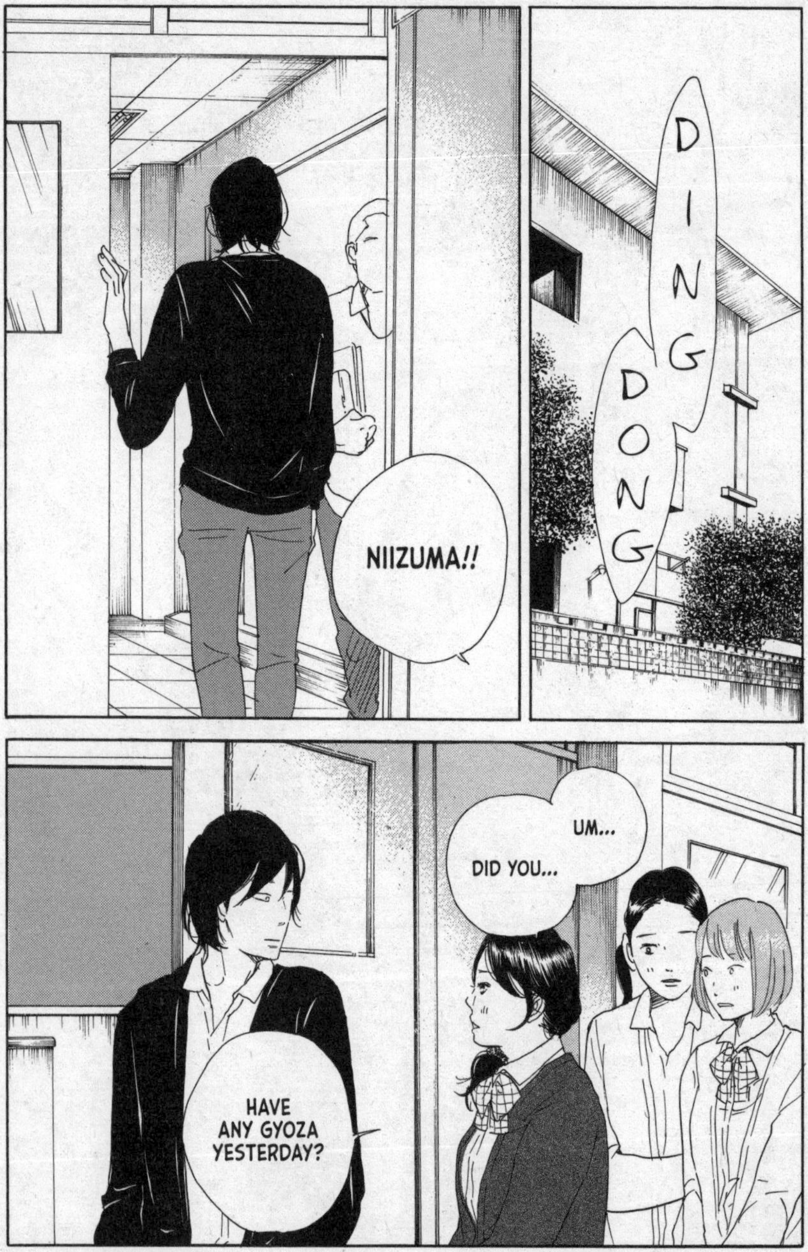
DING DONG
NIIZUMA!!
UM... DID YOU...
HAVE ANY GYOZA YESTERDAY?

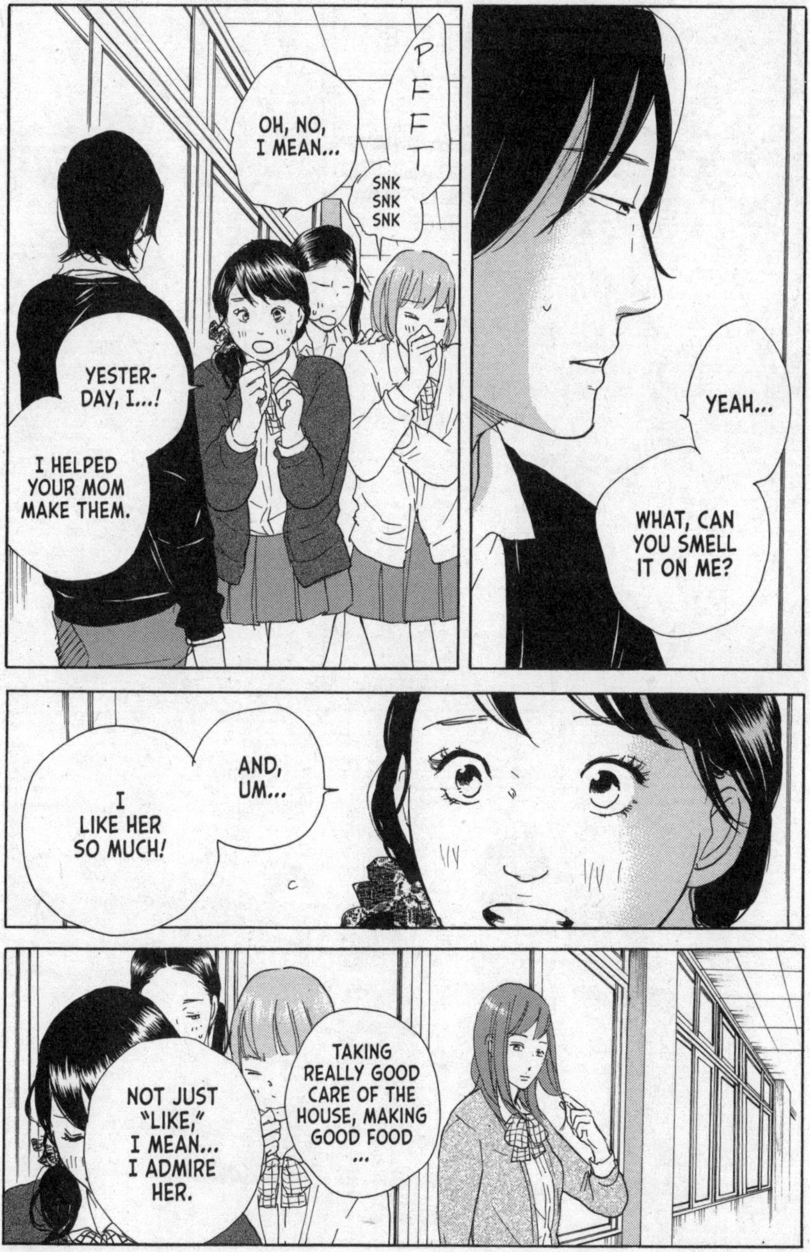
YEAH...
WHAT, CAN YOU SMELL IT ON ME?
PFFT
OH, NO, I MEAN...
SNK SNK SNK
YESTER-DAY, I...!
I HELPED YOUR MOM MAKE THEM.
AND, UM...
I LIKE HER SO MUCH!
TAKING REALLY GOOD CARE OF THE HOUSE, MAKING GOOD FOOD ...
NOT JUST "LIKE," I MEAN... I ADMIRE HER.

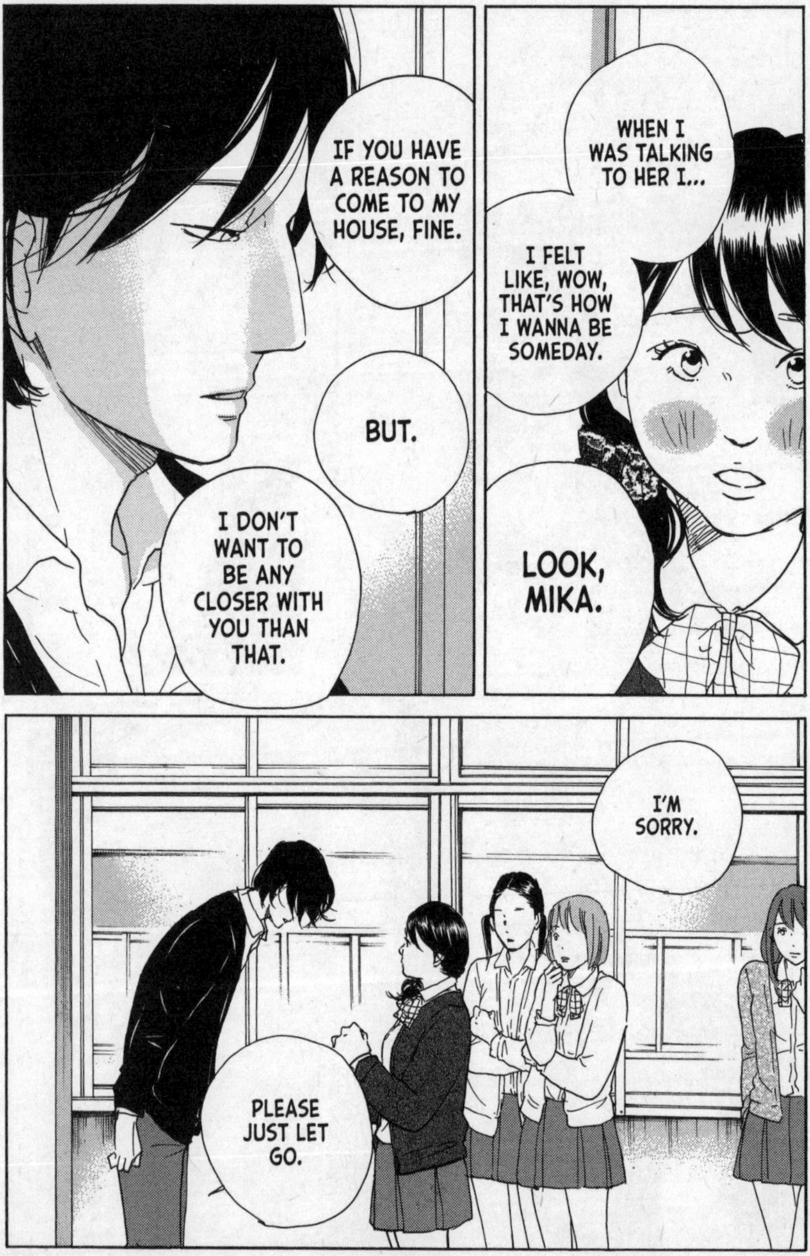
WHEN I WAS TALKING TO HER I...
I FELT LIKE, WOW, THAT'S HOW I WANNA BE SOMEDAY.
LOOK, MIKA.
IF YOU HAVE A REASON TO COME TO MY HOUSE, FINE.
BUT.
I DON'T WANT TO BE ANY CLOSER WITH YOU THAN THAT.
I'M SORRY.
PLEASE JUST LET GO.

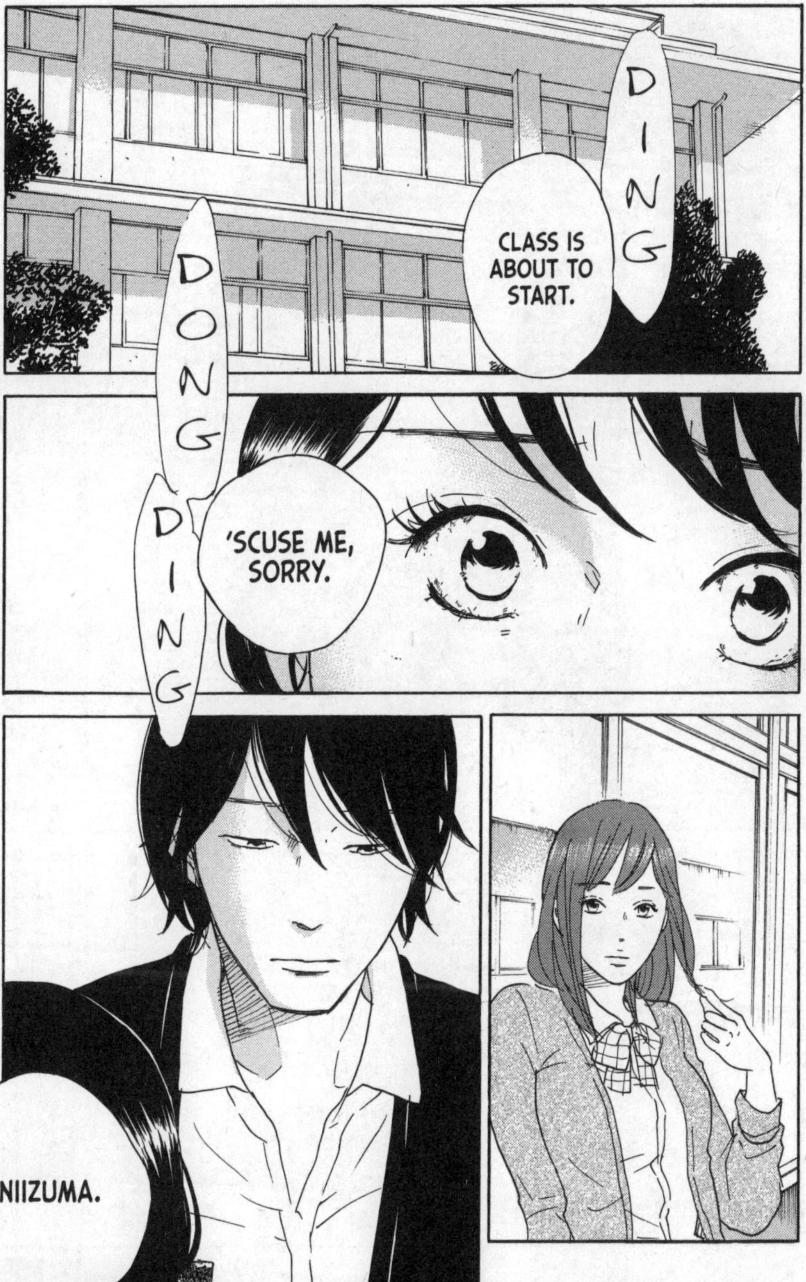
DING
CLASS IS ABOUT TO START.
DONG
'SCUSE ME, SORRY.
DING
NIIZUMA.

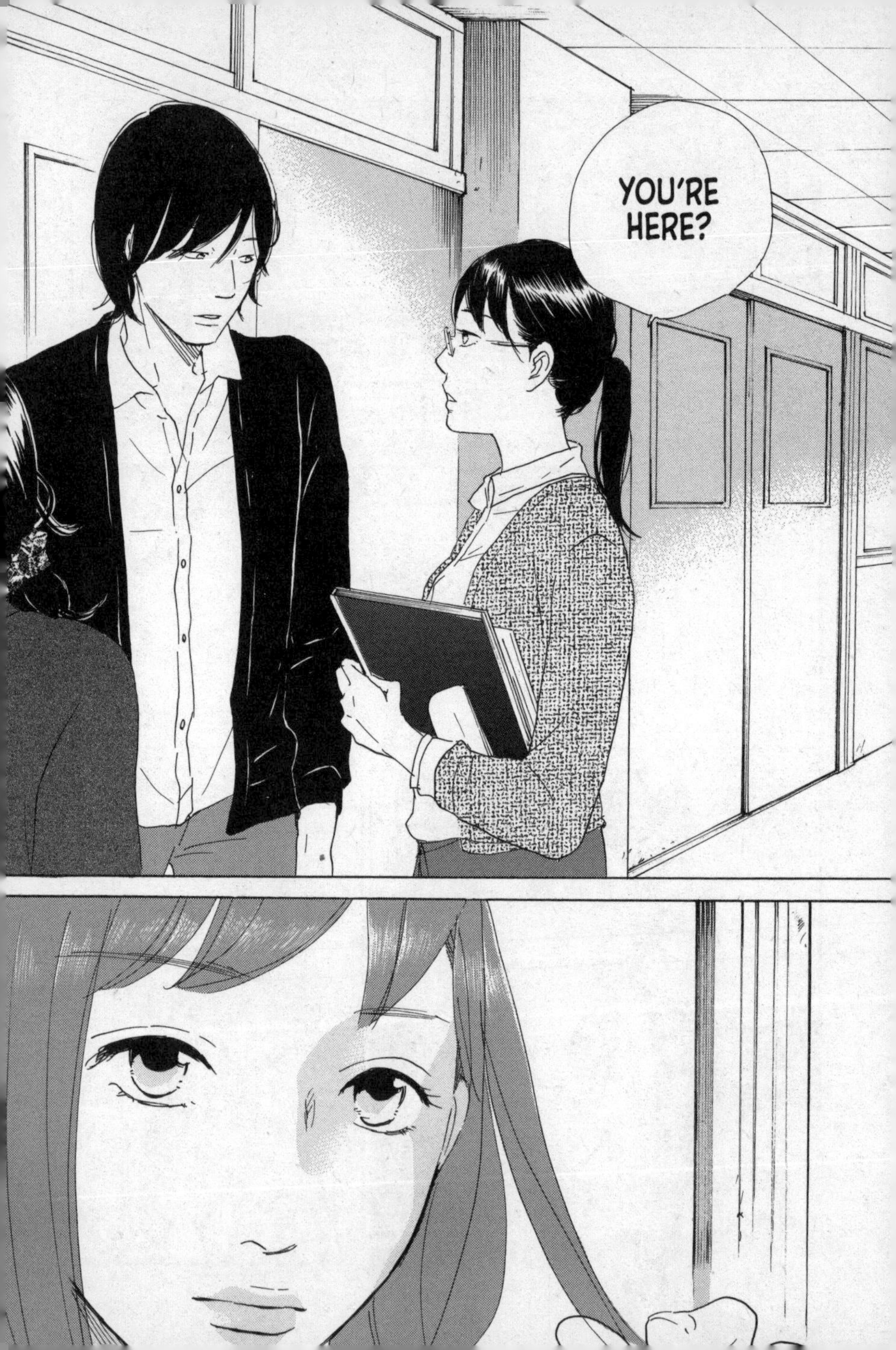
YOU'RE HERE?

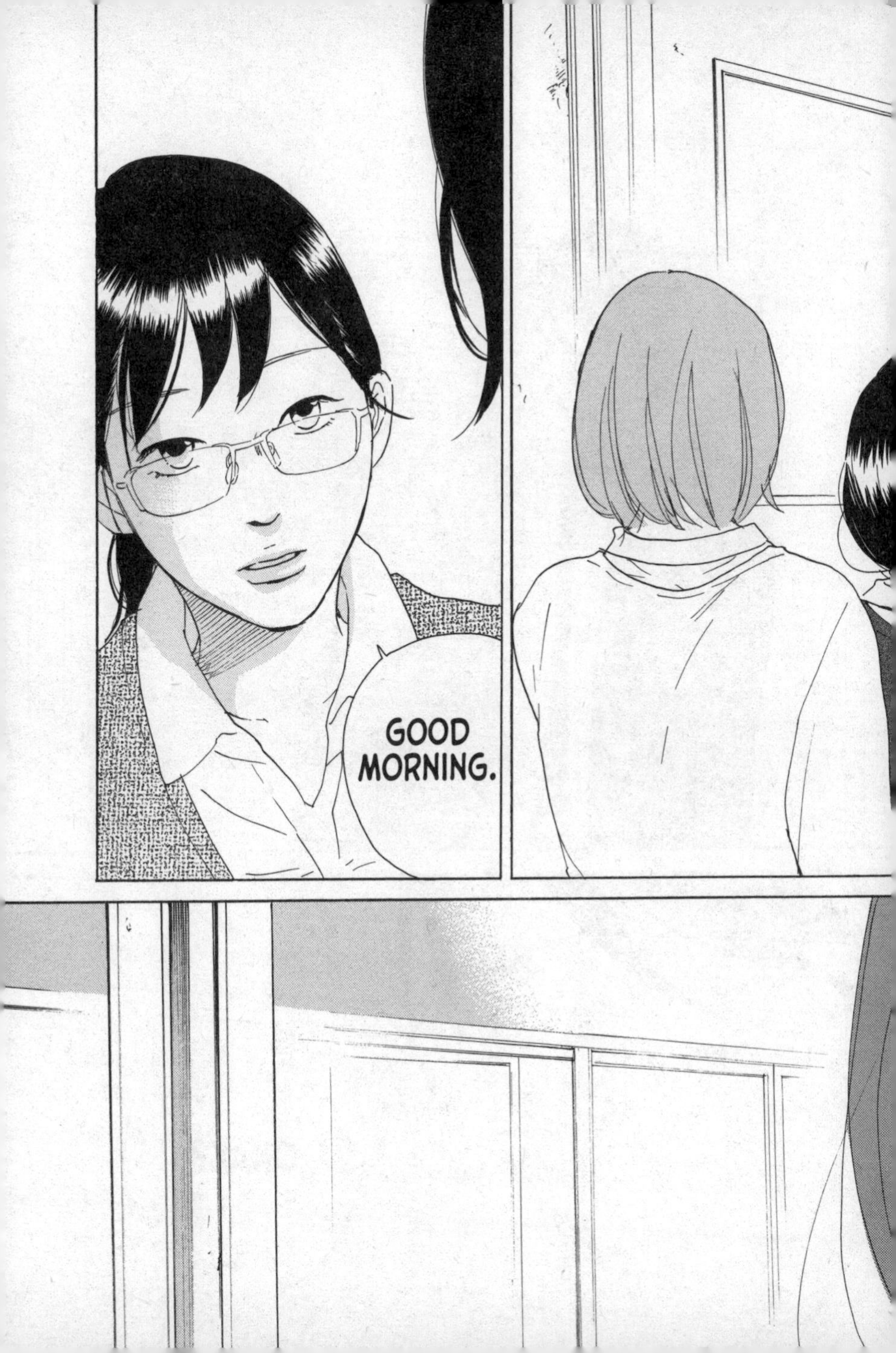
GOOD MORNING.

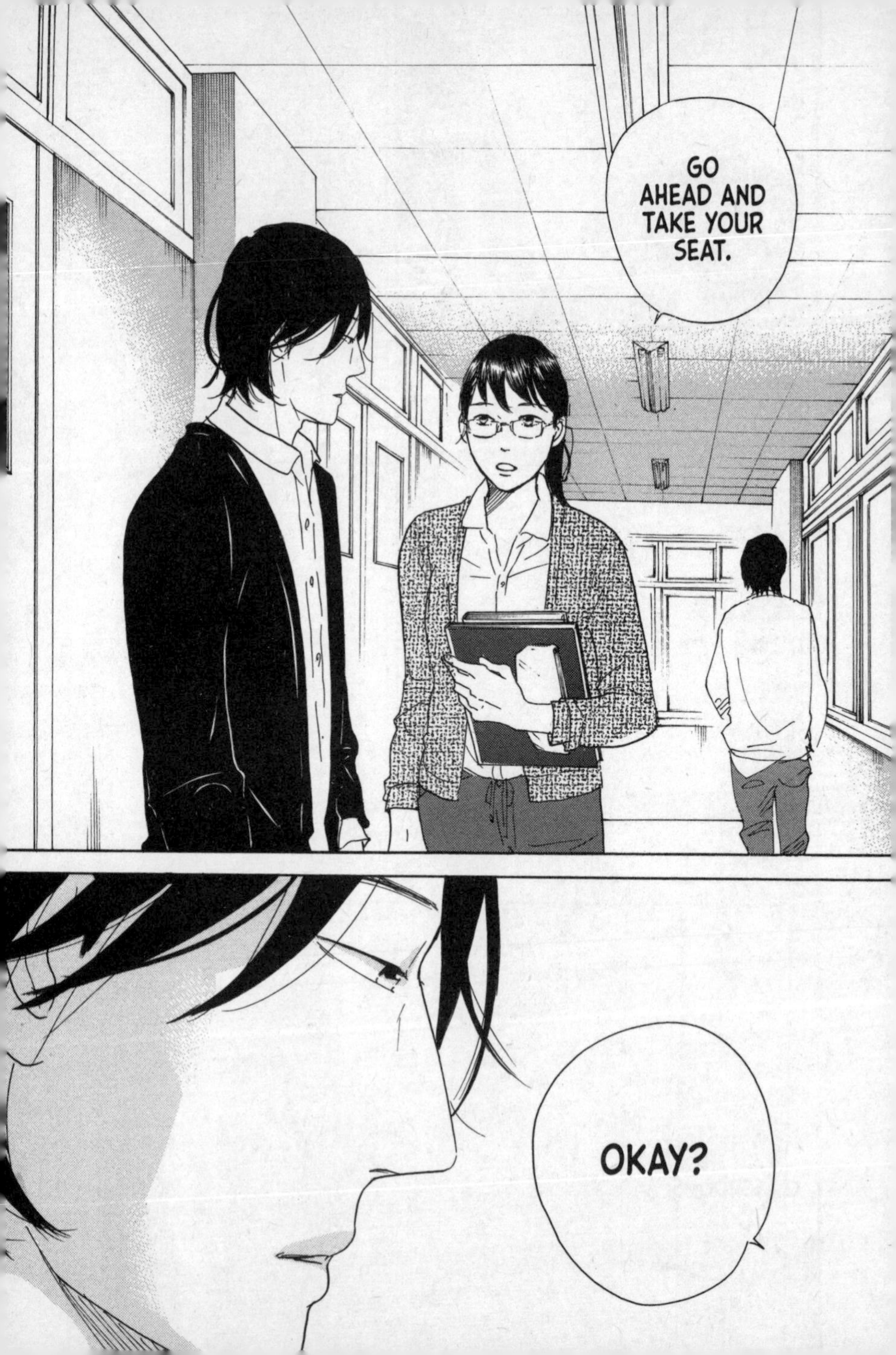
GO AHEAD AND TAKE YOUR SEAT.
OKAY?

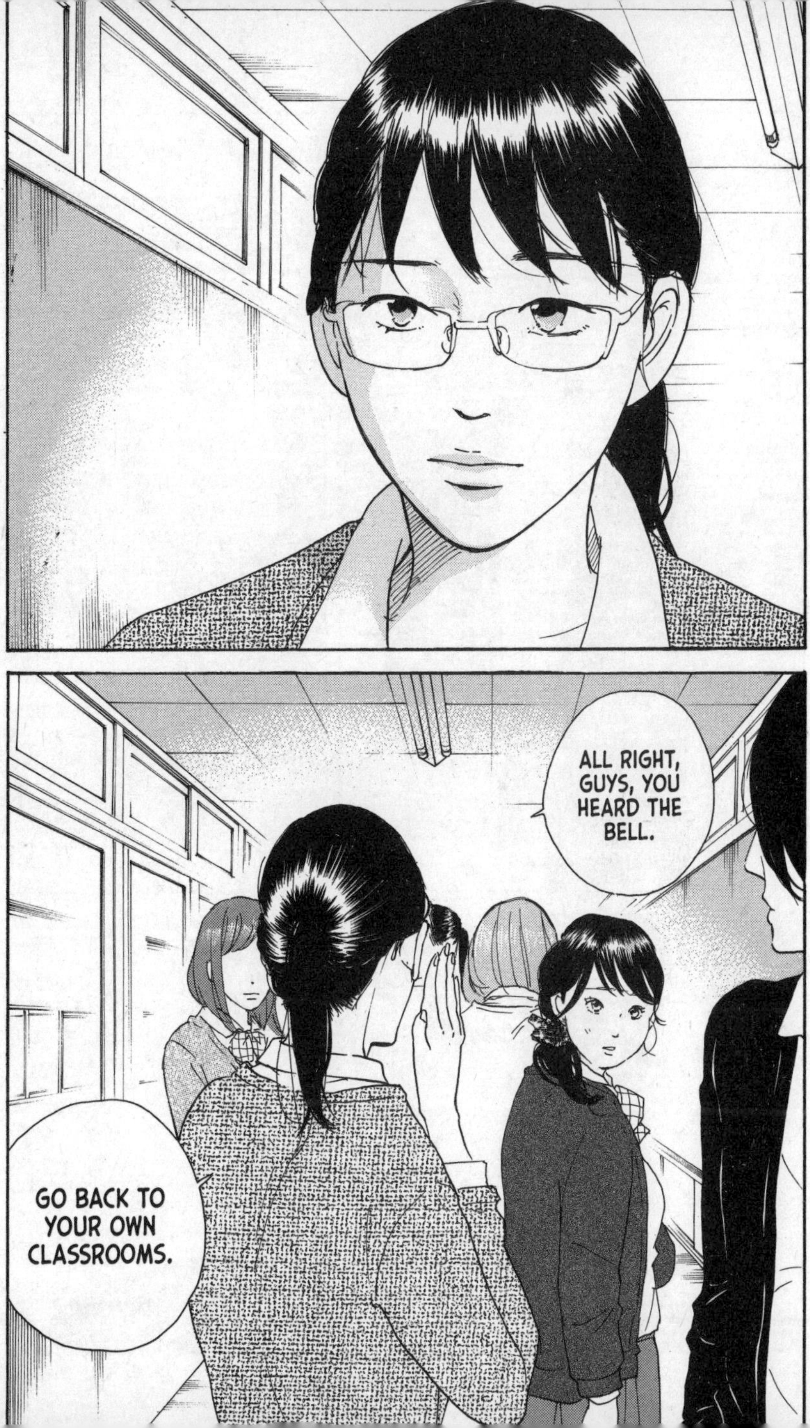
ALL RIGHT, GUYS, YOU HEARD THE BELL.
GO BACK TO YOUR OWN CLASSROOMS.

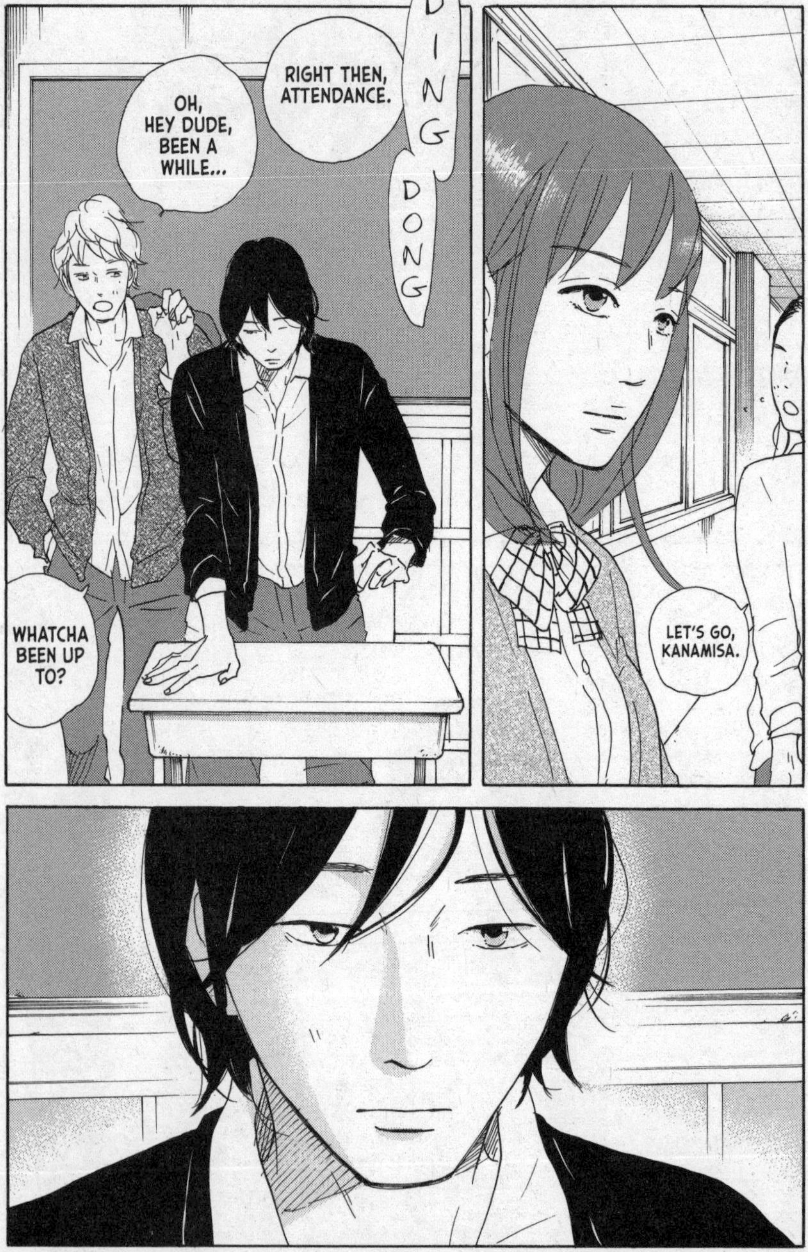
LET'S GO, KANAMISA.
DING DONG
RIGHT THEN, ATTENDANCE.
OH, HEY DUDE, BEEN A WHILE...
WHATCHA BEEN UP TO?

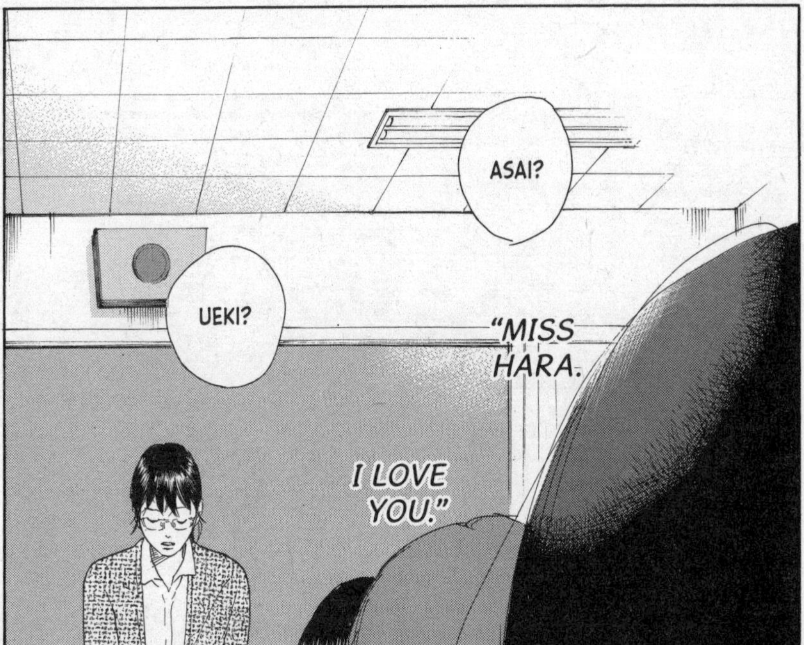
ASAI?
UEKI?
"MISS HARA.
I LOVE YOU."

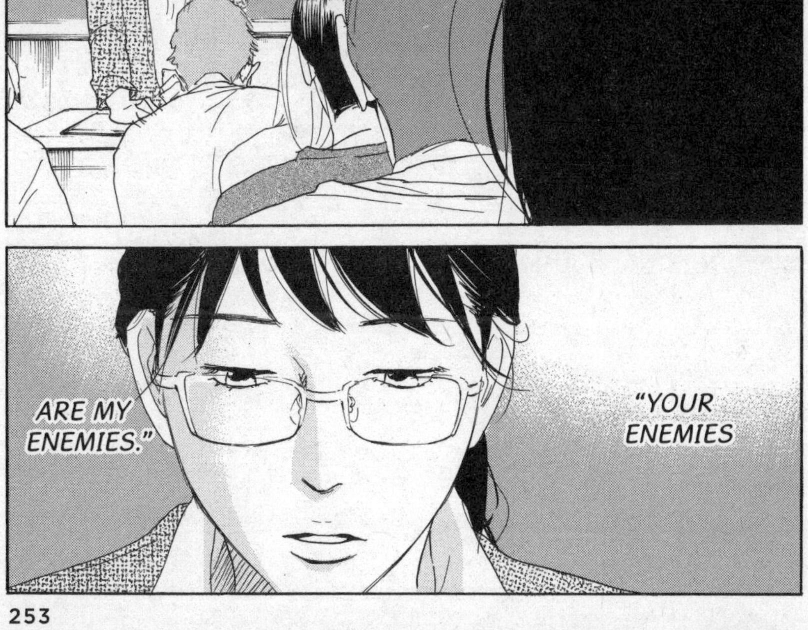
"YOUR ENEMIES
ARE MY ENEMIES."

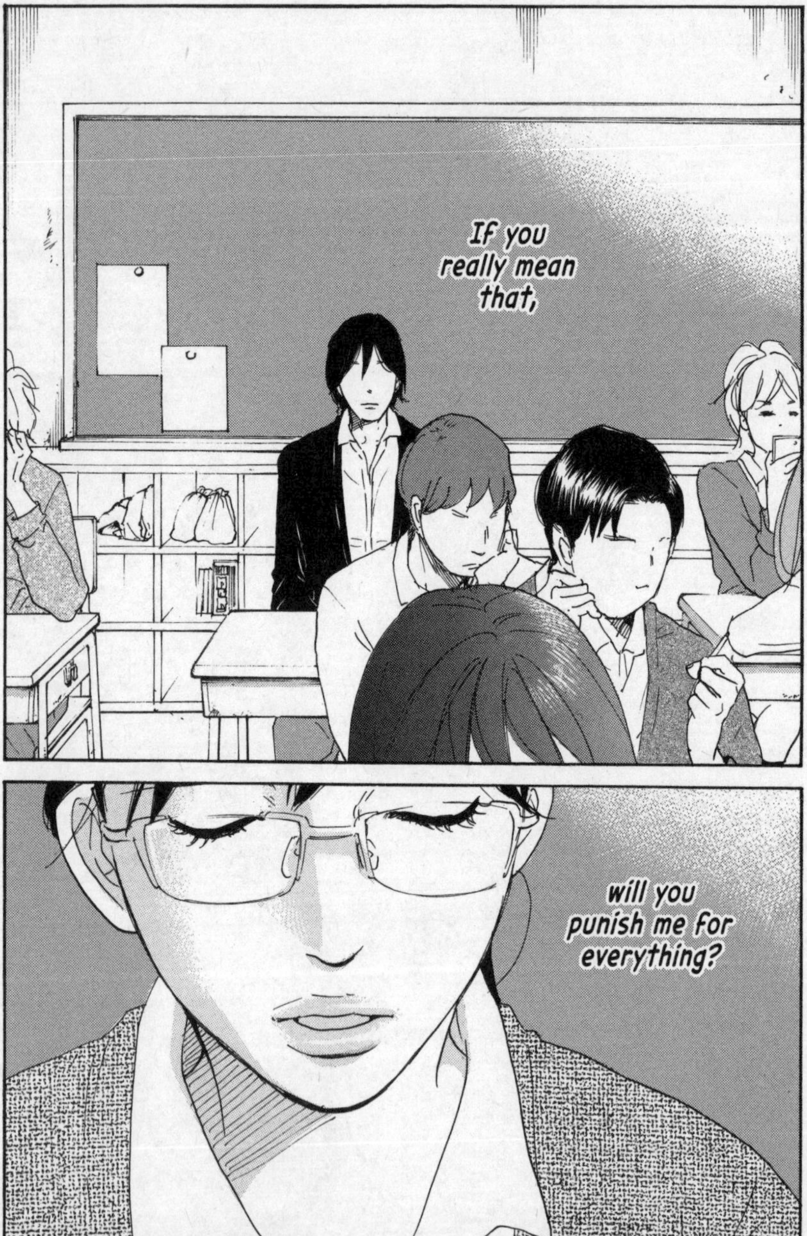
If you really mean that,
will you punish me for everything?
END

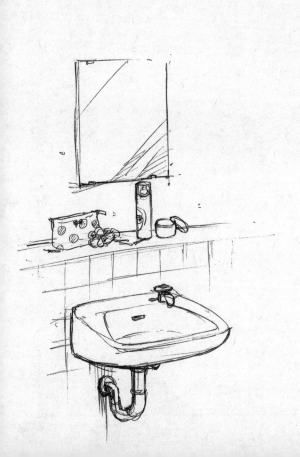

CHAPTER 21. WE CAN STILL WORK IT OUT

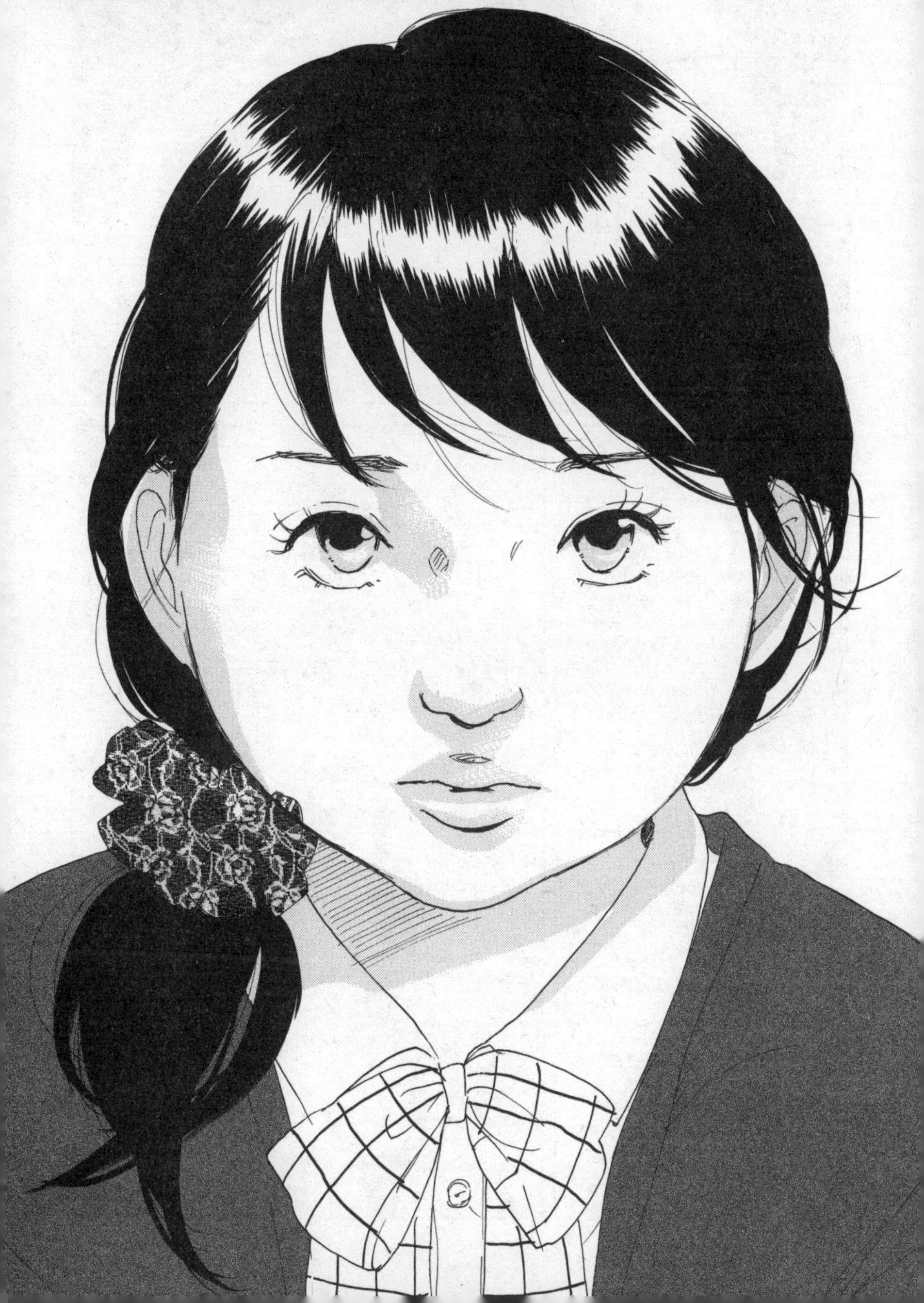

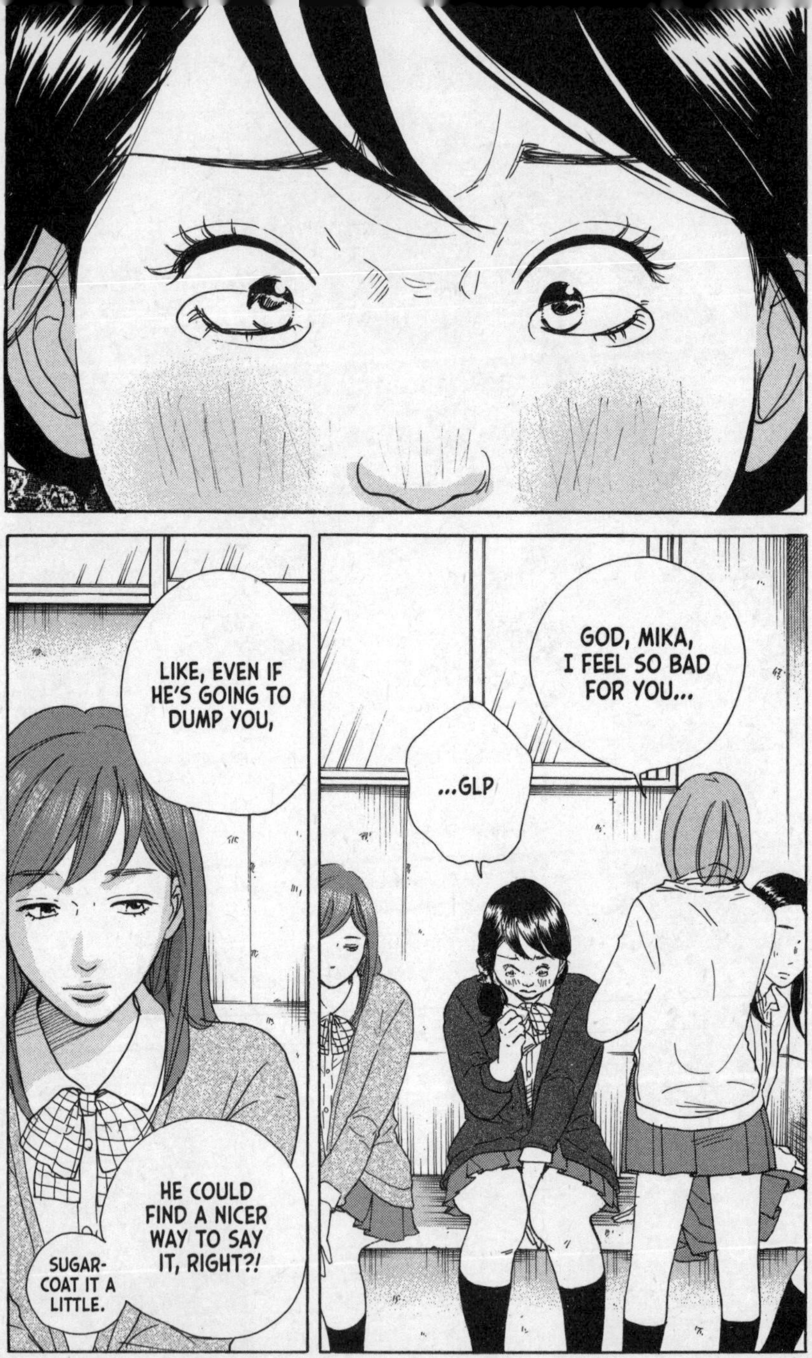
GOD, MIKA, I FEEL SO BAD FOR YOU...
...GLP
LIKE, EVEN IF HE'S GOING TO DUMP YOU,
HE COULD FIND A NICER WAY TO SAY IT, RIGHT?!
SUGAR-COAT IT A LITTLE.

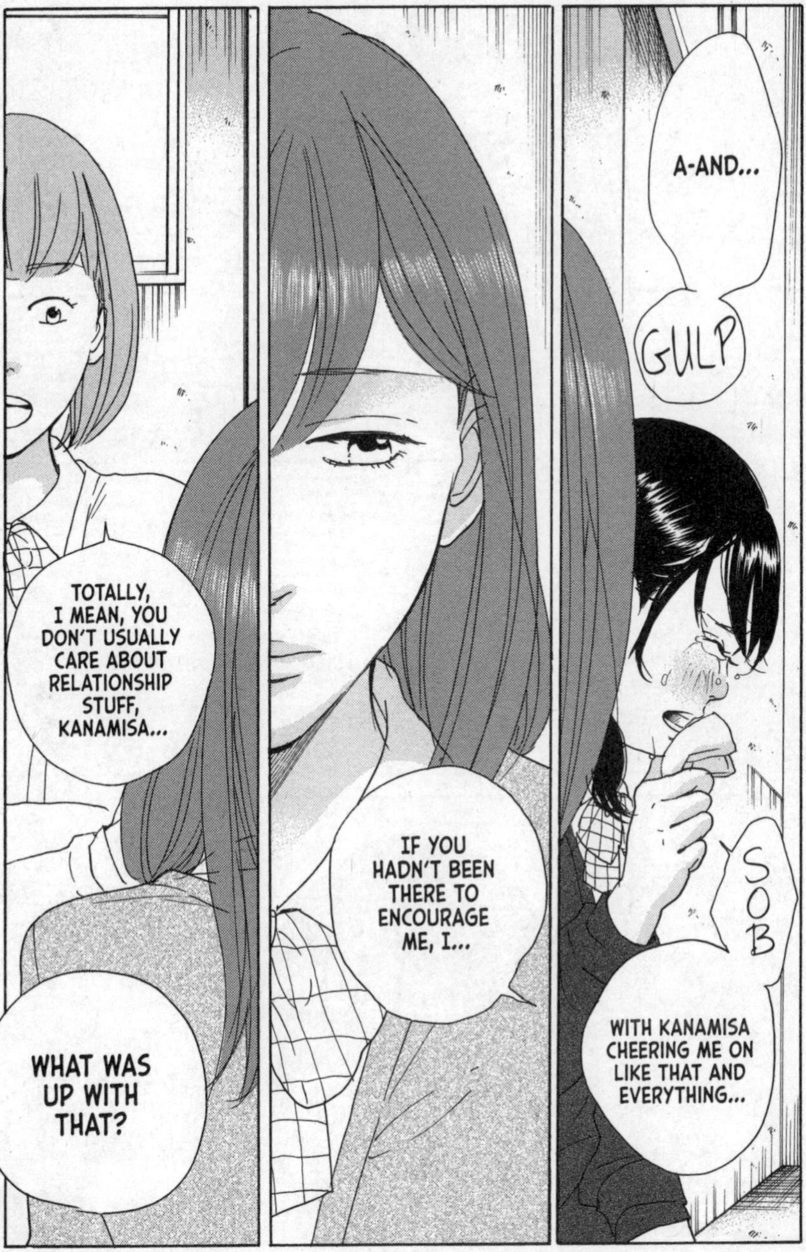
A-AND...
GULP
SOB
WITH KANAMISA CHEERING ME ON LIKE THAT AND EVERYTHING...
IF YOU HADN'T BEEN THERE TO ENCOURAGE ME, I...
TOTALLY, I MEAN, YOU DON'T USUALLY CARE ABOUT RELATIONSHIP STUFF, KANAMISA...
WHAT WAS UP WITH THAT?

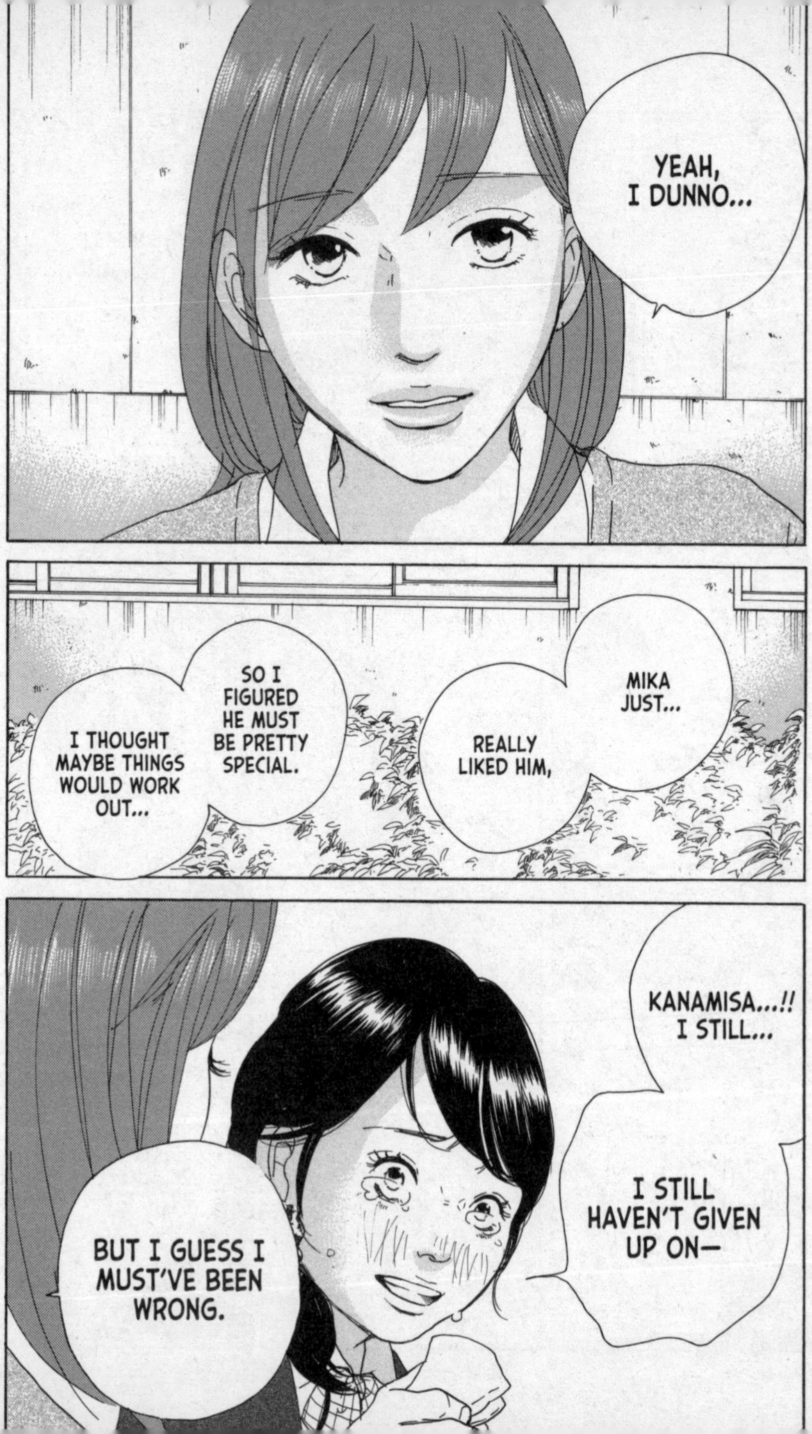
YEAH, I DUNNO...
MIKA JUST...
REALLY LIKED HIM,
SO I FIGURED HE MUST BE PRETTY SPECIAL.
I THOUGHT MAYBE THINGS WOULD WORK OUT...
KANAMISA...!! I STILL...
I STILL HAVEN'T GIVEN UP ON—
BUT I GUESS I MUST'VE BEEN WRONG.

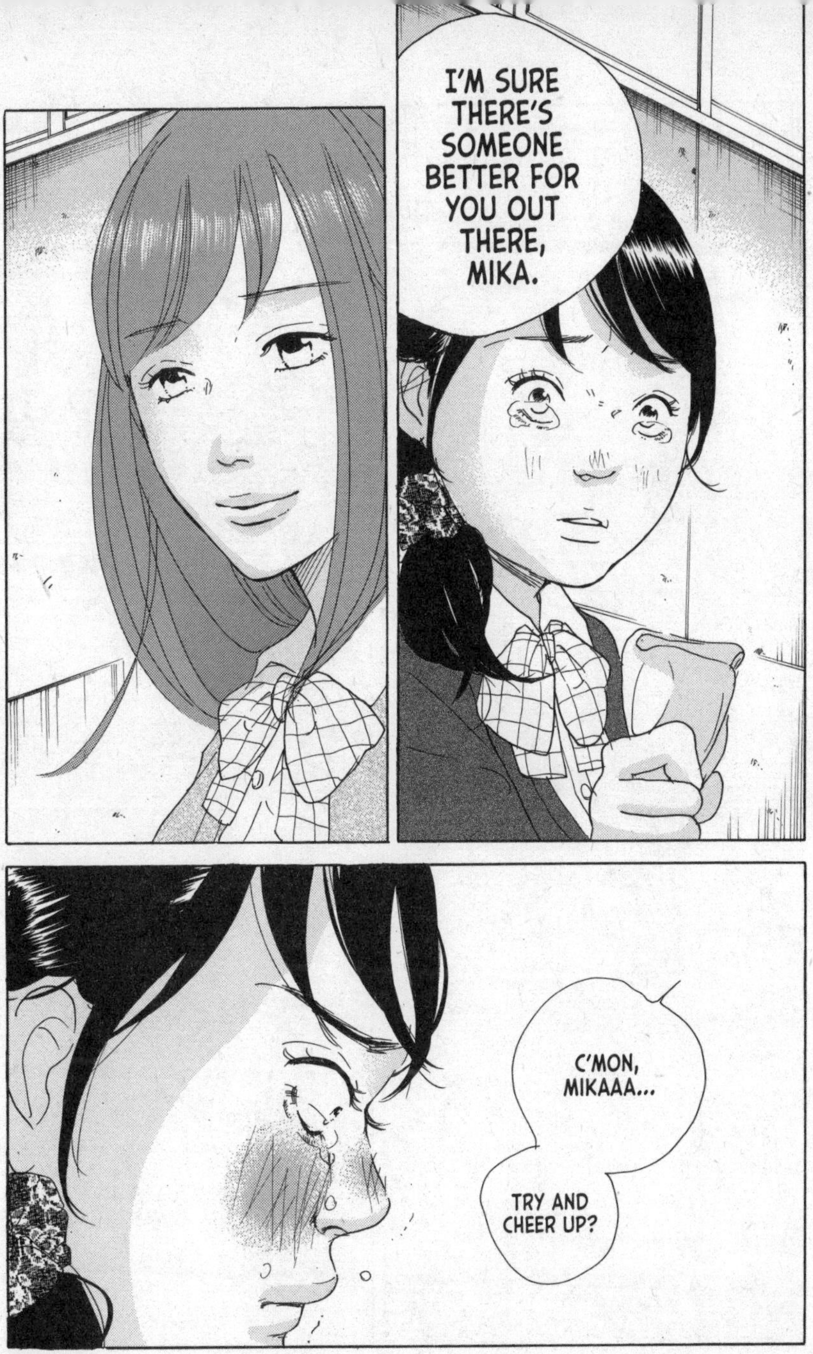
I'M SURE THERE'S SOMEONE BETTER FOR YOU OUT THERE, MIKA.
C'MON, MIKAAA...
TRY AND CHEER UP?

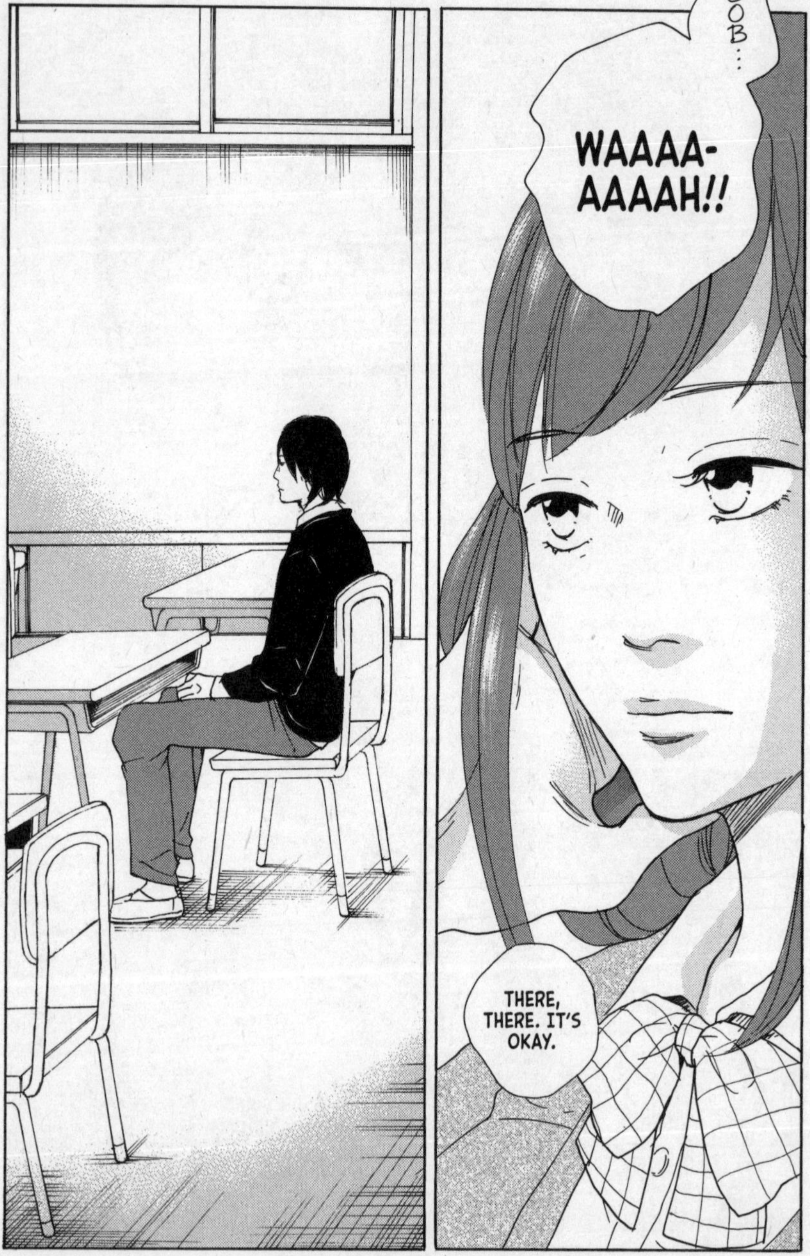
SOB...
WAAAA-AAAAH!!
THERE, THERE. IT'S OKAY.

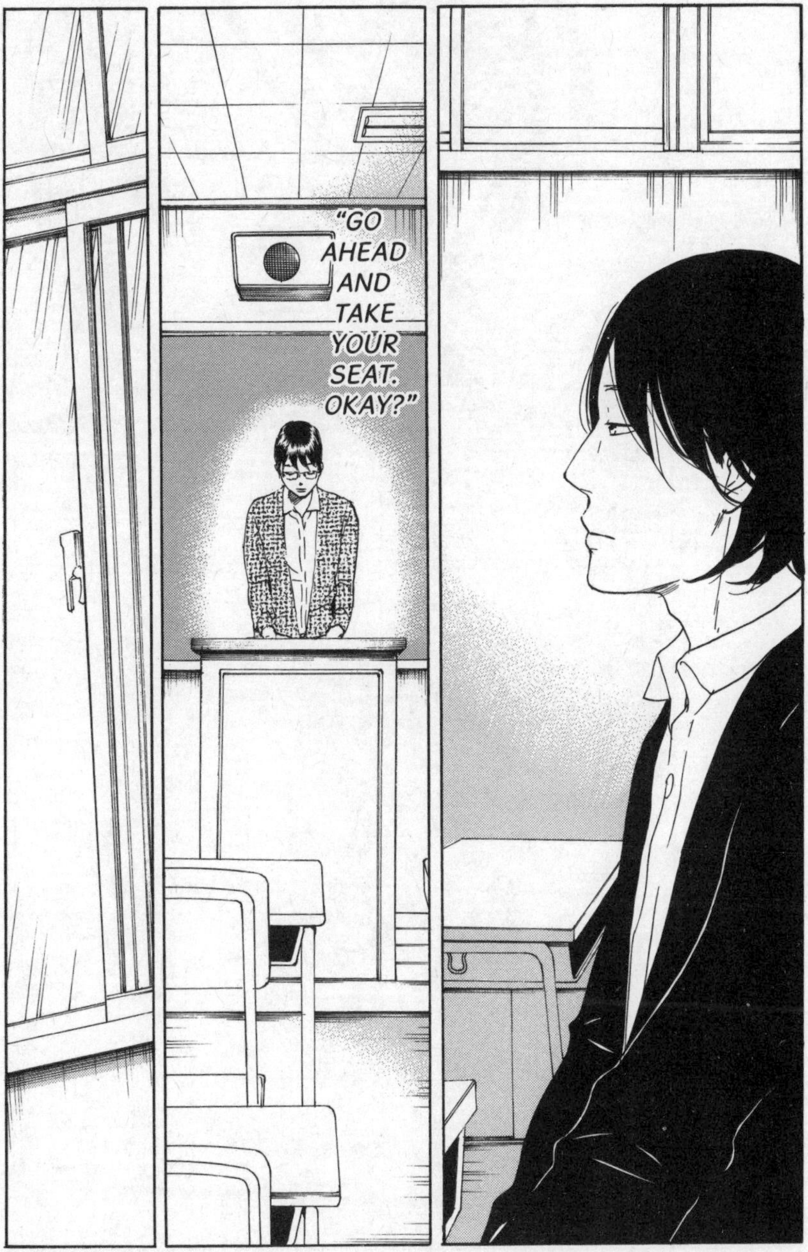
"GO AHEAD AND TAKE YOUR SEAT. OKAY?"

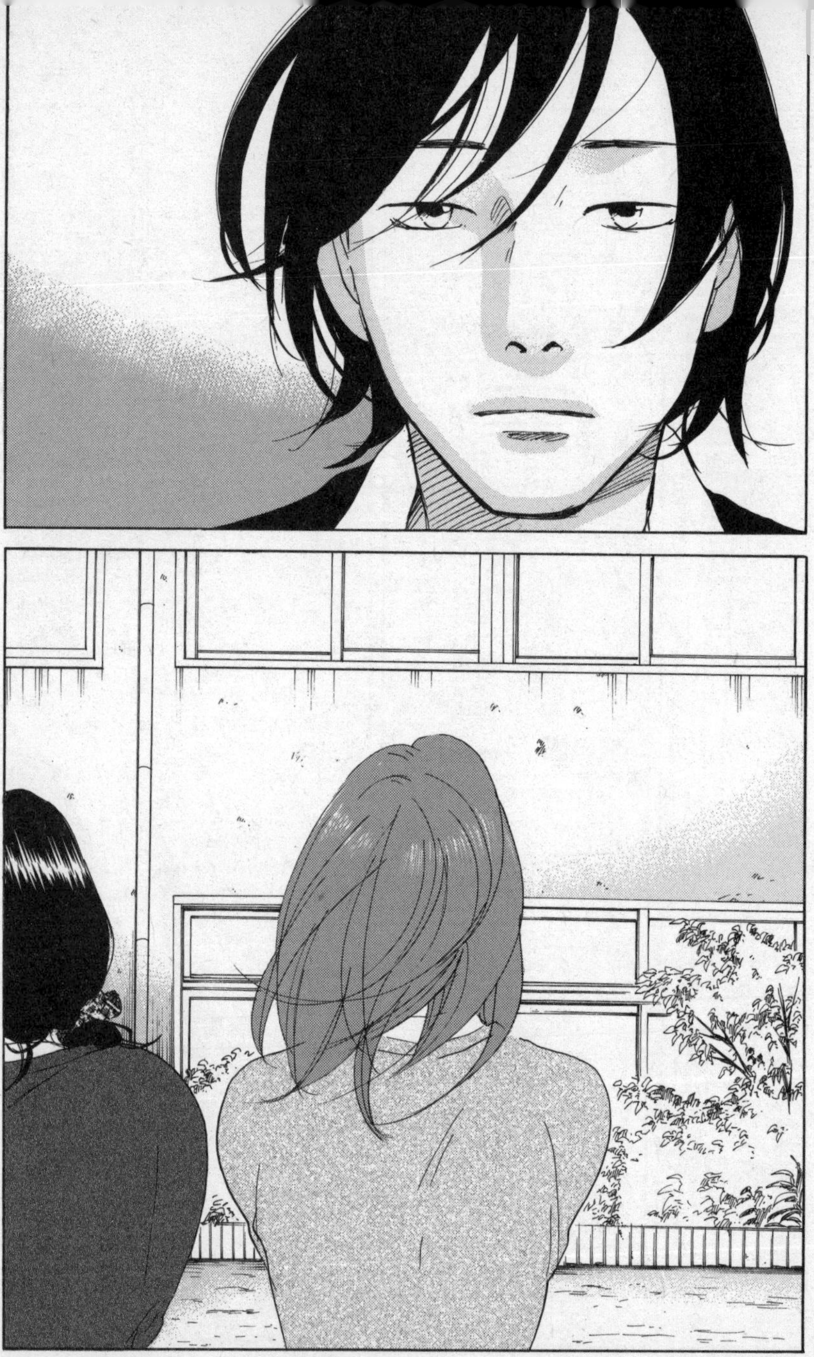

SHUWA REALTY
SHUWA REALTY

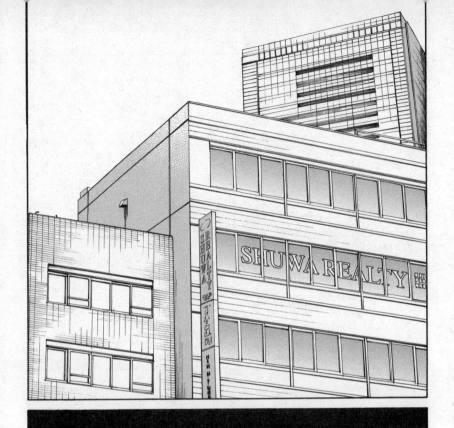

AYAKA

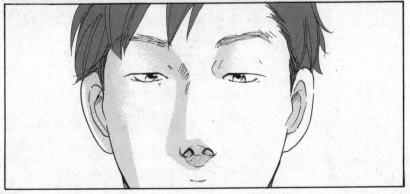

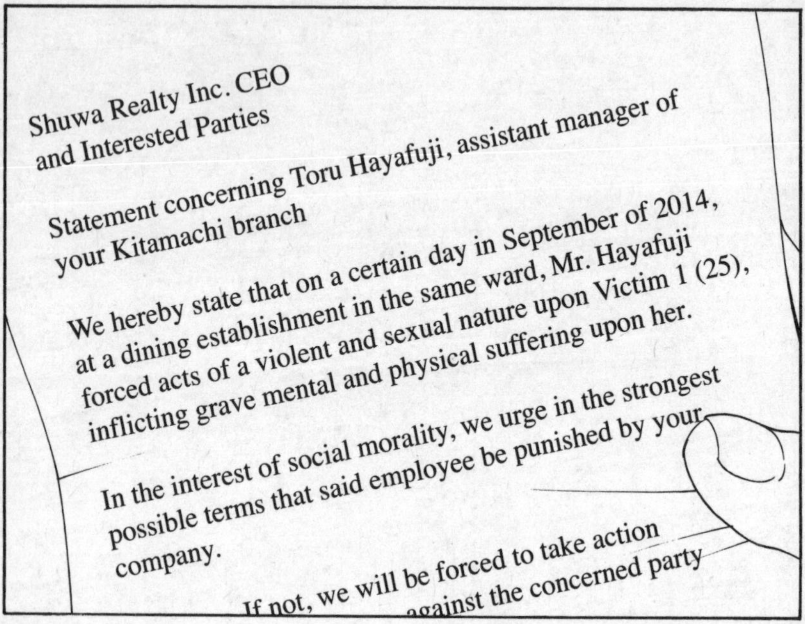
Shuwa Realty Inc. CEO
and Interested Parties
Statement concerning Toru Hayafuji, assistant manager of
your Kitamachi branch
We hereby state that on a certain day in September of 2014,
at a dining establishment in the same ward, Mr. Hayafuji
forced acts of a violent and sexual nature upon Victim 1 (25),
inflicting grave mental and physical suffering upon her.
In the interest of social morality, we urge in the strongest
possible terms that said employee be punished by your
company.
If not, we will be forced to take action
against the concerned party

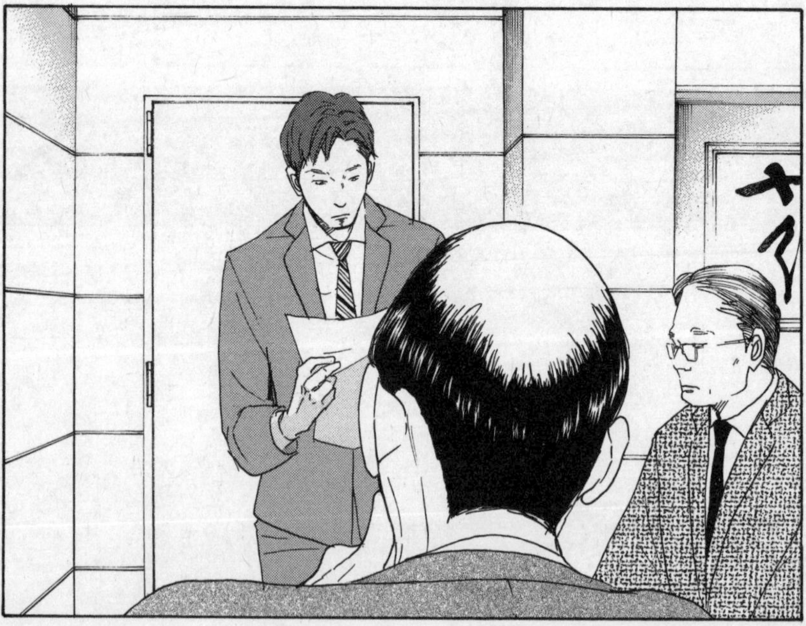

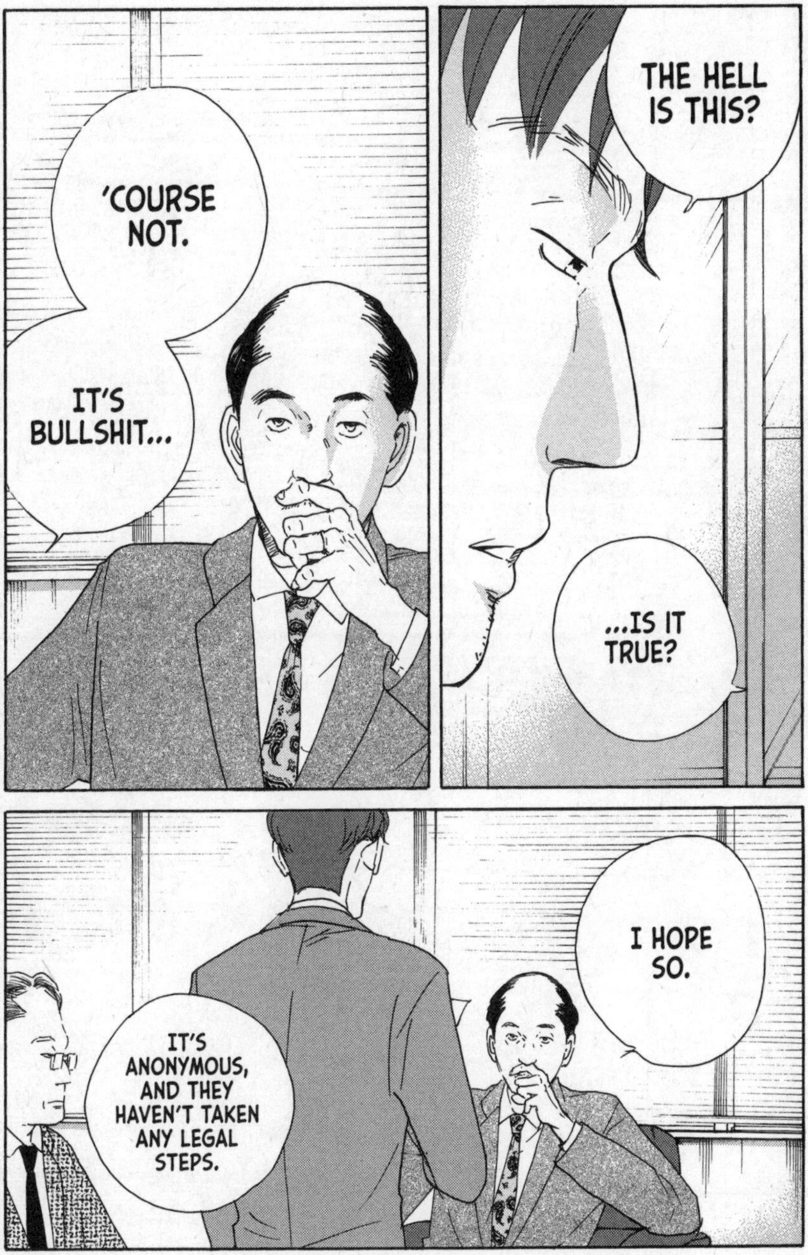
THE HELL IS THIS?
...IS IT TRUE?
'COURSE NOT.
IT'S BULLSHIT...
I HOPE SO.
IT'S ANONYMOUS, AND THEY HAVEN'T TAKEN ANY LEGAL STEPS.

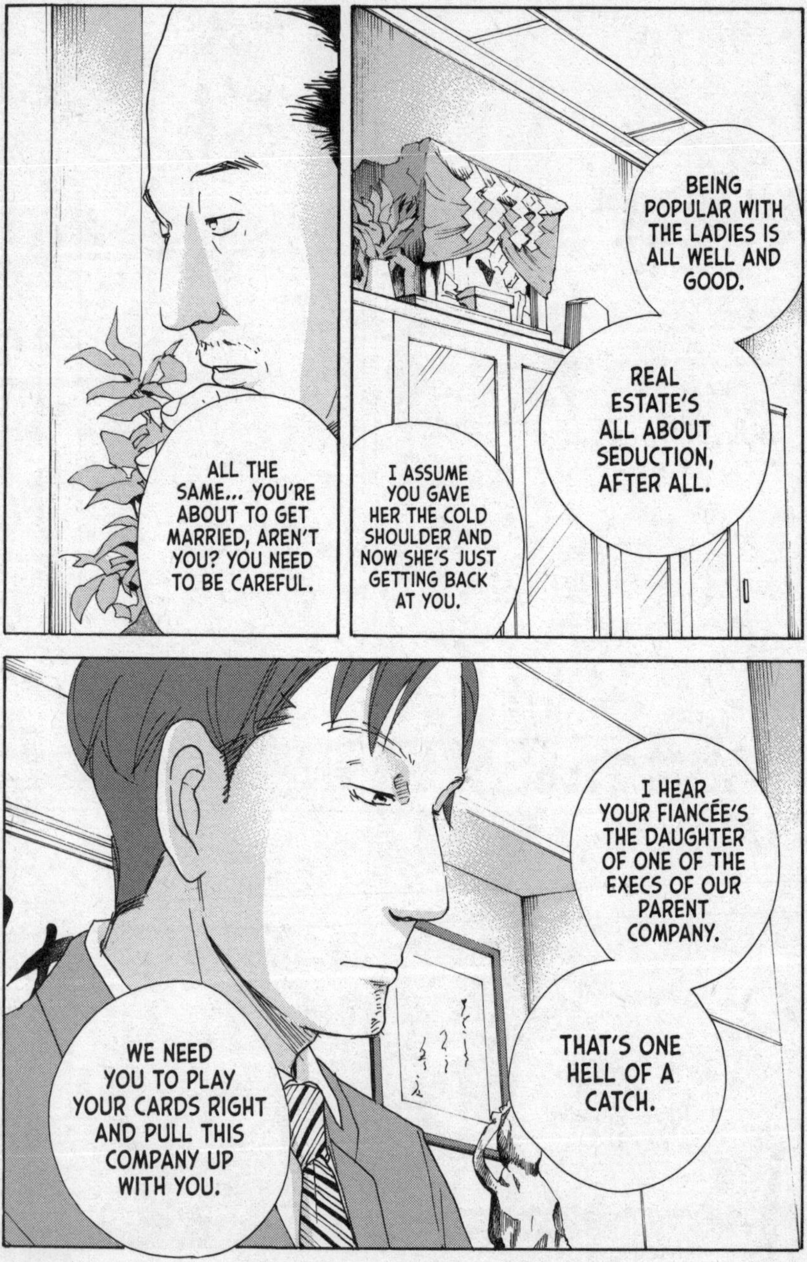
BEING POPULAR WITH THE LADIES IS ALL WELL AND GOOD.
REAL ESTATE'S ALL ABOUT SEDUCTION, AFTER ALL.
I ASSUME YOU GAVE HER THE COLD SHOULDER AND NOW SHE'S JUST GETTING BACK AT YOU.
ALL THE SAME... YOU'RE ABOUT TO GET MARRIED, AREN'T YOU? YOU NEED TO BE CAREFUL.
I HEAR YOUR FIANCÉE'S THE DAUGHTER OF ONE OF THE EXECS OF OUR PARENT COMPANY.
THAT'S ONE HELL OF A CATCH.
WE NEED YOU TO PLAY YOUR CARDS RIGHT AND PULL THIS COMPANY UP WITH YOU.

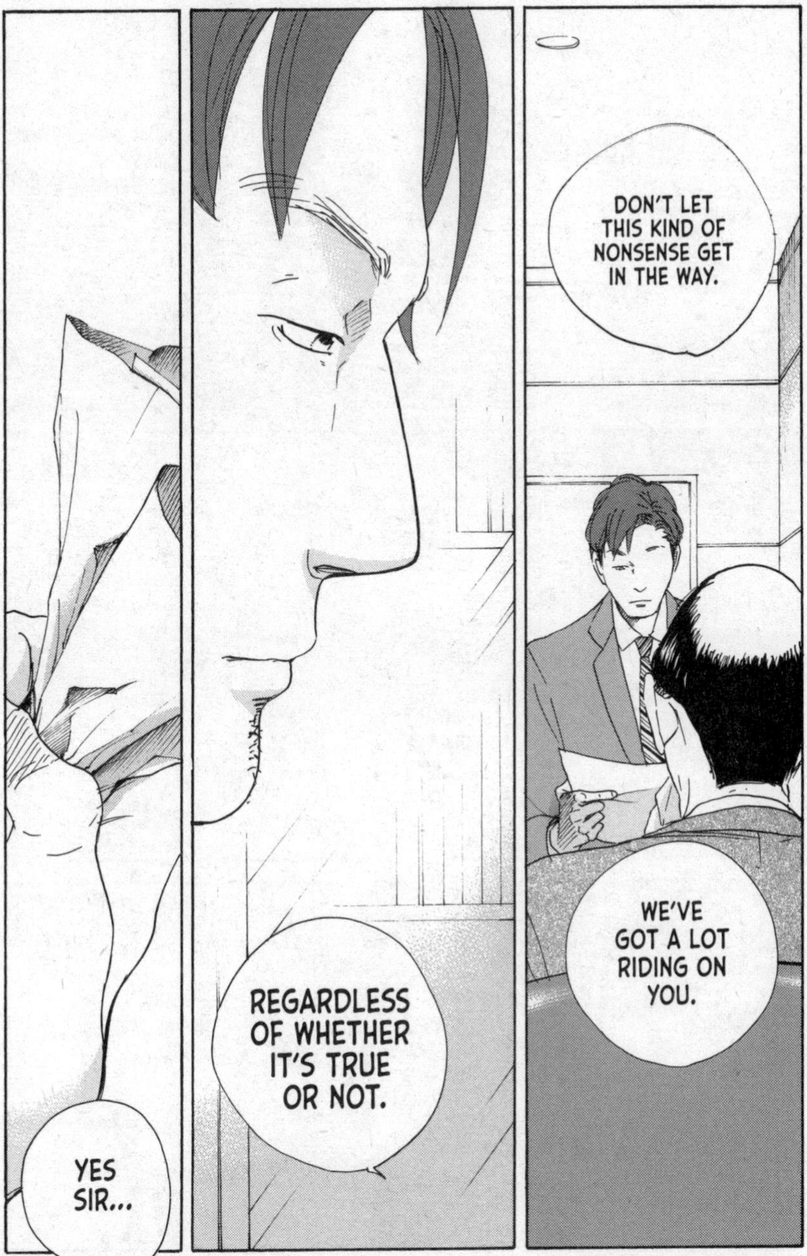
DON'T LET THIS KIND OF NONSENSE GET IN THE WAY.
WE'VE GOT A LOT RIDING ON YOU.
REGARDLESS OF WHETHER IT'S TRUE OR NOT.
YES SIR...

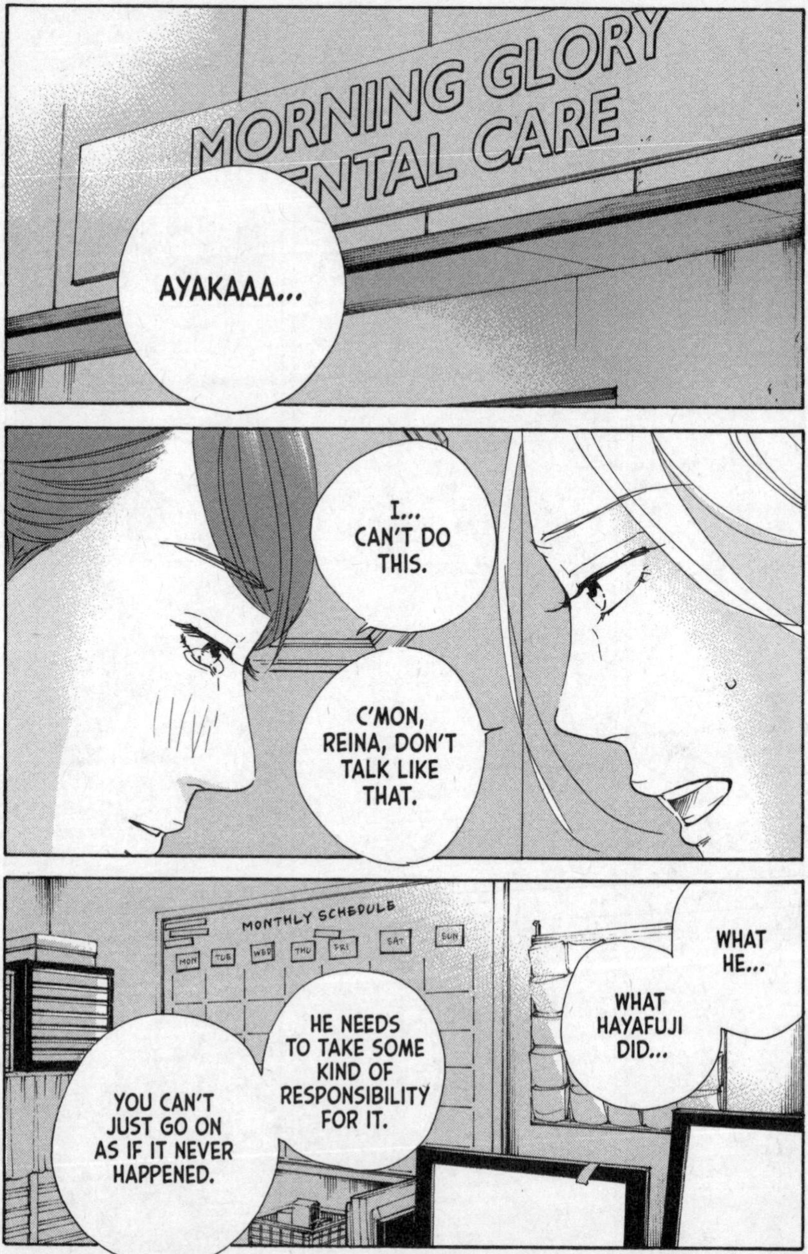
MORNING GLORY
ENTAL CARE
AYAKAAA...
I... CAN'T DO THIS.
C'MON, REINA, DON'T TALK LIKE THAT.
WHAT HE...
WHAT HAYAFUJI DID...
HE NEEDS TO TAKE SOME KIND OF RESPONSIBILITY FOR IT.
YOU CAN'T JUST GO ON AS IF IT NEVER HAPPENED.
MONTHLY SCHEDULE
MON TUE WED THU FRI SAT SUN

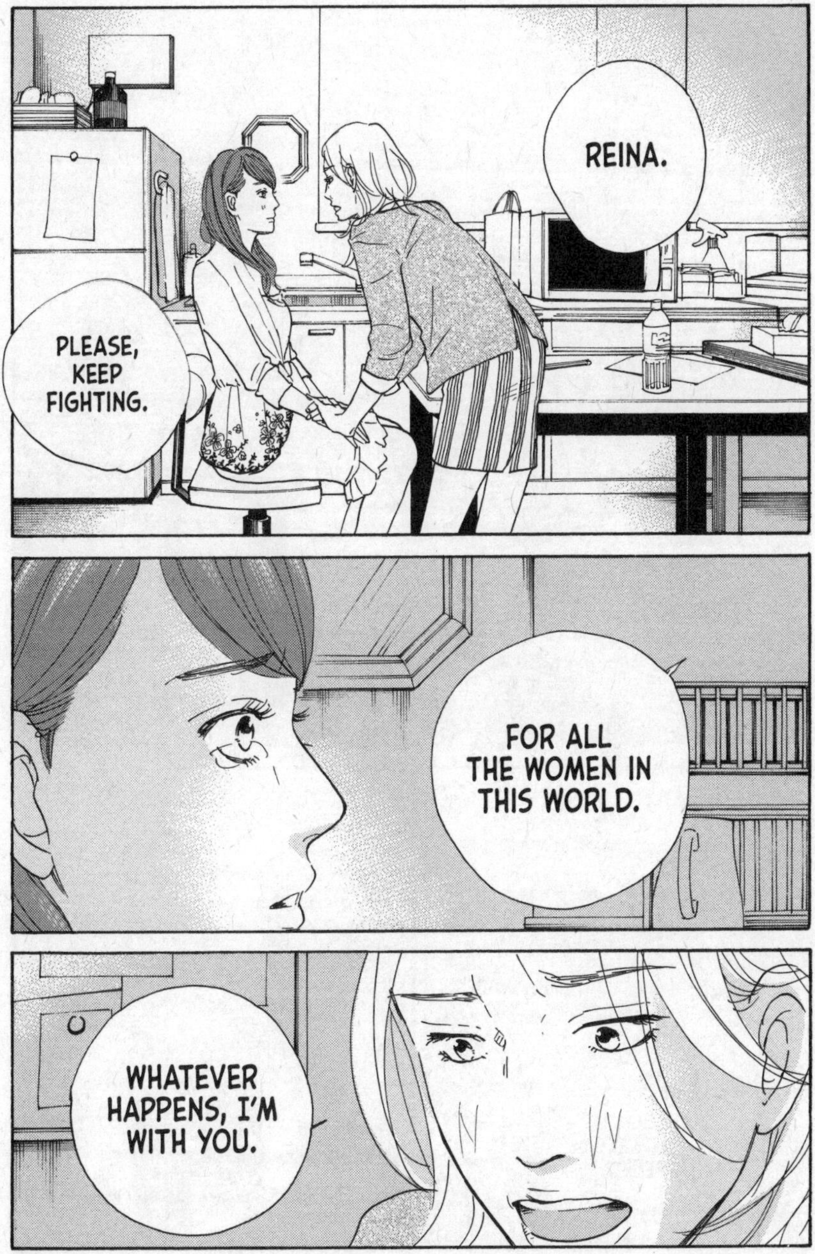
REINA.
PLEASE, KEEP FIGHTING.
FOR ALL THE WOMEN IN THIS WORLD.
WHATEVER HAPPENS, I'M WITH YOU.

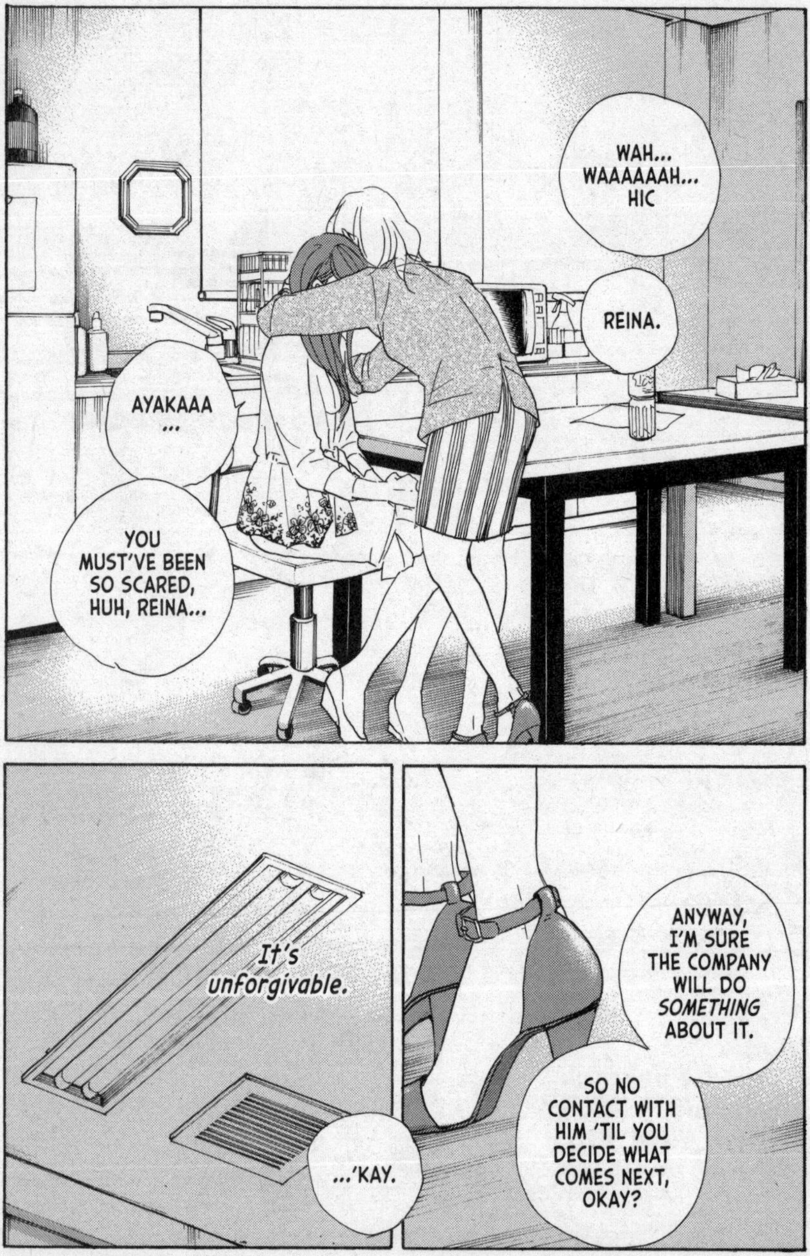
WAH... WAAAAAAH... HIC
REINA.
AYAKAAA ...
YOU MUST'VE BEEN SO SCARED, HUH, REINA...
ANYWAY, I'M SURE THE COMPANY WILL DO *SOMETHING* ABOUT IT.
SO NO CONTACT WITH HIM 'TIL YOU DECIDE WHAT COMES NEXT, OKAY?
It's unforgivable.
...'KAY.

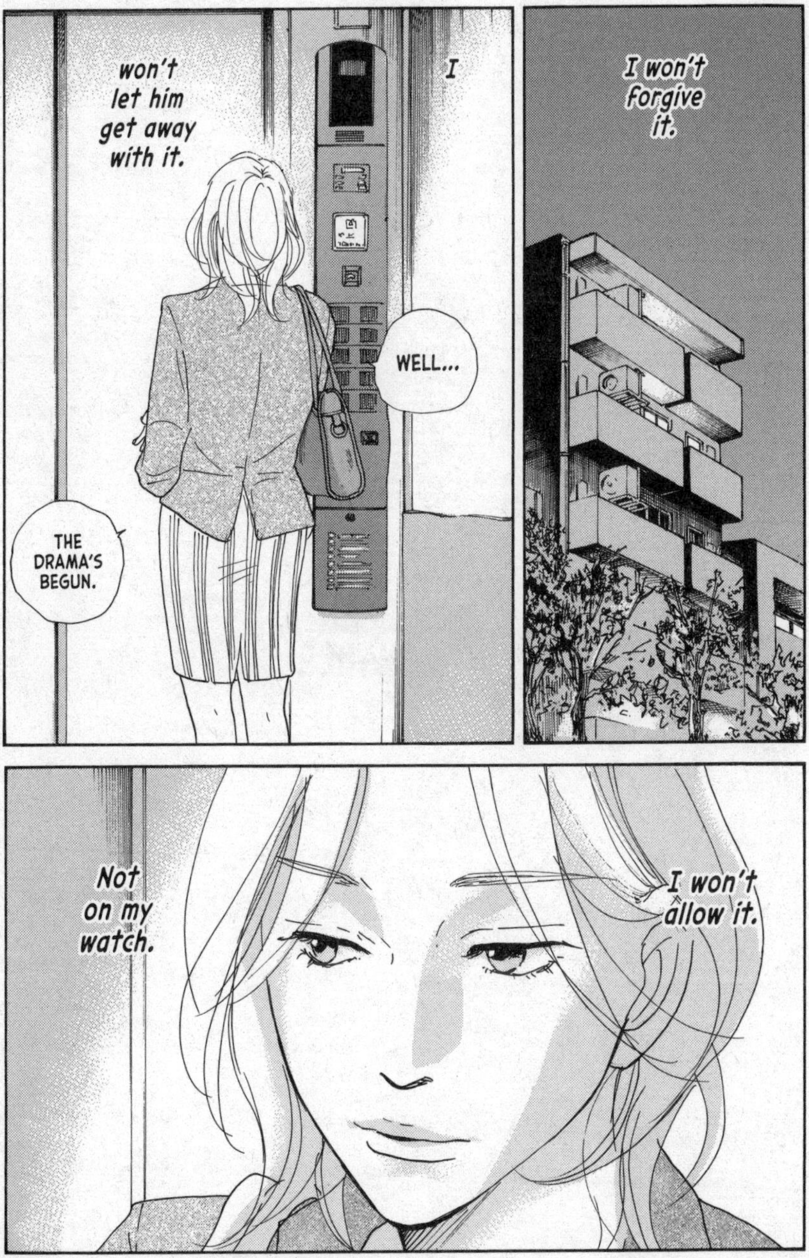
I won't forgive it.
I
won't let him get away with it.
WELL...
THE DRAMA'S BEGUN.
I won't allow it.
Not on my watch.

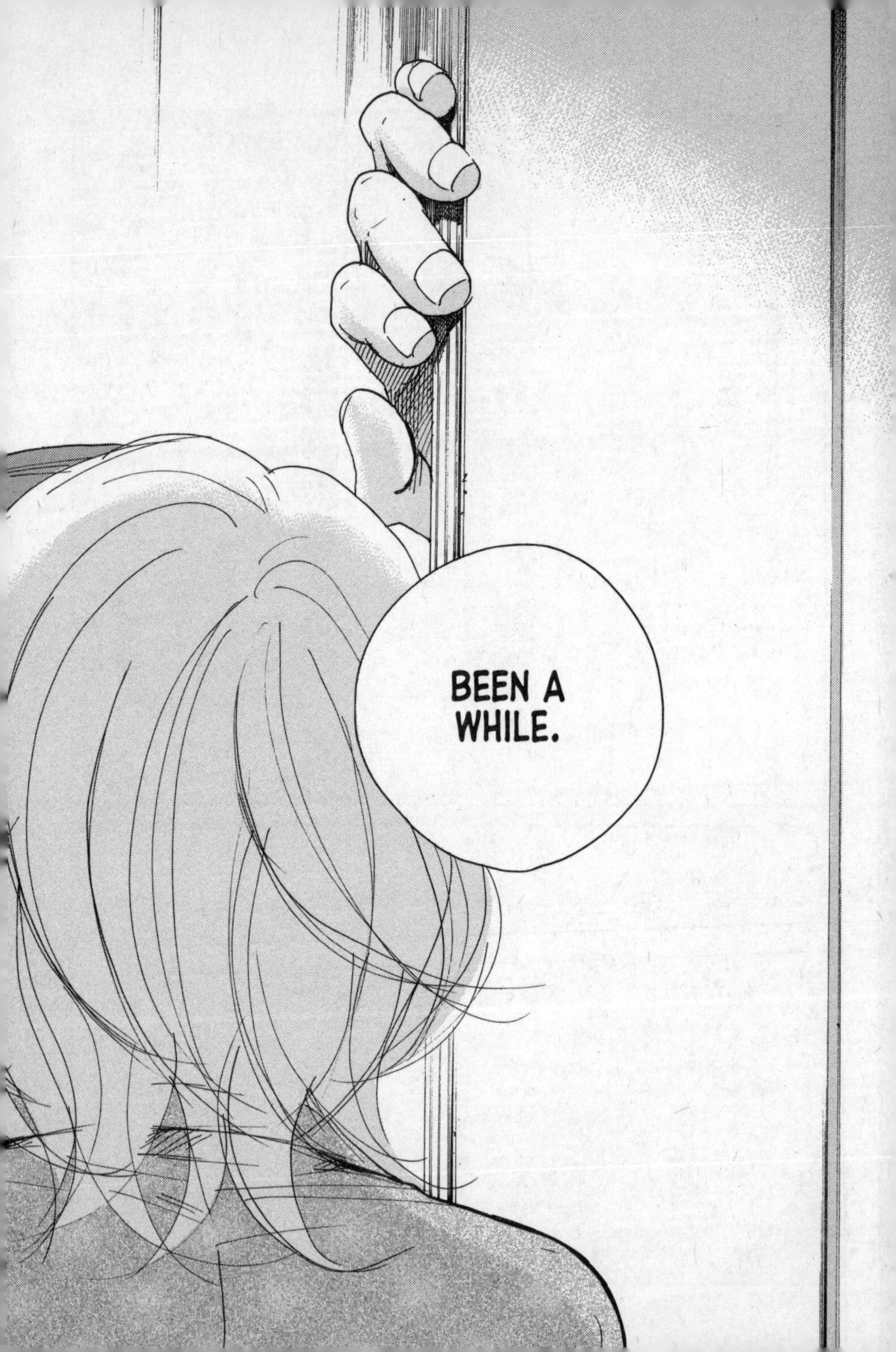
BEEN A WHILE.

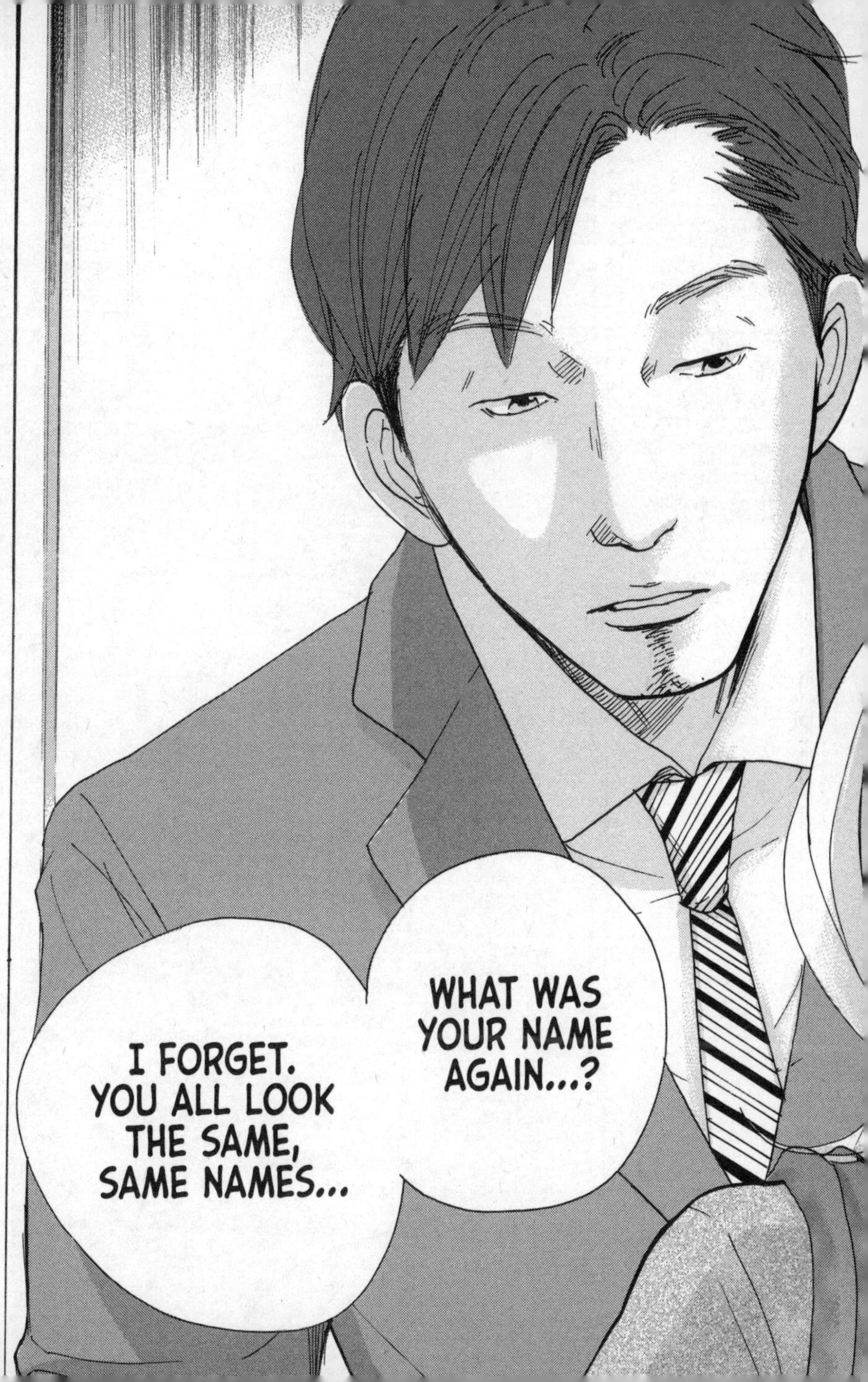
WHAT WAS YOUR NAME AGAIN...?
I FORGET. YOU ALL LOOK THE SAME, SAME NAMES...

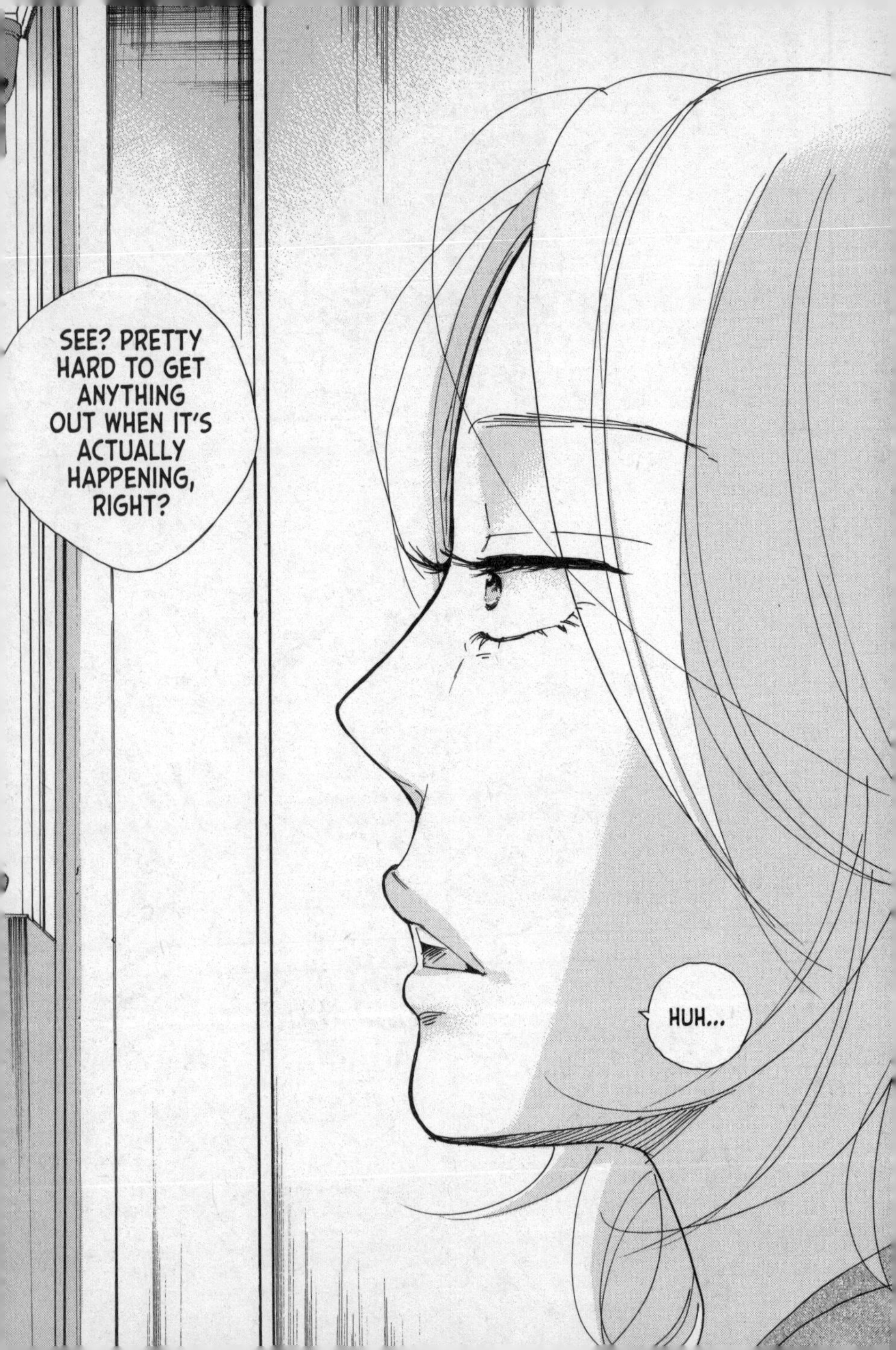
SEE? PRETTY HARD TO GET ANYTHING OUT WHEN IT'S ACTUALLY HAPPENING, RIGHT?
HUH...

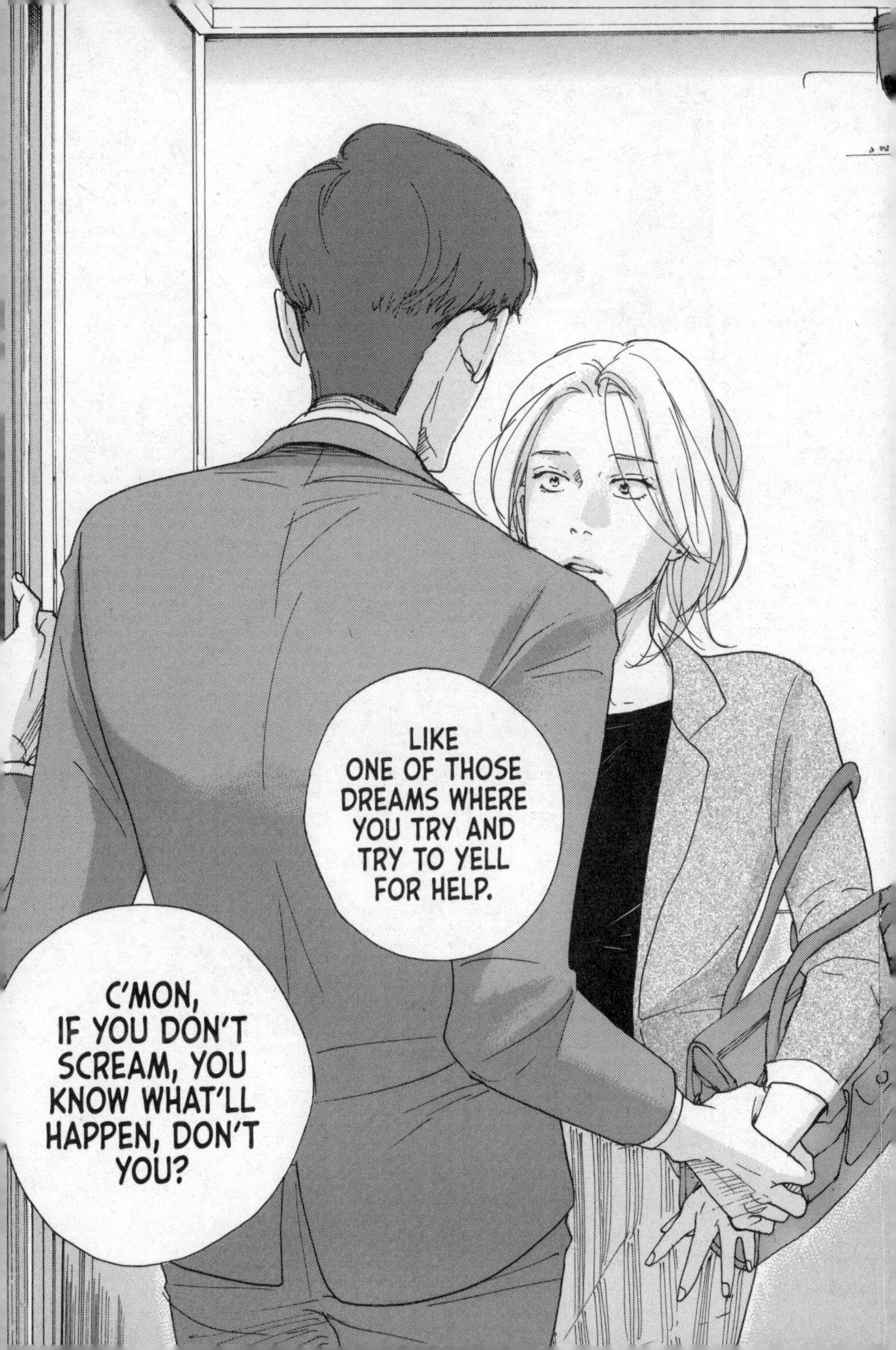
LIKE ONE OF THOSE DREAMS WHERE YOU TRY AND TRY TO YELL FOR HELP.
C'MON, IF YOU DON'T SCREAM, YOU KNOW WHAT'LL HAPPEN, DON'T YOU?

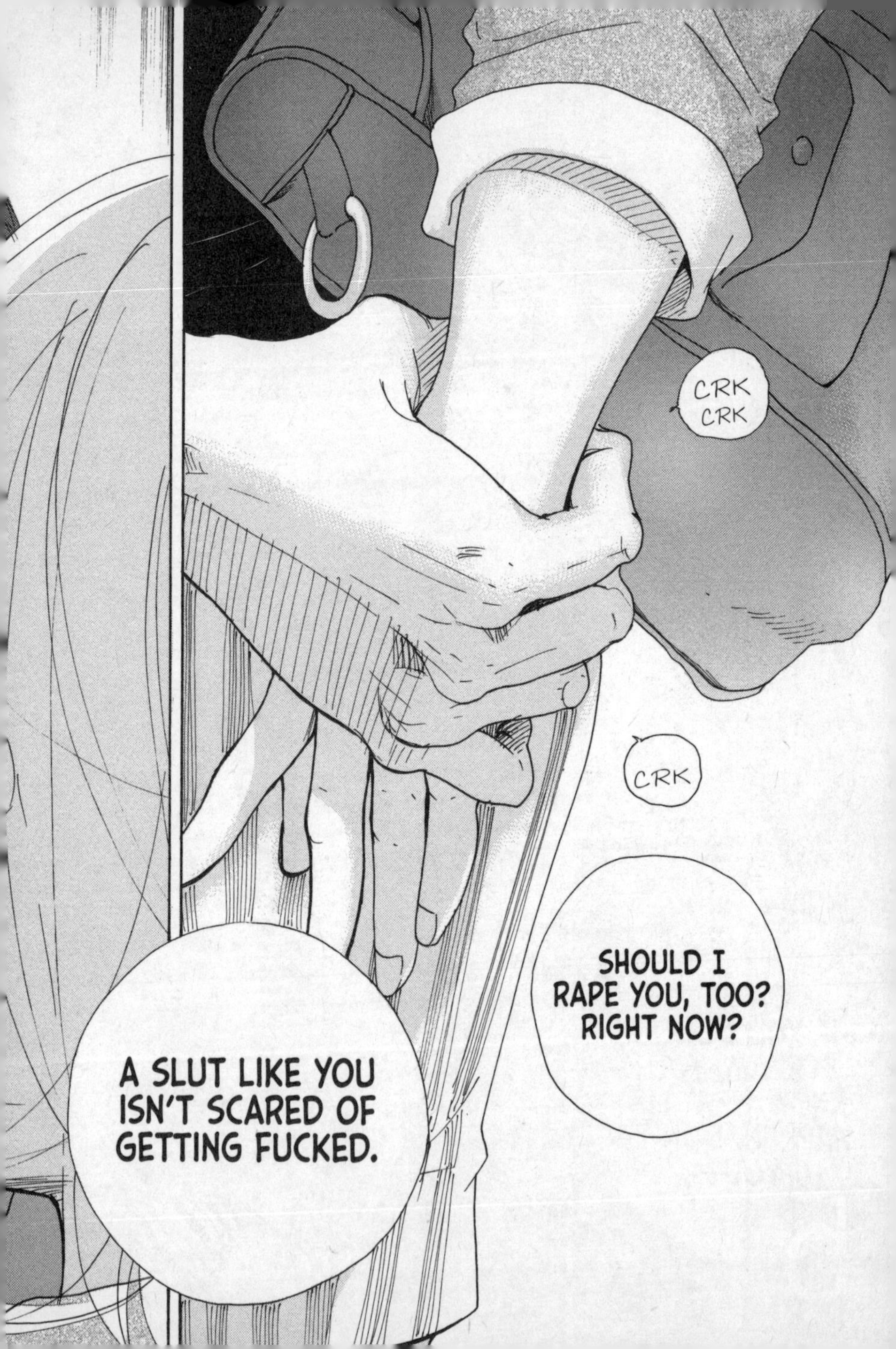
CRK CRK
CRK
SHOULD I RAPE YOU, TOO? RIGHT NOW?
A SLUT LIKE YOU ISN'T SCARED OF GETTING FUCKED.

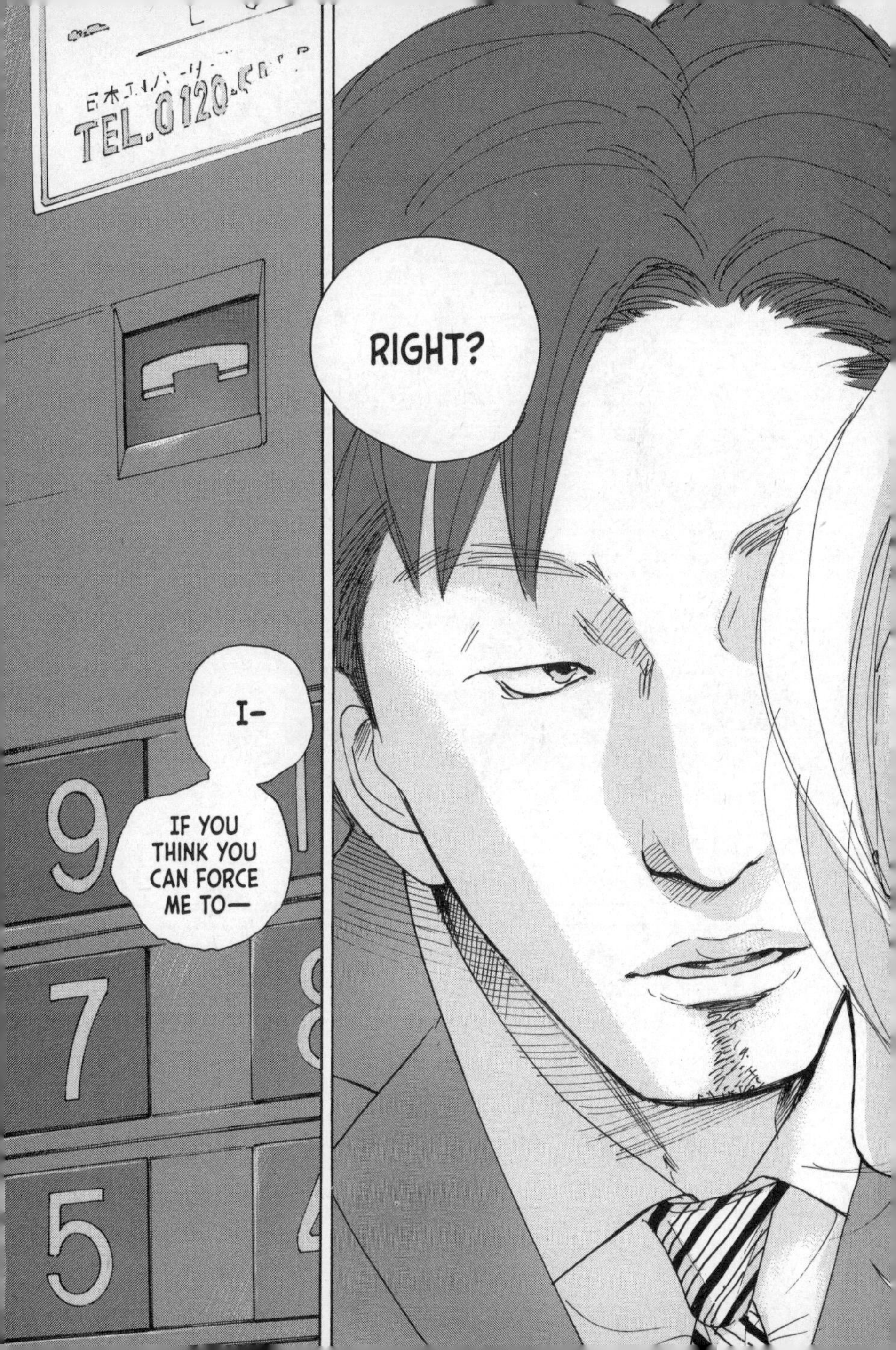
RIGHT?
I-
IF YOU THINK YOU CAN FORCE ME TO—

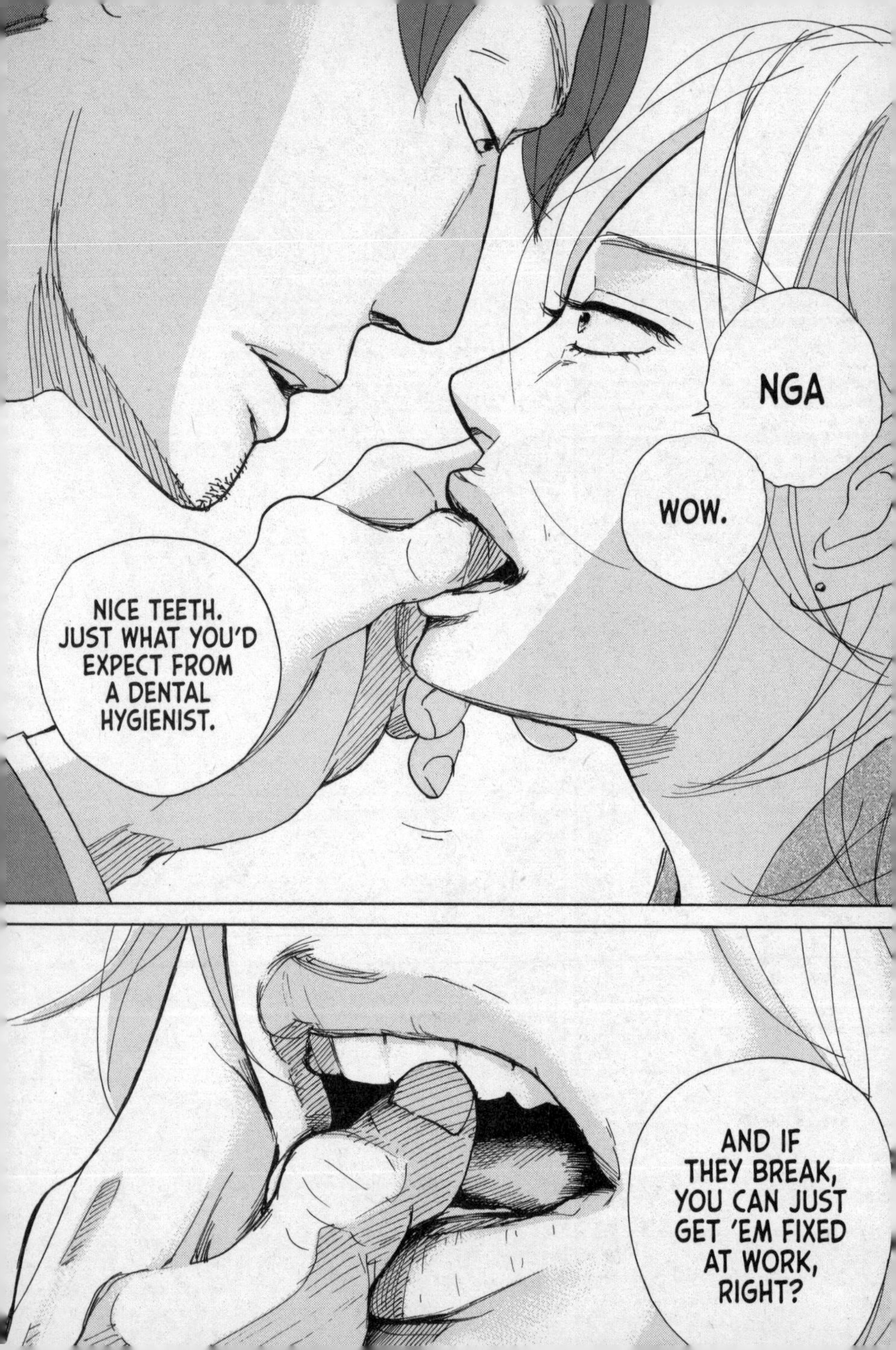
NGA
WOW.
NICE TEETH. JUST WHAT YOU'D EXPECT FROM A DENTAL HYGIENIST.
AND IF THEY BREAK, YOU CAN JUST GET 'EM FIXED AT WORK, RIGHT?

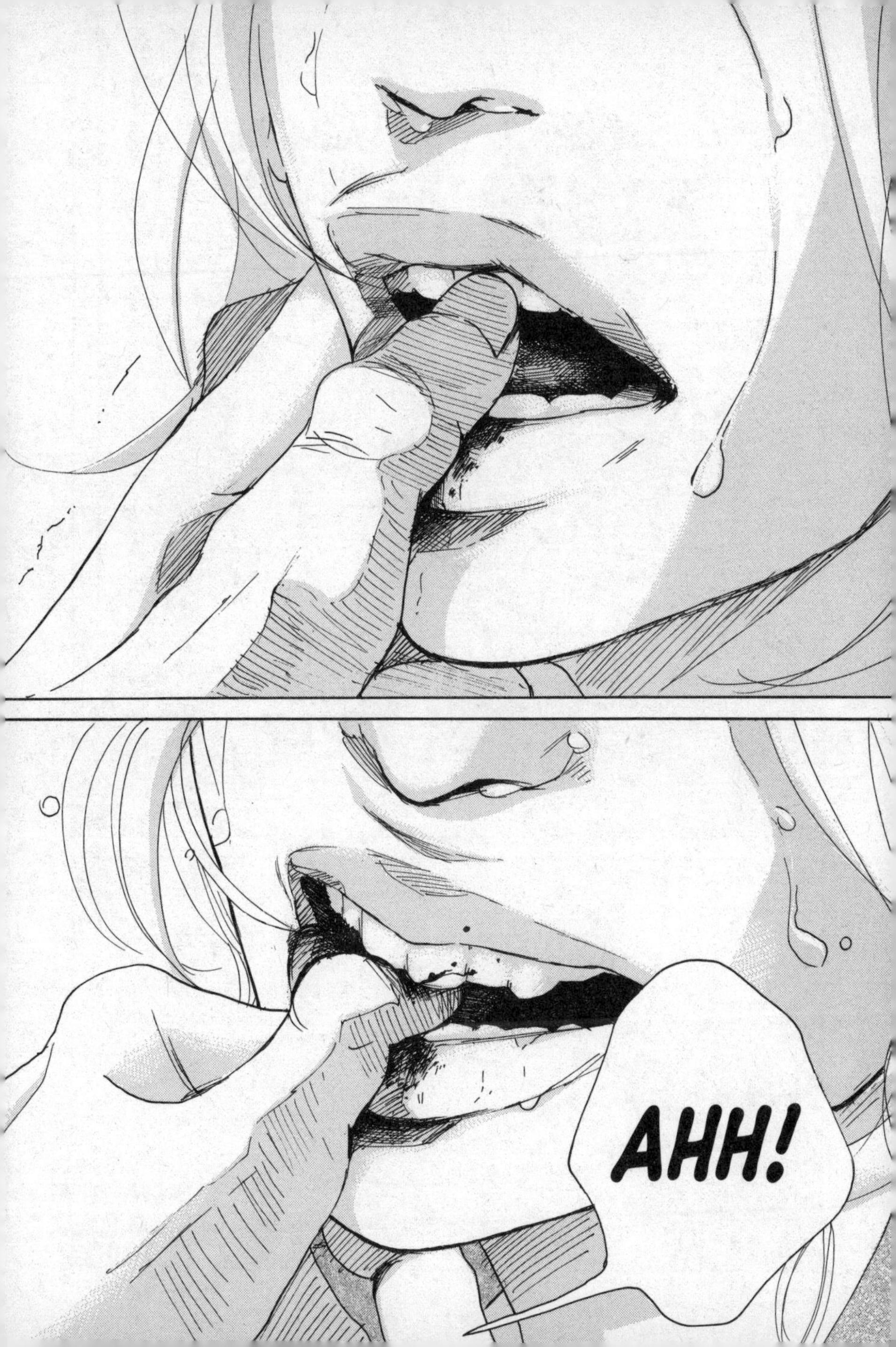
AHH!

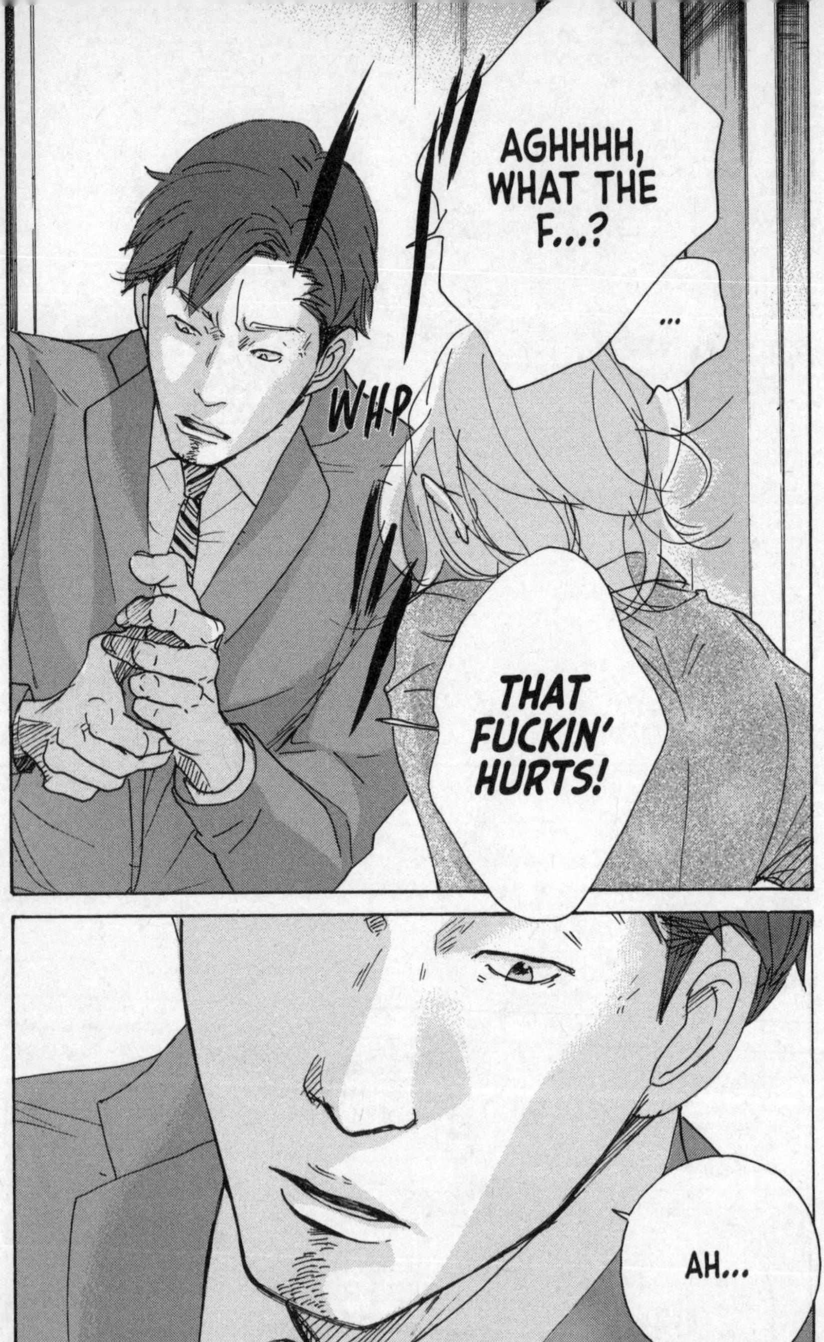
AGHHHH, WHAT THE F...?
...
WHP
THAT FUCKIN' HURTS!
AH...

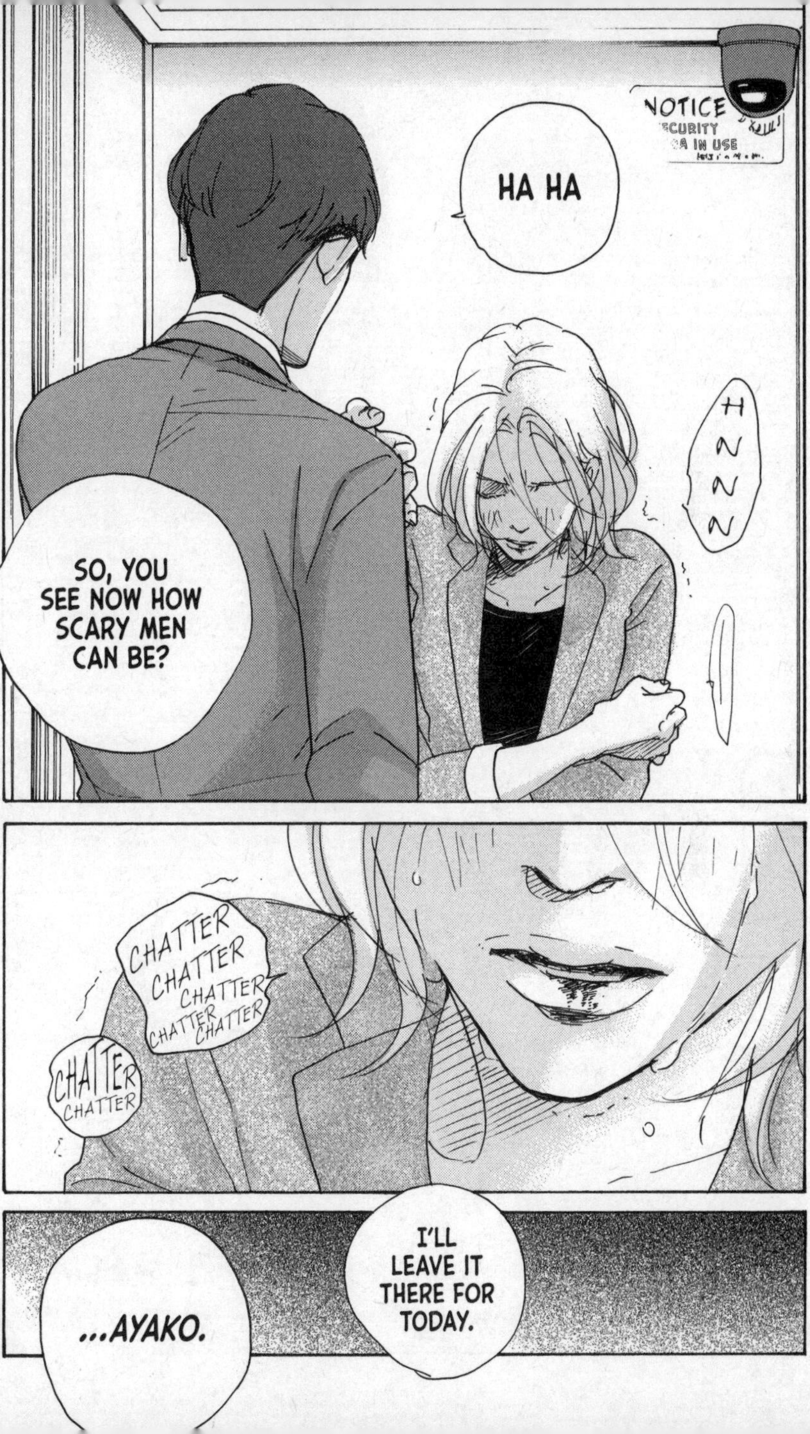
NOTICE
HA HA
HNNN
...
SO, YOU SEE NOW HOW SCARY MEN CAN BE?
CHATTER CHATTER CHATTER CHATTER CHATTER
CHATTER CHATTER
I'LL LEAVE IT THERE FOR TODAY.
...AYAKO.

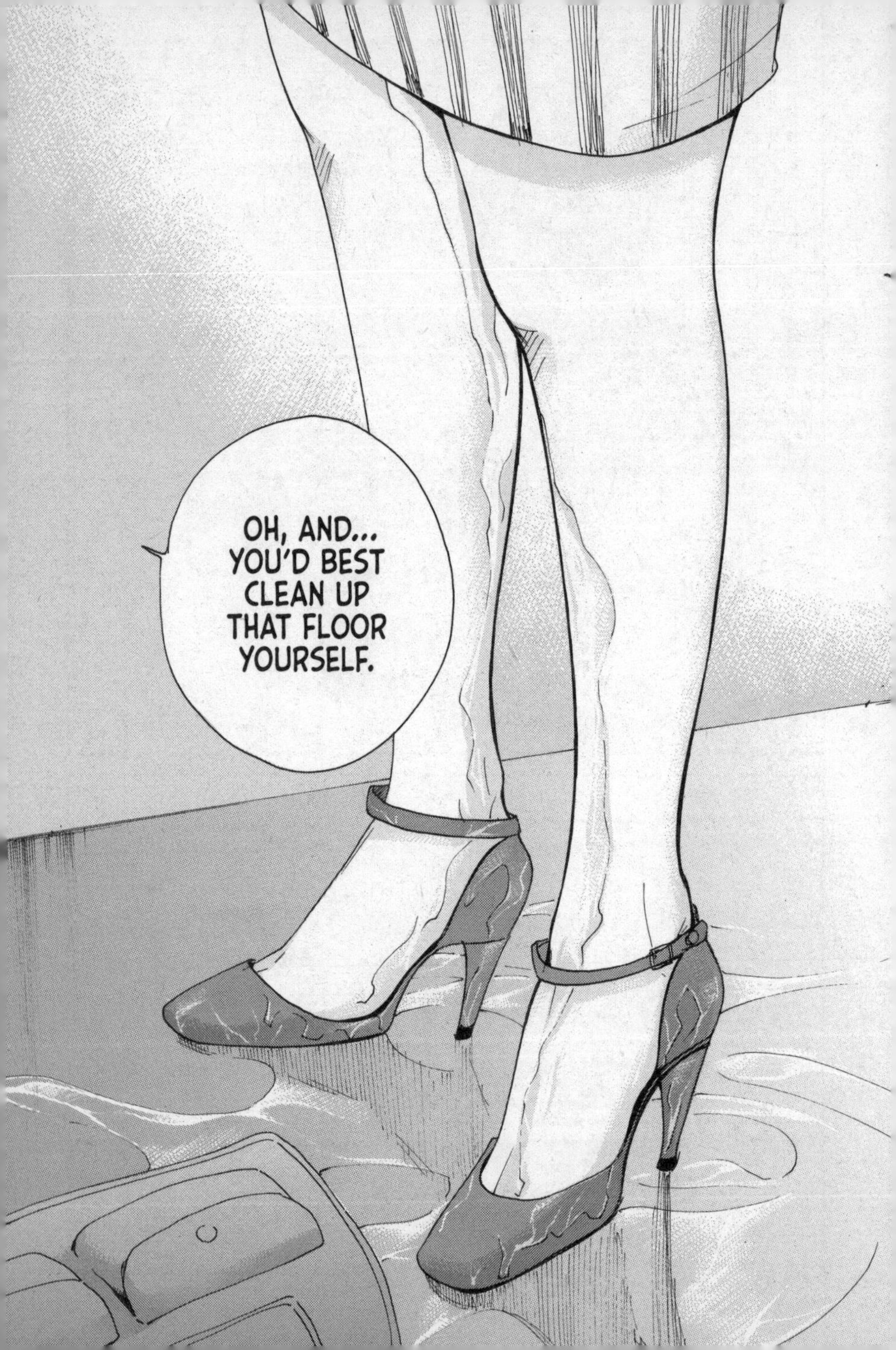
OH, AND... YOU'D BEST CLEAN UP THAT FLOOR YOURSELF.

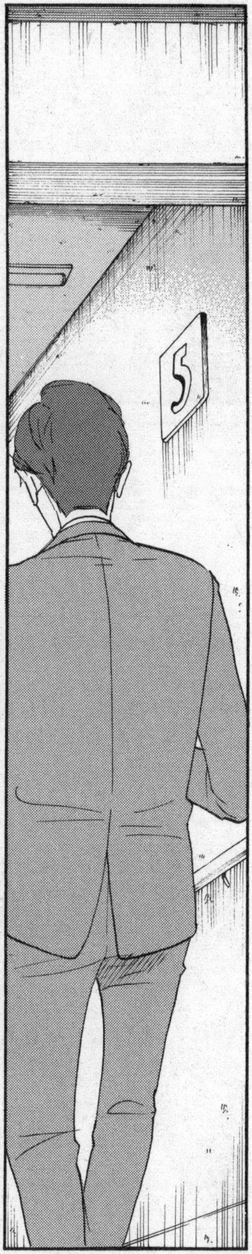
5
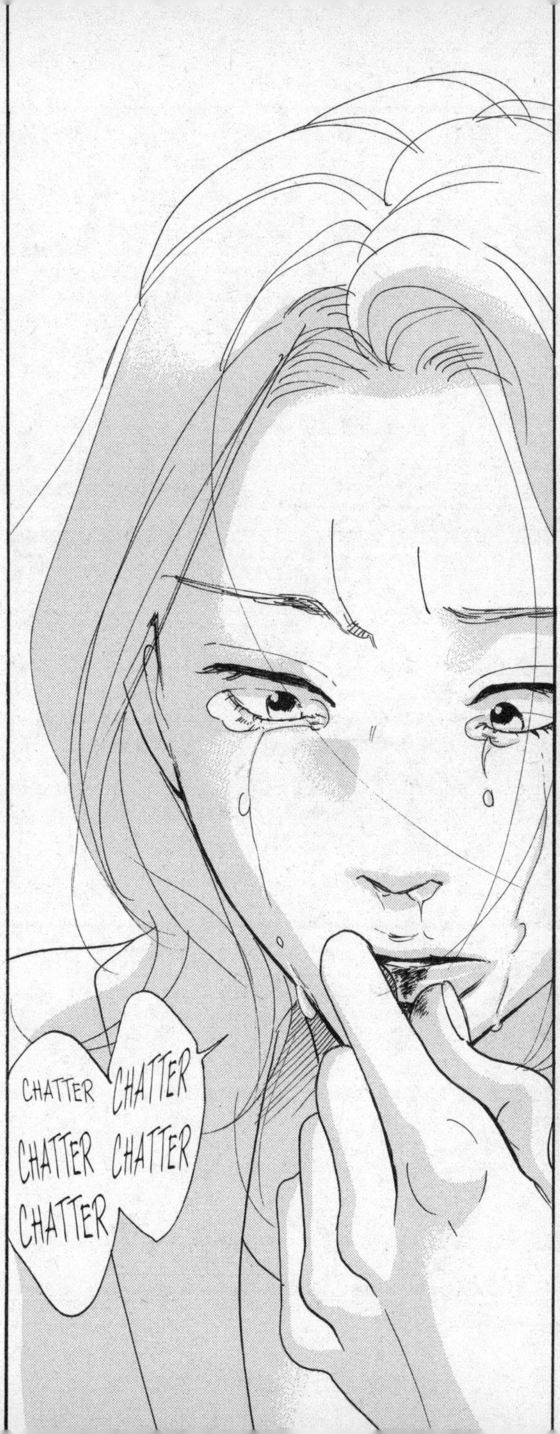
CHATTER CHATTER
CHATTER CHATTER
CHATTER

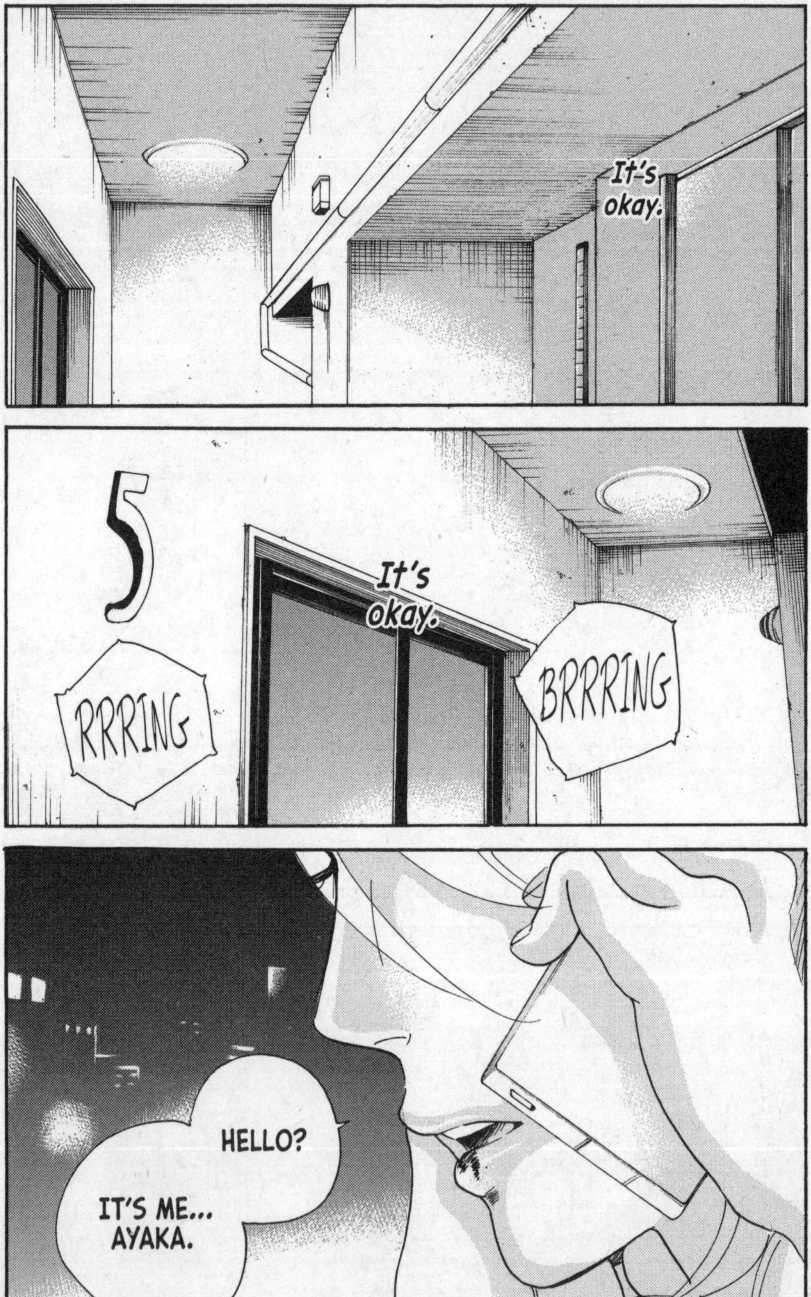
It's okay.
5
It's okay.
BRRRING
RRRING
HELLO?
IT'S ME... AYAKA.

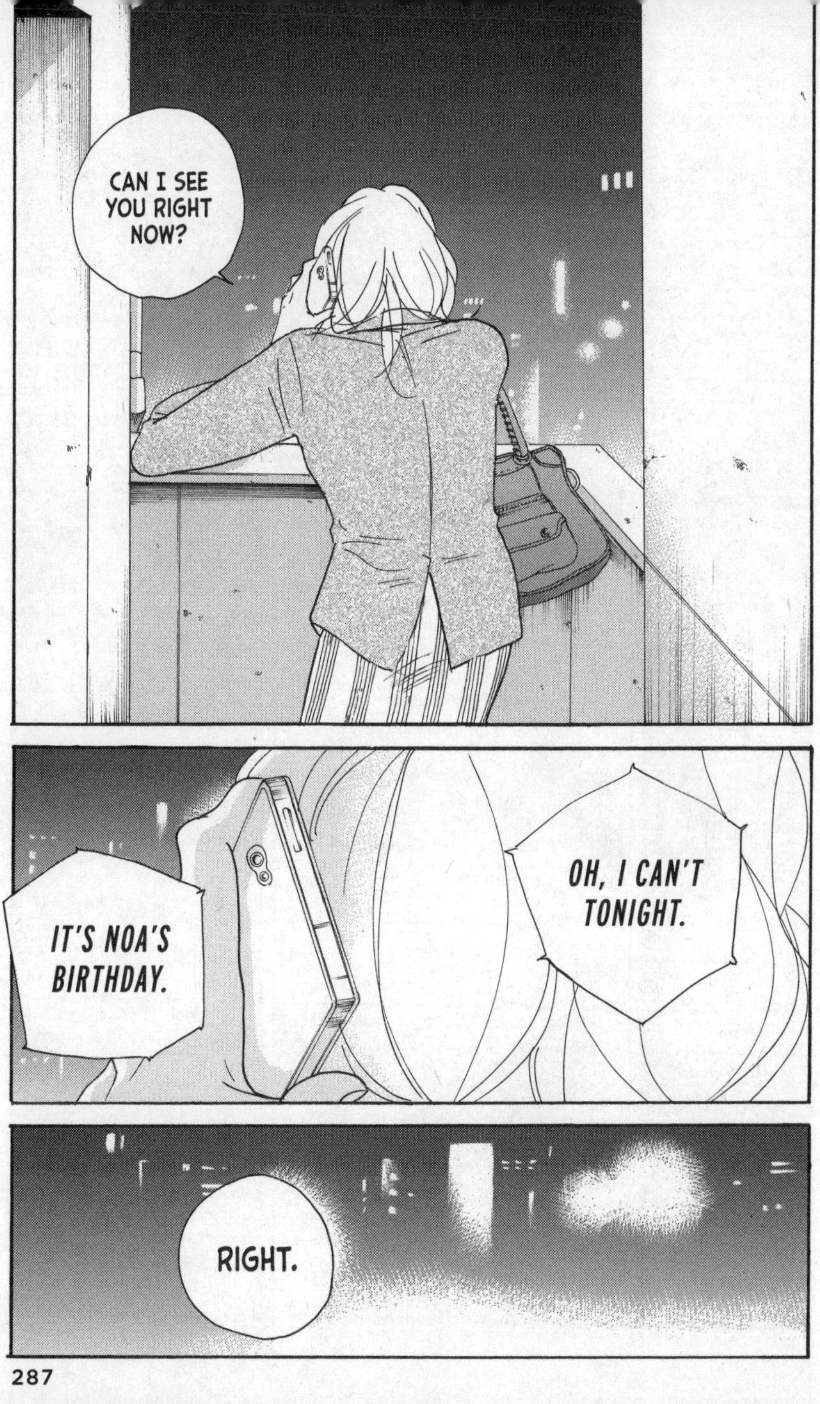
CAN I SEE YOU RIGHT NOW?
OH, I CAN'T TONIGHT.
IT'S NOA'S BIRTHDAY.
RIGHT.

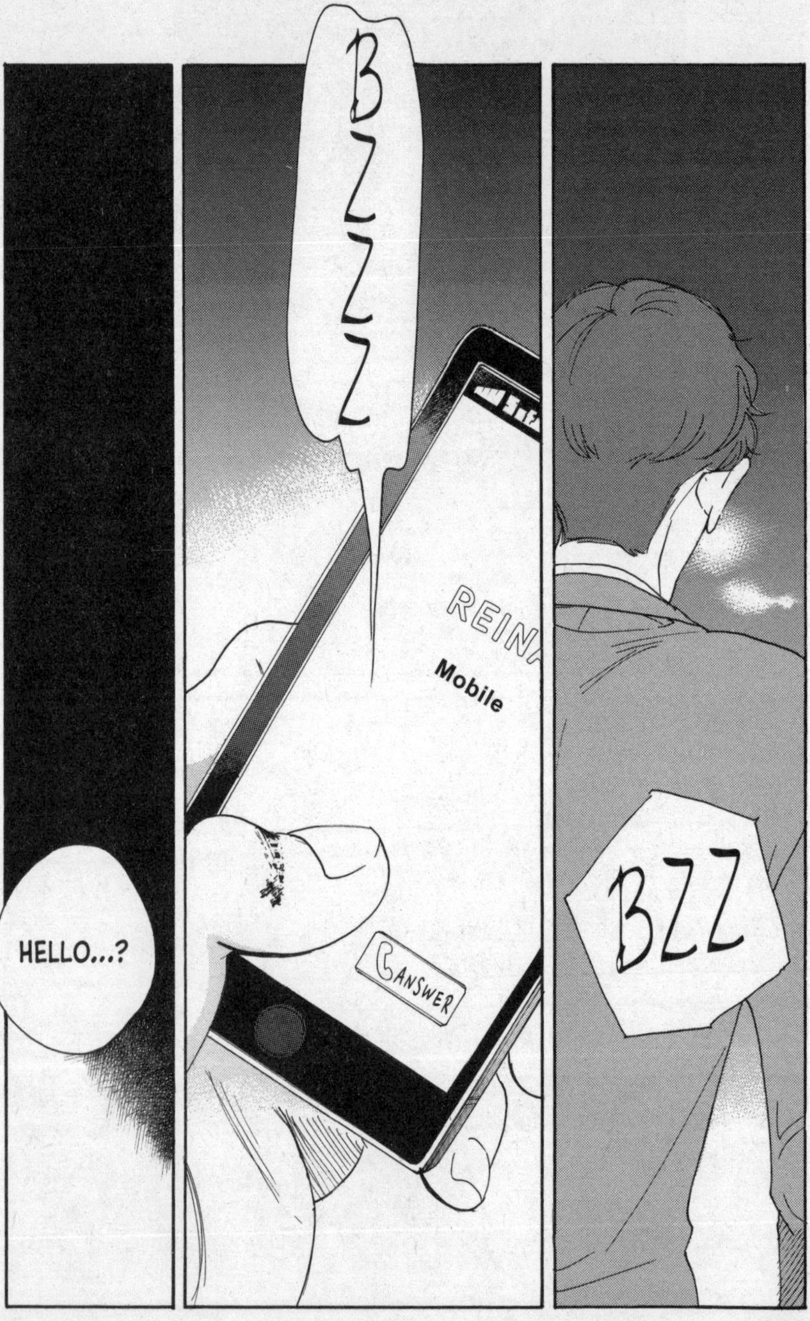
BZZ
BZZZZ
REINA
Mobile
ANSWER
HELLO...?

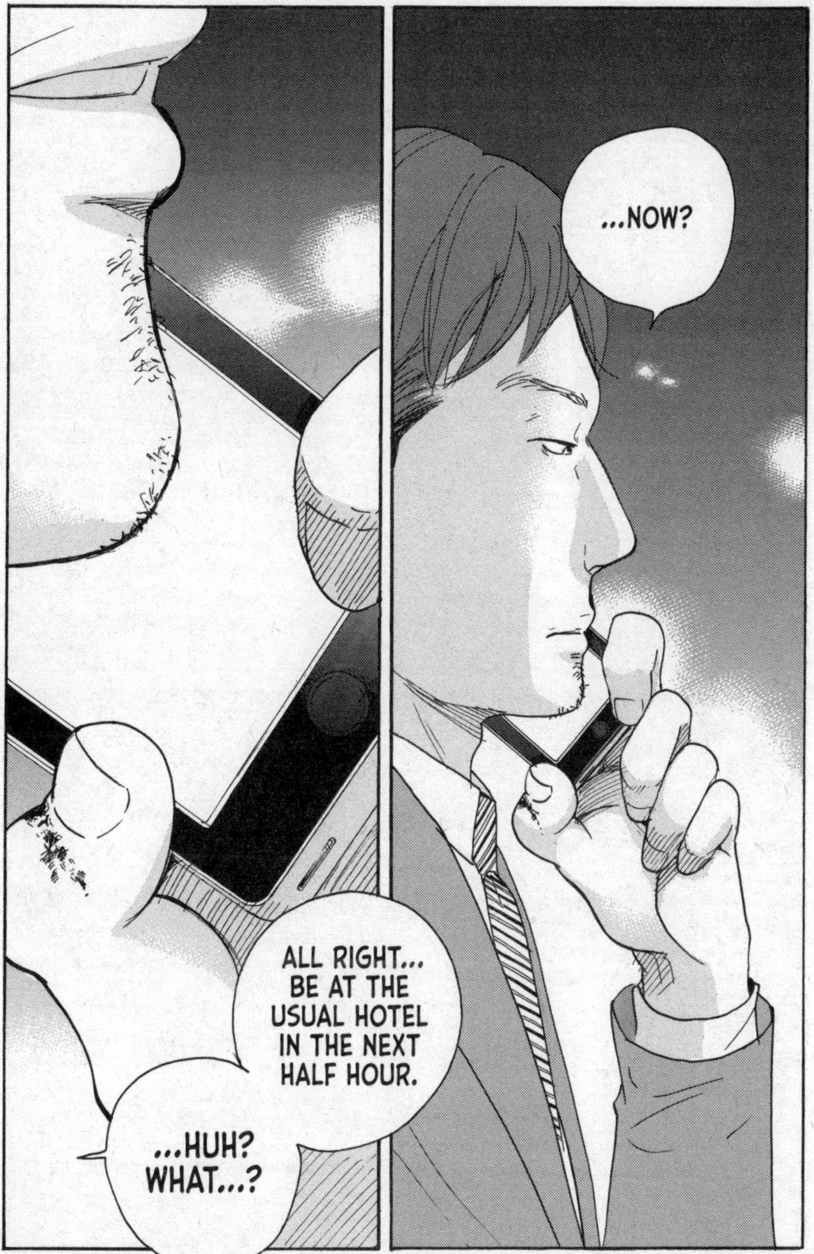
...NOW?
ALL RIGHT... BE AT THE USUAL HOTEL IN THE NEXT HALF HOUR.
...HUH? WHAT...?

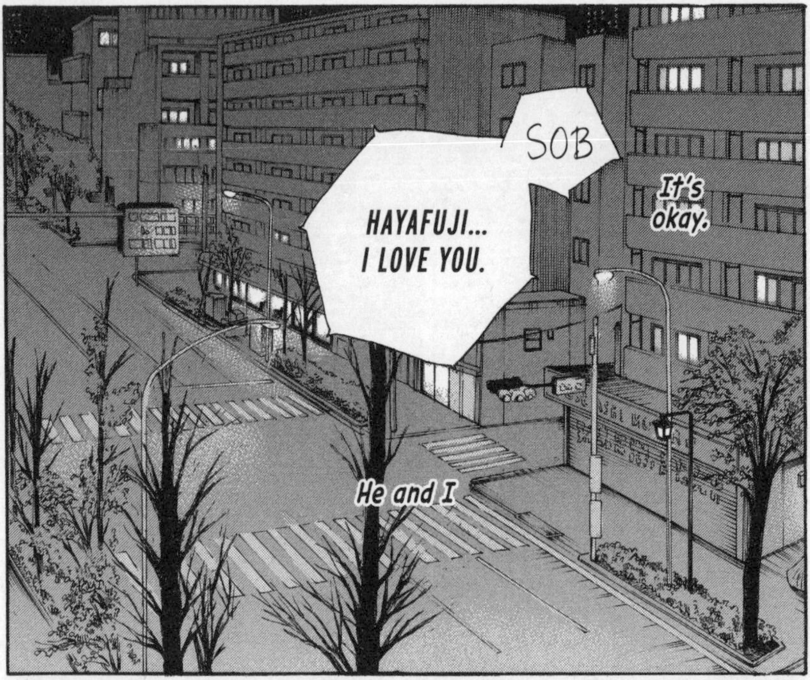
SOB
It's okay.
HAYAFUJI... I LOVE YOU.
He and I

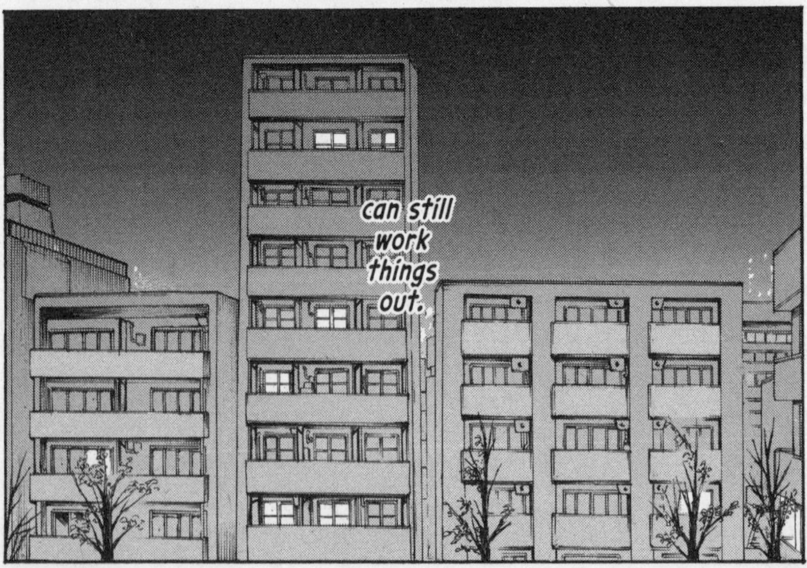
can still work things out.

END

CHAPTER 22. CONGRATULATIONS

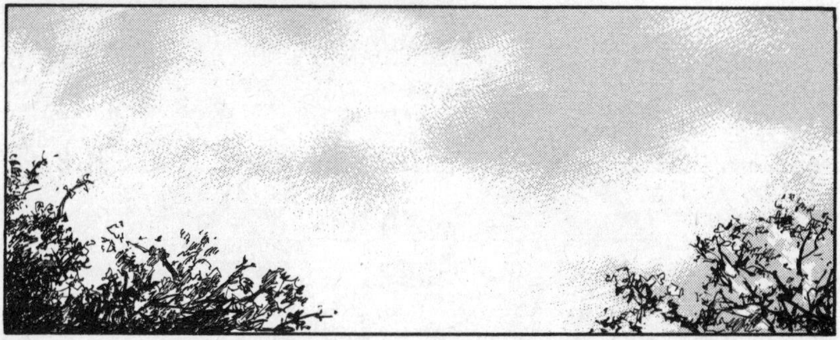

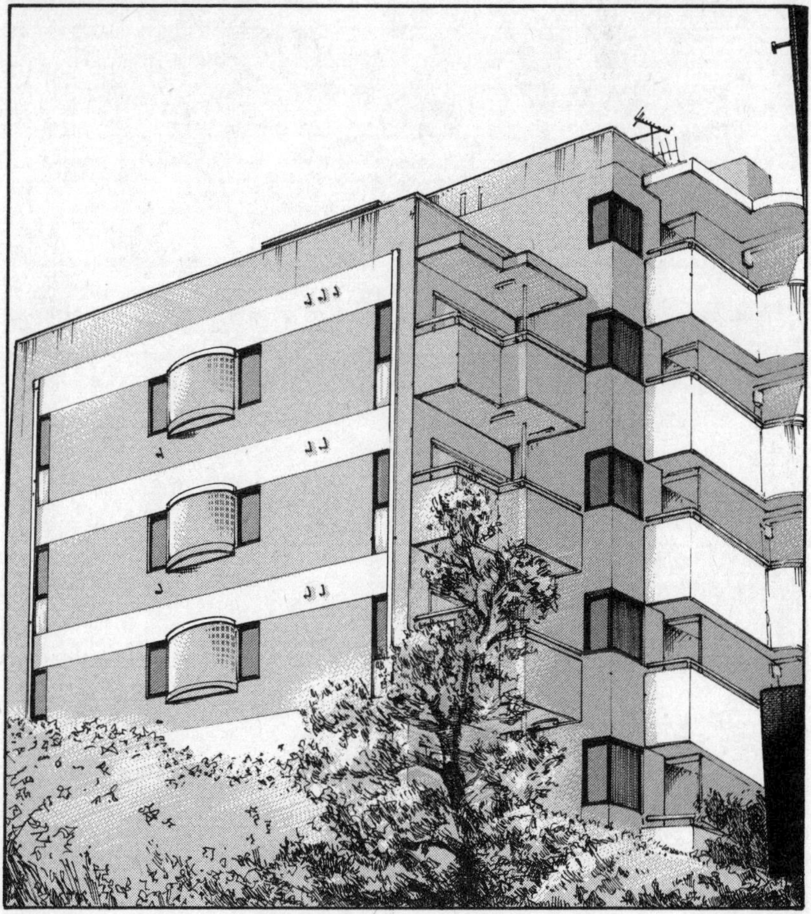

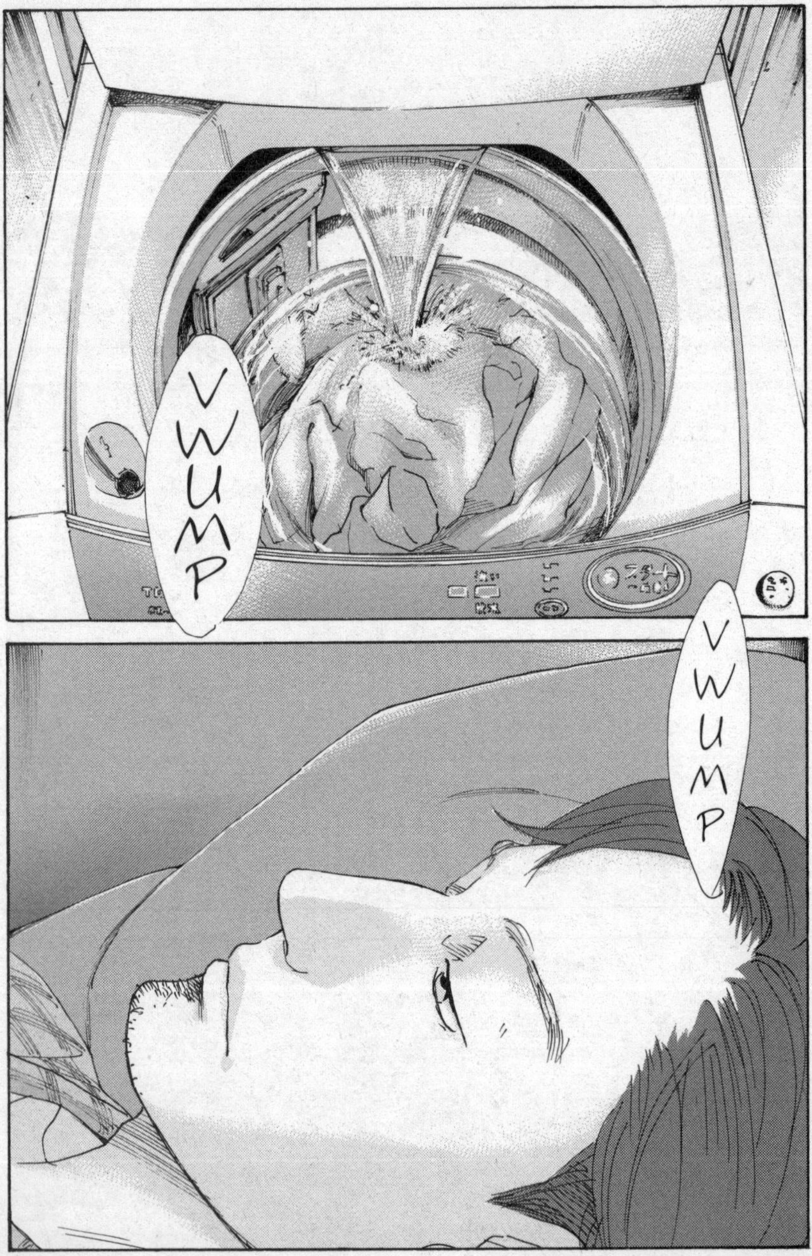
VWUMP
VWUMP

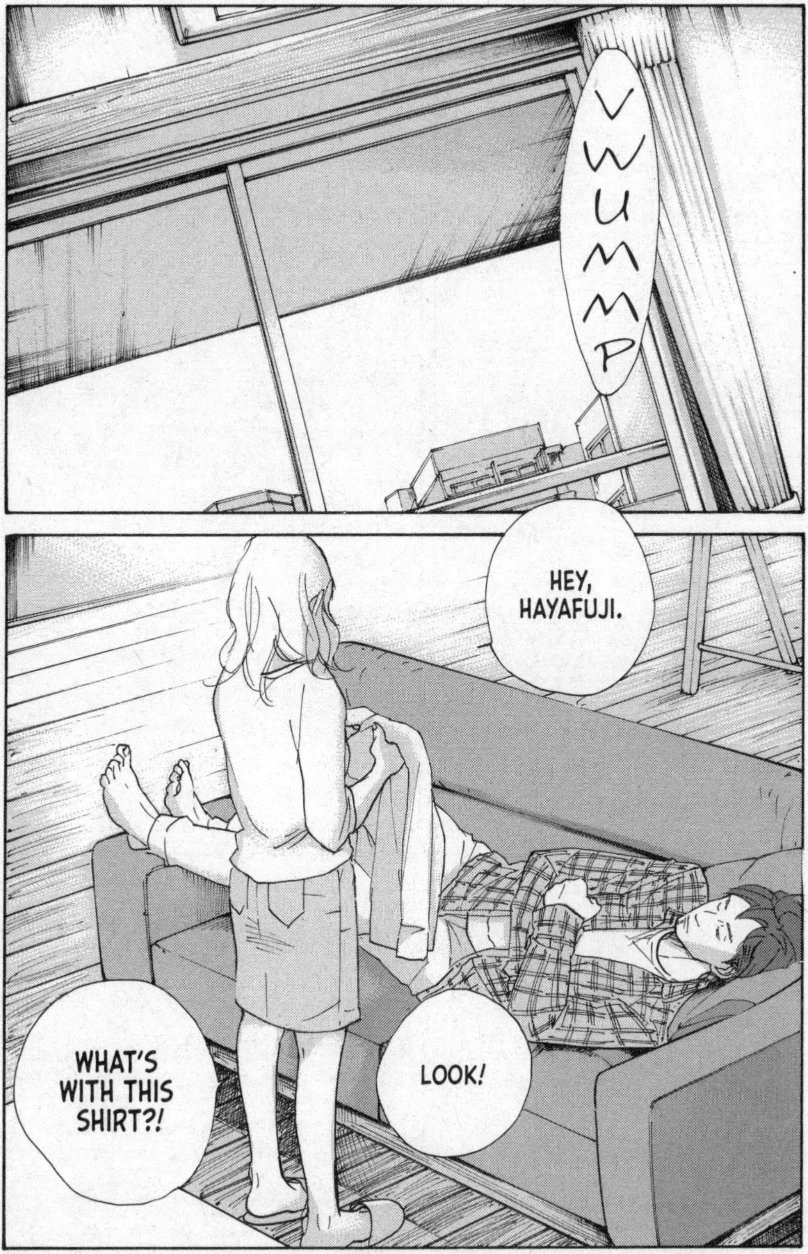
VWUMMP
HEY, HAYAFUJI.
LOOK!
WHAT'S WITH THIS SHIRT?!

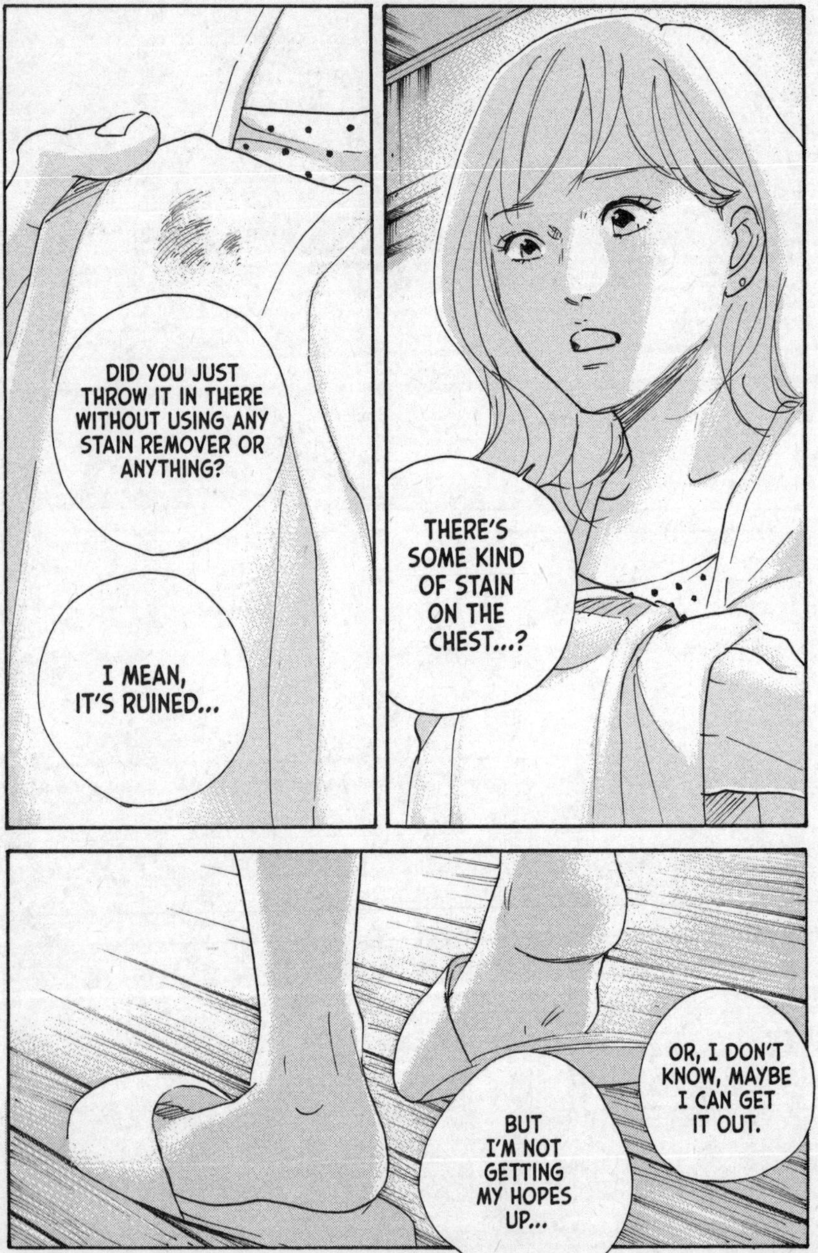
THERE'S SOME KIND OF STAIN ON THE CHEST...?
DID YOU JUST THROW IT IN THERE WITHOUT USING ANY STAIN REMOVER OR ANYTHING?
I MEAN, IT'S RUINED...
OR, I DON'T KNOW, MAYBE I CAN GET IT OUT.
BUT I'M NOT GETTING MY HOPES UP...

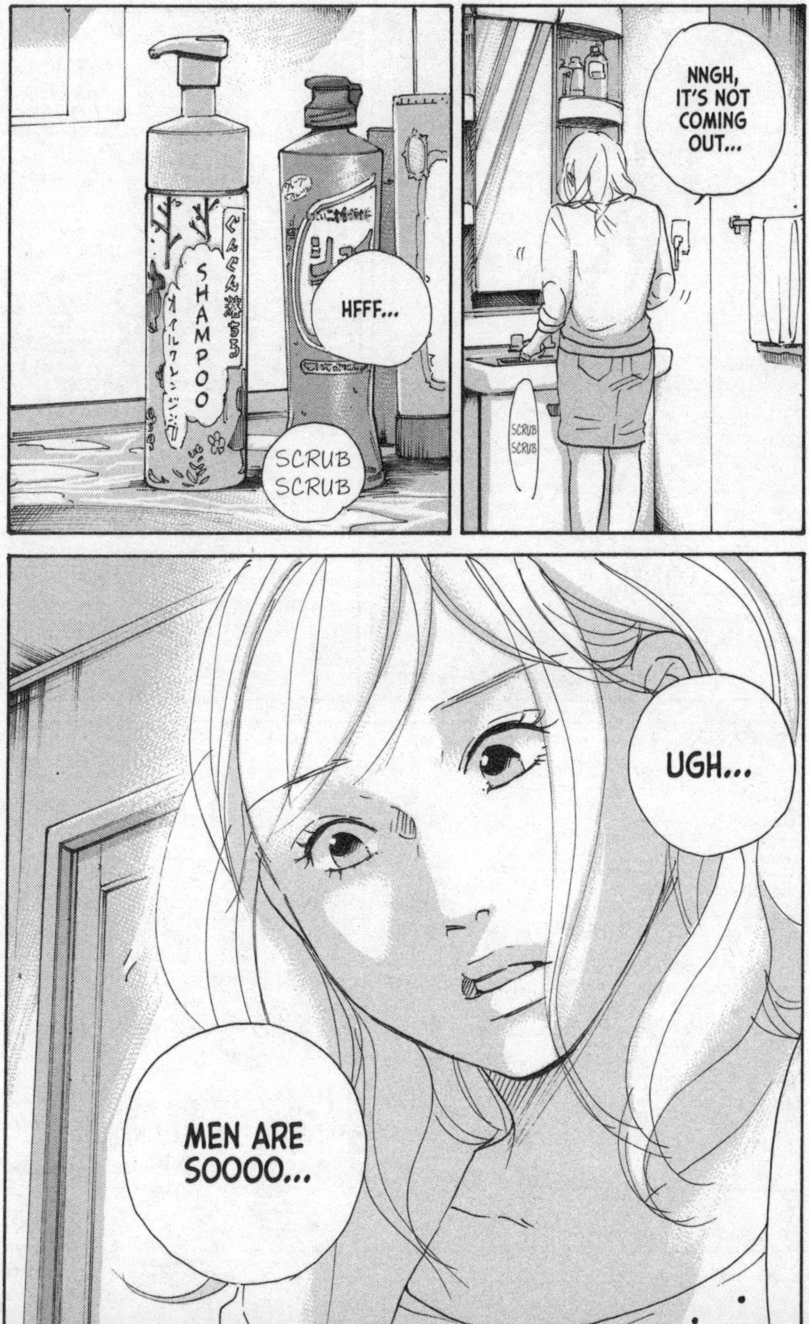
NNGH, IT'S NOT COMING OUT...
SCRUB SCRUB
HFFF...
SHAMPOO
SCRUB SCRUB
UGH...
MEN ARE SOOOO...

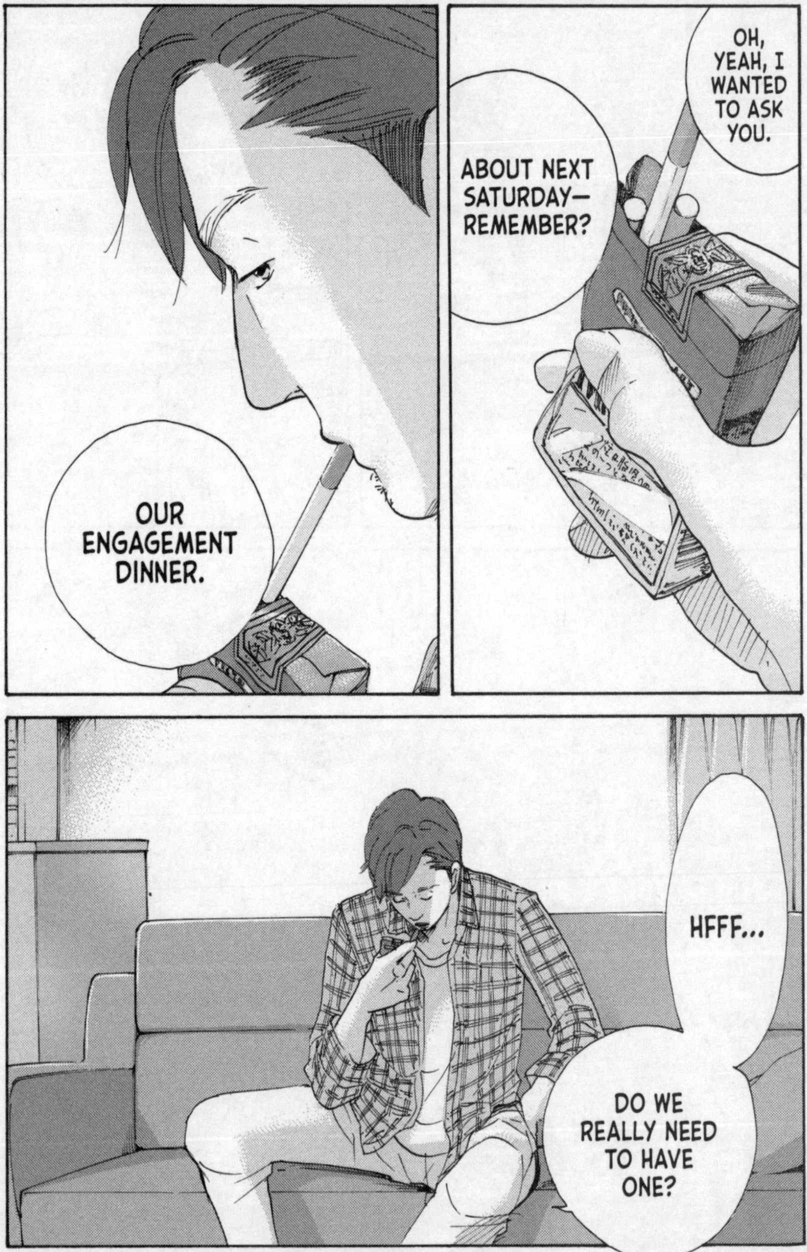
OH, YEAH, I WANTED TO ASK YOU.
ABOUT NEXT SATURDAY—REMEMBER?
OUR ENGAGEMENT DINNER.
HFFF...
DO WE REALLY NEED TO HAVE ONE?

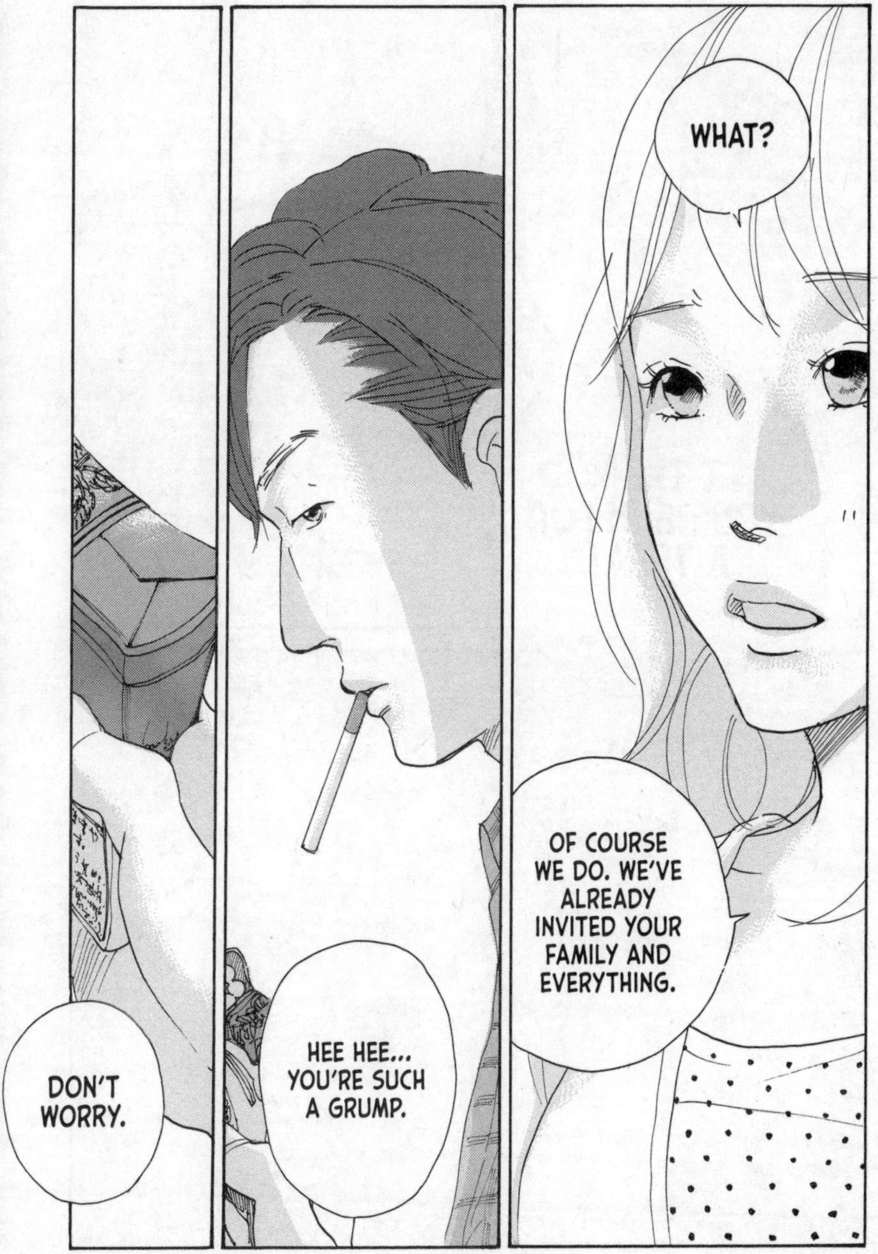
WHAT?
OF COURSE WE DO. WE'VE ALREADY INVITED YOUR FAMILY AND EVERYTHING.
HEE HEE... YOU'RE SUCH A GRUMP.
DON'T WORRY.

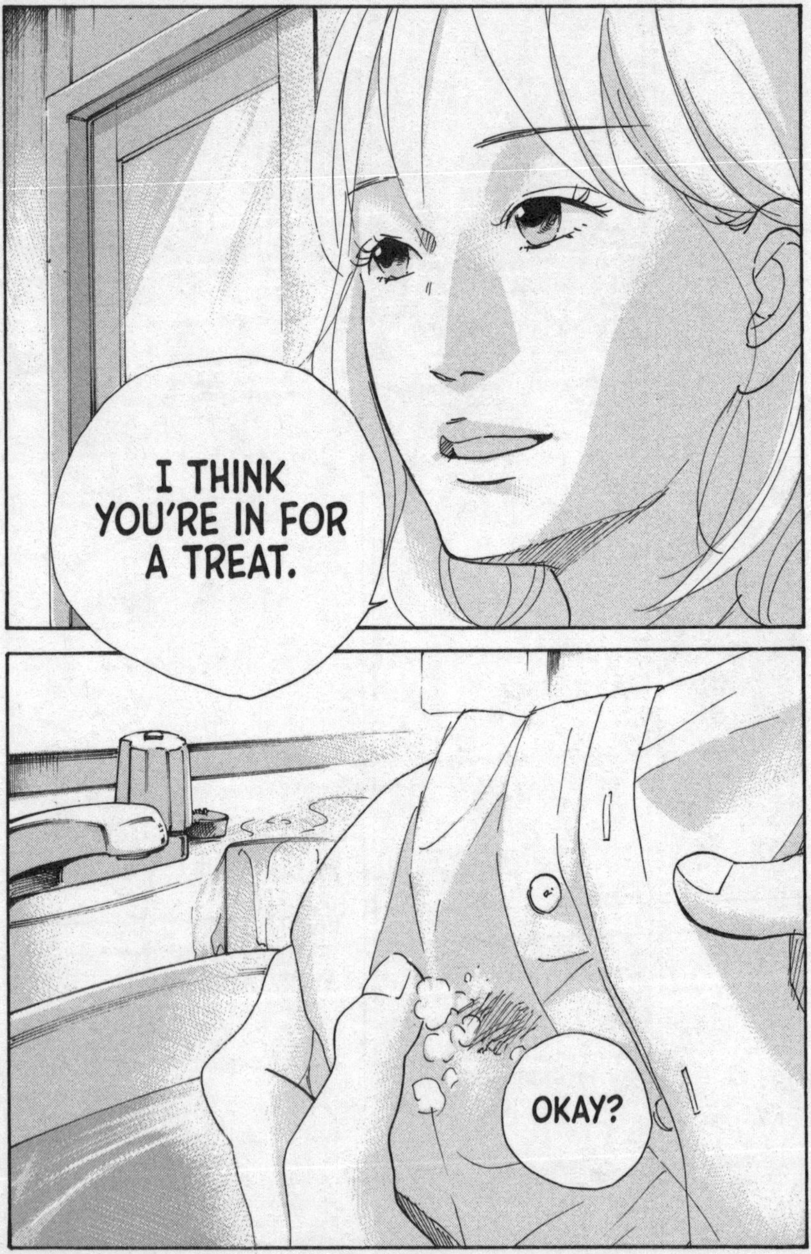
I THINK YOU'RE IN FOR A TREAT.
OKAY?

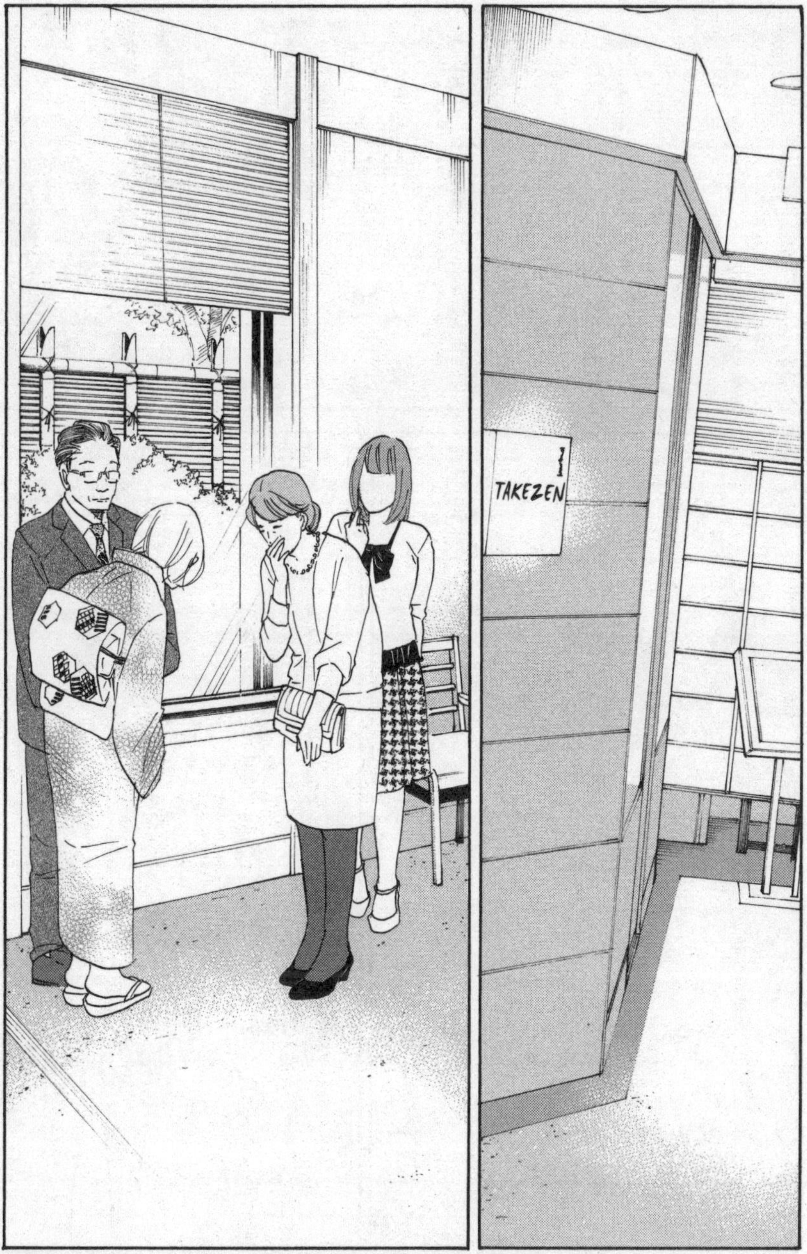
TAKEZEN

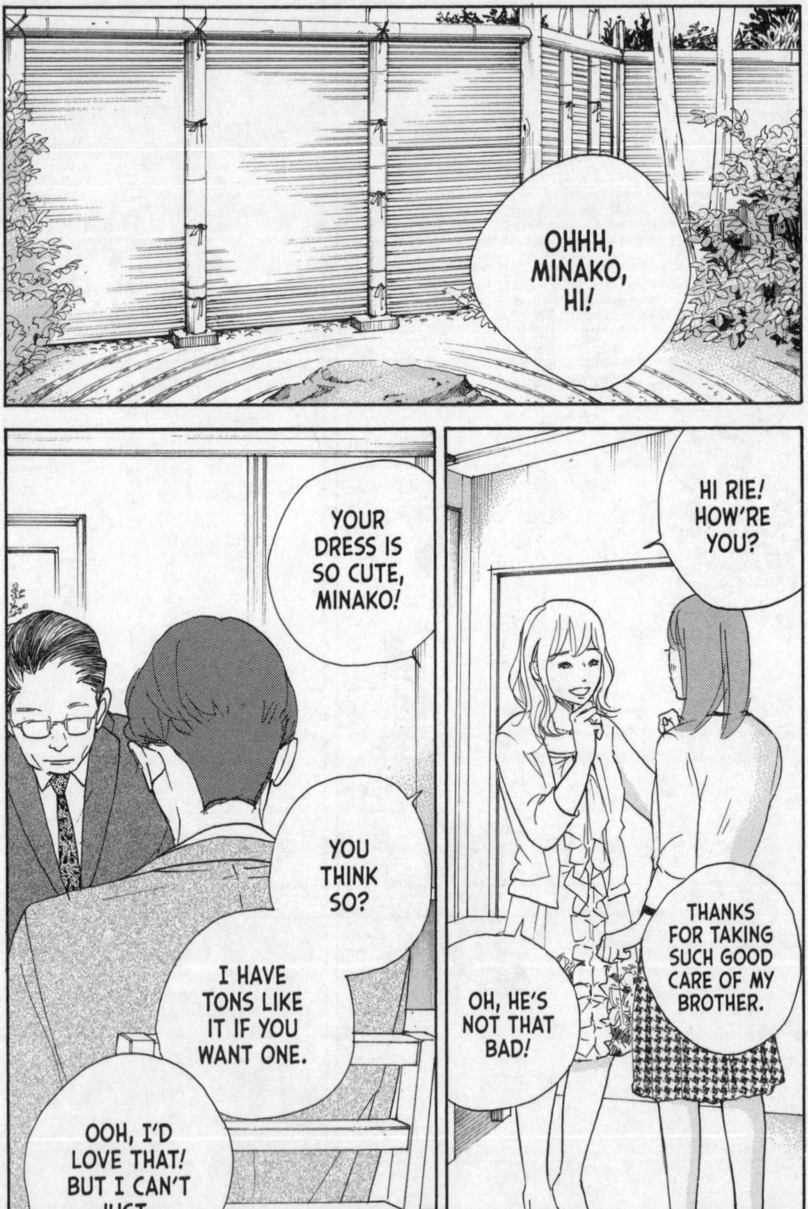
OHHH, MINAKO, HI!
HI RIE! HOW'RE YOU?
THANKS FOR TAKING SUCH GOOD CARE OF MY BROTHER.
OH, HE'S NOT THAT BAD!
YOUR DRESS IS SO CUTE, MINAKO!
YOU THINK SO?
I HAVE TONS LIKE IT IF YOU WANT ONE.
OOH, I'D LOVE THAT! BUT I CAN'T JUST...

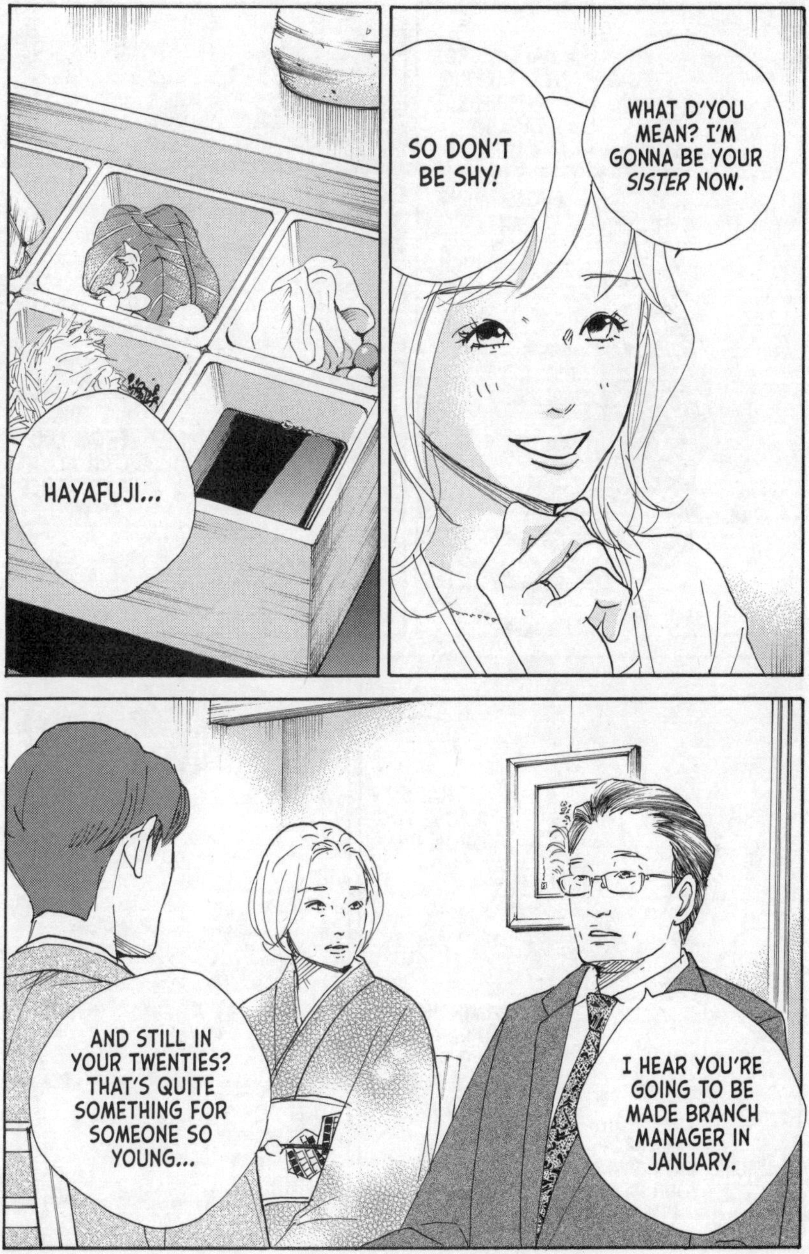
WHAT D'YOU MEAN? I'M GONNA BE YOUR *SISTER* NOW.
SO DON'T BE SHY!
HAYAFUJI...
I HEAR YOU'RE GOING TO BE MADE BRANCH MANAGER IN JANUARY.
AND STILL IN YOUR TWENTIES? THAT'S QUITE SOMETHING FOR SOMEONE SO YOUNG...

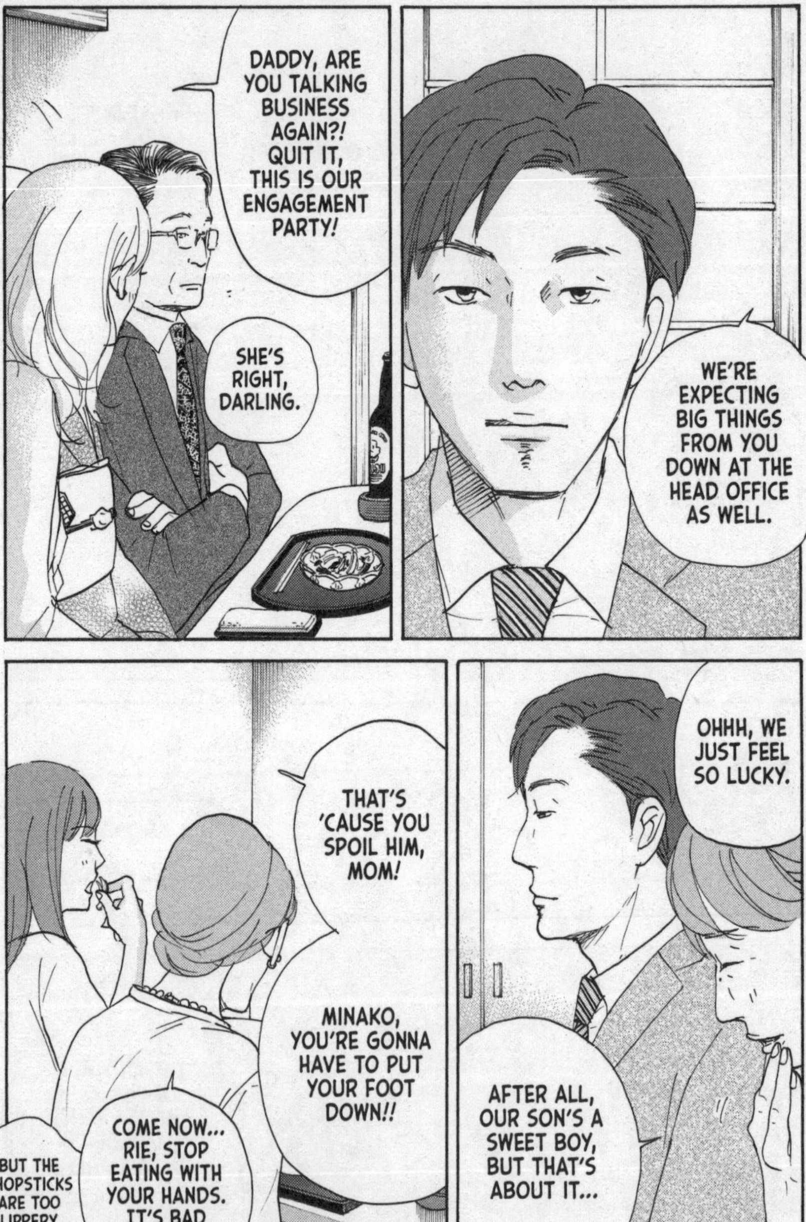
WE'RE EXPECTING BIG THINGS FROM YOU DOWN AT THE HEAD OFFICE AS WELL.
DADDY, ARE YOU TALKING BUSINESS AGAIN?! QUIT IT, THIS IS OUR ENGAGEMENT PARTY!
SHE'S RIGHT, DARLING.
OHHH, WE JUST FEEL SO LUCKY.
AFTER ALL, OUR SON'S A SWEET BOY, BUT THAT'S ABOUT IT...
THAT'S 'CAUSE YOU SPOIL HIM, MOM!
MINAKO, YOU'RE GONNA HAVE TO PUT YOUR FOOT DOWN!!
COME NOW... RIE, STOP EATING WITH YOUR HANDS. IT'S BAD MANNERS.
BUT THE CHOPSTICKS ARE TOO SLIPPERY...

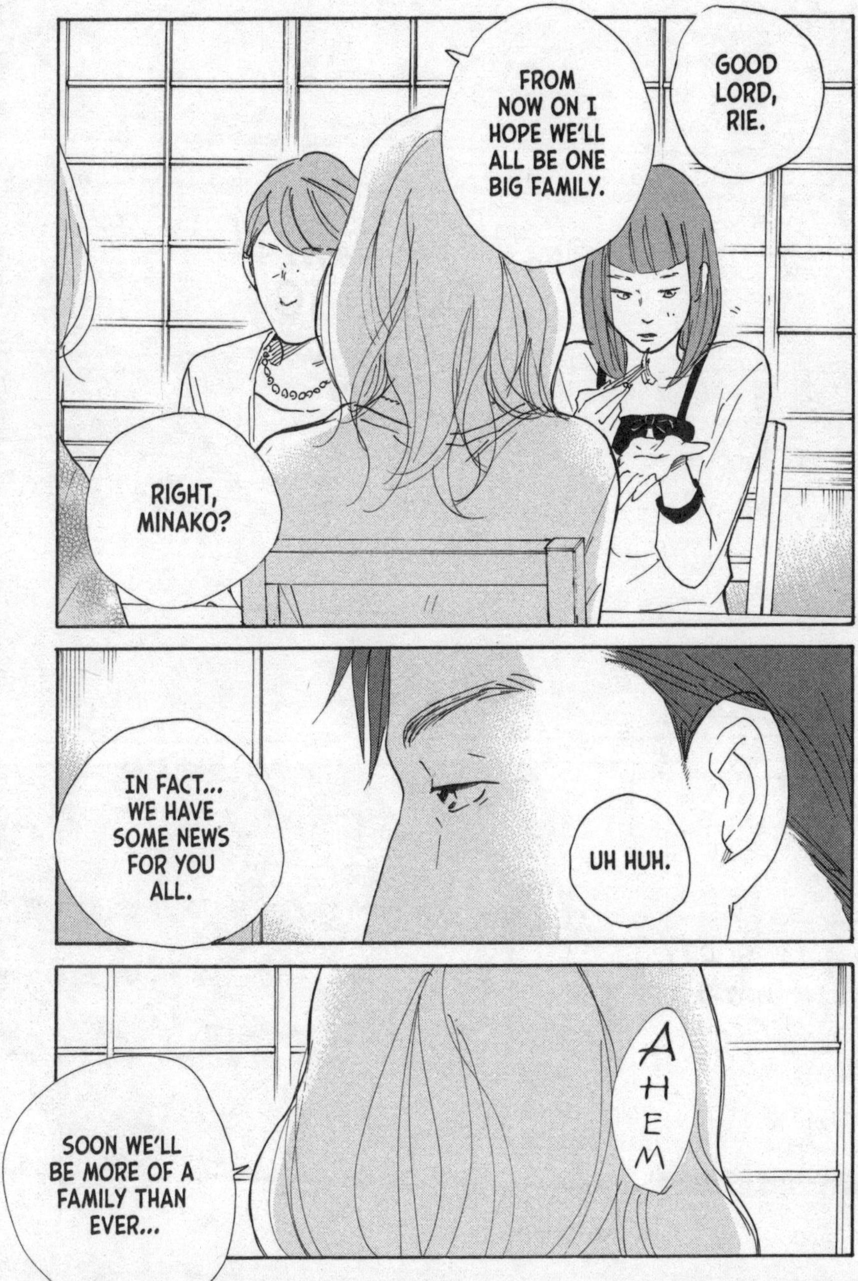
GOOD LORD, RIE.
FROM NOW ON I HOPE WE'LL ALL BE ONE BIG FAMILY.
RIGHT, MINAKO?
UH HUH.
IN FACT... WE HAVE SOME NEWS FOR YOU ALL.
AHEM
SOON WE'LL BE MORE OF A FAMILY THAN EVER...

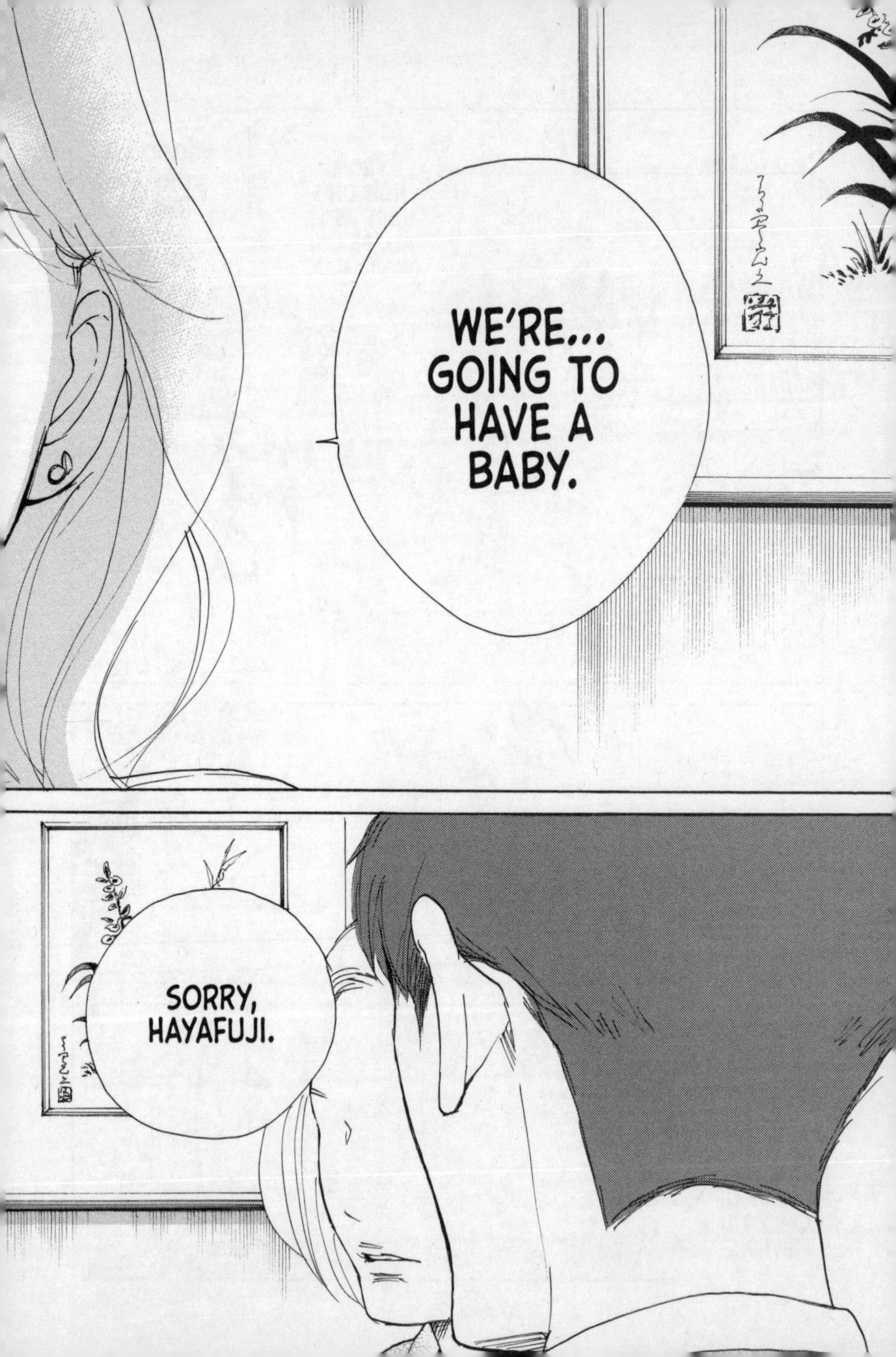
WE'RE... GOING TO HAVE A BABY.
SORRY, HAYAFUJI.

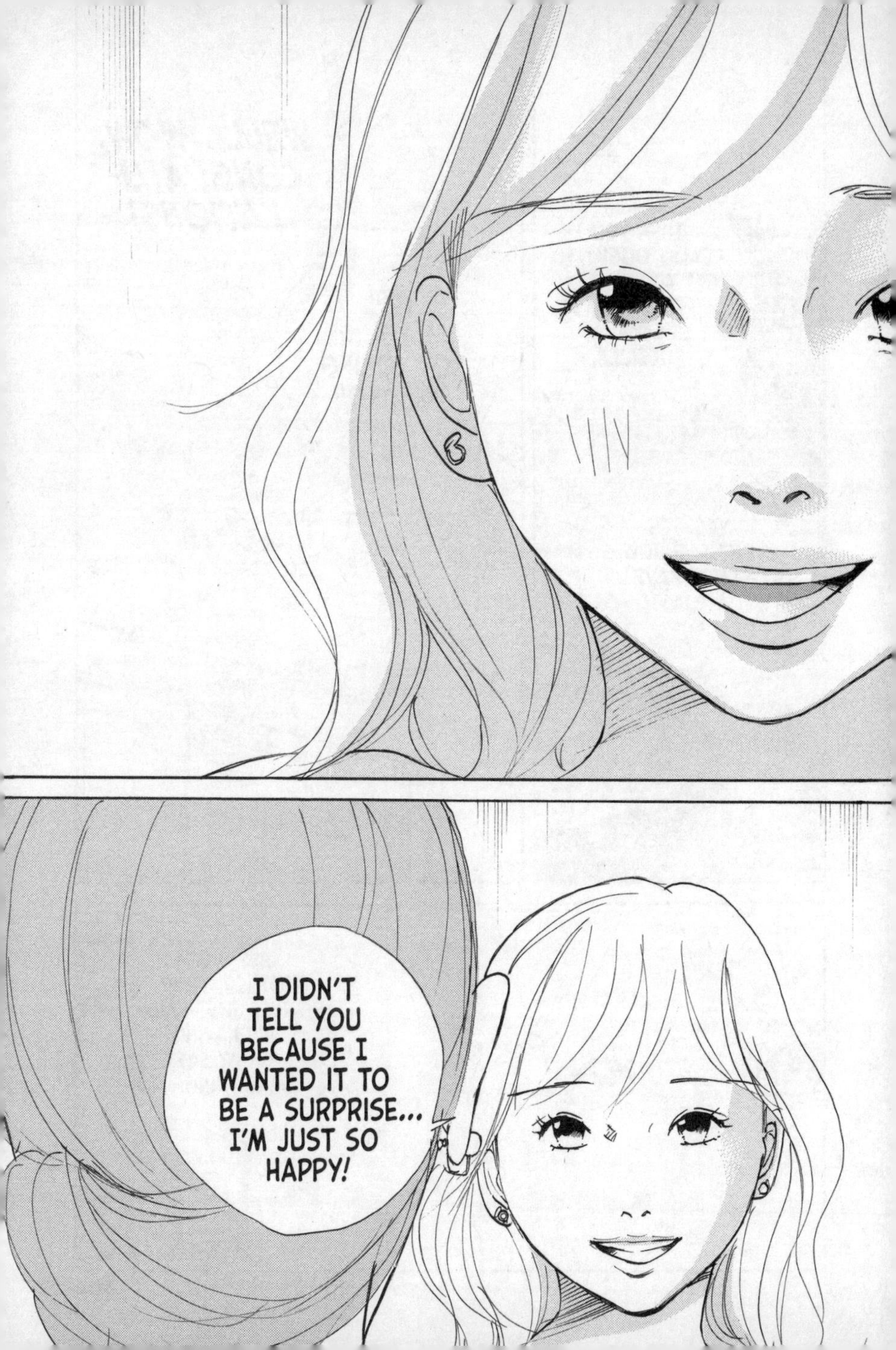
I DIDN'T TELL YOU BECAUSE I WANTED IT TO BE A SURPRISE... I'M JUST SO HAPPY!

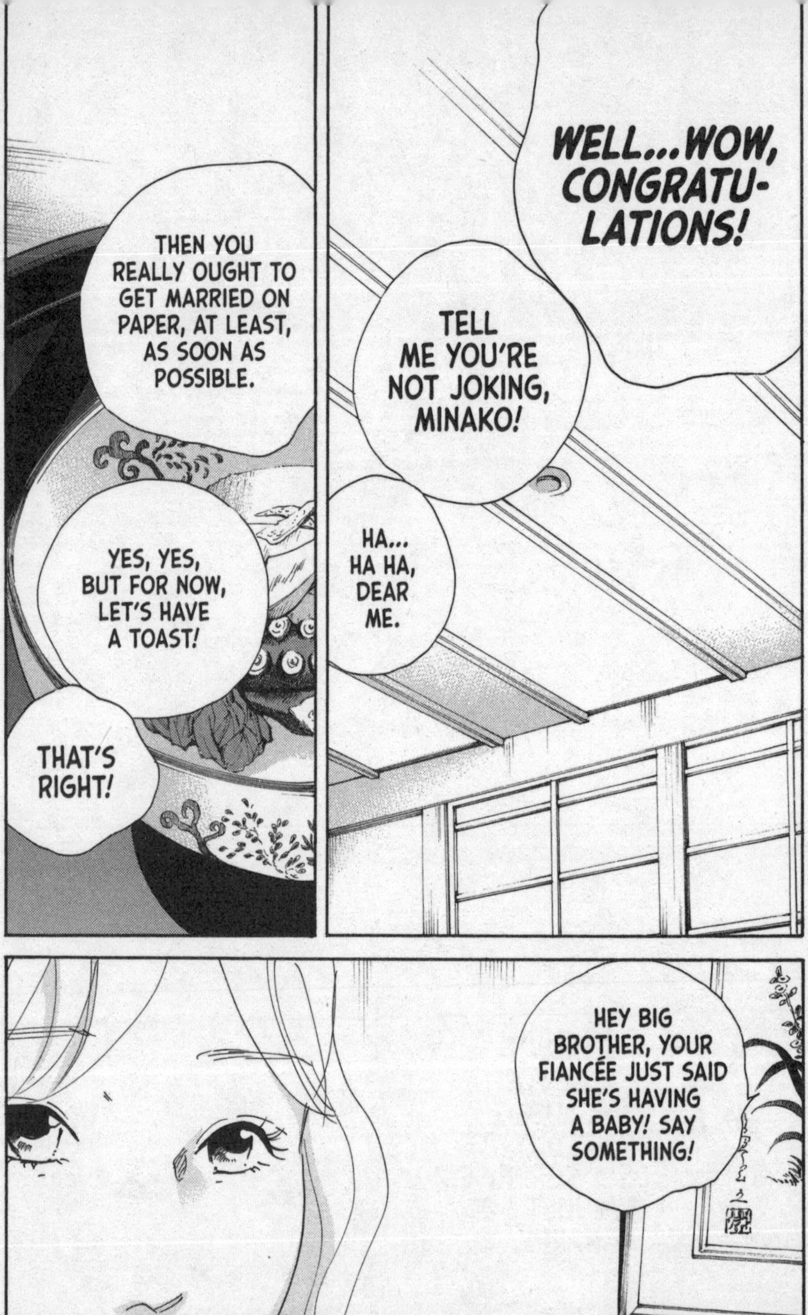
WELL...WOW, CONGRATU-LATIONS!
TELL ME YOU'RE NOT JOKING, MINAKO!
HA... HA HA, DEAR ME.
THEN YOU REALLY OUGHT TO GET MARRIED ON PAPER, AT LEAST, AS SOON AS POSSIBLE.
YES, YES, BUT FOR NOW, LET'S HAVE A TOAST!
THAT'S RIGHT!
HEY BIG BROTHER, YOUR FIANCÉE JUST SAID SHE'S HAVING A BABY! SAY SOMETHING!

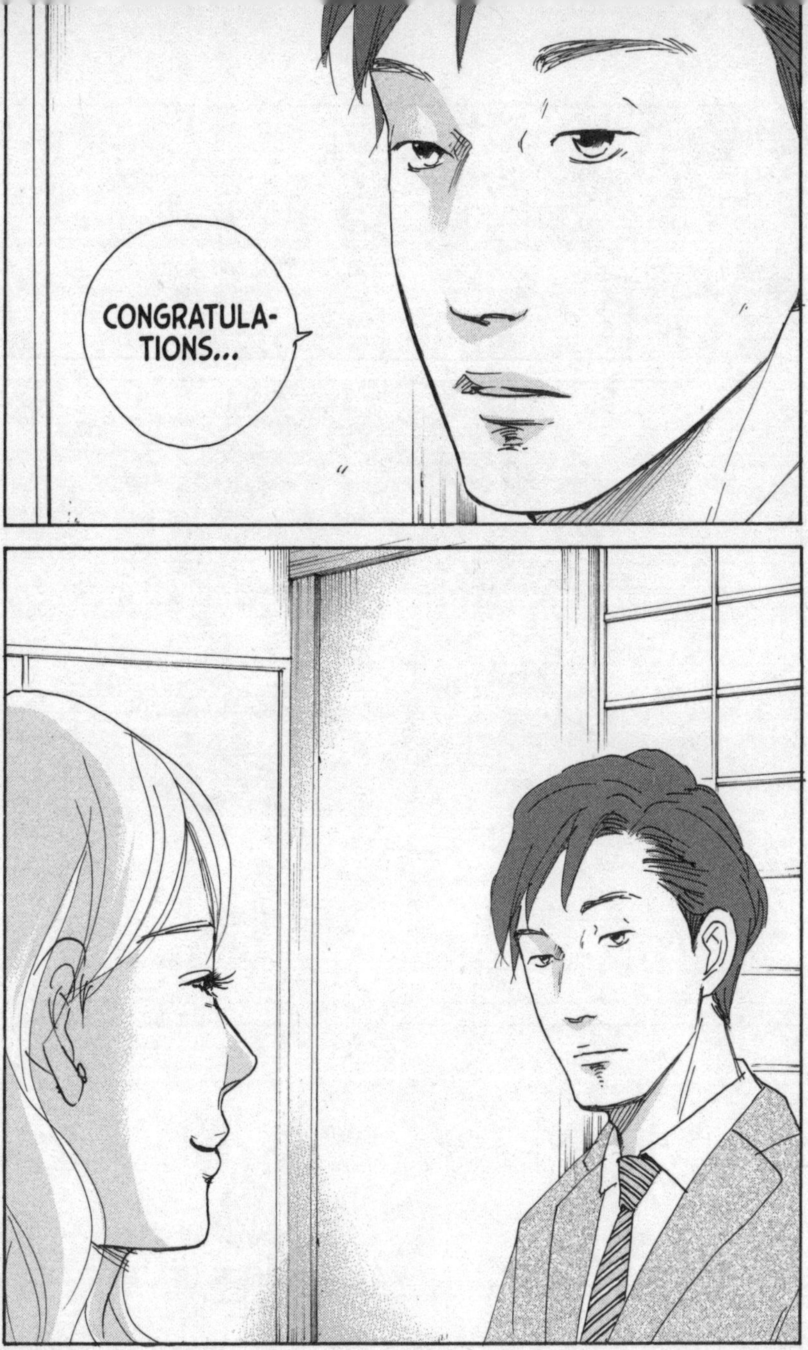
CONGRATULA-
TIONS...

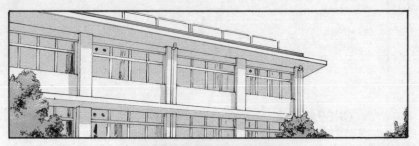

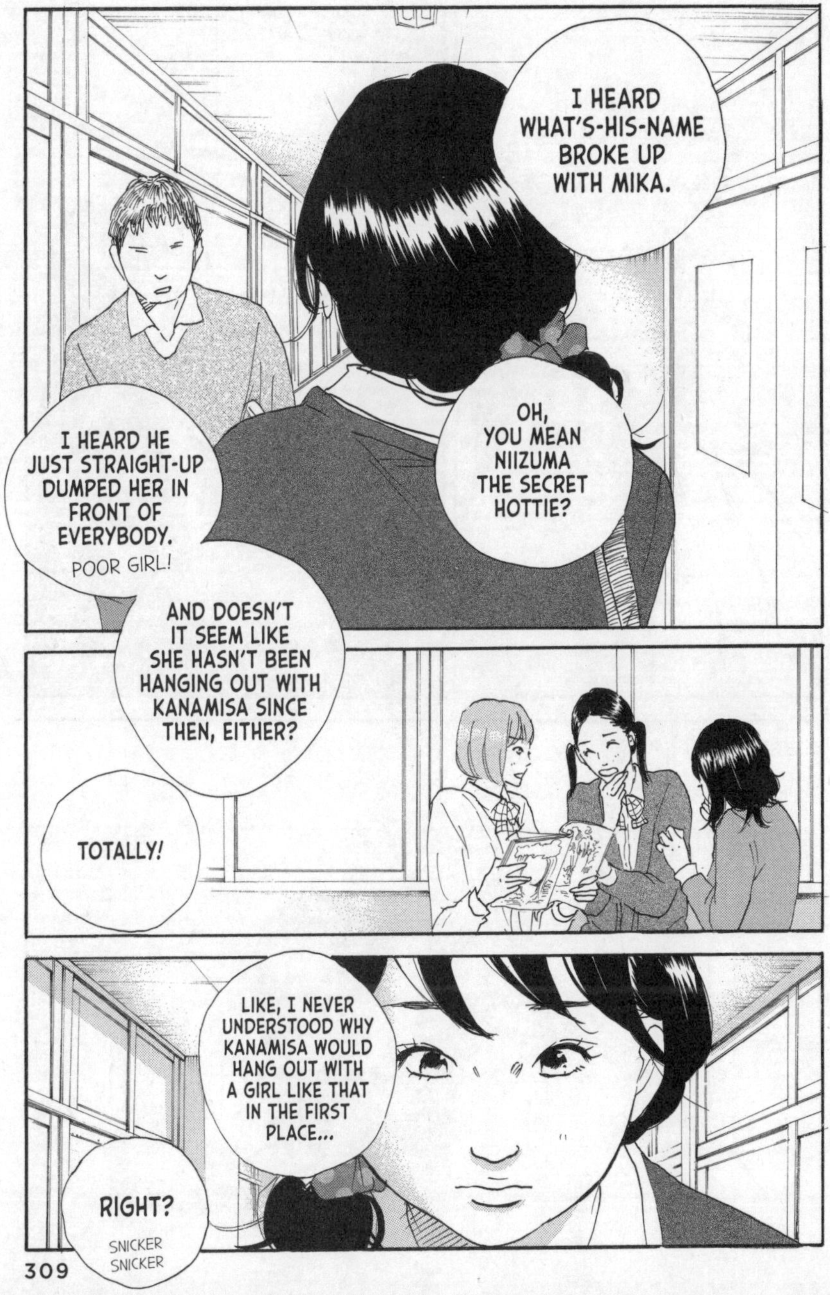
I HEARD WHAT'S-HIS-NAME BROKE UP WITH MIKA.
OH, YOU MEAN NIIZUMA THE SECRET HOTTIE?
I HEARD HE JUST STRAIGHT-UP DUMPED HER IN FRONT OF EVERYBODY.
POOR GIRL!
AND DOESN'T IT SEEM LIKE SHE HASN'T BEEN HANGING OUT WITH KANAMISA SINCE THEN, EITHER?
TOTALLY!
LIKE, I NEVER UNDERSTOOD WHY KANAMISA WOULD HANG OUT WITH A GIRL LIKE THAT IN THE FIRST PLACE...
RIGHT?
SNICKER SNICKER

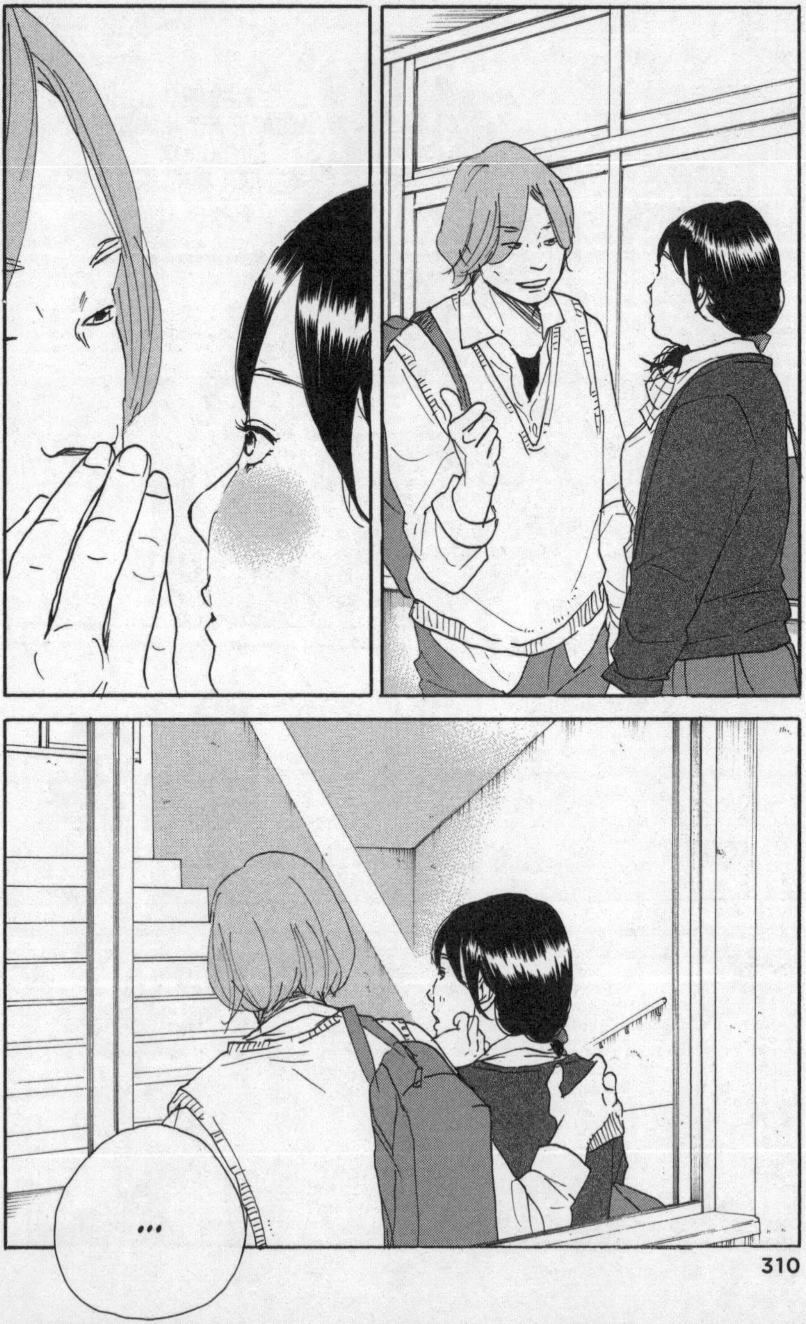
...

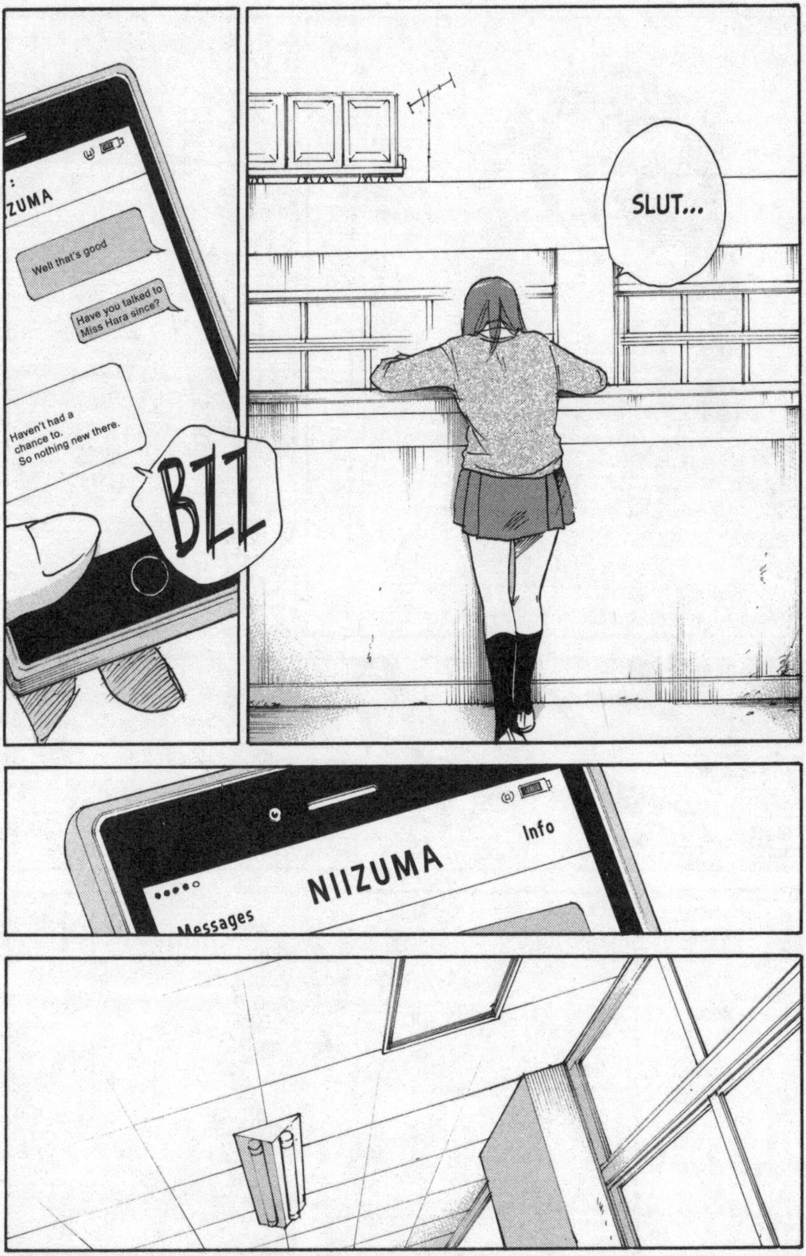
SLUT...
ZUMA
Well that's good
Have you talked to Miss Hara since?
Haven't had a chance to. So nothing new there.
BZZ
Info
NIIZUMA
Messages

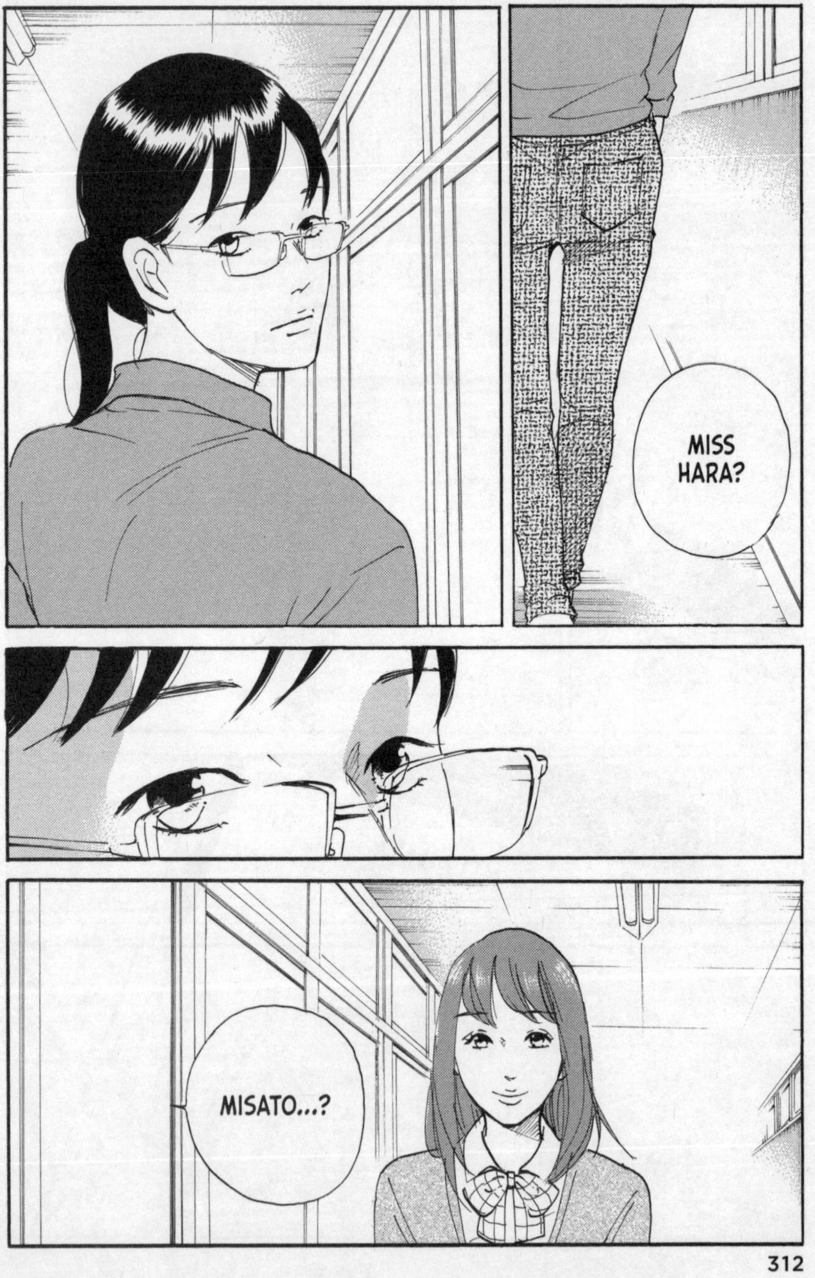
MISS HARA?
MISATO...?

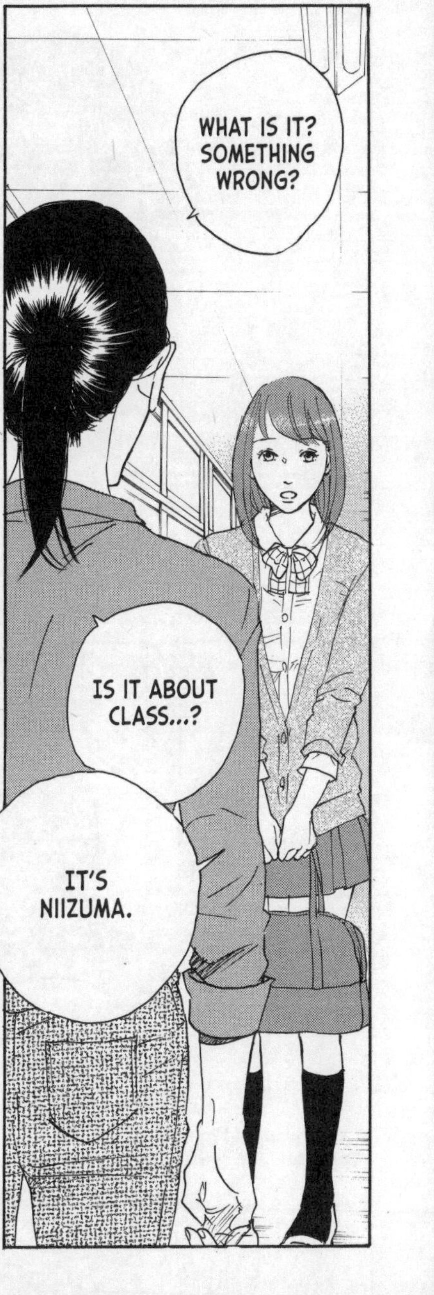
WHAT IS IT? SOMETHING WRONG?
IS IT ABOUT CLASS...?
IT'S NIIZUMA.

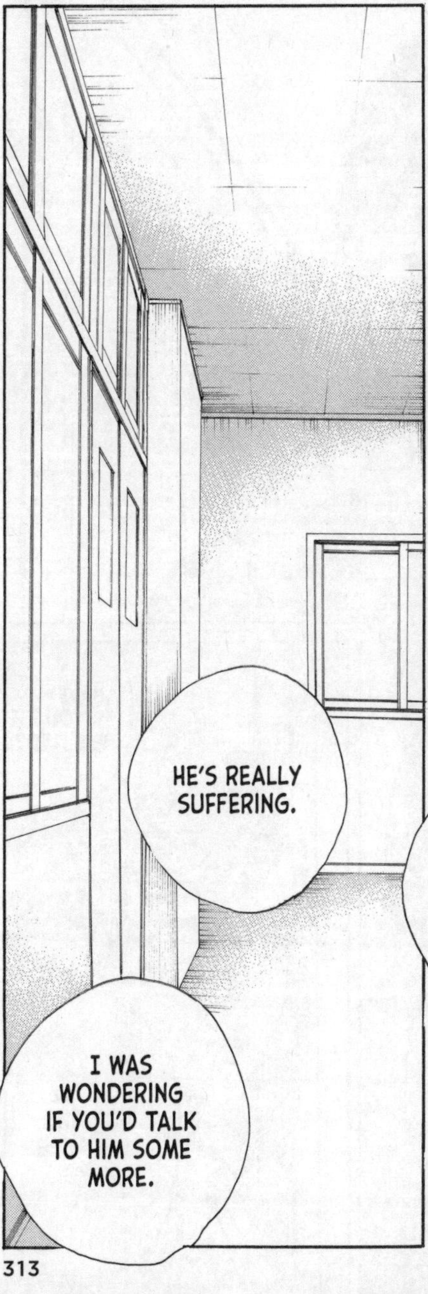
HE'S REALLY SUFFERING.
I WAS WONDERING IF YOU'D TALK TO HIM SOME MORE.

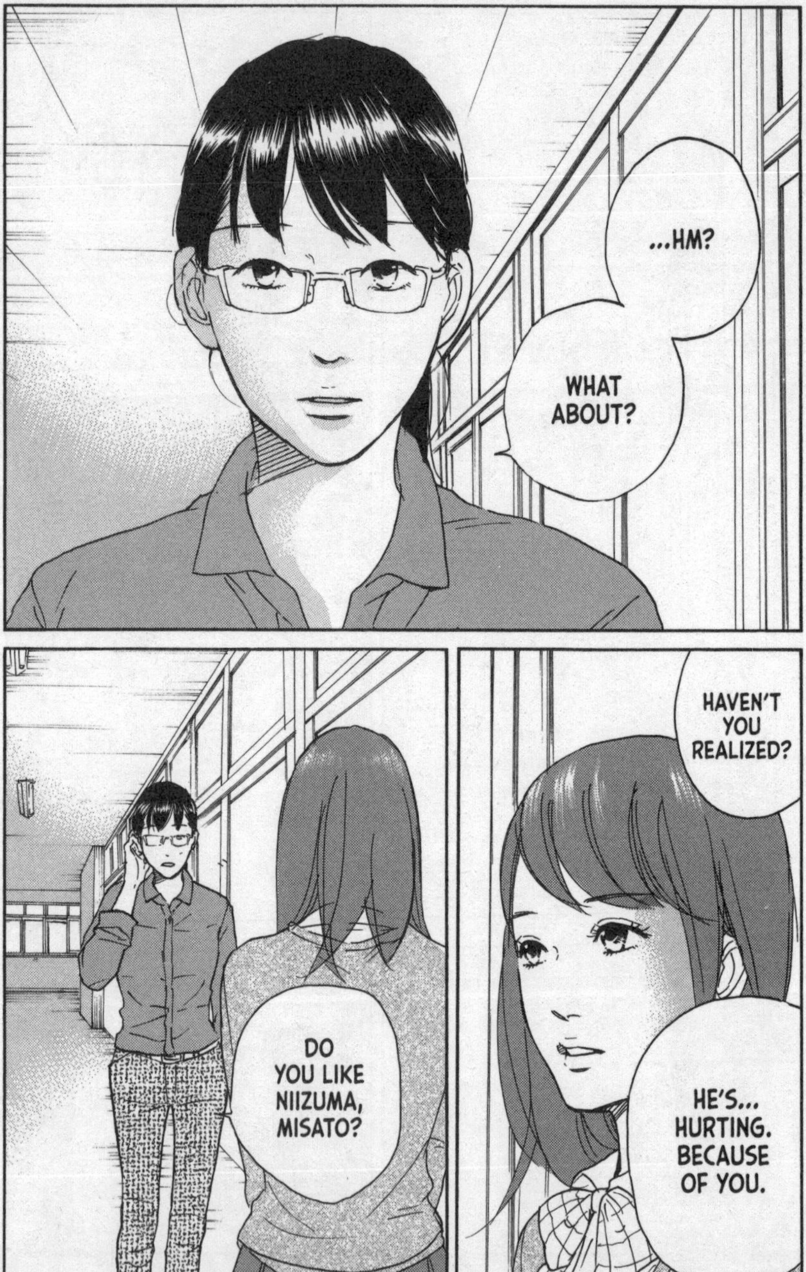
...HM?
WHAT ABOUT?
HAVEN'T YOU REALIZED?
HE'S... HURTING. BECAUSE OF YOU.
DO YOU LIKE NIIZUMA, MISATO?

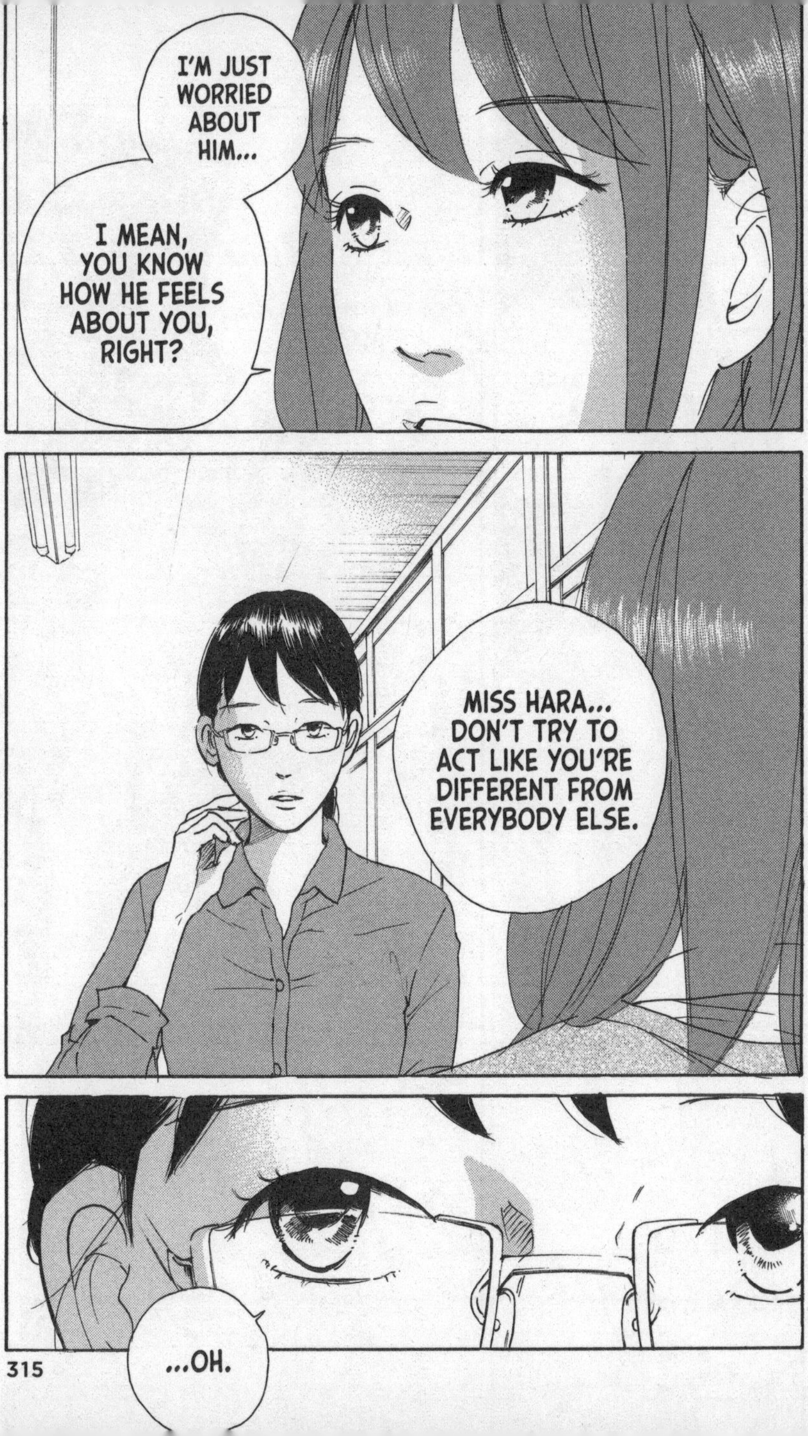
I'M JUST WORRIED ABOUT HIM...
I MEAN, YOU KNOW HOW HE FEELS ABOUT YOU, RIGHT?
MISS HARA... DON'T TRY TO ACT LIKE YOU'RE DIFFERENT FROM EVERYBODY ELSE.
...OH.

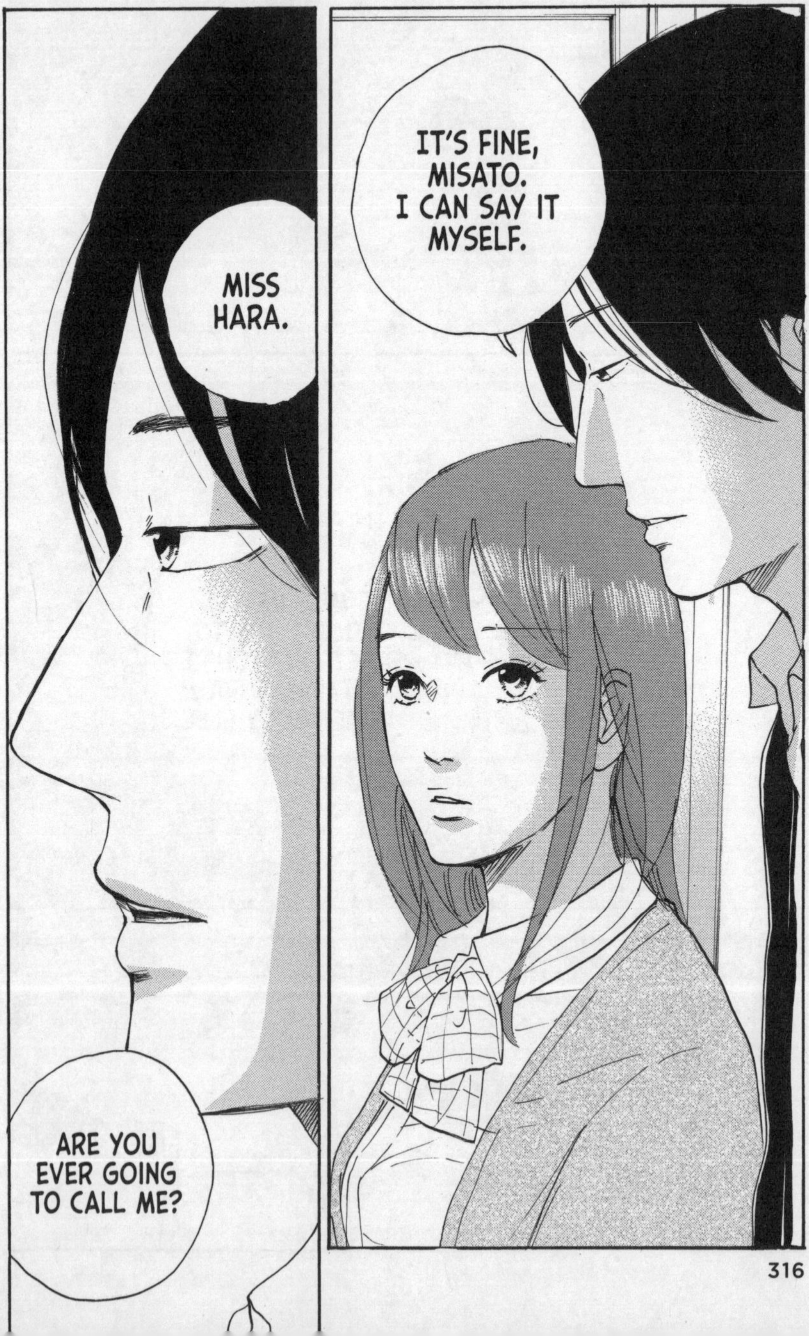
IT'S FINE, MISATO. I CAN SAY IT MYSELF.
MISS HARA.
ARE YOU EVER GOING TO CALL ME?

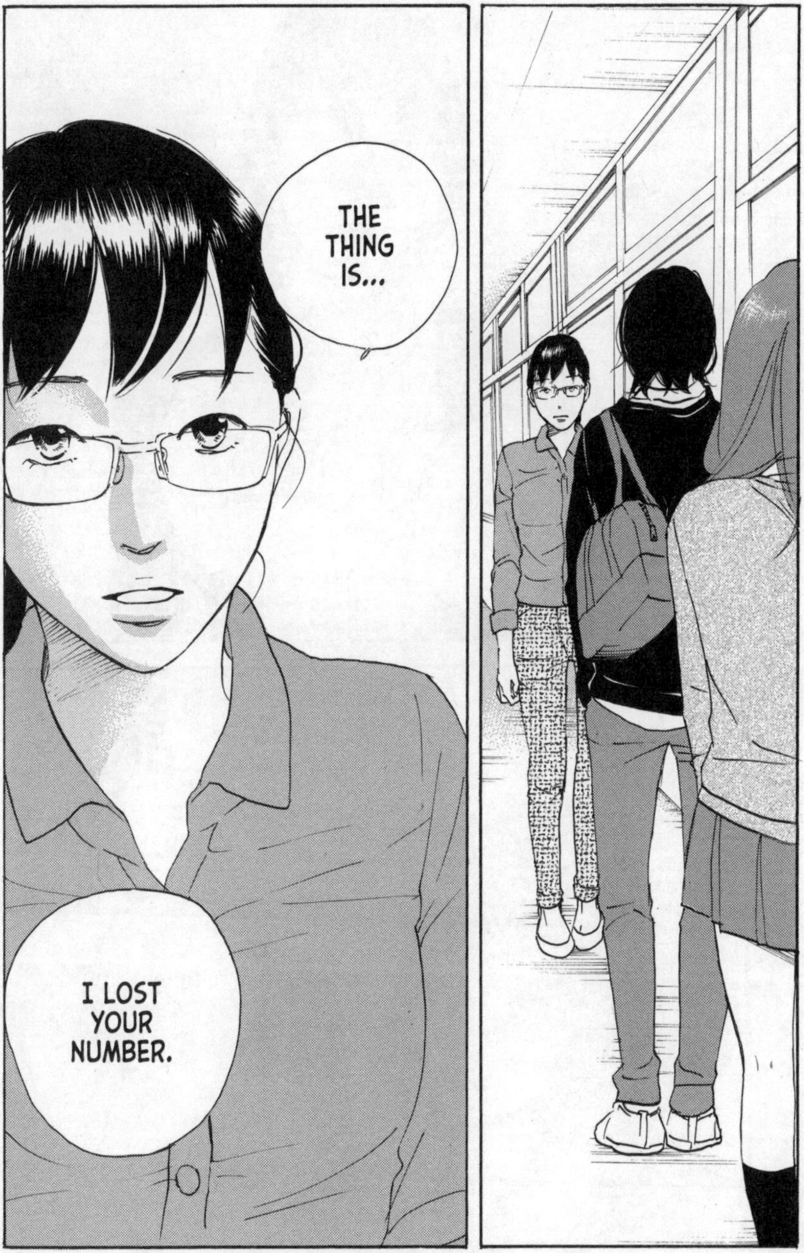
THE THING IS...
I LOST YOUR NUMBER.

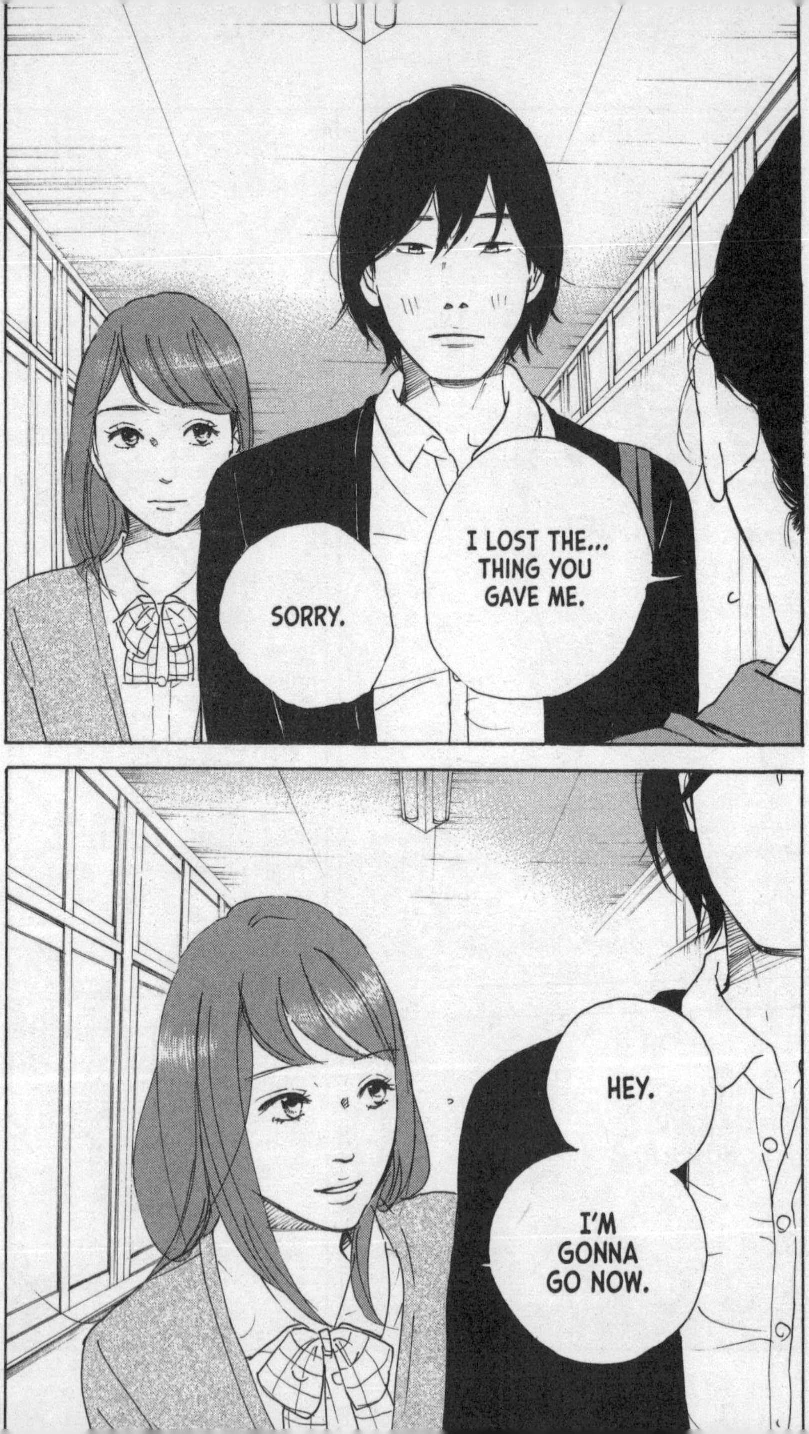
I LOST THE... THING YOU GAVE ME.
SORRY.
HEY.
I'M GONNA GO NOW.

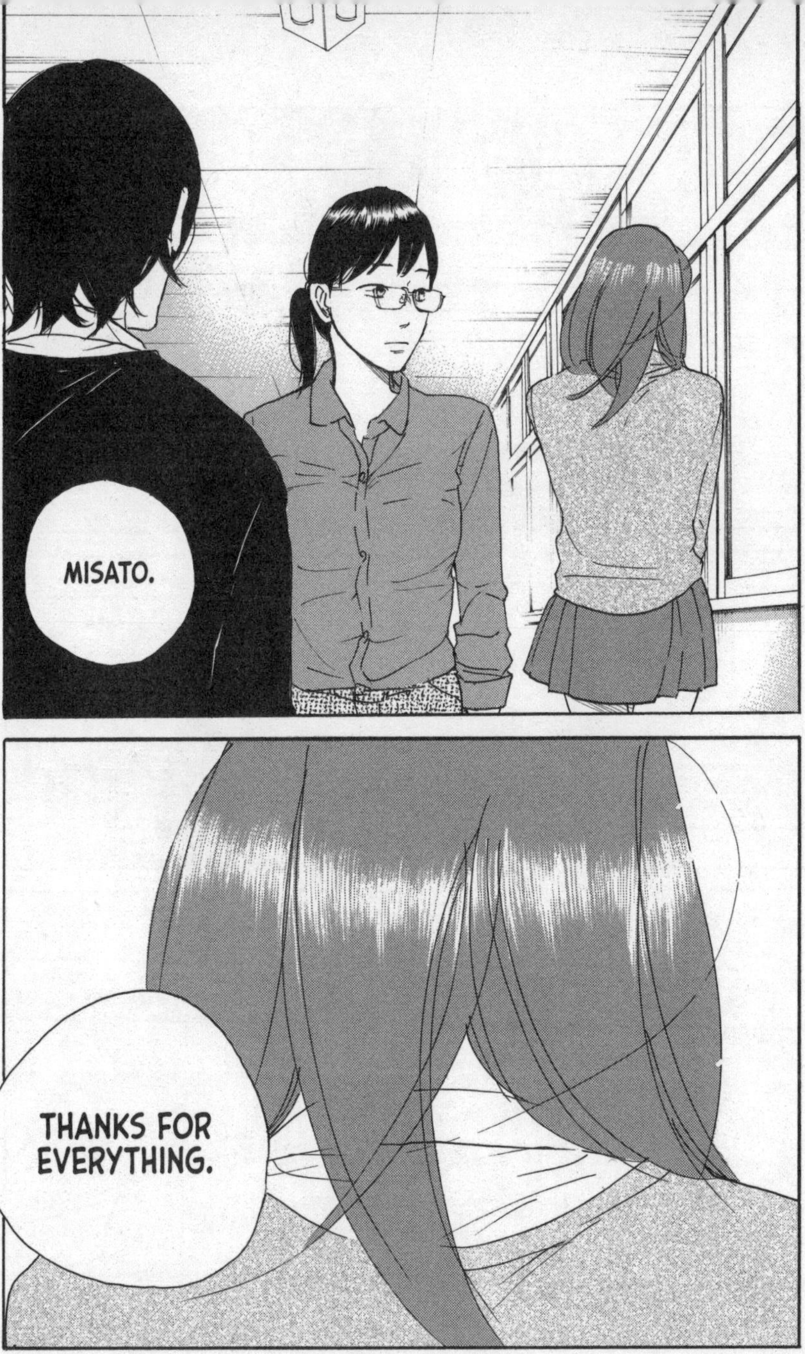
MISATO.
THANKS FOR EVERYTHING.

THEN...

I'LL BUY YOU ANOTHER ONE. ANOTHER ALARM.

I TOLD YOU, I DON'T NEED IT...

END

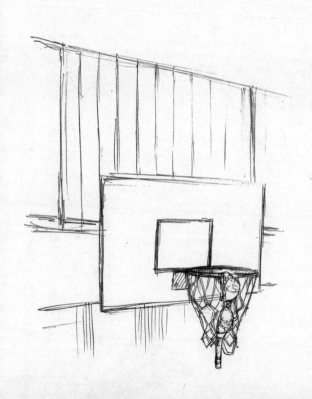

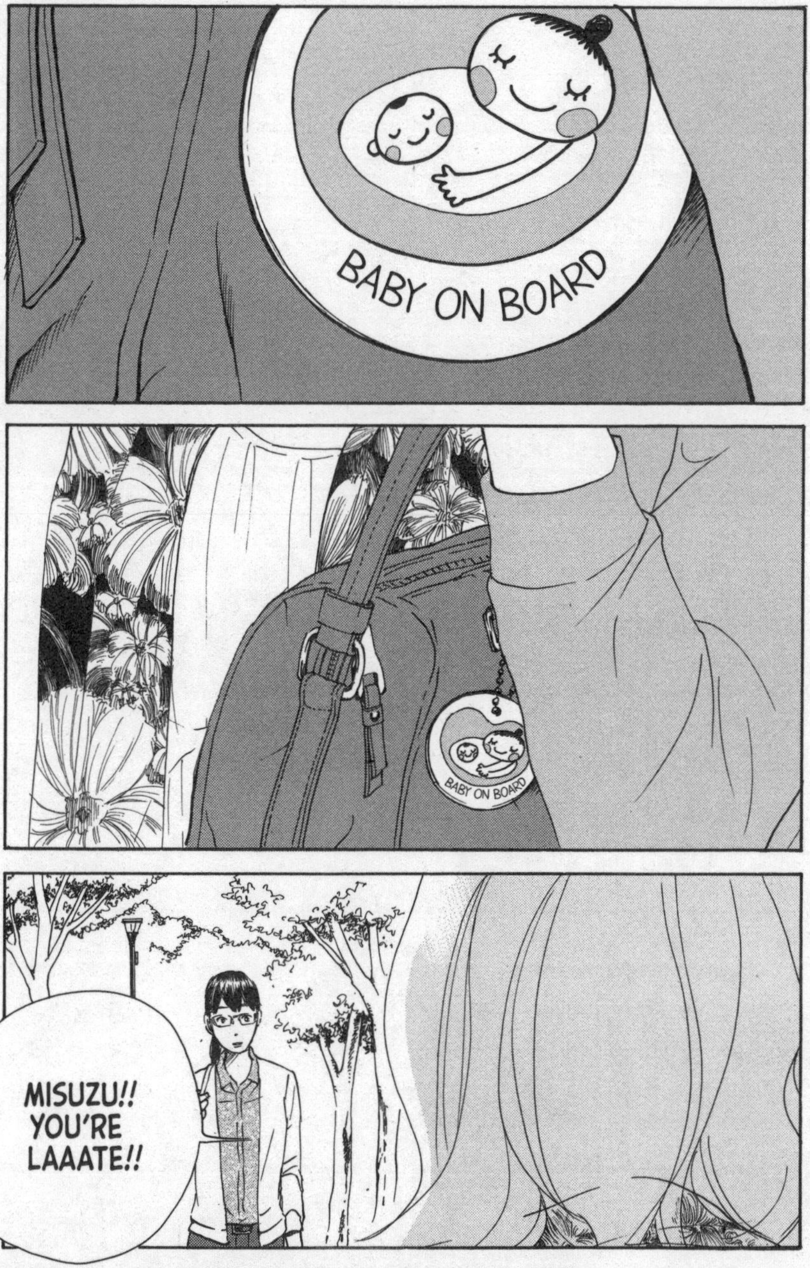
BABY ON BOARD
BABY ON BOARD
MISUZU!! YOU'RE LAAATE!!

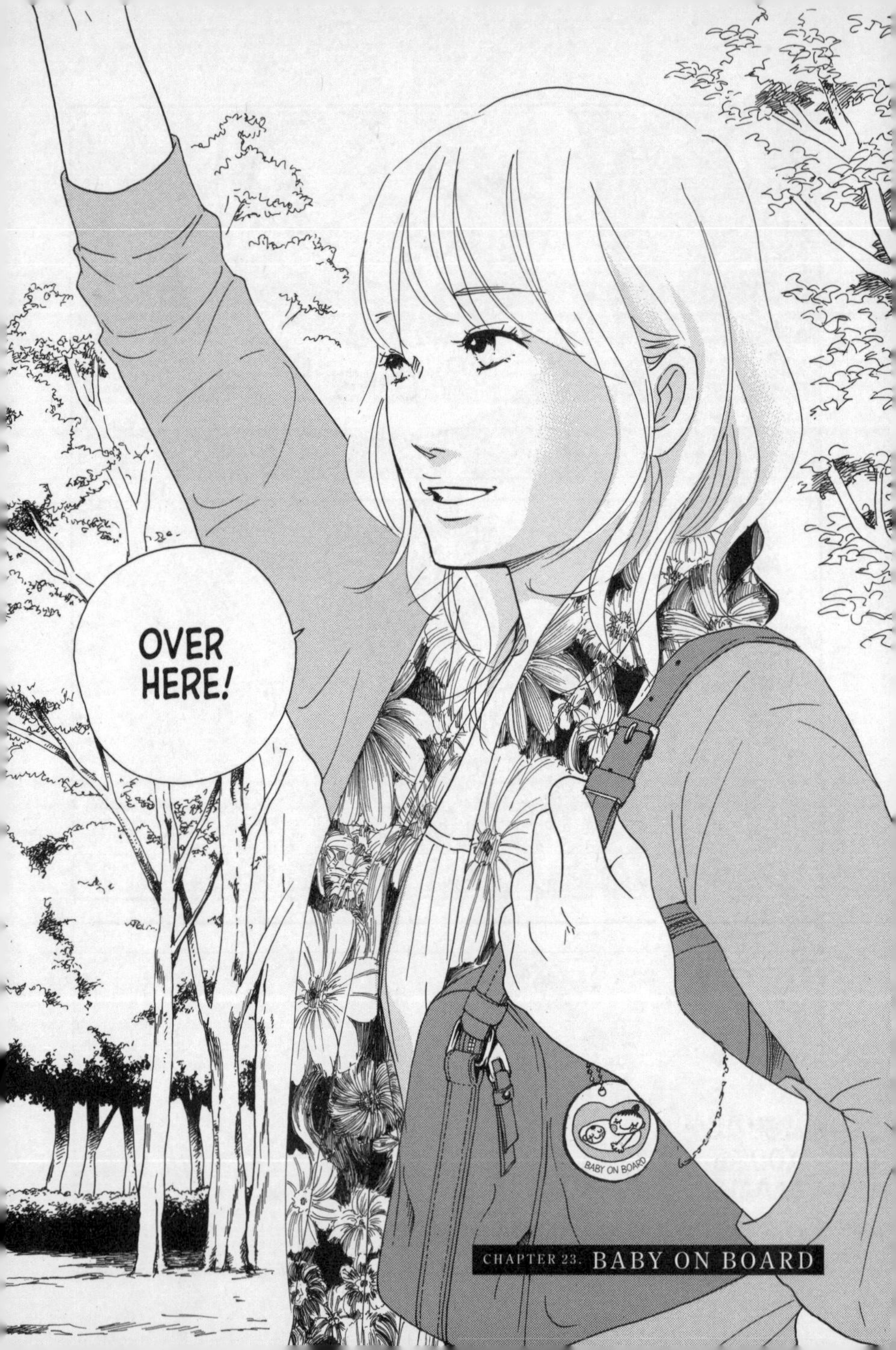
OVER HERE!
BABY ON BOARD

CHAPTER 23. BABY ON BOARD

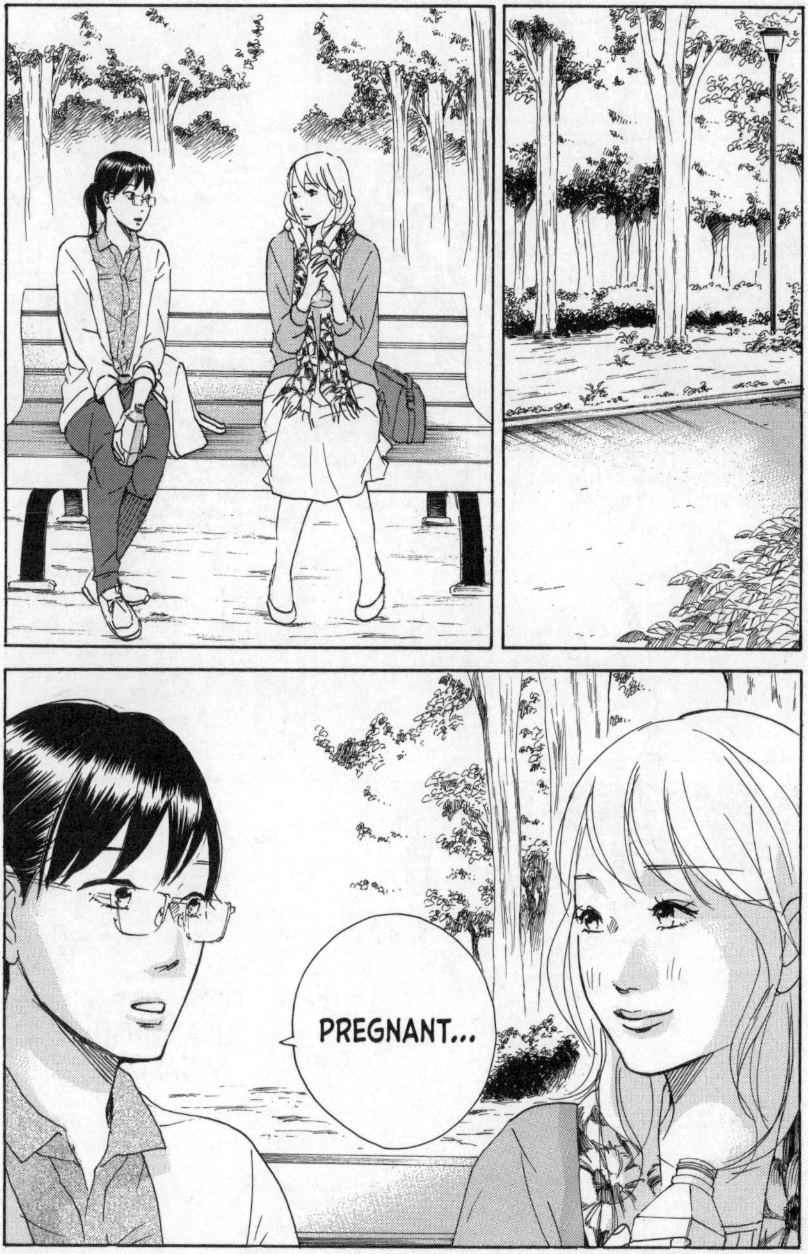
PREGNANT...

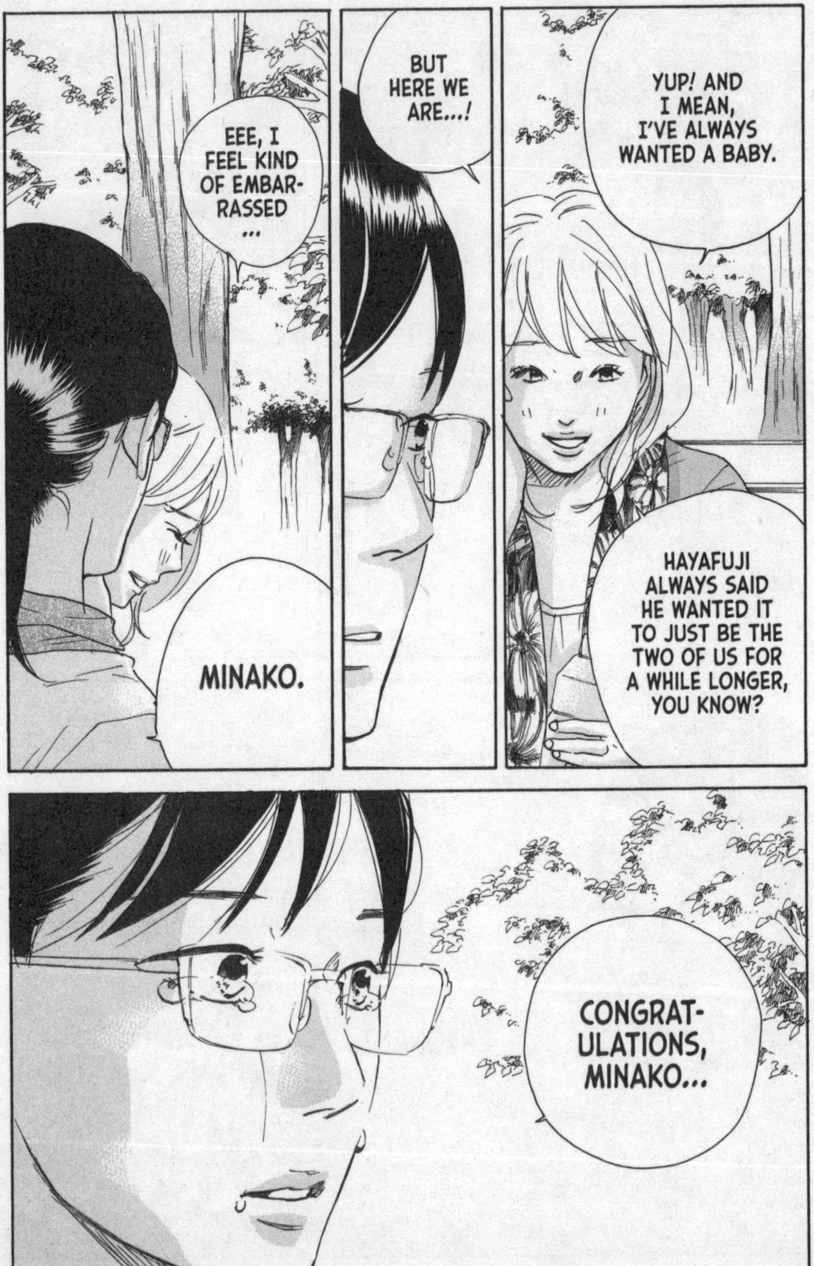
YUP! AND I MEAN, I'VE ALWAYS WANTED A BABY.
HAYAFUJI ALWAYS SAID HE WANTED IT TO JUST BE THE TWO OF US FOR A WHILE LONGER, YOU KNOW?
BUT HERE WE ARE...!
EEE, I FEEL KIND OF EMBAR-RASSED ...
MINAKO.
CONGRAT-ULATIONS, MINAKO...

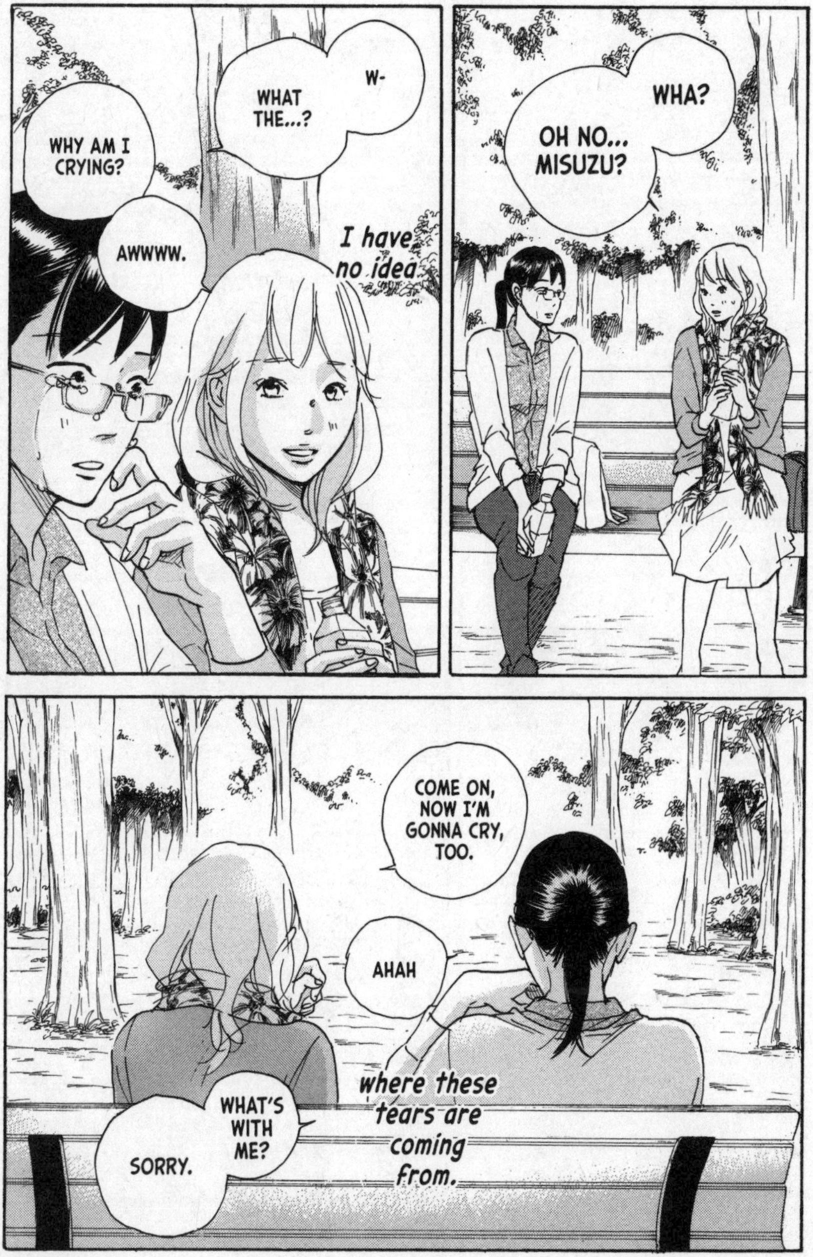
WHA?
OH NO... MISUZU?
W-
WHAT THE...?
WHY AM I CRYING?
AWWWW.
I have no idea
COME ON, NOW I'M GONNA CRY, TOO.
AHAH
where these tears are coming from.
WHAT'S WITH ME?
SORRY.

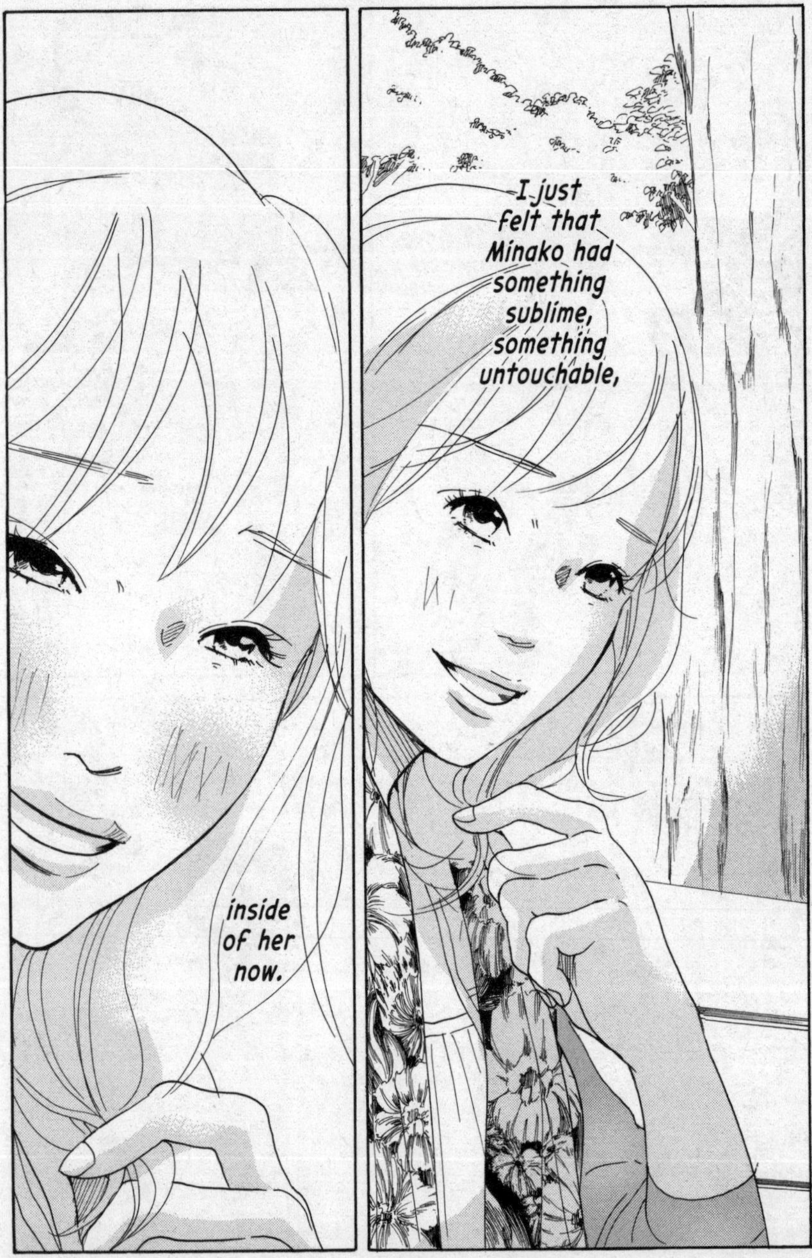
I just felt that Minako had something sublime, something untouchable,
inside of her now.

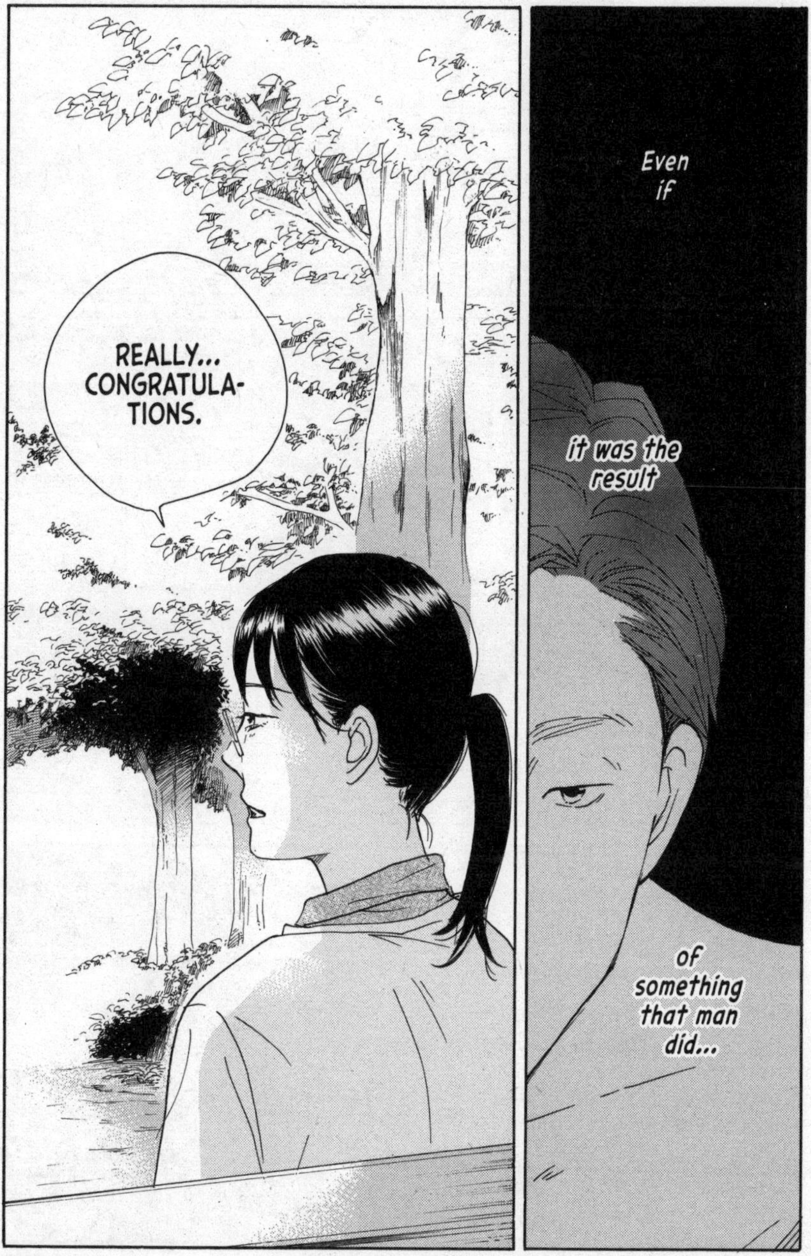
Even if
it was the result
of something that man did...
REALLY... CONGRATULA-TIONS.

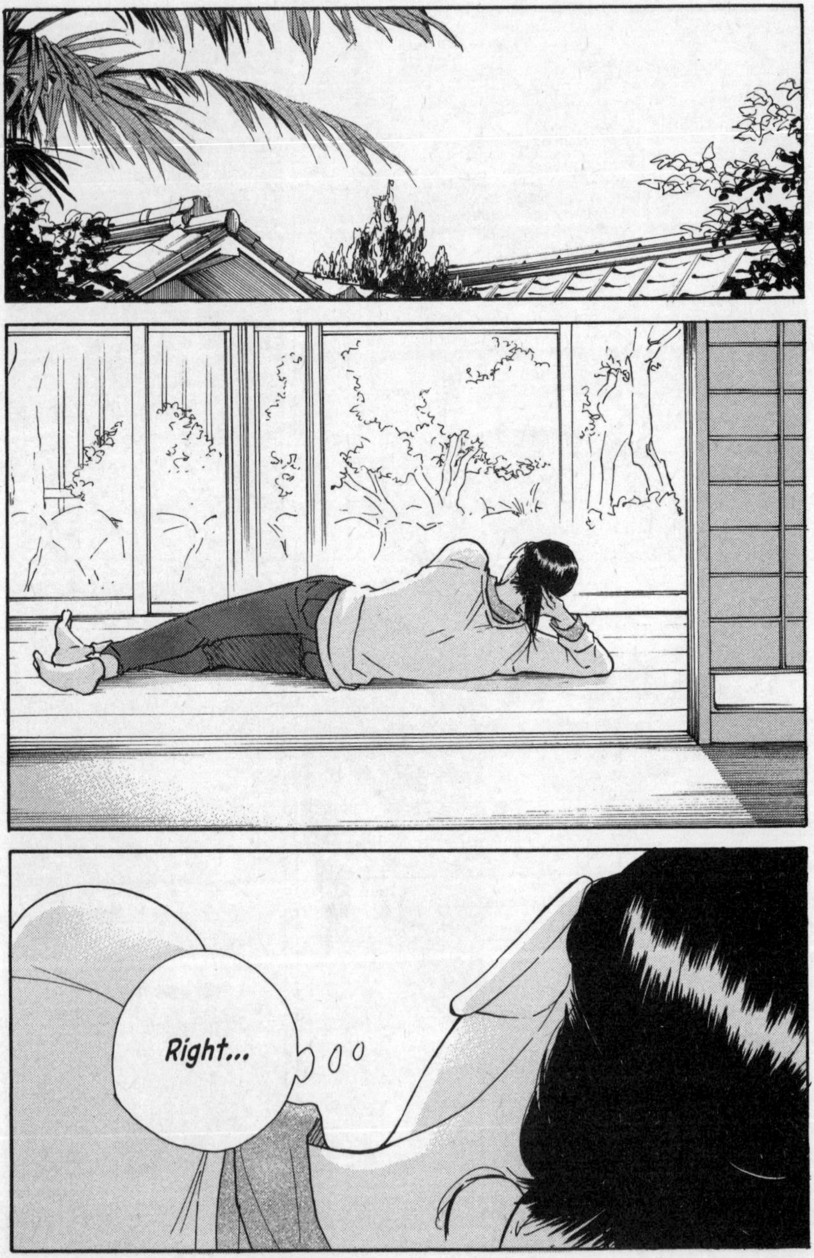
Right...

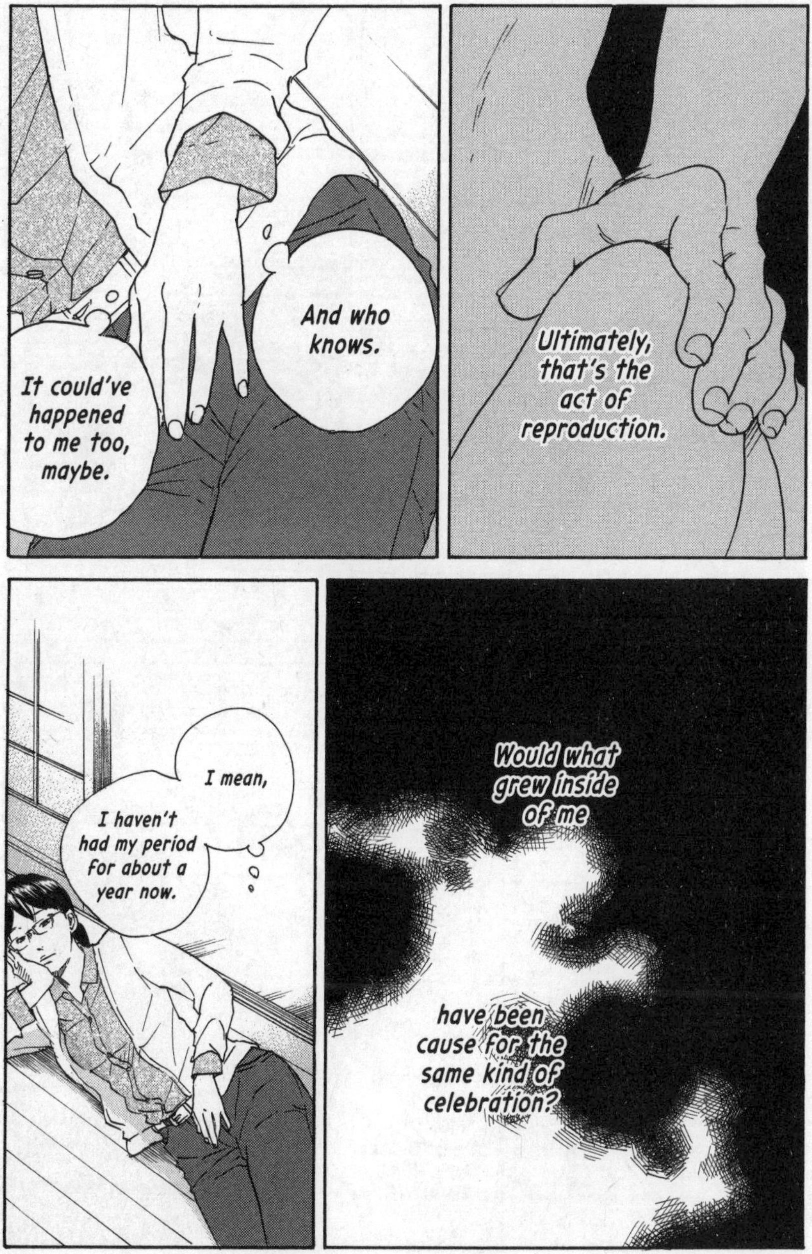
Ultimately, that's the act of reproduction.
And who knows.
It could've happened to me too, maybe.
Would what grew inside of me
have been cause for the same kind of celebration?
I mean,
I haven't had my period for about a year now.

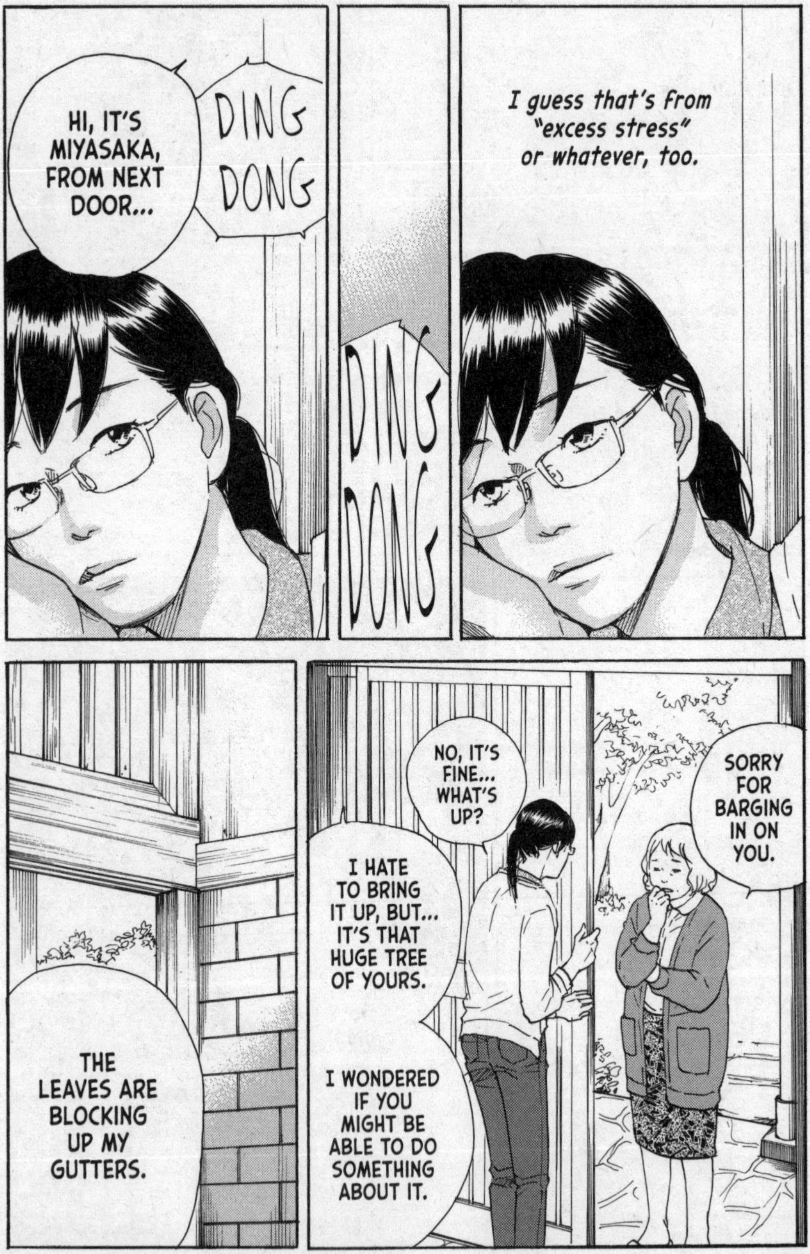
I guess that's from "excess stress" or whatever, too.
DING DONG
DING DONG
HI, IT'S MIYASAKA, FROM NEXT DOOR...
SORRY FOR BARGING IN ON YOU.
NO, IT'S FINE... WHAT'S UP?
I HATE TO BRING IT UP, BUT... IT'S THAT HUGE TREE OF YOURS.
I WONDERED IF YOU MIGHT BE ABLE TO DO SOMETHING ABOUT IT.
THE LEAVES ARE BLOCKING UP MY GUTTERS.

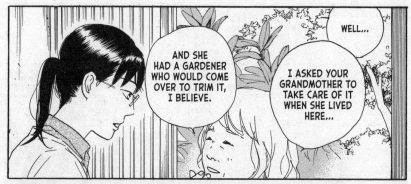

WELL...
I ASKED YOUR GRANDMOTHER TO TAKE CARE OF IT WHEN SHE LIVED HERE...
AND SHE HAD A GARDENER WHO WOULD COME OVER TO TRIM IT, I BELIEVE.
A GARDENER...?
THAT'S RIGHT.
YOU REMEMBER THAT BIG RAINSTORM THE OTHER DAY?
THAT'S WHEN IT REALLY GOT BAD.
OH,
SPEAKING OF THE OTHER DAY.
THERE WAS A YOUNG MAN... CROUCHED OUTSIDE YOUR HOUSE.

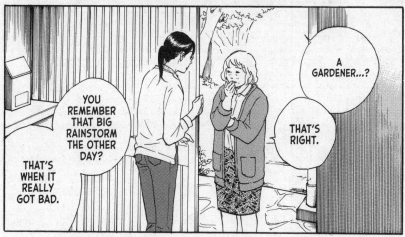

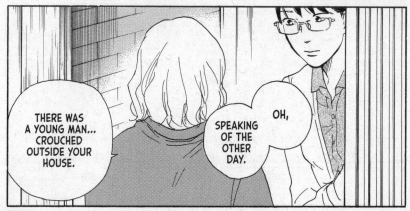

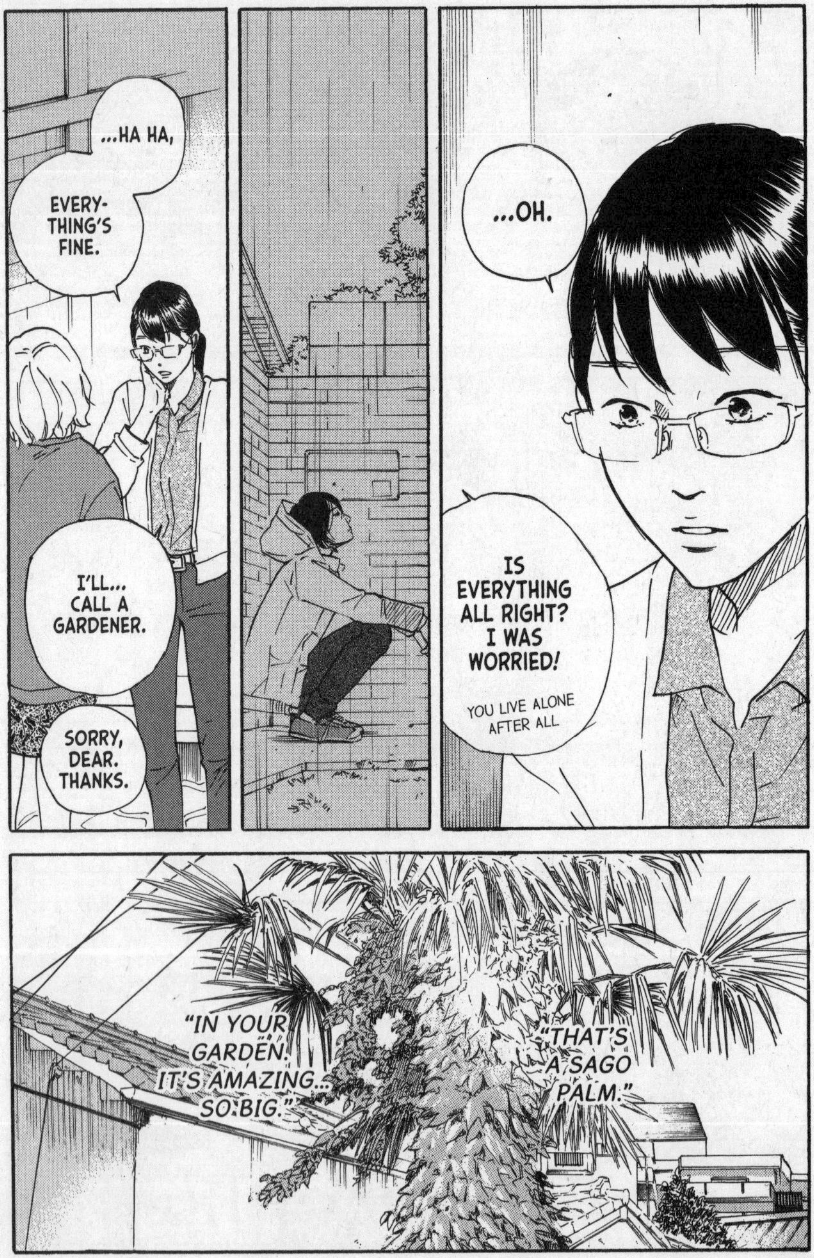

...OH.
IS EVERYTHING ALL RIGHT? I WAS WORRIED!
YOU LIVE ALONE AFTER ALL
...HA HA,
EVERY-THING'S FINE.
I'LL... CALL A GARDENER.
SORRY, DEAR. THANKS.
"THAT'S A SAGO PALM."
"IN YOUR GARDEN. IT'S AMAZING... SO BIG."

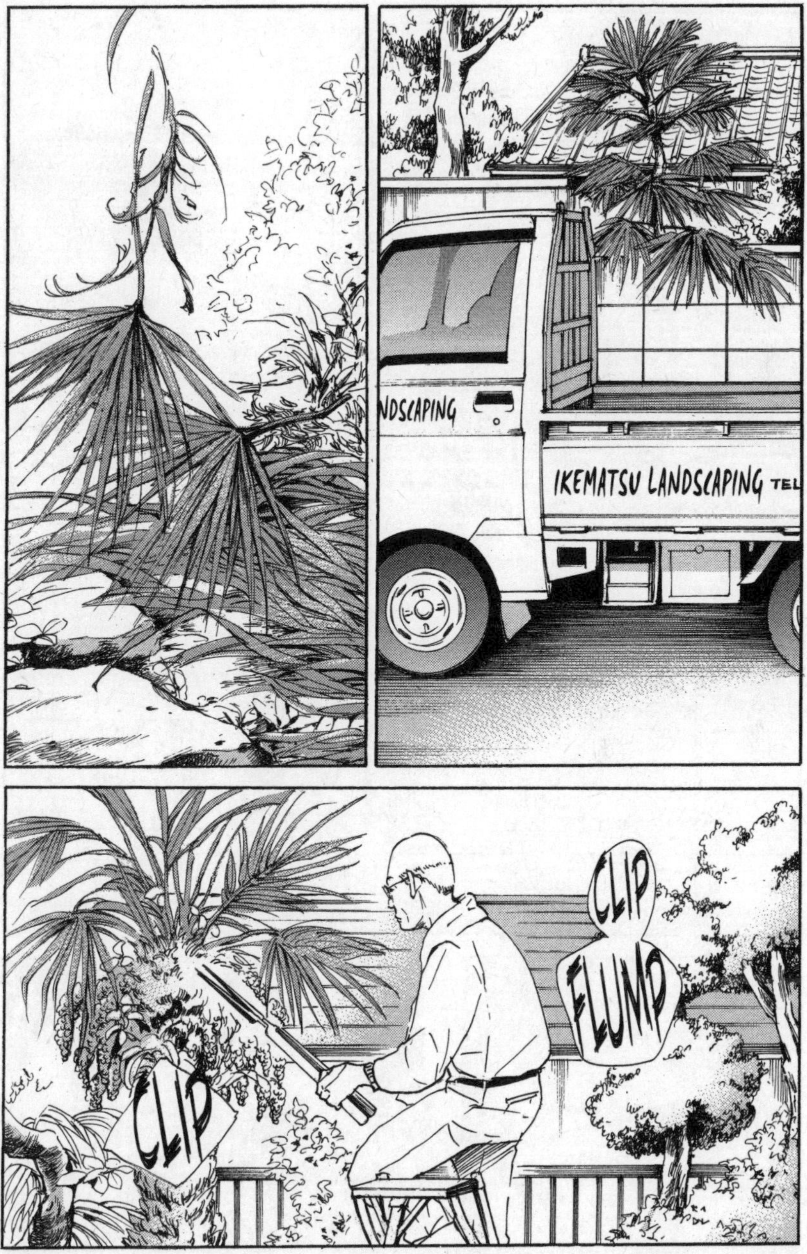
NDSCAPING
IKEMATSU LANDSCAPING TEL
CLIP
FLUMP
CLIP

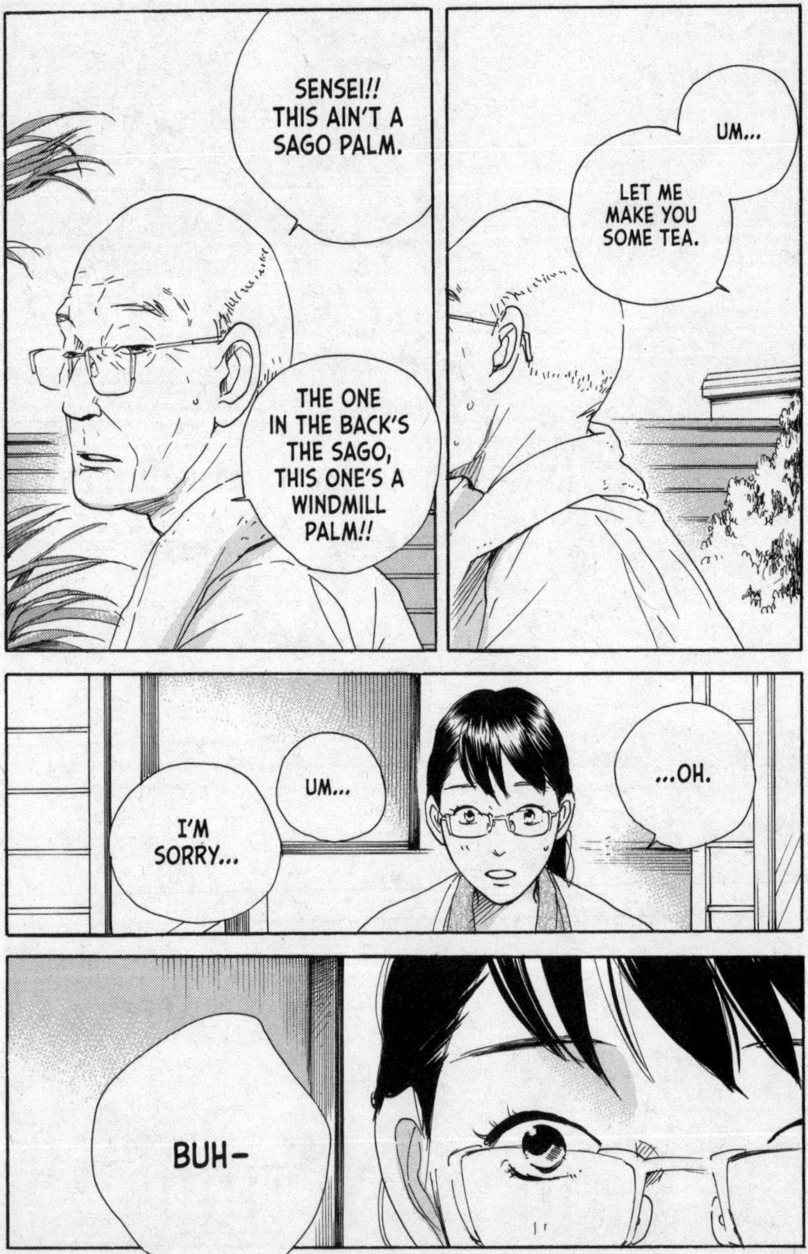
UM...
LET ME MAKE YOU SOME TEA.
SENSEI!! THIS AIN'T A SAGO PALM.
THE ONE IN THE BACK'S THE SAGO, THIS ONE'S A WINDMILL PALM!!
...OH.
UM...
I'M SORRY...
BUH-

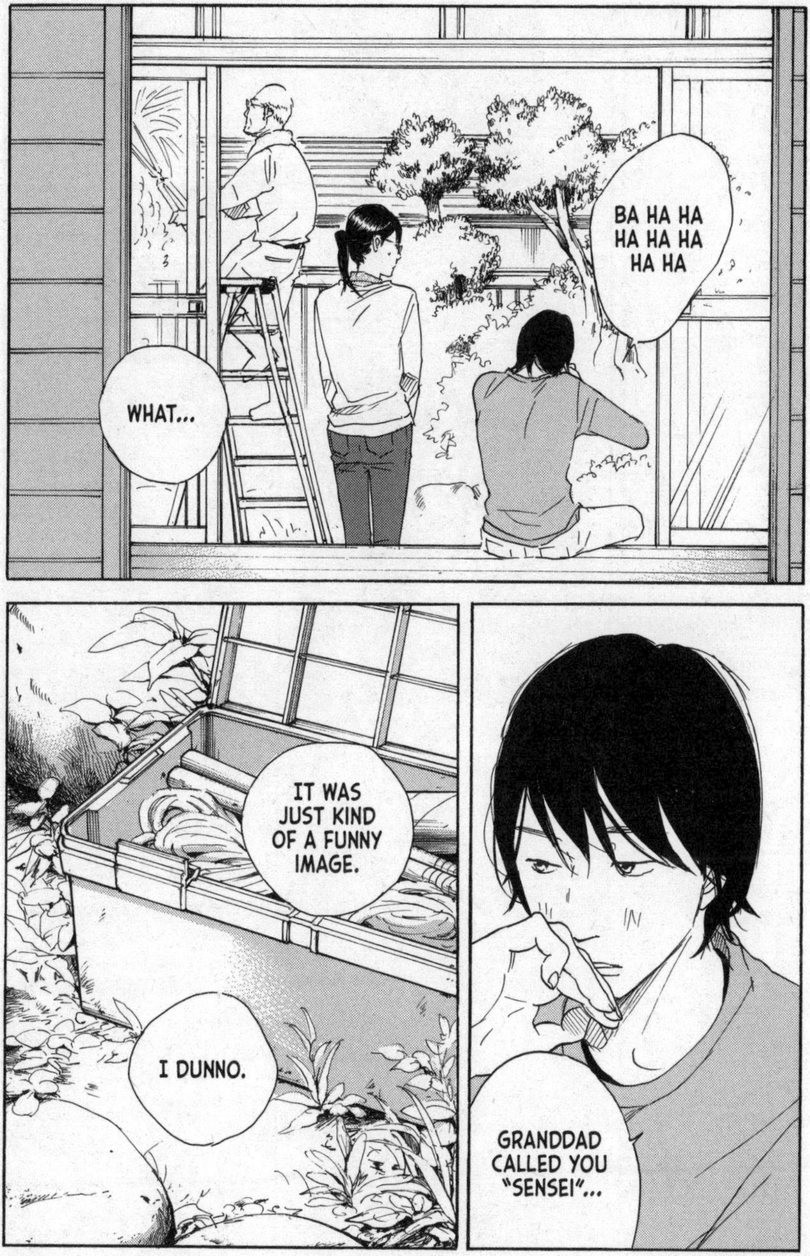
BA HA HA HA HA HA HA HA
WHAT...
GRANDDAD CALLED YOU "SENSEI"...
IT WAS JUST KIND OF A FUNNY IMAGE.
I DUNNO.

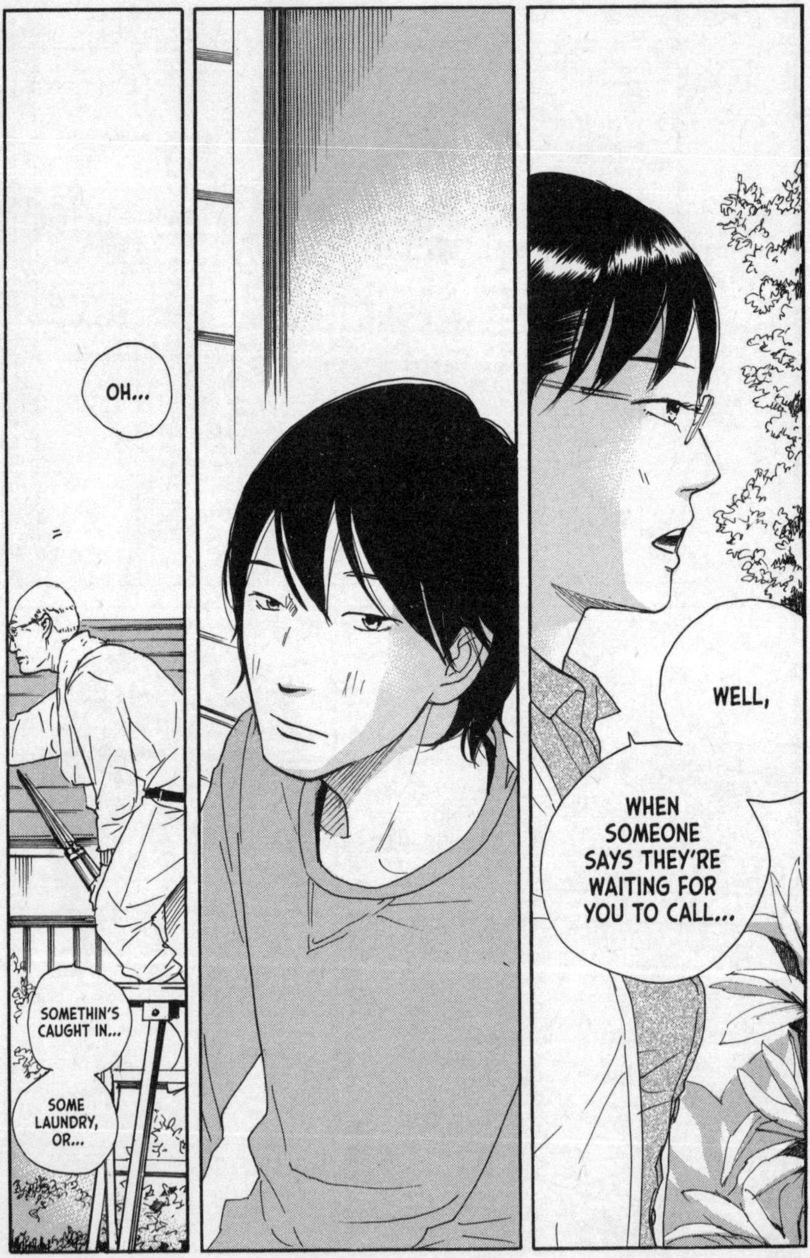
WELL,
WHEN SOMEONE SAYS THEY'RE WAITING FOR YOU TO CALL...
OH...
SOMETHIN'S CAUGHT IN...
SOME LAUNDRY, OR...

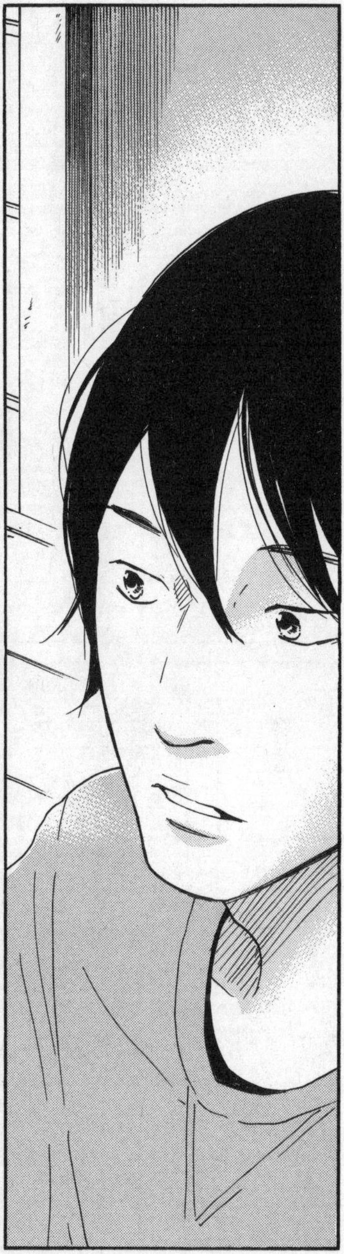

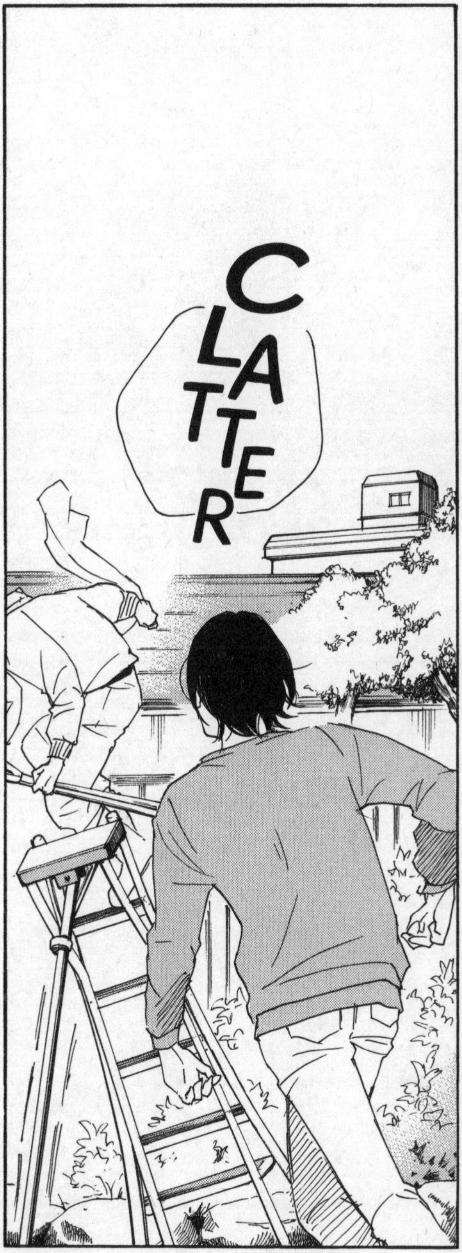
CLATTER

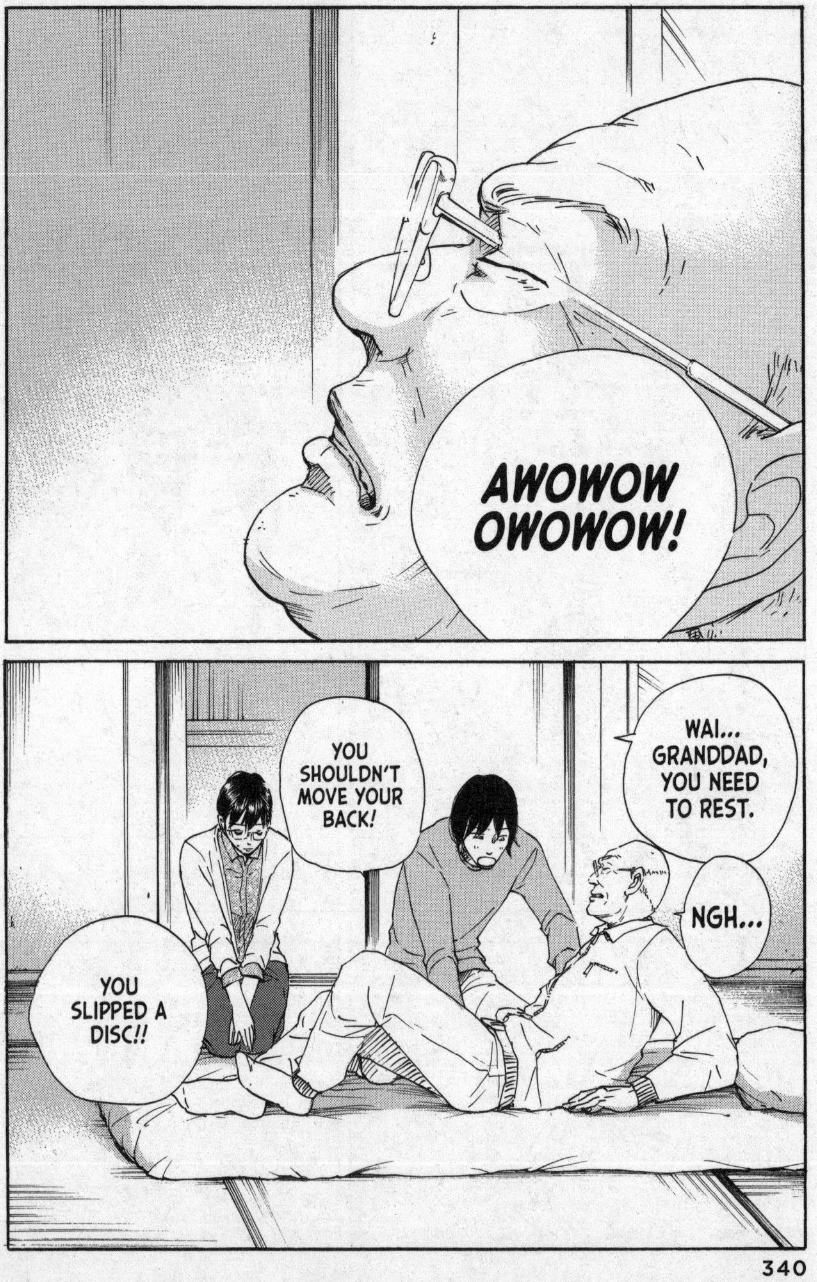
AWOWOW OWOWOW!
WAI... GRANDDAD, YOU NEED TO REST.
NGH...
YOU SHOULDN'T MOVE YOUR BACK!
YOU SLIPPED A DISC!!

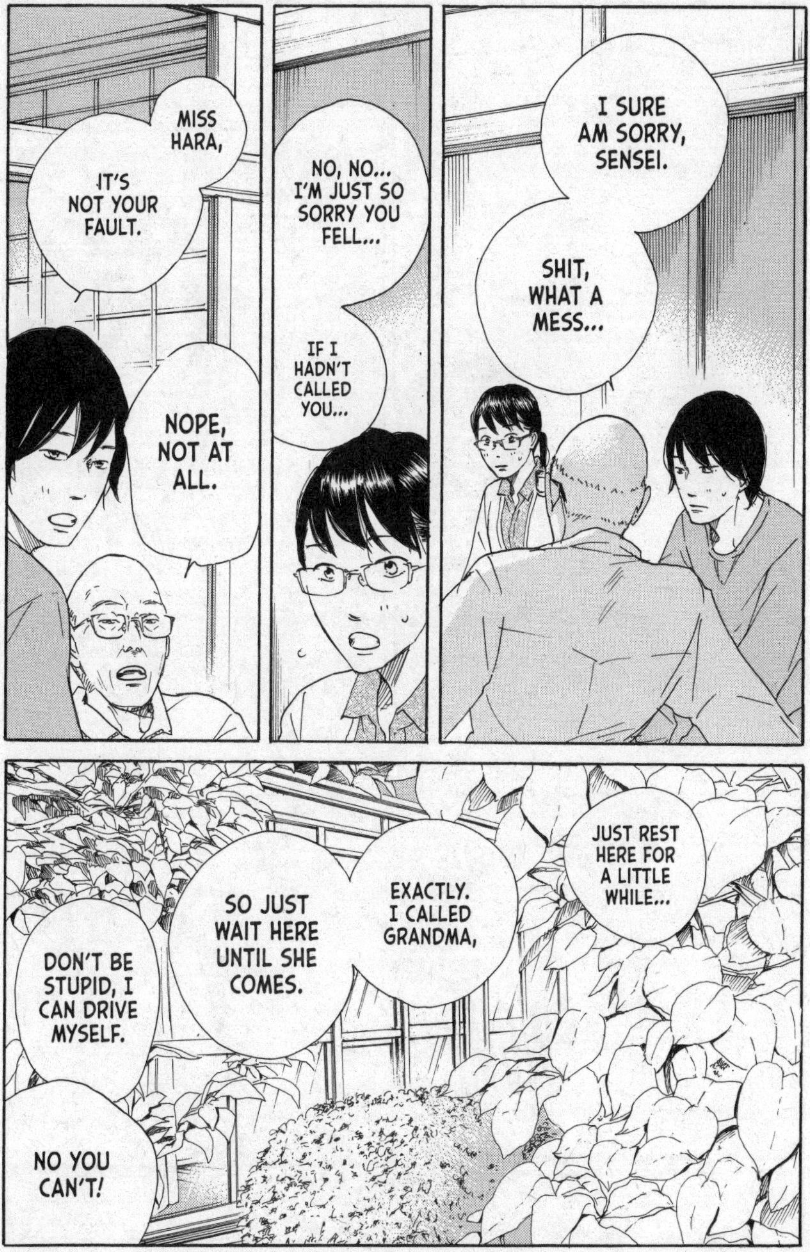
I SURE AM SORRY, SENSEI.
SHIT, WHAT A MESS...
NO, NO... I'M JUST SO SORRY YOU FELL...
IF I HADN'T CALLED YOU...
MISS HARA, IT'S NOT YOUR FAULT.
NOPE, NOT AT ALL.
JUST REST HERE FOR A LITTLE WHILE...
EXACTLY. I CALLED GRANDMA, SO JUST WAIT HERE UNTIL SHE COMES.
DON'T BE STUPID, I CAN DRIVE MYSELF.
NO YOU CAN'T!

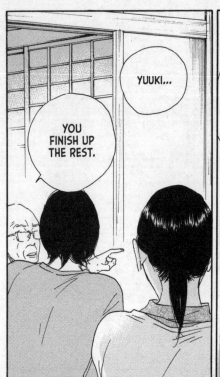

PLEASE...
AT LEAST GIVE YOUR-SELF A FEW MINUTES.
YUUKI...
YOU FINISH UP THE REST.
FWUMP

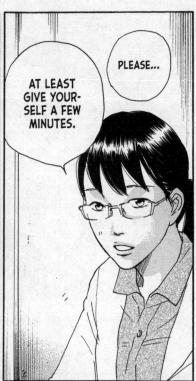

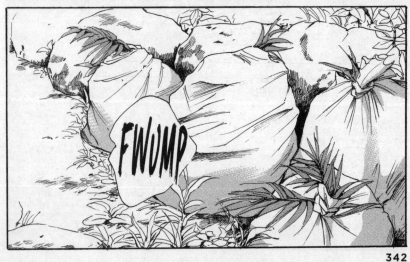

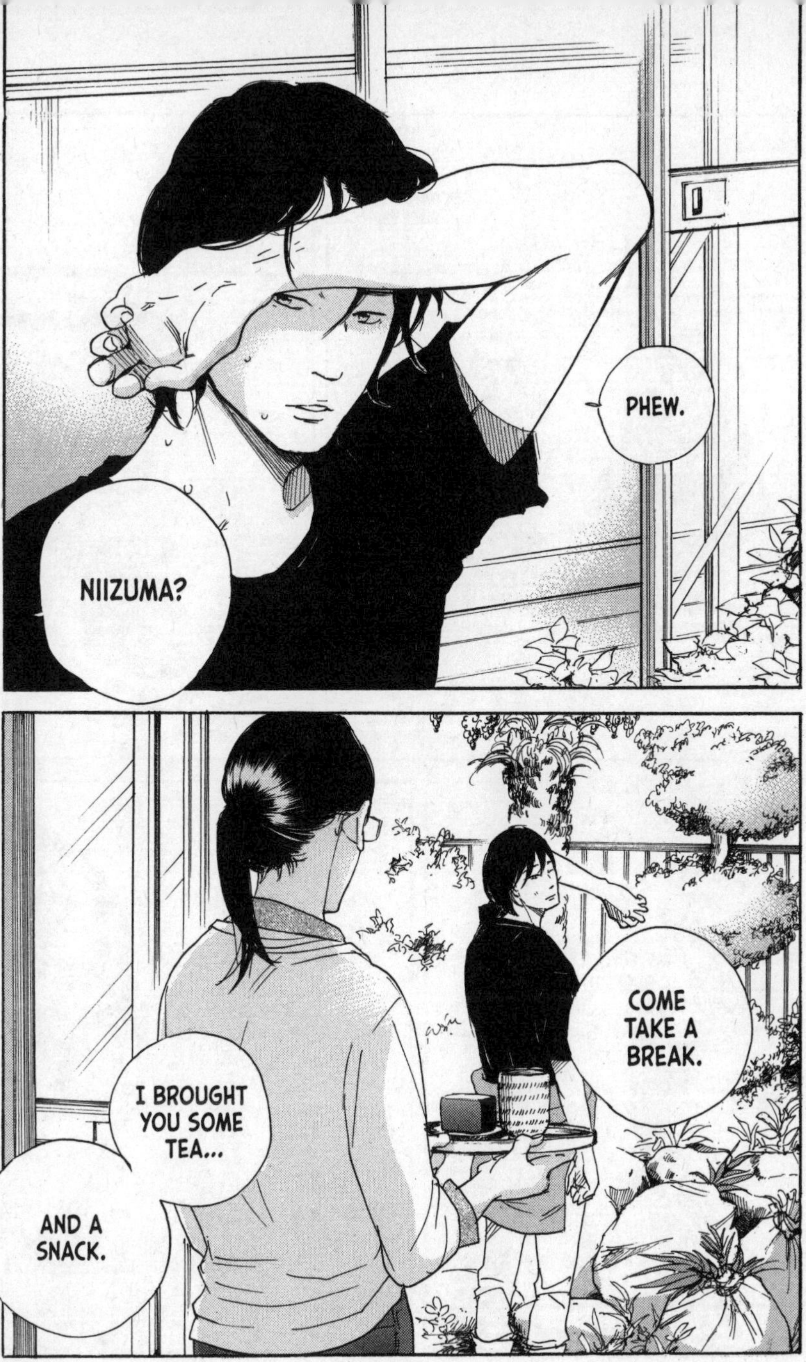
PHEW.
NIIZUMA?
COME TAKE A BREAK.
I BROUGHT YOU SOME TEA...
AND A SNACK.

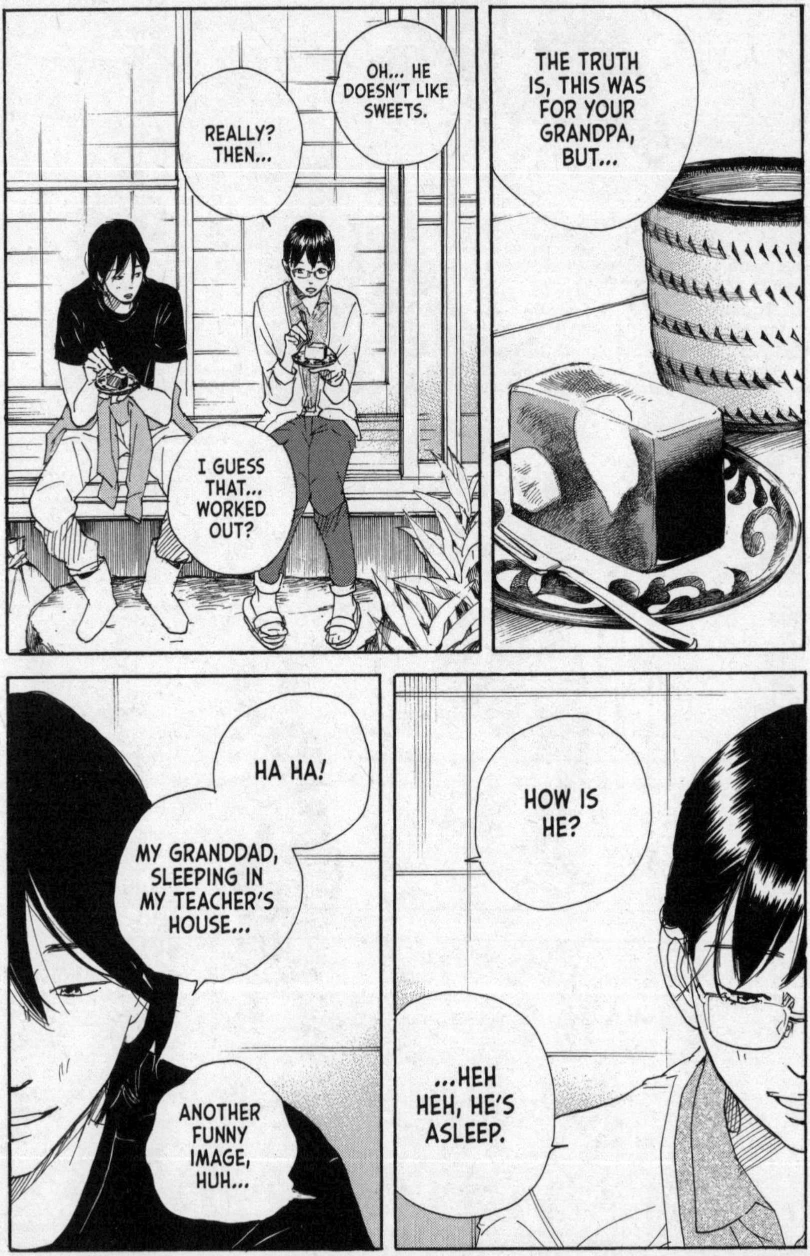
THE TRUTH IS, THIS WAS FOR YOUR GRANDPA, BUT...
OH... HE DOESN'T LIKE SWEETS.
REALLY? THEN...
I GUESS THAT... WORKED OUT?
HOW IS HE?
...HEH HEH, HE'S ASLEEP.
HA HA!
MY GRANDDAD, SLEEPING IN MY TEACHER'S HOUSE...
ANOTHER FUNNY IMAGE, HUH...

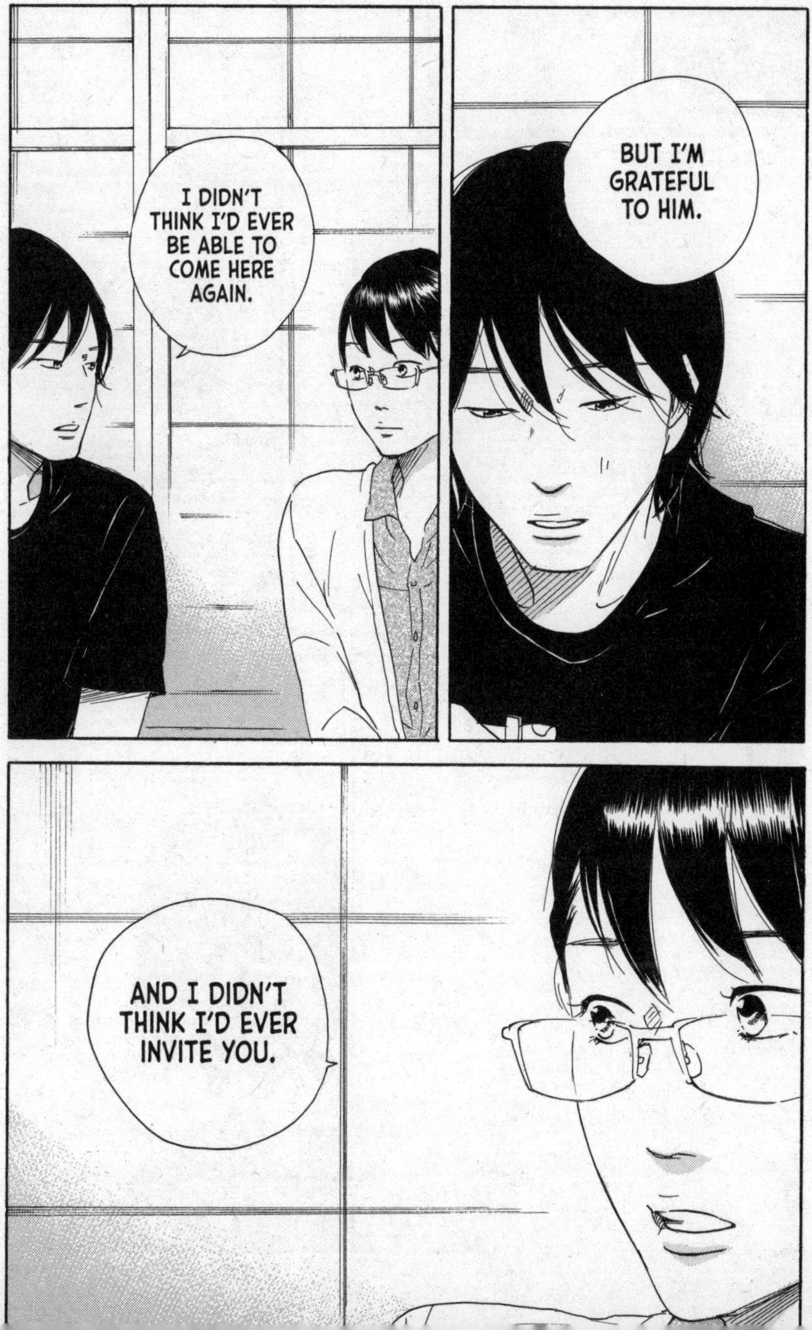
BUT I'M GRATEFUL TO HIM.
I DIDN'T THINK I'D EVER BE ABLE TO COME HERE AGAIN.
AND I DIDN'T THINK I'D EVER INVITE YOU.

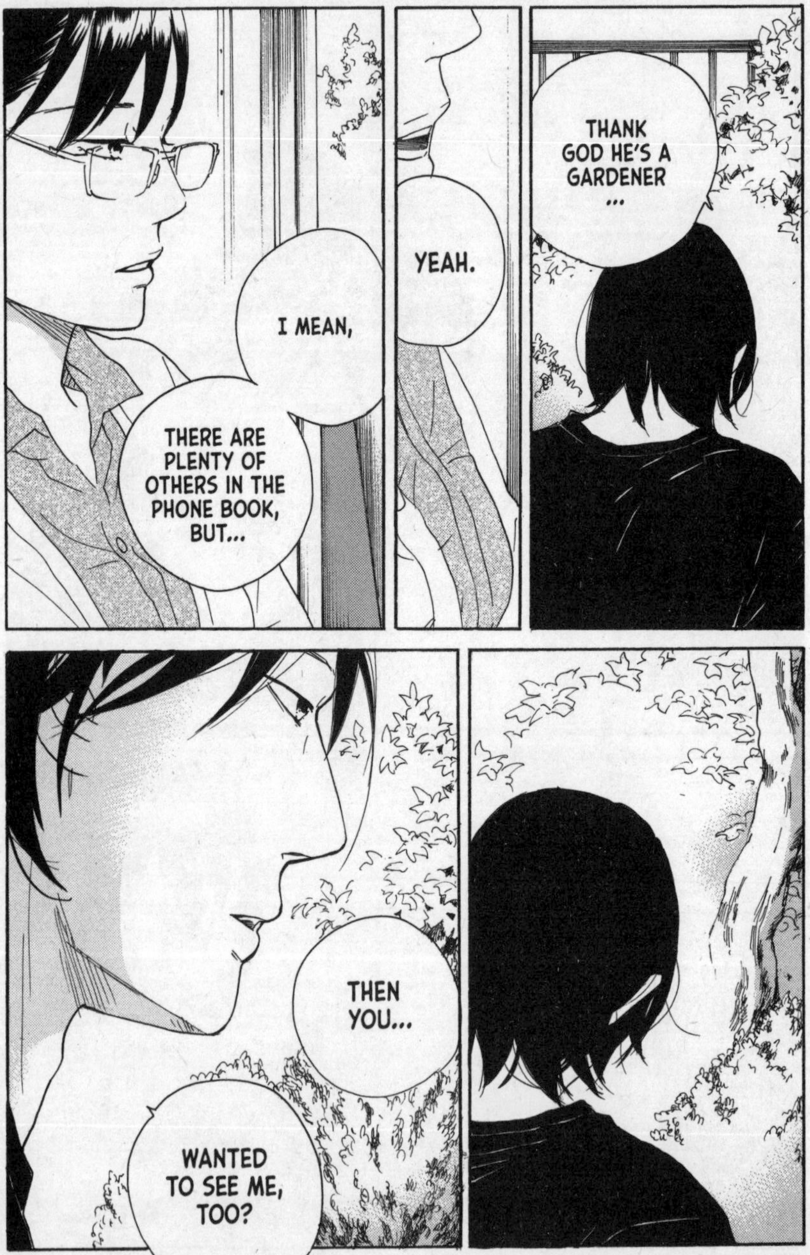
THANK GOD HE'S A GARDENER ...
YEAH.
I MEAN,
THERE ARE PLENTY OF OTHERS IN THE PHONE BOOK, BUT...
THEN YOU...
WANTED TO SEE ME, TOO?

I'M...
PRETTY SURE I DID, YES.

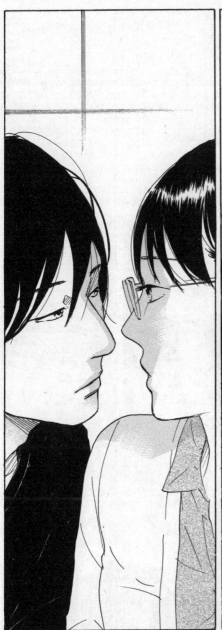

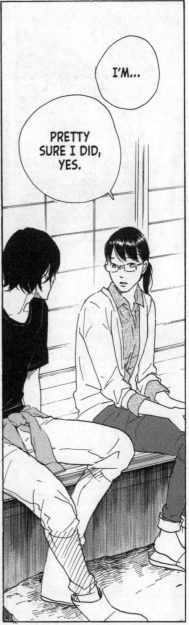

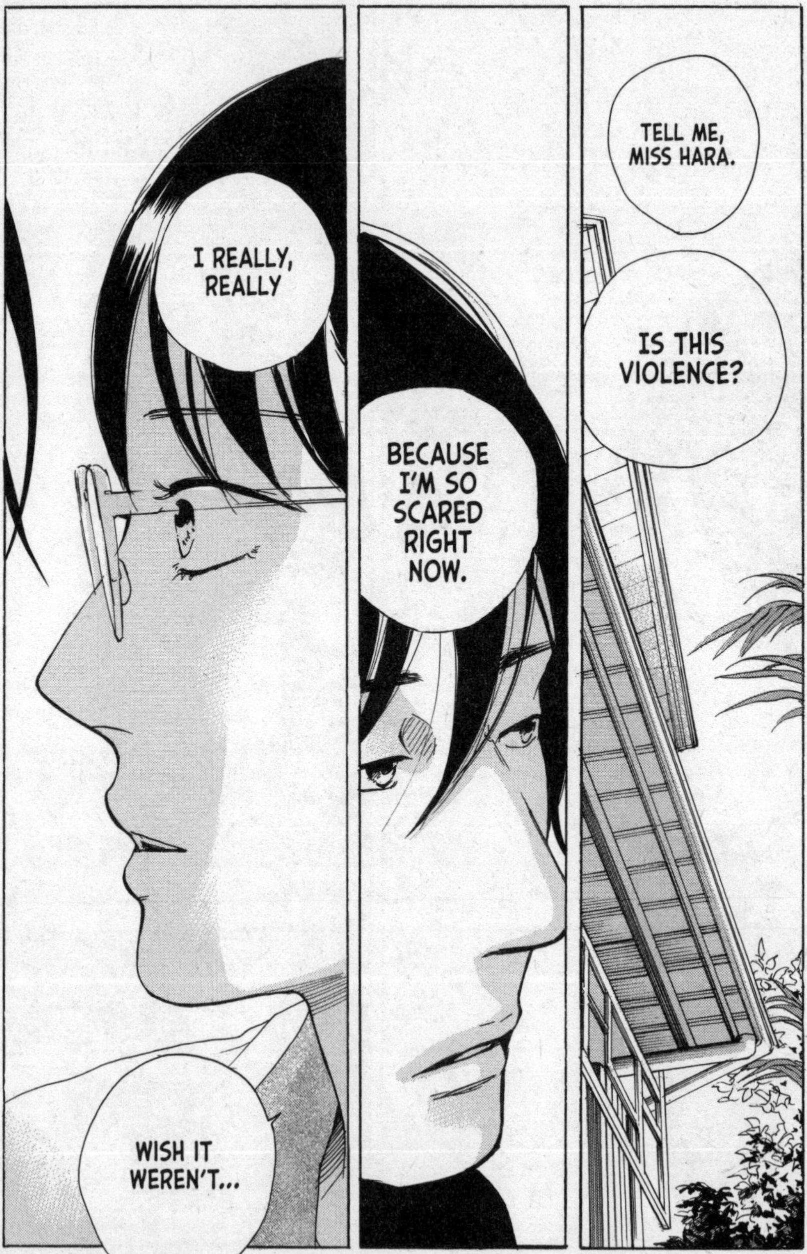
TELL ME, MISS HARA.
IS THIS VIOLENCE?
BECAUSE I'M SO SCARED RIGHT NOW.
I REALLY, REALLY
WISH IT WEREN'T...

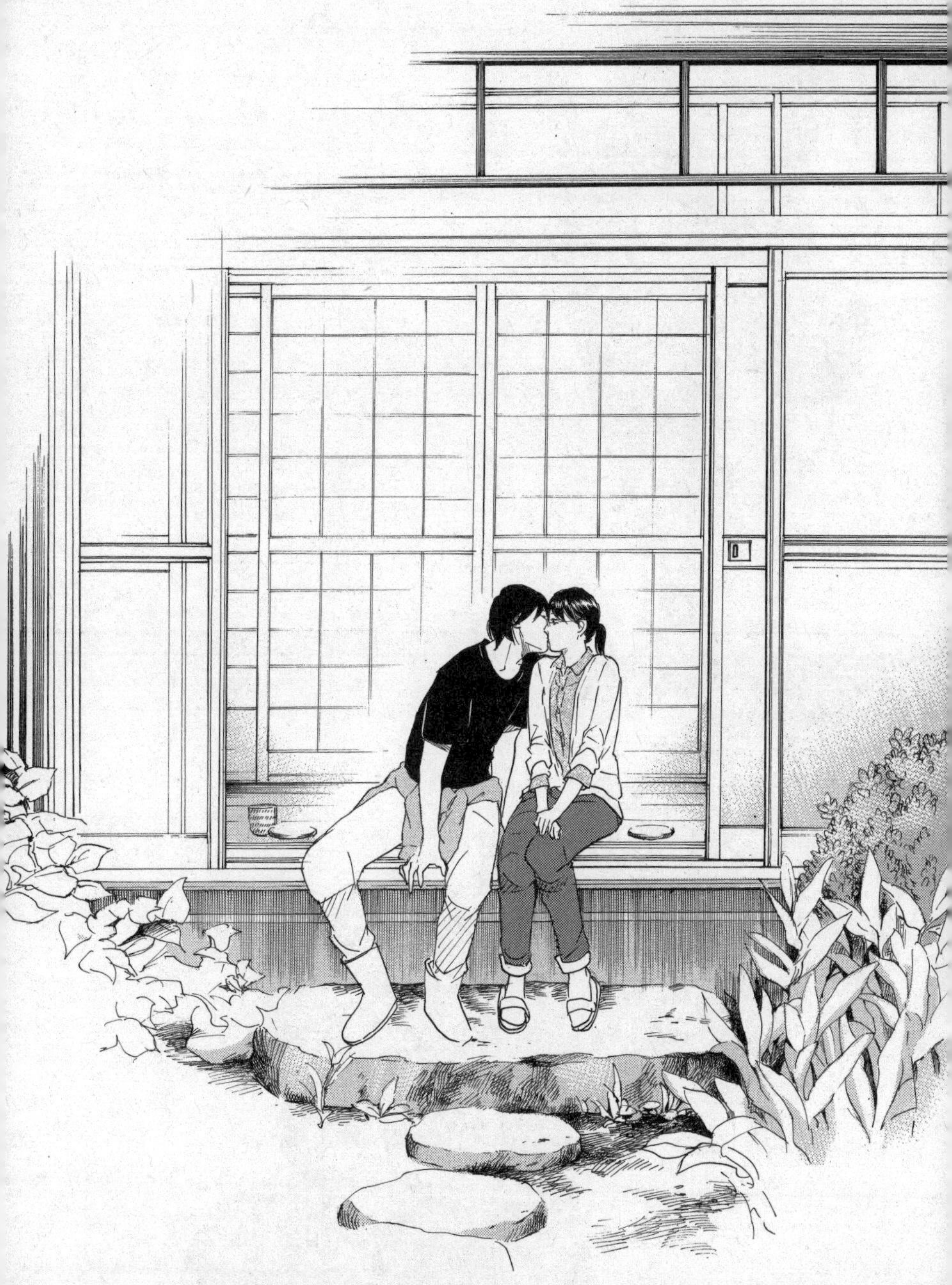

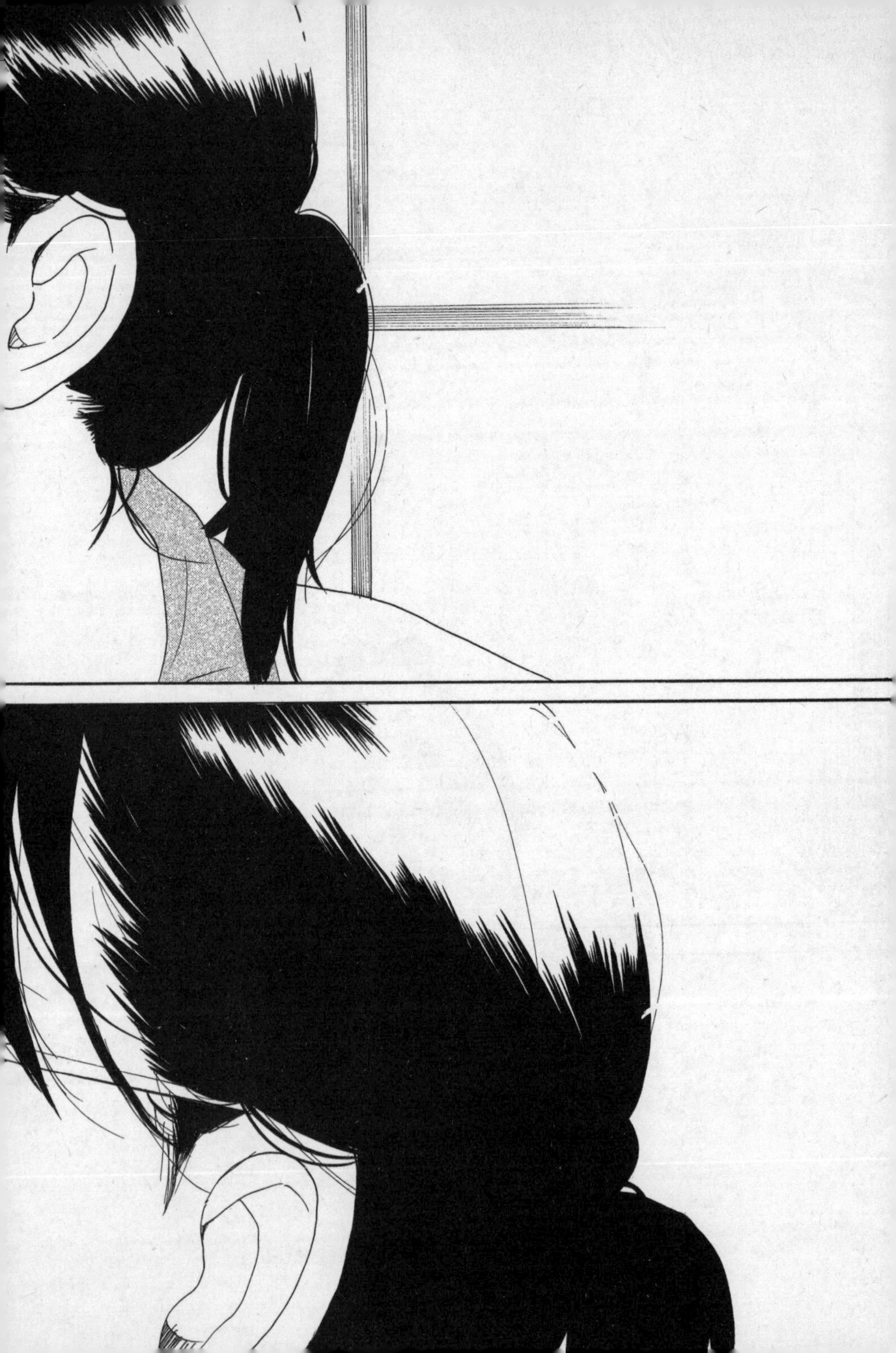

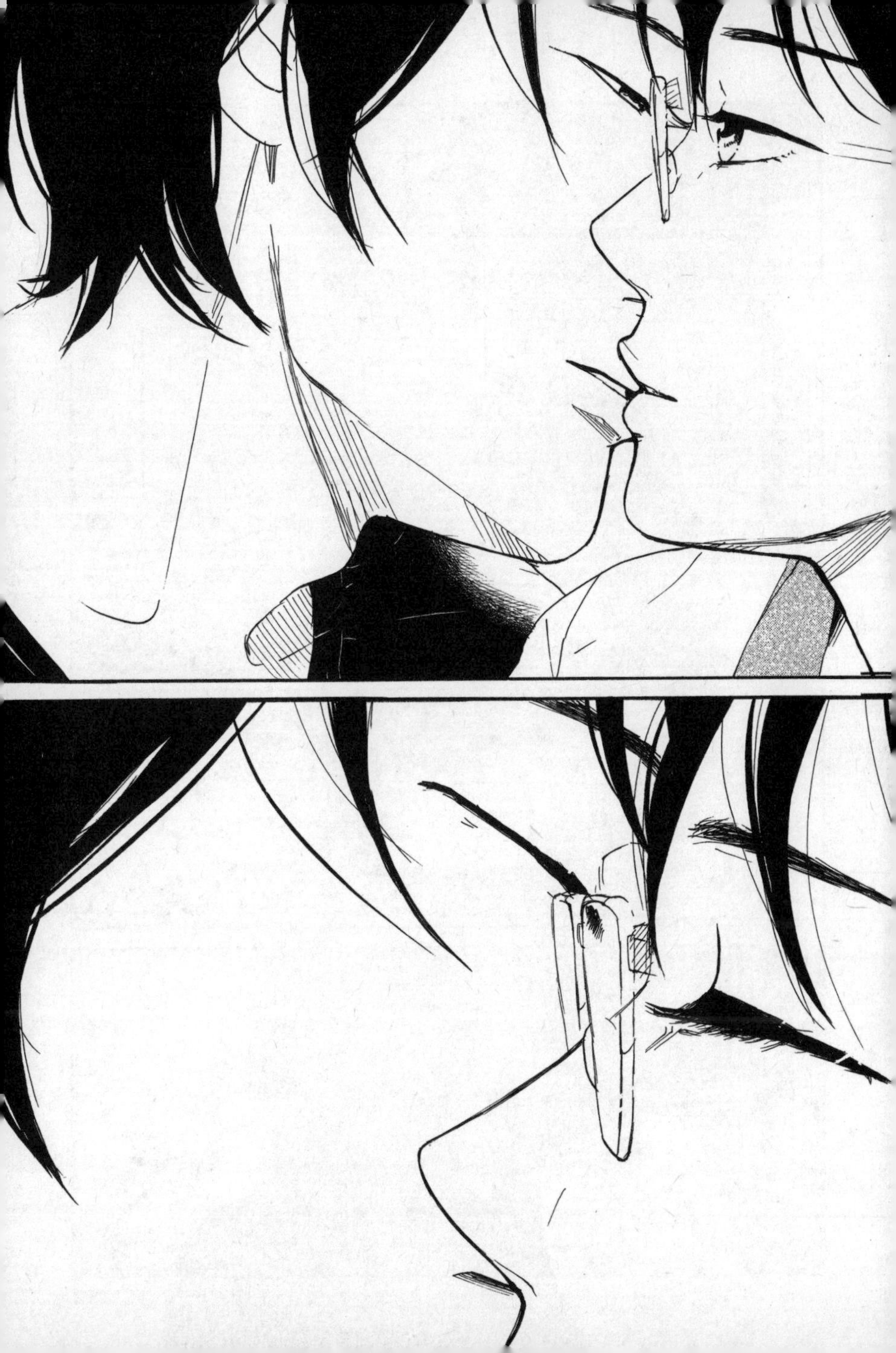

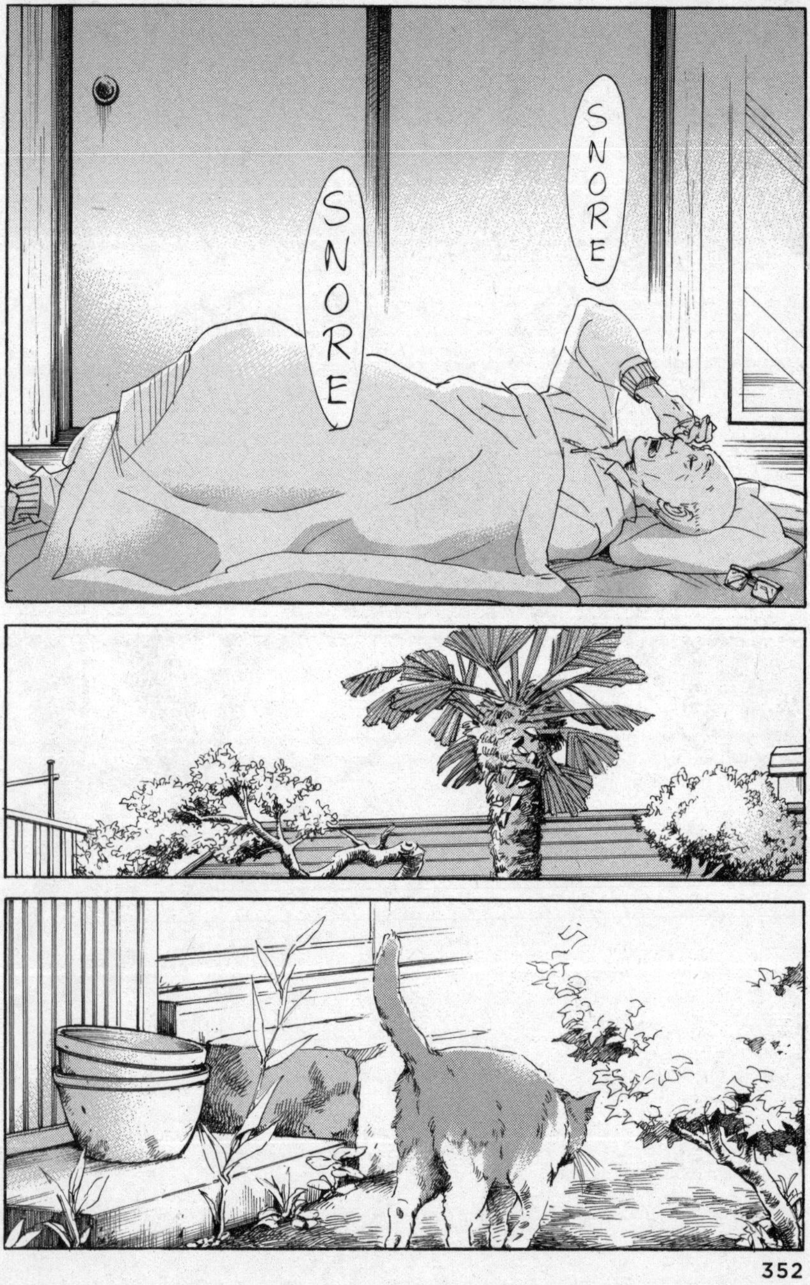
SNORE
SNORE

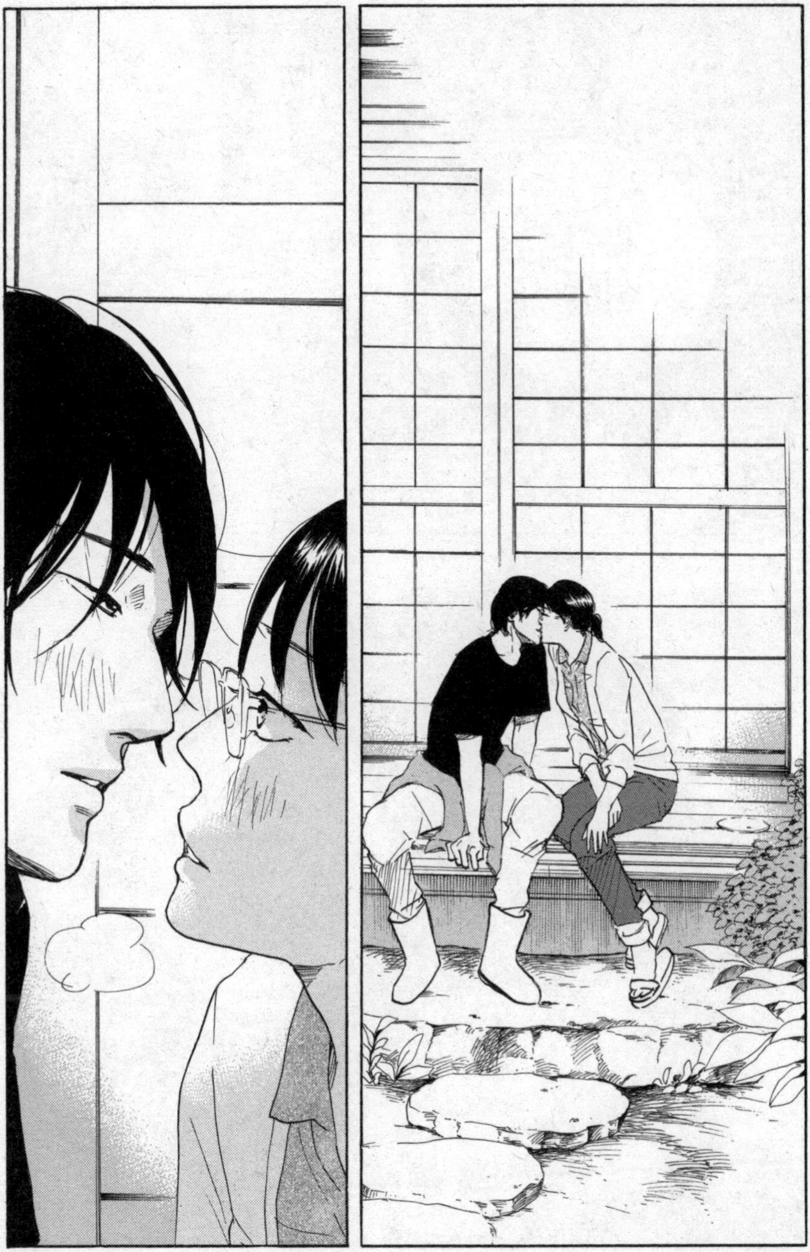

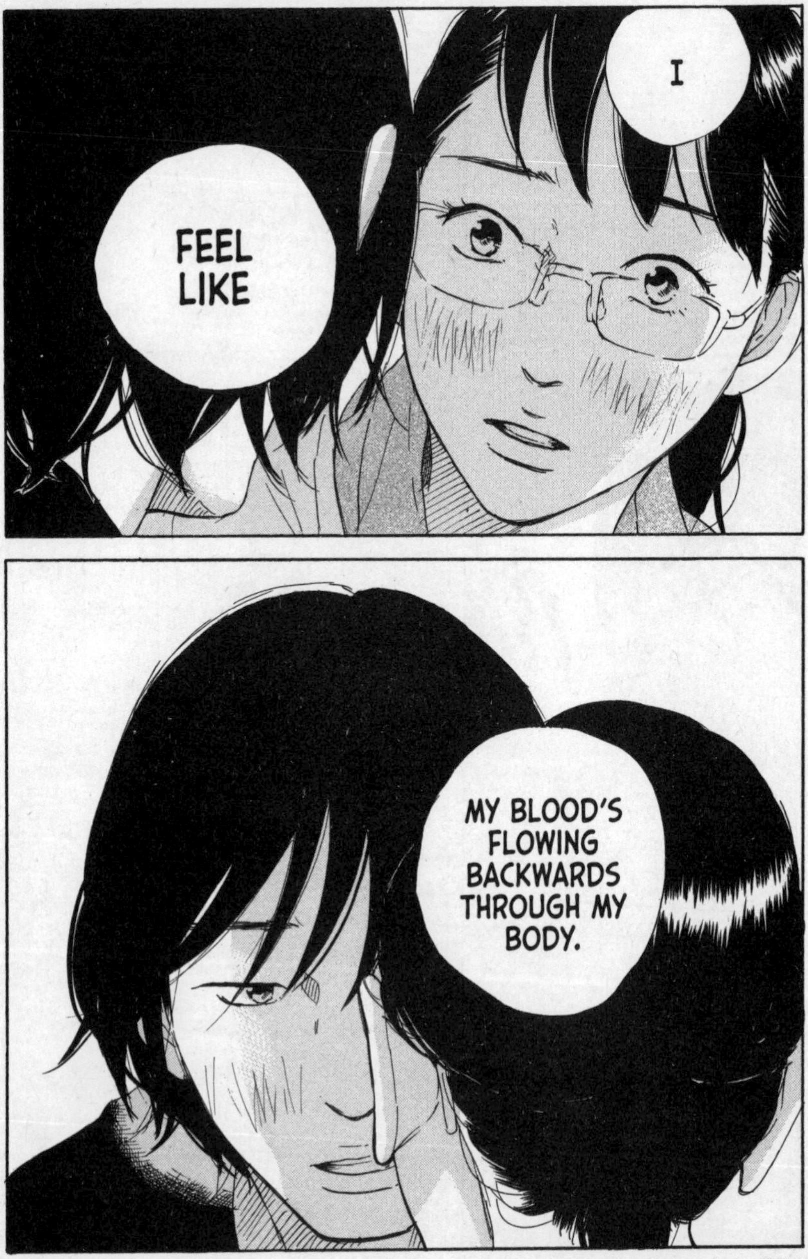
I
FEEL LIKE
MY BLOOD'S FLOWING BACKWARDS THROUGH MY BODY.

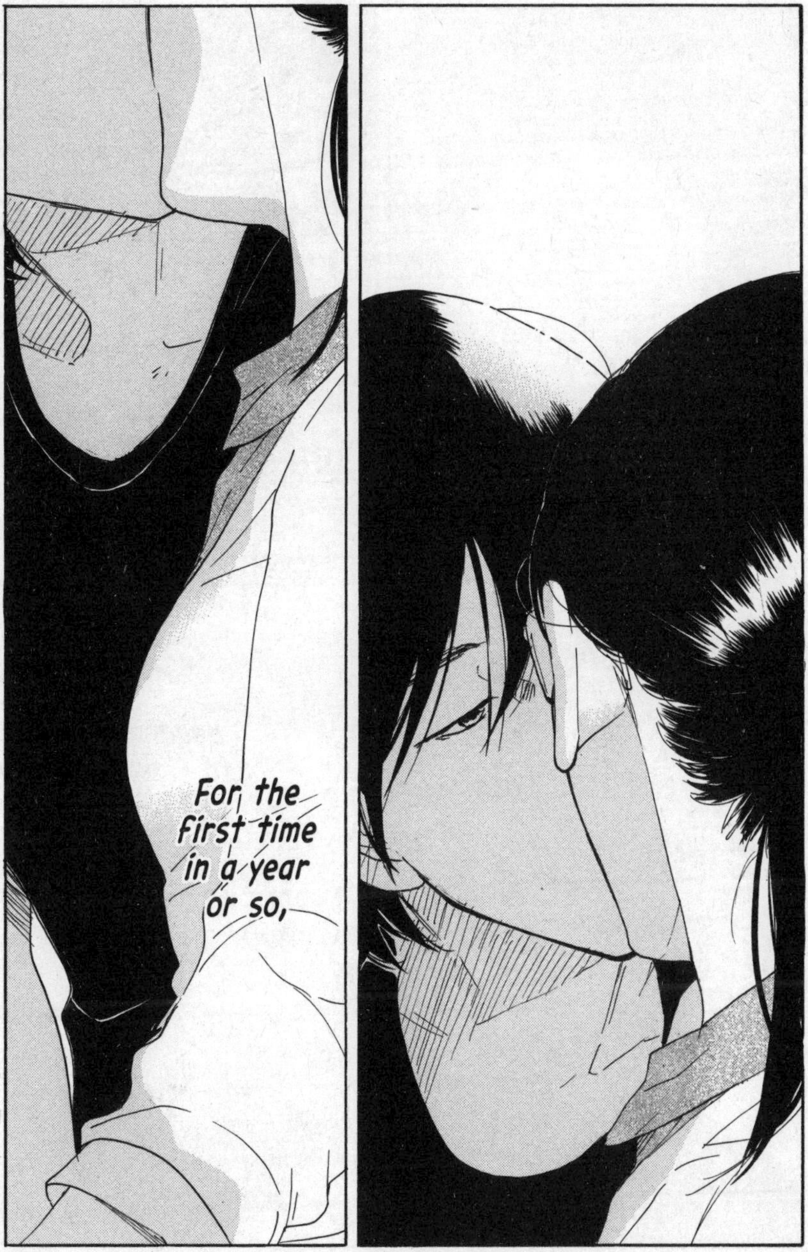
For the first time in a year or so,

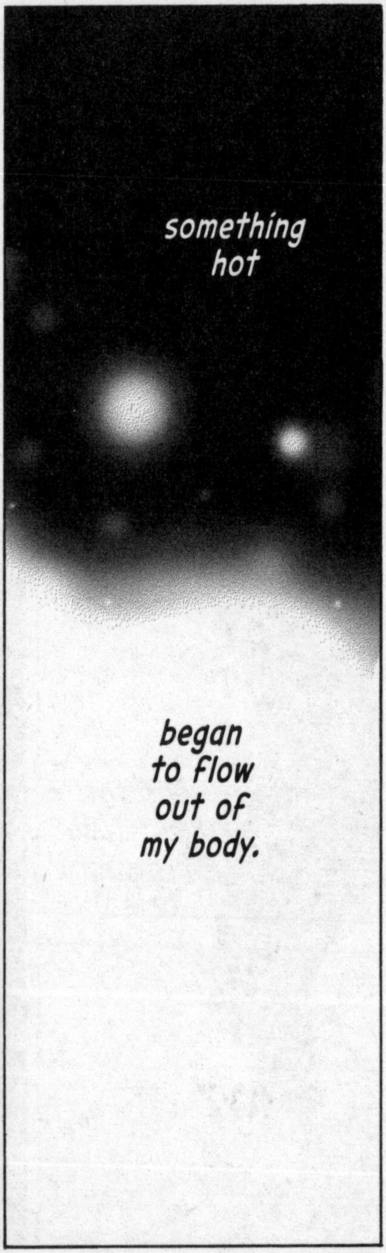
something hot
began to flow out of my body.

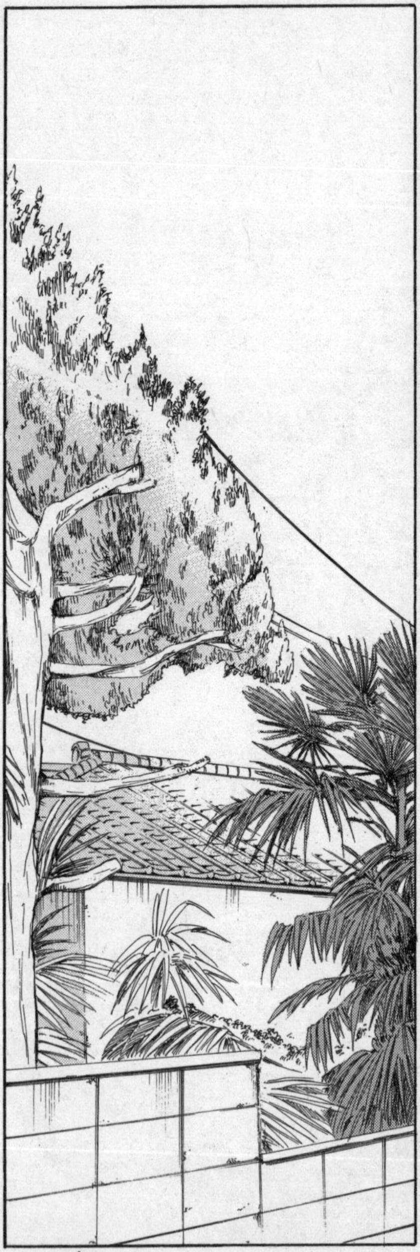

END

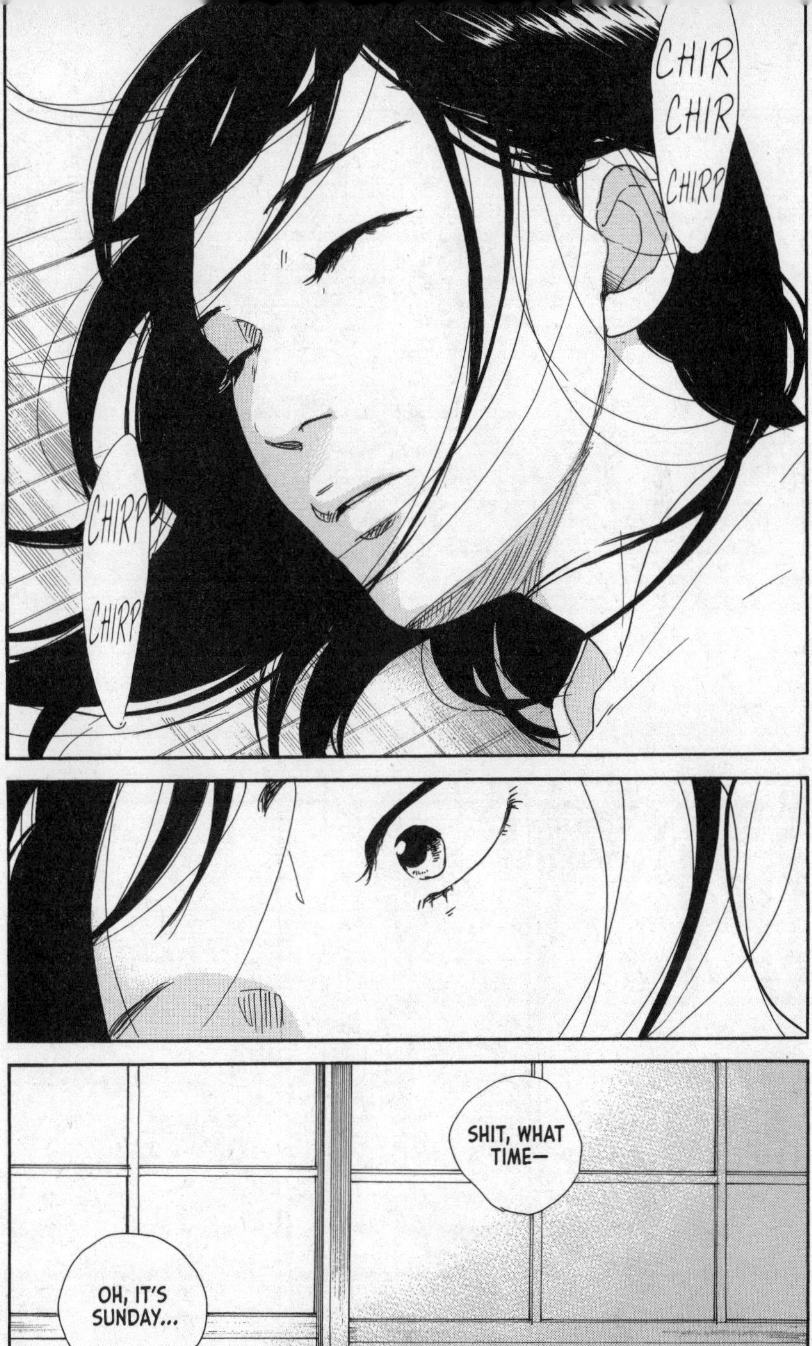
CHIR
CHIR
CHIRP
CHIRP
CHIRP
SHIT, WHAT TIME—
OH, IT'S SUNDAY...

CHAPTER 24. WHAT'S HAPPINESS, AGAIN?

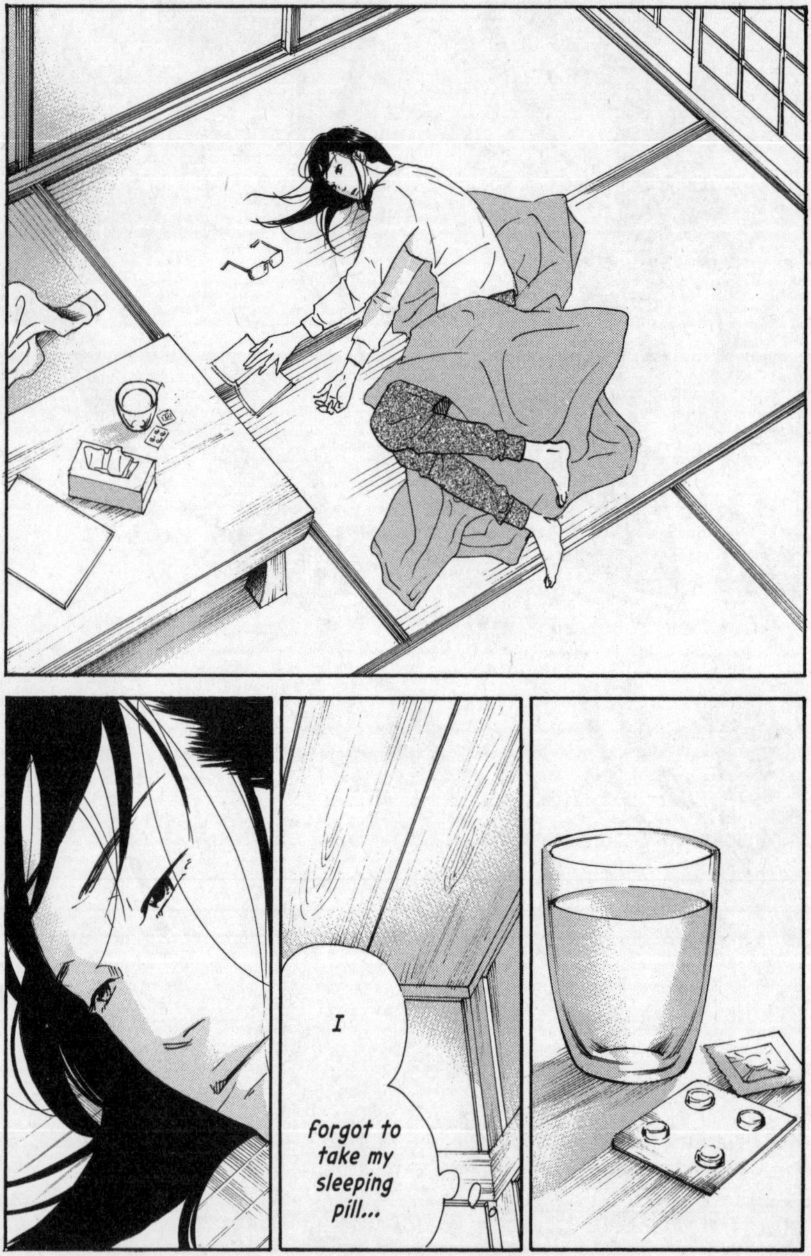
I forgot to take my sleeping pill...

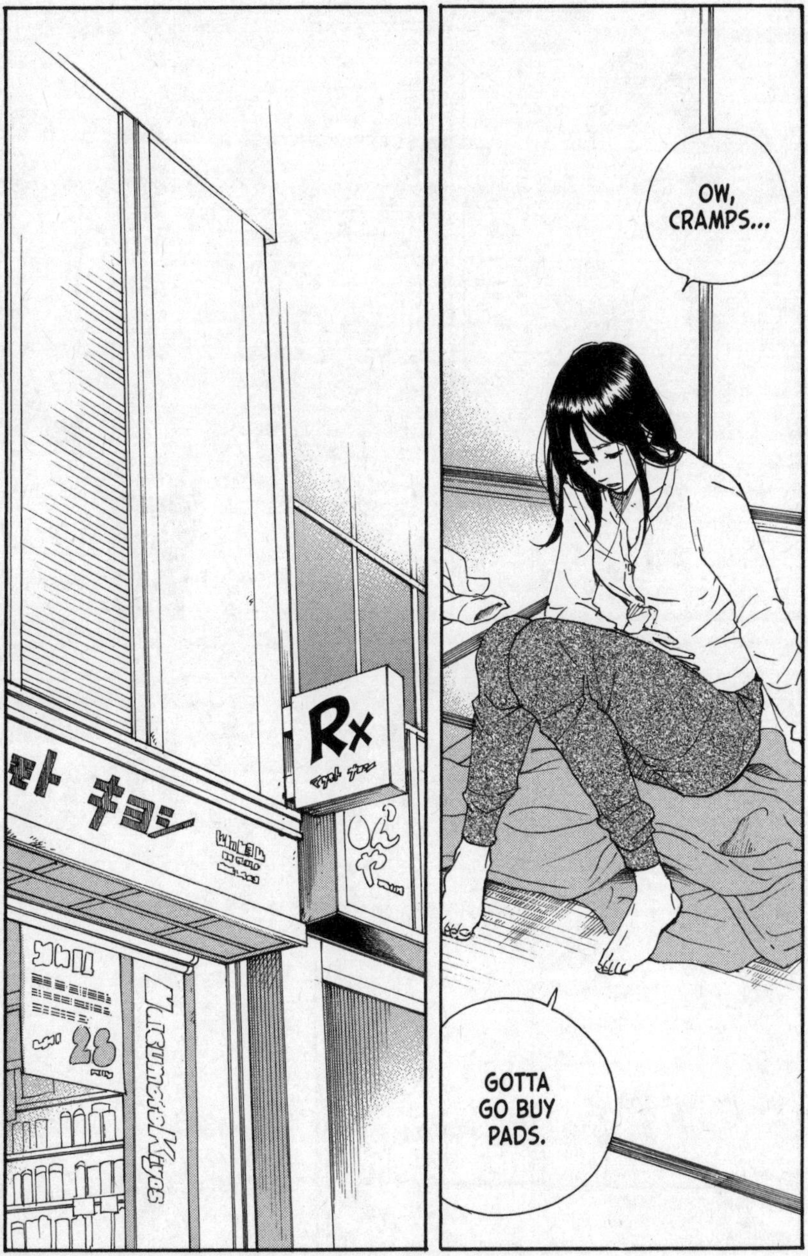
OW, CRAMPS...
GOTTA GO BUY PADS.
Rx

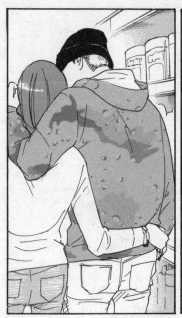

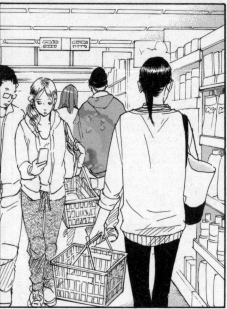

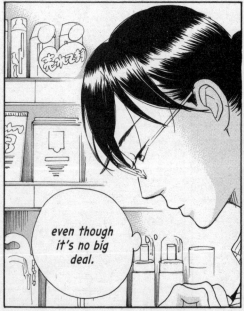

This place is full of couples...
even though it's no big deal.

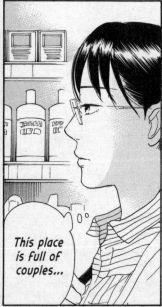

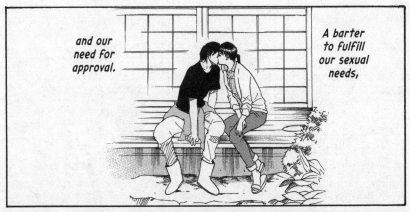

A barter to fulfill our sexual needs,
and our need for approval.
003
BABY & CHILD
BABY & CHILD

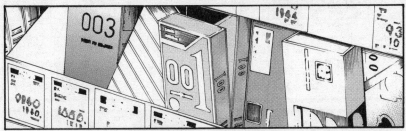

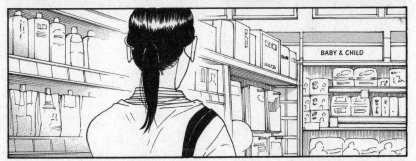

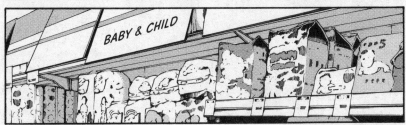

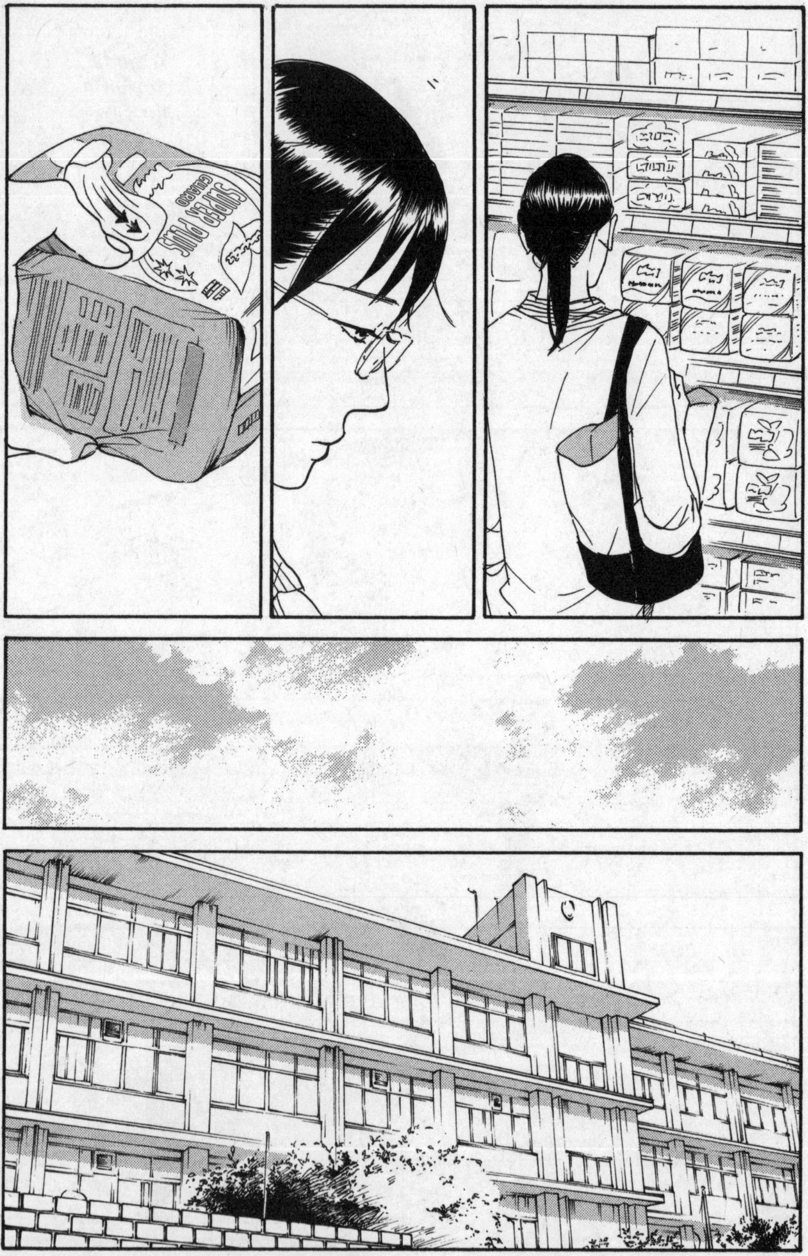
SUPER PLUS
CHIARO

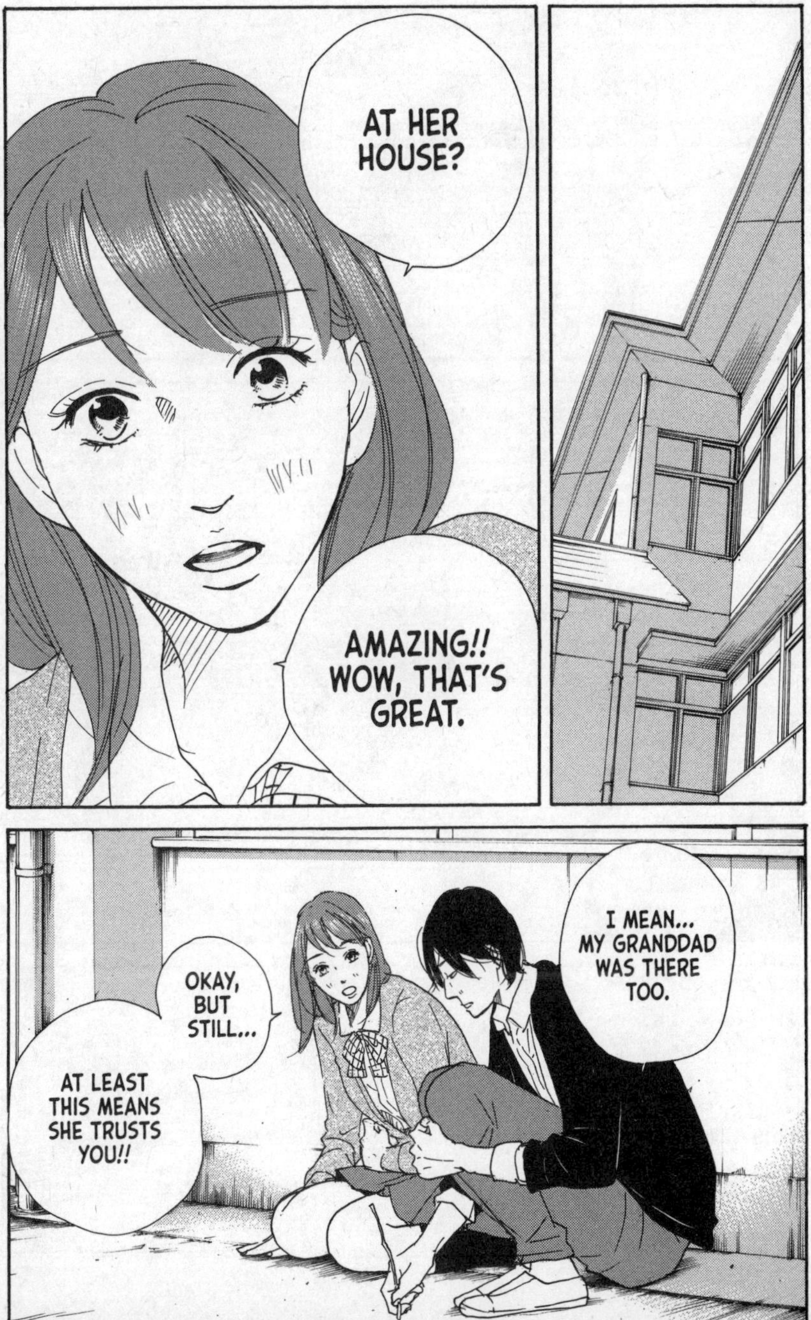
AT HER HOUSE?
AMAZING!! WOW, THAT'S GREAT.
I MEAN... MY GRANDDAD WAS THERE TOO.
OKAY, BUT STILL...
AT LEAST THIS MEANS SHE TRUSTS YOU!!

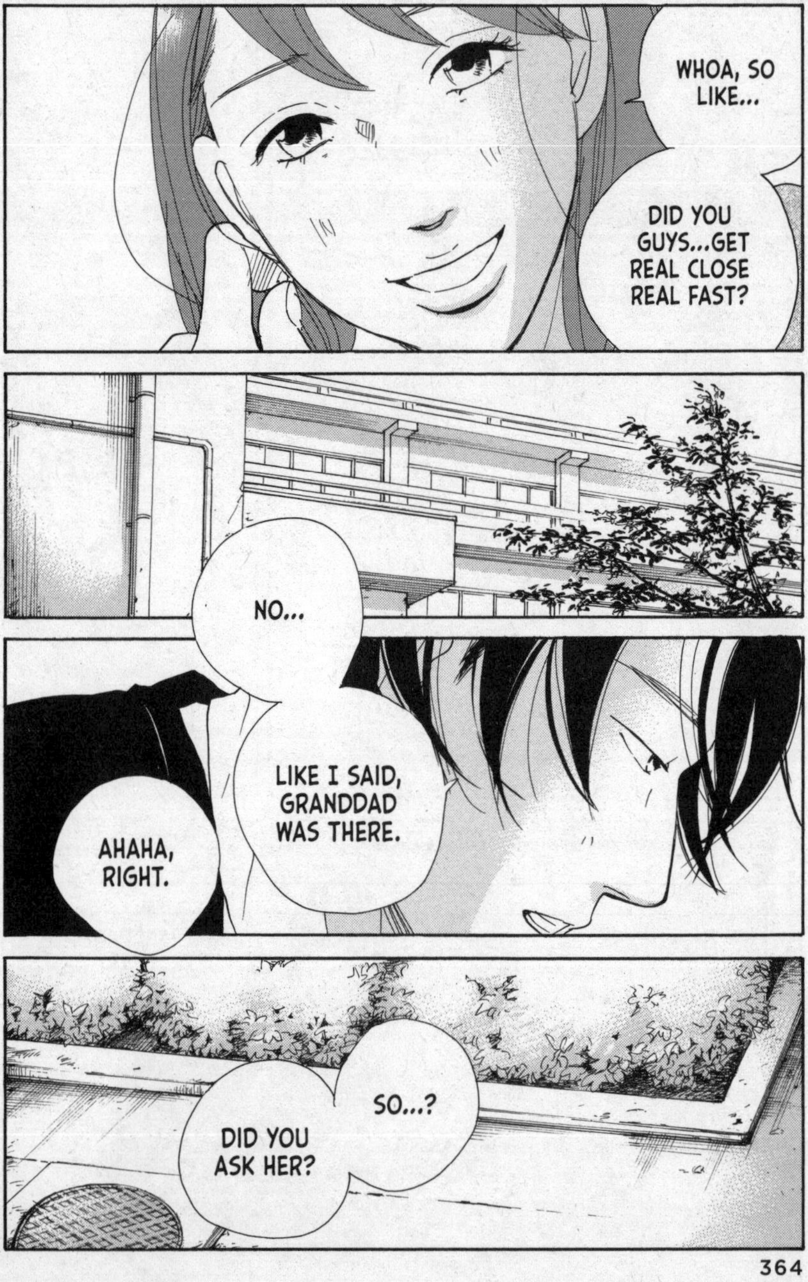
WHOA, SO LIKE...
DID YOU GUYS...GET REAL CLOSE REAL FAST?
NO...
LIKE I SAID, GRANDDAD WAS THERE.
AHAHA, RIGHT.
SO...?
DID YOU ASK HER?

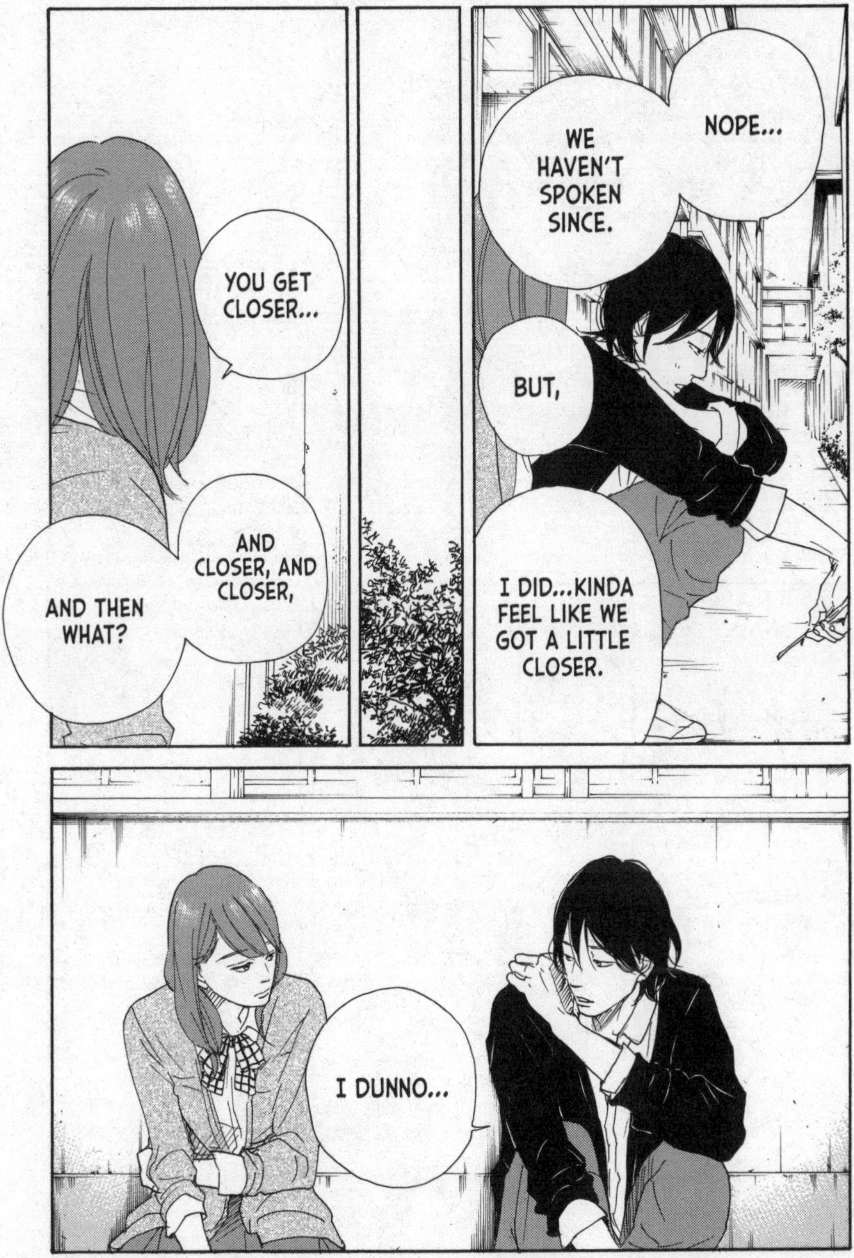
NOPE...
WE HAVEN'T SPOKEN SINCE.
BUT,
I DID...KINDA FEEL LIKE WE GOT A LITTLE CLOSER.
YOU GET CLOSER...
AND CLOSER, AND CLOSER,
AND THEN WHAT?
I DUNNO...

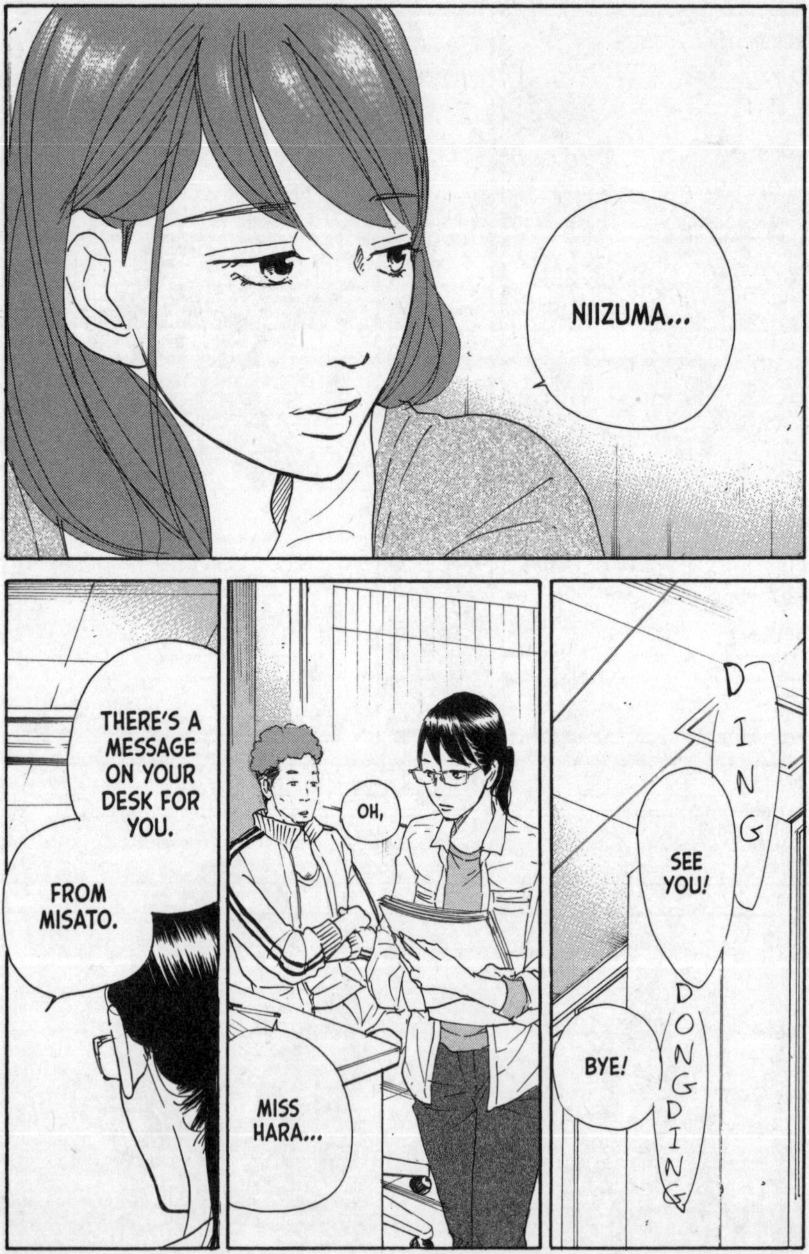
NIIZUMA...
DING
SEE YOU!
DONGDING
BYE!
OH,
MISS HARA...
THERE'S A MESSAGE ON YOUR DESK FOR YOU.
FROM MISATO.

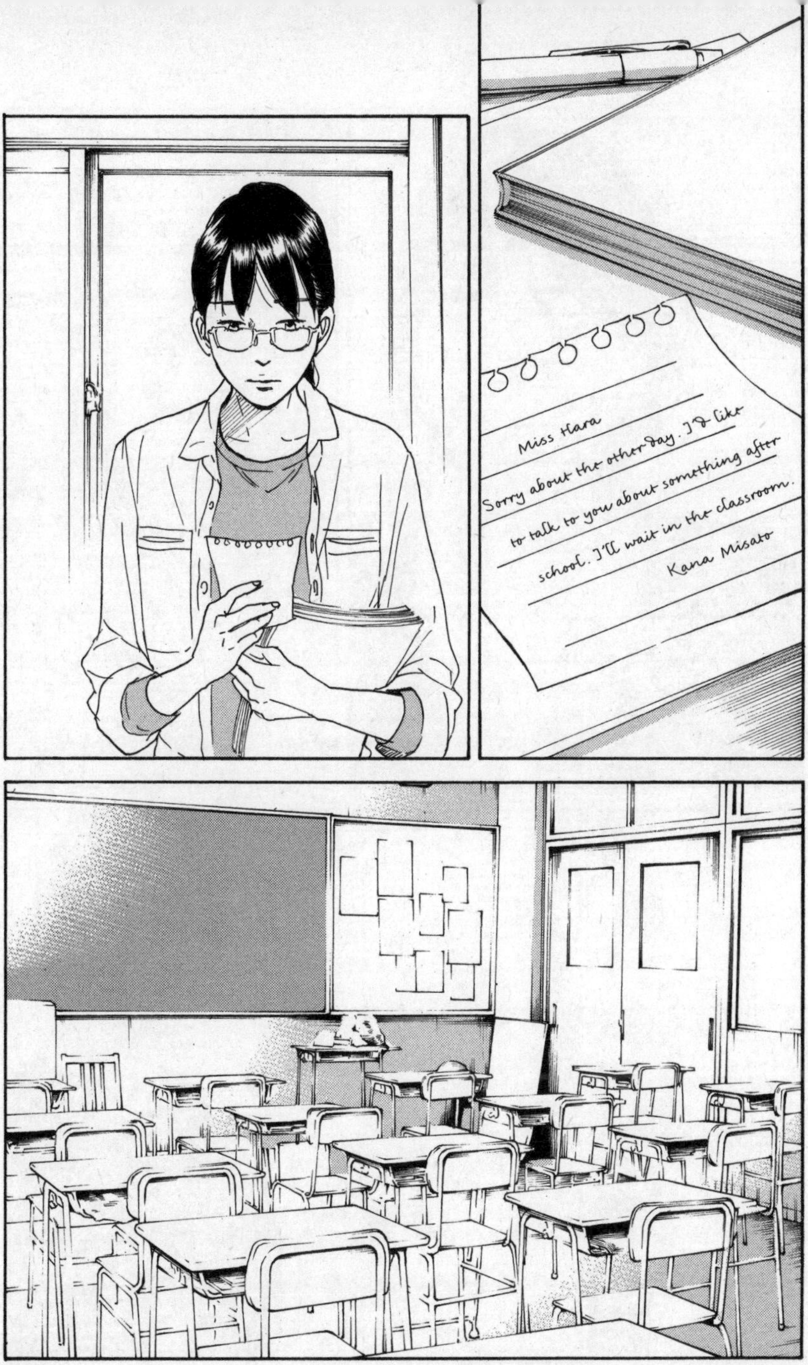
Miss Hara
Sorry about the other day. I'd like
to talk to you about something after
school. I'll wait in the classroom.
Kana Misato

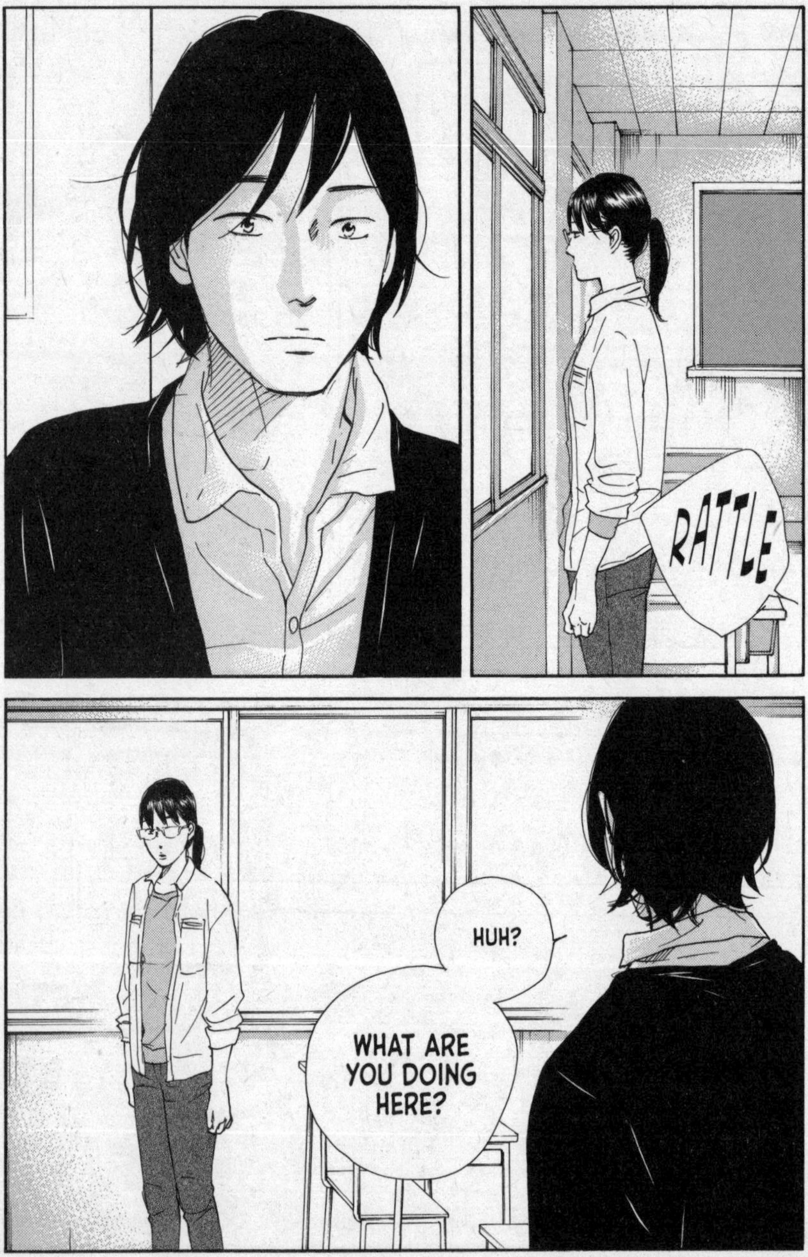
RATTLE
HUH?
WHAT ARE YOU DOING HERE?

HAAH...

GIMME A BREAK...

I'M LEAVING.

"NIIZUMA'S SUFFERING."

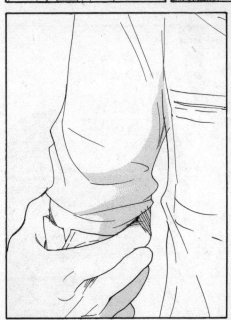

AND TELL MISATO THAT HER TEACHERS

DON'T HAVE AS MUCH SPARE TIME AS SHE MIGHT THINK.

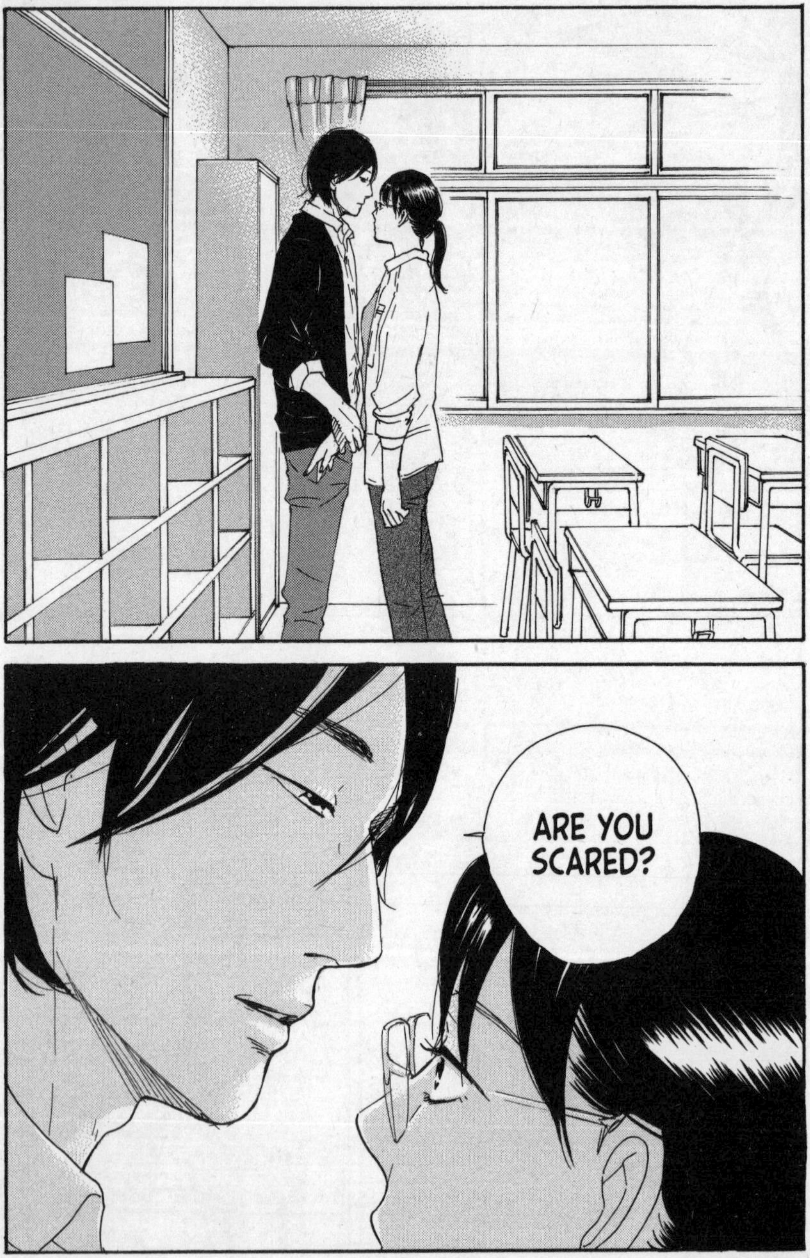
ARE YOU SCARED?

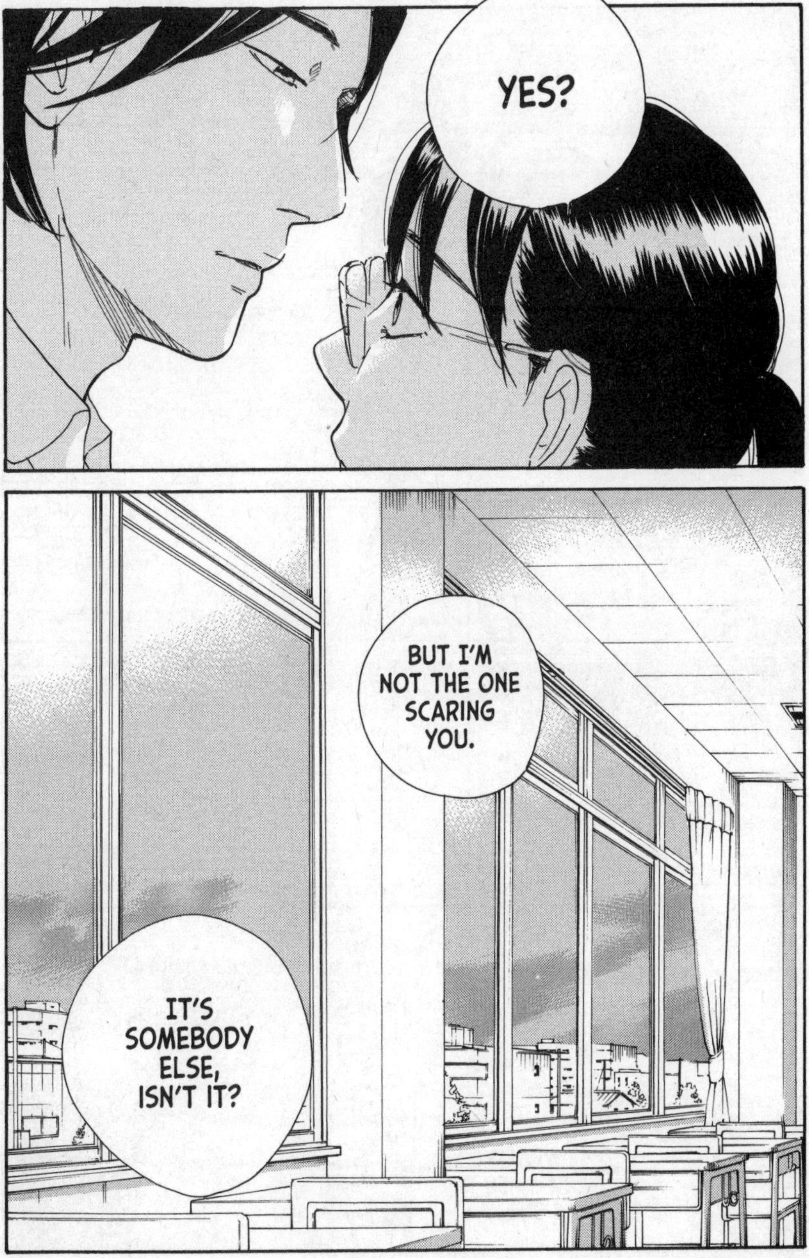
YES?
BUT I'M NOT THE ONE SCARING YOU.
IT'S SOMEBODY ELSE, ISN'T IT?

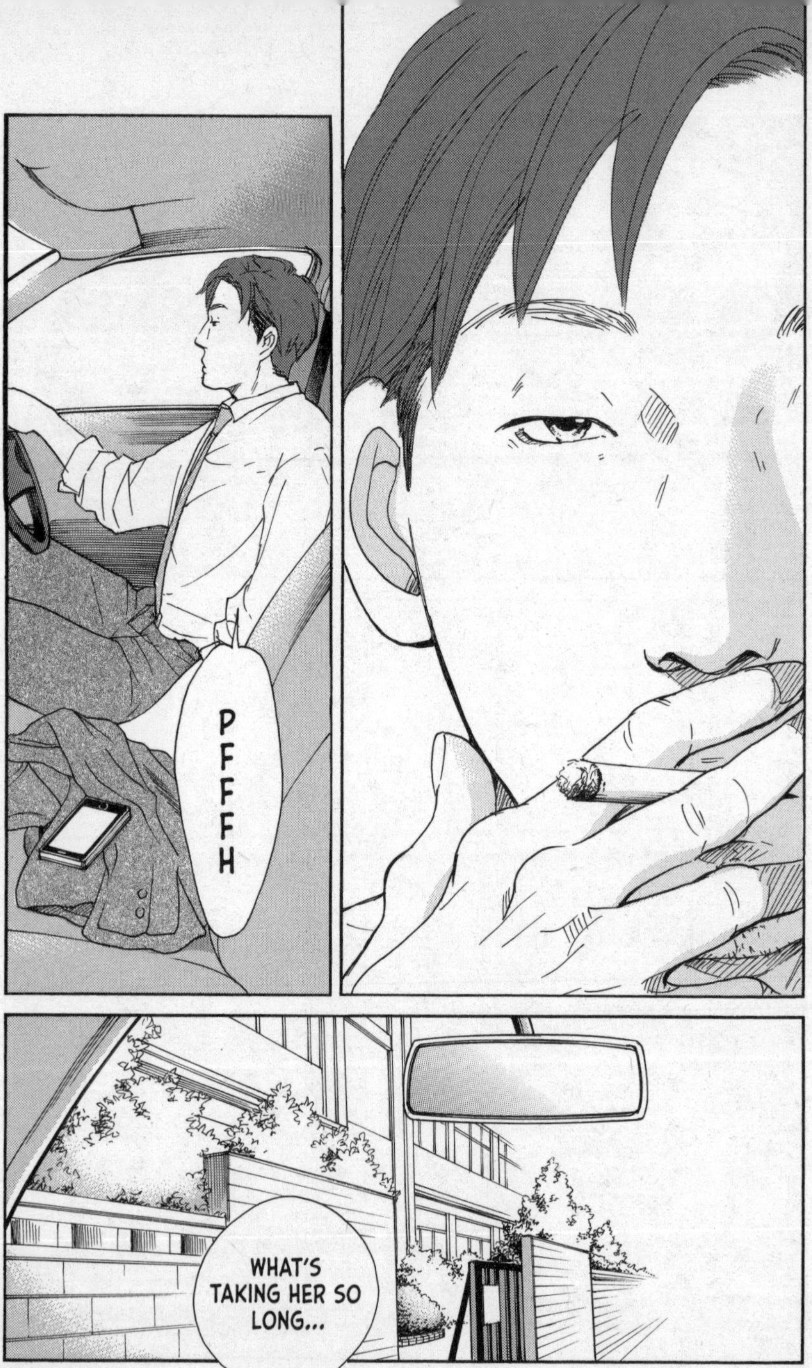
PFFFH
WHAT'S TAKING HER SO LONG...

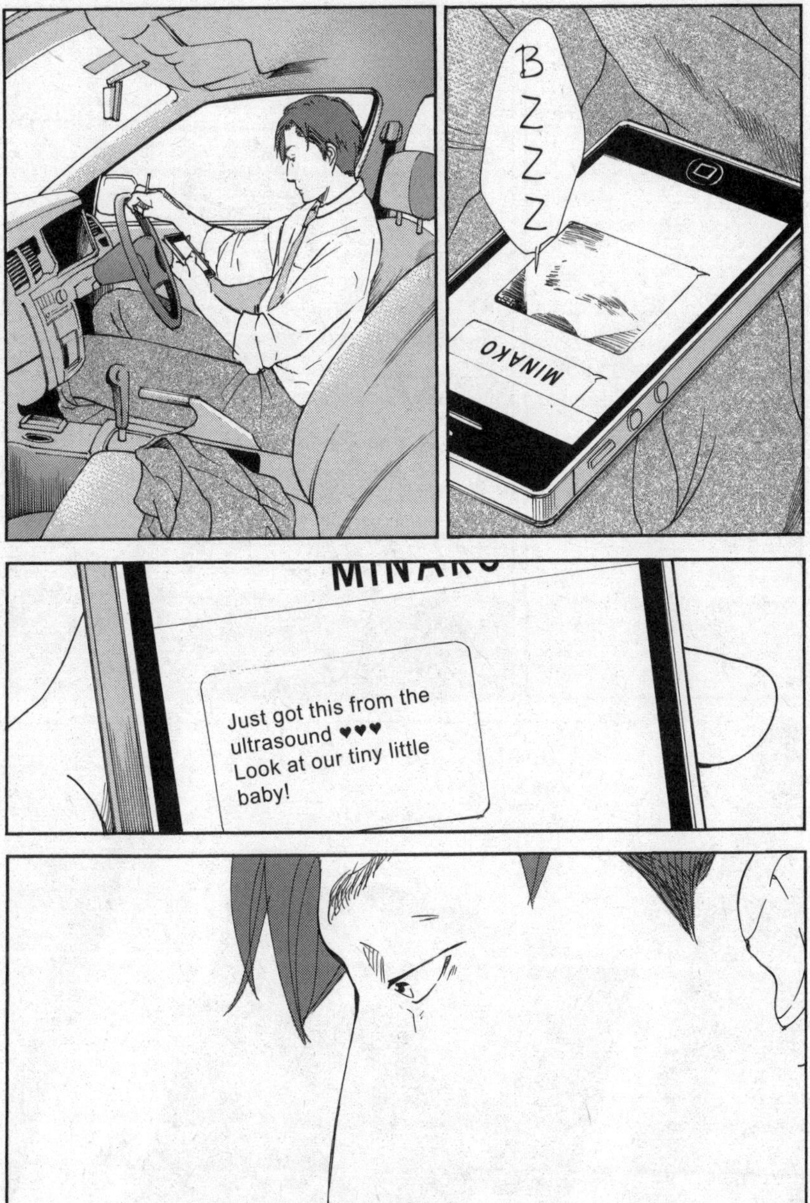
BZZZ
MINAKO
Just got this from the ultrasound ♥♥♥ Look at our tiny little baby!

UHG...
BLWAHH
KOFF
KOFF
KOFF
HUFF
HUFF
HUFF
Just got this from the ultrasound ♥♥♥ Look at our tiny little baby!

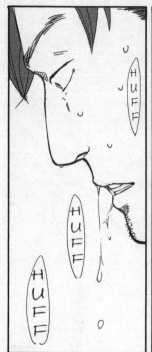

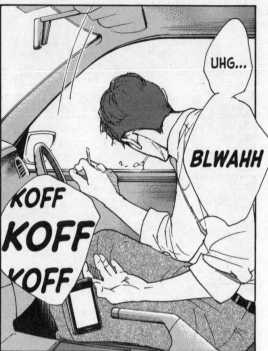

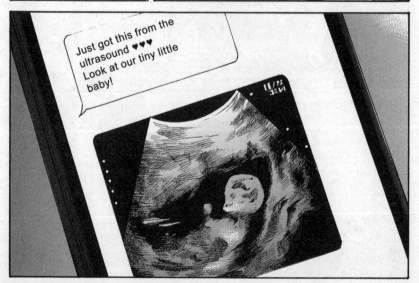

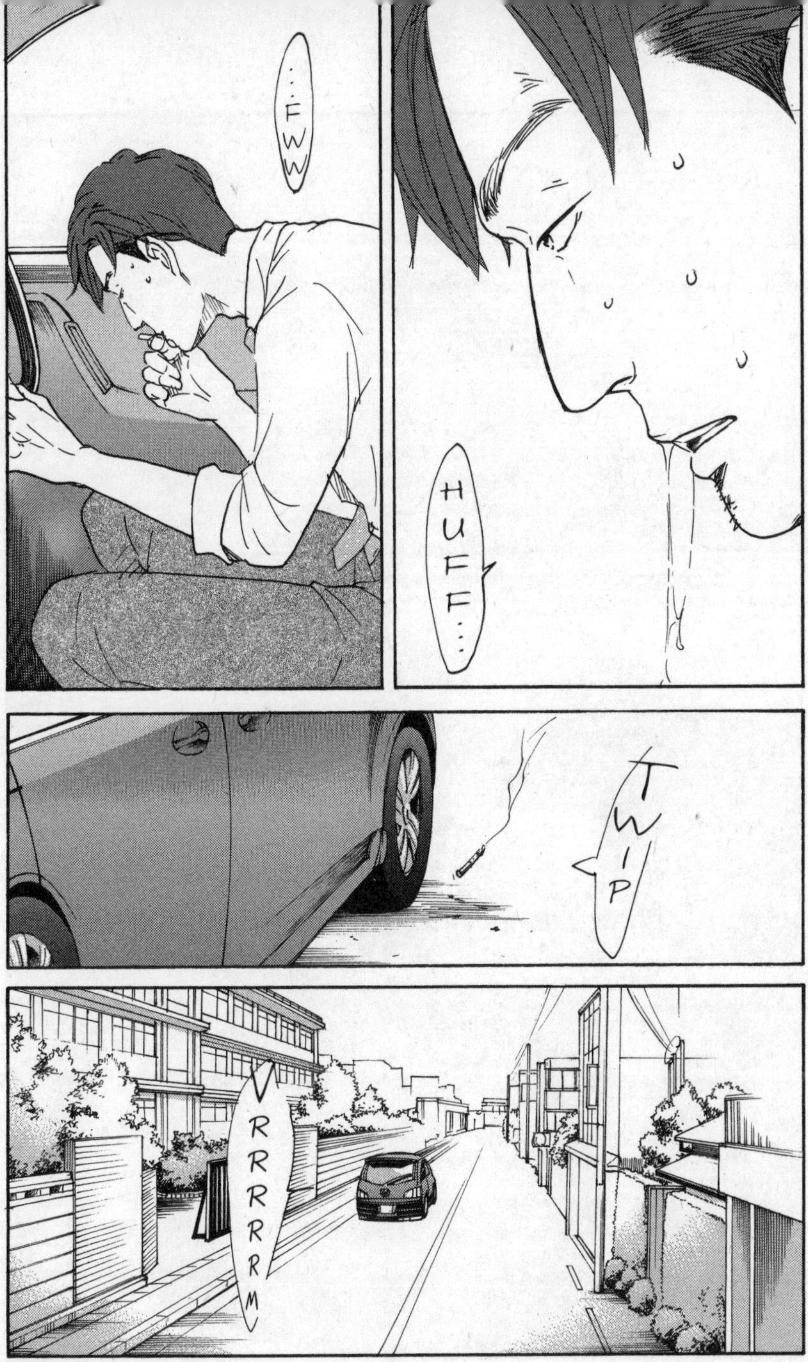
HUFF...
...FWW
TWIP
VRRRRRM

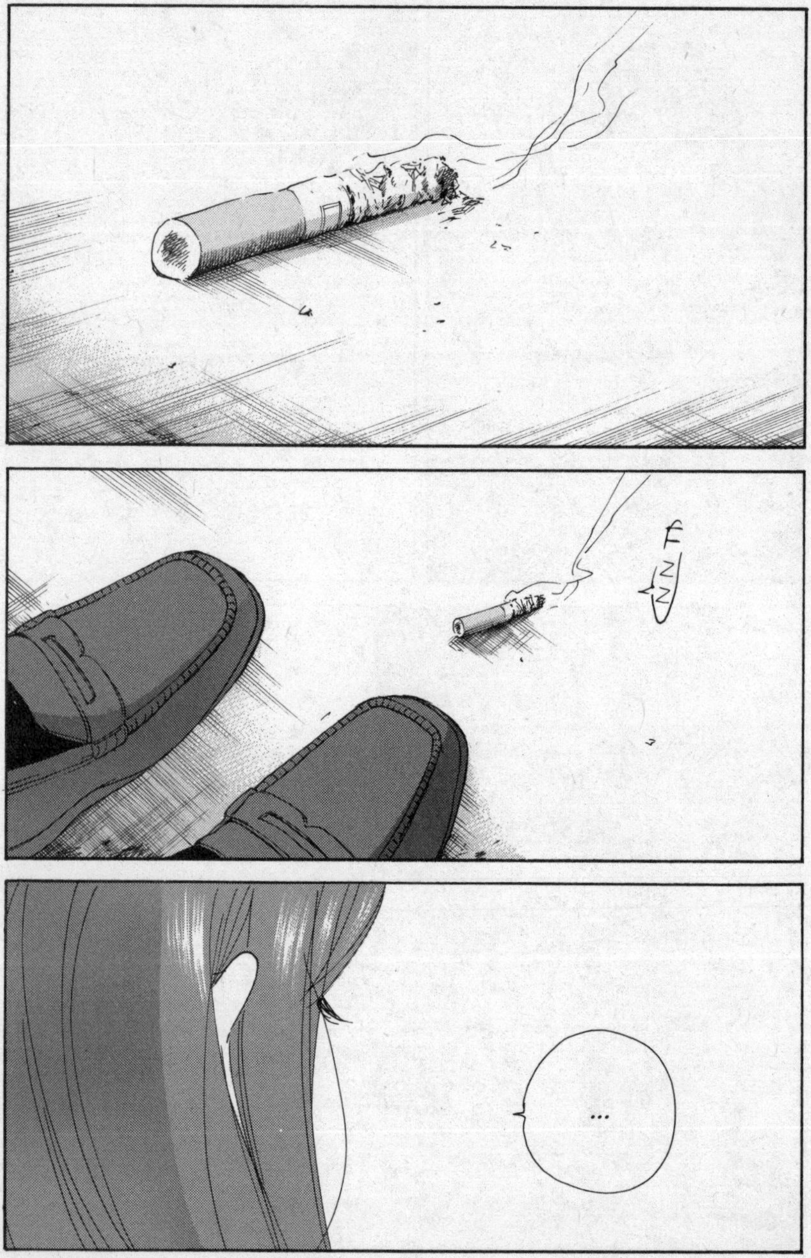
FZZ
...

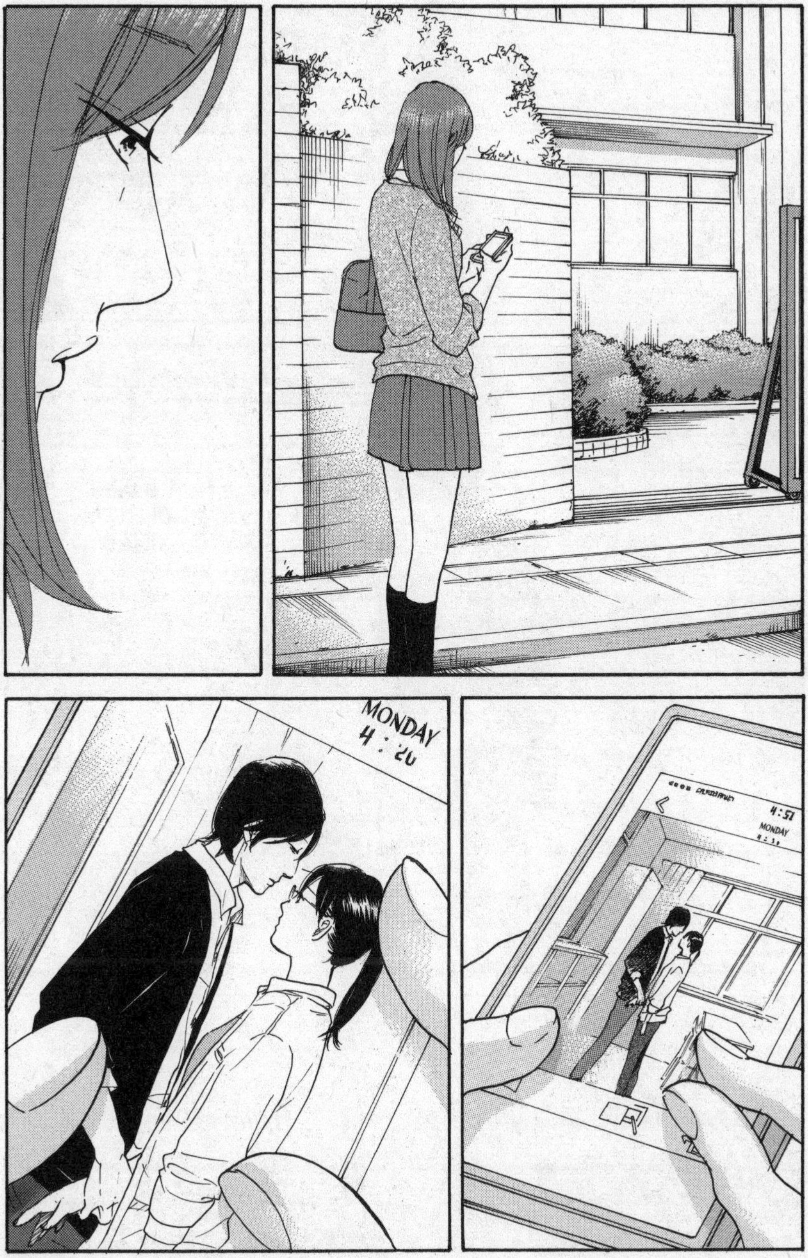
4:57
MONDAY
MONDAY
4 : 20

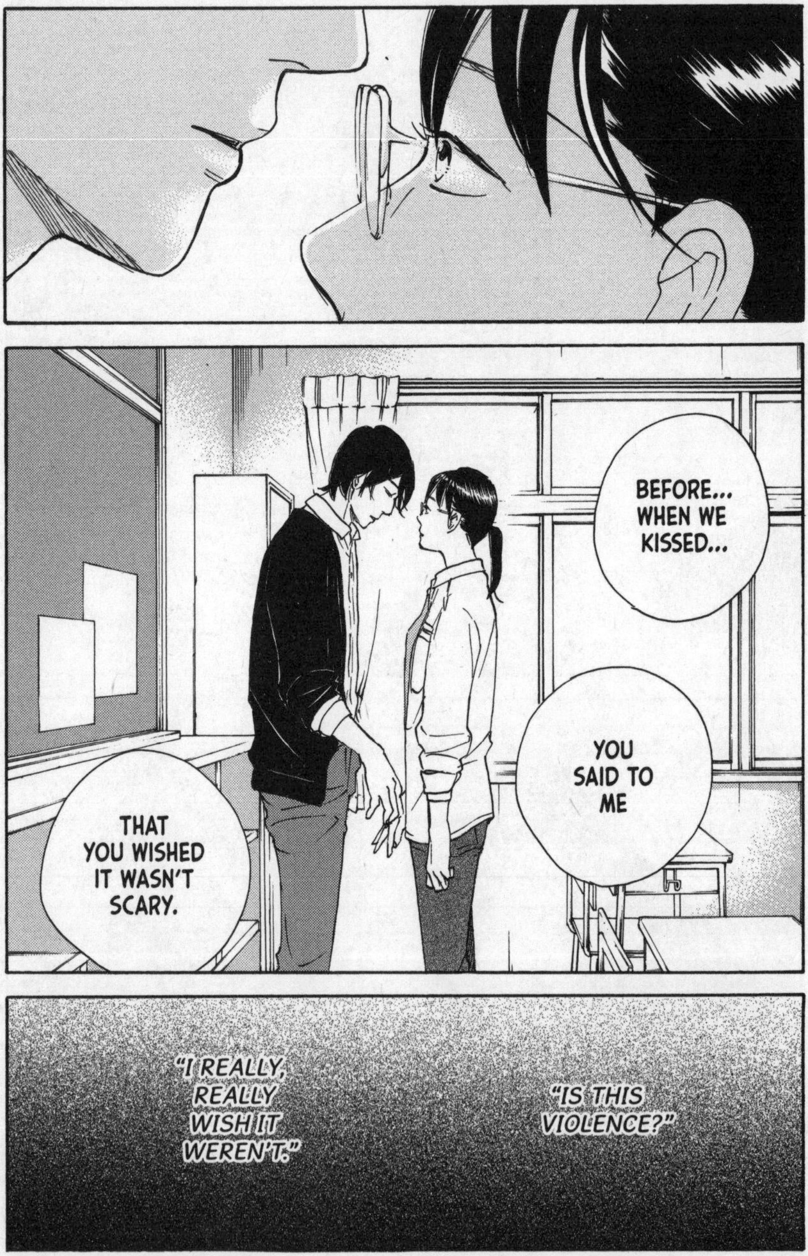
BEFORE... WHEN WE KISSED...
YOU SAID TO ME
THAT YOU WISHED IT WASN'T SCARY.
"IS THIS VIOLENCE?"
"I REALLY, REALLY WISH IT WEREN'T."

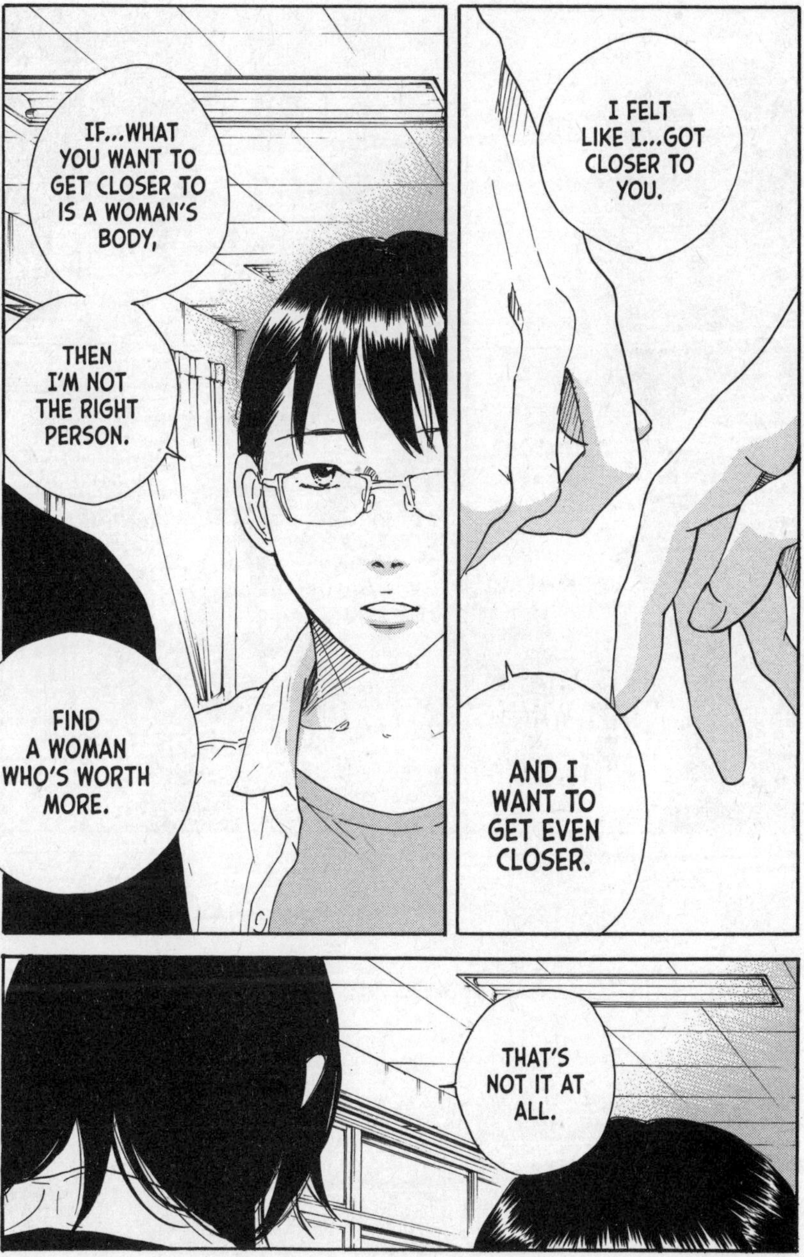
I FELT LIKE I...GOT CLOSER TO YOU.
AND I WANT TO GET EVEN CLOSER.
IF...WHAT YOU WANT TO GET CLOSER TO IS A WOMAN'S BODY,
THEN I'M NOT THE RIGHT PERSON.
FIND A WOMAN WHO'S WORTH MORE.
THAT'S NOT IT AT ALL.

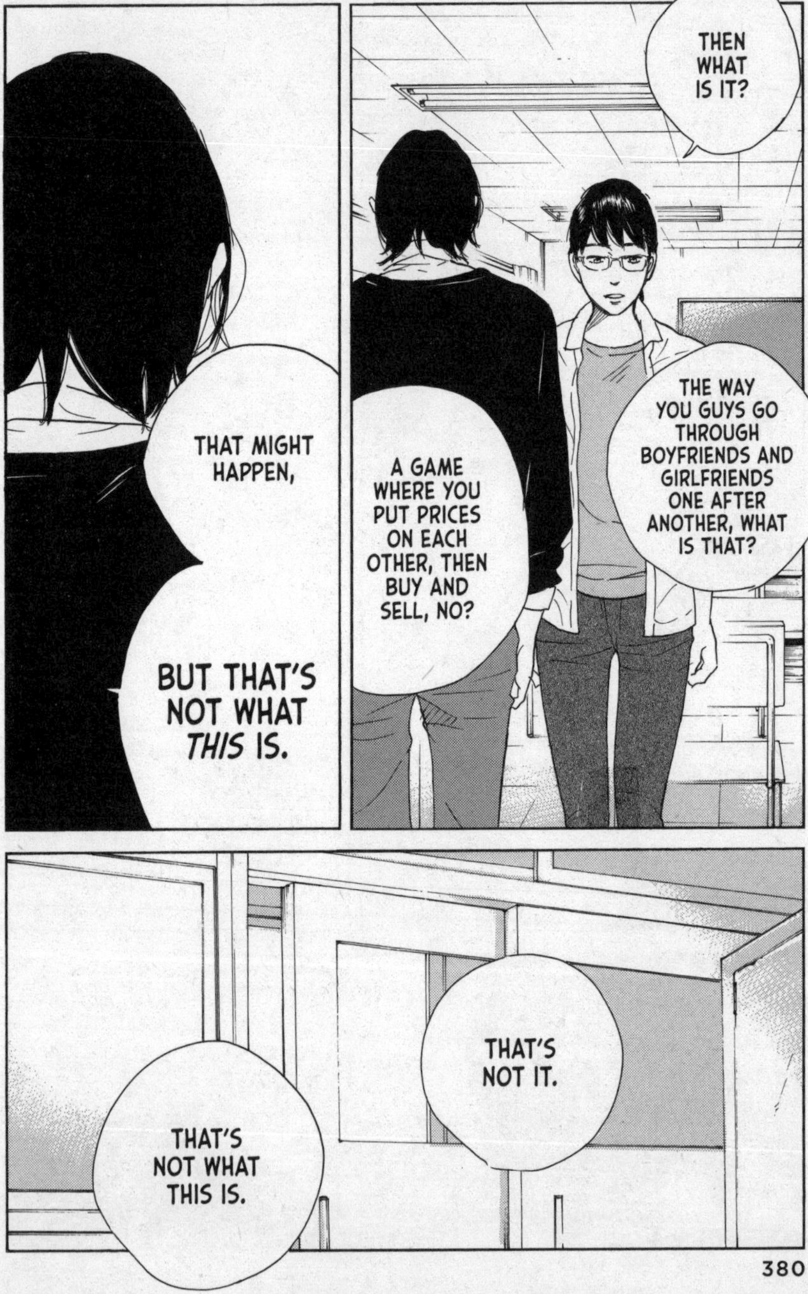
THEN WHAT IS IT?
THE WAY YOU GUYS GO THROUGH BOYFRIENDS AND GIRLFRIENDS ONE AFTER ANOTHER, WHAT IS THAT?
A GAME WHERE YOU PUT PRICES ON EACH OTHER, THEN BUY AND SELL, NO?
THAT MIGHT HAPPEN,
BUT THAT'S NOT WHAT *THIS* IS.
THAT'S NOT IT.
THAT'S NOT WHAT THIS IS.

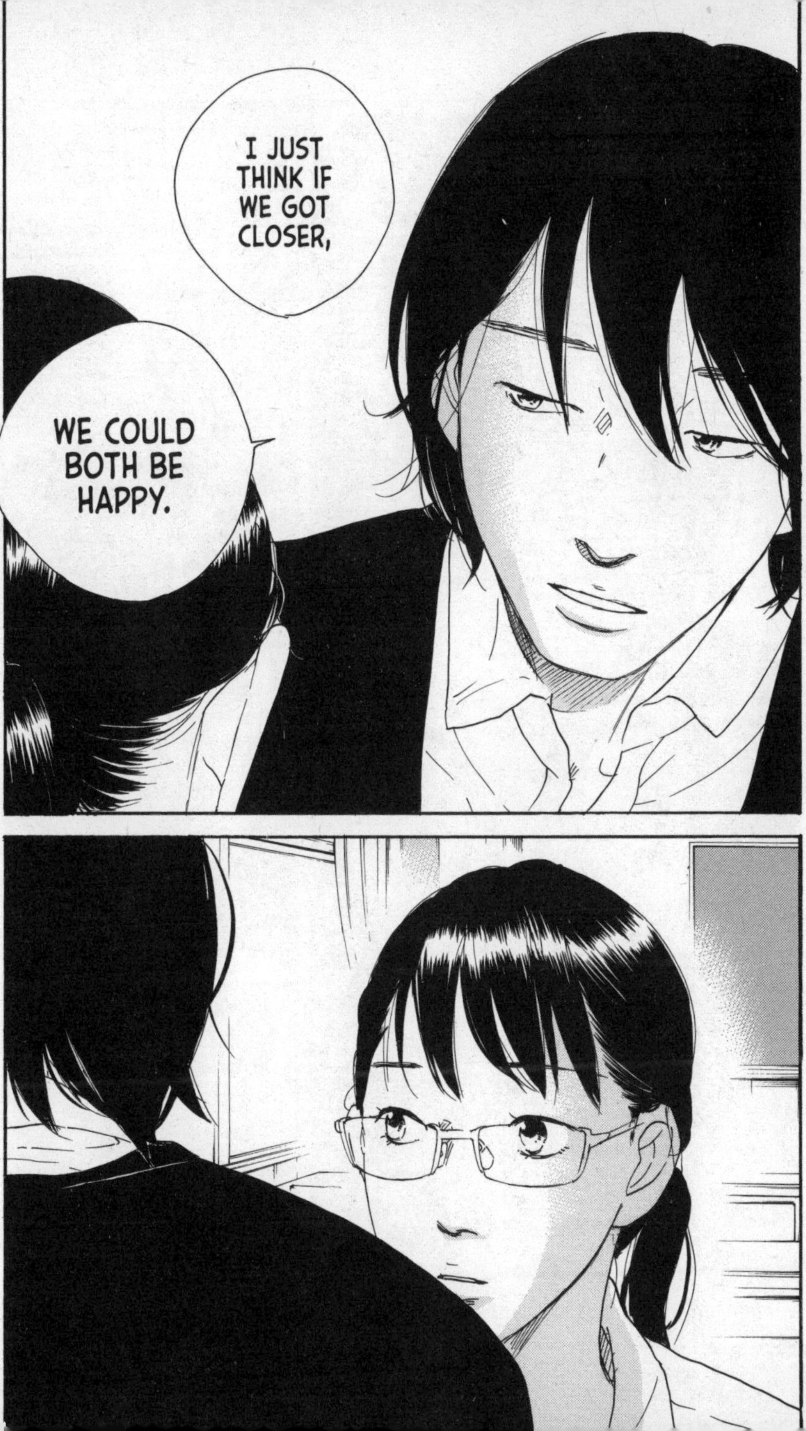
I JUST THINK IF WE GOT CLOSER,
WE COULD BOTH BE HAPPY.

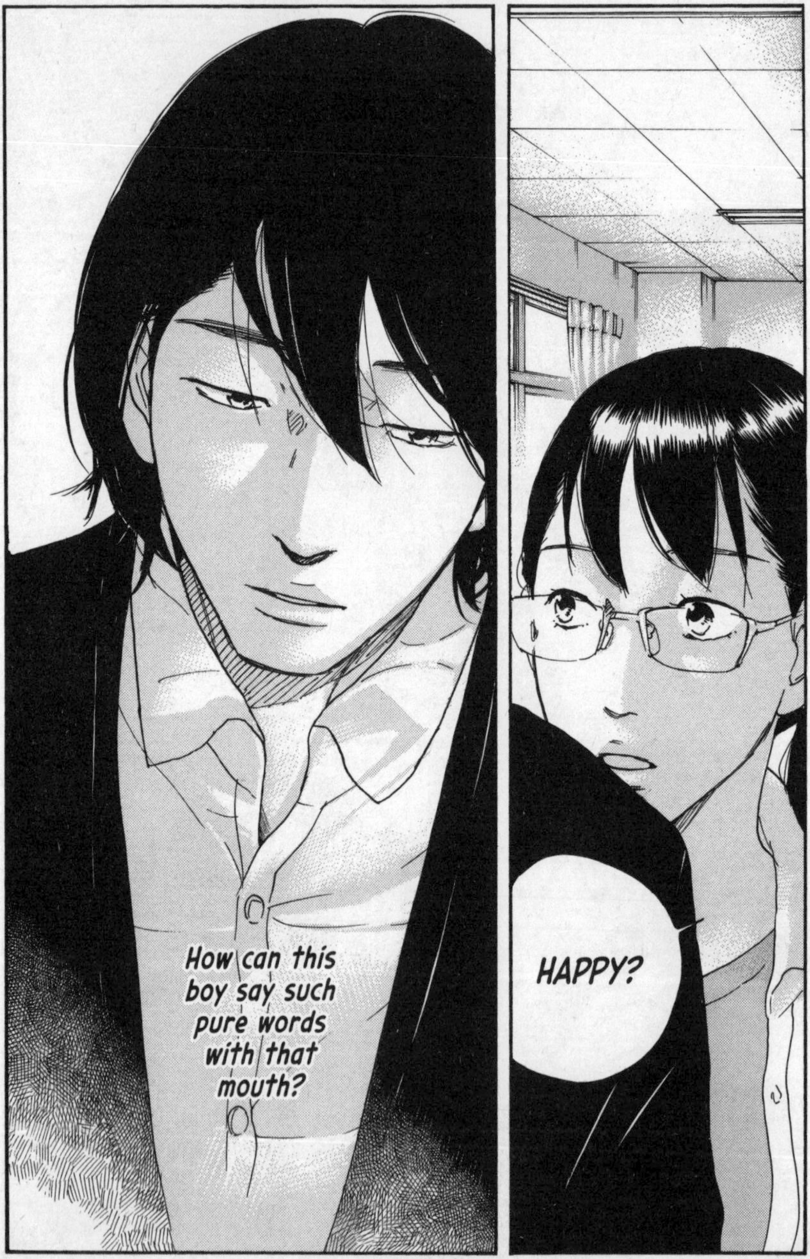
HAPPY?
How can this boy say such pure words with that mouth?

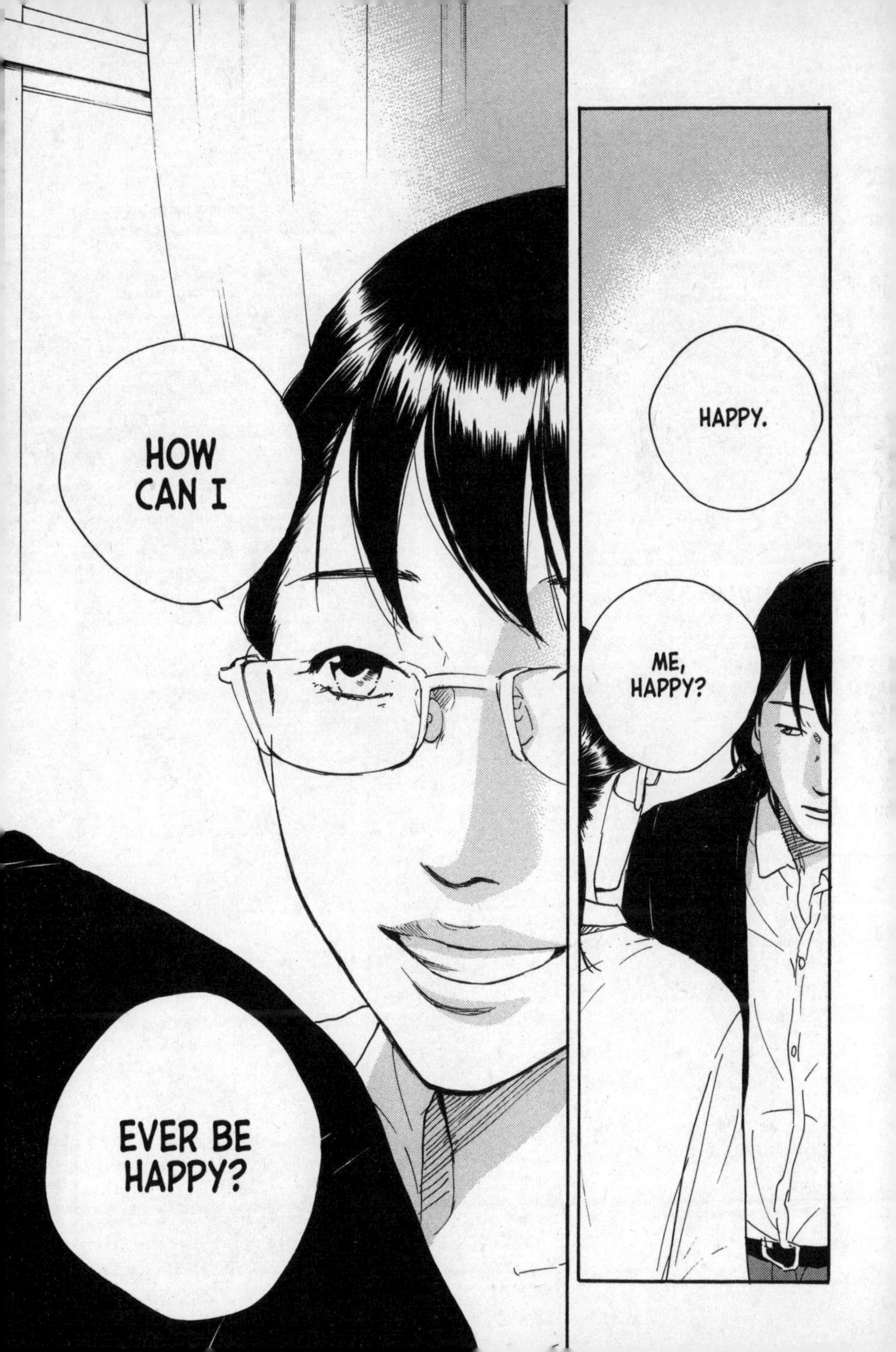
HAPPY.
ME, HAPPY?
HOW CAN I
EVER BE HAPPY?

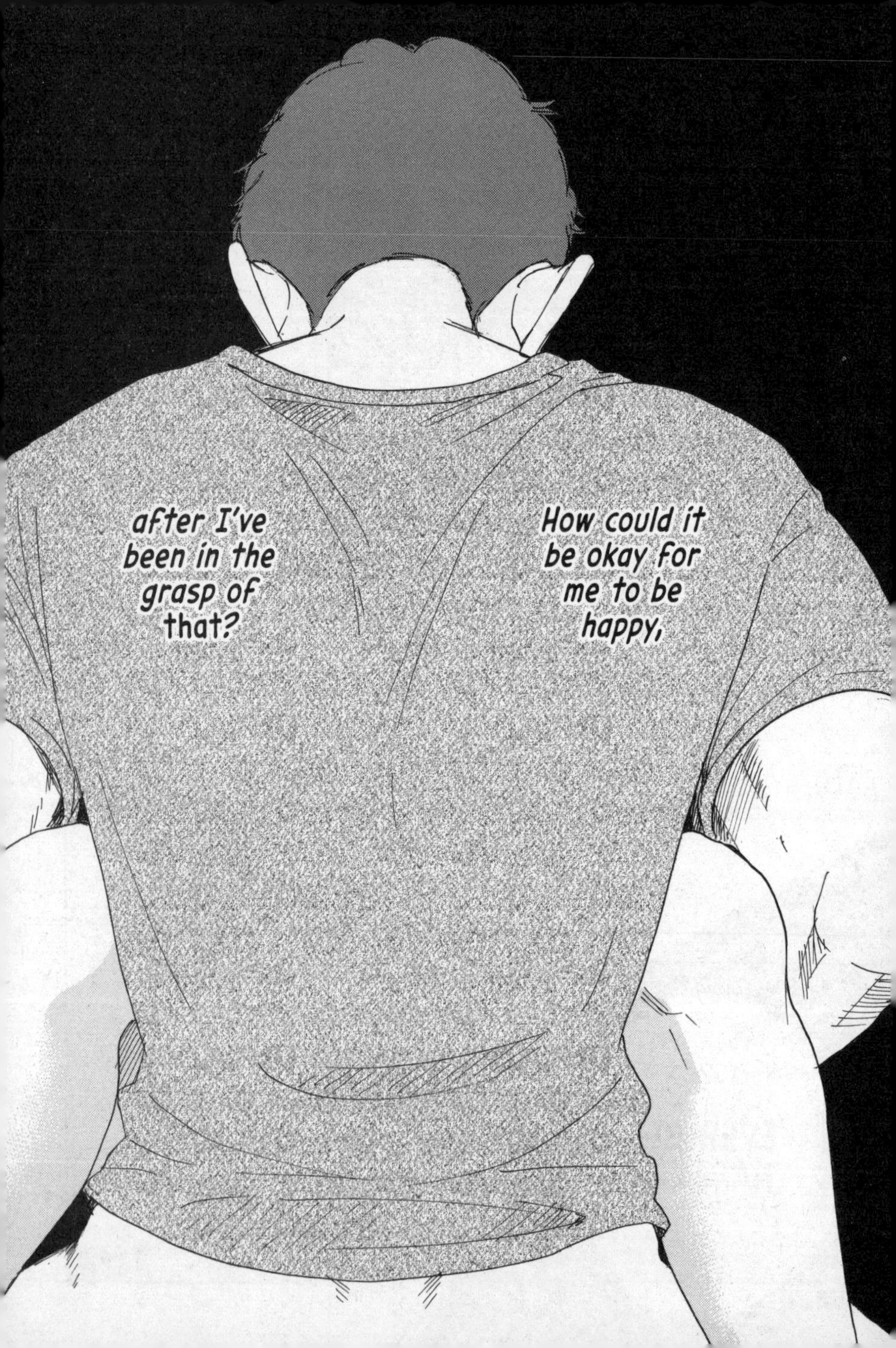
How could it be okay for me to be happy,
after I've been in the grasp of that?

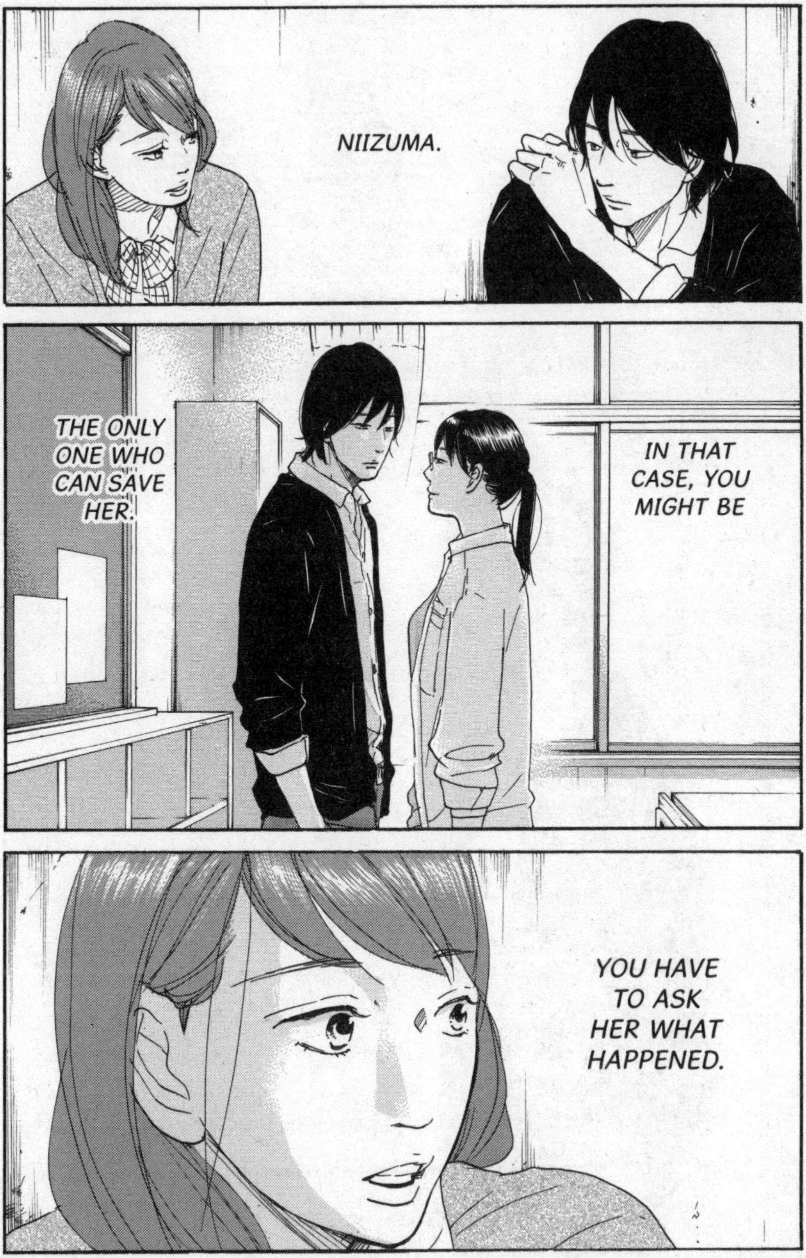
NIIZUMA.
IN THAT CASE, YOU MIGHT BE
THE ONLY ONE WHO CAN SAVE HER.
YOU HAVE TO ASK HER WHAT HAPPENED.

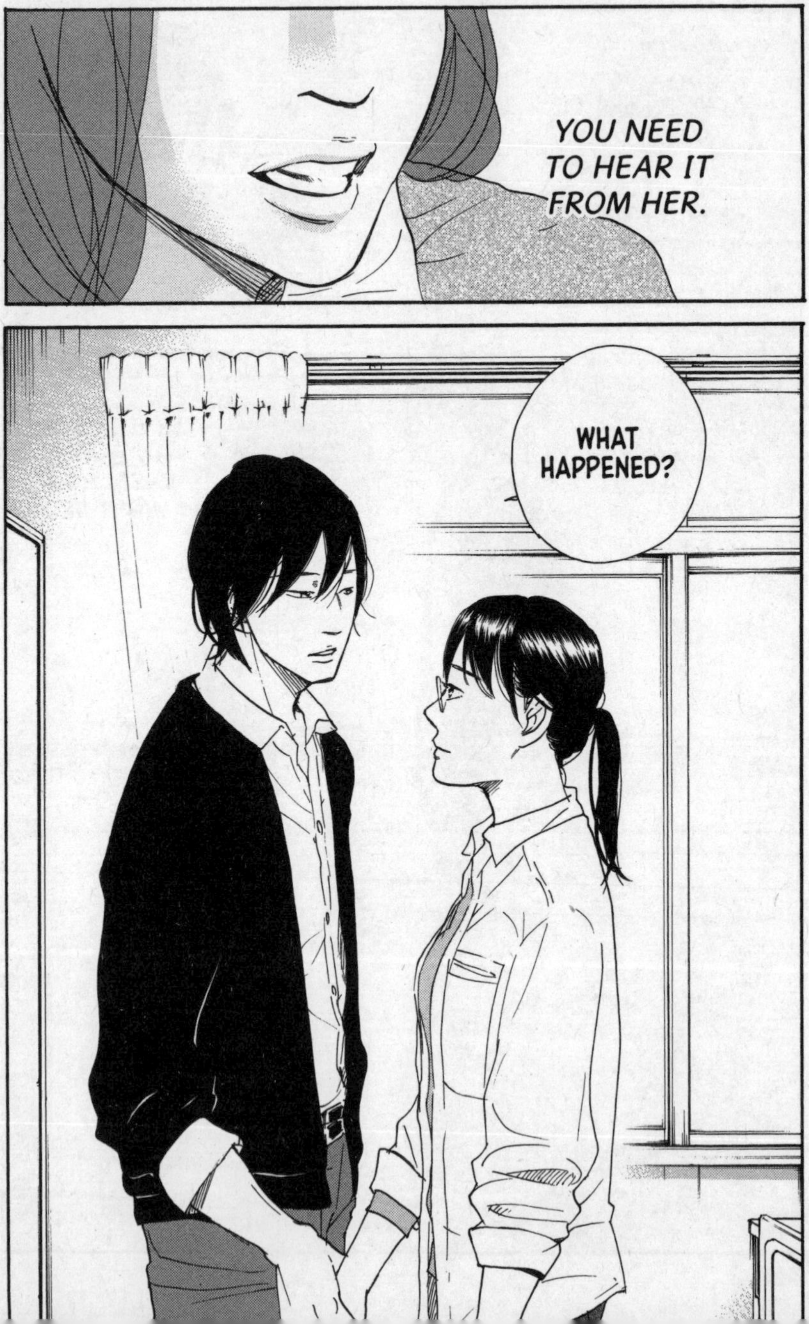
YOU NEED TO HEAR IT FROM HER.
WHAT HAPPENED?

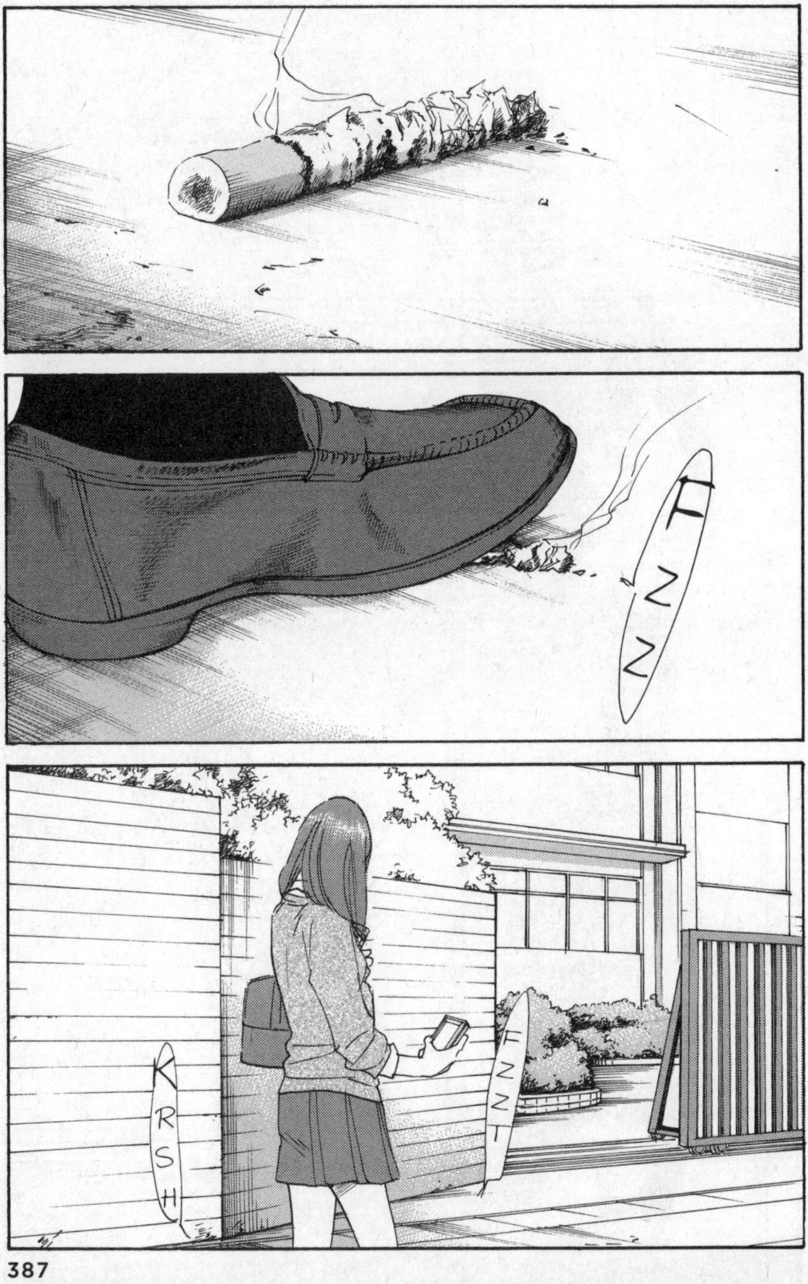
FZZ
FZZT
KRSH

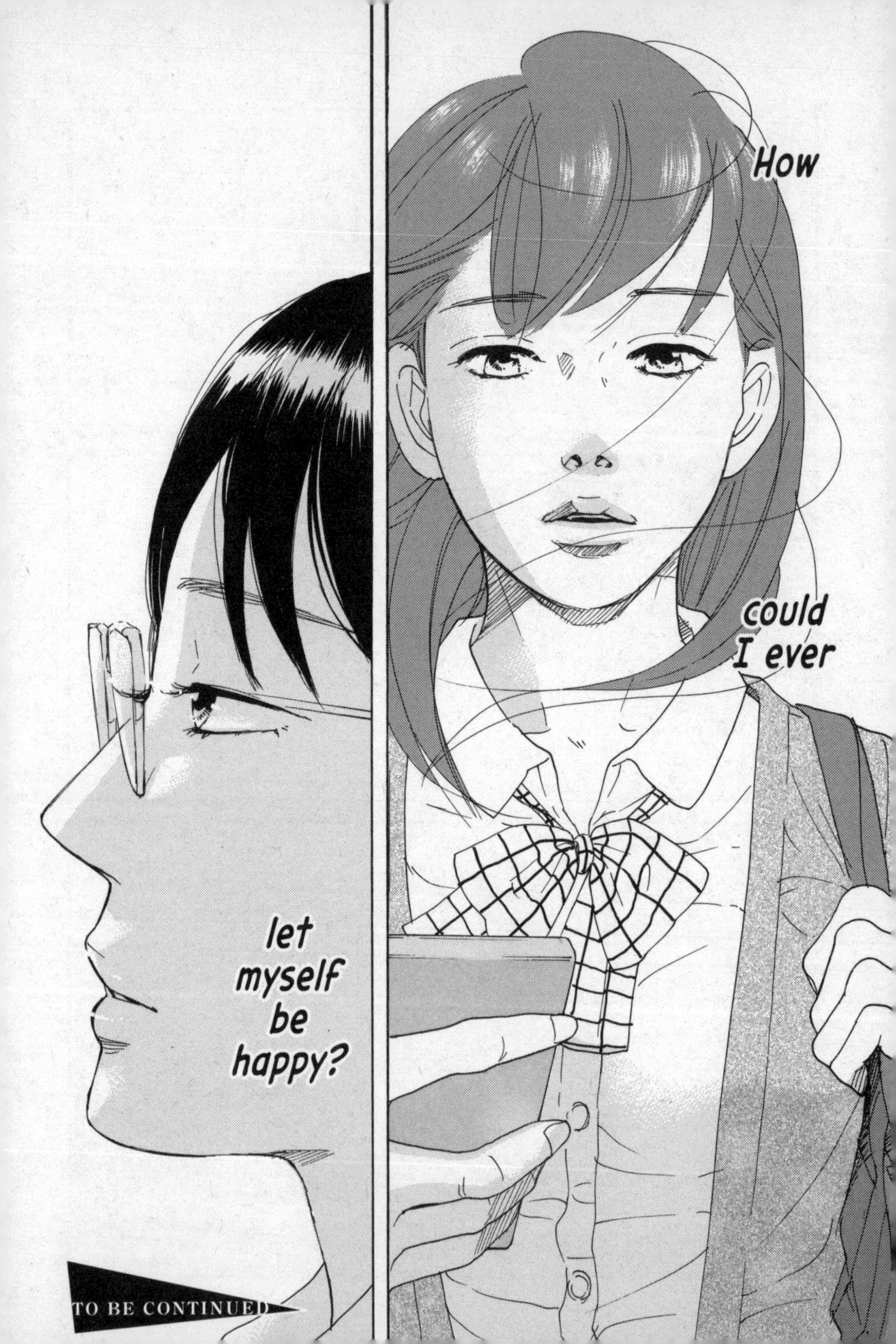
How
could I ever
let myself be happy?
TO BE CONTINUED

Sensei's Pious Lie 2

A VERTICAL Book

Editor: Daniel Joseph
Translation: Morgan Giles
Production: Risa Cho, Pei Ann Yeap, Lorina Mapa
Proofreading: Micah Q. Allen

First published in Japan in 2015 by Kodansha, Ltd., Tokyo
Publication for this English edition arranged through Kodansha, Ltd., Tokyo
English language version produced by Kodansha USA Publishing, LLC, 2022

Originally published in Japanese as *Sensei No Shiroi Uso 3* and *4* by Kodansha, Ltd.
Sensei No Shiroi Uso first serialized in *Gekkan Morning Two*, Kodansha, Ltd., 2013-2017

ISBN: 978-1-64729-113-6

Printed in the United States of America

First Edition

Kodansha USA Publishing, LLC
451 Park Avenue South
7th Floor
New York, NY 10016
www.kodansha.us

KODANSHA

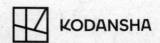

pink
kyoko okazaki

Yumi moonlights as a call girl because her day job doesn't pay enough for her to feed Croc, her voracious pet. Haru, an aspiring novelist who has nothing to say, sleeps with a woman his mother's age not just for the money but to work on his "powers of observation." When Yumi's step-mom turns out to be Haru's sugar mommy, it's time for—new shenanigans.

Published at the zenith of the Bubble era, women's comics legend Kyoko Okazaki's representative work captures, like no other graphic novel, the spirit of its times, when a nation lost something for good amidst the prosperity that made her the envy of the world. While the Bubble burst, that cynicism— and *pink*—have endured to this day.

256 pages | U.S. $16.95 / CAN $17.95
Ages 18 and up

Two from legend
kyoko okazaki

After cutting-edge full-body plastic surgery, supermodel Liliko's career is white-hot. But as her body begins to break down, she grows desperate and unhinged, lashing out as she realizes her expiration date as a product of pop culture is dangerously close. A surreal examination of the human cost of fame and the ugly side of glossy celebrity cultures, *Helter Skelter* won the 2004 Osamu Tezuka Cultural Prize and has been adapted into a film directed by Mika Ninagawa.

320 pages | U.S. $16.95 / CAN $17.95
Ages 18 and up

© Kyoko Okazaki

and Coming Winter 2022...*River's Edge*!